Lifetimes

The Great War to the Stock Market Crash

Lifetimes

The Great War to the Stock Market Crash

American History Through Biography and Primary Documents

Edited by Neil A. Hamilton

Writers

Mark LaFlaur

James M. Manheim

Renée Miller

Greenwood Press
Westport, Connecticut • London

© 2002 by The Moschovitis Group, Inc.

Greenwood Press
88 Post Road West
Westport, Connecticut 06881
www.greenwood.com
An imprint of Greenwood Publishing Group, Inc.

Produced by The Moschovitis Group, Inc.
339 Fifth Avenue
New York, New York 10016
www.mosgroup.com

Publisher	Valerie Tomaselli
Executive Editor	Hilary W. Poole
Project Editor	Stephanie Schreiber
Writers	Mark LaFlaur, James M. Manheim, Renée Miller
Design and Layout	Annemarie Redmond
Editorial Coordinator	Sonja Matanovic
Copyediting	Carole Campbell
Proofreading	Paul Scaramazza
Editorial Assistant	Colleen Sullivan
Production Assistant	Rashida Allen
Photo Research	Gillian Speeth
Index	AEIOU, Inc.

Printed and Bound in the United States of America
British Library Cataloguing in Publication Data is available.

Library of Congress Cataloguing-in-Publication Data
Lifetimes : the Great War to the stock market crash : American history through biography and
primary documents / edited by Neil A. Hamilton.
p. cm.
Includes bibliographical references and index.
ISBN 0-313-31799-2 (alk. paper)
1. United States—History—1913–1921—Sources. 2. United States—History—1919–1933—Sources.
3. United States—Biography. I. Title: Great War to the stock market crash. II. Hamilton, Neil A., 1949–
E766 .L48 2002   973.91—dc21   2001054700

Contents

Preface vii

Introduction 1

The Biographies

The Appendices, Bibliography, and Index

Preface

An expansion of the traditional biographical encyclopedia, *Lifetimes: The Great War to the Stock Market Crash* explores United States history through biography and primary source material. This book presents a complete portrait of the era from World War I to the stock market crash through the stories of those who created, criticized, and lived it.

To address the major themes and components of United States society during this period, we worked to include individuals from a wide variety of disciplines and spheres: activists, politicians, business leaders, sports figures, entertainers, writers, intellectuals, scientists, and so forth. Often, we could include only a few representative figures from each field, and in choosing our aim was to cover as many of these different experiences and perspectives as possible.

Each profile includes an original biography of the individual, discussing the subject's entire life, but with particular emphasis on the era covered by the book. Articles consider the overall influence of the individual and discuss his or her contributions to—or, in some cases, divergence from—the broader scene. Names appearing in boldface indicate other profiles included in the volume that can be consulted for additional information.

Each biography is followed by a section of primary source material, which further illuminates both the individual's life and the major themes of the era. Possible primary documents include: photographs, treaties, amendments, speeches, writings, lyrics, political cartoons, and other relevant material. Whenever possible, the selected documents originate from the period; some exceptions have been made to include pieces that cover an individual's defining moment or major contribution. Space constraints often caused us to excerpt material; all efforts have been made to provide the most informative, relevant, and noteworthy portions of the text. The header of the document indicates whether the material has been excerpted. To retain the integrity of the primary source material, we have kept the original language and spelling of the document text.

The biographical articles end with bibliographies that include print material for additional research. Most of these are autobiographical or biographical sources; the extensive bibliography in the back of the book can be consulted for historical sources, which are organized according to thematic categories. The appendix section includes a historical timeline, featuring brief descriptions of the important and influential events of the period. This section pulls together the many events and topics mentioned in the individual biographies, providing a broader picture of the era. A list of primary documents from the profiles completes the appendix; these are listed chronologically under the name of the biography in which they appear. The index offers a further means of locating topics of interest.

All efforts have been made to contact the copyright holders of the primary sources included in this publication. We apologize if we have inadvertently missed anyone and published material that is under copyright.

Introduction

Within the events that unfolded during World War I, or the Great War, and the 1920s, there pulsated the important contributions of individuals; these people, rather than theoretical social forces, are the heartbeat of this volume.

In attempting to communicate individual achievements and their dynamics, the editors have combined biographical essays—history's secondary sources—with evidence from the time—history's primary sources. We have chosen to focus primarily on the period from 1917 to 1930 as a crucial demarcation between prewar society, still largely isolated from European conflicts, and the beginning of the Great Depression was founded on modern consumerism and the optimism that fed it.

This book looks at 60 individuals, ranging from scientists to musicians, from radicals to sports figures, who exemplify the political, economic, and cultural developments of the era. Readers may find reasons to disagree with who was included and who was omitted, but it is hoped they will agree that the essays and primary material give a compelling and firsthand story of the times.

WORLD WAR I AND ISOLATIONISM

When people think of a castle surrounded by a moat, they think of a formidable structure protected from invaders, secure in an insecure world. Wars might rage beyond the castle's walls, yet it stands strong; its inhabitants might have their patience tried and their relations with people elsewhere altered, but their home remains safe.

From its beginning in 1776 into the early 1900s, the United States had its own moat—the Atlantic Ocean. While Americans had diplomatic relations with European countries, the moat almost always protected the United States from any direct entanglement in distant continental wars. World War I changed that. It brought the United States into intimate involvement with Europe and was only the first installment in a long chain of events that committed American troops to fight overseas. Writing in *The Great Departure: The United States and World War I, 1914–1920* (1965), David M. Smith argues that in this era the United States realized that "the nation could not be isolated from the effects of a major world war and that, in contrast to the past, a much higher cost in manpower and money would have to be paid for national security in a turbulent age." More than just a question of money and manpower, "World War I marked a great departure for the United States from the less-demanding world of the past and into the more dangerous but challenging world of the twentieth century."

When President **Woodrow Wilson** led the United States into World War I in 1917, it was, he claimed, "to make the world safe for democracy." Despite the idealistic proclamation, Americans were far from united. Many thought the country's entry unnecessary; they believed that Germany posed little threat to the United States. Still, Americans had their war heroes, notably **John J. Pershing**, who became a five-star general. A contributor to this volume, Mark LaFlaur, writes that Pershing "received the highest military ranking of any . . . general since George Washington." LaFlaur adds that "Pershing excelled not only as a field commander but also as an administrator of an international military coalition, and is widely regarded as the first of the modern generals."

Despite United States participation, immediately following the war Americans stepped back from European affairs. Dismayed by the war's failure to ensure that Wilson's idealistic goal would be reached, they tried once again to treat the ocean as a protective moat. President Wilson had envisioned a new world order led by the League of Nations, but Americans rejected that vision and turned inward. The United States signed the Kellogg-Briand Pact in 1928, a toothless international pact that renounced war, and it sent observers to the League of Nations (though not actual delegates, as the United States never joined the organization) but this was clearly an era where normality—or "normalcy" as President **Warren G. Harding** said—meant a detachment from Europe and an immersion in everything deemed American.

Americans immersed themselves in a consumer culture and in crusades that fought racism, on the one hand, and sought to oppress blacks and restrict immigration on the other. They fought for women's rights; traveled newly paved roads in cars being mass produced for the first time; flocked to theaters to see movies; and grouped around another technological marvel, the radio, to hear baseball games and boxing matches, along with news of **Charles Lindbergh**'s solo flight across the Atlantic in 1927.

The period from the end of World War I to the stock market crash in 1929 was energetic, materialistic, explosive, and freewheeling; it bounced and jumped and turned to the beat of jazz, and swayed to the wail of the saxophone. Frederick Lewis Allen notes in *Only Yesterday* (1931) that when couples took to the floor "No longer did even an inch of space separate them; they danced as if glued together, body to body, cheek to cheek." The *Catholic Telegraph* of Cincinnati, Allen reported, denounced the "sensuous" music and said that "the embracing of partners—the female only half dressed—is absolutely indecent; and the motions—they are such as may not be described, with any respect for propriety, in a family newspaper." As much as Harding may have presented "normalcy" as a concept set in stone, the definition of normality was undergoing a complete transformation; traditional and modern values and practices clashed sharply in the postwar period, with defenders of the "good old fashioned ways" finding themselves under assault from technology and an economy that stimulated progress and prosperity.

BOOM TIMES FOR THE ECONOMY AND THE BUSINESSMAN IS WORSHIPED

After World War I, Americans embraced business in an economy so expansive and heated that it engendered the phrase "Roaring Twenties." At first inflation hampered economic growth as prices more than doubled between 1915 and 1920. Then a recession took hold, lasting from 1919 into 1921. But in the 1920s the country's gross national product (GNP) grew by 40 percent. Wages and salaries also improved while inflation subsided. With more purchasing power, Americans spent money as if keeping it were a sin, a behavior that contrasted sharply with society's earlier emphasis on thrift, which many had labeled a virtue.

In 1919 Americans spent $2.5 billion on leisure activities; in 1929 this sum reached $4.3 billion, 21 percent of which was spent on movies, music, and sports. The number of telephones doubled, jumping from 10 million in 1915 to 20 million in 1929. Appliances such as washing machines, vacuum cleaners, and electric toasters became common sights in middle-class households.

The economic boom occurred as Republicans occupied the White House and dominated Congress. Under Presidents Warren G. Harding, **Calvin Coolidge**, and Herbert Hoover, multimillionaire businessman Andrew Mellon served as secretary of the treasury, and he crafted policies that sharply reduced taxes overall, but more so for the rich. Surtaxes (additional taxes imposed on individuals after net income has surpassed a particular amount) on the highest income bracket went from 65 percent in 1920 to 20 percent in 1928, inheritance taxes dropped, and gift and excess profits taxes came to an end.

Coolidge was, as Mark LaFlaur writes, "an honest, frugal, and efficient administrator," and pro-business to a fault. With the president proclaiming that "the business of America is business," regulatory agencies were dominated by former corporate executives and lawyers, and court decisions invariably went against labor unions. In 1922 Congress acceded to business demands and passed the Fordney-McCumber Tariff that protected domestic industries by imposing the highest duties ever on imports.

That Americans were so infatuated with business explains why, in 1925 and in 1926, **Bruce Barton**'s book *The Man Nobody Knows* topped the nonfiction best-seller lists. Barton argued that Jesus Christ should be best remembered as a successful businessman. "He picked up twelve men from the bottom ranks of business and forged them into an organization that conquered the world," Barton wrote. He added that Jesus "would be a national advertiser today" and that he was "the founder of modern business." As Frederick Lewis Allen stated in *Only Yesterday*, "Business had become almost the national religion of America. Millions of people wanted to be reassured that this religion was altogether right and proper, and that in the rules for making big money lay all the law and the prophets." Mark LaFlaur observes that Barton "conveyed a form of secular religion for a consumer society in which material success and spiritual development had become indistinguishable."

Barton may have exaggerated in saying Jesus would be a national advertiser, but without a doubt, advertising fueled the consumer spending spree on which 1920s economic growth depended. In that development, **Albert Lasker** was instrumental. As James M. Manheim writes in this volume, Lasker "came to believe that advertising copy should imaginatively promote products rather than just politely inform readers of their presence on the market." Modern advertising involved using psychological devices, clever slogans, and outrageous claims, all of which appealed to the decade's audience—so receptive to most anything promoting business.

The good times did, however, have limits. Not every American could indulge in the technological inventions. At least 50 percent of all farm and nonfarm workers barely earned a subsistence income, while the top five percent of Americans received about 33 percent of the nation's personal income. Unemployment remained high throughout the 1920s, hovering between seven and 12 percent of all nonfarm workers.

Minorities generally suffered more than whites. Three million African Americans, or 25 percent of the country's total black population, lived in Alabama, Georgia, and Mississippi in 1930; 80 percent of them in poverty while working as farmers, sharecroppers, and farm workers. Mexican Americans, for the most part, also had only low-paid and menial work. They made up three-quarters of all the farm laborers in the Southwest and California; those who lived in cities were segregated in barrios known for their dilapidated housing, poor sanitation, and inferior schools.

For the most part, labor unions refused to admit blacks and Mexican Americans to their ranks; in any event, unions faced a hard struggle just to survive, let alone win any big concessions for workers. From 1920 to 1929, union membership declined from five million to 3.5 million, partly as a result of many businesses establishing open shops. Ostensibly this arrangement gave workers complete freedom to choose whether to join a union. With the open shop, unions could not demand that every worker at a company site be a member. But in actuality the open shop allowed companies to harass and to fire those who supported unions.

The economic boom depended on significant buying on credit. Because consumers lacked the money to pay cash for items, they were encouraged to put some money down initially and pay the rest later. The danger inherent in this practice became evident when consumers overextended themselves, and then cut back on credit buying with damaging effects to the economy. They reduced buying on credit so extensively in the late 1920s that the economic boom gave way to the Great Depression.

Despite its problems, the economy generated enough wealth to assure that increasing numbers of Americans possessed more material goods than ever before. The economic engine was so strong that it made the United States dominant in international trade. According to historian William E. Leuchtenburg, "By the late 1920s the United States not only produced most of the world's manufactured goods but was by far the world's leading creditor nation."

POLITICS AND RADICALISM

Despite the postwar period's immersion in materialism and indulgence, political reformers and radicals offered alternatives. Progressive reform, the largely middle-class effort to correct the worst abuses wrought by America's industrial, corporate, and urban growth, lost the vitality of the early 1900s. Pushed into the background by the conservative reaction of the 1920s, Progressivism nevertheless remained strong locally and was promoted nationally by Wisconsin Senator **Robert La Follette**.

Republicans smeared the Progressives when they portrayed them as associates of communists, but La Follette actually distanced himself from such leftist radicalism, advising his supporters that Marxists wanted a totalitarian government. When La Follette ran for president in 1924 he proposed nationalizing railroads and raising taxes for the wealthy. The voters remained solidly Republican, however, embracing the combination of support for business and traditional values that the GOP advocated. Nevertheless, as contributing writer Renée Miller observes, La Follette battled admirably during World War I and in the 1920s as he "proposed reform measures in an atmosphere of national patriotism and political conservatism."

Radicalism expressed itself most vociferously during World War I in the form of those who spoke out against the United States entering the conflict. Suffragists and labor leaders, for example, **William "Big Bill" Haywood** of the Industrial Workers of the World, condemned the war for a variety of reasons ranging from pacifist principles to the belief, which Haywood stated, that the war benefited the rich at the cost of workingmen's lives. But in the 1920s, radicalism was most notable for being on the defensive in a conservative era. This was evident when Haywood, fleeing from a potential jail sentence, left the United States for the Soviet Union in 1921. Mark LaFlaur writes that had Haywood stayed in America he might well have "felt useless and out of place."

COMMUNISM AND THE RED SCARE

At the end of World War I capitalism came under assault from what most Americans labeled an invidious force, namely communism or Bolshevism. The ideological menace, which actually had been a worry since at least the late 1800s, metamorphosed into the Red Scare on the heels of the communist revolution in Russia in 1917. Bolshevism meant more than a threat to the existing economic system; it meant a radical challenge to those who held power and an assault on traditional values. Could a Bolshevik revolution erupt in the United States and ruin the country?

In 1919 the Red Scare caused 29 states to pass laws making it illegal to fly a red flag or any other symbol of Russia's communist revolution; a few years later six female counselors were arrested for displaying such a banner at a summer camp for children. They were sentenced to jail terms ranging from six months to 10 years. In New York, the government prohibited five socialists from taking their seats in the state legislature.

Columnist Walter Lippmann wrote, "The people are shivering in their boots over Bolshevism. They are far more afraid of [Russian leader Vladimir] Lenin than they ever were of the Kaiser." Labor strife made the threat seem all the more real. In January 1919, shipyard workers in Seattle walked off their jobs; when workers in other industries joined them, they paralyzed the city. The mayor and corporate managers labeled the strikers "anarchists," and Seattle newspapers printed bold headlines such as

REDS DIRECTING SEATTLE STRIKE—TO TEST CHANCE FOR REVOLUTION, thus magnifying the claim heard time and again that unions were dangerous and subversive. Although the Seattle strike failed, others followed that same year: theater actors in New York City, textile workers in New England and New Jersey, police in Boston.

Terrorists contributed to the hysteria. In the tumultuous year of 1919, they sent package bombs to the Seattle mayor and to a former senator, whose maid and wife were injured when it exploded. The police intercepted other bombs, 36 in all. On June 2, bombs planted in eight cities exploded; in the most spectacular incident, one ripped through Attorney General **A. Mitchell Palmer**'s house in Washington, D.C.

In September more than 300,000 steel workers walked off their jobs. The strike ended nearly all steel production and crippled the economy. The steel companies, however, fought back. In Gary, Indiana, U.S. Steel imported blacks from the South as strikebreakers and the strike turned violent after federal troops reinforced the local police. Steel workers, without income and unable to feed their families, began to riot. The companies and the government bombarded the public with propaganda about how the strikers wanted to ignite a Bolshevik revolution.

On the heels of the steel strike came a coal strike. It began in November, only to be called off by John L. Lewis, head of the United Mine Workers, after a judge issued an injunction against it. The workers continued to strike on their own, however, returning to the mines in December only after they had won a 14 percent wage increase.

Also in November, Attorney General Palmer—who, Mark LaFlaur points out, used the domestic crisis for political gain—added to the tension when he began arresting radicals, getting 39 of them deported. The next month, the government sent 249 aliens to Russia, including anarchist **Emma Goldman**.

In January 1920, FBI agents acted at the behest of Palmer and raided Communist Party headquarters, as well as homes, pool halls, and other places where Reds and radicals gathered. Both citizens and aliens were arrested without warrants—part of the "gross violations of civil liberties" discussed in LaFlaur's essay on Palmer—as the country committed itself to stamping out communism. Even liberal newspapers supported the attorney general's action.

Americans soon began tiring of the Red Scare, and the reactionary movement had lost its energy by 1921. Nevertheless, it combined with nativism and racism and, in so doing, cloaked attacks on immigrants and blacks with the American flag, making the attacks seem patriotic.

NATIVISM AND RACISM

In California, Democratic and Republican political leaders issued a joint declaration in September 1919 that maintained that the Japanese then settling in the state were more loyal to Japan than to the United States. The following year, the state legislature prohibited Japanese Americans from buying land. Congress responded to the nativist campaign by passing two bills that restricted immigration, one in 1921 and the other in 1924. The legislation set high quotas for people living in northwestern Europe, but reduced to a trickle the immigration permitted from Asia and from eastern and southern Europe—in effect shutting out Italians, Greeks, and Poles, among others, who brought with them "alien" practices and languages.

The trial of anarchists **Nicola Sacco and Bartolomeo Vanzetti** permitted the labeling of radical ideas as un-American, and it reflected a distaste for those immigrants from eastern and southern Europe who did manage legal entry into the United States. Many contemporaries considered the trial unfair for its bias against those who held unpopular views and those with immigrant backgrounds. LaFlaur states that the two men "were executed during a time of increasing political conservatism and a turning inward that marked America's desire for stability in the 1920s."

The Ku Klux Klan found overwhelming support when it shifted its emphasis from intimidating blacks to discriminating against immigrants and Roman Catholics. The Klan's effort to "protect" traditional Protestant values, which seemed threatened by social and cultural transformations, resulted in millions of Americans joining their cause. But more influential than the Ku Klux Klan in the nativist crusade were the Americanization study groups that met in public schools. Immigrants were encouraged to attend these meetings and shed their ethnic cultural practices for American ones. Many immigrants, however, held onto the languages and traditions of their homelands.

Whites attacked another kind of immigrant as well: blacks who were moving from the South into northern cities. African Americans later referred to summer 1919 as "red summer"—not because of communism, but because of bloody race riots. Hundreds of blacks were killed and thousands injured, with widespread property damage in black ghettos.

The riots were one reason why many African Americans supported black nationalist **Marcus Garvey**. When Garvey said "I am the equal of any white man," he spoke for resistance in the face of violence and oppression. His separatism proclaimed that African Americans could stand on their own, independent of white society. He provided, writes James M. Manheim in this volume, "a fundamental message of pride."

SUFFRAGISM AND WOMEN'S RIGHTS

During World War I the women's rights and suffragist movements—once symbolized by the moderate politics of **Carrie Chapman Catt** and the National American Woman Suffrage Association—entered a more militant phase led by **Alice Paul** and her National Woman's Party. "At the core of Paul's convictions," writes Renée Miller, "was the belief that women should be in charge of their own lives." Paul and her supporters picketed the White House and criticized President Wilson as a "hypocrite" for saying the United States was fighting the war to make the world safe for democracy while in practice the country was denying women the right to vote.

Paul's stand got a strong reaction—at one point a mob attacked the picketers—partly because it was seen as disloyal to voice such criticism during the war, but also because her demand for voting rights challenged male power and traditional values. Conservatives argued that women's proper place was in the home acceding to the man's wishes and serving as the family's moral and spiritual protector, and that, by voting, women would develop too much independence and would sully themselves with the tawdry world of politics. Despite this resistance, women won the right to vote when the Nineteenth Amendment was ratified and took effect in 1920.

As much as traditionalists wanted women to stay at home, economics pulled them into the workplace. Between 1900 and 1930 women filled the ranks of waitresses, hair dressers, and other jobs being created in the service sector. The number of women in clerical positions grew tenfold; by 1930 over one million women were working as bookkeepers, cashiers, and office clerks. Socially, more women began to drink, smoke, and experiment sexually—about half of all women lost their virginity before marriage.

MODERNITY VS. TRADITION

The clash between modernity and tradition grabbed national headlines in 1925 with the Scopes, or "Monkey," trial in Dayton, Tennessee. Schoolteacher John Scopes was charged with having violated state law by presenting the theory of evolution in his classroom. Christian fundamentalists called the theory, and Scopes's action, blasphemous. The trial attracted two prominent lawyers, **Clarence Darrow** for the defense and **William Jennings Bryan** for the prosecution. Bryan argued for the literal interpretation of the Bible; the debate over that point garnered the most attention. Darrow lost the case but prevailed in the court of public opinion; as Mark LaFlaur writes, Bryan spent the rest of his life defending "a simpler, fundamentalist view of a bygone world."

Scientific ideas and new academic inquiries also entered the battlefield between traditionalists and modernists. Anthropologists, sociologists, psychologists, biologists, and historians assaulted the prevailing faith in white supremacy. Anthropologist Franz Boas, for example, dismantled the idea that blacks had smaller and inferior brains than whites, and he asserted that environment was more important than heredity in shaping human beings. As new theories of genetics, relativity, and quantum mechanics challenged biblical assumptions, fundamentalist Christians accused universities of undermining religious beliefs.

Prohibition contained much of the same conflict between old and new and revolved around the issue of morality. In January 1920 the Eighteenth Amendment took effect, making it illegal to produce, sell, transport, or import any intoxicating beverage with an alcohol level of 0.5 percent or more. The amendment cut the consumption of liquor by about half, but many people defied it, and illegal taverns, called speakeasies, thrived. By the late 1920s, New York City had 32,000. Gangsters such as **Al Capone** made fortunes through bootlegging in Chicago, while moonshiners produced hard liquor that sometimes caused blindness. Renée Miller says in this volume that Capone "[c]ontributed significantly to the lawless reputation during the Prohibition era."

Many city residents disliked Prohibition, but evangelical Baptists and Methodists enthusiastically supported it. Some Americans saw it as an attack on immigrant culture, for example, the German practice of brewing beer and socializing in beer gardens.

TECHNOLOGY AND THE AUTOMOBILE

Technology provided its own challenge to traditional values, and none greater than the automobile. Car registrations soared from fewer than 500,000 in 1910 to 15 million in 1923; by 1929 there was one car for every six Americans. As **Henry Ford** lowered the price of his Model T to less than $300 in 1926, working-class families could afford to buy cars, particularly as they could use the new installment plans that allowed a customer to put some money down and pay the rest later.

The spread of car ownership caused the federal government to provide money for highway construction and stimulated the oil industry, and it boosted the economy through the jobs created at auto plants and steel and rubber factories. One out of every eight workers was employed in an automobile-related job.

Autos encouraged tourism and also enabled the birth of the suburbs by making commuting to work possible. In addition, the widespread use of automobiles resulted in the first shopping center opening in Kansas City, Missouri, in 1922, the first national road atlas being published by Rand McNally in 1924, the first motel operating in San Luis Obispo, California, in 1925, and the first public parking garage appearing in Detroit, Michigan, in 1929. Automobiles also gave more independence to women who could drive, and they allowed young people to socialize and date away from the watchful eyes of their parents. One judge called the horseless carriages "houses of prostitution on wheels."

POPULAR CULTURE, SPORTS, AND ENTERTAINMENT

"Ev'ry morning, ev'ry evening, ain't we got fun," blared a popular song, and as Americans reveled in 1920s prosperity, they indulged in fads, the result of an increasingly integrated national media that made the United States "smaller." Frederick Lewis Allen observed in *Only Yesterday* that "it was now possible . . . for more people to enjoy the same good show at the same time than in any other land on earth or at any previous time in history." Flagpole sitting, goldfish swallowing, marathon dance contests—all received extensive coverage from newspapers that were now part of large consolidated chains.

A favorite of newspapers and their readers was sports, whose immediacy combined with constantly changing scores fit the format of radio and of those papers being printed with multiple daily editions. Historian Guy Lewis has labeled the 1920s the "Golden Age of Sport." Americans spent 300 percent more on amusements and recreation at the end of the decade than at the beginning. Newspapers heaped enormous coverage on golf—men and women were spending more than $500 million a year on the game—as well as on prizefights, baseball, tennis, and football. In tennis, **Helen Wills** earned national acclaim. Renée Miller writes that Wills "[p]roved to America and the world that women could be more than gentle nurturers. Rising to the status of a sports celebrity . . . [she] dazzled fans, made young men swoon, and, most important, excelled at the game she loved."

University of Illinois football player Red Grange became an icon, as did Notre Dame football coach **Knute Rockne** and his backfield players from 1922 to 1924, called the "Four Horsemen." As Miller writes, Rockne trained the Fighting Irish "to use wits and speed over pure brawn."

In 1921 about 60,000 fans watched **Jack Dempsey** fight Georges Carpentier. Renée Miller states it was "the first million-dollar gate . . . in boxing history." An even larger audience listened on the radio when Dempsey fought Gene Tunney in 1927. At the same time, major league baseball attracted more spectators, with attendance topping 9.5 million in 1924. Fifteen of the 16 clubs made money during the decade, and the New York Yankees chalked up a $3.5 million profit.

Sports revealed the tension between tradition and modernity; for instance, baseball promoted itself as a game firmly rooted in small-town America but built its ever-greater following on urban audiences tied to a faster-paced world. With speed consuming society through rapid communications, action-packed movies, frenetic dances, and jazz music, baseball shifted into high gear. The major leagues used a livelier ball, phased out the spitball—which had given pitchers an advantage—and glorified the heavy hitters. **Babe Ruth** epitomized the new offense, swinging, as Renée Miller writes, "the bat with confidence and power." Ruth set major league records with 29 home runs in 1919, 54 in 1920, and 59 in 1921. In 1927 he set the record of 60 homers in a single season that stood until Roger Maris broke it 34 years later with 61.

Jazz permeated the new era. Having appeared as a music form a few decades earlier, it traveled with African Americans from the South to Chicago. The music evolved into a "swing" sound and became easier to dance to. With his virtuoso performances on cornet, and later trombone, **Louis Armstrong** captivated listeners. Another culturally significant jazz composer from this period was **Duke Ellington**, whose innovations broke with the form of music then being played in New Orleans. Many traditional Americans neither understood jazz nor welcomed it— they labeled it "sinful," and some whites criticized it for its connection to black society.

Radio, as an essay in this book notes, has **Edwin Armstrong** to thank for his invaluable improvements; the medium created a larger audience for music and other forms of entertainment. In Pittsburgh, KDKA signed on the air in 1920 as the country's first licensed station. The claim was made about early radio that "The air is your theater, your college, your newspaper, your library." In 1926, though, the radio library turned commercial when the NBC network began broadcasting advertisements for Dodge cars during a variety show.

Movies emerged as a major attraction in the changing world of consumer entertainment. Pioneering film director **D. W. Griffith**'s *The Birth of a Nation*, released in 1915, was controversial for its racist slurs against African Americans, but as contributing writer James M. Manheim states, it "dwarfed all previous productions, not only in size but also in range of technique and visual imagination."

The stars of silent movies became idols: **Clara Bow**— "whose sex appeal and spirited personality epitomized the liberated female" says Renée Miller—Joan Crawford, Theda Bara, Douglas Fairbanks, and the heartthrob Rudolph Valentino. **Louis B. Mayer** built MGM studios into an industry giant; as Miller notes, he entertained audiences "with extravagant sets and ravishing stars."

The movie theaters themselves offered escape. Many were built as grand palaces, presenting royal treatment to everyday workers and housewives. The Roxy, which opened in New York City in 1926, began each show with the ringing of chimes.

The first sound movies, or "talkies," appeared in 1927, inaugurated by *The Jazz Singer*. By 1930, weekly attendance at movie theaters had reached 100 million, compared to 60 million at churches. Several religious organizations complained about the celluloid assault on traditional morality that had been accompanied by sensational motion picture magazines; pressure from the federal government caused Hollywood studios to stress moral messages in their productions. (In 1930 Hollywood established a production code to govern the content of movies.) The newspapers, airwaves, and movies made famous those who accomplished great feats. The decade's infatuation with the famous—and its hunger for heroes—was evident with **Charles Lindbergh**. His solo flight across the Atlantic enthralled millions and, according to Renée Miller, "marked him as a leader among the decade's daring youth." On Lindbergh's arrival in Washington, D.C., following his return from France, the aviator was greeted with 55,000 congratulatory telegrams.

LITERATURE AND THE DISILLUSIONED

If traditionalists had problems with modernity, intellectuals often did too, though for different reasons. Many prominent writers expressed disillusionment with postwar society and its materialism, though at the same time they often sought wealth and the limelight. **F. Scott Fitzgerald**, says Mark LaFlaur, "was a serious moralist who distrusted the rich as much as he admired wealth and its privileges." **Ernest Hemingway**, LaFlaur states, "depicted the numbed nihilists of the Lost Generation, the 'walking wounded' survivors of the modern age." Sherwood Anderson assaulted traditional small-town values, Eugene O'Neill attacked puritanical restraints on sexual freedom; other writers added their criticism of society, including William Faulkner, e. e. cummings, Theodore Dreiser, Ring Lardner, and **H. L. Mencken**.

Black writers flourished after World War I as they portrayed the search for individual identity among African Americans torn between being black and being American, and as they extolled African culture. **Langston Hughes** became the leading figure of the Harlem Renaissance, a literary and artistic flourishing among blacks in New York City's Harlem district. According to Renée Miller, Hughes wrote an essay in 1926 in which he "eloquently expresses the values of this movement and urges blacks to create from their own experiences rather than assimilate into the dominant white culture."

The Roaring Twenties was a decade in which Americans attempted to return to the days of the Atlantic moat, raising the drawbridge and holding the rest of the world at bay. But the inward turn may well have worsened the conflict between tradition and modernity by magnifying internal differences and external threats. Americans desired stability, but the moat was an illusion in a world soon shaken by an international economic depression and another world war.

—*Neil A. Hamilton*

The Biographies

Edwin Armstrong

1890–1954
Inventor and
Electrical Engineer

Edwin Armstrong was an American inventor and electrical engineer who helped lay the foundation for modern radio. Revolutionizing wireless communication, his innovations profoundly affected popular culture from the 1920s onward.

Edwin Howard Armstrong was born into an affluent Presbyterian family in New York City on December 18, 1890. From childhood, he was fascinated with trains, automobiles, and all types of mechanical devices. Armstrong delved into the study of technology and, at the age of 14, became inspired by the feats of Guglielmo Marconi, an Italian inventor who a few years earlier sent the first wireless telegraph signals across the Atlantic. Armstrong, too, desired the challenges of experimentation and the rewards of discovery. Pursuing his boyhood dreams, he enrolled in Columbia University's School of Engineering in 1909. Three years later he developed one of his most significant inventions—the regenerative, or feedback, circuit, which vastly amplified radio reception and eventually transmitted continuous radio waves. After graduating in June 1913, Armstrong filed for two patents on his regeneration methods and remained at Columbia as an instructor and research assistant.

Courtesy, Armstrong Memorial Research Foundation; Columbia University, New York.

In 1917, during World War I, Armstrong's knowledge of wireless communication brought him to Paris as a captain in the U.S. Army Signal Corps' division of research and inspection. He installed and tested radio sets for airplanes, solved wireless communication problems for the Allies, and attempted to intercept high-frequency wireless messages of the Germans. While setting to work on this last assignment, Armstrong made another important breakthrough with the creation of the superheterodyne circuit, a mechanism used to convert high-frequency signals into audible sounds. Today this circuit provides the basis for 98 percent of radio and television reception. Foreseeing its potential, Armstrong filed for a patent in France in 1918 and the United States in 1919. Both countries immediately recognized his achievements: in 1918, Armstrong received the Institute of Radio Engineers'

Medal of Honor for his first invention of the regenerative circuit, and the following year, he was promoted to major and awarded France's Legion of Honor.

Unfortunately for Armstrong, the regenerative circuit also initiated the most bitter and emotional court case in the history of radio. Beginning in 1914, he began a 20-year legal dispute over the rights to the discovery of regeneration with Lee De Forest, the inventor of the audion. De Forest's audion served primarily as a telephone circuit until Armstrong uncovered its capacity for radio amplification, leading to his development of the regenerative circuit. When Armstrong returned to the United States after the war, the federal court ruled in his favor. De Forest then decided to take the case to the Supreme Court, where he won Armstrong's patent rights to regeneration in 1924 and retained them after a final court battle a decade later. Although the loss humiliated Armstrong, the scientific world still acknowledged him as the true originator.

As radio popularity exploded throughout the 1920s, Armstrong became a millionaire and a valuable resource for Radio Corporation of America (RCA). David Sarnoff, then vice president of RCA, quickly beat out rival companies for rights to Armstrong's 1921 superregeneration circuit, which improved regeneration's amplifying methods by increasing radio signals up to 100,000 times their original power. For $200,000 and 60,000 shares of RCA stock, Armstrong sold superregeneration to RCA and agreed to consult with them before selling future innovations. Superregeneration never achieved the commercial success of Armstrong's other inventions, but it did make him RCA's top private shareholder. In the process of his deal with RCA, Armstrong met Sarnoff's secretary Marion MacInnis, whom he married in 1923 and surprised with a unique wedding present—the first portable radio.

From Morse code signals to commercial broadcasting, radio advances were transforming the lives of Americans. Families began gathering less around the hearth and more around the radio, listening to music, sporting events, political speeches, stock market quotes, and the daily news. Radio connected the public to the outside world and offered instantaneous information and entertainment. Instead of reading yesterday's highlights in the paper, people could hear the current details of **Charles Lindbergh**'s historic transatlantic flight or a play-by-play description of one of **Babe Ruth**'s record-setting home runs. The demand for this new form of entertainment grew rapidly. Eight broadcasting stations were operating at the end of 1921; more than 550 were licensed less than a year later. Armstrong foresaw radios in every home and broadcasting stations in every city. As a result of this widespread growth, radio created a sense of a common popular culture among varied economic classes and regions.

Constantly trying to improve upon wireless communication, Armstrong tried to change the entire way radio worked by replacing amplitude modulation (AM) with frequency modulation (FM). Whereas AM varied the amplitude, or height, of radio waves, FM varied their frequency, or length. Armstrong spent the last half of the 1920s researching this field, and in 1933, he introduced an FM system that eliminated AM's static interference and produced a higher sound quality. In the Depression of the 1930s, though, major corporations like RCA were not prepared to restructure the radio industry. Determined to

promote his findings, Armstrong set up his own FM station, W2XMN, in Alpine, New Jersey, in 1939. Two years later the Franklin Institute awarded him the Franklin Medal—the highest honor in U.S. science and technology.

During World War II, when Armstrong permitted the military to use his FM system royalty-free, the benefits of FM became apparent. Yet, after the war, Armstrong faced more legal disputes over patent rights with RCA and other companies, resulting in financial, health, and marital problems. Driven to suicide, he jumped from the thirteenth floor of his New York City apartment building on January 31, 1954.

An accomplished inventor, Armstrong opened the airways to radio—one of the first modern mass media. In the 1920s the power of sound captured the human imagination as the era's celebrities entered the American home. With the turn of a dial, historic events and live entertainment engaged listeners in both small towns and large cities. Armstrong's genius was often envied and attacked, but even today his inventions continue to dominate the world of communication and popular culture.

Renée Miller

For Further Reading

Erickson, Don V. *Armstrong's Fight for FM Broadcasting: One Man vs Big Business and Bureaucracy.* Tuscaloosa: University of Alabama Press, 1973.

Lessing, Lawrence. *Man of High Fidelity: Edwin Howard Armstrong, a Biography.* New York: Bantam Books, 1969.

Lewis, Tom. *Empire of the Air: The Men Who Made Radio.* New York: Edward Burlingame Books, 1991.

"THE MAN WHO MADE BROADCASTING POSSIBLE" from *The Literary Digest* (1922)

Armstrong revolutionized wireless communication and opened the airways to modern radio. Published in a 1922 issue of The Literary Digest, *"The Man Who Made Broadcasting Possible" discusses his first major discovery of the regenerative circuit and initial court triumph against Lee De Forest, which was overturned in 1924.*

Source: *"The Man Who Made Broadcasting Possible." The Literary Digest, April 29, 1922.*

Every one who has passed beyond the novice stage in radio lore has heard of the "feed-back" system which enables a local battery to contribute energy for the amplification of a signal received at a wireless station. But until very recently no one could be quite sure as to who was to be officially credited with the invention of the method, as the matter had been subject of legal controversies since 1914. Now, however, the courts have handed down a final decision in favor of Mr. Edwin H. Armstrong, whose popular sobriquet, "Feed-back Armstrong," thus receives substantial authentication. The New York *Tribune*, after remarking that the decision of the courts would not only have a far-reaching effect upon all forms of radio communication, but also upon every industry to which an electrical oscillator may be used in the future, makes this explicative comment:

"Stript of its legal and technical verbiage, the decision of the court, which is final, means that no transatlantic telephone conversation can be carried on without the Armstrong principle, nor can any of the big radiophone broadcasting stations now sending music nightly through the ether operate without using the Armstrong patent. Even the modern multiplex forms of wire telegraphy and telephony must use the Armstrong method.

"The decision of the court is very broad. It confirms Armstrong in his patent and recognizes the fact that he

conceived the idea which revolutionized radio and made broadcasting possible as early as January 31, 1912, and in this confirms the sweeping decision previously handed down by Federal Judge Julius M. Mayer."

The decision hinged on a simple diagram, clearly showing the feed-back principle, which young Armstrong drew and had witnessed before a notary in January, 1913, at which time he was a student at Columbia. The few simple lines, which any one versed in the art will readily understand, make record of an invention which professor Michael I. Pupin, of Columbia University, characterizes as "one of the most important inventions, if not the most important, in the wireless art." As quoted in the *Tribune*, Professor Pupin, after referring to Armstrong's invention of the feed-back circuit, says:

"The invention enabled him to make another most important step in wireless telegraphy, and that is the construction of a vacuum tube oscillator. When the feed-back circuit energized by the local source contributes more than a certain definite amount, then the system of circuits becomes an electrical oscillator, oscillating at the perfectly definite period which depends upon the inductance and the capacity of the controlling circuit. By varying either the inductance or the capacity, we can produce any period of oscillation between a few periods per second and many millions per second, and the oscillation once established maintains its pitch indefinitely.

"It is a generator of electrical oscillations, maintaining its pitch with a degree of accuracy never before obtained by any apparatus constructed by man.

"The importance of the feed-back circuit in the reception of wireless signals and the importance of the electrical oscillator, not only in wireless telegraphy but also in wire telegraphy and other departments of applied electricity, can not be overestimated.

"It is admitted by those skilled in the wireless art that the ordinary electromagnetic generator of high power will before long be superseded by the vacuum tube oscillator, which also will bring about more or less reconstruction of wireless transmitting stations. I am particularly pleased that this decision gives the credit for the invention to a man who is a former student of mine and a student of Columbia University, and who has made a deal of his work in the Marcellus Hartley Research Laboratory of Columbia University. It goes without saying that long-distance radio communication and radiophone broadcasting would be impossible without this invention."

In an interview published in the *Evening Post* (New York), the young inventor himself forecasts the future of the new art for which his own work is so largely responsible. What he has to say about prospective receiving outfits has interest for every amateur:

"'The time is not far off,' said Armstrong, 'when the radiophone receiver will be as common as the victrola now is. Not every home will have the radio-phone, of course, but I can predict that every home now having a phonograph will be equipped with wireless.'

"This equipment will consist of none of the outside and unsightly wires, switchboards, and batteries now seen in every radio station, he maintains. The whole radiophone receiver, horn and all, will be no larger than the now ordinary music box, and the current to operate it will be supplied by an electric cord connected with the nearest wall plug.

"'Instead of the aerial wires now used,' he said, 'the radiophone receiver will have a small coil of wire, or a metal rod five or six feet long, something no more conspicuous than the ordinary curtain rod. Outside wires will be unnecessary.'

"Armstrong can do this very thing now. At his home at 1032 Warburton Avenue, Yonkers, he has set up in his room a small receiver, employing no outside wires, which picks up music and other signals from the Westinghouse station at Newark with such strength that they may be heard for half a mile—if the window be opened.

"In every city he believes there will be one or more broadcasting stations, constantly sending out entertainment and information. The finest concerts can be provided by the city, and sent out free to every citizen who cares to turn on his receiver. There could be baseball reports, stock market quotations, weather predictions, the news of the day, educational lectures, even political speeches, sermons on Sunday, grand opera at night—everything, in short, for the complete recreation or edification of the people. That is to say, if political speeches may be said to do either of these things.

"Would anybody read newspapers then?

"Armstrong grinned in non-committal silence."

EDWIN ARMSTRONG AND MARION MACINNIS (1923)

In the 1920s, radio transformed the lives of Americans by offering instantaneous communication and entertainment. A leader in wireless technology, Armstrong constantly sought ways to advance this medium. In this 1923 honeymoon shot at Palm Beach, Armstrong and wife Marion MacInnis display his wedding present to her of the first portable radio.

Source: Courtesy, Armstrong Memorial Research Foundation; Columbia University, New York.

Although this speech was delivered on behalf of the Institute of Radio Engineers in 1934, it demonstrates how the scientific community backed Armstrong despite the Supreme Court's 1924 decision to grant Lee De Forest the patent rights to regeneration. Here, the Institute's President C. M. Jansky refuses to take back Armstrong's award for his first invention of regeneration.

Source: Lewis, Tom. *Empire of the Air: The Men Who Made Radio.* New York: Edward Burlingame Books, 1991.

Speech by the Institute of Radio Engineers (1934)

Sixteen years ago you received from the Institute of Radio Engineers its Medal of Honor in recognition of your outstanding contributions to the radio art. Because of a chain of circumstances well known to many of us, you came to this convention with the intention of returning this medal to us.

The impulse which prompted this decision on your part clearly demonstrates how deeply you feel your obligations to the Institute. The Board of Directors has been informed by me of your views to which it has given full and complete consideration.

Major Armstrong, by unanimous opinion of the members of the Board, I have been directed to say to you

First: That it is their belief that the Medal of Honor of the Institute was awarded to you by the Board with a citation of substantially the following import; namely,

"That the Medal of Honor be awarded Edwin Howard Armstrong for his engineering and scientific achievements in relation to regeneration and the generation of oscillations by vacuum tubes,"

Second: That the present Board of Directors, with full consideration of the great value and outstanding quality of the original scientific work of yourself and of the present high esteem and repute in which you are held by the membership of the Institute and themselves, hereby strongly reaffirms the sense of what it believes to have been the original citation.

Louis Armstrong

One of the most innovative figures in jazz, Louis Armstrong inspired musical trends and played the trumpet with peerless talent.

Armstrong claimed that his birthday was July 4, 1900, but he actually was born on August 4, 1901, in New Orleans, Louisiana. He grew up in one of its poorest sections, which nevertheless created some of its richest sounds: music emanated from picnics, dances, parades, funerals, saloons, brothels, and riverboats. On New Year's Eve, at age 12, he participated in the street festivities by shooting blanks from his stepfather's shotgun; Armstrong was arrested and spent a year and a half at the Colored Waif's Home for Boys, a reform school where he received his first formal lessons in music. Learning to play the snare drum, alto horn, bugle, and cornet, he became the home's bandleader. After his release, his talents further progressed under the guidance of jazz great Joe "King" Oliver, who gave him cornet lessons and eventually sent him out on local gigs. When Oliver left for Chicago in 1918, Armstrong replaced him as cornetist in the Kid Ory Band, the best-known jazz ensemble in New Orleans.

After World War I, many Southern blacks migrated to the North in search of social and economic opportunities, among them many jazz musicians. Armstrong became part of this cultural movement—described by historians as the Great Migration. In 1922, he joined Oliver's Creole Jazz Band and settled in Chicago's South Side, which hosted a growing community of African-American artists and entrepreneurs. The Chicago nightclub scene thrived in these days, and the Creole Jazz Band entertained at the city's most popular venues. Playing second cornet, Armstrong attracted the greatest attention during his duets with Oliver, in which they created sophisticated breaks that seemed to harmonize spontaneously. Armstrong made his recording debut with Oliver's band in 1923, and within a year, he moved to New York and contributed to more than 50 records with blues vocalists

Hulton/Archive.

Bessie Smith and Ma Rainey, and saxophonist Sidney Bechet. Although labeled "race records" and marketed only to black customers, these blues and jazz tunes rapidly gained a racially diverse audience. In this period, jazz began its transition from a novelty genre to a genuine art form, and few played as significant a role in this evolution as did Armstrong.

By the 1920s, phonograph records and radio enabled musicians to reach a significantly larger number and wider range of listeners than ever before. After 14 months as sideman with the Fletcher Henderson Band in New York, Armstrong returned to Chicago in 1925 to make a series of recordings as the leader of the Hot Five. The group highlighted their individual talents on the piano, trombone, clarinet, banjo, and the trumpet. Armstrong's solos on the trumpet, an instrument he had recently switched to from the cornet, dumbfounded the music world with their unprecedented virtuosity and creativity. Never before had instrumental solos overpowered the collective sound of the ensemble. Departing from the traditional New Orleans musical format, Armstrong forged the future of jazz.

Armstrong also introduced vocals known as scatting or scat singing, a blend of nonsense syllables and guttural sounds sung in place of words. Scatting greatly caught on after his first Hot Five release, "Heebie Jeebies," became a hit in 1926. In his everyday discourse, Armstrong was equally inventive and coined many slang phrases. He addressed people as "Pops," "Cat," and "Daddy" and commanded his band to "swing it" and "play that thing." Romanian poet Tristan Tzara once remarked that the poetry of Armstrong's "personal language . . . touches the sensitivity of individuals from all four corners of the world."

The Hot Five later increased to the Hot Seven, adding the drums and tuba to their repertoire of sounds. Between 1925 and 1928, Armstrong exhibited the depth of his originality on the Hot Five and Hot Seven records "Savoy

Blues," "Potato Head Blues," and "West End Blues." The last in particular remains a landmark in jazz.

Armstrong entered another stage in his career in 1929, when he relocated to New York and performed at the chic Harlem nightclub Connie's Inn with the Carroll Dickerson Orchestra. He appeared on Broadway that year in the show *Hot Chocolates* and produced the popular songs "Ain't Misbehavin" and "Black and Blue." He soon began making films and marketing his songs to mainstream audiences. Although jazz purists criticized this transition, Armstrong's ability to merge pop and jazz helped influence the Swing era of the mid-1930s to early 1940s. In 1947, a revival of traditional New Orleans jazz persuaded Armstrong to form the All-Stars band. The All-Stars toured the United States, Europe, Australia, the Far East, and Africa; as a result, Armstrong was dubbed the "Ambassador of Jazz." He recorded his last hit, "What a Wonderful World," in 1968 and made his last famous film *Hello, Dolly!* in 1969. On June 6, 1971, he died at his home in New York.

With the growth of technology in the 1920s and increasing opportunities for minority performers, music evolved from a regional dialect to a universal language. Armstrong filled the nightclubs of Chicago and New York as well as the homes of America and Europe. His authentic voice displayed musical genius and invented a new vocabulary for modern jazz.

Renée Miller

For Further Reading

Armstrong, Louis. *Satchmo: My Life in New Orleans.* 1954. Reprint, Introduction by Dan Morgenstern. New York: Da Capo Press, 1986.

Bergreen, Laurence. *Louis Armstrong: An Extravagant Life.* New York: Broadway Books, 1997.

Jones, Max, and John Chilton. *Louis: The Louis Armstrong Story, 1900–1971.* Boston: Little, Brown, 1971.

LETTER FROM LOUIS ARMSTRONG TO ISADORE BARBARIN (1922)

The traditions of jazz are tied to the rituals of life in New Orleans. Feeling homesick after moving to Chicago in 1922, Armstrong reminisces about the New Orleans brass bands and funeral parades in this letter to friend and musician Isadore Barbarin.

Source: Giddins, Gary. *Satchmo.* New York: Doubleday, 1988.

Mr Barbarin.
Dear Friend.

Yours of this afternoon has been received. And I take great pleasure in letting you know that I was glad to hear from you. I'm well as usual and also doing fine as usual. Hoping you and your family are well. Pops I just had started to wondering what was the matter with you. You takin' so long to answer: Well I know just how it is when a fellow is playing with a red hot brass band and they have all the work he don't have time to be bothered with writing no letters.

Well I understand that Pops. I heard all about you all having all those funerals down there. I'm sorry that I ain't down there to make some of them with you all. The boys give me H. . . all the time because [I'm] forever talking about the Brass Band and how I used to like to make those parades. They say I don't see how a man can be crazy about those hard parades. I told them that they don't go hard with you when you are playing with a good band. Joe Oliver is here in my room now and he sends you his best regards. Also all the boys. I heard the Celestin lost his sister. Well that's too bad. I feel sorry for the poor fellow. I will tell Paul what you said when I see him again. The next time you meet Nenest ask him what is the matter with him he don't answer my letter. Ask him [if] he needs any writing paper-stamps to let me know at once and I'll send him some at once. . Ha. . Ha. . Well Old pal I tell you the news some other time. I have to go to work now. Good knight.,

All from Louis Armstrong.
459 East 31 St. Chicago, Ill.

"HEEBIE JEEBIES" (1926)

Say, I've got the heebies,
I mean the jeebies
Talking about
The dance, the heebie jeebies,
Do, because they're boys,
Because it pleases me to be joy!

Say, don't you know it?
You don't know how, don't be blue
Someone will teach you;
Come on, and do that dance,
They call the heebie jeebies dance,
Yes, ma'am,
Papa's got the heebie jeebies dance!

Skatting:

Say, come on, now, and do that dance,
They call the heebie jeebies dance,
Sweet mama!
Papa's go to do the heebie jeebies dance!

Spoken:
Wooh! Got the heebie jeebies!
Whatcha doin' with the heebies?
I just have to have the heebies!

The Hot Five's recording of "Heebie Jeebies," by Boyd Atkins, popularized scatting in 1926. A story circulated that when Armstrong dropped his lyric sheet while recording, he replaced the words with nonsense syllables and guttural sounds. Armstrong later told a jazz scholar that he had been scat singing since his street quartet days in New Orleans. With this old trick, Armstrong started a new trend.

Source: Heptune Jazz and Blues Lyrics Page. *www.heptune.com /heebieje.html* (August 28, 2001). Reprinted with permission from Universal MCA Music Publishing.

LOUIS ARMSTRONG AND THE CARROLL DICKERSON ORCHESTRA (1929)

Harlem was a cultural center for art and entertainment in the 1920s, and Armstrong was a headliner at the city's hottest nightspots. This photo of Armstrong (standing center) and the Carroll Dickerson Orchestra commemorates their 1929 appearance at Connie's Inn, a popular venue in Harlem.

Source: From the collections of the Louisiana State Museum.

Josephine Baker

1906–1975

Expatriate African-American Performer

Josephine Baker was an African-American performer whose vivacious and sensual dancing electrified the French in the 1920s.

Baker was born Freda J. McDonald in a St. Louis, Illinois, slum on June 3, 1906. Educated only up to the fourth grade, she relied on her street savvy to counter her harsh poverty. Baker experienced the daily injustice of racism and witnessed widespread persecution of African Americans during the East St. Louis Race Riot of 1917, which left 40 blacks dead and thousands homeless. At 13, she left home and married Willie Wells. Their marriage dissolved within a few weeks, and Baker supported herself as a waitress and a street entertainer in the Jones Family Band. She soon left St. Louis to travel with a performance troupe called the Dixie Steppers on the Theatre Owners Booking Association (TOBA) circuit. She worked as a dresser for the troupe star Clara Smith, but Baker desired the limelight for herself.

In Philadelphia in 1921, Baker went from dresser to dancer with the Dixie Steppers and entered another short marriage, this time to William H. Baker, whose name she retained throughout her career. By 1923, her persistence led to a part in a road tour of Noble Sissle and Eubie Blake's musical *Shuffle Along*. She drew notice as a funny chorus girl who improvised exaggerated movements and crossed her eyes at the climax in the music. Baker applied these same comic techniques the next year on Broadway in her second Sissle and Blake production *Chocolate Dandies*; she primarily played a vagabond in bright cotton frocks, clown shoes, and blackface makeup. Such caricatures of the minstrel tradition reinforced racial stereotypes, but at the same time they offered black performers a chance to succeed in a racist America that provided limited opportunities for African Americans.

On September 15, 1925, Baker set sail for France with more than 20 other black dancers, musicians, and singers recruited by Caroline Dudley for a new Parisian show. Two weeks later, she mesmerized the audience at the opening

©*Bettmann/Corbis.*

night of *La Revue Nègre* at the Théâtre des Champs-Élysées. Baker made her final entrance seminude in a skirt of feathers, carried upside down while balancing on the shoulders of dance partner Joe Alex. This began their provocative performance "Danse Sauvage." Baker shimmied and gyrated to the intense cadence of drums and blues; she thrilled some, offended others, and surprised everyone. Her uninhibited dance—which provoked wild cheers and hisses as the curtain closed—created a box-office sensation. Baker quickly became one of the most celebrated entertainers in France and the star of the Folies-Bergère, where the next year she again astonished audiences in *La Folie du Jour* by dancing in only a girdle adorned with bananas.

Baker's performances catered to French notions of black women's sexuality; she was perceived as "primitive," exotic, and carnal. Critics and spectators compared her to a snake, giraffe, and kangaroo as well as glorified her as an "ebony statue" and a "black Venus." Of these mythical depictions, Baker remarked that "the white imagination sure is something when it comes to blacks." Baker's free and festive spirit appealed to Parisians who prided themselves on their hedonistic society; in contrast, the French viewed American culture as puritanical and oppressive. Although France harbored its own racial prejudices that contributed to Baker's popularity, America blatantly discriminated on the basis of race and overlooked some of its finest talent and emerging artistic traditions. Like many black artists of the 1920s, Baker discovered new freedoms and immense fame in Paris where African-American jazz music and dance as well as African sculpture were highly valued and deemed fashionable.

Baker especially realized the limits of her career in America after an unfavorable reception in the New York *Ziegfeld Follies* in 1936. The next year Baker became an official citizen of France, where she was a respected dancer, singer, and actor. During World War II, Baker worked as a nurse for the Red Cross, a spy for the French Resistance, and an entertainer with the Free French forces for the troops in North Africa and the Middle East. Her wartime contributions earned her the Croix de Guerre, the Legion of Honor, and the Rosette of the Résistance. From 1954 to 1965, she adopted 12 children of different nationalities—known as her "Rainbow Tribe." An advocate of universal brotherhood, she also participated in several civil rights marches in the United States during the 1960s. Baker died in Paris on April 12, 1975—50 years after her arrival in France and four days after the opening of her last show, *Joséphine*.

When Baker moved from America to France, she was transformed from a comedic chorus girl into a sex symbol. She dared to wear immodest costumes, perform risqué numbers, and become part of the Paris vogue. Although some critics accused her of corrupting their French traditions and classic civilization, others praised Baker for revitalizing their dormant culture. Baker achieved stardom in the 1920s by enchanting audiences with exotic beauty and frenetic energy, lifting barriers for black female entertainers to come.

Renée Miller

For Further Reading

Baker, Jean-Claude, and Chris Chase. *Josephine: The Hungry Heart.* New York: Random House, 1993.

Haney, Lynn. *Naked at the Feast: A Biography of Josephine Baker.* New York: Dodd, Mead, 1981.

Rose, Phyllis. *Jazz Cleopatra: Josephine Baker in Her Time.* New York: Vintage Books, 1991.

JOSEPHINE BAKER IN *CHOCOLATE DANDIES* (1924)

Following the Civil War, blackface minstrel shows, which reinforced existing stereotypes of African Americans, were among the limited opportunities for gifted black performers. In the 1924 musical Chocolate Dandies, *Josephine Baker first caught the attention of audiences for her comedic talents, rather than for her sexuality. One of her favorite ways to amuse was to cross her eyes at the climax in the music, which was one of her early trademark expressions.*

Source: Billy Rose Theater Collection, The New York Public Library for the Performing Arts, Astor, Lenox and Tilden Foundations.

POSTER FOR *LA REVUE NÈGRE* (1925)

"THE NEGRO DANCE: UNDER EUROPEAN EYES" by André Levinson (1927) [EXCERPT]

. . . Negro dancing may suggest at once any one of a variety of quite separate problems. The student of aesthetics may be interested in defining the indigenous principles of the dance and of judging its intrinsic artistic value. The moralist, on the other hand, in his search for an explanation of our times, may be more concerned with the effect of this black virus upon European civilization. The ethnologist, comparing the aborigines of the Ivory Coast and the cotton pickers of the plantations of Louisiana, may find the Negro dance of primary importance as an organic phenomenon. While, as it is found in our present-day dance halls, it may appear as a symptom of an epidemic contagion of society which should concern the pathologist. It is, therefore, necessary to set down in the beginning that this article is merely attempting to present a European interpretation of the Negro dance as it has lately been demonstrated by the colored artists of the "Revue Negre" at the Champs Elysées. . .

Josephine Baker, who was responsible for the Charleston rage in Paris, is an extraordinary creature of simian suppleness—a sinuous idol that enslaves and incites mankind. Thanks to her carnal magnificence and her impulsive vehemence, her unashamed exhibition comes close to pathos. As I wrote, when she first appeared at the Champs Elysées, there seemed to emanate from her violently shuddering body, her bold dislocations, her springing movements, a gushing stream of rhythm. It was she who led the spellbound drummer and the fascinated saxophonist in the harsh rhythm of the "blues." It was as though the jazz, catching on the wing the vibrations of this mad body, were interpreting, word by word, its fantastic monologue. This music is born from the dance, and what a dance! The gyrations of this cynical yet merry mountebank, the good-natured grin on her large mouth, suddenly give way to visions from which good humor is entirely absent. In the short *pas de deux* of the savages, which came as the finale of the "Revue Nègre", there was a wild splendor and magnificent animality. Certain of Miss Baker's poses, back arched, haunches protruding, arms entwined and uplifted in a phallic symbol, had the compelling potency of the finest examples of Negro sculpture. The plastic sense of a race of sculptors came to life and the frenzy of the African Eros swept over the audience. It was no longer a grotesque dancing girl that stood before them, but the black Venus that haunted Baudelaire. The dancer's personality had transcended the character of her dance. . . .

The road is long indeed from the valley of the Niger to the lights of Broadway; from the primeval forest to Upton Sinclair's jungle in Chicago. The savage has turned into a city rowdy. The ceremonial, sacred character of the dance ritual has entirely evaporated from what has become a mere divertissement, offered to the white idlers of the world's capitals. The grandeur of those ancient observances dedicated to Priape and Hecate, pure rhythmic orgies induced by a panic terror of the demons who inhabit the night; those symbolic ceremonies with dancers dressed in stags' antlers or flamingos' claws, are only the symbols of a gay and remunerative extravaganza.

Although Josephine Baker, by her extraordinary and disturbing genius, is able with one bound to join her savage forefathers and with another to go back to our common animal ancestors, the Negro dancers of today are no longer beings possessed by devils, but merely professionals. The really devil-ridden today are those European idlers who passively give themselves up to an enjoyment of the Negro dance without setting up any barriers to its atavistic, demoralizing appeal.

"Topic of the Day" Dedication by Josephine Baker (1927)

Then the rage was in New York of colored people
Monsieur Siegfied of Ziegfied Follies said its getting
darker and darker on old broadway"
Since the La Revue Nagri "came to Gai Paree,
I'll say its geting darker and darker in Paris.
In a little while it shall be so dark untill one shall
light a match then light another to see if the first
is lit are not.
As the old saying is I may be a dark horse but you "will
never be a black mare,
By the way we can't forget the "charleston" that mad
dance
A friend ask me to pay them a visite,
But when I went to there home, people were in front of
the house, and dogs were barking, I dident know what
to think
but on the second thought I decided to inter,
On intering the cat was hanging on the chandlier the
birds cage
turned over, dishes were broken and the two people
looked as
if a terrible storm had happened, of course with this
sight
I did know again what to do, go in or go out, but by me
being
so curious I intered, When they saw me, both stopped
the wife saying witch is right, Josephine this way or that

then the husband said, no it isn't I tell you this the
right way, isn't it Josephine!? As a matter of fact I
dident
know what to say, so I ask if they would try to cool down
a bit, I would try to see, all this time I dident know what
they
Were talking about, on this idear they stopped, told me
they were
dancing the Charleston, and to make peace in the family
I said both were right.
Its not safe to walk in the streets now,
When the driver says Hey "Hey" to make his horse
stop, the people think he means "Charleston" and
start Dancings, dont stop untill each fall out and
faint.

The new way of meeting a friend

Marcel   Hey "Hey"
Jocky.   Charleston
Marcel,   Did you hear the scandle that happened
        Yesterday?
Jock – –   Why no, What happened?
Marcel   My fathers secretary and foreman
        Was caught in the office
Jocky   doing what??????????
Marcel   The Charleston of course idiot."

Josephine Baker

A craze for black music, art, and dance swept through Paris in the 1920s. In this hand-written preface to Paul Colin's 1927 portfolio Le Tumulte Noir, *Baker humorously describes the French and their fascination with the Charleston. She jokes that "that mad dance" has invaded the home, the streets, and even the office. Note: Language and spelling from original document has been retained.*

Source: *Paul, Colin. Josephine Baker and La Revue Negre: Paul Colin's Lithographs of Le Tumulte Noir in Paris, 1927.* New York: Harry N. Abrams, 1998.

Autobiographical Prose Poem by Josephine Baker (1931)

At the age of eight I was already working to calm the
    hunger of my family.
I have suffered: hunger, cold—
I have a family
They said I was homely
That I danced like an ape
Then I was less homely—Cosmetics
I was hooted
Then I was applauded—The crowd
I continued to dance—I loved jazz
I continued to sing—I loved sadness; my soul is sick
I had an opportunity—Destiny
I had a mascot—a panther—Ancestral superstition—
I made a tour of the world—In third class and in Pullman
I am moral
They said I was the reverse
I do not smoke—I have white teeth
I do not drink—I am an American
I have a religion
I adore children
I love flowers
I aid the poor—I have suffered much
I love the animals—they are the sincerest
I sing and dance still—Perseverance
I earn much money—I do not love money
I save my money—for the time when I am no longer an
    attraction.

In 1931, a collection of Baker's press clippings and autographs was published in Joséphine Baker vue par la presse francaise. *This autobiographical prose poem written by Baker was included in the book and describes her transformation from an awkward chorus girl to a controversial sex symbol.*

Source: *Rose, Phyllis. Jazz Cleopatra: Josephine Baker in Her Time.* New York: Doubleday, 1989.

Roger Nash Baldwin

Best remembered as the founder of the American Civil Liberties Union (ACLU), Roger Nash Baldwin exemplified the spirit of activism that arose after World War I in response to the restrictions on individual liberty and the general conservatism of the time. As director of the ACLU through the 1920s and 1930s, Baldwin stood at the center of several key court cases that laid the groundwork for a renewed emphasis on civil rights and freedom of expression in the United States.

Baldwin was born on January 21, 1884, in Wellesley, Massachusetts, into a wealthy family. His parents were members of the free-thinking Unitarian church. A sensitive youth, he was known as a nonconformist in school and developed a general sympathy for those less fortunate than himself. Baldwin attended Harvard University, studying social sciences and earning a bachelor's degree in 1904 and a master's degree in 1905. In 1906, he moved to St. Louis and became noted as a social worker and educator and was influenced by Progressive reforms. But an important second phase of his education began in 1909 when he met the lecturer **Emma Goldman** and began to spend time with political reformers and radicals. Political idealism and civil liberties first became linked in his mind in 1912 when St. Louis police blocked a speech by birth control advocate **Margaret Sanger**.

The imminent entry of the United States into World War I drew Baldwin back to the East Coast in 1917. He joined a pacifist group called the American Union Against Militarism (AUAM) as its secretary and worked in a division of the group, the National Civil Liberties Bureau (NCLB), that helped to defend draft resisters and peace activists against government prosecution. As U.S. involvement in the war deepened, the government sharply restricted dissent. The Espionage Act of 1917, among other things, prescribed a 20-year prison term and a $10,000 fine for the vague offense of interfering with the recruitment of troops, and the Sedition Act of 1918 severely restricted criticism of the government itself. Baldwin's office broadened its mission to include the protection of basic freedoms. Drafted for military service in

©Bettmann/Corbis.

1918, Baldwin put his beliefs on the line and registered as a conscientious objector, for which he was sentenced to a year in prison (but served only nine months). He became further radicalized after his release by a four-month trek around the Midwest, during which he took various blue-collar jobs and became supportive of labor unions' efforts to improve the quality of life of ordinary workers. After the war, Baldwin took the lead in reorganizing the NCLB into the American Civil Liberties Union (ACLU). In 1920, at the height of the anticommunist "Red Scare," marked by the fear that the Bolshevik Revolution would spread communism from Russia to the United States, Baldwin was named the executive director of the ACLU.

Although the ACLU often faced accusations of being anti-American in its early years, the group nevertheless helped to chip away at some of the speech restrictions that the government had established during and after the war. Long sympathetic to the struggles of African Americans, Baldwin often found common cause with the young National Association for the Advancement of Colored People (NAACP) in the 1920s. Under Baldwin's directorship, the ACLU also worked on behalf of labor unions and had some success in restricting the powers of the notorious company police forces that attempted to thwart union organizing drives. The ACLU resisted the censorship of material in the arts considered obscene by the government with a long struggle to overturn a ban (eventually lifted in 1933) on the importation of James Joyce's novel *Ulysses*.

The ACLU first etched itself on a broad public consciousness, however, with its 1925 defense of Tennessee schoolteacher John T. Scopes in the so-called "Monkey Trial." Scopes was charged with teaching the theory of evolution, then illegal under Tennessee law. Although the ACLU and its lawyer **Clarence Darrow** were defeated by prosecutor **William Jennings Bryan**, the group made great advances in the court of public opinion. Another high-profile trial in which Baldwin became personally involved was that of the anarchists **Nicola Sacco and Bartolomeo Vanzetti**, who were executed for murder in 1927 even though many believed they were falsely accused.

Baldwin's own politics tended toward radicalism; he traveled twice to the Soviet Union in the late 1920s and early 1930s and flirted with communism until disillusioned by Russian cooperation with Hitler in 1940. Yet his devotion to the principle of freedom of expression was complete, and he felt no guilt about causing dismay among his allies on the left by using the ACLU's resources to defend right-wing individuals and organizations whose free-speech rights were threatened. The ACLU defended the racist Ku Klux Klan and later antagonized Jewish supporters by working to permit the distribution of anti-Semitic pamphlets by the industrialist **Henry Ford**. Baldwin believed that open discussion was the best way to root out noxious ideas. (At the same time, however, in his book *Liberty Under the Soviets* [1927] he accepted the suppression of free speech to further the revolution, and in 1940 he removed activist Elizabeth Gurley Flynn from the ACLU board because of her communist beliefs.)

Baldwin remained in the ACLU directorship until the end of 1949. In later life he worked to spread the concept of civil liberties protections internationally; he remained active until his death on August 26, 1981, at the age of 97.

In an attempt to combat the restrictions arising out of the anticommunist Red Scare and the remnants of a wartime mentality, Baldwin organized the ACLU, a body whose name became synonymous with the protection of civil rights. With a crusading spirit forged at a time when basic American liberties came under unprecedented attack, Baldwin helped to make civil liberties a basic feature of the social and political landscape of the United States.

James M. Manheim

For Further Reading

Cottrell, Robert. *Roger Nash Baldwin and the American Civil Liberties Union.* New York: Columbia University Press, 2001.

Lamson, Peggy. *Roger Baldwin: Founder of the American Civil Liberties Union.* Boston: Houghton Mifflin, 1976.

Macdonald, Dwight. "The Defense of Everybody." *New Yorker*, July 11, 1953, pp. 31ff, and July 18, 1953, pp. 29ff.

"CONSCIENCE AT THE BAR" by Roger Nash Baldwin (November 9, 1918) [EXCERPT]

Mr. Baldwin's Statement

I am before you as a deliberate violator of the draft act. On October 9, when ordered to take a physical examination, I notified my local board that I declined to do so, and instead presented myself to the United States district attorney for prosecution. I submit herewith for the record a copy of the letter of explanation which I addressed to him at the time. . . .

The compelling motive for refusing to comply with the draft act is my uncompromising opposition to the principle of conscription of life by the state for any purpose whatever, in time of war or peace. I not only refuse to obey the present conscription law, but I would in future refuse to obey any similar statute which attempts to direct my choice of service and ideals. I regard the principle of conscription of life as a flat contradiction of all our cherished ideals of individual freedom, democratic liberty, and Christian teaching.

I am the more opposed to the present act, because it is for the purpose of conducting war. . . . I am opposed to this and all other wars. I do not believe in the use of physical force as a method of achieving any end, however good.

The district attorney calls your attention, your Honor, to the inconsistency in my statement to him that I would under extreme emergencies as a matter of protecting the life of any person use physical force. I don't think there is an argument that can be used in support of the wholesale organization of men who achieve political purposes in nationalistic or domestic war. I could accept no service therefore under the present act, regardless of its character.

Holding such profound convictions I determined, while the new act was pending, that it would be more

honest to make my stand clear at the start and therefore concluded not even to register, but to present myself for prosecution. I therefore resigned my position as director of the National Civil Liberties Bureau to be free to follow that personal course of action. But on the day my resignation took effect (August 31) agents of the Department of Justice began an examination of the affairs of that organization, and I was constrained to withdraw my resignation and register in order to stand by the work at a critical moment. With that obligation discharged, I resigned, and took the next occasion, the physical examination, to make my stand clear.

I realize to some this refusal may seem a piece of wilful defiance. It might well be argued that any man holding my views might have avoided the issue, by obeying the law either on the chance of being rejected on physical grounds, or on the chance of the war stopping before a call to service. I answer that I am not seeking to evade the draft; that I scorn evasion, compromise and gambling with moral issues.

It may further be argued that the War Department's liberal provision for agricultural service on furlough for conscientious objectors would be open to me if I obey the law and go to camp, and that there can be no moral objection to farming, even in time of war. I answer first, that I am opposed to any service under conscription, regardless of whether that service is in itself morally objectionable; and second, that, even if that were not the case, and I were opposed only to war, I can make no moral distinction between the various services which assist in prosecuting the war—whether rendered in the trenches, in the purchase of bonds or thrift stamps at home or in raising farm products under the lash of the draft act. All serve the same end—war. Of course all of

Baldwin's statement delivered during his trial for disobeying the new Selective Service Act, on November 9, 1918.

Source: Baldwin, Roger. "Conscience at the Bar." *The Survey,* November 9, 1918.

us render involuntary assistance to the war in the processes of our daily living. I refer only to those direct services undertaken by choice.

I am fully aware that my position is extreme, that it is shared by comparatively few, and that in the present climate it is regarded either as unwarranted egotism or a species of feeblemindedness. . . .

When the war came to America, it was an immediate challenge to me to help protect those ideals of liberty which seemed to me not only the basis of the radical economic view, but of the radical political view of the founders of this republic, and of the whole medieval struggle for religious freedom. Before the war was declared, I severed all my connections in St. Louis, and offered my services to the American Union Against Militarism to help fight conscription. Later that work developed into the National Civil Liberties Bureau, organized to help maintain the rights of free speech and free press, and the Anglo-Saxon tradition of liberty of conscience, through liberal provisions for conscientious objectors. This work has been backed by both pro-war liberals and so-called pacifists. It is not anti-war in any sense. It seemed to me the one avenue of service open to me, consistent with my views, consistent with the country's best interest, and with the preservation of the radical minority for the struggle after the war.

Even if I were not a believer in radical theories and movements, I would justify the work I have done on the ground of American ideals and traditions alone—as do many of those who have been associated with me. They have stood for those enduring principles which the revolutionary demands of war have temporarily set aside. We have stood against hysteria, mob violence, unwarranted prosecution, the sinister use of patriotism to cover attacks on radical and labor movements, and for the unabridged right of a fair trial under the statutes. We have tried to keep open those channels of expression which stand for the kind of world order for which the President is battling today against the tories and militarists.

Now comes the government to take me from that service and to demand of me a service I cannot in conscience undertake. I refuse it simply for my own peace of mind and spirit, for the satisfaction of that inner demand more compelling than any consideration of punishment or the sacrifice of friendship and reputation.

I seek no martyrdom, no publicity. I merely meet as squarely as I can the moral issue before me, regardless of consequences. . . .

I am not complaining for myself or others. I am merely advising the court that I understand full well the penalty of my heresy, and am prepared to pay it. The conflict with conscription is irreconcilable. Even the liberalism of the President and the secretary of war in dealing with objectors leads those of us who are

"absolutists" to a punishment longer and severer than that of desperate criminals.

But I believe most of us are prepared even to die for our faith, just as our brothers in France are dying for theirs. To them we are comrades in spirit—we understand one another's motives, though our methods are wide apart. We both share deeply the common experience of living up to the truth as we see it, whatever the price.

Though at the moment I am of a tiny minority, I feel myself just one protest in a great revolt surging up from among the people—the struggle of the masses against the rule of the world by the few—profoundly intensified by the war. It is a struggle against the political state itself, against exploitation, militarism, imperialism, authority in all forms. It is a struggle to break in full force only after the war. Russia already stands in the vanguard, beset by her enemies in the camps of both belligerents; the Central empires break asunder from within; the labor movement gathers revolutionary force in Britain, and in our own country the Nonpartisan league, radical labor and the Socialist party hold the germs of a new social order. Their protest is my protest. Mine is a personal protest at a particular law, but it is backed by all the aspirations and ideals of the struggle for a world freed of our manifold slaveries and tyrannies.

I ask the court for no favor. I could do no other than what I have done, whatever the court's decree. I have no bitterness or hate in my heart for any man. Whatever the penalty, I shall endure it, firm in the faith that whatever befalls me, the principles in which I believe will bring forth out of this misery and chaos a world of brotherhood, harmony and freedom for each to live the truth as he sees it.

I hope your Honor will not think that I have taken this occasion to make a speech for the sake of making a speech. I have read you what I have written, in order that the future record for myself—my friends—may be perfectly clear, and in order to clear up some of the matters to which the district attorney called your attention. I know that it is pretty nigh hopeless in times of war and hysteria to get across to any substantial body of people the view of an out-and-out heretic like myself. I know that so far as my principles are concerned, they seem to be utterly impractical—mere moonshine. They are not the views that work in the world today. I fully realize that. But I fully believe that they are the views which are going to guide in the future.

Having arrived at that point of mind in which those views mean the dearest things in life to me, I cannot consistently, with self-respect, do other than I have, namely, to deliberately violate this act, which seems to me to be a denial of everything which ideally and in practice I hold sacred.

REUNION AT CALDWELL PENITENTIARY (1923)

"AMERICAN CIVIL LIBERTIES UNION" from *Reds in America* (1924) [EXCERPT]

. . .The American Civil Liberties Union is definitely linked with Communism through the system of interlocking directorates, so successfully used by the Communist party of America in penetrating into every possible organization with a view to getting control so that when the time comes for the great general strike which, they believe and hope, will lead to the overthrow of the United States Government by violence, they will already have these bodies definitely aligned with them. The party has several members in the American Civil Liberties Union and the constant activities of that body are proving of great moral and financial benefit to the Communists. . . .

Complaint has frequently been made that the American Civil Liberties Union is never exercised about predicaments in which poor men, who are not radicals, find themselves. Their interests and activities are always, without exception, in behalf of lawbreakers of the radical criminal class. A survey of the National Committee of this Union shows at once that practically the entire membership is made up of radicals of one stripe or another. They solicit funds from every class, exactly as do the Communists, to be devoted to the defence or other assistance of criminals, never to aid a man who steals a loaf of bread for himself or his hungry family or who commits a crime of this nature. Of course in soliciting funds from the public it does not always admit that the money is to be thus used; many people contribute with the hazy idea of uplifting the downtrodden. This Union busily sought aid for those of its own members and others who, caught in the Bridgman raid, were actually engaged in a criminal conspiracy against the United States Government. . . .

The American Civil Liberties Union owes its existence to the notorious pacifist organizations of war-time fame, which were presumably financed by German agents in this country working desperately, and for a time successfully, to keep the United States from entering the war. To be sure, in its present form it has existed only since January 12, 1920, when it was formed as an outgrowth and with the merging of various organizations which were developed during the World War, dating from October, 1914, and the members of which were pacifists, defeatists, German agents, radicals of many hues, Communists, I.W.W. and Socialists. . . .

The gradual evolution of the various anti-war and other subversive organizations into the American Civil Liberties Union brought quick results. Radicals of every stripe found a haven in this body, each where he could help his particular friends who were in trouble because of infractions of the laws of the country. Soon after the formation of the Union we find the names of Amos Pinchot, brother of Governor Gifford Pinchot of Pennsylvania, as vice-chairman, and Scott Nearing and Max Eastman on the Executive Committee. And in the two years of its existence it has been used by all radicals to fight the existing Government of the United States. The rallying cry of "free speech and free press" brought many well-intentioned people into its ranks and hundreds of others to place their names on the lists of contributors. The difference between free speech and the conspiracy to overthrow the Government is not drawn by the leaders of the movement. Freedom to them means the license of treason and sedition. Zacharia Chaffee, colleague at Harvard of Felix Frankfurter, writes, preaches and presumably teaches that there should be no law against anarchy or sedition.

The directors of the American Civil Liberties Union hold that citizenship papers should not be refused an alien because of his radicalism, no matter of what degree. They profess to believe that no persons should be refused admission to the United States, especially radicals, and that aliens should not be deported for expression of opinion or for membership in radical or even revolutionary organizations, even if they aim at the destruction of the Government and social system of the United States.

The methods to be employed in securing civil liberties by this Union, they contend, is through maintaining an aggressive policy. This can be obtained by unions of organized labor, farmers, radical and liberal movements, free speech demonstrations (as they interpret free speech), publicity through circulars and posters, but more particularly through personal influence with editors or subordinates on reputable newspapers, which is also their chief means of spreading subversive propaganda, and legal defence work. Thus the Union creates in the minds of communists, Anarchists and all classes of radicals the idea that it is improper for anyone to interfere with their activities aimed at the destruction of American institutions.

The activities of this organization are extensive. It assists any radical movement through publications of high standing in order to influence public sympathy toward the radical organizations, furnishing attorneys for radical criminals, conscientious objectors and radical or foreign spies, "bores from within" in churches, religious and labor organizations, Women's Clubs, schools and colleges and the American Federation of Labor, in order to spread their radical ideas. The union maintains a staff of speakers, investigators and lawyers who are working in all sections of the country. Lawyers are furnished on short notice wherever a radical criminal gets into trouble. A press clipping service is maintained which keeps the organization in close touch with every radical criminal or group of radical criminals in trouble and immediate financial aid, publicity and counsel is offered. Aiding in this service are some 800 cooperating lawyers, and more than a thousand correspondents and investigators, representing 450 weekly labor, farmer and liberal papers with 420 speakers and writers.

The American Civil Liberties Union was particularly active in aiding the Communists caught in the Bridgman, Mich., raid. It was active in behalf of trouble makers in connection with, and prominently identified with the coal and railroad strikes, the Amalgamated Textile Worker's strike in Passaic, N.J., the National Committee for organizing Iron and Steel Workers in Duquesne, Pa., the Socialist party at Mt. Vernon, N.Y., and in fighting the State Supreme Court's rulings on free speech during 1920, and the Sacco-Vanzetti defense in 1921. An office is maintained in Washington with the *Federated Press* organization to handle matter requiring direct contact with the Government. A special drive was engineered and directed by the Union seeking amnesty for so-called "political" and industrial pris-

oners, people who had been duly convicted of crime against the laws of the country. The organization established branch offices and bodies were formed under other names. It maintains separate funds such as an "amnesty fund" and an "I.W.W. Publicity Fund."

In addition to the regular services already furnished, an extra program was put forth upon which special efforts were devoted. This program included: amnesty for 150 "political prisoners" of whom 103 were members of the I.W.W.; test meetings as a basis for getting laws before the courts on the question of free speech; a special campaign against the American Legion and the Ku Klux Klan; completing studies on injunctions and advising tactics for labor organizations; a campaign in schools and colleges for "academic freedom"; and further development of the National Bill Fund to reach all defendants in "civil liberty" cases. The policies of the organization are determined by the National Committee and the carrying out of them is left to the Executive Committee which meets weekly. Rose Pastor Stokes, a delegate at the illegal Communist convention at Bridgman, is in close contact and at times sits with this executive committee.

The Harvard Liberal Club, the I.W.W., the World War Veterans and many local "defense leagues" and "civil liberty" organizations are affiliated with the union. The directors of the union, who are members of the executive committee, are Roger N. Baldwin and Albert DeSilver. Baldwin has stated, in setting forth the purposes and principles of the Union, that "the advocacy of murder, unaccompanied by any act, is within the legitimate scope of free speech." And in telling the position of the members of the organization, he says:

"All of them believe in the right of persons to advocate the overthrow of government by force and violence. We want to, also, look like patriots in everything we do. We want to get a lot of good flags, talk a good deal about the Constitution and what our forefathers wanted to make of this country, and to show that we are the fellows that really stand for the spirit of our institutions."

It should not be forgotten that Baldwin refused to fight for the United States during the war and was sentenced and served time for "slacking." The above was the advice given by Baldwin to Louis P. Lochner, representative of the communistic *Federated Press* in Berlin, in reference to the methods to be employed in carrying out the propaganda of the People's Council which was organized to imitate in this country the Workmen's and Soldiers' Councils of Soviet Russia. And it is evident that these people see no crime in the advocacy of crime alone, even when that crime reaches the stage of treason and sedition. . . .

Bruce Barton

1886–1967
Advertising Executive and
Inspirational Writer

The work of Bruce Barton, a best-selling author and the best-known advertising man of the 1920s, radiated optimism and fueled that decade's commercial and religious spirit.

Bruce Fairchild Barton, the first of five children of a Congregationalist minister and a schoolteacher, was born on August 5, 1886, in Robbins, Tennessee. The family later moved to Oak Park, Illinois. Barton had a newspaper route at the age of nine, and by 16 he was earning $500 to $600 a year by selling maple syrup. He worked his way through Amherst College by selling pots and pans, was elected to Phi Beta Kappa (an undergraduate honors society), and was voted the most likely to succeed in the class of 1907.

From the collections of the Library of Congress.

He edited several small religious publications in Chicago, then moved to New York City in 1912. He found his first success in advertising at *Collier's* magazine, where he wrote advertising copy for the Harvard Classics book set. On October 2, 1913, he married Esther Maude Randall; they had three children.

Barton came of age at a time of great cultural energy: the nation's cities were booming; industry was mechanizing the production of goods formerly made by hand; and an increasing abundance of manufactured goods found a growing population eager to buy. Advertisements promised vitality and alertness—whether the product was orange juice, shredded wheat, or a laxative. Improvements in printing (including the introduction of color) and distribution of publications by air mail made possible a new age of mass advertising that used hard-sell seduction and persuasion.

During World War I Barton edited *Every Week* magazine and began writing uplifting, inspirational essays and articles for such national magazines as *Redbook*, *McCall's*, and *Good Housekeeping*. He was rejected for military service, but volunteered for the Salvation Army, where he coined his first famous slogan, "A man may be down but he is never out." In 1918 he was asked by the government to supervise publicity for the United War Work fund drive. He helped raise $220 million and met two future partners in advertising, Roy Durstine and Alex Osborn.

Among the casualties of World War I was America's traditional ethic of saving and self-denial—part of a national rejection of puritan conservatism. In its place grew a powerful, commerce-driven compulsion to buy and enjoy *now* the many new commodities streaming off the production lines, and, increasingly, available on the installment plan. After the war, advertising came into its own as a profession of highly paid specialists, basing national sales campaigns on market research statistics and using psychology to motivate the public to buy through appeals to vanity, ambition, and fear. The mass-circulation magazines' revenues swelled and pages were brightened by handsomely illustrated and slickly written ads for cigarettes, mouthwash, refrigerators, and even presidential candidates (**Albert Lasker**'s Lord & Thomas agency, for instance, sold **Warren G. Harding** in 1920).

The Barton, Durstine, and Osborn agency opened in January 1919, with Barton as president and lead writer. Within four years its clients included General Electric, General Motors, and Dunlop Tires. One of his enduring inventions is the character Betty Crocker, a typical American homemaker created for General Mills. In 1928 the firm merged with the George Batten Company and became Batten, Barton, Durstine, and Osborn (BBDO), one of the largest advertising agencies in the United States.

Barton came to national prominence with the publication in 1925 of *The Man Nobody Knows*, a reinterpretation of Jesus Christ as a super-successful salesman and advertising man. Barton discarded the "weak and sad-faced Savior" and presented Jesus as strong and masculine, the most popular dinner guest in Jerusalem and "the greatest advertiser of his own day." Barton wrote, "He picked up twelve men from the bottom ranks of business and forged them into an organization that conquered the world." Barton's simple and affirmative praise of everyday work through his portrayal of Jesus as doing "his Father's business" was just the message many Americans wanted to read. With its irresistible, upbeat message, *The Man Nobody Knows* topped the nonfiction best-seller list for two years.

A conservative Republican, Barton was elected to the first of two terms in Congress in 1936, and was a leading critic of Franklin D. Roosevelt's New Deal legislation. In 1941 he returned to advertising, serving as chairman of his agency until his retirement in 1961. He died in New York City in 1967.

Bruce Barton was one of the most successful advertisers of his time. His ad copy and inspirational articles and books encouraged consumer satisfaction, business success, and spiritual renewal with a sunny cheer that ran counter to the cynicism of the "Lost Generation," and conveyed a form of secular religion for a consumer society in which material success and spiritual development had become indistinguishable.

Mark LaFlaur

For Further Reading

Fox, Stephen. *The Mirror Makers: A History of American Advertising and Its Creators.* Urbana: University of Illinois Press, 1997.

Lears, Jackson. *Fables of Abundance: A Cultural History of Advertising in America.* New York: Basic Books, 1994.

Susman, Warren I. *Culture as History: The Transformation of American Society in the Twentieth Century.* New York: Pantheon Books, 1984.

SALVATION ARMY POSTER (1918)

After being rejected for military service in World War I, Barton did volunteer work for the Salvation Army and coined his first famous slogan, "A man may be down but he is never out." Here is another Salvation Army poster from the period.

Source: National Archives.

THE MAN NOBODY KNOWS by Bruce Barton (1925) [EXCERPT]

Theology has spoiled the thrill of his life by assuming that he knew everything from the beginning—that his three years of public work were a kind of dress rehearsal, with no real problems or crises. What interest would there be in such a life? What inspiration? You who read these pages have your own creed concerning him; I have mine. Let us forget all creed for the time being, and take the story just as the simple narratives give it—a poor boy, growing up in a peasant family, working in a carpenter shop; gradually feeling his powers expanding, beginning to have an influence over his neighbors, recruiting a few followers, suffering disappointments and reverses, finally death. Yet building so solidly and well that death was only the beginning of his influence! Stripped of all dogma this is the grandest achievement story of all! . . .

Success is always exciting; we never grow tired of asking what and how. What, then were the principal elements in his power over men? How was it that the boy from a country village became the greatest leader?

First of all he had the voice and manner of the leader—the personal magnetism which begets loyalty and commands respect. . . . We speak of personal magnetism as though there were something mysterious about it—a magic quality bestowed on one in a thousand and denied to all the rest. This is not true. The essential element in personal magnetism is a consuming sincerity—an overwhelming faith in the importance of the work one has to do. . . .

The second [secret of Jesus' success] was his wonderful power to pick men, and to recognize hidden capacities in them. It must have amazed Nicodemus when he learned the names of the twelve whom the young teacher had chosen to be his associates. What a list! Not a single well-known person on it. Nobody who had ever made a success of anything. A haphazard collection of fishermen and small-town businessmen, and one tax collector—a member of the most hated element in the community. What a crowd! . . .

Having gathered together his organization, there remained for Jesus the tremendous task of training it. And herein lay the third great element in his success—his vast unending patience. The Church has attached to each of the disciples the title of Saint and thereby done most to destroy the conviction of their reality. They were very far from sainthood when he picked them up.

For three years he had them with him day and night, his whole energy and resources poured out in an effort to create an understanding in them. . . .

The Bible presents an interesting collection of contrasts in this matter of executive ability. Samson had almost all the attributes of leadership. He was physically powerful and handsome; he had the great courage to which men always respond. No man was ever given a finer opportunity to free his countrymen from the oppressors and build up a great place of power for himself. Yet Samson failed miserably. He could do wonders singlehanded, but he could not organize. Moses started out under the same handicap. He tried to be everything and do everything; and was almost on the verge of failure. It was his father-in-law, Jethro, who saved him from calamity. Said that shrewd old man: "The thing that thou doest is not good. Thou wilt surely wear away, both thou and this people that is with thee, for this thing is too heavy for thee, for thou are not able to perform it thyself alone."

Moses took the advice and associated with himself a partner, Aaron, who was strong where he was weak. They supplemented each other and together achieved what neither of them could have done alone.

John, the Baptist, had the same lack. He could denounce, but he could not construct. He drew crowds who were willing to repent at his command, but he had no program for them after their repentance. They waited for him to organize them for some sort of effective service, and he was no organizer. So his followers drifted away and his movement gradually collapsed. The same thing might have happened to the work of Jesus. He started with much less reputation than John and a much smaller group of followers. He had only twelve, and they were untrained simple men, with elementary weakness and passions. Yet because of the fire of his personal conviction, because of his marvelous instinct for discovering their latent powers, and because of his unwavering faith and patience, he molded them into an organization which carried on victoriously. Within a very few years after his death, it was reported in a far-off corner of the Roman Empire that "these who have turned the world upside down have come hither also." A few decades later the proud Emperor himself bowed his head to the teachings of this Nazareth carpenter, transmitted through common men.

In this excerpt from The Man Nobody Knows, *Barton describes Jesus' "organizational skills" in terms that twentieth-century corporation employees would find familiar.*

Source: Bruce Barton, *The Man Nobody Knows: A Discovery of the Real Jesus.* Indianapolis, Ind.: Bobbs-Merrill, 1925.

Barton's "There Are Two Seas," written for McCall's in 1928, shows the touch of the minister's son as advertising man. This inspirational piece was written just a year after the publication of The Book Nobody Knows, *about the Bible.*

Source: Barton, Bruce. "There Are Two Seas." *McCall's,* April 1928.

"THERE ARE TWO SEAS" by Bruce Barton (1928)

There are two seas in Palestine.

One is fresh, and fish are in it. Splashes of green adorn its banks. Trees spread their branches over it and stretch out their thirsty roots to sip of its healing waters.

Along its shores the children play as children played when He was there. He loved it. He could look across its silver surface when He spoke His parables. And on a rolling plain not far away He fed five thousand people.

The river Jordan makes this sea with sparkling water from the hills. So it laughs in the sunshine. And men build their houses near to it, and birds their nests; and every kind of life is happier because it is there.

The river Jordan flows on south into another sea.

Here no splash of fish, no fluttering of leaf, no song of birds, no children's laughter. Travelers choose another route, unless on urgent business. The air hangs heavy above its water, and neither man nor beast nor fowl will drink.

What makes this mighty difference in these neighbor seas? Not the river Jordan. It empties the same good water into both. Not the soil in which they lie; not the country round about.

This is the difference. The Sea of Galilee receives but does not keep the Jordan. For every drop that flows into it another drop flows out. The giving and receiving go on in equal measure.

The other sea is shrewder, hoarding its income jealously. It will not be tempted into any generous impulse. Every drop it gets, it keeps.

The Sea of Galilee gives and lives. The other sea gives nothing. It is named The Dead.

There are two kinds of people in the world. There are two seas in Palestine.

Clara Bow 1905–1965

Silent Film Star

Clara Bow was a star in the silent film era whose sex appeal and spirited personality epitomized the liberated female of the Roaring Twenties.

Bow was born in Brooklyn on July 29, 1905, into extreme poverty. Her semi-invalid mother suffered from bouts of mental illness, while her father was an abusive alcoholic who barely earned enough money for food or clothing. Dressed in rags during her childhood, Bow played with the boys to avoid being ostracized by the girls. Out of place at school and unloved at home, Bow escaped her unhappiness at the movies, watching the slapstick comedian Roscoe "Fatty" Arbuckle, the handsome Wallace Reid, or "America's Sweetheart" Mary Pickford. At home, she mimicked the actors in front of her mirror and dreamed of starring in movies herself. Her unstable mother disapproved of such ambitions and threatened to kill her after Bow landed the part of Priscilla in the school play, *Miles Standish*. Bow was forced to leave the eighth grade early and never performed the role of Priscilla.

In 1921, Bow sought another chance to perform when she entered the Fame and Fortune Contest announced in *Motion Picture, Shadowland,* and *Motion Picture Classic* magazines. Impressing the judges with her photogenic features and animated expressions, Bow won a contract to appear in a motion picture. She landed her first role in *Beyond the Rainbow,* but to Bow's dismay, her scenes were cut before the film's release in 1922. Not long after, director Elmer Clifton discovered her contest photo and cast her as a spunky tomboy in his 1923 production *Down to the Sea in Ships.* Several reviews mentioned her performance favorably; *Variety* even suggested she stole the show.

Bow headed for Hollywood after she acquired a contract with independent producer B. P. Schulberg. Between 1923 and 1925, she acted in more than 20 films and most often played the role of the flapper, a young woman who strayed from conventions and exercised freedom in behavior and fashion. With women joining the workforce in World War I and winning voting rights in 1920 with the Nineteenth Amendment, the flapper represented the modern woman's new sense of identity that emerged from these social, economic, and legal changes. In the Prohibition era, during which the Eighteenth Amendment outlawed the manufacture and sale of alcohol, the flapper drank from flasks, danced all night, and flaunted her sexuality; she bobbed her hair, wore low heels, and abandoned petticoats and corsets for a loose dress with higher hemlines and lower necklines. Many of the titles of Bow's movies reflect this shift from the outmoded virtuousness of nineteenth-century womanhood to the liberated behavior of the modern woman— *Daughters of Pleasure* (1924), *The Adventurous Sex* (1925), *My Lady's Lips* (1925), and *Kiss Me Again* (1925). Through the escapades of the flapper, Bow presented a natural and carefree sexuality that contrasted with both the campy sex appeal of the vamp and the wholesome innocence of the girl next door.

From the collections of the Library of Congress.

Her popularity increased in 1926 when Schulberg arranged for her films *The Plastic Age* (1925) and *Mantrap* (1926) to premiere the same week in New York. *The Plastic Age* promoted her energy and sexuality by selling her as "the hottest jazz baby in films." A romantic story about youth and the dilemmas of love, the film exemplifies the type of character Bow typically played—a free spirit seeking excitement. From *Mantrap*, one of her first films for Paramount Pictures, she gained even more recognition; Bow played the central character that flirts outrageously with men and discards them at will. Both of these films simultaneously received excellent reviews and marked her rise to fame.

Bow experienced the height of her career and international stardom after making the 1927 film *It* based on Elinor Glyn's best-selling novel of the same name. Glyn believed that Bow embodied "It," the combination of sex appeal and self-confidence that set her apart from other women. "It," as explained in the movie's titles, allures others with its "magnetic force" while remaining "absolutely unself-conscious." Through slight gestures—an enticing glance, a coquettish head toss, or a playful pout—Bow played her role with remarkable success. This film grossed over a million dollars for Paramount and defined Bow as Hollywood's "It Girl." Her fashion, hairstyle, and makeup were widely imitated by women, and a 1928 national poll pronounced her America's most popular female movie star. In one week, she averaged over 8,000 fan letters, double the number of any other Paramount performer.

Although she continued to charm audiences, Bow experienced several nervous breakdowns in 1928 and 1929. Her fast-paced lifestyle of drinking, gambling, and promiscuity began to overtake her and led to Hollywood gossip. The president of Paramount Pictures, Adolph Zukor, stated she was "exactly the same off the screen as on." Bow, indeed, lived wildly but she sarcastically refuted Zukor's claim, suggesting that her characters were much happier. Yet, even in this period of distress she managed to portray giddy enthusiasm in movies like *Red Hair* (1928), one of her last silent films.

In the 1930s, Bow faded from the screen as the popularity of the flapper declined and she struggled with the advent of sound. Personal scandals also damaged her reputation. When her former secretary, Daisy De Voe, attempted blackmail after being discharged, Bow retaliated by suing her in court. The 1931 trial damaged Bow with reports on her private life; De Voe was sentenced to one year in jail for embezzlement. That year Bow, released early from her Paramount contract, married cowboy actor Rex Bell and moved to his Nevada ranch. She bore two sons after officially retiring in 1933, but mental illness kept her in sanitariums and seclusion. Bow publicly appeared for the first time in 15 years at her husband's funeral in 1962 and died three years later of a heart attack in Los Angeles on September 26, 1965.

Remembered as the "It Girl" of the Roaring Twenties, Bow symbolized the ultimate flapper who was sexy, young, and lively. She personified the independent modern woman with a new social awareness who dressed and behaved as she desired—both on-screen and off. Appearing in nearly 50 films in the 1920s, Bow worked as hard as she played, entertaining audiences with youthful mischief and convincing them that she was the happy flapper depicted on screen.

Renée Miller

For Further Reading

Basinger, Jeanine. *Silent Stars*. New York: Alfred A. Knopf, 1999.

Morella, Joe, and Edward Z. Epstein. *The "It" Girl: The Incredible Story of Clara Bow*. New York: Delacorte Press, 1976.

Stenn, David. *Clara Bow: Runnin' Wild*. New York: Penguin Books, 1990.

REVIEW OF *THE PLASTIC AGE* from *Variety* (1926)

The Plastic Age named Bow as "the hottest jazz baby in films" and captured the attention of audiences and critics. This 1926 Variety film review praises Bow for her role as a cute yet mischievous college girl and, in the slang of the day, markets the movie as perfect "For the flappers and their sundae buyers."

Source: Variety Film Reviews 1926–1929. Vol. 3. New York and London: Garland Publishing, 1983. Reprinted with permission from Variety Magazine.

A nifty picture. It's made that way and plays that way. In it are yaps, saps, flips and flaps. What more could be said for what is strictly a boy and girl-made film?

For the flappers and their sundae buyers, "The Plastic Age" is perfect. Probably the book hit them as hard as this film is bound to. And the home run hitter will be Clara Bow as Cynthia Day, a tough little baby to hang around a college campus, but her excuse can be that she had no mother to guide her. At least in this film. And her reward can stand on her feet which she never allowed to slip, but seemingly not particular otherwise.

Ben Schulberg must have selected this picture as sure-fire. It has been playing out of town for months. Schulberg has been with Famous Players (coast studios) for some time. Anytime would be the right time for this one. But perhaps Mr. Schulberg passed it over to the Commonwealth Film Corp., as a distributor, at its pleasure, with Samuel Zierler listed on the program as its president, if for no other identification or publicity purpose.

This story of college life abounds with girls, suggesting either a co-ed institution or else a seminary was planted in the next yard.

Donald Keith is the sap freshman of Prescott, who was the crack 440-yard flier in his home town high school, but he flopped at Prescott on the track after nearly making Cynthia and a few road houses. Without knowing it, Hugh Carver "busted" right into the class that holds Mickey Walker and Young Slattery. Though the picture fails to detail whether Carver ever won a foot race at Prescott after losing his first, he did win the big football match of the season for his college.

Mr. Keith does very well, as does Gilbert Roland, as a boyish semi-villain. All of the cast play well the young people, even "types," exceptionally so.

The picture takes its own jumping record, leaping three years over but one caption. The football game is excellent, and in the work out very much like Lloyd's "Freshman's" game, but without the ridiculousness, of course, that Lloyd stuck into his.

Somehow it appears easy to be a trainer in pictures. David Butler here is exemplary as the football coach, or maybe Wesley Ruggles so directed him he couldn't flop. Mr. Ruggles did very good directorial work in every way. His road house raid is a most logical bit of that kind of work, inclusive of the dancing preceding along with the fist fight between the two college rivals.

Laughs come out quite often, some very hearty, and others begotten by trivial snappy captions. Picture ends with a laugh, besides.

This film can't muff with the younger set. They'll sit glued to it. Clara Bow as a college cutie who knows all of the tricks, besides all of the boys, may set them a worst example than they ever believe a flapping kid could fall into. But for the boys it is proven here that the virtue of training brings its own reward to success, even though it is possible to get soused at a college ball.

How the adults will take to it is another thing. They will probably go solid against Clara and won't be so strong for Hughie. They may also wonder if Prescott College owned a faculty. For a go-as-you-please hall of learning Prescott is a prize pip.

But if Prescott did have a faculty it's odds on that Clara copped the pres and hid him under the bridge, too.

REVIEW OF *MANTRAP* from *Variety* (1926)

Clara Bow! And how! What a "mantrap" she is!

And how this picture is going to make her! It should do as much for this corking little ingénue lead as "Flaming Youth" did for Colleen Moore.

Miss Bow just walks away with the picture from the moment she walks into camera range. Every minute that she is in it she steals it from such a couple of corking troupers as Ernest Torrence and Percy Marmont. Any time a girl can do that she is going some. In this particular role, that of a fast-working, slang-slinging manicurist from a swell barber shop in Minneapolis, who marries the big hick from "Mantrap," she is fitted just like a glove.

The picture itself is a wow for laughs, action and corking titles.

The story deals with a lawyer who is a divorce specialist, sick and tired of vamping females who come to his office with their troubles. To be rid of them he decides to go up into the Canadian wilds. His office neighbor takes him on the trip and in less than a week the two are at loggerheads.

The contrast to the lawyer characterization is shown in the owner of a trading store in the lonely country, who is woman-hungry and who goes to Minneapolis, wins himself the flip little manicure girl and takes her back to the wilds. There she is a trig little flapper, bobbed tresses, lipstick and powder puff and all the usual rolled stocking touches, practicing her flirting on the "untamed hens of the wide open," and boy, how she vamps with her lamps! And how they fall!

It is the storekeeper who comes across the campers just about the time when they're ready to kill each other. He decides he'll take the lawyer back with him to the trading post. He figures the law shark will be good company for the wife. When the lawyer gets a flash at her he just about shrivels. He keeps battling her wiles as long as he can. Finally she is too much for him, and he decides to go back and rejoin his camping companion. She's going too. When he refuses to take her she marches off down to the trail herself and plants herself in his way as he comes along.

The two are finally lost when their Indian guide deserts them and are overtaken by the more or less irate husband, who sees the humor of the situation, although he has been played fast and loose with up to a certain point. Instead of shooting the man, he decides that he had better let his wife go to the big city for a vacation. This she does, stealing their boat and leaving both the men flat.

The final shot shows the lawyer back in civilization. A blond client is waiting for him in his private office, and it looks as though he is due to fall again. Back in the wilds the hick hubby is shown peeling his own potatoes while a neighboring trader and his wife are telling him he should be glad that he is rid of the flapper wife, he in turn defending her when she opens the door in all her flapper glory and applauds hubby.

While still in his arms receiving her return greeting she looks over his shoulder and spies a good-looking Royal Mounted Policeman and immediately starts giving him the eye. It is a wow of a finish.

Torrence is the hick hubby, while Marmont is the lawyer. These three carry all the principal action, with the balance of the cast doing fill-in bits.

In this 1926 review, Variety accurately predicted that Mantrap would elevate Bow to star status. According to the opening lines of the review, the title of the film exhibits the essence of her character—an outrageous flirt who traps men. Bow's role, which "fitted just like a glove," shows the spirit of the era's emancipated woman, actively influencing the events in the story.
Source: Variety Film Reviews 1926–1929. Vol. 3. New York and London: Garland Publishing, 1983. Reprinted with permission from *Variety Magazine.*

STILL OF CLARA BOW AND ANTONIO MORENO FROM *IT* (1927)

In this photo taken from the 1927 film It, *Bow approaches the desk of her boss, played by Antonio Moreno, in an attempt to focus his attention on her and away from his work. She undoubtedly wins his affections and those of audiences with "It," her trademark sexuality that defined her as an icon for the era.*
Source: Hulton/Archive.

"CLARA BOW: MY LIFE STORY, PART THREE " by Clara Bow (1928) [EXCERPT]

Appearing in three consecutive issues of Photoplay *in 1928, this autobiography by Bow reveals the raw facts of her life through the polished interpretation of Adela Rogers St. Johns. In their interview, Bow vividly described her unhappy childhood and rise to stardom. This final feature relates the success, romances, and attitudes of the real Bow rather than her public persona.*

Source: *Bow, Clara, "Clara Bow: My Life Story, Part Three," interview by Adela Rogers St. Johns,* Photoplay, *April 1928.*

. . . I don't believe anybody had a harder time getting started in pictures than I did.

You see, I had to make a niche for myself. If I am different, if I'm the "super-flapper" and "jazz-baby" of pictures, it's because I had to create a character for myself. Otherwise, I'd probably not be in pictures at all. They certainly didn't want me.

I was the wrong type to play ingenues. I was too small for a leading woman and too kiddish for heavies. I had too much of what my wonderful friend Elinor Glyn calls "It," apparently, for the average second role or anything of that sort. I got turned down for more jobs, I guess, than any other girl who ever tried to break into pictures.

Finally I did get a lead with Glenn Hunter. The girl was a little rough-neck, and somehow they thought I fitted into it. I guess I did. I'd always been a tomboy, and at heart I still was. I worked in a few pictures around New York and by that time Down to the Sea in Ships, which had been held up for such a long time, was released and that helped me. . . .

You know enough about me to realize that I'd never "had things." I'm not going to pretend that I had. Everything was new and wonderful to me. It was wonderful to have the things I wanted to eat, not to have to scrimp on dessert and be able to order the best cuts of meat. It was wonderful to have silk stockings, and not cry if they happened to get a run in them. It was wonderful to have a few dollars to spend, just as I liked, without having to worry about the fact that they ought to be used to pay the gas bill.

Maybe other people don't realize that, don't get the kick out of those things that I do. Of course I still can't exactly understand the money that is coming and is going to make my Dad and me comfortable and happy all the rest of our lives. When I bought my first home, the one I still live in, a little bungalow in Beverly Hills, when I signed the check, I couldn't possibly appreciate what the figures meant. I knew I had that much in the bank—me, little Clara Bow—and that the home was mine and I'd actually earned it. But the figures were just too big for my comprehension.

But I do know what a hundred dollars is. That used to be a dream to me—to have a hundred dollars. I never thought I would, not all at once—have a hundred dollars, and certainly not to do something I really wanted to do with. So now I get more thrill out of a hundred dollars that I can go and buy a present for a friend with, or do something for Dad, or get myself something

awfully feminine and pretty with, than I do out of my salary check. . . .

All this time I was "running wild," I guess, in the sense of trying to have a good time. I'd never had any fun in my life, as you know. And I was just a kid, under twenty, with a background of grief and poverty that I've tried to make you understand, even though I've had to bare my whole soul to do it. Why, I'd never been to a real party, a real dance. I'd never had a beautiful dress to wear, never had anyone send me flowers. It was like a new world to me, and I just drank it all in with that immense capacity of youth for understanding and loving excitement, I tried to make up for all my barren, hungry, starved-for-beauty years in no time at all.

Maybe this was a good thing, because I suppose a lot of that excitement, that joy of life, got onto the screen, and was the sort of flame of youth that made people enjoy seeing me. A philosopher might call it the swing of the pendulum, from my early years of terror and lack, to this time when all the pleasures of the world opened before me. . . .

Somehow, I had managed to make a niche for myself. I'd created a Clara Bow by being myself largely I guess, who fitted the public desire and the public imagination. I hope they'll go on loving me a long time. I don't know.

I live in my little bungalow in Beverly Hills with my father. I work very, very hard. I like young people and gaiety, and have a lot of both around me whenever I have time. I like to swim and ride and play tennis. I have a few close friends, but not many acquaintances. I don't have time. I am happy—as happy as anyone can be who believes that life isn't quite to be trusted. I give everything I can to my pictures and the rest to being young and trying to make my father happy, and filling up the gaps in my education.

I don't think I'm very different from any other girl—except that I work harder and have suffered more. And I have red hair.

All in all, I guess I'm just Clara Bow. And Clara Bow is just what life made her. That's what I've tried to tell you in this story. I'm terribly grateful and still a little incredulous of my success. It seems like a dream. But—I'm willing to work just as hard as ever to go on having it. Beyond that, I haven't yet evolved any plans or desires.

After all, I'm still only twenty-two. That isn't so very old, is it?

Louis Brandeis

1856–1941
Supreme Court Justice

Louis Brandeis was a progressive lawyer, Zionist leader, and the first Jewish associate justice of the U.S. Supreme Court. Throughout his career, he used his legal expertise to limit the power of big business and protect civil liberties.

Louis Dembitz Brandeis was born on November 13, 1856, in Louisville, Kentucky, to Jews who had emigrated from Prague to the United States in search of economic growth and social freedom. A brilliant scholar, Brandeis graduated at the top of his class from Harvard Law School in 1877 and formed his own legal practice in Boston in 1879. As his business prospered, he became an unpaid counsel for many public causes and a leader of Progressivism, a movement that worked to improve conditions in government and society. Two of his early triumphs for the public included the preservation of the Boston subway system against the threat of corporate monopoly (1893–1902) and the creation of the Massachusetts savings-bank life insurance system (1905–07), both of which protected communities from the encroachment of wealthy corporations. On behalf of laborers, he devised the 1908 Brandeis brief to defend an Oregon statute limiting working hours for women and mediated the 1910 New York garment workers' strike to improve working conditions in the textile industry. His brief, setting a legal precedent, introduced a model for constitutional litigation by using economic and sociological data, including facts and figures, to demonstrate a law's relevance to society and relation to the Constitution. Instead of the typical two-page legal citations, the 1908 Brandeis brief contained more than 100 pages of information pertaining to the Oregon labor law. This approach was used frequently thereafter, including in *Brown* v. *Board of Education of Topeka* (1954), and is still in use today.

Brandeis's experience with Jewish immigrant workers during the 1910 garment workers' strike sparked his interest in Zionism, a movement for the establishment of a national Jewish state in Palestine. Two years later his devotion deepened when he met Jacob deHaas, founder of

From the collections of the Library of Congress.

modern Zionism. Although Brandeis was an assimilated Jew, his interest in his cultural and religious heritage had been awakened. In 1914, Brandeis became the chairman of the Provisional Executive Committee for General Zionist Affairs; while touring Palestine in 1919, Brandeis was honored in every Jewish city and settlement he visited for his leadership in the American Zionist movement.

Known as the "people's lawyer," Brandeis was admired by minorities, laborers, social workers, and progressive politicians. He had earned a national reputation for defending civil liberties and attacking large enterprises through his pro bono (free of charge) court cases and notable publications. In his 1914 book *Other People's Money, and How the Bankers Use It,* based on a series of articles for *Harper's Weekly* called "Breaking the Money Trust," Brandeis particularly criticized investment banking companies such as J. P. Morgan & Company, the National City Bank, and the First National Bank of New York for their control over American corporations. To break down economic monopolies, he proposed to eliminate interlocking directorates (in which an individual is director of two competitive organizations) and publicize bankers' earnings and practices. His theories on big business helped persuade Congress to pass in 1914 the Clayton Antitrust Act and the Federal Trade Commission Act. These antitrust laws, intended to prevent monopolies and foster competition, became part of President **Woodrow Wilson**'s reform program.

In 1916, Wilson showed his appreciation to Brandeis by nominating him associate justice of the Supreme Court. However, the country's racist and conservative attitudes led to a four-month heated debate over his nomination in the Senate Judiciary Committee. Brandeis's Jewish ancestry and Zionist advocacy made him a victim of anti-Semitism; some members of the Protestant elite resented the idea of a Jew receiving such a prestigious position. Right-wing politicians maintained that his radical views would alter the American legal system, while businessmen claimed that his pro-labor policies would hurt company profits. Nevertheless, on June 1, 1916, the Senate confirmed the appointment of Brandeis to the Supreme Court by a vote of 47 to 22.

As the bench's most liberal jurist, Brandeis emphasized the need to protect civil liberties and respect the concerns of all citizens. His belief that the centralization of power threatened these very principles led him to condemn unlimited governmental control. For instance, Brandeis dissented on several of the Supreme Court's decisions to uphold the Espionage Act of 1917, which ruled it illegal to protest the war. A fervent proponent of free speech, he viewed this act as a direct violation of the First Amendment. Brandeis strongly objected to laws restricting personal expression, but if laws benefited individual rights, he actively encouraged state and federal legislatures to experiment with new policies. In the 1921 case *Truax* v. *Corrigan*, where the Supreme Court struck down an Arizona law limiting injunctions (court orders prohibiting specific actions) in labor disputes, Brandeis argued that such a law enabled unions to demonstrate peacefully and served as a valuable social experiment. Brandeis insisted that laws must adapt to the changing times and relate to present rather than past social conditions.

Brandeis's judicial opinions, while often in the minority, concurred with those of his colleague Justice **Oliver Wendell Holmes, Jr.**, on most major issues. During the 1930s many of the Supreme Court's majority positions began reflecting Brandeis and Holmes's former dissenting positions on issues involving free speech, personal privacy, and labor relations. Brandeis also had a profound influence on President Franklin D. Roosevelt's New Deal legislation, including the 1933 Public Securities Act, the 1934 Securities Exchange Act, and the 1935 National Labor Relations Act. Brandeis retired in 1939, and died in Washington, D.C., on October 5, 1941.

Through both his court cases and his political causes, Brandeis stressed the importance of just treatment and equal opportunity. He believed that laws should protect and enhance the lives of all individuals, and he promoted his concept of the legal system as a continuously evolving entity that should strive toward social progress.

Renée Miller

For Further Reading

Dawson, Nelson L., ed. *Brandeis and America*. Lexington: The University Press of Kentucky, 1989.

Mason, Alpheus Thomas. *Brandeis: A Free Man's Life*. New York: Viking Press, 1966.

Strum, Philippa. *Brandeis: Beyond Progressivism*. Lawrence: University Press of Kansas, 1993.

"A 'People's Lawyer' for the Supreme Court" from *The Literary Digest* (February 12, 1916) [Excerpt]

Published in The Literary Digest *on February 12, 1916, the article "A 'People's Lawyer' for the Supreme Court" reviews the opposing opinions surrounding President Woodrow Wilson's appointment of Brandeis to the Supreme Court.*

Source: "A 'People's Lawyer' for the Supreme Court." The Literary Digest, February 12, 1916.

No appointment to the Supreme Court could have created a greater sensation or caused more talk than the one actually made by President Wilson. So several Washington correspondents rather sweepingly aver. In any list of eligibles for the vacancy caused by the death of Mr. Justice Lamar, observes the Rochester *Post Express* (Rep.), Louis Dembitz Brandeis "would probably have been fiftieth if he had figured into the list at all." If there were a million lawyers in the United States, says the Charleston (W. Va.) *Mail* (Ind. Rep.), the thought of the choice of Mr. Brandeis would not have occurred to more than one of them; hence we can easily appreciate "the astounded sensibilities of the members of the United States Senate" when the President submitted the nomination to them. To Wall Street, we read in the New York *Sun*, the announcement "came as a surprise and a shock." But a few days later there met in New York a board of arbitration which has for six years preserved a friendly understanding between 100,000 garment-workers and their employers. And at this meeting it was remarked as the most natural thing in the world that the President of the United States should promote their chairman from "the position of chief judge of our supreme court to that of the highest court in the nation." On the whole, agrees the New York *World* (Dem.), "a 'people's lawyer' will not be out of place on the United States Supreme Court. It is the people's court." Nine out of eleven members of the faculty of the Harvard Law School have, according to the Boston *Post*, exprest unqualified approval of the selection of this brilliant graduate of their institution. In the editorial columns of the New York *Times*, which, like most other conservative newspapers, does not approve of this nomination to the Supreme Court, Mr. Brandeis's qualifications are acknowledged in these ungrudging words:

"There will be universal agreement that the President has conferred the honor of this nomination upon a very distinguished member of the bar, a man learned in the law, extraordinarily well-informed as to the conditions of life throughout the country, deeply interested in the public affairs and the infinite private activities of the people, full of energy and capable of taking his full share in the arduous labor of the great tribunal. It can not be doubted that Mr. Brandeis, should the Senate confirm the nomination, would be a conspicuous member of the court. Because of his ability, his intense interest in the tasks to which he applies himself, and his fearlessness in the expression of opinion, he would be heard from, he would of a certainty attain to great distinction. His legal qualifications are attested by the nature of his practise or occupation in recent years. His services and his knowledge have been availed of in matters where only lawyers of great ability would be called into council."

Why, then was the President's choice of Mr. Brandeis received with universal surprise, and why did it at once arouse wide-spread and vigorous editorial opposition, and a Senatorial context of almost unprecedented violence? Mr. Louis Seibold, writing from Washington to the New York *World*, thus states, "crystallized in general terms," the objections to the Brandeis nomination:

"That Mr. Brandeis is a radical, a theorist, impractical, with strong socialistic tendencies.

"That he is given to extravagances of utterance, inspired by prejudice and intolerance.

"That he is a 'self-advertiser,' reckless in his methods of seeking personal exploitation.

"That he does not possess the 'judicial temperament' that would fit him for the duties of a Supreme Court judge, in that he would be influenced by personal considerations rather than the merits of the causes submitted for impartial analysis and exact judgment.

"That Mr. Brandeis is not a Democrat, and that prior to 1912 he was active in the organization and promotion of 'Progressive sentiment' that eventuated in the candidacy of Colonel Roosevelt, of whom he was once a strong admirer.

"That the vacancy on the Supreme Court bench 'belonged to the South,' as but two of the present Justices were appointed from that section of the country, and that the late Justice Lamar's successor should have been taken from it."

The fact that Mr. Brandeis is a Jew, his lack of judicial experience, and some charges of departure from the strictest standards of professional ethics seem also to influence critics of this Wilson appointment. But the greatest objection of all, held by many editors who approve of Mr. Brandeis on all other counts, is his supposed lack of "judicial temperament." This is the chief basis of editorial disapproval on the part of such diversely minded papers as the Boston *Herald* (Ind. Rep.), New Haven *Journal-Courier* (Ind.), Hartford *Courant* (Rep.), Lowell *Courier-Citizen*, New York *Press* (Rep.), Philadelphia *Press* (Rep.), Syracuse *Post-Standard* (Rep.), Rochester *Post-Express*, *Herald* (Dem.), and *Democrat and Chronicle* (Rep.), Washington *Herald* (Ind.), and *Times* (Ind.), Nashville *Banner* (Ind.), Chicago *News* (Ind.), and St. Louis *Globe Democrat* (Rep.).

The trouble with Mr. Brandeis, as the otherwise complimentary Nashville *Banner* puts it, is that "he is a man who 'starts things,' not one who weighs or ponders facts and questions in the light that precedents, the Constitution, and the laws may determine." The fact "that he is a man of furious partizanship, of violent antagonism, and of irredeemable prejudices," utterly disqualifies him, in the opinion of Mr. Munsey's New York *Press*, from acting in a judicial capacity; "the American people don't want to have the Supreme Court of the United States converted into a china-shop with a bull turned loose in it."

The combination of the Brandeis "temperament" and the Brandeis "radical" view-point is altogether too much for papers like the New York *Sun* and the Boston *News Bureau*. The Boston daily calls the nomination "an insult to New England and the business interests of the country," and asks those favoring the nomination to "visit Boston for a day and learn how Brandeis has garnered his wealth." The appointee is "negatively" unfit, according to *The Commercial and Financial Chronicle*, "because Mr. Brandeis is without judicial experience and has given no evidence of possessing" the requisite ability, while "his positive unfitness lies in the association he has already had in the very gravest matters which are still far from being finally settled and must come again before the Court, and also in the bias under which he lies." Brandeis, observes the indignant Charleston *Mail*, "has appeared conspicuously time and time again, during the last five years, as a loud expounder of new-fangled or demagogic doctrines and as a know-it-all publicist to whom the solution of every industrial and political problem is as simple as is the curing of bodily ills to the quack doctor. . . . On the bench of the United States Supreme Court this flighty and dangerous doctrinaire would write his opinions into the lasting body of law of his country; and there would be no appeal." And in the course of an angry, satiric and denunciatory editorial the conservative Detroit *Free Press* (Ind.) asks:

"What motive could have influenced a President to appoint such a man to such a position? Brandeis, a socialist or a Progressive, used his influence in 1912 to have Progressives vote for Woodrow Wilson. But was there no less reward that he would have taken for his service? Must the security of life and property of every inhabitant of the country be jeopardized because a political debt had to be paid?"

In spite of the assurances of Senator James (Dem., Kentucky), *The Florida Times-Union* (Dem.) does "not believe that Brandeis is a Democrat," and since, in addition to that, "he is not a lawyer of known ability, he is not a man of judicial temperament," the Jacksonville daily finds it difficult "to conceive of the selection of a man less fit than he for the position to which he has been appointed."

Surprizing as the Brandeis appointment was to all editors, yet it is hard to escape the conviction that the ayes outnumber the noes. None of Mr. Brandeis's friends in editorial sanctums can pay higher tribute to his abilities than does the New York *Times*. But they, unlike the papers just quoted, are dismayed neither by his "radicalism" nor his "unjudicial temperament." That President Wilson has chosen a Jew of high legal attainments to sit in the Supreme Court is generally held wise and commendable. Mr. Brandeis is the second of his faith to receive nomination at the hands of an American Chief Magistrate, and if the Senate confirms the choice he will be the first to sit in the Court. The remark of the Columbus *Dispatch* is typical:

"With a Catholic as Chief Justice and a Jew as an associate Justice, each appointed by a President of a different faith, the Supreme Court will be a shining example of what religious liberty in the American Republic really is and ought to be. . . ."

From the White House to Wall Street, conservative politicians and businessmen feared Brandeis's appointment to the Supreme Court. Appearing in The Literary Digest *on February 12, 1916, this political cartoon entitled "The Blow That Almost Killed Father" illustrates the perceived threat of the radical views and pro-labor policies of Brandeis—the "people's lawyer."*

Source: Reproduced from Lewis J. Paper, *Brandeis*. Englewood Cliffs, N.J.: Prentice-Hall, 1983.

As the acknowledged leader of the American Zionist movement, Brandeis dedicated himself to the establishment of a national Jewish state in Palestine. Delivered by Brandeis at a 1918 convention for the Zionist Organization of America, these five principles pledge the group's commitment to a Jewish homeland that protects and benefits all citizens in Palestine.

Source: Urofsky, Melvin I. *Brandeis and American Reform: A Mind of One Piece.* New York: Charles Scribner's Sons, 1971.

"THE BLOW THAT ALMOST KILLED FATHER" POLITICAL CARTOON (1916)

PITTSBURGH PLATFORM (1918)

First: We declare for the political and civil equality irrespective of race, sex, or faith of all the inhabitants of the land.

Second: To insure in the Jewish National Home of Palestine equality of opportunity we favor a policy which, with due regard to existing rights, shall tend to establish the ownership and control by the whole people of the land, of all natural resources and of all public utilities.

Third: All land, owned or controlled by the whole people, should be leased on such conditions as will insure the fullest opportunity for development and continuity of possession.

Fourth: The cooperative principle should be applied so far as feasible in the organization of all agricultural, industrial, commercial, and financial undertakings.

Fifth: The system of free public instruction which is to be established should embrace all grades and departments of education.

DISSENT BY LOUIS BRANDEIS IN *SCHAEFER V. UNITED STATES* (1920) [EXCERPT]

With the opinion and decision of this court, reversing the judgment against Schaefer and Vogel on the ground that there was no evidence legally connecting them with the publication, I concur fully. But I am of opinion that the judgments against the other three defendants should also be reversed, because either the demurrers to the several counts should have been sustained or a verdict should have been directed for each defendant on all of the counts.

The extent to which Congress may, under the Constitution, interfere with free speech, was in Schenck v. United States, 249 U.S. 47, 52, 39 S. Sup. Ct. 247, 249 (63 L. Ed. 470), declared by a unanimous court to be this:

> The question in every case is whether the words . . . are used in such circumstances and are of such a nature as to create a clear and present danger that they will bring about the substantive evils that Congress has a right to prevent. It is a question of proximity and degree.

This is a rule of reason. Correctly applied, it will preserve the right of free speech both from suppression by tyrannous, well-meaning majorities, and from abuse by irresponsible, fanatical minorities. Like many other rules for human conduct, it can be applied correctly only by the exercise of good judgment; and to the exercise of good judgment calmness is, in times of deep feeling and on subjects which excite passion, as essential as fearlessness and honesty. The question whether in a particular instance the words spoken or written fall within the permissible curtailment of free speech is, under the rule enunciated by this court, one of degree; and because it is a question of degree the field in which the jury may exercise its judgment is necessarily a wide one. But its field is not unlimited. The trial provided for is one by judge and jury, and the judge may not abdicate his function. If the words were of such a nature and were used under such circumstances that men, judging in calmness, could not reasonably say that they created a clear and present danger that they would bring about the evil which Congress sought and had a right to prevent, then it is the duty of the trial judge to withdraw the case from the consideration of the jury; and, if he fails to do so, it is the duty of the appellate court to correct the error. . . .

The constitutional right of free speech has been declared to be the same in peace and in war. In peace, too, men may differ widely as to what loyalty to our country demands; and an intolerant majority, swayed by passion or by fear, may be prone in the future, as it has often been in the past to stamp as disloyal opinions with which it disagrees. Convictions such as these, besides abridging freedom of speech, threaten freedom of thought and of belief.

A fervent proponent of free speech, Brandeis dissented on several of the Supreme Court's decisions to uphold the Espionage Act of 1917. The following dissenting statement from the 1920 case Schaefer v. United States *exemplifies his belief that true democracy should enable personal expression in times of peace and war.*

Source: Lief, Alfred, ed. *The Brandeis Guide to the Modern World.* Boston: Little, Brown, 1941.

William Jennings Bryan

William Jennings Bryan, a three-time presidential candidate and an eloquent force in the Democratic Party for nearly 20 years, served as President **Woodrow Wilson**'s secretary of state and defended the biblical account of creation in the highly publicized 1925 Scopes "Monkey" trial.

Bryan was born in Salem, Illinois, on March 19, 1860, and was raised as a devout Christian by his Methodist mother and his Baptist father; at the age of 14 he became a Presbyterian, and throughout his life he was an active churchgoer. After graduating from Illinois College in 1881 he studied law at the Union College of Law in Chicago. In 1884 he married Mary Baird of Perry, Illinois, with whom he would have a son and two daughters, and in 1887 they moved to Lincoln, Nebraska.

During the election of 1888, Bryan's gift for oratory attracted attention at rallies for presidential candidate Grover Cleveland and the Democrats, and in 1890 he defied expectations by winning a seat in the U.S. House of Representatives in the heavily Republican Lincoln and Omaha district. He supported many ideas of Nebraska's new Independent (Populist) Party, including relief for farmers and prohibition of alcohol. He also was a strong supporter of the Free Silver Movement, which advocated the coinage of silver along with gold—known as bimetallism—in order to cause currency inflation. Silver miners, mostly in the West, complained that the powerful Eastern bankers (Wall Street in particular) dominated the national economy and hurt the common man through their insistence on basing the value of money on the price of gold.

He was reelected in 1892, but failed in his bid for a seat in the U.S. Senate in 1894. He spent the next two years as editor-in-chief of the Omaha *World-Herald*, where he continued to advocate bimetallism. Bryan's support of bimetallism, as well as his later involvement in the Scopes trial, demonstrated his commitment to protecting traditional society from the effects of industrialism. At the 1896 Democratic convention, Bryan electrified the audience with his "cross of gold" speech in which he criticized the gold-standard capi-

From the collections of the Library of Congress.

talists and voiced his support of agrarian causes. He so impressed the delegates that they nominated him as the Democratic presidential candidate. Bryan's themes and his deep, resonant voice mesmerized overflowing crowds, but he failed to unite rural and urban interests, and his Republican opponent William McKinley won with 7.1 million votes to Bryan's 6.5 million. Bryan ran again in 1900 and 1908 against McKinley and William H. Taft, respectively, but was defeated both times and vowed not to run for president again.

Nonetheless, Bryan remained a power in the Democratic Party. After he helped Woodrow Wilson gain victory in the three-way presidential race of 1912 against Taft and Theodore Roosevelt, Wilson appointed Bryan secretary of state, even though Bryan was an anti-imperialist pacifist with no diplomatic experience. Bryan's proudest achievement in his two years as secretary of state (1913–15) was the negotiation of treaties with some 30 nations to provide for arbitration of international disputes and, it was hoped, to avert war. He also persuaded the congressional Democrats to pass many of the bills in Wilson's New Freedom program, such as the Federal Reserve Act (1913), which established a Federal Reserve Board to stabilize the national economy and protect the currency from wild fluctuations in value, and the Underwood Tariff Act (1913), which lowered import duties and levied the first federal income tax.

When World War I began in Europe in 1914, Wilson declared that the United States would remain neutral, a stance Bryan wholeheartedly supported. Neutrality became harder to maintain, however, as German submarines repeatedly sank American vessels in the Atlantic. (Bryan argued in vain that Americans should temporarily yield the right to travel in perilous waters.) When the British liner *Lusitania* was sunk on May 7, 1915, drowning 1,198 passengers, including 128 Americans, Wilson wrote several stern warnings to the German government. Unable to support what he regarded as a violation of neutrality, and frustrated by Wilson's bypassing him and conducting foreign policy on his own, Bryan resigned on June 9, 1915. Bryan remained loyal to the president, however, and, once war was declared, asserted that Germany must be defeated "at all costs."

Bryan continued speaking and writing, but was less directly involved in politics. He made his last campaign against the teaching of evolution as scientific fact (rather than theory) in public schools. In the Scopes "Monkey" trial of 1925, John T. Scopes, a teacher in Dayton, Tennessee, was charged with violating the state's law by teaching evolution (as opposed to the biblical account of creation as told in Genesis). The American Civil Liberties Union had engaged Scopes to allow himself to be arrested, in order to stage a "test case" of the law. With Bryan arguing for the prosecution and **Clarence Darrow** the defense, the stage was set for a highly publicized battle that pitted traditional belief (and literal interpretation of the Bible) against modern, scientific rationalism.

The trial was also a media spectacle in which everyone involved ultimately appeared either ridiculous or mean-spirited. Bryan was subjected to a withering cross-examination by Darrow, the sharpest courtroom attorney of the day and a longtime political enemy. Bryan was a devout believer, but his attempts to defend literal interpretation of the Bible's account of creation could not stand up under Darrow's interrogation. The 100-degree heat and the strain of the trial exhausted Bryan; Darrow's questions (and big-city newspapers accounts) made him look foolish. Soon after the trial (Scopes was found guilty and fined $100, though the verdict was later overturned), Bryan died in his sleep in Dayton, Tennessee, on July 26, 1925.

In his early political career, William Jennings Bryan was the most prominent Democrat in the nation and a pioneering advocate of many social and political reforms that would eventually become standard. These causes and the assistance he gave to Wilson's New Freedom legislation helped modernize the nation; paradoxically, at the end of his life he was struggling to defend a simpler, fundamentalist view of a bygone world that, in part, his work had helped to weaken.

Mark LaFlaur

For Further Reading

Allen, Frederick Lewis. *Only Yesterday: An Informal History of the 1920s.* New York: Perennial Classics, 2000.

Ashby, LeRoy. *William Jennings Bryan: Champion of Democracy.* Boston: Twayne, 1987.

Cherny, Robert W. *A Righteous Cause: The Life of William Jennings Bryan.* Edited by Oscar Handlin. Boston: Little, Brown, 1985.

Coletta, Paolo E. *William Jennings Bryan.* 3 vols. Lincoln: University of Nebraska Press, 1964–69.

"CROSS OF GOLD" SPEECH by William Jennings Bryan (JULY 8, 1896) [EXCERPT]

... Never before in the history of this country has there been witnessed such a contest as that through which we have just now passed. Never before in the history of American politics has a great issue been fought out as this issue has been, by the voters of a great party. On the fourth of March, 1895, a few Democrats, most of them members of Congress, issued an address to the Democrats of the nation, asserting that the money question was the paramount issue of the hour; declaring that a majority of the Democratic party had the right to control the action of the party on this paramount issue; and concluding with the request that the believers in the free coinage of silver in the Democratic party should organize, take charge of, and control the policy of the Democratic party. Three months later, at Memphis, an organization was perfected and the silver Democrats went forth openly and courageously proclaiming their belief, and declaring that, if successful, they would crystallize into a platform the declaration which they had made.

Then began the conflict. With a zeal approaching the zeal of Peter the Hermit, our Silver Democrats went forth from victory into victory until they are now assembled not to discuss, not to debate, but to enter upon the judgment already entered by the plain people of this country. In this contest brother has been arrayed against brother, father against son. The warmest ties of love, acquaintance, and association have been disregarded; old leaders have been cast aside when they refused to give expression to the sentiments of those whom they would lead, and new leaders have sprung up to give direction to this cause of truth. Thus has the contest been waged, and we have assembled here under as binding and solemn instructions as were ever imposed upon the representatives of the people....

If they ask us why it is that we say more on the money issue than we say upon the tariff question, I reply that, if protection has slain its thousands, the gold standard has slain its tens of thousands. If they ask us why we do not embody in our platform all the things that we believe in, we reply that when we have restored the money of the Constitution all other necessary reforms will be possible; but until this is done there is no other reform that can be accomplished.

Why is it that within three months such a change has come over the country? Three months ago, when it was confidently asserted that those who believe in the gold standard would frame our platform and nominate our candidates, even the advocates of the gold standard did not think that we could elect a President. And they had good reason for their doubt, because there is scarcely a state here today asking for the gold standard which is not in the absolute control of the Republican party....

We go forth confident that we shall win. Why? Because on the paramount issue of this campaign there is not a spot of ground upon which the enemy will dare to challenge battle. If they tell us that the gold standard is a good thing, we shall point to their platform and tell them that their platform pledges the party to get rid of the gold standard and substitute bimetallism. *If the gold standard is a good thing, why try to get rid of it?...*

An excerpt from the New York Times *account of William Jennings Bryan's "Cross of Gold" speech at the Democratic National Convention in Chicago on July 8, 1896.*

Source: Wilson, Charles Morrow. *The Commoner: William Jennings Bryan.* Garden City, N.Y.: Doubleday, 1970.

Mr. Carlisle said in 1878 that this was a struggle between "the idle holders of idle capital" and "the struggling masses, who produce the wealth and pay the taxes of the country"; and, my friends, the question we are to decide is: Upon which side are we, [the side of] "the idle holders of idle capital" or upon the side of "the struggling masses"? This is the question which the party must answer first, and then it must be answered by each individual hereafter. The sympathies of the Democratic party, as shown by the platform, are on the side of the struggling masses, who have ever been the foundation of the Democratic party. There are two ideas of government. There are those who believe that, if you will only legislate to make the well-to-do prosperous, their prosperity will leak through on those below. The Democratic idea, however, has been that if you legislate to make the masses prosperous, their prosperity will find its way up through every class that rests upon them.

You come to us and tell us that the great cities are in favor of the gold standard; we reply that the great cities rest upon our broad and fertile prairies. Burn down your cities and leave our farms, and your cities will spring up again as if by magic; but destroy our farms, and the grass will grow in the streets of every city in the country. . . .

Our ancestors, when but three million in number, had the courage to declare their political independence of every other nation; shall we, their descendants, when we have grown to seventy millions, declare that we are less independent than our forefathers? No, my friends, that will never be the verdict of our people. Therefore, we care not upon what lines the battle is fought. If they say bimetallism is good, but that we cannot have it until other nations help us, we reply that, instead of having a gold standard because England has, we will restore bimetallism, then let England have bimetallism because the United States has it. If they dare come out in the open field and defend the gold standard as a good thing, we will fight them to the uttermost. Having behind us the producing masses of this nation and the world, supported by the commercial interests, and the toilers everywhere, we will answer their demand for a gold standard by saying to them: You shall not press down upon the brow of labor the crown of thorns, you shall not crucify mankind upon a cross of gold.

"GATHERING DATA FOR THE TENNESSEE TRIAL" POLITICAL CARTOON (1925)

As the prosecuting attorney in the 1925 Scopes "Monkey" trial, Bryan became an important player in the sensational case that pitted traditional belief against scientific rationalism. In this political cartoon, published in the N.Y. World on May 19, 1925, Rollin Kirby shows Bryan observing organgutans in a zoo "in preparation" for his defense of the Bible's account of creation.

Source: From the collections of the Library of Congress.

ORANG-UTANS HABITAT

BRYAN

ROLLIN KIRBY

"Mr. Bryan's Last Speech" from the Scopes Trial (1925) [Excerpt]

May It Please the Court,
and Gentlemen of the Jury:

Demosthenes, the greatest of ancient orators, in his "Oration on The Crown," the most famous of his speeches, began by supplicating the favor of all the gods and goddesses of Greece. If, in a case which involved only his fame and fate, he felt justified in petitioning the heathen gods of his country, surely we, who deal with the momentous issues involved in this case, may well pray to the Ruler of the Universe for wisdom to guide us in the performance of our several parts in this historic trial. . . .

Can any Christian remain indifferent? Science needs religion to direct its energies and to inspire with lofty purpose those who employ the forces that are unloosed by science. Evolution is at war with religion because religion is supernatural; it is, therefore, the relentless foe of Christianity, which is a revealed religion.

Let us, then, hear the conclusion of the whole matter. Science is a magnificent material force, but it is not a teacher of morals. It can perfect machinery, but it adds no moral restraints to protect society from the misuse of the machine. It can also build gigantic intellectual ships, but it constructs no moral rudders for the control of storm-tossed human vessels. It not only fails to supply the spiritual element needed but some of its unproven hypotheses rob the ship of its *compass* and thus endanger its cargo.

In war, science has proven itself an evil genius; it has made war more terrible than it ever was before. Man used to be content to slaughter his fellowmen on a single plain—the earth's surface. Science has taught him to go down into the water and shoot up from below, and to go up into the clouds and shoot down from above, thus making the battlefield three times as bloody as it was before; but science does *not* teach brotherly love. Science has made war so hellish that civilization was about to commit suicide; and now we are told that newly discovered instruments of destruction will make the cruelties of the late war seem trivial in comparison with the cruelties of wars that may come in the future. If civilization is to be saved from the wreckage threatened by intelligence not consecrated by love, it must be saved by the moral code of the meek and lowly Nazarene. His teachings, and His teachings alone, can solve the problems that vex the heart and perplex the world. . . .

It is for the jury to determine whether this attack upon the Christian religion shall be permitted in the public schools of Tennessee by teachers employed by the State and paid out of the public treasury. This case is no longer local; the defendant ceases to play an important part. The case has assumed the proportions of a battle-royal between unbelief that attempts to speak through so-called science and the defenders of the Christian faith, speaking through the Legislators of Tennessee. . . .

Again force and love meet face to face, and the question, "What shall I do with Jesus?" must be answered. A bloody, brutal doctrine—Evolution—demands, as the rabble did nineteen hundred years ago, that He be crucified. That cannot be the answer of this jury representing a Christian State and sworn to uphold the laws of Tennessee. Your answer will be heard throughout the world; it is eagerly awaited by a praying multitude. If the law is nullified, there will be rejoicing wherever God is repudiated, the Saviour scoffed at and the Bible ridiculed. Every unbeliever of every kind and degree will be happy. If, on the other hand, the law is upheld and the religion of the school children protected, millions of Christians will call you blessed and, with hearts full of gratitude to God, will sing again that grand old song of triumph:

"Faith of our fathers, living still,
In spite of dungeon, fire and sword;
O how our hearts beat high with joy
Whene'er we hear that glorious word—
Faith of our fathers—holy faith;
We will be true to thee till death!"

Bryan's closing remarks in the Scopes trial were never delivered in court—the case was submitted to the jury without argument. However, Bryan intended to publish the speech and had just finished his revision before his sudden death.

Source: Bryan, William Jennings, and Mary Baird Bryan. *The Memoirs of William Jennings Bryan.* New York: Haskell House Publishers Ltd., 1925.

Anti-Evolution League Book Sale (1925)

At the beginning of the Scopes trial in Dayton, Tennessee, the Anti-Evolution League held a book sale featuring some of Bryan's books.
Source: ©Bettmann / Corbis.

"BRYAN AND THE DOGMA OF MAJORITY RULE" by Walter Lippmann (1926) [EXCERPT]

An excerpt from Walter Lippmann's 1926 essay "Bryan and the Dogma of Majority Rule" on William Jennings Bryan's defense in the 1925 Scopes trial in Dayton, Tennessee, from Men of Destiny.

Source: Lippmann, Walter. Men of Destiny. New York: Macmillan, 1927. Reprinted with the permission of Scribner, a division of Simon & Schuster, Inc., from Men of Destiny by Walter Lippmann. ©1927 by the Macmillan Company, copyright renewed ©1955 by Walter Lippmann.

During the Dayton trial there was much discussion about what had happened to Mr. Bryan. How had a progressive democrat become so illiberal? How did it happen that the leader of the hosts of progress in 1889 was the leader of the hosts of darkness in 1925?

It was said that he had grown old. It was said that he was running for President. It was said that he had the ambition to lead an uprising of fundamentalists and prohibitionists. It was said that he was a beaten orator who had found his last applauding audience in the backwoods. And it was said that he had undergone a passionate religious conversion.

No matter whether the comment was charitable or malicious, it was always an explanation. There was always the assumption that Mr. Bryan had changed, and that, in changing, he had departed from the cardinal tenets of his political faith. Mr. Bryan vehemently denied this and, on reflection, I am now inclined to think he was right. We were too hasty. Mr. Bryan's career was more logical and of a piece than it looked. There was no such contradiction, as most of us assumed, in the spectacle of the Great Commoner fighting for the legal suppression of scientific teaching.

He argued that a majority of the voters in Tennessee had the right to decide what should be taught in their schools. He had always argued that a majority had the right to decide. He had insisted on their right to decide on war and peace, on their right to regulate morals, on their right to make and unmake laws and lawmakers and executives and judges. He had fought to extend the suffrage so that the largest possible majority might help to decide; he had fought for the direct election of senators, for the initiative and referendum and direct primary, and for every other device which would permit the people to rule. He had always insisted that the people should rule. And he had never qualified this faith by saying what they should rule and how. It was no great transformation of thought, and certainly it was not for him an abandonment of principle to say that, if a majority in Tennessee was fundamentalist, then the public schools in Tennessee should be conducted on fundamentalist principles.

To question this right of the majority would have seemed to him as heretical as to question the fundamentalist creed. Mr. Bryan was as true to his political as he was to his religious faith. He had always believed in the sanctity of the text of the Bible. He had always believed that a majority of the people should rule. Here in Tennessee was a majority which believed in the sanctity of the text. To lead this majority was the logical climax of his career, and he died fighting for a cause in which the two great dogmas of his life were both at stake.

Given his two premises, I do not see how it is possible to escape his conclusions. If every word of the first chapter of Genesis is directly inspired by an omniscient and omnipotent God, then there is no honest way of accepting what scientists teach about the origin of man. And if the doctrine of majority rule is based on the eternal and inherent rights of man, then it is the only true basis of government, and there can be no fair objections to the moral basis of a law made by a fundamentalist majority in Tennessee. It is no answer to Mr. Bryan to say that the law is absurd, obscurantist, and reactionary. It follows from his premises, and it can be attacked radically only by attacking his premises.

This first premise—that the text of the Bible was written, as John Donne put it, by the Secretaries of the Holy Ghost—I shall not attempt to discuss here. There exists a vast literature of criticism. I am interested in his second premise: that the majority is of right sovereign in all things. And here the position is quite different. There is a literature of dissent and of satire and denunciation. But there exists no carefully worked-out higher criticism of a dogma which, in theory at least, constitutes the fundamental principle of nearly every government in the Western World. On the contrary, the main effort of political thinkers during the last few generations has been devoted to vindicating the rights of masses of men against the vested rights of clerics and kings and nobles and men of property. There has been a running counter attack from those who distrusted the people, or had some interest in opposing their enfranchisement, but I do not know of any serious attempt to reach a clear understanding of where and when the majority principle applies.

Mr. Bryan applied it absolutely at Dayton, and thereby did a service to democratic thinking. For he reduced to absurdity a dogma which had been held carelessly but almost universally, and thus demonstrated that it was time to reconsider the premises of the democratic faith. Those who believed in democracy have always assumed that the majority should rule. They have assumed that, even if the majority is not wise, it is on the road to wisdom, and that with sufficient education the people would learn how to rule. But in Tennessee the people used their power to prevent their own children from learning, not merely the doctrine of evolution, but the spirit and method by which learning is possible. They had used their right to rule in order to weaken the agency which they had set up in order that they might learn how to rule. They had founded popular government on the faith in popular education, and they had used the prerogatives of democracy to destroy the hopes of democracy. . . .

Annie Jump Cannon

Annie Jump Cannon was the most famous American female astronomer in the first half of the twentieth century. She devised the classification system of stellar spectra and identified more stars than anyone in history.

Born in Dover, Delaware, on December 11, 1863, Cannon became fascinated by the night sky during her childhood. One of the first Delaware women to attend college, she graduated with a bachelor of science degree from Wellesley College in Massachusetts in 1884 and spent the next 10 years at her family home in Dover. Her major scientific work didn't begin until after her mother's death in 1893. In 1894 Cannon returned to Wellesley as a physics assistant and graduate student, and the following year she enrolled as a special student of astronomy at Radcliffe, where she studied under Edward C. Pickering, director of the Harvard College Observatory. In 1896, she became an assistant at the Harvard Observatory on Pickering's project to classify and catalogue stars from data on photographic plates according to their spectra, the distinct features of a

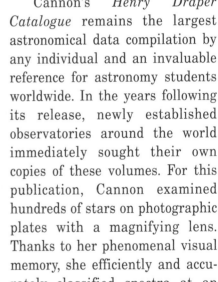

From the collections of the Library of Congress.

star's radiation such as color and brightness. Cannon published her initial findings on bright southern stars in the Harvard *Annals* in 1901, and a decade later, she began her most extensive research as curator of astronomical photographs. In 1914, having gained international recognition in the scientific community, Cannon was made an honorary member of the Royal Astronomical Society in England.

Between 1918 and 1924, Cannon's revolutionary investigations on stellar spectra appeared in nine volumes of the *Henry Draper Catalogue,* published in the *Annals* of the Harvard Observatory. The catalogue contains a record of 225,300 stars with each star's spectral classification, position in the sky, and visual and photographic magnitude. To document her observations, Cannon applied the classification system that she had developed earlier from spectra photographed at the Harvard station in Arequipa, Peru. Her system, modifying

previous methods used at Harvard by Williamina P. Fleming and Antonia C. Maury, represented a class sequence descending from hotter to cooler temperatures: O, B, A, F, G, K, M. Ranging from type O at 70,000 degrees Fahrenheit to type M at 4,000 degrees Fahrenheit, the temperature of a star corresponds to its color with types O and B blue, A white, F and G yellow, K orange, and M red. In 1922, the International Astronomical Union adopted this order, known as the "Harvard System," as the official classification system of stellar spectra.

Cannon's *Henry Draper Catalogue* remains the largest astronomical data compilation by any individual and an invaluable reference for astronomy students worldwide. In the years following its release, newly established observatories around the world immediately sought their own copies of these volumes. For this publication, Cannon examined hundreds of stars on photographic plates with a magnifying lens. Thanks to her phenomenal visual memory, she efficiently and accurately classified spectra at an average of three stars per minute. The catalogue, in which Cannon designated every classification, holds immense value in its consistent format and detailed attention to the peculiarities of particular stars.

After completing the *Henry Draper Catalogue,* Cannon started exploring fainter stars for the *Henry Draper Extension.* This two-volume set, published between 1925 and 1936, classifies 130,000 stars from select regions such as the Milky Way areas in Cygnus, Sagittarius, and Carina. In addition to her *Henry Draper* research, Cannon discovered approximately 300 variable stars, which change in brightness, and five novas, which grow intensely bright and then gradually dim. All of these achievements earned her numerous honors in the United States and abroad. In 1925, she became one of the few women to be elected to the American Philosophical Society and the first woman ever to receive an honorary doctoral degree from Oxford University. Cannon also held five other honorary degrees from the University of Delaware (1918), Groningen University in Holland (1921), Wellesley College (1925), Oglethorpe University (1935), and Mount Holyoke College (1937). In 1924, at the end of an era that had come to know her priceless contributions, the National League of Women Voters named her one of the 12 greatest living women in America.

A pioneer in astronomy, Cannon helped establish greater acceptance of and opportunities for women scientists at a time when women generally found most professions closed to them. Mainstream society still believed that women were intellectually inferior to men and that they could not handle the demands imposed by politics, higher education, and the sciences. Only in 1920 had women gained the right to vote, an accomplishment won in part by the efforts of the same National League of Women Voters that honored Cannon. The sciences, in particular, had long been dominated by men and perceived as a rational, arduous, and impersonal subject. Women, often depicted as emotional and delicate, were traditionally excluded from this field and directed toward more "nurturing" roles. Women scientists, consequently, faced severe prejudices and challenges because they defied popular conceptions about a woman's feminine nature. When Cannon entered astronomy in the late nineteenth century, women had just begun to gain acceptance in the astronomical community because of the development of women's colleges and the need for new types of research characterized as "women's work," such as routine calculations, measurements, and data entry. Cannon and other Harvard Observatory women, placed in low-paying, subordinate positions, performed these jobs with patience and diligence and, in the process, made significant contributions to astronomy.

Throughout the 1930s, Cannon continued to break down barriers of sexism and discrimination in science. In 1931, Cannon was the first woman awarded the Henry Draper Medal of the National Academy of Sciences, one of the most prestigious astronomical awards in the United States, and, in 1932, she was the laureate of the $1,000 Ellen Richards Prize. A year later she donated this prize money to the American Astronomical Society to establish the Annie J. Cannon triennial award recognizing important contributions by women astronomers around the world. In 1938, after working over 40 years at the Harvard Observatory, Cannon received an appointment as the William Cranch Bond Astronomer. She retired from the observatory in 1940 but continued her research until shortly before her death in Cambridge, Massachusetts, on April 13, 1941.

The greatest female astronomer of her time, Cannon laid the groundwork for the exploration of stellar evolution. On a clear night, the human eye may possibly discern 2,000 stars; through persistent research, she identified some 400,000. Uncovering some of the celestial mysteries of the universe, Cannon helped increase the status of her generation and future generations of women scientists.

Renée Miller

For Further Reading

Kass-Simon, G., and Patricia Farnes, eds. *Women of Science: Righting the Record.* Bloomington and Indianapolis: Indiana University Press, 1993.

Rossiter, Margaret W. *Women Scientists in America: Struggles and Strategies to 1940.* Baltimore, Md.: Johns Hopkins University Press, 1982.

Yost, Edna. *American Women of Science.* Philadelphia: Lippincott, 1955.

"FRIEND TO THE STARS" by Kate M. Tucker (June 14, 1924) [EXCERPT]

Cannon hoped to expand common knowledge of the celestial world. In this excerpt from Kate M. Tucker's article "Friend to the Stars," Cannon remarks on the probability of making errors in her work, society's relation to the stars, and the challenges of popularizing astronomy.

Source: Tucker, Kate M. "Friend to the Stars." *Woman Citizen* 9, no. 13, June 14, 1924.

. . . Annie Jump Cannon has been listed among the twelve great women of the world. It is difficult to discover if this listing has pleased her or overwhelmed her. That it has made an impression, one realizes merely because she speaks of the League of Woman Voters, which collected the votes that named the twelve, as one refers to a familiar face—a friend. But she has not taken the compliment personally: rather as a recognition of the work which she believes has merely carried her along on its tide of progress. . . .

The work which Miss Cannon does now is almost entirely with photographs of the stars. The first successful plate was obtained in 1890, and the perfecting of the dry process has materially aided in keeping the plates free from injury. The rays of the star are passed through a prism and the image is piled up upon the plate, which is left exposed for days. From this plate Miss Cannon takes her readings with the aid of a magnifying glass, calling her observations to a recorder who repeats. The width, the intensity, and the distance apart of the bright lines all have a meaning to her which she detects at a glance.

"For one becomes used to the stars," she says. "In this way I have covered the sky. . . . It is quite a problem to cover the sky.

"In astronomy," she continued, "a worker is never allowed to change an observation. All errors must stand and be acknowledged as such. Other astronomers must know the probable error of observation. The stars stay on forever, we are the ones who grow old.

"I often wonder how many mistakes I have made in my catalogue. I may have duplicated some of the stars. It would be difficult not to, for the plates overlap in the sky and the duplicate stars have to be eliminated. Then there are the figures to consider—and the printer makes many errors, which all have to be checked so carefully. I asked a visiting astronomer one day if he thought I could have made mistakes in my recording. 'Of course, you probably have,' he answered. 'But if you have made a mistake in about three or four thousand stars we won't mind.'

"This catalogue, you see, is the basis from which the astronomers all over the world start. They take data, figures and observations from it, and on these records build up their theories and, eventually, facts.

"It must be remembered when the work first started here no records existed anywhere. We had nothing to guide us; all our observations had to be duplicated again and again until definitely proved, before they could be accepted. Even in the work of the catalogue the sky was drawn off into rectangular squares, each square photographed and each star in each square classified and listed. And each one had to be checked. It has all required much patience." And the vision in her eyes mocked the word patience, even as she used it.

"Too few people care about the stars. Sometimes I have wondered if it were possible to popularize astronomy. Old people know the stars and children love them. Working men ask about them. These people are the ones who come to me seeking—when they learn that I know the stars. Astronomy has been given up in our school curriculums for domestic science and stenography. Stars are no longer regarded as useful, therefore, they have been abandoned. A century ago people knew them better. Men were closer to the sea and learned their value in steering ships. Houses were lit by lamps and the stars could be seen by their inhabitants at night. Culture was given precedence in the schools over practicality and stars all had names to the students. That is why at the receptions here at the Observatory I find the old people can call the stars by name, the young people do not know them.

"Now we have electric lights, and the great cities of Boston and Cambridge are so brilliantly lighted that the stars are hard to see. At sea we hide in luxurious cabins and do not even question the machinery which holds us so steadily to our course.

"Children still love the stars. They grasp the idea of the fairy-tale—the might-be of the star so far away. They are closer to the stars, for all things are possible to them.

"The trouble is not with the American people themselves, for the American observatories and astronomers rank very high. The only other peoples who can compete with them are the English. English women are very well up on astronomy.

"It is just the difficulty of popularizing real learning. People are too busy just getting on in the world to stop and wonder. Astronomy appeals to the imagination and is interesting most, perhaps, to people who are drawn into daily contact with the stars, those whose work leads them to where the stars are still to be seen. They are vital to the working classes, to gardeners and to chauf-feurs. A chauffeur asked me one day: 'At night I have seen a cluster of stars in the East, later at dawn I have seen a cluster in the West that looks the same—why is this? And when I explained to him that they were the same, and told him the theory of the rotation of the earth on its axis, he was most grateful. He seemed to me like the primitive man—observing and wondering." A free masonry exists with great people—they never stoop to teach those who ask—they merely share.

"Marriage does interfere with this work, especially for women. Like all intensive work it must be carried on in groups to be really successful. Many women here at the Observatory have married, fully intending to keep on—but they rarely do. Their interests become diversified, they have not the instruments, the materials nor the incentive to keep on alone. It is work that demands isolation—and, if you would call it so, sacrifice. But the reward is worth it. Perhaps," —and, again, Miss Cannon's rare humor lighted her face—"the proximity of Harvard with its numberless youths is a bad influence in keeping women astronomers at work here permanently. However, very few women care for research work. They would rather teach or hold executive positions where they come into contact with more people."

For as Annie Jump Cannon says: "It might seem that examining an hourly average of 200 streaks with vertical lines through them would not be interesting work. I know that if my whole heart were not in such a task it would be monstrous. But they aren't just streaks to me—each new spectrum is a gateway to a wonderful new world."

And this is her message to the world which has dubbed her great.

"When first I started I studied the bright stars—and the methods opened up. An old-line astronomer, one who studied the solar system, laughed at my classifying the stars: 'It is a pleasing pastime,' he said, for he thought that it could not be done."

It is done—the word finis is written at the bottom of volume 99. And for each new spectrum Annie Jump Cannon has entered through a gateway into a new world.

"And now," she said, "I am planning an extension to the work. I am starting to classify the variable stars. I am searching for the fainter ones, those farther away in space. I have listed about 3,400 of these, twice as many as are in the bowl of the dipper. The fifth magnitude is the farthest which can be seen with the naked eye. We have discovered stars in the twelfth. Not so long ago I had a European astronomer ask me if I had ever located a star in the fifteenth magnitude.

She smiled and shrugged her shoulders.

"So far, I think we have done very well."

So far. . . .

ANNIE JUMP CANNON WITH OTHER HARVARD COLLEGE OBSERVATORY STAFF (c. 1925)

Cannon's pioneering work in astronomy opened avenues for women scientists. Taken in about 1925, this photo shows Cannon (fifth from left) with her female colleagues at the Harvard College Observatory. Left to right: (front) Irene Crossman, Mary B. Howe, Harvia H. Wilson, Margaret L. Walton (Mayall), Antonia C. Maury; (middle) Lillian L. Hodgdon, Annie J. Cannon, Evelyn F. Leland, Ida E. Woods, Mabel A. Gill, Florence Cushman; (rear) Margaret Harwood, Cecilia H. Payne (Gaposchkin), Arville D. Walker, Edith F. Gill.

Source: Harvard College Observatory.

"THE AWARD OF THE DRAPER MEDAL TO DR. ANNIE J. CANNON" from *Scientific Monthly* (1932)

Over her lifetime, Cannon earned numerous honors for her contributions to astronomy. Appearing in Scientific Monthly *in April 1932, this article describes her research on stellar spectra in the* Henry Draper Catalogue *and commends her on winning the Henry Draper Medal of the National Academy of Sciences.*

Source: Reprinted with permission from J. M. Cattell, "The Award of the Draper Medal to Dr. Annie J. Cannon." *Scientific Monthly*, April 1932. ©1932, American Association for the Advancement of Science.

One of the most marked distinctions in the American astronomical world was recently conferred on Dr. Annie Jump Cannon, of the Harvard College Observatory at a meeting of the National Academy of Sciences in New Haven last November, when she was awarded the Henry Draper Medal for outstanding achievement in astronomical physics.

Perhaps no single item of information about the stars finds its way into so many different aspects of astronomical research as does the knowledge of their spectra. In problems of distance, brightness, temperature, size, motions, distribution in space, variation, and physical structure, the spectrum of a star plays a revealing role. And it is to Miss Cannon's untiring work during the past thirty years that much of the present knowledge of stellar spectra owes its existence.

Dr. Cannon, who was born in Dover, Delaware, graduated from Wellesley College. She has received honorary degrees from Wellesley, from Groningen and from Oxford, where she was the first woman to receive the honorary degree of Doctor of Science.

The work which was, in the course of time, to provide such a powerful instrument for astronomers in their analysis of stellar structure, was begun at the instigation of Professor Pickering, then director of the Harvard Observatory. A considerable amount of work had been done on classifying spectra on the Harvard photographs. Miss Cannon re-organized the classification, and so effective was the result that it has, with few additions, remained ever since the internationally accepted basis for stellar analysis.

The most distinguishing characteristic of Miss Cannon's classification of stars is the fact that it reveals a continuous sequence throughout the entire gamut of stellar types. This relationship exhibited among all classes of stars shows the possibility of an evolutionary progress, and offers much in the way of explaining the history and development of the stars.

During a period of fifteen years Miss Cannon devoted her energies to analyzing and classifying 225,000 stars, over the whole sky. Her results were published in a series of nine volumes of the Harvard Observatory Annals, in which are given not only the stars' spectra, but their positions and magnitudes as well.

Since completion of this catalogue, Miss Cannon has demonstrated her remarkable energy and enthusiasm by undertaking an extension to the catalogue, comprising stars of magnitudes fainter than those earlier classified. This extension already contains the classification of over a hundred thousand stars.

The catalogue itself is a memorial to Henry Draper. It is peculiarly fitting that the valuable work of Dr. Cannon should be acknowledged by the conferring on her of the Henry Draper Medal.

Al Capone

1899–1947

Organized Crime Boss

Al Capone was a famous gangster who controlled organized crime in Chicago and contributed significantly to the city's lawless reputation during the Prohibition era.

Alphonse Capone was the fourth of nine children born to Italian immigrants in Brooklyn, New York, on January 17, 1899. Raised in a rough neighborhood, he belonged to two juvenile gangs, the Brooklyn Rippers and the Forty Thieves Juniors. After dropping out of school in the seventh grade, he joined the notorious Five Points Gang, managed by the racketeer Johnny Torrio. Capone, loyal and reliable, became Torrio's protégé. After Torrio relocated to Chicago, Capone became the bartender and bouncer at gangster Frankie Yale's Brooklyn nightclub. One night at the club, Capone received three slashes across his left cheek in a brawl, leading to his later nickname "Scarface." In 1919, Capone was invited to Chicago to assist Torrio with underworld operations.

The Eighteenth Amendment, or Prohibition, took effect in 1920; the Amendment criminalized the manufacture, sale, and transportation of alcoholic beverages but, of course, did not eliminate the public's demand for booze. The distribution of liquor provided lucrative opportunities for crooks in Chicago, where its citizens had voted against Prohibition by six to one and politicians and police were easily corrupted. Capone quickly became Torrio's right-hand man and manager of his headquarters, the Four Deuces. A saloon, gambling den, and brothel, it was an infamous underworld attraction. Capone used his physical strength to intimidate and punish rivals, and his combination of cunning and violence eventually rewarded him with a share of the business and a quarter of the weekly profits of the Four Deuces. Torrio and Capone also organized a bootlegging syndicate in the Chicago Loop, the Levee, and the western and southern suburbs of the city, gaining power by providing highly valued goods to the public. Capone soon became a new kind of celebrity—one who intrigued people with his notorious reputation and, in effect, glamorized crime.

From the collections of the Library of Congress.

After Torrio's retirement from the Chicago rackets in 1925, Capone emerged as the city's chief vice lord. Besides the Four Deuces, Capone had suburban headquarters at the Anton Hotel and the Hawthorne Inn. His speakeasies, gambling dens, brothels, distilleries, breweries, and other illicit enterprises earned approximately $100,000,000 per year. Often boasting that he "owned" Chicago, Capone secured his control by tampering with local elections. His armed gangsters would frighten voters into selecting corrupt candidates and batter, kidnap, or kill those who refused to cooperate. Everyone from political leaders to police officers protected the Capone empire.

The reign of Capone, however, was never fully safeguarded from competitors. During the 1920s, fighting among bootleggers and their gangs resulted in hundreds of deaths in the streets of Chicago. Capone engaged in ruthless violence and his enemies retaliated with similar cold-bloodedness. One of the most infamous attempts on Capone's life, called the "Bootleg Battle of the Marne" after the 1914 World War I battle, occurred on September 20, 1926. In broad daylight, the O'Banion gang from Chicago's North Side machine-gunned more than 1,000 rounds at the Hawthorne Inn. The bullets shattered all the windows and destroyed the outside doorway, but Capone and others inside were unharmed. After this shootout, Capone successfully eliminated two of the men who launched the attack, arranging the murders of Earl "Hymie" Weiss and Vincent "the Schemer" Drucci. Only one lead member of the O'Banion gang remained—George "Bugs" Moran.

The St. Valentine's Day Massacre, an event planned to assassinate Moran, was Capone's most notorious slaughter. Jack "Machine Gun" McGurn set the plan in motion by hiring a middleman to entice Moran and his mob with high-quality whiskey at an unusually low price. On February 14, 1929, minutes after the whiskey was delivered to Moran's main bootlegging headquarters, four Capone men exited from a stolen police car and entered the O'Banion storage garage. Two of these men wore police uniforms, thus the seven already inside assumed it was a routine raid and surrendered their weapons. Capone's men frisked them and then opened fire with two machine guns and two shotguns, killing the seven men with more than 150 bullets. Yet their central target, Moran, was not among the victims.

Even though Capone had gone to Florida to establish an alibi, Moran immediately knew who was behind the attack, telling reporters "only Capone kills like that." Capone attempted to keep a low profile and feign innocence, but this proved nearly impossible in the spotlight of international publicity and police inquiry. The public was appalled by Capone's violence and President Herbert Hoover wanted him in prison. Although the nation once romanticized the image of the smartly dressed and coolly authoritative gangster, it now awakened to the reality of the brutal criminal world. Even the country's racketeers believed that Capone had crossed the line and they united to disband his monopoly. Seeking a safe hideout, Capone arranged to be arrested on a minor weapons charge and went behind bars for 10 months.

Capone left his cell in 1930 only to face heightened governmental pressures from "The Untouchables," a special justice squad designed to combat organized crime and police corruption. The Justice Department successfully weakened Capone's "outfit," but, ironically, it was the Treasury Department that finally destroyed him. In 1931, Capone was convicted, not for murder and mayhem, but for federal income-tax evasion. He was sentenced to $80,000 in fines and 11 years in prison. He served two years at the Atlanta Penitentiary before transferring to California's Alcatraz, a maximum-security prison built in response to high crime levels during the 1920s and 1930s. Released early on medical orders in 1939, Capone underwent hospitalization for syphilis, and his mental and physical health deteriorated. With the end of Prohibition in 1933, Capone's time had passed, and his particular brand of malfeasance went out of style. On January 25, 1947, the now-penniless and insane Capone died of syphilis at his Palm Island estate in Florida.

At the prime of Capone's rule in the middle and late 1920s, he dominated organized crime in Chicago and profited from the public's demand for illegal liquor. The Eighteenth Amendment, which was enacted to promote health and morality, brought with it corruption and murder. Capone once remarked about the hypocrisy of Prohibition: "Everybody calls me a racketeer. I call myself a businessman. When I sell liquor it's bootlegging. When my patrons serve it on a silver tray on Lake Shore Drive, it's hospitality." Capone capitalized on these social contradictions in a city and an era where politics, the law, and crime worked together as a corrupt trinity.

Renée Miller

For Further Reading

Bergreen, Laurence. *Capone: The Man and the Era.* New York: Simon and Schuster, 1994.

Kobler, John. *Capone: The Life and World of Al Capone.* New York: Da Capo Press, 1992.

Schoenberg, Robert J. *Mr. Capone: The Real and Complete Story of Al Capone.* New York: Morrow, 1992.

The Eighteenth Amendment, which outlawed the manufacture, sale, or transportation of alcohol, became a part of the Constitution on January 29, 1919. It became operative one year after ratification, initiating an era of Prohibition that allowed gangsters like Capone to thrive off the public's demand for illegal alcohol.

Source: The Constitution of America as Amended. 102d Cong., 2d sess. 1992, House Doc. 102–188.

EIGHTEENTH AMENDMENT TEXT (January 29, 1919)

Section 1. After one year from the ratification of this article the manufacture, sale, or transportation of intoxicating liquors within, the importation thereof into, or the exportation thereof from the United States and all territory subject to the jurisdiction thereof for beverage purposes is hereby prohibited.

Section 2. The Congress and the several States shall have concurrent power to enforce this article by appropriate legislation.

Section 3. This article shall be inoperative unless it shall have been ratified as an amendment to the Constitution by the legislatures of the several States, as provided in the Constitution, within seven years from the date of the submission hereof to the States by the Congress.

Rap Sheet of Al Capone (1919–31)

Admission: 1919; Arrested at N.Y. City. Disorderly Conduct. (Fighting) Discharged.

1923,? Arrested, Chicago, Ill. Traffic Violation (Collision) Dismissed.

1923,? (Denied) Fined $150.00. Operating disorderly House, Gambling at Chicago, Ill.

9-5-23; Arrested. Pistol in Car. Discharged.

3-5-24; (Denies) Arrested, Chicago, Ill. Witness—Johnnie Duffey. Murder. Released.

5-8-24; Arrested, Chicago, Ill. Witness—murder Joe Howard.

1925,? Arrested, Olean, N.Y. (Denied) Disorderly. Released.

6-7-26; Indicted at Chicago, Ill. Viol. Nat'l Pro. Act—Dismissed.

7-15-26; Indicted, Stickney, Ill. Vote Fraud. Dismissed in Dec, 1926.

7-28-26; Arrested, Chicago, Ill. Murder. Charge withdrawn.

10-1-26; Indicted, Chicago, Ill. Viol. N.P. Act (With 78 others) Dismissed.

11-12-27; Arrested, Chicago, Ill. Refusal to Testify. Dismissed.

12-22-27; Fined $2600.00, Joliet, Ill., with 5 other Henchmen. Concealed weapons.

May 17, 1929; Received at Eastern State Pen., Philadelphia, Pa. to serve 12 months for Concealed Weapons. Disch. By Exp. Sentence 3-17-30.

5-8-30; Arrested at Miami, Fla. Suspicion. Kept in jail over night and released.

May 1930; Arrested several times at Miami, Fla., from May 8th to May 17th. Suspicion, Vagrancy, Perjury. Consolidated and dismissed.

2-27-31; Sentenced at Chicago, Ill. To serve 6 months for Contempt. Appealed the case. Conviction affirmed (part of this sentence)

Indictment pending, Chicago, Ill. Cons. Viol. Nat'l Pro, Act.

Capone, a feared gangster and skilled manipulator, managed to avoid conviction for his heinous crimes from his first charge in 1919 to the St. Valentine's Day Massacre in 1929, probably as the result of crooked police and politicians. When he arrived at the Atlanta Penitentiary, his rap sheet, which contained numerous errors, showed the omission of his major felonies and revealed his repeated discharges.

Source: Bergreen, Laurence. Capone: The Man and the Era. New York: Simon & Schuster, 1994.

St. Valentine's Day Massacre (1929)

The St. Valentine's Day Massacre on February 14, 1929, was considered Capone's most notorious slaughter and monumental blunder. This famous photo shows the aftermath of the massacre that left seven men dead but failed to assassinate the primary target, George "Bugs" Moran. Although Capone secured his alibi by going to Florida, Moran knew the true perpetrator of the crime.

Source: From the collections of the Library of Congress.

MUG SHOT OF AL CAPONE (1931)

"WALTER WINCHELL ON BROADWAY: PORTRAIT OF A MAN TALKING TO CAPONE" by Walter Winchell (1931)

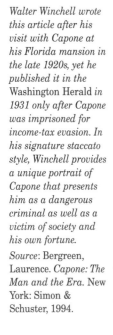

A mutual friend asked me if I would like to meet Capone, and I said I would . . . Might have made a lot of coin from all those magazines that asked for an article on the visit with "The Capones at Home". . . But I told Capone I wouldn't go commercial on the call—and I didn't . . . He said that he didn't care whether I did or not—that he never met a newspaper man yet who didn't cross him . . . Wonder is it true what I heard about him? . . . That before retiring each night he cried like a baby.

I had always pictured him as a small and fat person . . . He's over six feet! . . . When I was entering his place, he saw me coming up the three steps leading to the parlor . . . He was playing cards with three huskies . . . Their backs were to the door—Capone faced it! . . . "Oh, come in," he called as he saw me, and in the same breath he must have said to the others, "Scram" because they disappeared quicker than the birds . . . He was sweeping the table clean of cards and chips as I sat down on a settee near his side of the table. . . "Sit over here," he said . . . "No, this is all right," I countered . . . "No, sit over here, please." He persisted but I didn't move . . . My orbs had caught sight of the largest automatic I ever saw . . . He covered the gun with one of his immense paws and hid it on the other side of the table. . . . "I don't understand that," I said, "Here you are play-

ing a game of cards with your friends, but you keep a gun handy" . . . "I have no friends," he said as he handed me a glass of grand beer.

Among other things I learned during that call was that every time you referred to it as his gang, he corrected you with "my organization" . . . He argued long and loud about being blamed for everything—most of which he never did . . . "All I ask is that they leave me alone," he said once . . . I didn't tell him so, but I thought of a lot of people who wished he would leave them alone . . . His beautiful mansion was really another prison for him . . . He couldn't leave it without a heavy guard . . . When he moved it was done secretly—by plane or boat—both of which were anchored in the waters adjacent to his home there . . . He told me of a doctor down in Miami who crossed him for the Government—who told the officials he wasn't sick at all when all the while he thought he'd die from pneumonia . . . "Once," he was saying, "I was so sick I fell down a whole flight of stairs!" . . . The doctor's fee, he thought, was too stiff, and he paid him only half . . . "So he told the Government," said Capone, "that I was never sick" . . . He sighed heavily, and, with a prop smile, added: "That's the funniest thing. Anybody I have wined and dined right in my own house crossed me" . . . He handed me the third beer... Swelegant!

Carrie Chapman Catt

1859–1947
Suffragist Leader

Carrie Chapman Catt was a dynamic activist whose practical politics and shrewd strategies helped secure passage of the Nineteenth Amendment, which granted women a political voice.

Born Carrie Lane on January 9, 1859, in Ripon, Wisconsin, Catt was a precocious child who spent most of her youth in the prairie town of Charles City, Iowa. Graduating from Iowa State College with a bachelor of science degree in 1880, Catt worked as a high school principal in Mason City, Iowa, where in 1883, she became superintendent of schools. Shortly thereafter, she resigned from her position and joined her new husband, Leo Chapman, as coeditor of the local newspaper, the *Mason City Republican*, installing a weekly feature on women's issues called "Woman's World."

After her husband's death in 1886, Catt struggled to support herself. In 1887 she directed her attention to the cause of equal suffrage and served as secretary of the Iowa Woman Suffrage Association. In 1890, she married George W. Catt, who signed a prenuptial legal contract entitling her to devote four months of each year to suffrage work. Catt chaired the organization committee of the National American Woman Suffrage Association (NAWSA) in 1895, and she succeeded Susan B. Anthony as president of the association in 1900. As her husband's health deteriorated in 1904, Catt resigned her presidency to care for him until his death in 1905. For the next nine years, she frequently traveled abroad as leader of the newly formed International Woman Suffrage Alliance (IWSA).

Persuaded by her peers in 1915, Catt resumed the presidency of the NAWSA and proceeded to coordinate her most powerful campaign—the "Winning Plan." At a 1916 emergency conference in Atlantic City, New Jersey, Catt unveiled her platform of political action that required pragmatism, cohesion, and momentum. She worked to combine lobbying efforts at the state level with a broadminded national strategy. To secure voting rights for women, she insisted that NAWSA must seek passage of a federal amendment. Catt

From the collections of the Library of Congress.

believed that Congress would acquiesce to their demands before many of the resistant states would give in, yet she knew that final ratification depended upon the consent of at least 36 state legislatures. Consequently, she called for continued agitation in states with strong pro-suffrage influences, less focus on states with high anti-suffrage sentiments, and more pressure from existing suffrage states to push for a federal amendment. The "Winning Plan" received approval from NAWSA delegates and remained confidential for maximum effectiveness.

During World War I, suffragists in the United States were attacked for fighting for their own causes while the country was at war. Critics accused suffragists of exhibiting disloyal and pro-German sentiments, branding them as un-American pacifists because many promoted international peace. Catt compromised her antiwar principles to soften the anti-suffrage opposition. She drafted a letter announcing her party's support of the war cause, promoted Liberty Loan drives, which raised money for the war effort, and served on the Woman's Committee of the Council of National Defense. She also solicited women to participate in the Red Cross, canteen service, and other patriotic activities. Catt hoped that women's wartime efforts would be reciprocated with the vote.

A brilliant strategist, Catt aligned the policies of the NAWSA with popular sentiments to attract rather than alienate supporters. She incorporated patriotic ideals in her suffrage arguments, reminding the country that true democracy enfranchised all citizens. Woman suffrage, she contended, was a necessary "war measure." Her moderate approach differed vastly from the militant tactics of suffragist leader **Alice Paul** and the National Woman's Party (NWP). Paul and the NWP waged hunger strikes, picketed the White House, and publicly burned copies of President **Woodrow Wilson**'s speeches. In Catt's opinion, their civil disobedience only antagonized opponents and diminshed vital Democratic votes. Although Catt resented Paul for isolating suffragists from the mainstream, she hoped to avoid conflict between the NAWSA and the NWP and recognized their common battle.

Following the path set forth by her great predecessor Susan B. Anthony, Catt was nonpartisan in her appeal to both Democrats and Republicans. She claimed neither as ally nor enemy but networked with both parties. Catt and associates Maud Wood Park and Helen Gardener lobbied tirelessly in Congress for a federal amendment; this strategy was nicknamed the "Front Door Lobby." Catt's nonthreatening activism earned President Wilson's respect and eventually helped convert him to the suffragist cause. Meanwhile, anti-suffragist men and women used sexist and religious arguments in an attempt to block ratification of a federal amendment, believing that women's lives should revolve around the church and family. The possibility of woman suffrage threatened the existing male-dominated power structure, as many anti-suffragists feared that women's votes, by enacting social reforms, would dismantle the economic and political status quo. In 1919, the House and Senate passed the Nineteenth Amendment, also known as the Susan B. Anthony Amendment. Suffragists then rallied for state ratification, celebrating the end of their 72-year struggle when Tennessee became the 36th state to ratify. On August 26, 1920, the Nineteenth Amendment became a part of the Constitution of the United States.

A new era had arrived giving women a political voice, yet in a male-dominated world, this voice did not immediately increase their political status. In the following years, few female candidates held office, and overall voter turnout declined. Conventional societal views still considered men to be the leaders of business and women to be the guardians of the household. In fact, many suffragists shared this very view, claiming that their votes should focus on social issues, such as neighborhood sanitation and education reform, which they felt would improve their domestic lives. Even Catt, who had no children and two unorthodox marriages, stressed that equal suffrage would sustain traditional gender roles. Although support of these views was partly an attempt to sway public opinion toward the suffragist cause, Catt did consider women to be the reformers of society. Historically, women had pursued their civic goals through social reform, a pattern that continued in the 1920s. Organizations like the Women's International League for Peace and Freedom (WILPF) and the National Congress of Parents and Teachers Associations (PTA) strengthened in membership and momentum. Female political activity centered less on electoral offices and more on health, safety, moral, and education issues. Catt, for instance, defended Prohibition—which made the manufac-

ture, sale, or distribution of alcohol illegal—not only because of alcohol's debilitating effects but also because liquor proprietors corrupted the political system by bribing politicians and fixing the outcomes of elections.

Whereas Catt's political causes dealt with social reform and reflected Victorian norms such as traditional gender roles and sexual conservatism, radical feminists desired a female revolution and embraced sexual liberation. Anarchist **Emma Goldman** and activist **Margaret Sanger** advocated birth control, the former idealizing sexual freedom and the latter believing women deserved control over their reproductive abilities. Catt, too, agreed that women had a right to control births, but she usually avoided tackling sexual and reproductive issues and considered "free love" to be a detriment to women and the community, as well as to the suffragist movement as it antagonized the middle class. Her traditional notion of womanhood also continued to clash with Paul's radical politics. For instance, with the rising number of female workers in the 1920s, Catt highly criticized Paul and the NWP's proposal of an Equal Rights Amendment, contending that its passage would eliminate protective labor laws for women.

During the 1920s, Catt sought to improve the lives of all women by continuing work with the IWSA and establishing the League of Women Voters (LWV), the successor of NAWSA. Her main concern, though, became the promotion of world peace. Catt spoke throughout the country on behalf of the Versailles Treaty and the League of Nations; in 1925, she founded the Committee on the Cause and Cure of War, the largest women's peace organization of the decade.

Catt began working for the relief of Jews in Germany in the 1930s. She lobbied for the United States to aid Jewish refugees and formed the Protest Committee of Non-Jewish Women Against the Persecution of Jews in Germany. This coalition gathered over 9,000 signatures for a letter protesting the Nazi pogrom and distributed copies to the League of Nations and women's groups around the world. In honor of this undertaking, Catt became the first woman to receive the American Hebrew Medal in 1933. Her last major enterprise was organizing the 1940 Woman's Centennial Congress that commemorated women's past achievements and future aspirations. A year later Eleanor Roosevelt presented Catt with the Chi Omega gold medal. At 88, Catt died in New Rochelle, New York, on March 9, 1947.

Catt dedicated her life to improving the welfare of women. With forethought and fortitude, she led suffragists in their struggle to achieve passage of the Nineteenth Amendment. She maintained that equal suffrage marked the evolution of the human race and initiated women's independence. In her pursuit of female emancipation and international unity, she exhibited both the pragmatism and idealism that are marks of a dynamic leader.

Renée Miller

For Further Reading

Catt, Carrie Chapman, and Nettie Rogers Shuler. *Woman Suffrage and Politics: The Inner Story of the Suffrage Movement*. New York: Charles Scribner's Sons, 1923.

Fowler, Robert Booth. *Carrie Catt: Feminist Politician*. Boston: Northeastern University Press, 1986.

Peck, Mary Gray. *Carrie Chapman Catt: A Biography*. New York: Octagon Books, 1975.

Van Voris, Jacqueline. *Carrie Chapman Catt: A Public Life*. New York: The Feminist Press at the City University of New York, 1986.

"Woman Suffrage Must Win" by Carrie Chapman Catt (1915)

The woman suffrage amendments which will soon be voted on in New York, Pennsylvania, Massachusetts and New Jersey bring two questions prominently to the front. 1. For what reasons was the vote extended to the men of this country? 2. Do those reasons apply to women?

Governments have been instituted among men to serve the common welfare of the people. It follows therefore that he who pays a tax to support that welfare is given a ballot's share in the disbursement of the money he pays, and he who obeys the laws which regulate that welfare is given a ballot's share in the making of those laws. For these reasons and for no other the vote has been given to men.

These reasons assuredly apply to women. They are not only taxpayers but they pay enormous taxes. They are also affected as closely as men by the nature of the government under which they live. No one will deny these facts. The opponents of woman suffrage for three generations have evaded the fundamental reasons for extending the vote to women and have attempted to discover some cause which would place them outside the pale of these reasons.

They have so far failed that constitutions have been amended in eleven states to grant complete suffrage to women. In Illinois the municipal and presidential franchise has been conferred, and full suffrage in Alaska. Suffragists hold that they have a demonstration complete and overwhelming in behalf of their cause in the following facts: Woman suffrage has spread from state to neighboring state where people know best what woman suffrage means. No anti-suffrage movement exists in any suffrage state. No person who advocated the enfranchisement of women before its adoption has changed his mind, while the number of those who did oppose it and who are now enthusiastic supporters is legion.

Yet despite logic that no one attempts to deny, and the practically unanimous approval of the great West, a struggle to obtain woman suffrage is now in progress in four states of the East which finds no equal in world campaigns. In the center of the stage where the limelight is most brilliant stand women, respectable and doubtless conscientious women, who to the superficial observer seem to be the chief opponents.

These women have two lines of appeal. They eloquently plead: "Do not thrust the ballot upon us; we do not want it," and there are those who believe this to be a valid excuse for withholding it from the entire sex. There are two classes of men who vote in the United States; those who have been born here and those who have been naturalized here. Is any boy of twenty-one or any man who steps forth from a naturalization court ever asked whether he wants to vote? Has the vote been given to any man because he wanted it? Never. The vote is given to use or not to use as the individual chooses. It is permissive, never compulsory. It can be no burden to those to whom it is extended, for such persons as possess no patriotic desire to serve in this manner the country under which they live are free to remain away from the ballot box.

The other appeal put forth by women anti-suffragists is one to the world not to trust their sex. Men were a thousand years in reaching the ballot. The cause of delay was on the one hand the distrust which governing classes had of those whom they governed and on the other the distrust which disfranchised men had of members of their own class. So it is not strange perhaps that women plead with men not to trust women. Anti-suffragists appeal to the distrust which those who govern have always shown to the governed and try to strengthen it. It is their claim that women are so lacking in patriotism that they do not want to vote and will not vote when the opportunity is given. They claim that women care so little for the moral development of society that they will not trouble to vote even for good causes. It is their plea that women are so deficient in intelligent understanding of public measures that their votes will weaken any government which admits them.

As men have ever been their own worst enemies, so women have been a potent power to retard the advancement of their own sex. It was women as well as men who were scandalized at the idea of taxing the public to maintain public schools for the education of "shes." It was women who regarded the high school, the college and the university education as indelicate for women. It was women who refused to speak to Dr. Elizabeth Blackwell, the first woman physician. It was women who cried "shame" at Susan B. Anthony when she arose to address a teachers' convention in the State of New York. It was women who cried "served them right" when several of the leading newspapers of this country editorially stigmatized the first women who attempted to speak in public as "she hyenas." It was wives, when the first petition to the legislature for property rights for women was circulated, who refused to sign it upon the ground that the control of property was the just privilege of husbands.

Yet, tho women opposed each step of the progress of their sex in turn, they have not failed to avail themselves of every privilege when it has been won, and no man or woman would now claim that the gain of any of them was a mistake. So it happens that in the year 1915 all women have practically complete emancipation from the old traditions and occupy their present advanced positions because some women were willing

With firm resolution, Catt fought for her cause and foresaw victory. In the essay "Woman Suffrage Must Win," published in a 1915 edition of The Independent, *Catt questions why the United States has granted men voting rights that have been denied to women. Criticizing the irrational reasoning of her opponents, she stresses the logic of woman suffrage.*

Source: Chapman, Carrie. "Woman Suffrage Must Win." The Independent, October to December, 1915.

to demand each right when all the world was against them and to stand by that demand until the world caught up with them. The same type of women who opposed education, property rights, public speech, organization, accept all the privileges won for them by the struggle of other women and from that position of vantage turn to oppose as best they can the logical, inevitable next step in the evolution of women.

The number of women who are demanding the vote grows enormously year by year. I cannot speak with authority as to the number of the disfranchised women in the United States who want to vote, but in the State of New York, where I am familiar with conditions and can speak, 1,000,000 women—a big majority of those who would be eligible to vote—is a conservative estimate.

The handwriting on the wall of human destiny announces the inevitable coming of woman suffrage. All signs point in that direction and none points the other way.

New York City

During World War I, Catt used patriotic messages in order to attract supporters to the suffragist cause. This suffragist poster, circulated by the National Woman Suffrage Publishing Company during the war, suggested that woman suffrage would help the war effort.

Source: Courtesy of the Library of Virginia.

"STAND BY THE COUNTRY" POSTER (c. 1917)

Stand by the Country

TO DEFEND THE NATION all its resources are needed. Women must be mobilized equally with men.

As a measure of Preparedness Give Women the Vote.

England has had to do it. The new franchise bill will give the vote to 6,000,000 women.

Canada has done it. Since the war began five big Canadian provinces have given women the vote.

France is going to do it. The Chamber of Deputies has announced that the municipal vote will be given at once to women.

Denmark did it in 1915; when threatened by war, she gave the vote to women.

Russia is basing her new government on universal suffrage.

THE UNITED STATES HAS BEGUN. Since January **North Dakota, Ohio, Indiana, Rhode Island, Michigan and Nebraska** have been added to the twelve woman suffrage states by giving the Presidential vote to Women. **Arkansas** has broken the ranks of the Solid South and given women primary suffrage.

Don't wait for the tragedies of War to prove that the Country belongs to **both men** and **women.**

It is **our Country** as well as yours. Give us the vote that we may **support** it **most effectively** in both **war and peace.**

NATIONAL WOMAN SUFFRAGE PUBLISHING COMPANY, INC.

171 Madison Avenue 151 **New York City**

DECLARATION OF PRINCIPLES **from the Southern Women's League (c. 1917)**

DECLARATION OF PRINCIPLES OF THE SOUTHERN WOMEN'S LEAGUE FOR THE REJECTION OF THE PROPOSED SUSAN B. ANTHONY AMENDMENT TO THE CONSTITUTION OF THE UNITED STATES

1. We believe in the political principle of Local Self Government and that **State Sovereignty is essential** to the Liberty, Happiness, True Progress, and Welfare of the American People.

2. **WE ARE UNALTERABLY OPPOSED TO THE ADOPTION OF THE SUSAN B. ANTHONY AMENDMENT TO THE CONSTITUTION OF THE UNITED STATES,** which Amendment will force the unrestricted ballot upon unwilling majorities in Southern States, and will place the control of the electorate outside the Sovereign State.

3. We deny the Justice of the Compulsory Regulation of the Electorate of our States by a **combination** of other States, who have no sympathetic understanding of our peculiar Social and Racial problems.

4. We oppose any measure that threatens the continuation of **Anglo-Saxon** domination of Social and Political affairs in each and every State of the Union without strife and bloodshed which would inevitably follow an attempt to overthrow it.

5. We oppose **SOCIALISM, BOLESHVISM, RADICALISM** and all the Social disorders that are now disturbing the world and are rapidly encroaching upon our own Republic, and believe that these disorders will be aided and multiplied and more effectually forced upon the Conservative States such as we represent, through the adoption of the Susan B. Anthony Amendment.

6. We declare that the REJECTION of the Susan B. Anthony Amendment to the Constitution of the United States, in **NO** way affects the rights of the several individual States. **TO SO AMEND THEIR CONSTITUTIONS**, as to enfranchise the women of those States, where a majority so elect; and to throw safeguards and limitations upon electoral qualifications as local conditions demand.

7. We believe that in its present form, we live under the fairest and most liberal Government in the world, and desire to see it perpetuated in order that generations coming after us may enjoy the same Liberty in the Pursuit of Happiness we have enjoyed; and to that end we pledge our most earnest and continued efforts in behalf of the **Rejection of the Susan B. Anthony Amendment to the Constitution of the United States**, and call upon **all true Americans** to join us in this fight.

Anti-suffragists employed various tactics to restrict female voting rights, from racial arguments defending the principles of white supremacy, to biblical arguments proclaiming the sins of woman suffrage. In this Declaration of Principles, *the Southern Women's League opposes the constitutional adoption of the Susan B. Anthony Amendment, asserting that its passage would create social havoc and inhibit their states' rights.*

Source: Wheeler, Marjorie Spruill, ed. *Votes For Women: The Woman Suffrage Movement in Tennessee, the South, and the Nation.* Knoxville: The University of Tennessee Press, 1995.

WOMEN IN THE HOME (c. 1917)

The place of the Woman is in the Home. But merely to stay in the Home is not enough. She must care for the health and welfare, moral as well as physical, of her family.

SHE is responsible for the cleanliness of the house.

SHE is responsible for the wholesomeness of the food.

SHE is responsible for the children's health.

SHE is responsible above all for their morals.

How far can the mother control these things?

She can clean her own rooms and care for her own plumbing and refuse, BUT if the building is unsanitary, the streets filthy, and the garbage allowed to accumulate, she cannot protect her children from the sickness that will result.

She can cook her food well, BUT if dealers are permitted to sell adulterated food, unclean milk, or short weight or measure, she cannot provide either wholesome or sufficient feeding for her family.

She can open her windows to give her children air, BUT if the air is laden with infection, she cannot protect her children from disease.

She can send her children out for exercise, BUT if the conditions on the streets are immoral and degrading, she cannot shield them from these dangers.

It is the government of the town or city that controls these things and the officials are controlled by the men who elect them.

Women do not elect these officials, yet we hold the women responsible for the results of—

Unclean Houses, Defective Sewerage, Unwholesome Food, Fire Risks, Danger of Infection, Immoral Influence on the Streets. If women are responsible for the results, let them have something to say as to what the conditions shall be. There is one simple way to do this. **GIVE THEM THE VOTE.**

Women are by nature and training housekeepers. Let them help in the city housekeeping. They will introduce an occasional spring cleaning.

VOTES FOR WOMEN
Equal Suffrage Association of North Carolina
Raleigh

Suffragists across the country, including Catt, often rallied for their cause on behalf of family needs and social reform. The text from this Women in the Home *brochure, distributed by state suffrage associations, illustrates how women's votes would improve their local conditions and domestic lives.*

Source: Wheeler, Marjorie Spruill, ed. *Votes For Women: The Woman Suffrage Movement in Tennessee, the South, and the Nation.* Knoxville: The University of Tennessee Press, 1995.

On August 18, 1920, suffragists held their breath as Tennessee approved the Nineteenth Amendment by the narrow margin of 50 to 46, becoming the 36th, and final, state needed for ratification. This cartoon from the Chicago Tribune conveys the tensions between suffragist women and Southern anti-suffragist men, who feared that women's voting rights would destabilize traditional gender roles.

Source: Carrie Chapman Catt Papers. Tennessee State Library and Archives. Courtesy of the Tennessee Historical Society.

"SOUTHERN CHIVALRY ISN'T WHAT IT USED TO BE" POLITICAL CARTOON (1920)

NINETEENTH AMENDMENT TEXT (1920)

Section 1. The right of citizens of the United States to vote shall not be denied or abridged by the United States or by any State on account of sex.

Section 2. Congress shall have power to enforce this article by appropriate legislation.

After years of working toward woman suffrage, on August 26, 1920, Catt was finally able to celebrate the ratification of the Nineteenth Amendment. Here is the text of that amendment.

Source: The Constitution of the United States of America as Amended. 102d Cong., 2d sess. 1992, House Doc. 102–188.

Charlie Chaplin

1889–1977

Silent Film Actor and Director

Charlie Chaplin was a silent film actor and director whose comic pantomime and tramp character helped make him the first international movie star. His work combined a quiet social commentary with a gentle humor that endeared him to worldwide audiences.

On April 16, 1889, Charles Spencer Chaplin was born to music-hall performers in London, England. Shortly after his birth, Chaplin's father abandoned the family; he later died of alcoholism when Chaplin was 12. His mother's mental illness and financial misfortunes caused young Chaplin to spend much of his childhood in boarding schools and orphanages. He got his first break in 1898, landing a part with the clog-dancing act "Eight Lancashire Lads." At 17, he joined the Fred Karno Company, a vaudeville comedy troupe that performed musical skits filled with miming, acrobatics, and burlesque. While touring with Karno in New York City, Chaplin attracted the attention of director and producer Mack Sennett and secured a movie contract for $150 a week with the Keystone Film Company. Chaplin moved to Los Angeles in December of 1913 and released his first film, *Making a Living*, in February 1914.

Hulton / Archive.

Chaplin entered the movie industry at an opportune time. Studios had started promoting the star performers of the films, rather than titles or story lines. This "star system" elevated the actor's status and increased the public's fascination with screen personas. By 1914, the industry also advertised features, the principal motion picture in a series of shorter pictures. Feature films marked a new form of entertainment among the middle class and proved profitable. Moreover, movie houses became fashionable with both the economic elites and the poor, serving as a temporary escape for audiences. Chaplin's career benefited from these changes, which increased the feature films' appeal to the masses and created movie stars.

In his second film, *Kid Auto Races at Venice* (1914), Chaplin introduced his famous tramp costume: bowler hat, tight jacket, baggy trousers, floppy shoes, tiny mustache, and cane. After Chaplin signed a one-year contract with Essanay Film Company in 1915, he explored the emotional qualities of his tragicomic tramp character. A classic example of this style was *The Tramp* (1915), where Chaplin plays a fumbling prankster whose love is unrequited. Moving beyond pure slapstick, Chaplin charmed audiences with comedy and raised sympathy for the common man. With his comical mannerisms, Chaplin's tramp character mocked the pretensions of upper-class society.

By 1915, "Chaplinitis" had infected the country, and this talented British youth had become an American icon.

Chaplin achieved every artist's desire—fame, fortune, and artistic freedom. He soon began directing all of his pictures, and his next contract with Mutual Film Corporation guaranteed him $10,000 a week plus a $150,000 signing bonus. He made 12 two-reel films for Mutual between 1916 and 1917, including the memorable *The Pawnshop* (1916), *The Rink* (1916), *Easy Street* (1917), *The Cure* (1917), and *The Immigrant* (1917). In the summer of 1917, he signed a contract with First National to make eight pictures for a staggering $1,000,000 salary and complete artistic control. His second major film for First National, *Shoulder Arms* (1918), was his biggest achievement to date. Released three weeks before the end of World War I, Chaplin plays an American soldier who dreams about capturing the Kaiser and the crown prince of Germany. In 1919, Chaplin, along with leading screen stars Mary Pickford and Douglas Fairbanks and director D. W. Griffith, formed United Artists to independently produce and distribute their own films—thus following the trend of business consolidation in the movie industry, but also breaking free from the Hollywood tradition of keeping businessmen on one side and artists on the other. Chaplin and friends took their financial *and* artistic destinies into their own hands—an act that would serve as inspiration to independent-minded actors and directors in the future.

Beginning in the 1920s, Chaplin received recognition as a serious filmmaker; he presented an in-depth view of the tramp in his feature-length comedies that contained humorous antics and insights on life. In *The Kid* (1921), Chaplin addresses the social problem of parental neglect, as the tramp is transformed into a doting caregiver after discovering an abandoned baby. In *The Gold Rush* (1925), Chaplin creates one of the most unforgettable food scenes in film history, in which the famished tramp savors his shoe like a gourmet Thanksgiving meal. Although the film is lighthearted in tone, it contains an undercurrent of social commentary, as Chaplin seems to compare the class exploitation of the 1898 Klondike Gold Rush to the capitalistic greed of the 1920s.

Chaplin's later films exposed his growing concern with contemporary social issues. *City Lights* (1931), which brought together the tramp's love for a young, blind flower seller with his tempestuous friendship with a millionaire, blended a sweet romance with an exploration of class issues. In *Modern Times* (1936), Chaplin humorously critiques the technological advances in society, perhaps in response to the rise of talking pictures, which took Hollywood by storm in the late 1920s. Chaplin resisted using dialogue until *The Great Dictator* (1940), a satirical commentary on Nazi Germany that demonstrated Chaplin's growing political concerns. His movies and views became associated with the leftist politics that were on the rise at the time.

Chaplin's personal life gained much attention in the 1940s and 1950s. His well-known image as a womanizer grew in 1943 as he entered his fourth marriage, to 18-year-old Oona O'Neill while embroiled in a paternity suit brought by actress Joan Barry. In 1952, at the height of the McCarthy era, Chaplin's reentry permit was revoked by the United States. Publicly attacked because of his political views and support of subversive causes, Chaplin moved to Europe where he enjoyed a warm welcome. He returned to the United States only once, to accept a special Oscar from the Academy of Motion Picture Arts and Sciences in 1972. Chaplin was knighted by Queen Elizabeth II at Buckingham Palace in 1975 and died in Corsier-sur-Vevey, Switzerland, on December 25, 1977.

Chaplin's silent films remain classics. He engaged audiences worldwide in over 70 pictures through the art of pantomime. The tramp—his universal common man—characterized the complexities of humanity. The public loved the vanity of his mustache, the dignity of his cane, and the absurdity of his baggy trousers. Even more, they revered the man behind the costume for his ability to simultaneously convey high-minded satire, low-brow slapstick, and poignant drama. Chaplin was the foremost international star of the silent film era.

Renée Miller

For Further Reading

Chaplin, Charlie. *My Autobiography*. New York: Simon & Schuster, 1964.

Lynn, Kenneth S. *Charlie Chaplin and His Times*. New York: Simon & Schuster, 1997.

Milton, Joyce. *Tramp: The Life of Charlie Chaplin*. New York: HarperCollins, 1996.

Robinson, David. *Chaplin, His Life and Art*. New York: Da Capo Press, 1994.

REVIEW OF THE TRAMP from *Little Review* (1915)

"Chaplinitis" spread throughout America in early 1915. Published that year in the Little Review, *this caustic prose piece scoffs at the public's exultance of Chaplin and his latest movie* The Tramp. *The article labels him the "Mob-God," the dichotomy of vulgar comedian and eminent artist.*

Source: Lynn, Kenneth S. *Charlie Chaplin and His Times.* New York: Simon & Schuster, 1986.

The seats creak expectantly. The white whirr of the movie machine takes on a special significance. In the murky gloom of the theater you can watch row on row of backs becoming suddenly enthusiastic, necks growing suddenly alive, heads rising to a fresh angle. Turning around you can see the stupid masks falling, vacant eyes lighting up, lips parting and waiting to smile. . . . The lights dance on the screen in front. Letters appear in two short words (i.e., *The Tramp*) and a gasp sweeps from mouth to mouth.

The name of a Mob-God flashes before the eyes. Suddenly the screen in front vanishes. In its place appears a road stretching away to the sky and lined with trees. . . . The road smiles like an old friend. And far in the distance a speck appears and moves slowly and jerkily. . . . It takes the form of a man, a little man with a thin cane. . . .

Charlie Chaplin is before them, Charles Chaplin with the wit of a vulgar buffoon and the soul of a world artist. He walks, he stumbles, he dances, he falls. His inimitable gyrations release torrents of mirth clean as spring freshets. He is cruel. He is absurd; unmanly; tawdry; cheap; artificial. And yet behind his crudities, his obscenities, his inartistic and outrageous contortions, his "divinity" shines. He is the Mob-God. He is a child and a clown. He is a gutter snipe and an artist. He is the incarnation of the latent, imperfect, and childlike genius that lies buried under the fiberless flesh of his worshippers. They have created Him in their image. He is the Mob on two legs. They love him and laugh.

"Fruits to Om."

"Glory to Zeus."

"Mercy, Jesus."

"Praised be Allah."

"Hats off to Charlie Chaplin."

REVIEW OF *THE KID* from *Variety* (January 21, 1921)

Charlie Chaplin, after a long absence, comes back in "The Kid." It is a six-reeler, 6,300 feet long, and a corker. It will be called better than "Shoulder Arms" or "A Dog's Life," and is to be sent forth by Associated First National.

In this, the longest subject he has ever released, Chaplin is less of the buffoon and more of the actor, but his comedy is all there and there is not a dull moment, once the comedian comes into the picture, which is along about the middle of the first reel.

"The Kid," for which a year's labor is claimed by the distributors, has all the earmarks of having been carefully thought out and painstakingly directed, photographed and assembled. The cutting, in some places, amounts almost to genius. Introduced as "a picture with a smile—perhaps a tear," it proves itself just that. For while it will move people to uproarious laughter and keep them in a state of unceasing delight, it also will touch their hearts and win sympathy, not only for the star, but for his leading woman, and little Jackie Coogan.

It is almost impossible to refrain from superlatives in referring to this child. In the title role his acting is so smooth as to give him equal honors with the star. Usually Chaplin is the picture; but in "The Kid" he has to divide with the boy, whose character work probably never has been equaled by a child artist. Edna Purviance is attractive as the unmarried mother of the kid, but hers is comparatively a small role.

Chaplin indulges in the usual broad references where he handles a moist infant, and rather overdoes it. Some of this play could be cut out to advantage, and he might also eliminate the flash of the Savior bearing the cross, a piece of symbolism flashed on the screen to emphasize the burden of "the woman whose sin was motherhood," and, perhaps, to give the film tone.

Outside of these two spots, the picture is flawless in treatment and has so many good points, artistically and dramatically, it would seem the better discretion if the cited spots, potential points of attack, were discarded. The action is lightning-fast and the tempo never lags.

The picture, as is to be expected, does not have its action in regal splendors, but in tenements, police stations and back alleys. So there are no "sets" to it. But the photography is sharp all the way and the lightings, especially in the night scenes, are splendid.

There are characteristic "Chaplin touches." A fine instance of imagination is where he dreams of Heaven. His slum alley is transformed into a bit of Paradise, with everybody—including his Nemesis, the cop, and a big bully who had wrecked a brick wall and bent a lamppost swinging at Charlie—turned into angels. Here, with Satan doing a Tex Rickard, a cockfight between Charlie and the bully is promoted and pulled off and feathers fly freely. At another point, Charlie has

"the kid," an infant, in a hammock with an ingeniously arranged coffee pot serving as a nursing bottle. Some of the best business is here.

"The Kid" starts with "the woman" issuing from a maternity hospital, bearing her child in her arms. She is distraught and, after scribbling a note, "please love and care for this orphan," abandons the infant in a limousine. Auto thieves get away with the car, unaware of its cargo. They drive to the slum district, where a wail attracts them to the child and they toss it in an alley. Charlie, ragged but debonair, finds the baby, and tries to get rid of it by putting it in a perambulator with another. But the mother objects and Charlie returns to leave it where he found it. A policeman makes him change his mind. He then hands it to an old man, but the latter drops it into the original perambulator. Charlie is blamed and beaten by the woman, and forced to take the child to his garret house. Five years pass and the boy, devoted to his foster parent, is an enthusiastic assistant in his business, which is glazing. The boy breaks windows and Charlie, "happening" along at the right psychological moment, repairs them.

Meantime, the mother of Jackie has risen to fame as an actress and when visiting the slums, gives the boy a toy without knowing it is her lost child. Subsequently, she holds the child in her arms after he has had a fight and urges Charlie to get a doctor. The latter sends the county authorities after the child, but they get him only after a terrific battle in which little Jackie wields a sledge hammer with all the delightful zest that Chaplin himself could have put into it. As the boy is carried to a waiting auto truck, Chaplin flees over roofs, then drops into the truck and rescues the child. The doctor, who has taken the identification slip from Charlie, is at the house when the mother arrives. Seeing the note, she realizes Jackie is her own boy, and puts a reward offer in the newspapers. This excites the cupidity of the keeper of a lodging house where Charlie and the boy are asleep. He steals the boy and takes him to the police station, where the mother comes and claims him.

Chaplin wanders all night seeking the boy in vain and returns to his slum, worn out. It is then he has his dream of heaven. He is awakened by the policeman, who takes him to the home of the actress, where Jackie and his mother greet him and drag him into the house. This is the end of the picture, the star's back being to the audience at the fade-out.

Chaplin, in his more serious phases, is a revelation; and his various bits of laugh-making business the essence of originality. No better satire has ever been offered by the comedian than the introduction of his ragamuffin kid seated on a curbstone manicuring his nails: and his instruction of the boy in table etiquet will register as one of the best things he has done.

The Kid signaled a turning point for Chaplin as he moved to feature-length comedies and gained acceptance as a serious filmmaker. This review of the film by Variety from January 21, 1921, remarks on his transformation from slapstick clown to sophisticated satirist. In this longer production, Chaplin further develops the fusion of comedy and pathos and comes close to artistic and dramatic perfection.

Source: *Variety Film Reviews* (1907–1980). New York: Garland Publishing, 1983–1985.

CHARLIE CHAPLIN MOVIE POSTERS (1925)

This 1925 photo, which shows a selection of French posters advertising Charlie "Charlot" Chaplin's movies, demonstrates his popularity with international audiences. Alfred Reeves, the production manager of The Gold Rush, *is standing in front of the posters.*
Source: Hulton/Archive.

STILL FROM *THE GOLD RUSH* (1925)

Variety *claimed that* The Gold Rush *(1925) was to comedy what* The Birth of a Nation *(1915) was to drama, and the* New York Times *called the film "the outstanding gem of all Chaplin's pictures." In this classic food scene from the movie, Chaplin feasts on his boiled shoe for Thanksgiving dinner: eating his laces like spaghetti, cutting his boot like tender meat, and relishing the nails of the sole like flavorful bones.*
Source: ©Bettmann/ Corbis.

Calvin Coolidge

President Calvin Coolidge, the cool-mannered and businesslike successor to **Warren G. Harding**, restored discipline to the White House after a series of scandals and presided over an extraordinary business boom in the 1920s nicknamed the "Coolidge prosperity."

John Calvin Coolidge was born in the small town of Plymouth Notch, Vermont, on July 4, 1872. After graduating from the Black River Academy in 1890, Coolidge took an interest in Republican Party politics. He entered Amherst College in 1891, graduating cum laude with the class of 1895.

Coolidge was admitted to the bar in 1897, and opened his own practice early in 1898, at the age of 25. He entered politics as a city councilman in Northampton, Massachusetts, in 1898, and rose steadily in the ranks; he would win 19 out of 20 races in his career. In October 1905 Coolidge married Grace Anna Goodhue of Burlington, Vermont, a lively, popular teacher at a school for the deaf. (Coolidge, nicknamed "Silent Cal," dryly joked that, "having taught the deaf to hear, Miss Goodhue might perhaps cause the mute to speak.") Elected mayor of Northampton in 1909 and 1910, Coolidge lowered taxes, reduced the city's debt, and raised the pay of schoolteachers and other public employees. He was elected state senator (1911–15), appointed president of the state senate in 1913, and served as the lieutenant governor from 1915 to 1918.

Coolidge was elected governor of Massachusetts in 1918 and served most of his term quietly, reducing taxes and trimming the state bureaucracy, until the Boston police strike of September 1919 brought him to national prominence. During the "Red Scare"—a year of nationwide labor strikes and a growing fear of communist influence following the Bolshevik Revolution in Russia—the Boston police walked off the job after the police commissioner denied their right to unionize. Looting and riots broke out across the city, and Coolidge brought in 5,000 National Guards to restore order. Coolidge had hesitated

From the collections of the Library of Congress.

to intervene in a dispute between the police commissioner and the mayor of Boston, but sided with the commissioner in banning the strikers from returning to their old jobs. Replying to labor leader **Samuel Gompers**'s appeal for arbitration, Coolidge stated flatly, "There is no right to strike against the public safety by anybody, anywhere, any time." This clear formulation of public disgust with striking workers as a subversive menace was printed in newspapers across the nation, and Coolidge was hailed as a hero. It was also typical of Coolidge: he didn't waste his words.

He was soon chosen as the running mate to Republican Warren G. Harding in the 1920 presidential election against Ohio governor James M. Cox, whose running mate was Franklin D. Roosevelt; some political wits called the contest a "kangaroo race," in which the hind legs were stronger than the front. Although 1920 was the first year that women nationwide could vote—having finally won the right through the Nineteenth Amendment passed that year—turnout at the polls was under 50 percent, the lowest in U.S. history. Harding and Coolidge trounced the Democrats with 60 percent of the popular vote and 404 electoral votes.

Coolidge kept a low profile during the first two years of the administration, while Harding's old "Ohio Gang" pals went about making secret deals that soon exploded into a scandal. Harding himself was not personally involved in the deals, but he did little to prevent the corruption of his cronies. On August 3, 1923, during a summer vacation at his father's home in Plymouth, Vermont, Coolidge was awakened to learn that Harding had died in the middle of the night in San Francisco. By the light of kerosene lamps, Coolidge took the oath of office administered by his father, a notary, and became the thirtieth president of the United States.

The Harding administration's scandals were just beginning to break around the time of Harding's death. The worst was the Teapot Dome affair, in which Interior

Secretary Albert B. Fall took $400,000 for illegally leasing federal petroleum reserves to oil companies. It is not clear what Vice President Coolidge had known of the "Ohio Gang's" sly dealings, but he kept quiet. No one ever suspected Coolidge of graft or greed—he was respected as a "straight arrow" who lived simply and economically—and the foul smell of corruption surrounding the White House soon cleared as Coolidge took command. He appointed investigating committees, cooperated with the Senate investigators, and demanded the resignations of Fall, Attorney General Harry M. Daugherty, and Secretary of the Navy Edwin Denby.

Coolidge continued the conservative, pro-business policies of his predecessor, focusing on cutting taxes and reducing the national debt. He easily won election in 1924 with the slogan "Keep Cool with Coolidge" and on a platform of tax reduction, lower government spending, a protective tariff, and limited aid to farmers. He was the first president whose inaugural address was broadcast over the radio and the first to hold regular press conferences with reporters. The financial prosperity of the Roaring Twenties was helped along by the president's friendliness to big business: he stacked the Federal Trade Commission, established in 1914 to regulate business and industry, with corporate executives, and Coolidge and Treasury Secretary Andrew Mellon encouraged speculation (anticipation of future profits) in the stock market. "The man who builds a factory," Coolidge wrote, "builds a temple, and the man who works there worships there."

The 1920s saw a rapid growth of advertising and the art of salesmanship and a flood of new consumer items. The Ford Motor Company was rolling out a new car every 10 seconds. Sales of radios, the hot new mass medium of the period, reached $60 million in 1922; by 1929, radio sales topped $842.5 million—an increase of 1,400 percent. Much of this business, however, was built on the unsteady foundations of speculation and buying on credit.

Although business was booming—corporate profits rose 80 percent between 1923 and 1929, industrial output grew by 40 percent, and in that time the number of millionaires increased from 75 to more than 300—there were ominous economic signs. The cost of living was rising, yet industrial wages grew by only 8 percent. Between 1921 and 1929, personal debt rose from $3.1 billion to $6.9 billion. On Wall Street, industrial stocks—which tripled in value between 1921 and 1928—were selling at roughly 10 times a company's earnings, and a speculator needed to put down only 20 percent of the stock's cost.

Not all Americans enjoyed the boom times, certainly not textile workers, miners, and some 30 million farm-

ers—a quarter of the nation's population. American farmers had geared up to feed Europe during World War I, but now European farmers were planting again, so demand fell. Farm incomes dropped by half in 1921 alone. Overproduction only made the problem worse. In the 1920s farm bankruptcies multiplied fivefold, and hundreds of rural banks failed. Coolidge vetoed two bills (in 1927 and 1928) that would have aided farmers by establishing a government corporation to purchase surplus crops. In 1925 he told the Farm Bureau Federation that farmers must compete "on an independent business basis," and the federal government had no business tampering with farm prices.

The administration's greatest foreign policy achievement, through Secretary of State Frank Kellogg, was the signing of the Kellogg-Briand Pact of 1928, a multilateral security treaty (initiated by French foreign minister Aristide Briand) intended to prohibit wars of aggression. Even though the pact was soon violated by Japan (in Manchuria) and Germany (in Europe), it laid a legal foundation for the post–World War II Nuremberg War Trials.

Coolidge was still very popular when he decided not to run for reelection in 1928. Tightlipped as ever, he made his announcement by handing reporters, as they filed past him, a slip of paper with the simple statement, "I do not choose to run for President in 1928." He had nothing more to say.

In retirement in Northampton, the former president wrote his memoirs, *The Autobiography of Calvin Coolidge* (1929), and a syndicated column on current affairs (1930–31). In the fall of 1932, when his own hometown bank was failing in the midst of the Great Depression (1929–39), he made a campaign speech in New York City at Madison Square Garden, two-thirds empty, trying to rally support for Herbert Hoover's desperate bid for reelection against Franklin D. Roosevelt. He died 15 weeks later, on January 5, 1933.

Coolidge was admired as an honest, frugal, and efficient administrator, but his reputation has suffered from an over-reliance on laissez-faire, or "hands-off," treatment of business that allowed imprudent market speculation to plunge the nation into an economic abyss.

Mark LaFlaur

For Further Reading
Allen, Frederick Lewis. *Only Yesterday: An Informal History of the 1920s.* New York: Wiley, 2000.
Ferrell, Robert H. *The Presidency of Calvin Coolidge.* Lawrence: University Press of Kansas, 1998.
McCoy, Donald R. *Calvin Coolidge: The Quiet President.* Lawrence: University Press of Kansas, 1988.
Sobel, Robert. *Coolidge: An American Enigma.* Washington, D.C.: Regnery Publishing, 1998.

NATIONAL GUARDS DURING BOSTON POLICE STRIKE (1919)

Coolidge rose to national prominence in his stand against the Boston police strike in 1919. In this photo, National Guards called in by Coolidge protect a sporting goods store that had been looted. The nation applauded his assertion that "There is no right to strike against the public safety by anybody, anywhere, any time."

Source: ©Bettmann/Corbis.

CALVIN COOLIDGE'S FIRST INAUGURAL ADDRESS (March 4, 1925) [EXCERPT]

In his first inaugural address, broadcast to the nation by radio on March 4, 1925, Coolidge discusses tax reform.

Source: Inaugural Addresses of the Presidents of the United States, 1789–1985. Washington, D.C.: U.S. Government Printing Office, 1989.

. . . This Administration has come into power with a very clear and definite mandate from the people. The expression of the popular will in favor of maintaining our constitutional guarantees was overwhelming and decisive. There was a manifestation of such faith in the integrity of the courts that we can consider that issue rejected for some time to come. Likewise, the policy of public ownership of railroads and certain electric utilities met with unmistakable defeat. The people declared that they wanted their rights to have not a political but a judicial determination, and their independence and freedom continued and supported by having the ownership and control of their property, not in the Government, but in their own hands. As they always do when they have a fair chance, the people demonstrated that they are sound and are determined to have a sound government.

When we turn from what was rejected to inquire what was accepted, the policy that stands out with the greatest clearness is that of economy in public expenditure with reduction and reform of taxation. The principle involved in this effort is that of conservation. The resources of this country are almost beyond computation. No mind can comprehend them. But the cost of our combined governments is likewise almost beyond definition. Not only those who are now making their tax returns, but those who meet the enhanced cost of existence in their monthly bills, know by hard experience what this great burden is and what it does. No matter what others may want, these people want a drastic economy. They are opposed to waste. They know that extravagance lengthens the hours and diminishes the

rewards of their labor. I favor the policy of economy, not because I wish to save money, but because I wish to save people. The men and women of this country who toil are the ones who bear the cost of the Government. Every dollar that we carelessly waste means that their life will be so much the more meager. Every dollar that we prudently save means that their life will be so much the more abundant. Economy is idealism in its most practical form.

If extravagance were not reflected in taxation, and through taxation both directly and indirectly injuriously affecting the people, it would not be of so much consequence. The wisest and soundest method of solving our tax problem is through economy. Fortunately, of all the great nations this country is best in a position to adopt that simple remedy. We do not any longer need wartime revenues. The collection of any taxes which are not absolutely required, which do not beyond reasonable doubt contribute to the public welfare, is only a species of legalized larceny. Under this republic the rewards of industry belong to those who earn them. The only constitutional tax is the tax which ministers to public necessity. The property of the country belongs to the people of the country. Their title is absolute. They do not support any privileged class; they do not need to maintain great military forces; they ought not to be burdened with a great array of public employees. They are not required to make any contribution to Government expenditures except that which they voluntarily assess upon themselves through the action of their own representatives. Whenever taxes become burdensome a remedy can be applied by the people; but if they do not act for themselves, no one can be very successful in acting for them.

The time is arriving when we can have further tax reduction, when, unless we wish to hamper the people in their right to earn a living, we must have tax reform. The method of raising revenue ought not to impede the transaction of business; it ought to encourage it. I am opposed to extremely high rates, because they produce little or no revenue, because they are bad for the country, and, finally, because they are wrong. We can not finance the country, we can not improve social conditions, through any system of injustice, even if we attempt to inflict it upon the rich. Those who suffer the most harm will be the poor. This country believes in prosperity. It is absurd to suppose that it is envious of those who are already prosperous. The wise and correct course to follow in taxation and all other economic legislation is not to destroy those who have already secured success but to create conditions under which every one will have a better chance to be successful. The verdict of the country has been given on this question. That verdict stands. We shall do well to heed it.

These questions involve moral issues. We need not concern ourselves much about the rights of property if we will faithfully observe the rights of persons. Under our institutions their rights are supreme. It is not property but the right to hold property, both great and small, which our Constitution guarantees. All owners of property are charged with a service. These rights and duties have been revealed, through the conscience of society, to have a divine sanction. The very stability of our society rests upon production and conservation. For individuals or for governments to waste and squander their resources is to deny these rights and disregard these obligations. The result of economic dissipation to a nation is always moral decay....

"Third Annual Message" by Calvin Coolidge (December 8, 1925) [Excerpt]

In his "Third Annual Message" to the members of Congress, delivered on December 8, 1925, Coolidge discusses immigration, agriculture, prohibition, and the railroads.

Source: Coolidge, Calvin. "3rd Annual Message to Congress." *Congressional Record*. 69th Cong., 1st sess. 1926, Vol. 67.

IMMIGRATION

While not enough time has elapsed to afford a conclusive demonstration, such results as have been secured indicate that our immigration law is on the whole beneficial. It is undoubtedly a protection to the wage earners of this country. The situation should, however, be carefully surveyed, in order to ascertain whether it is working a needless hardship upon our own inhabitants. If it deprives them of the comfort and society of those bound to them by close family ties, such modifications should be adopted as will afford relief....

AGRICULTURE

No doubt the position of agriculture as a whole has very much improved since the depression of three and four years ago. But there are many localities and many groups of individuals, apparently through no fault of their own, sometimes due to climatic conditions and sometimes to the prevailing price of a certain crop, still in a distressing condition. This is probably temporary, but it is none the less acute. National Government agencies, the Departments of Agriculture and Commerce, the Farm Loan Board, the intermediate credit banks, and the Federal Reserve Board are all cooperating to be of assistance and relief. On the other hand, there are localities and individuals who have had one of their most prosperous years. The general price level is fair, but here again there are exceptions both ways, some items being poor while others are excellent. In spite of a lessened production the farm income for this year will be about the same as last year and much above the three preceding years.

Agriculture is a very complex industry. It does not consist of one problem, but of several. They can not be solved at one stroke. They have to be met in different ways, and small gains are not to be despised.

It has appeared from all the investigations that I have been able to make that the farmers as a whole are determined to maintain the independence of their business. They do not wish to have meddling on the part of the Government or to be placed under the inevitable restrictions involved in any system of direct or indirect price-fixing, which would result from permitting the Government to operate in the agricultural markets. They are showing a very commendable skill in organizing themselves to transact their own business through cooperative marketing, which will this year turn over about $2,500,000,000, or nearly one-fifth of the total agricultural business. In this they are receiving help from the Government. The Department of Agriculture should be strengthened in this facility, in order to be able to respond when these marketing associations want help. While it ought not to undertake undue regulation, it should be equipped to give prompt information on crop prospects, supply, demand, current receipts, imports, exports, and prices.

A bill embodying these principles, which has been drafted under the advice and with the approval of substantially all the leaders and managers in the cooperative movement, will be presented to the Congress for its enactment. Legislation should also be considered to provide for leasing the unappropriated public domain for grazing purposes and adopting a uniform policy relative to grazing on the public lands and in the national forests....

PROHIBITION

Under the orderly processes of our fundamental institutions the Constitution was lately amended providing for national prohibition. The Congress passed an act for its enforcement, and similar acts have been provided by most of the States. It is the law of the land. It is the duty of all who come under its jurisdiction to observe the spirit of that law, and it is the duty of the Department of Justice and the Treasury Department to enforce it....

RAILROADS

The railroads throughout the country are in a fair state of prosperity. Their service is good and their supply of cars is abundant. Their condition would be improved and the public better served by a system of consolidations. . . .

It is gratifying to report that both the railroad managers and railroad employees are providing boards for the mutual adjustment of differences in harmony with the principles of conference, conciliation, and arbitration. . . .

A strike in modern industry has many of the aspects of war in the modern world. It injures labor and it injures capital. If the industry involved is a basic one, it reduces the necessary economic surplus and, increasing the cost of living, it injures the economic welfare and general comfort of the whole people. It also involves a deeper cost. It tends to embitter and divide the community into warring classes and thus weakens the unity and power of our national life. . . .

"CALVIN COOLIDGE: PURITANISM DE LUXE" by Walter Lippmann (1926) [EXCERPT]

. . . Mr. Coolidge may be a great captain but he has never been to sea. He came into office after the great postwar deflation had run its course, and the postwar scandals had run theirs. He inherited a war-time system of taxation which his predecessors had had the pain of imposing. He had the delightful problem of dealing with a surplus and not a deficit, and the pleasure of reducing taxes. A foolish man might have squandered the surplus and not reduced the taxes. Mr. Coolidge took good care of the surplus. Except for the inter-Allied debts, Mr. Coolidge has fortunately not had a single problem in statesmanship of the first order to deal with. As I write it is still uncertain whether he has settled the debts; it is very certain that he has failed to convince anyone in Europe that the United States is generous, although the terms of the Italian debt settlement are very generous indeed.

For the rest, he has approached but done nothing about coal, agriculture or shipping, the three domestic questions which trouble the placid waters. There is no great insistence anywhere that he do anything. These problems produce a certain amount of local inconvenience, but no widespread distress and discontent. It is not imperative that anything should be done. On the contrary, a widespread distaste of political activity is the controlling mood of public life in this country to-day.

Mr. Coolidge's genius for inactivity is developed to a very high point. It is far from being an indolent inactivity. It is a grim, determined, alert inactivity which keeps Mr. Coolidge occupied constantly. Nobody has ever worked harder at inactivity, with such force of character, with such unremitting attention to detail, with such conscientious devotion to the task. Inactivity is a political philosophy and a party program with Mr. Coolidge, and nobody should mistake his unflinching adherence to it for a soft and easy desire to let things slide. Mr. Coolidge's inactivity is not merely the absence of activity. It is on the contrary a steady application to the task of neutralizing and thwarting political activity wherever there are signs of life.

The White House is extremely sensitive to the first symptoms of any desire on the part of Congress or of the executive departments to do something, and the skill with which Mr. Coolidge can apply a wet blanket to an enthusiast is technically marvelous. There have been Presidents in our time who knew how to whip up popular enthusiasm. There has never been Mr. Coolidge's equal in the art of deflating interest. This mastery of what might be called the technique of anti-propaganda is worthy of prolonged and profound study by students of public opinion. The naïve statesmen of the pre-Coolidge era imagined that it was desirable to interest the people in their government, that public discussion was a good thing, that indignation at evil was useful. Mr. Coolidge is more sophisticated. He has discovered the value of diverting attention from the government, and with an exquisite subtlety that amounts to genius, he has used dullness and boredom as political devices.

I do not know whether Mr. Coolidge was born with this gift or whether he developed it by necessity in the absence of certain other political gifts. But I do know that in its present development it is no mean gift. The Democratic Party has good reason to know this, for the Democrats have been flabbergasted and routed by Mr. Coolidge's skill in destroying issues. The Democrats are simple folks used to heating themselves up to a terrific temperature over any issue. They only feel at peace with themselves when they are in an ecstatic broil. They simply do not know what to do with Mr. Coolidge. They hit his party an awful blow. They knocked three members out of his Cabinet and covered them with disgrace. And what happened? Did Mr. Coolidge defend his Cabinet? He did not. Did he prosecute the grafters? Not very fiercely. He managed to get the public so bored that they could bear it no longer, and to make the Democrats thoroughly disliked for raising such a dull row. It was superb. To every yawp Mr. Coolidge can match a yawn. He has had the country yawning over the outcry against relieving the super-rich of taxes, yawning over Colonel Mitchell, yawning over the World Court, yawning over the coal strike. He has brought his technique to such perfection that one paper announced the conclusion of the coal strike in streamer headlines, saying "Coolidge Wins Coal Victory; Denies He Interfered."

This active inactivity suits the mood and certain of the needs of the country admirably. It suits all the business interests which want to be let alone. It suits everybody who is making money who wants to let well enough alone. And it suits all those who have become convinced that government in this country has become dangerously complicated and top-heavy, and that it is important to reduce and decentralize the Federal power. Mr. Coolidge, though a Republican, is no Hamiltonian Federalist. Mr. Slemp is right in saying that he has stopped, if not reversed, the Republican nationalizing tendency which runs from Hamilton to Roosevelt. He has just stopped it, mind you. He has not replaced it with anything. He has just stopped it while business is good.

In his 1926 essay, "Calvin Coolidge: Puritanism De Luxe," Walter Lippmann assesses Coolidge's presidency and critiques his political technique of "active inactivity"— which served business interests and the needs of the consuming public.

Source: Lippmann, Walter. Men of Destiny. New York: Macmillan, 1927. Reprinted with the permission of Scribner, a division of Simon & Schuster, Inc., from Men of Destiny by Walter Lippmann. ©1927 by the Macmillan Company, copyright renewed ©1955 by Walter Lippmann.

The politicians in Washington do not like Mr. Coolidge very much, for they thrive on issues, and he destroys their business. But the people like him, not only because they like the present prosperity, and because at the moment they like political do-nothingism, but because they trust and like the plainness and nearness of Calvin Coolidge himself. This is one of the most interesting conjunctions of our age.

As a nation we have never spent so much money on luxury and pleasure as we are spending now. There has never in all history been such a widespread pursuit of expensive pleasure by a whole people. The American people can afford luxury and they are buying it furiously, largely on the instalment plan. And in the White House they have installed a very frugal little man who in his personal life is the very antithesis of the flamboyant ideal that everybody is frantically pursuing. They have not only installed him in the White House, but they trust him utterly as they hear his voice on expensive radio sets; they praise him as they ride in expensive motor cars; they toast him at banquets where there is more food than can be eaten. At a time when Puritanism as a way of life is at its lowest ebb among the people, the people are delighted with a Puritan as their national symbol.

They are delighted with the oil lamps in the farmhouse at Plymouth, and with fine old Colonel Coolidge and his chores and his antique grandeur. They haven't any of them the slightest intention of living in such a farmhouse if they can escape from it, or of doing the chores if they can buy a machine to do them, or of holding themselves aloof like Colonel Coolidge. But they are delighted that the President comes of such stock, and they even feel, I think, that they are stern, ascetic, and devoted to plain living because they vote for a man who is. The Coolidges are really virtuous people in the old American sense, and they have provided this generation, which is not virtuous in that sense, with an immense opportunity for vicarious virtue.

Thus we have attained a Puritanism de luxe in which it is possible to praise the classic virtues while continuing to enjoy all the modern conveniences.

"FIFTH ANNUAL MESSAGE" by Calvin Coolidge (December 6, 1927) [EXCERPT]

In his "Fifth Annual Message" to the members of Congress, delivered on December 6, 1927, Coolidge addresses issues relating to African Americans and Native Americans.

Source: Coolidge, Calvin. "5th Annual Message to Congress." *Congressional Record.* 70th Cong., 1st sess. 1928, Vol. 69.

THE NEGRO

History does not anywhere record so much progress made in the same length of time as that which has been accomplished by the Negro race in the United States since the Emancipation Proclamation. . . .They have especially been made the target of the foul crime of lynching. For several years these acts of unlawful violence had been diminishing. In the last year they have shown an increase. Every principle of order and law and liberty is opposed to this crime. The Congress should enact any legislation it can under the Constitution to provide for its elimination.

AMERICAN INDIAN

The condition of the American Indian has much improved in recent years. Full citizenship was bestowed upon them on June 2, 1924, and appropriations for their care and advancement have been increased. Still there remains much to be done.

Notable increases in appropriations for the several major functions performed by the Department of the Interior on behalf of the Indians have marked the last five years. In that time, successive annual increases in appropriations for their education total $1,804,325; for medical care $578,000; and for industrial advancement, $205,000; or $2,582,325 more than would have been spent in the same period on the basis of appropriations for 1923 and the preceding years.

The needs along health, educational, industrial, and social lines, however, are great, and the Budget estimates for 1929 include still further increases for Indian administration.

To advance the time when Indians may become self-sustaining, it is my belief that the Federal Government should continue to improve the facilities for their care, and as rapidly as possible turn its responsibility over to the States.

Clarence Darrow

Clarence Darrow, the foremost courtroom lawyer of his time, was known as "the attorney for the damned" because of his defense of anarchists, murderers, and underdogs. He is best remembered for his defense of a science teacher in the famous Scopes "Monkey" trial of 1925.

Clarence Seward Darrow was born on April 18, 1857, near Kinsman, Ohio. After briefly studying law at the University of Michigan, he practiced as a small town lawyer in Ohio for several years. He married Jessie Ohl in 1880; they had one son, moved to Chicago in 1887, and divorced in 1897.

In Chicago he soon became involved in a campaign to secure amnesty for the eight anarchists charged with murder in the 1886 Haymarket riot, a violent confrontation between police and labor protesters. Darrow was an attorney for the Chicago & North Western Railway (1891–94), but resigned to defend American Railway Union president **Eugene V. Debs** and others against federal charges of conspiring against interstate commerce during the Pullman strike, a nationwide boycott initiated by unions that disrupted rail service. Darrow lost the case, but gained a reputation as a forceful defender of workers' rights.

His reputation continued to grow as he represented striking coal miners (1902–03); won the acquittal of labor leader **William "Big Bill" Haywood**, who had been charged with assassinating the governor of Idaho (1908); and defended the McNamara brothers (1911). The McNamaras were accused of dynamiting the antiunion *Los Angeles Times* building and causing the death of 21 people. After a member of Darrow's defense team was arrested for attempting to bribe a potential juror, Darrow changed their plea to guilty. Darrow was later charged with attempted bribery of jurors; he was acquitted ater a three-month trial. His reputation was sullied, but he restored his good name during World War I (1914–18) by supporting the war effort.

In 1924 he took on one of his most notorious cases, the defense of two wealthy Chicago college students, Richard Loeb and Nathan Leopold, who had murdered a 14-year-

From the collections of the Library of Congress.

old simply for the thrill of getting away with a "perfect crime." Darrow saved them from execution by urging them to plead guilty and by arguing against capital punishment based on evidence of their psychological disturbance.

The following year he argued his most celebrated case when he defended a Dayton, Tennessee, teacher named John Thomas Scopes, charged with violating a state prohibition against the teaching of evolution in public schools. The American Civil Liberties Union had encouraged Scopes to allow himself to be arrested, in order to stage a "test case" of the law. The Scopes (or "Monkey") trial was a hot and highly publicized clash of modern rationalism and traditional faith, of science and religion, city and country. Darrow's father had graduated from a theological seminary, but preached no more than a year, and raised his children in an agnostic, rationalist household. Darrow had made his career arguing cases on the basis of reason and logic, and he defended Scopes as a matter of principle—the right to think freely—and took no fee. He argued that the Tennessee legislature had violated academic freedom and the separation of church and state with the antievolution law.

The special prosecutor was **William Jennings Bryan**. A three-time Democratic presidential candidate, former secretary of state, and America's most famous orator, Bryan had grown up as a devout Christian and had recently campaigned throughout the South against the teaching of evolution. In the 100-degree summer heat, Darrow placed Bryan on the stand and shredded his halting defense of a fundamentalist, literal interpretation of the Bible. ("Do you think the Earth was made in six days?" Darrow asked. "Not in six days of twenty-four hours.") Scopes was found guilty, though the verdict was later overturned.

After the Scopes trial, Darrow handled a few high profile cases, most notably his successful defense (1925–26) of Ossian Sweet, a black physician who had fired into a mob gathered to evict him from his new home in a white neighborhood in Detroit. In 1934 President Franklin Roosevelt appointed Darrow chairman of the National Recovery

Review Board, but his report, critical of the administration's New Deal (an economic relief program), was unwelcome. Darrow died of heart disease in Chicago on March 13, 1938.

Clarence Darrow was a complex man who encompassed many of the social and intellectual trends of his time, some of them contradictory. He defended the rights of African Americans and striking workers, but had no interest in women's rights; he was a pacifist who championed U.S. intervention in World War I. He used the cases he took on to publicize larger issues, in part to win sympathy for his clients but also to educate the public toward a more humane, civilized treatment of fellow citizens.

Mark LaFlaur

For Further Reading:
Darrow, Clarence. *The Story of My Life.* New York: Da Capo Press, 1996.
Stone, Irving. *Clarence Darrow for the Defense.* Garden City, N.Y.: Garden City Publishing, 1943.
Tierney, Kevin. *Darrow: A Biography.* New York: Crowell, 1979.
Weinberg, Arthur, and Lila Weinberg. *Clarence Darrow: A Sentimental Rebel.* New York: Putnam, 1980.

CLARENCE DARROW'S LETTER TO THE *CHICAGO TRIBUNE* (July 4, 1923) [EXCERPT]

In a July 4, 1923, letter to the Chicago Tribune, *Clarence Darrow responds to a letter from William Jennings Bryan regarding the teaching of science in the public schools. His letter foreshadows the questions he would later pose to Bryan in the Scopes trial in Dayton, Tennessee, 1925.*

Source: Chicago Tribune, *July 4, 1923.*

Editor of the Tribune: I was very much interested in Mr. Bryan's letter to *The Tribune* and in your editorial reply. I have likewise followed Mr. Bryan's efforts to shut out the teaching of science from the public schools and his questionnaires to various college professors who believe in evolution and still profess Christianity. No doubt his questions to the professors, if answered, would tend to help clear the issue, and likewise a few questions to Mr. Bryan and the fundamentalists, if fairly answered, might serve the interests of reaching the truth—all of this assumes that truth is desirable.

For this reason I think it would be helpful if Mr. Bryan would answer the following questions:

Do you believe in a literal interpretation of the whole Bible?

Is the account of the creation of the earth and all life in Genesis literally true, or is it an allegory?

Was the earth made in six literal days, measured by the revolution of the earth on its axis?

Was the sun made on the fourth day to give light to the earth by day and the moon made on the same day to give light to the night, and were the stars made for the benefit of the earth?

Did God create man on the sixth day?

Did God rest on the seventh day? . . .

Under the biblical chronology, Was not the earth created less than 6,000 years ago?

Were there not many flourishing civilizations on the earth 10,000 years ago?

According to the same chronology, Was not Adam created less than 6,000 years ago?

Are there not evidences in writing and hieroglyphics and the evidence of man's handiwork which show that man has been on the earth more than 50,000 years?

Are there no human remains that carry their age on the earth back to at least 100,000 years?

Has not man probably been on earth for 500,000 years?

Does not geology show by fossil remains, by the cutting away of rock from river beds, by deposit of all sorts, that the earth is much more than a million years and probably many million years old?

Did Christ drive devils out of two sick men and did the devils request that they should be driven into a large herd of swine and were the devils driven into the swine and did the swine run off a high bank, and were they drowned in the sea?

Was this literally true, or does it simply show the attitude of the age toward the cause of sickness and affliction?

Can one not be a Christian without believing in the literal truth of the narrations of the Bible here mentioned?

Would you forbid the public schools from teaching anything in conflict with the literal statement referred to?

Questions might be extended indefinitely, but a specific answer to these might make it clear what one must believe to be a "fundamentalist."

Very truly yours,
Clarence Darrow

"MERCY FOR LEOPOLD AND LOEB" by Clarence Darrow (1924) [EXCERPT]

An excerpt from Darrow's eloquent 1924 defense of Nathan Leopold and Richard Loeb, in which he argues against capital punishment on grounds of mercy and the boys' psychological disturbance. His defense spared the Chicago youths from execution. Darrow argued this sensational case just a year before the Scopes trial.

Now, your Honor, I have spoken about the war. I believed in it. I don't know whether I was crazy or not. Sometimes I think perhaps I was. I approved of it; I joined in the general cry of madness and despair. I urged men to fight. I was safe because I was too old to go. I was like the rest. What did they do? Right or wrong, justifiable or unjustifiable—which I need not discuss to-day—it changed the world. For four long years the civilized world was engaged in killing men. Christian against Christian, barbarian uniting with Christians to kill Christians; anything to kill. It was taught in every school, aye in the Sunday schools. The little children played at war. The toddling children on the street. Do you suppose this world has ever been the same since then? How long, your Honor, will it take for the world to get back the humane emotions that were slowly growing before the war? How long will it take the calloused hearts of men before the scars of hatred and cruelty shall be removed?

We read of killing one hundred thousand men in a day. We read about it and we rejoiced in it—if it was the other fellows who were killed. We were fed on flesh and drank blood. Even down to the prattling babe. I need not tell your Honor this, because you know; I need not tell you how many upright, honorable young boys have come into this court charged with murder, some saved and some sent to their death, boys who fought in this war and learned to place a cheap value on human life. You know it and I know it. These boys were brought up in it. The tales of death were in their homes, their playgrounds, their schools; they were in the newspapers that they read; it was a part of the common frenzy—what was a life? . . .

Your Honor knows that in this very court crimes of violence have increased growing out of the war. Not necessarily by those who fought but by those that learned that blood was cheap, and human life was cheap, and if the State could take it lightly why not the boy? There are causes for this terrible crime. There are causes, as I have said, for everything that happens in the world. War is a part of it; education is a part of it; birth is a part of it; money is a part of it—all these conspired to compass the destruction of these two poor boys. Has the court any right to consider anything but these two boys? The State says that your Honor has a right to consider the welfare of the community, as you have. If the welfare of the community would be benefited by taking these lives, well and good. I think it would work evil that no one could measure. Has your Honor a right to consider the families of these two defendants? I have been sorry, and I am sorry for the bereavement of Mr. and Mrs. Frank, for those broken ties that cannot be healed. All I can hope and wish is that some good may come from it all. But as compared with the families of Leopold and Loeb, the Franks are to be envied—and everyone knows it.

I do not know how much salvage there is in these two boys. I hate to say it in their presence, but what is there to look forward to? I do not know but what your Honor would be merciful if you tied a rope around their necks and let them die; merciful to them, but not merciful to civilization, and not merciful to those who would be left behind. To spend the balance of their days in prison is mighty little to look forward to, if anything. Is it anything? They may have the hope that as the years roll around they may be released. I do not know. I do not know. I will be honest with this court as I have tried to be from the beginning. I know that these boys are not fit to be at large. I believe they will not be until they pass through the next stage of life, at forty-five or fifty. Whether they will then, I cannot tell. I am sure of this, that I will not be here to help them. So far as I am concerned, it is over. . . .

But there are others to consider. Here are these two families, who have led honest lives, who will bear the name that they bear, and future generations must carry it on. . . .

The easy thing and the popular thing to do is to hang my clients. I know it. Men and women who do not think will applaud. The cruel and thoughtless will approve. It will be easy to-day; but in Chicago, and reaching out over the length and breadth of the land, more and more fathers and mothers, the humane, the kind and the hopeful, who are gaining an understanding and asking questions not only about these poor boys, but about their own—these will join in no acclaim at the death of my clients. These would ask that the shedding of blood be stopped, and that the normal feelings of man resume their sway. And as the days and the months and the years go on, they will ask it more and more. But, your Honor, what they shall ask may not count. I know the easy way. I know your Honor stands between the future and the past. I know the future is with me, and what I stand for here; not merely for the lives of these two unfortunate lads, but for all boys and all girls; for all of the young, and as far as possible, for all of the old. I am pleading for life, understanding, charity, kindness, and the infinite mercy that considers all. I am pleading that we overcome cruelty with kindness and hatred with love. I know the future is on my side. Your Honor stands between the past and the future. You may hang these boys; you may hang them by the neck until they are dead. But in doing it you will turn your face toward the past. In doing it you are making it harder for every other boy who in ignorance and darkness must grope his way through the mazes which only childhood knows. In doing it you will make it harder for unborn children. You may save them and make it easier for every child that sometime may stand where these boys stand. You will make it easier for every human being with an aspiration and a vision and a hope and a fate. I am pleading for the future; I am pleading for a time when hatred and cruelty will not control the hearts of men. When we can learn by reason and judgment and understanding and faith that all life is worth saving, and that mercy is the highest attribute of man. . . .

Source: Byron, Basil Gordon, and Frederic René Coudert. *America Speaks*. New York: Modern Eloquence, 1928.

CLARENCE DARROW AT THE SCOPES TRIAL (1925)

In July 1925, at the Scopes trial in Dayton, Tennessee, Darrow defended a high school teacher charged with violating a state law by teaching the theory of evolution. In this photo, Darrow (center) is shown with his defense team in the crowded courtroom.

Source: From the collections of the Library of Congress.

"DARROW'S ELOQUENT APPEAL" by H. L. Mencken (July 14, 1925) [EXCERPT]

Baltimore Sun *editor and correspondent H. L. Mencken took particular pleasure in reporting on the follies of the Scopes trial. In this editorial published in the* Baltimore Sun *on July 14, 1925, he applauds Darrow's blistering attack on prosecuting attorney William Jennings Bryan's fundamentalist beliefs.*

Source: Mencken, H. L. *Baltimore Sun*, July 14, 1925. Reprinted with permission from the *Baltimore Sun*.

Dayton, Tenn., July 14. — The net effect of Clarence Darrow's great speech yesterday seems to be precisely the same as if he had bawled it up a rainspout in the interior of Afghanistan. That is, locally, upon the process against the infidel Scopes, upon the so-called minds of these fundamentalists of upland Tennessee. You have but a dim notion of it who have only read it. It was not designed for reading, but for hearing. The clanging of it was as important as the logic. It rose like a wind and ended like a flourish of bugles. The very judge on the bench, toward the end of it, began to look uneasy. But the morons in the audience, when it was over, simply hissed it.

During the whole time of its delivery the old mountebank, Bryan, sat tight-lipped and unmoved. There is, of course, no reason why it should have shaken him. He has those hill billies locked up in his pen and he knows it. His brand is on them. He is at home among them. Since his earliest days, indeed, his chief strength has been among the folk of remote hills and forlorn and lonely farms. Now with his political aspirations all gone to pot, he turns to them for religious consolations. They understand his peculiar imbecilities. His nonsense is their ideal of sense. When he deluges them with his theological bilge they rejoice like pilgrims disporting in the river Jordan. . . .

The talk of the lawyers, even the magnificent talk of Darrow, is so much idle wind music. The case will not be decided by logic, nor even by eloquence. It will be decided by counting noses — and for every nose in these hills that has ever thrust itself into any book save the Bible there are a hundred adorned with the brass ring of Bryan. These are his people. They understand him when he speaks in tongues. The same dark face that is in his own eyes is in theirs, too. They feel with him, and they relish him.

I sincerely hope that the nobility and gentry of the lowlands will not make the colossal mistake of viewing this trial of Scopes as a trivial farce. Full of rustic japes and in bad taste, it is, to be sure, somewhat comic on the surface. One laughs to see lawyers sweat. The jury, marched down Broadway, would set New York by the ears. But all of that is only skin deep.

Deeper down there are the beginnings of a struggle that may go on to melodrama of the first caliber, and when the curtain falls at least all the laughter may be coming from the yokels. You probably laughed at the prohibitionists, say, back in 1914. Well, don't make the same error twice.

As I have said, Bryan understands these peasants, and they understand him. He is a bit mangey and flea-bitten, but no means ready for his harp. He may last five years, ten years or even longer. What he may accomplish in that time, seen here at close range, looms up immensely larger than it appears to a city man five hundred miles away. The fellow is full of such bitter, implacable hatreds that they radiate from him like heat from a stove. He hates the learning that he cannot grasp. He hates those who sneer at him. He hates, in general, all who stand apart from his own pathetic commonness. And the yokels hate with him, some of them almost as bitterly as he does

himself. They are willing and eager to follow him—and he has already given them a taste of blood.

Darrow's peroration yesterday was interrupted by Judge Raulston, but the force of it got into the air nevertheless. This year it is a misdemeanor for a country school teacher to flout the archaic nonsense of Genesis. Next year it will be a felony. The year after the net will be spread wider. Pedagogues, after all, are small game; there are larger birds to snare—larger and juicier. Bryan has his fishy eye on them. He will fetch them if his mind lasts, and the lamp holds out to burn. No man with a mouth like that ever lets go. Nor ever lacks followers.

Tennessee is bearing the brunt of the first attack simply because the civilized minority, down here, is extraordinarily pusillanimous.

I have met no educated man who is not ashamed of the ridicule that has fallen upon the State, and I have met none, save only judge Neal, who had the courage to speak out while it was yet time. No Tennessee counsel of any importance came into the case until yesterday and then they came in stepping very softly as if taking a brief for sense were a dangerous matter. When Bryan did his first rampaging here all these men were silent.

They had known for years what was going on in the hills. They knew what the country preachers were preaching—what degraded nonsense was being rammed and hammered into yokel skulls. But they were afraid to go out against the imposture while it was in the making, and when any outsider denounced it they fell upon him violently as an enemy of Tennessee.

Now Tennessee is paying for that poltroonery. The State is smiling and beautiful, and of late it has begun to be rich. I know of no American city that is set in more lovely scenery than Chattanooga, or that has more charming homes. The civilized minority is as large here, I believe, as anywhere else.

It has made a city of splendid material comforts and kept it in order. But it has neglected in the past the unpleasant business of following what was going on in the cross roads Little Bethels.

The Baptist preachers ranted unchallenged.

Their buffooneries were mistaken for humor. Now the clowns turn out to be armed, and have begun to shoot.

In his argument yesterday judge Neal had to admit pathetically that it was hopeless to fight for a repeal of the anti-evolution law. The Legislature of Tennessee, like the Legislature of every other American state, is made up of cheap job-seekers and ignoramuses.

The Governor of the State is a politician ten times cheaper and trashier. It is vain to look for relief from such men. If the State is to be saved at all, it must be saved by the courts. For one, I have little hope of relief in that direction, despite Hays' logic and Darrow's eloquence. Constitutions, in America, no longer mean what they say. To mention the Bill of Rights is to be damned as a Red.

The rabble is in the saddle, and down here it makes its first campaign under a general beside whom Wat Tylor seems like a wart beside the Matterhorn.

Eugene V. Debs

1855–1926
Socialist Party Leader

A popular left-wing leader, Eugene V. Debs ran for the presidency five times as the candidate of the Socialist Party. During World War I, his pacifist views clashed with the nation's rising intolerance of dissent, and after the war, imprisoned as part of a widespread crackdown on civil liberties, he conducted his last campaign from his cell.

Eugene Victor Debs was born in Terre Haute, Indiana, on November 5, 1855. He dropped out of high school to work in a local rail yard and was anything but radical. He joined a union, the Brotherhood of Locomotive Firemen, which was oriented more toward mutual aid and social support rather than toward militant labor action. Debs opposed the strikes that began to break out in the 1870s and 1880s, but the increasing ruthlessness of the industrial businessmen, or "robber barons," of the day gradually changed his mind. A gifted orator, he rose to prominence in the labor movement when he led a successful strike against the Great Northern Railroad in Illinois in 1893, and was imprisoned in connection with the Pullman railroad car factory strike in Chicago in 1894. Debs became acquainted with European socialist thought, which merged with his vision of the United States as a place where workers might pursue equality. At the dawn of the twentieth century, several new political parties coalesced out of the labor unrest of the preceding years, and Debs emerged as the leader of the largest of them, the Social Democratic Party of America. American socialism served as a political challenge to capitalism, yet party members were split on the best approach to transforming society; some, such as Debs, supported revolutionary change while others endorsed a more reformist approach. Debs first ran for the office of president in 1900, receiving only 100,000 votes, but by 1912 he had garnered 10 times that figure and a promising 6 percent of the popular vote.

Debs and his compatriots looked forward to a peaceful socialist revolution, a transfer of power from the wealthy classes to the nation's working people effected through elec-

From the collections of the Library of Congress.

toral means. He was an idealist who believed that socialism represented a new way of life, and he had no appetite for compromise with established political parties. Unlike anarchists such as **Emma Goldman**, Debs consistently refused to advocate violence. When the repressive direction of Soviet Russian communism became apparent in the 1920s, he condemned that movement even though he had hailed the communists' rise to power in 1917 and despite the praise and support of the Russian communist leader, Vladimir Lenin. Debs was in poor health by 1916, and declined to run for president a fifth time. He had become increasingly preoccupied by the deepening mire of World War I in Europe. Most of his socialist associates opposed United States entry into the war, and Debs joined in supporting an antiwar resolution adopted at the party's annual convention in 1917. Many socialists, as well as other radicals and anarchists, were harassed and even thrown into prison in 1917 and 1918 as the government clamped down on dissent; the Sedition Act of 1918 was the most restrictive of several measures, proscribing a range of expression that went beyond views specifically related to the war. Mailings of socialist newspapers were banned by some post offices, and Debs, although largely confined to home by illness, felt compelled to speak out against the government's harsh treatment of party members and labor leaders. He embarked on a speaking tour, and was arrested and charged with impeding the war effort after delivering a speech at Ohio's Socialist Party state convention on June 16, 1918, in which he called for an end to the persecutions. Debs's speech at the subsequent trial was eloquent and widely reprinted: "While there is a lower class," he thundered, "I am in it; while there is a criminal element, I am of it; while there is a soul in prison, I am not free." He was sentenced to 10 years in prison and an appeal to the U.S. Supreme Court failed. Debs began serving his term in West Virginia; he was soon transferred to a penitentiary in Atlanta.

The Socialist Party nominated Debs for president for the fifth and final time in 1920, and he accepted and campaigned from his prison cell. Once again Debs rose to the occasion with words of the hour: "There are no bars and no walls for the man who in his heart is free, and there is no freedom for the man who in his heart is a slave." His followers printed campaign buttons that read, "VOTE FOR PRISONER 9653," and Debs gained a respectable 3.5 percent of the November popular vote, eclipsing his 1912 raw total (although the percentage dropped as a result of the increase in the number of ballots cast). But the U.S. socialist movement, under the twin drags of the postwar desire for stability and rising fear of Soviet communism, was running out of steam. The Palmer Raids of 1919 and 1920, in which Attorney General (and presidential hopeful) **A. Mitchell Palmer** deported hundreds of suspected communists, marked the rise of a "Red Scare" that would not abate until well into the 1920s. President **Warren G. Harding** correctly sensed that Debs no longer posed much of a threat and pardoned him on Christmas Day of 1921. His personal popularity and his ability to connect with ordinary people undimmed, Debs was greeted after his release by large crowds in Chicago and in his hometown of Terre Haute.

Debs donated the small sum he received upon his release to the defense fund of anarchists **Nicola Sacco and Bartolomeo Vanzetti**, accused of robbery and murder. At 66 years old, he plunged back into the fray, discouraged but undaunted by the country's increasing conservatism and xenophobic aversion to progressive international ideals. He embarked on a national speaking tour in 1923 and the following year joined with a group of socialist leaders in making common cause with Wisconsin Senator **Robert Marion La Follette**'s Progressive Party. For a time he edited a socialist weekly paper called the *American Appeal*, but his health was failing and he spent much of his time in a Chicago sanatorium. He died there on October 20, 1926.

Eugene Debs fought for economic equality, social justice, and labor reforms; he struggled to transform existing political and legal structures. The harassment and imprisonment of Debs during his life shows much about the direction in which the United States was headed. Those who resisted the mainstream risked their very liberty, and the idea that government might improve the conditions under which common people lived and worked had been nearly stamped out. That idea would emerge once again, in a vastly altered form, only after the onset of the Great Depression (1929–39), when the U.S. government borrowed many of the ideas of leftists like Debs, whom they had once persecuted.

James M. Manheim

For Further Reading

Ginger, Ray. *Eugene V. Debs: A Biography.* New York: Collier, 1980.

Salvatore, Nick. *Eugene V. Debs: Citizen and Socialist.* Urbana: University of Illinois Press, 1982.

Young, Marguerite. *Harp Song for a Radical: The Life and Times of Eugene Victor Debs.* New York: Knopf, 1999.

SPEECH FROM THE CANTON, OHIO, SOCIALIST PARTY CONVENTION by Eugene V. Debs (June 16, 1918) [EXCERPT]

The speech that led to Debs's imprisonment was delivered at a Canton, Ohio, Socialist Party convention on June 16, 1918. The speech embodied many of the qualities that had always made Debs such a powerful orator: it was humorous, it engaged its audience on a personal level, and it rose and fell in grand rhetorical waves. Its notes of bitterness and sarcasm, however, reflected Debs's anger over the government's repression of the socialist-led antiwar movement.

Source: Schlesinger, Arthur, ed. Writings and Speeches of E. V. Debs. New York: Hermitage Press, 1948.

Comrades, friends and fellow-workers, for this very cordial greeting, this very hearty reception, I thank you all with the fullest appreciation of your interest in and your devotion to the cause for which I am to speak to you this afternoon. [Applause.]

To speak for labor; to plead the cause of the men and women and children who toil; to serve the working class, has always been to me a high privilege; [Applause] a duty of love.

I have just returned from a visit over yonder [pointing to the workhouse], where three of our most loyal comrades are paying the penalty for their devotion to the cause of the working class. [Applause.] They have come to realize, as many of us have, that it is extremely dangerous to exercise the constitutional right of free speech in a country fighting to make democracy safe in the world. [Applause.]

I realize that, in speaking to you this afternoon, there are certain limitations placed upon the right of free speech. I must be exceedingly careful, prudent, as to what I say, and even more careful and prudent as to how I say it. [Laughter.] I may not be able to say all I think; [Laughter and applause] but I am not going to say anything that I do not think. [Applause.] I would rather a thousand times be a free soul in jail than to be a sycophant and coward in the streets. [Applause and shouts.]

They may put those boys in jail—and some of the rest of us in jail—but they can not put the Socialist movement in jail. [Applause and shouts.] Those prison bars separate their bodies from ours, but their souls are here this afternoon. [Applause and cheers.] They are simply paying the penalty that all men have paid in all the ages of history for standing erect, and for seeking to pave the way to better conditions for mankind. [Applause.] . . .

There is but one thing you have to be concerned about, and that is that you keep foursquare with the principles of the international Socialist movement. [Applause.] It is only when you begin to compromise that trouble begins. [Applause.] So far as I am concerned, it does not matter what others may say, or think, or do, as long as I am sure that I am right with myself and the cause. [Applause.] There are so many who seek refuge in the popular side of a great question. As a Socialist, I have long since learned how to stand alone. [Applause.] For the last month I have been traveling over the Hoosier State; and, let me say to you, that, in all my connection with the Socialist movement, I have never seen such meetings, such enthusiasm, such unity of purpose; never have I seen such a promising outlook as there is today, notwithstanding the statement published repeatedly that our leaders have deserted us. [Laughter.] Well, for myself, I never had much faith in leaders. [Applause and laughter.] I am willing to be charged with almost anything, rather than to be charged with being a leader. I am suspicious of leaders, and especially of the intellectual variety. [Applause.] Give me the rank and file every day in the week. If you go to the city of Washington, and you examine the pages of the Congressional Directory, you will find that almost all of those corporation lawyers and cowardly politicians, members of Congress, and misrepresentatives of the masses - you will find that almost all of them claim, in glowing terms, that they have risen from the ranks to places of eminence and distinction. I am very glad I cannot make that claim for myself. [Laughter.] I would be ashamed to admit that I had risen from the ranks. When I rise it will be with the ranks, and not from the ranks. [Applause.] . . .

Why should a Socialist be discouraged on the eve of the greatest triumph in all the history of the Socialist movement? [Applause.] It is true that these are anxious, trying days for us all—testing days for the women and men who are upholding the banner of labor in the struggle of the working class of all the world against the exploiters of all the world [applause]; a time in which the weak and cowardly will falter and fail and desert. They lack the fiber to endure the revolutionary test; they fall away; they disappear as if they had never been. On the other hand, they who are animated by the unconquerable spirit of the social revolution; they who have the moral courage to stand erect and assert their convictions; stand by them; fight for them; go to jail or to hell for them, if need be [applause and shouts]—they are writing their names, in this crucial hour—they are writing their names in faceless letters in the history of mankind. [Applause.]

Those boys over yonder—those comrades of ours— and how I love them! Aye, they are my younger brothers [laughter and applause]; their very names throb in my heart, thrill in my veins, and surge in my soul. [Applause.] I am proud of them; they are there for us; [applause] and we are here for them. [Applause, shouts and cheers.] Their lips, though temporarily mute, are more eloquent than ever before; and their voice, though silent, is heard around the world. [Great applause.]

Are we opposed to Prussian militarism? [Laughter.] [Shouts from the crowd of "Yes. Yes."] Why, we have been fighting it since the day the Socialist movement was born; [applause] and we are going to continue to fight it, day and night, until it is wiped from the face of the earth. [Thunderous applause and cheers.] Between us there is no truce—no compromise. . . .

Socialism is a growing idea; an expanding philosophy. It is spreading over the entire face of the earth: It is as vain to resist it as it would be to arrest the sunrise on the morrow. It is coming, coming, coming all along the line. Can you not see it? If not, I advise you to consult an oculist. There is certainly something the matter with your vision. It is the mightiest movement in the history of mankind. What a privilege to serve it! I have regretted a thousand times that I can do so little for the movement that has done so much for me. [Applause.] The little that I am, the little that I am hoping to be, I owe to the Socialist movement. [Applause.] It has given me my ideas and ideals; my principles and convictions, and I would not exchange one of them for all of Rockefeller's bloodstained

dollars. [Cheers.] It has taught me how to serve—a lesson to me of priceless value. It has taught me the ecstasy in the handclasp of a comrade. It has enabled me to hold high communion with you, and made it possible for me to take my place side by side with you in the great struggle for the better day; to multiply myself over and over again, to thrill with a fresh-born manhood; to feel life truly worthwhile; to open new avenues of vision; to spread out glorious vistas; to know that I am kin to all that throbs; to be class-conscious, and to realize that, regardless of nationality, race, creed, color or sex, every man, every woman who toils, who renders useful service, every member of the working class without an exception, is my comrade, my brother and sister—and that to serve them and their cause is the highest duty of my life. [Great applause.]

And in their service I can feel myself expand; I can rise to the stature of a man and claim the right to a place on earth—a place where I can stand and strive to speed the day of industrial freedom and social justice.

Yes, my comrades, my heart is attuned to yours. Aye, all our hearts now throb as one great heart responsive to the battle cry of the social revolution. Here, in this alert and inspiring assemblage [applause] our hearts are with the Bolsheviki of Russia. [Deafening and prolonged applause.] Those heroic men and women, those unconquerable comrades have by their incomparable valor and sacrifice added fresh luster to the fame of the international movement. Those Russian comrades of ours have made greater sacrifices, have suffered more, and have shed more heroic blood than any like number of men and women anywhere on earth; they have laid the foundation of the first real democracy that ever drew the breath of life in this world. [Applause.] And the very first act of the triumphant Russian revolution was to proclaim a state of peace with all mankind, coupled with a fervent moral appeal, not to kings, not to emperors, rulers or diplomats but to the people of all nations. [Applause.] Here we have the very breath of democracy, the quintessence of the dawning freedom. The Russian revolution proclaimed its glorious triumph in its ringing and inspiring appeal to the peoples of all the earth. In a humane and fraternal spirit new Russia, emancipated at last from the curse of the centuries, called upon all nations engaged in the frightful war, the Central Powers as well as the Allies, to send representatives to a conference to lay down terms of peace that should be just and lasting. Here was the supreme opportunity to strike the blow to make the world safe for democracy. [Applause.] Was there any response to that noble appeal that in some day to come will be written in letters of gold in the history of the world? [Applause.] Was there any response whatever to that appeal for universal peace? [From the crowd. "No!"] No, not the slightest attention was paid to it by the Christian nations engaged in the terrible slaughter. . . .

Wars throughout history have been waged for conquest and plunder. In the Middle Ages when the feudal lords who inhabited the castles whose towers may still be seen along the Rhine concluded to enlarge their domains, to increase their power, their prestige and their wealth they declared war upon one another. But they themselves did not go to war any more than the modern feudal lords, the barons of Wall Street go to war. [Applause.] The feudal barons of the Middle Ages, the economic predecessors of the capitalists of our day, declared all wars. And their miserable serfs fought all the battles. The poor, ignorant serfs had been taught to revere their masters; to believe that when their masters declared war upon one another, it was their patriotic duty to fall upon one another and to cut one another's throats for the profit and glory of the lords and barons who held them in contempt. And that is war in a nutshell. The master class has always declared the wars; the subject class has always fought the battles. The master class has had all to gain and nothing to lose, while the subject class has had nothing to gain and all to lose—especially their lives. [Applause.]

They have always taught and trained you to believe it to be your patriotic duty to go to war and to have yourselves slaughtered at their command. But in all the history of the world you, the people, have never had a voice in declaring war, and strange as it certainly appears, no war by any nation in any age has ever been declared by the people.

And here let me emphasize the fact—and it cannot be repeated too often - that the working class who fight all the battles, the working class who make the supreme sacrifices, the working class who freely shed their blood and furnish the corpses, have never yet had a voice in either declaring war or making peace. It is the ruling class that invariably does both. They alone declare war and they alone make peace.

Yours not to reason why;

Yours but to do and die.

That is their motto and we object on the part of the awakening workers of this nation.

If war is right let it be declared by the people. You who have your lives to lose, you certainly above all others have the right to decide the momentous issue of war or peace. [Applause.] . . .

Now what you workers need is to organize, not along craft lines but along revolutionary industrial lines. [Applause.] All of you workers in a given industry, regardless of your trade or occupation, should belong to one and the same union.

Political action and industrial action must supplement and sustain each other. You will never vote the Socialist republic into existence. You will have to lay its foundations in industrial organization. The industrial union is the forerunner of industrial democracy. In the shop where the workers are associated is where industrial democracy has its beginning. Organize according to your industries! Get together in every department of industrial service! United and acting together for the common good your power is invincible.

When you have organized industrially you will soon learn that you can manage as well as operate industry. You will soon realize that you do not need the idle masters and exploiters. They are simply parasites. They do not employ you as you imagine but you employ them to take from you what you produce, and that is how they function in industry. You can certainly dispense with them in that capacity. You do not need them to depend upon for your jobs. You can never be free while you work and live by their sufferance. You must own your own tools and then you will control your own jobs, enjoy the products of your own labor and be free men instead of industrial slaves.

Organize industrially and make your organization complete. Then unite in the Socialist Party. Vote as you strike and strike as you vote.

Your union and your party embrace the working class. The Socialist Party expresses the interests, hopes and aspirations of the toilers of all the world.

Get your fellow workers into the industrial union and the political party to which they rightly belong, especially this year, this historic year in which the forces of labor will assert themselves as they never have before. This is the year that calls for men and women who have courage, the manhood and womanhood to do their duty.

Get into the Socialist Party and take your place in its ranks; help to inspire the weak and strengthen the faltering, and do your share to speed the coming of the brighter and better day for us all. [Applause.]

When we unite and act together on the industrial field and when we vote together on election day we shall develop the supreme power of the one class that can and will bring permanent peace to the world. We shall then have the intelligence, the courage and the power for our great task. In due time industry will be organized on a cooperative basis. We shall conquer the public power. We shall then transfer the title deeds of the railroads, the telegraph lines, the mines, mills and great industries to the people in their collective capacity; we shall take possession of all these social utilities in the name of the people. We shall then have industrial democracy. We shall be a free nation whose government is of and by and for the people.

And now for all of us to do our duty! The clarion call is ringing in our ears and we cannot falter without being convicted of treason to ourselves and to our great cause.

Do not worry over the charge of treason to your masters, but be concerned about the treason that involves yourselves. [Applause.] Be true to yourself and you cannot be a traitor to any good cause on earth.

Yes, in good time we are going to sweep into power in this nation and throughout the world. We are going to destroy all enslaving and degrading capitalist institutions and re-create them as free and humanizing institutions. The world is daily changing before our eyes. The sun of capitalism is setting; the sun of socialism is rising. It is our duty to build the new nation and the free republic. We need industrial and social builders. We Socialists are the builders of the beautiful world that is to be. We are all pledged to do our part. We are inviting—aye challenging you this afternoon in the name of your own manhood and womanhood to join us and do your part.

In due time the hour will strike and this great cause triumphant—the greatest in history—will proclaim the emancipation of the working class and the brotherhood of all mankind. [Thunderous and prolonged applause.]

EUGENE V. DEBS DELIVERING CANTON, OHIO, SPEECH (JUNE 16, 1918)

Debs speaking in Canton, Ohio. Photographs of Debs in action in front of a crowd reveal a charismatic speaker of limitless energy and a boundless desire to connect with and inspire common people.

Source: Courtesy Eugene V. Debs Foundation, Terre Haute, Indiana.

EUGENE V. DEBS'S CAMPAIGN BUTTON (1920)

Debs conducted his fifth and final run for the presidency from an Atlanta prison cell. His followers printed these buttons, which now command a premium price among collectors of political memorabilia.

Source: Courtesy Eugene V. Debs Foundation, Terre Haute, Indiana.

TERRE HAUTE CITIZENS SIGNING PETITIONS (1921)

Debs commanded extraordinary loyalty among his followers. In 1921 they agitated for his release from prison; 21,000 residents of his hometown of Terre Haute, Indiana, signed petitions demanding that he be freed. President Warren Harding commuted Debs's 10-year sentence on Christmas Day of 1921.

Source: Courtesy Eugene V. Debs Foundation, Terre Haute, Indiana.

Jack Dempsey

Jack Dempsey was a world heavyweight boxing champion whose mammoth strength and savage aggression made him a leading box office attraction during the 1920s, an era that craved the excitement of sports extravaganzas and celebrities.

Born William Harrison Dempsey on June 24, 1895, in Manassa, Colorado, he was the ninth of 11 children raised by sharecroppers on the Western frontier. His childhood included minimal schooling and much labor. The young Dempsey farmed, hauled coal, chopped trees, waited tables, and shined shoes to help support his family. Eager to escape, he left home at the age of 16. For the next five years, with little education and no training, he wandered through mining camps and hobo jungles in search of work and food. Dempsey ultimately relied on brute force for survival, fighting for money in barrooms and later in the boxing ring.

Historically, boxing has tended to attract men from lower-income communities, and in the early twentieth century, many of these men were immigrants with few opportunities. Enduring the physical demands and persistent dangers of the sport, these athletes viewed boxing as a way out of poverty.

Assuming the name "Kid Blackie," Dempsey fought his first professional fight in 1914. He quickly developed his skills competing against veterans like Jack Downey and Andy Malloy in mining towns. By the end of 1916, he had knocked out both of these men as well as other rivals such as "Two-Round Gillian," "One-Punch Hancock," and the "Boston Bearcat." About this time he dropped his own colorful title for Jack Dempsey, the ring name of a former middleweight champion. In 1917, under the direction of manager John Leo McKernan, known as "Doc" Kearns, Dempsey began winning bouts that attracted the press and ignited the crowds. A year later his 22 matches—21 victories that included 11 first-round knockouts—qualified him as a chief contender for the heavyweight championship.

On July 4, 1919, 20,000 fight fans watched Dempsey challenge the reigning champion Jess Willard in Toledo, Ohio. Willard was an inch and a half taller and 70 pounds heavier,

but Dempsey was quicker on his feet and fiercer with his punches. In the first round, Dempsey knocked Willard down seven times and crushed his cheekbone: a white towel tossed from Willard's corner into the ring indicated the fight had ended after the third round. Frenzied spectators rushed to carry Dempsey—the new heavyweight champion of the world—on their shoulders. The American public now knew him as the "Manassa Mauler," a ruthless attacker with rugged looks and coarse manners.

Hulton/Archive.

Celebrated by the public, Dempsey suddenly entered a Hollywood world of exclusive parties and glamorous socialites. Pathé Studios signed him to a $1,000 weekly contract with a $10,000 advance to star in the film serial *Daredevil Jack.* The project was postponed, however, when scandalous accusations were brought against Dempsey by former wife and dance-hall prostitute Maxine Cates. In a January 1920 letter to the *San Francisco Chronicle,* she claimed that Dempsey had dodged the draft and failed to financially support her during World War I. After many of Cates's statements were shown to conflict with her grand jury testimony later that year, the San Francisco U.S. District Court acquitted Dempsey of draft evasion. Whether guilty or innocent, he continued to suffer from his reputation as a draft dodger. The media accused Dempsey of protecting himself while other men died defending their country.

Public opinion of Dempsey wavered until his grand-scale bout with French war hero Georges Carpentier. Publicized by Kearns and fight promoter George "Tex" Rickard, their 1921 match in Jersey City, New Jersey, drew the first million-dollar gate (income from ticket sales) in boxing history. Famous attendees from industrialist **Henry Ford** to singer Al Jolson witnessed Dempsey redeem himself as the American champion by knocking out the French contender in the fourth round. In 1923, Dempsey's popularity again soared with his fans' nationalistic pride after he defeated Argentinean Luis Angel Firpo, the "Wild Bull of the Pampas," at the Polo Grounds in New York City. The fight climaxed when Dempsey fell backward through the ropes and ended when Firpo fell to the canvas for the tenth time. In two rounds spanning less than four minutes, they delivered one of the most sensational fights of the twentieth century. Dempsey's power appeared superhuman, symbolizing the vitality of the times. The Jazz Age generation found both stimulation and solace through the individual boxer's strength, which contrasted with the dehumanizing aspects of industrialism.

The 1920s witnessed a surge in the popularity of sports. The government had established extensive athletic programs on its military bases in an effort to keep soldiers occupied and physically fit during World War I. As soldiers returned home, their interest in sports spread. Thanks to economic prosperity and an increase in leisure time, Americans spent greater amounts of money on recreational activities—approximately 300 percent more at the end of the decade than at the beginning. Meanwhile, radio usage increased exponentially, and the over-the-air coverage of sports events only fueled the nation's obsession.

Dempsey held his heavyweight crown for seven years before finally being dethroned by Gene Tunney in 1926. At Philadelphia's Sesquicentennial Stadium wealthy gamblers, actors, politicians, and other spectators formed a crowd of over 120,000 and paid nearly $2,000,000 in total. An estimated 39,000,000 other fans, who could not afford to see the fight live, gathered in private and public establishments to listen to the event's radio broadcast. Much to the surprise of audiences, Dempsey lost in a 10-round decision. Acknowledging his defeat like a dignified sportsman, he congratulated Tunney at the last bell and heard his name cheered by fans despite the loss.

Whereas the 1926 battle between Dempsey and Tunney had stunned the sports community, their 1927 fight sparked debate. In round seven at Chicago's Soldier Field, Dempsey stood over the collapsed Tunney before retreating to a neutral corner, delaying the referee's count by about five extra seconds. (The rules required that box-

ers withdraw immediately to the farthest corner from their fallen opponents.) Once Dempsey was in a neutral corner, Tunney recovered his feet on the referee's ninth count, approximately 14 seconds after he had fallen, and fought on for three more rounds to retain his title. Dempsey, by violating the rules, sacrificed his chances for making a comeback by allowing Tunney more time to recover. The legitimacy of what came to be called the "long count" became a controversial question debated by sportswriters and fans across the nation.

Retiring after this dramatic defeat, Dempsey refereed boxing matches and fought exhibition bouts. His career had made him a millionaire, but the 1929 stock market crash and ensuing Great Depression depleted his funds. He went on to open Jack Dempsey's Restaurant in New York City in 1935 and continued to greet customers until its close in 1974. Although his image as a draft dodger had long been forgotten, he joined the Coast Guard and headed its physical training program during World War II. Dempsey, named the Fighter of the Half Century by the Associated Press in 1950 and honored by the Boxing Hall of Fame in 1990, died in his Manhattan apartment on May 31, 1983.

Dempsey rose from humble beginnings to conquer the boxing world as the leading prizefighter in an era captivated by spectator sports. Between his first and last championship fight, Dempsey's purse increased from $27,500 to $450,000 and attendance expanded from 20,000 to 100,000, as prosperity and leisure time drew Americans to the fights. For a generation filled with restless energy, Dempsey electrified fight fans with raucous and ferocious ring power.

Renée Miller

For Further Reading

Dempsey, Jack. *Dempsey, by the Man Himself.* As told to Bob Considine and Bill Slocum. New York: Simon & Schuster, 1960.

Kahn, Roger. *A Flame of Pure Fire: Jack Dempsey and the Roaring '20s.* New York: Harcourt Brace, 1999.

Roberts, Randy. *Jack Dempsey: The Manassa Mauler.* Baton Rouge: Louisiana State University Press, 1984.

JACK DEMPSEY'S FIGHT RECORD (1914–27)

Year	Date	Opponent	Location	W/L/D	Round
1914		Andy Malloy		L	10
1914	Aug. 17	Young Herman	Ramona, CO	D	6
1915	Apr. 5	Jack Downey	Salt Lake City, UT	L	4
1915	Apr. 26	Anamas Campbell	Reno, NV	KO	3
1915	June 13	Johnny Sudenberg	Tonopah, NV	W	10
1915	July 3	Johnny Sudenberg	Goldfield, NV	D	10
1915	Dec. 13	Jack Downey	Salt Lake City, UT	D	4
1915	Dec. 20	Two Round Gillian	Salt Lake City, UT	KO	1
1916	Jan.	Boston Bearcat	Ogden, UT	KO	1
1916	Feb.	Johnny Sudenberg	Ely, NV	KO	2
1916	Feb. 21	Jack Downey	Salt Lake City, UT	KO	2
1916	Mar. 9	Cyril Kohn	Provo, UT	KO	4

Year	Date	Opponent	Location	W/L/D	Round
1916	Apr. 8	Joe Bond	Ely, NV	W	10
1916	May 3	Terry Keller	Ogden, UT	W	10
1916	May 17	Dan Ketchell	Provo, UT	KO	3
1916	May	George Christian	Price, UT	KO	1
1916	June	Bob York	Price, UT	KO	4
1916	June 24	Andre Anderson	New York, NY	ND	10
1916	July 8	Wild Bert Kenny	New York, NY	ND	10
1916	July 14	John L. Johnson	New York, NY	ND	10
1916	Sept. 28	Young Hector	Salida, UT	KO	3
1916	Oct. 7	Terry Keller	Ely, NV	W	10
1916	Oct. 16	Dick Gilbert	Salt Lake City, UT	W	10
1917	Feb. 13	Jim Flynn	Murray, UT	KO by	1

Dempsey's powerful knockouts captivated thrill-seeking crowds and created an impressive fight record. The following list of Dempsey's fights between 1914 and 1927 provides the result of each match and the round in which it ended.

Source: Record adapted from Nathaniel Fleischer, Jack Dempsey. New Rochelle, N.Y.: Arlington House, 1972 and The Internet Boxing Records Archive. 1998. www2.xtdl.com/~brasslet/index.html (September 21, 2001).

Year	Date	Opponent	Location	W/L/D	Round
1917	Mar. 28	Willie Meehan	Oakland, CA	L	4
1917	Apr. 11	Al Norton	Oakland, CA	D	4
1917	May 21	Al Norton	Oakland, CA	D	4
1917	July 25	Willie Meehan	San Francisco, CA	W	4
1917	Aug. 1	Al Norton	San Francisco, CA	KO	1
1917	Aug. 10	Willie Meehan	San Francisco, CA	D	4
1917	Sept. 7	Willie Meehan	San Francisco, CA	D	4
1917	Sept. 19	Charley Miller	Oakland, CA	KO	1
1917	Sept. 26	Bob McAllister	Oakland, CA	W	4
1917	Oct. 2	Gunboat Smith	San Francisco, CA	W	4
1917	Oct. 16	Gunboat Smith	San Francisco, CA	ND	4
1917	Nov. 2	Carl Morris	San Francisco, CA	W	4
1918	Jan. 24	Homer Smith	Racine, WI	KO	1
1918	Feb. 4	Carl Morris	Buffalo, NY	WF	6
1918	Feb. 14	Jim Flynn	Fort Sheridan, IL	KO	1
1918	Feb. 25	Bill Brennan	Milwaukee, WI	KO	6
1918	Mar. 16	Fred Saddy	Memphis, TN	KO	1
1918	Mar. 25	Tom Riley	Joplin, MO	KO	1
1918	May 3	Bill Miske	St. Paul, MN	ND	10
1918	May 22	Dan Ketchell	Excelsior Springs, CO	KO	2
1918	May 29	Arthur Pelkey	Denver, CO	KO	1
1918	July 1	Kid McCarthy	Tulsa, OK	KO	1
1918	July 4	Bob Devere	Joplin, MO	KO	1
1918	July 6	Porky Flynn	Atlanta, GA	KO	1
1918	July 27	Fred Fulton	Harrison, NJ	KO	1
1918	Aug. 17	Terry Keller	Dayton, OH	KO	5
1918	Sept. 13	Willie Meehan	San Francisco, CA	L	4
1918	Sept. 14	Jack Moran	Reno, NV	KO	1
1918	Nov. 6	Battling Levinsky	Philadelphia, PA	KO	3
1918	Nov. 18	Porky Flynn	Philadelphia, PA	KO	1
1918	Nov. 28	Billy Miske	Philadelphia, PA	ND	6
1918	Dec. 16	Carl Morris	New Orleans, LA	KO	1
1918	Dec. 20	Clay Turner	New York, NY	Exh.	4
1918	Dec. 30	Gunboat Smith	Buffalo, NY	KO	2

Year	Date	Opponent	Location	W/L/D	Round
1919	Jan. 22	Big Jack Hickey	Harrisburg, PA	KO	1
1919	Jan. 23	Kid Harris	Reading, PA	KO	1
1919	Jan. 29	Kid Henry	Easton, PA	KO	1
1919	Feb. 13	Eddy Smith	Altoona, PA	KO	1
1919	Apr. 2	Tony Drake	New Haven, CT	KO	1
1919	May 1	Terry Keller	Washington, DC	Exh.	3
1919	July 4	Jess Willard	Toledo, OH	KO	3
1919	Aug. 24	One Round Garrison	St. Louis, MO	Exh.	4
1920	Mar. 5	Terry Keller	Los Angeles, CA	Exh.	3
1920	Sept. 6	Billy Miske	Benton Harbor, MI	KO	3
1920	Dec. 14	Bill Brennan	New York, NY	KO	12
1921	July 2	Georges Carpentier	Jersey City, NJ	KO	4
1922	July 18	Elziar Rioux	Montreal, Que.	Exh. KO	1
1922	July 19	Jack Renault	Ottawa, Ont.	Exh.	3
1922	Sept. 4	Jack Thompson	Michigan City, IN	Exh.	2
1922	Sept. 7	Andre Anderson	Michigan City, IN	Exh.	2
1922	Oct. 7	Jack Thompson	Boston, MA	Exh.	3
1923	July 4	Tommy Gibbons	Shelby, MT	W	15
1923	Sept. 14	Luis Firpo	New York, NY	KO	2
1924	Feb. 10	Dutch Seifert	Memphis, TN	Exh. KO	1
1924	Feb. 11	Martin Burke	New Orleans, LA	Exh.	2
1924	Feb. 11	Tommy Marvin	New Orleans, LA	Exh. KO	2
1924	June 3	Rock Stragmalia	Los Angeles, CA	Exh. KO	2
1924	June 3	Joe Ryan	Los Angeles, CA	Exh. KO	1
1924	June 3	Eli Stanton	Los Angeles, CA	Exh. KO	1
1925	Engaged in 8 exhibitions				
1926	Feb. 8	Jack League	Memphis, TN	Exh. KO	1
1926	Feb. 8	Tony Catalina	Memphis, TN	Exh. KO	1
1926	Feb. 8	Cowboy Warner	Memphis, TN	Exh. KO	1
1926	Feb. 8	Marty Cuyler	Memphis, TN	Exh. KO	1
1926	Feb. 12	Boxed 6 opponents			
1926	Sept. 23	Gene Tunney	Philadelphia, PA	L	10
1927	July 21	Jack Sharkey	New York, NY	KO	7
1927	Sept. 22	Gene Tunney	Chicago, IL	L	10

Key: W=Win, L=Loss, D=Draw, KO=The fighter won by knockout or technical knockout, KO by=The fighter lost by knockout or technical knockout, ND=No Decision, Exh.= Exhibition bout

---

"THE WAR-RECORD OF DEMPSEY" from *The Literary Digest* (February 14, 1920)

Shortly after becoming the world heavyweight champion, Dempsey faced scandal and a trial for draft evasion. This article, "The War-Record of Dempsey," published in The Literary Digest *on February 14, 1920, examines popular sentiments regarding these charges and their effects on the upcoming bout between Dempsey and war hero Georges Carpentier.*

Source: "The War-Record of Dempsey." The Literary Digest, *February 14, 1920.*

A fighter who didn't fight when fighters were needed most may have a first-class explanation, but he can hardly wonder if those who did fight are a little prejudiced about his case. One of the two men who will meet for the world championship has a war-record made in the trenches; the other has a war-record which was made far in the rear of the fighting-line. Georges Carpentier pulled off the gloves, picked up the bayonet, faced the German shells, and won the war-cross for gallantry in action; Jack Dempsey dropt his mitts to handle tools in a shipyard. Dempsey has his friends, who say that he was under no peculiar obligation because of his profession to enlist, and that he did not fail in his duty in waiting to be drafted. The American Legion is not among those who regard Dempsey's record with favor. There are two sides to every question, and this case, too, has its other side. It may be developed and be shown with good face in the Federal investigation in San Francisco into the champion's war record.

Concerning Dempsey Herbert Reed ("Right Wing") has this to say in *The Evening Post (New York)*:

> There is a great host of followers of sport that believes that in time of war such a man should not wait for a draft, but should volunteer. That host will never be satisfied with any excuse whatever. That host will never believe that the preeminent athlete, ready to accept the rewards of peace, has not put himself under obligation to accept the hazards of war. He owes that, from their point of view, to the men he represents, consciously or unconsciously. If he has accepted these things without that idea of obligation, then he has done something that is ill-thought out and essentially careless.
>
> Amateurs who went into the "big show" stood to lose as much as any professional, yet in most cases they hesitated not at all, least of all in the case of men who had played games in which personal physical contact was predominant. It seems to be the feeling, as far as I can gage it, among amateurs, that the obligations of excellence in physical build as well as skill should apply as well to the professional as to the amateur. The thing went even deeper than that. There were oarsmen, who indulge in a form

of sport in which cold patience and blind courage are paramount, who went into the service, and the most perilous forms thereof, in advance of the first call.

Just now there is a movement to extend the scope of compulsory physical development in and out of colleges. This movement will succeed beyond a doubt, but it is worth while inquiring whether the men benefited by such training will have a sufficiently profound idea of their obligations to those who work immediately with them and to a system that makes it possible.

To return for the moment to the status of Dempsey. Will a clean bill of health from any draft board in the world quite clear him? Will the statement, easy enough to make, that other men did what he did without so much excuse, quite clear him? Will he be forgiven for not knowing any better, when he knows enough now to get the biggest purse in the world for a few minutes in the ring? Professional prizefighters were in the war in large numbers. Many of them were volunteers. They had no such reputation as Dempsey's, no such gorgeous opportunities, it is true. Yet some of them had to forego what to them was as big a thing as the greatest purse in the world is to Dempsey.

It has been said in defense of Dempsey that he is a boxer, that boxing *per se* involved no particular obligation. Yet anyone who knows boxing as it should be, knows that one can not even just box and hit "soft." The blows are not the same. Right here I shall venture to lay down this law, and shall be glad to abide by it. You can not box without hitting, in the accepted sense, and the man who tries to box "softly" might as well give up the game. In common with other sports, the boxing, the fighting game, carries the obligation of fighting in the larger sense, and I am convinced that the balance of any supporters of first-class sports will feel that the man who works up to the top in the representative sense must accept obligations that less gifted members of his class and country would be only too glad to assume had they the equipment.

As a matter of fact, these less gifted men who were not athletes did assume these obligations to an extent unforeseen and rather astonishing. Unless an athlete volunteers to fight when the time comes he might better give way to those who will. This is a point of view gained by contact with one side of the controversy, it must be admitted. The other side has its own case to prove.

It may be hard to prove to the soldier who went out and had a jab at the Hun that Dempsey, a trained athlete and physically fit to undergo the toil and moil of war, was not under moral obligation to shoulder a rifle and harness himself in the habiliments of battle. So Dempsey must expect not to go unchallenged. Such a view is taken in an editorial appearing in the Chicago *Tribune*:

> Jack Dempsey and his manager, Mr. Kearns, are beginning to feel that the American Legion must be brought to view the war-record of the champion in a more favorable light. The members of the Legion are appropriating money to bet on Carpentier and they are breaking Dempsey's heart by proclaiming him a slacker who fought in the shipyards.
>
> Mr. Kearns wants a hearing before the Legion for Mr. Dempsey, who was ready to go to the front as soon as the draft finally got him. If the war had lasted longer the draft probably would have got him. In the meanwhile Mr. Dempsey contained himself the best he could, made ships to carry the boys across, supported his dependents, and almost ruined his constitution boxing in the training-camps and for soldiers' benefits, paying his own expenses and not taking a cent of remuneration. Mr. Kearns thinks it is a fine record, and that if the veterans look it over they will not be so unkind as to knock Dempsey and bet their money foolishly on Carpentier.

THE LONG-COUNT (1927)

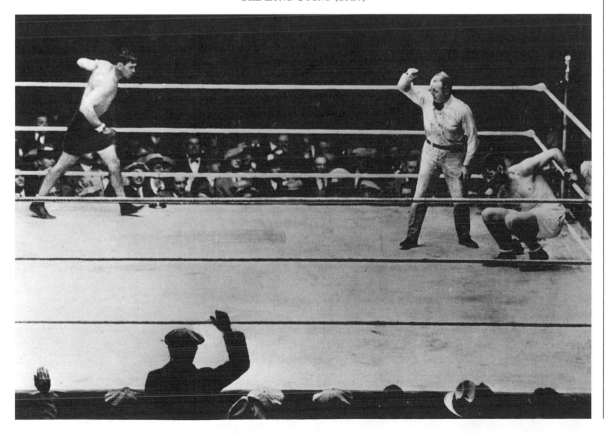

Debate over the justice and duration of the "long-count" continued for years after the final match between Dempsey and Gene Tunney in 1927. Here, Tunney rises to his feet on the referee's ninth count while Dempsey eagerly attacks from a neutral corner. By not promptly retreating, Dempsey gave Tunney more time to recover.

Source: ©Bettmann/ Corbis.

"FIGHT FAST AND FURIOUS" by James P. Dawson (September 23, 1927) [EXCERPT]

Following the last Dempsey-Tunney fight, sportswriters and newspapers across the nation addressed the legitimacy of the "long-count." In this September 23, 1927, article from the New York Times, entitled "Fight Fast and Furious," James P. Dawson describes the monumental mistake that sacrificed Dempsey's chances for a comeback and secured Tunney's heavyweight championship title.

Source: Dawson, James P. "Fight Fast and Furious." New York Times, September 23, 1927.

Ringside, Soldier Field, Chicago, Sept. 22—
His refusal to observe the boxing rules of the Illinois State Athletic Commission, or his ignorance of the rules, or both, cost Jack Dempsey the chance to regain the world's heavyweight championship here tonight in the ring at Soldier Field.

By the same token this disregard of the rules of ring warfare, or this surprising ignorance, saved the title for Gene Tunney, the fighting ex-marine, who has been king of the ring for just a year. . . .

DEMPSEY'S FURIOUS PLUNGE.

In that seventh round Dempsey was being peppered and buffeted about on the end of Tunney's left jabs and hooks and sharp though light right crosses as he had been in every preceding round, with the exception of the third.

In a masterful exhibition of boxing Tunney was evading the attack of his heavier rival and was countering cleanly, superbly, skillfully, accurately the while for half of the round or so.

Then Dempsey, plunging in recklessly, charging bull-like, furiously and with utter contempt for the blows of the champion, since he had tasted of Tunney's best previously, suddenly lashed a long, wicked left to the jaw with the power of old. This he followed with a right to the jaw, the old "iron mike" as deadly as ever, and quickly drove another left hook to the jaw, under which Tunney toppled like a falling tree, hitting the canvas with a solid thud near Dempsey's corner, his hand reaching blindly for a helping rope which somehow or other refused to be within clutching distance.

Then Dempsey made his mistake, an error which, I believe, cost him the title he values so highly.

COUNT BEGUN AND HALTED.

The knockdown brought the knockdown timekeeper, Paul Beeler, to his feet automatically, watch in hand, eyes glued to the ticking seconds and he bawled "one" before he looked upon the scene in the ring.

There he saw Dempsey in his own corner, directly above the prostrate, brain-numbed Tunney, sitting there looking foolishly serious, his hand finally resting on the middle ring strand. Beeler's count stopped. Referee Barry never started one.

It is the referee's duty to see to it that a boxer scoring a knockdown goes to the corner fartherest from his fallen foe and it is the duty of the knockdown timekeeper to delay the count from the watch until this rule is obeyed. Beeler was simply observing the rule, which Dempsey either forgot to observe or refused to observe.

The challenging ex-champion stood there, arms akimbo on the top ropes of the ring in his own corner, watching his fallen rival, the characteristic Dempsey snarl o'erspreading his countenance, his expression saying more plainly than words: "Get up and I'll knock you down again, this time for keeps."

DEMPSEY FINALLY MOVES.

Dempsey had no eyes for Referee Barry, who was waving frantically for the former titleholder to run to a neutral corner, even as he kept an eye on the fallen Tunney. Instead, Dempsey merely looked down at Tunney squatting there, striving instinctively to regain his feet and waiting for his whirling brain to clear.

Finally, Dempsey took cognizance of the referee's frantic motions. He was galvanized into action and sped hurriedly to a neutral corner, away from Tunney.

If he had observed the rule to the letter, Dempsey should, in fact, have gone to Tunney's corner, which was furthest removed from the fallen champion.

But three or four, or possibly five precious seconds had elapsed before Dempsey realized at all what he should do. In that fleeting time of the watch Tunney got the advantage. No count was proceeding over him, and quickly his senses were returning. When Referee Barry started counting along with Timekeeper Beeler, Tunney was in a state of mental revival where he could keep count with the tolling seconds and did, as his slowly moving lips revealed.

Slowly the count proceeded. It seemed an eternity between each downward sweep of the arm of Referee Barry and the steady pounding of the fist of Timekeeper Beeler.

Seconds are like that in a crisis, and here was one if ever one existed.

Tunney's senses came back to him. He got to his feet with the assistance of the ring ropes and with visible effort at the count of "nine." He was groggy, stung, shaken, his head was whirling as so many other heads have whirled under the Dempsey punch.

But Dempsey was wild in this crisis, a floundering, plodding man-killer, as Tunney, back pedaling for dear life, took to full flight, beating an orderly, steady retreat with only light counter moves in the face of the plunging, desperate, vicious Dempsey, aroused now for the kill.

Dempsey plodded on so futilely and ineffectively that he tired from his own exertions. The former champion stopped dead in his tracks in mid-ring and with a smile spreading over his scowling face, motioned disgustedly, daringly, for Tunney to come on and fight.

But Tunney was playing his own game, and it was a winning game. He did not want to expose himself to that deadly Dempsey punch again, and he would not. . . .

George and Gladys Dick

1881–1967; 1881–1963

Physicians and Microbiologists

Scientists George and Gladys Dick determined the cause of and developed preventive treatment for scarlet fever, an acute contagious disease that had affected thousands in Europe and North America. In the 1920s, their profound discoveries helped transform scarlet fever from a life-threatening disease to a preventable illness.

George Frederick Dick was born on July 21, 1881, in Fort Wayne, Indiana. He decided in his adolescence to become a doctor, attended Indiana University, and in 1905 graduated from Rush Medical College in Chicago. Born December 18, 1881, in Pawnee City, Nebraska, Gladys Henry also grew up wanting a career in medicine. She received a bachelor's degree from the University of Nebraska in 1900 and her medical degree from Johns Hopkins University School of Medicine in 1907, one of the few prestigious medical schools of the era to accept women. Mary Garrett, the daughter of one of the school's original trustees, donated $350,000 for its opening on the condition that men and women would be admitted on equal terms, an unusual policy as medical science had been traditionally categorized as a male preserve. Henry's education, therefore, differed from that of most women of the time who were encouraged to study only subjects related to nurturing and care-taking such as teaching and nursing. In 1911, these two physicians met while working as pathologists at the University of Chicago. They married in January 1914.

At the McCormick Memorial Institute for Infectious Diseases, the Dicks worked together to identify the bacteria that produces scarlet fever. Deriving its name from the characteristic red rash that surfaces on the body of an infected individual, the disease primarily

National Library of Medicine.

National Library of Medicine.

struck children in Europe and North America, killing a quarter of those infected and leaving others severely crippled. At the turn of the nineteenth century, scarlet fever accounted for about 25 percent of all children's deaths in Europe and North America. Previous laboratory studies had pointed to the *streptococcus* family as the probable cause, but scientists could not find conclusive evidence. The Dicks began exploring this elusive field by injecting animals (guinea pigs, mice, pigeons, dogs, and rabbits) with culture fluid from scarlet-fever patients. When the animals showed no diagnostic symptoms, the Dicks found it necessary to use human subjects. Before making significant headway, though, World War I delayed their joint efforts. George oversaw an army medical unit overseas, while Gladys continued research in the United States.

The Dicks continued their investigation after the war with patience and precision. Friends, acquaintances, and people who had lost loved ones to scarlet fever volunteered for their experiment. The Dicks inoculated volunteers and themselves with throat mucus, blood serums, and whole blood from critical cases of scarlet fever. Yielding negative results, the Dicks ultimately narrowed their test group to include those who had never been exposed to the disease. These subjects were inoculated with a pure culture of *hemolytic streptococcus*, which, in 1923, was verified by the Dicks as the bacteria that causes scarlet fever. Now knowing the source of infection, they began to focus on prevention and treatment.

In 1924, they devised the "Dick test" to indicate an individual's immunity or susceptibility to scarlet fever. This test involved injection of a small solution of the scarlet-fever bacteria under the skin. If the individual was susceptible, the punctured area was inflamed within 24 hours. People with a positive skin test were then gradually given larger doses of toxin that, in turn, created vital antitoxins needed for immunization. The Dicks immediately supplied the toxin to the New York City Board of Health, Harvard University, and the University of Iowa. They also patented their procedure in the United States and England to ensure the quality of preparation and distribution. Some in the medical profession, particularly the Health Organization of the League of Nations, argued that their patent placed needless restrictions on the drug and accused them of commercial opportunism. The Dicks countered these arguments by claiming that their patent was not for financial profit but for product safety and standards.

In addition to preventing scarlet fever, their test could reveal a pregnant woman's risk of developing puerperal fever, an infection in the female reproductive organs occurring after abortion or childbirth. Although the Dicks were nominated for the 1925 Nobel Prize in Medicine, the Nobel committee could not agree upon a prize winner and presented no award that year. In 1926, their discovery earned them the Mickel Prize of the University of Toronto and in 1933 they received the Cameron Prize of the University of Edinburgh.

After contributing greatly to the understanding of scarlet fever, Gladys pursued the study of polio, another highly contagious disease usually striking children and leaving them disabled; George headed the department of medicine at the University of Chicago from 1933 to 1945. The Dicks adopted two children in 1930, and they published the book *Scarlet Fever* in 1938. Their work held importance for over two decades, but the arrival of antibiotics during World War II made their methods obsolete. In 1953, they retired to Palo Alto, California. Gladys died there on August 21, 1963; four years later, George died there on October 12, 1967.

Scarlet fever poses little threat today, but during the Dicks' lifetime, the disease could be deadly. At a time when physicians had no other choice but to isolate contagious patients to avoid further outbreak, the "Dick test" offered a greatly improved method of fighting an epidemic. Their preventive treatment drastically reduced child mortality and disabilities traced to a prior infection of scarlet fever.

Renée Miller

For Further Reading
Dick, George F., and Gladys Henry Dick. *Scarlet Fever.* Chicago: The Year Book Publishers, 1938.
Gruening, Ernest. "Another Germ Bites the Dust," *Colliers* 74, October 4, 1924.
Uhlenberg, Peter. "Death and the Family." In *Growing Up in America: Children in Historical Perspective*, edited by N. Ray Hiner and Joseph M. Hawes. Urbana and Chicago: University of Illinois Press, 1985.

"Scarlet Fever in a State Juvenile Home" from *The American Journal of Public Health* (1923) [Excerpt]

Before the "Dick test," doctors could fight outbreaks of scarlet fever only by isolating contagious patients. This excerpt from the June 1923 article "Scarlet Fever in a State Juvenile Home," featured in The American Journal of Public Health, *shows how rapidly the disease spread to create a serious epidemic.*

Source: Griswold, Don M. "Scarlet Fever in a State Juvenile Home." *The American Journal of Public Health,* June 1923. ©1923 by the American Public Health Association.

The State Juvenile Home was founded to care for normal children from three to sixteen years of age, who need a home. One hundred and fifty-nine of these children are housed in the buildings formerly used by the Leander Clark College. The main building is used as a dormitory, dining room, kitchen, laundry, and school for about one hundred and thirty of the younger children. About thirty of the older girls use the "Cottage" for a dormitory, but use the main building for all other purposes. To have this number of children housed under one roof means that they come in very intimate contact with each other many times each day. Likewise, when a disease appears that is spread by contact, the means of transportation is so ever-present that it is possible for a large number of exposures to be made very early in the outbreak. For this reason eternal vigilance must be exercised and prompt and adequate medical attention must always be at hand. . . .

Some time before Christmas, Christine P. was taken sick. She was one of the older girls who lived at the Cottage. The matron of the Cottage belonged to a peculiar religious sect that denies the existence of disease. This matron told the sick girl that she was in error about being sick and advised her not to report to the physician. Shortly after, a rash appeared over the child's neck and chest. At the onset of the rash, the child was secreted in the matron's room "so that the other children wouldn't get the false idea that she was sick." During this time, the child slept on the floor of the matron's room and ate such food as the matron could smuggle to her.

After the rash had disappeared the matron allowed her to go to her own room and mingle with the other children. On January 11 she was found to be desquamating. At that time, she gave a history of having headache, sore throat, fever and rash, over her neck and chest. She also told of the confinement in the matron's room during the acute stages of her illness. This matron is no longer employed at the Home. The child was likewise removed from the Home to avoid any further contact with the well children.

THE OUTBREAK

Evidently the infectious agent of scarlet fever was transmitted from this girl to a susceptible well child before her removal, for on January 13, Lucielle B., one of the older girls who lived at the Cottage and who had associated with Christine P., began to feel ill. It was not until January 15 that she was diagnosed scarlet fever and quarantined. This girl acted as a waitress in the main dining room.

January 17, Gayle P., a little girl who holds the door open between the dining room and kitchen, and who eats with the waitresses, developed scarlet fever.

January 20, Leona P., a sister of Gayle P., also a waitress in the main dining room, began to "feel bad." On the same day, Ethel R., who "plays with Gayle P. lots," reported as "feeling bad."

January 22 and 23, these girls were both diagnosed scarlet fever and quarantined.

January 26, Fay S., also a waitress, who was a chum of Leona P., was diagnosed scarlet fever and quarantined.

On the same day, Neva R. was diagnosed scarlet fever and quarantined. On the same day, Frank P. who sits near Neva R. in school was diagnosed scarlet fever and quarantined.

On this day Ruby B. who sat at the same table waited upon by Fay S. was diagnosed scarlet fever and quarantined. Clarence W. who also sat at this table began to "feel bad" this day. February 1, Clarence W. was diagnosed scarlet fever and quarantined. Likewise Martin P. who had been playing with Frank P. the day before he was quarantined, was diagnosed scarlet fever and quarantined. On the same day, Etta C., who had been playing with Ruby B. the day before she was quarantined, was diagnosed scarlet fever and quarantined.

February 2, Viola H. who had visited Neva R. between the time she was first "feeling bad" and the time she was quarantined, was diagnosed scarlet fever and quarantined.

February 3, Lilly T. who also visited Neva R. when she was "feeling bad" before she was quarantined, developed scarlet fever and was quarantined. On the same day, Minnie R. who sets and clears the tables in the main dining room, developed scarlet fever and was quarantined.

February 5, Noel P., Viola P. and Ruth P. were diagnosed scarlet fever and quarantined. Noel P. had been playing with Clarence W. on February 1. Viola P. gave a history of contact with Minnie R. She sits at table No. 2. Ruth P. gave a history of contact with Viola H. She sits at table No. 2. February 6, Agnes H. who sits at table No. 2 developed scarlet fever and was quarantined. She gave a history of contact with Lilly T.

On this date it was felt by the attending physicians that Lucielle B. and Gayle P. who had only mild cases and had been in quarantine for 22 and 20 days respectively, had ceased giving off infectious material. They were therefore released from quarantine and resumed their usual work. . . .

THE DICKS' UNITED STATES PATENT (July 28, 1925) [EXCERPT]

Patented July 28, 1925
UNITED STATES PATENT OFFICE
GEORGE F. DICK AND GLADYS HENRY DICK, OF EVANSTON, ILLNOIS.
SCARLET-FEVER TOXIN AND ANTITOXIN AND PROCESS FOR PRODUCING THE SAME.
To all whom it may concern:

Be it known that we, GEORGE F. DICK and GLADYS HENRY DICK, both citizens of the United States, residing at Evanston, Illinois, have invented certain new and useful Improvements in Scarlet-Fever Toxin and Antitoxin and Processes for Producing the Same, of which the following is a specification.

Our invention relates to a scarlet fever toxin, its applications to medical use, and to the process of producing it and also to a scarlet fever antitoxin, its applications to medical use and to the process of producing it.

Among the objects of our invention are to provide a scarlet fever toxin prepared in form suitable for medical use, as a means of identifying scarlet fever; as a skin test to determine susceptibility to scarlet fever; for use as an immunization to prevent scarlet fever, and as a means for producing scarlet fever antitoxin.

Prior to our invention and discovery, experimental scarlet fever had not been produced in animals or in man by inoculation of a pure culture of any organism. Attempts had been made to produce experimental scarlet fever in man, by inoculation with material from erythematous areas, with serum from miliary vesicles, from skin scales, from blood, from filtrates of throat mucus, and from pure cultures of organisms isolated from scarlet fever patients. Accidental inoculations of human beings with materials of scarlet fever origin had been reported but they had occurred under circumstances that threw no light on the origin and development of the disease.

We produced experimental scarlet fever by inoculation of human beings with a pure culture of hemolytic streptococcus. This was obtained by inoculating a volunteer with a pure culture of a hemolytic streptococcus isolated from a lesion on the finger of a scarlet fever patient. After numerous experiments we found that scarlet fever is caused by a specific hemolytic streptococcus.

We next discovered that the hemolytic streptococcus produced the scarlatinal rash when growing in the throat of human beings and that the filtered cultures of this hemolytic streptococcus contained a sterile toxin specific to scarlet fever. We also ascertained that when certain amounts of this toxin alone were injected into susceptible persons it caused general malaise, nausea, vomiting, fever, and a generalized scarlatinal rash.

In other words, we discovered that this sterile toxin itself is capable of producing the characteristic symptoms of scarlet fever, including the rash. . . .

What we claim is—
1. The process of isolating hemolytic streptococci specific to scarlet fever, growing them in a suitable medium, obtaining sterile toxin therefrom, injecting an animal with the sterile toxin, and obtaining therefrom a serum containing an antitoxin specific to scarlet fever.
2. The process of isolating hemolytic streptococci specific to scarlet fever, growing them in a suitable medium, obtaining the sterile toxin therefrom, injecting an animal with the sterile toxin and obtaining an antitoxin specific to scarlet fever.
3. The process of isolating hemolytic streptococci specific to scarlet fever, growing them in a suitable medium, obtaining the sterile toxin therefrom, injecting an animal with the sterile toxin, obtaining an antitoxin specific to scarlet fever, and inject-

The Dicks claimed that their patent for their toxin and antitoxin procedure would guarantee product safety and standards, but some in the medical profession perceived this as a means of commercial opportunism. On July 28, 1925, the following controversial patent was granted to the Dicks in the United States.

Source: United States Patent and Trademark Office.

ing the antitoxin into or through the skin of a human being.

4. An antitoxin specific to scarlet fever obtained from the blood of a animal which has been injected with sterile toxin grown from a pure culture of hemolytic streptococci specific to scarlet fever.

5. An antitoxin specific to scarlet fever obtained from the blood of an animal which has been injected with sterile toxin specific to scarlet fever.

6. The process of isolating hemolytic streptococci specific to scarlet fever growing them in a suitable medium and obtaining a sterile toxin therefrom.

7. The process of isolating hemolytic streptococci specific to scarlet fever, growing them in a suitable

medium, obtaining a sterile toxin therefrom, and injecting the toxin into or through the skin of a human being.

8. A sterile toxin specific to scarlet fever.

9. A sterile toxin specific to scarlet fever obtained from a pure culture of hemolytic streptococci specific to scarlet fever.

10. A sterile toxin specific to scarlet fever obtained from hemolytic streptococci specific to scarlet fever.

In witness whereof, we hereunto subscribe our names to this specification.

GEORGE F. DICK

GLADYS HENRY DICK

"No One Need Have Scarlet Fever!" by Gladys Dick (1930) [Excerpt]

To practically apply their findings, the Dicks educated both the general public and medical profession on their groundbreaking work with scarlet fever. In this article "No One Need Have Scarlet Fever!" from the May 1930 Parents' Magazine, *Gladys explains in simple terms how scarlet fever can be detected, prevented, and properly treated.*

Source: Dick, Gladys H. "No One Need Have Scarlet Fever!" Parents' Magazine, *May 1930.*

An epidemic of scarlet fever may be controlled in forty-eight hours.

If the present knowledge of scarlet fever were universally and intelligently applied, the disease and its consequences would be eliminated.

Most people know that something has been happening recently in the field of scarlet fever prevention and control. But they do not know what that "something" is or how they may benefit from it. Few realize that we now know the germ of scarlet fever; have an antitoxin for the disease; can make skin tests to tell which persons in any group are susceptible and have a method of immunizing susceptible persons so that they become immune to scarlet fever and are no longer in danger of catching it. If the announcements of these new developments, resulting in four different biological products, had been made one at a time, separated by intervals of some years, there would have been time to assimilate each. Coming all together, they have caused confusion which is not limited to the laity but extends to the medical profession and to the druggists.

How can scarlet fever be recognized? The first symptom is sore throat. The second symptom is nausea which usually results in vomiting. If a child complains of sore throat, seems feverish and vomits, the possibility of scarlet fever should be considered and a physician called.

The rash which gives the disease its name usually appears on the second day of illness. It begins as a flush on the chest and abdomen and spreads over the whole body except the face. The fully developed rash consists of minute pin points of bright red color thickly scattered over the flushed skin. If the hand with the fingers spread out is pressed on the skin and removed quickly, it leaves its print in white on the red background. As soon as the pressure is removed the blood begins to come back into the dilated vessels of the skin and the white print of the hand promptly disappears.

While the symptoms at the onset of an attack of scarlet fever are quite constant, it is impossible to predict what the subsequent course of the disease will be. Some attacks are mild. In others, the patient grows rapidly worse and dies in a few days. Between these extremes there is every gradation. In the ordinary, uncomplicated

attack of moderate severity, the rash stays about one week. The fever lasts about ten days and subsides gradually. During the third or fourth week of illness the top layer of the skin begins to peel off. This peeling, or desquamation, is most noticeable on the palms of the hands and soles of the feet.

If sore throat, rash and fever of about two weeks' duration exhausted the possibilities of scarlet fever, the disease would not cause so much concern. Even the mildest attack of scarlet fever may be accompanied or followed by complications which may cause death or permanent disability. The complications most frequently involve the ears, kidneys and heart. Scarlet fever is well known as one of the causes of partial or complete deafness. Many of the heart and kidney conditions which incapacitate useful citizens at the prime of life may be traced to an attack of scarlet fever in childhood.

In the immediate vicinity of the scarlet fever patient, the air is contaminated by minute droplets of moisture from the patient's breath. These droplets carry the microbe of scarlet fever. If the contaminated air is breathed by some one susceptible to the disease, the germs may lodge in the throat and grow there, producing the first symptom of scarlet fever—sore throat.

If the contaminated air is breathed by some one who is immune to the disease, the germs are not able to make the immune person sick, but such an infected immune person may carry the germs in his throat for a few days and pass them on to some one else who is not immune. It commonly happens that when one child in a family of several children develops scarlet fever and is quarantined in a room by himself, the mother who takes care of the sick child continues to cook the meals or eat with the rest of the family. Under these circumstances the mother either contracts the disease herself or becomes an immune carrier and may pass the germs on to the other children while she herself remains well. Such immune carriers together with the very mild, unrecognized cases of scarlet fever in persons who stay home for a day or so with sore throat and then go back to their school or business account for the development of typical attacks of scarlet fever in persons who have not been in contact with a scarlet fever patient. . . .

W. E. B. Du Bois

1868–1963

Civil Rights Leader and Author

W. E. B. Du Bois, author of *The Souls of Black Folk*, contributed to the founding of the National Organization for the Advancement of Colored People (NAACP) and was a longtime editor of its influential magazine, *The Crisis*.

William Edward Burghardt Du Bois was born on February 23, 1868, in Great Barrington, Massachusetts, the son of Mary Silvina Burghardt and Alfred Du Bois, a barber and former Union army soldier who left the family two years after his son's birth. W. E. B. Du Bois was educated in the small western Massachusetts town's racially integrated school and, in 1884, became its first African-American graduate. By that time he was already writing and publishing articles in regional newspapers, one of them the black-owned *New York Globe*.

Beginning in 1885 Du Bois studied at Fisk University in Nashville, Tennessee, and in the summers he taught school in eastern Tennessee. He entered Harvard in 1888, earning a bachelor's degree cum laude in 1890 and a master's degree in 1891. He studied economic history in Germany from 1892 to 1894, and in 1895 he was awarded a doctorate in history by Harvard.

In 1903 Du Bois published *The Souls of Black Folk*, perhaps his most important book. It established him as the main ideological rival of the conservative, accommodationist educator Booker T. Washington. Founder and head of the black school Tuskegee Normal and Industrial Institute (later Tuskegee University) in Alabama, Washington urged blacks to obtain a vocational education and focus first on economic self-improvement, and to let political and social equality come later. In his "Atlanta Compromise" speech in 1895, Washington had argued that it was useless to agitate for social and political equality until blacks had achieved economic equality. Du Bois, on the other hand, affirmed that African Americans should strive not for assimilation, nor for separatism, but, as he wrote in *The Souls of Black Folk*, "to be both a Negro and an American . . . to be a co-worker in the kingdom of cul-

Hulton/Archive.

ture." Warning against an overemphasis on the industrial training espoused by Washington, Du Bois asserted in a famous essay titled "The Talented Tenth" the necessity of educating "the best and most capable" African Americans to inspire the masses to excel, to rise up from second-class citizenship to political and civil equality: "The Talented Tenth of the Negro race must be made leaders of thought and missionaries of culture among their people."

In 1905, Du Bois became a cofounder of the Niagara Movement, which attacked Washington's accommodationist stance and demanded full voting rights for African Americans. This movement soon dissolved because of internal disputes, but it served as an impetus to the creation of a biracial organization, the National Association for the Advancement of Colored People, which Du Bois joined in 1910 as the director of research and publicity. The NAACP filed legal suits, launched publicity campaigns, and lobbied legislatures for protection from lynching and an end to racial segregation. Du Bois left his teaching position at Atlanta University (where he had taught sociology since 1897) to become the organization's director of publications and research, and founded its monthly magazine, *The Crisis*. The independent-minded editor was frequently in dispute with the more cautious board members, but the magazine's circulation rose steadily from a first printing of 1,000 in 1910 to a peak of 100,000 in 1919. Du Bois used *The Crisis* to rally support for NAACP initiatives, to show the richness and variety of black life in America, and to spread the word about another interest of his, Pan-Africanism—the struggle for liberation of black people around the world and the eviction of European colonial powers from Africa. While in London in 1900, he had attended the first international conference on the political and social condition of people of African descent, and in 1911 he was the joint secretary for the American delegation at the Universal Races Congress in London. He attended Pan-African Congresses in Europe in 1919, 1921, 1923, and in New York in 1927.

In May 1915 he wrote an article for the *Atlantic Monthly*, "The African Roots of War," linking World War I to colonialism and imperialism. Nevertheless, he supported U.S. intervention in the war and, in a *Crisis* editorial in 1918 titled "Close Ranks," he enraged many readers by urging black Americans to "forget our special grievances and close our ranks" with whites to defeat Germany. Many of those alienated by the NAACP's stand and outraged by the mistreatment of black soldiers in the armed forces during the war and after their return to the United States turned to **Marcus Garvey** and his Universal Negro Improvement Association (UNIA).

Du Bois wanted *The Crisis* not only to promote political ideas but also to enrich black culture. With the help of its literary editor Jessie Redmon Fauset, who selected works by **Langston Hughes**, Countee Cullen, Jean Toomer, and others, *The Crisis* became one of the nurturers of the flowering of black literary and musical talent in the 1920s known as the Harlem Renaissance. The magazine found itself in a healthy competition with *Opportunity*, a new magazine edited by Charles Spurgeon Johnson and published by the Urban League. Both magazines sponsored literary competitions and offered prizes to promote the writers and increase the magazines' circulation.

Du Bois edited *The Crisis* until 1934 when he broke with the NAACP, believing that the organization no longer represented the masses. He taught again at Atlanta University and continued writing and editing, and returned to the NAACP for a brief period (1944–48). He grew increasingly interested in socialism and Marxism and more and more disaffected with the United States. In 1961 he joined the Communist Party, moved to Ghana, and renounced his American citizenship. In 1963, he died in Ghana at age 95.

W. E. B. Du Bois was easily the most important African-American intellectual and protest leader in the first half of the twentieth century. He helped build the NAACP into a powerful instrument of social change, and through his writings and teachings he set an admirable example for African Americans wounded by lynchings, race riots, and everyday injustices.

Mark LaFlaur

For Further Reading

Lewis, David Levering. *W.E.B. Du Bois: Biography of a Race, 1868–1919*. New York: Henry Holt, 1993.

———. *W.E.B. Du Bois: The Fight for Equality and the American Century, 1919–1963*. New York: Henry Holt, 2001.

Rampersad, Arnold. *The Art and Imagination of W.E.B. Du Bois*. Cambridge, Mass.: Harvard University Press, 1976.

Zamir, Shamoon. *Dark Voices: W.E.B. Du Bois and American Thought, 1888–1903*. Chicago: University of Chicago Press, 1995.

"OF MR. BOOKER T. WASHINGTON AND OTHERS" by W. E. B. Du Bois (1903) [EXCERPT]

Du Bois's intense dissatisfaction with Booker T. Washington's industrial education program (and limited political aspirations for blacks) shows clearly in this powerful critique. Du Bois outlined his own educational vision in his famous essay "The Talented Tenth."

Source: Du Bois, W. E. Burghardt. Souls of Black Folk. Chicago: A. C. McClurg, 1903.

. . . Mr. Washington represents in Negro thought the old attitude of adjustment and submission; but adjustment at such a peculiar time as to make his programme unique. This is an age of unusual economic development, and Mr. Washington's programme naturally takes an economic cast, becoming a gospel of Work and Money to such an extent as apparently almost completely to overshadow the higher aims of life. Moreover, this is an age when the more advanced races are coming in closer contact with the less developed races, and the race-feeling is therefore intensified; and Mr. Washington's programme practically accepts the alleged inferiority of the Negro races. Again, in our own land, the reaction from the sentiment of war time has given impetus to race-prejudice against Negroes, and Mr. Washington withdraws many of the high demands of Negroes as men and American citizens. In other periods of intensified prejudice all the Negro's tendency to self-assertion has been called forth; at this period a policy of submission is advocated. In the history of nearly all other races and peoples the doctrine preached at such crises has been that manly self-respect is worth more than lands and houses, and that a people who voluntarily surrender such respect, or cease striving for it, are not worth civilizing.

In answer to this, it has been claimed that the Negro can survive only through submission. Mr. Washington distinctly asks that black people give up, at least for the present, three things,—

First, political power,

Second, insistence on civil rights,

Third, higher education of Negro youth,

—and concentrate all their energies on industrial education, the accumulation of wealth, and the conciliation of the South. This policy has been courageously and insistently advocated for over fifteen years, and has been triumphant for perhaps ten years. As a result of this tender of the palm-branch, what has been the return? In these years there have occurred:

1. The disfranchisement of the Negro.
2. The legal creation of a distinct status of civil inferiority for the Negro.
3. The steady withdrawal of aid from institutions for the higher training of the Negro.

These movements are not, to be sure, direct results of Mr. Washington's teachings; but his propaganda has, without a shadow of doubt, helped their speedier accomplishment. The question then comes: Is it possible, and probable, that nine millions of men can make effective progress in economic lines if they are deprived of political rights, made a servile caste, and allowed only the most meagre chance for developing their exceptional men? If history and reason give any distinct answer to these questions, it is an emphatic No. And Mr. Washington thus faces the triple paradox of his career:

1. He is striving nobly to make Negro artisans business men and property-owners; but it is utterly

impossible, under modern competitive methods, for workingmen and property-owners to defend their rights and exist without the right of suffrage.

2. He insists on thrift and self-respect, but at the same time counsels a silent submission to civic inferiority such as is bound to sap the manhood of any race in the long run.

3. He advocates common-school and industrial training, and depreciates institutions of higher learning; but neither the Negro common-schools, nor Tuskegee itself, could remain open a day were it not for teachers trained in Negro colleges, or trained by their graduates. . . .

[Washington's] doctrine has tended to make the whites, North and South, shift the burden of the Negro problem to the Negro's shoulders and stand aside as critical and rather pessimistic spectators; when in fact the burden belongs to the nation, and the hands of none of us are clean if we bend not our energies to righting these great wrongs.

The South ought to be led, by candid and honest criticism, to assert her better self and do her full duty to the race she has cruelly wronged and is still wronging. The North—her co-partner in guilt—cannot salve her conscience by plastering it with gold. We cannot settle this problem by diplomacy and suaveness, by "policy" alone. If worse comes to worst, can the moral fibre of this country survive the slow throttling and murder of nine millions of men?

The black men of America have a duty to perform, a duty stern and delicate,—a forward movement to oppose a part of the work of their greatest leader. So far as Mr. Washington preaches Thrift, Patience, and Industrial Training for the masses, we must hold up his hands and strive with him, rejoicing in his honors and glorying in the strength of this Joshua called of God and of man to lead the headless host. But so far as Mr. Washington apologizes for injustice, North or South, does not rightly value the privilege and duty of voting, belittles the emasculating effects of caste distinctions, and opposes the higher training and ambition of our brighter minds,—so far as he, the South, or the Nation, does this,—we must unceasingly and firmly oppose them. By every civilized and peaceful method we must strive for the rights which the world accords to men, clinging unwaveringly to those great words which the sons of the Fathers would fain forget: "We hold these truths to be self-evident: That all men are created equal; that they are endowed by their Creater with certain unalienable rights; that among these are life, liberty, and the pursuit of happiness."

COVER OF THE FIRST ISSUE OF *THE CRISIS* (1910)

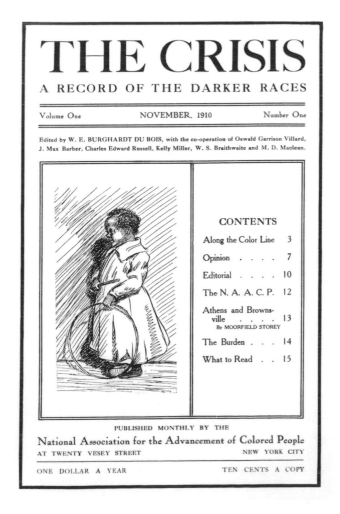

The first issue of the NAACP's monthly magazine, The Crisis, *was published in November 1910 and edited by Du Bois.* The Crisis *was a leading force in the Harlem Renaissance, building pride in black thought and culture and nurturing the careers of such talented writers as Arna Bontemps, Countee Cullen, Jean Toomer, and Langston Hughes.*

Source: ©Bettmann/ Corbis.

"THE AFRICAN ROOTS OF WAR" by W. E. B. Du Bois (May 1915) [EXCERPT]

In this excerpt from "The African Roots of War," Du Bois argues that World War I resulted from the colonial powers' "desperate struggle for Africa" and economic exploitation, and prophesied that a "War of the Color Line" could be avoided only if the European powers extended the "democratic ideal to the yellow, brown, and black peoples." Indeed, such an extension would be attempted by the ambitious provisions of the League of Nations following World War I.

Source: Du Bois, W. E. Burghardt, "The African Roots of War." *Atlantic Monthly*, May 1915.

. . . Hitherto the peace movement has confined itself chiefly to figures about the cost of war and platitudes on humanity. What do nations care about the cost of war, if by spending a few hundred millions in steel and gunpowder they can gain a thousand millions in diamonds and cocoa? How can love of humanity appeal as a motive to nations whose love of luxury is built on the inhuman exploitation of human beings, and who, especially in recent years, have been taught to regard these human beings as inhuman? I appealed to the last meeting of peace societies in St. Louis, saying, 'Should you not discuss racial prejudice as a prime cause of war?' The secretary was sorry but was unwilling to introduce controversial matters!

We, then, who want peace, must remove the real causes of war. We have extended gradually our conception of democracy beyond our social class to all social classes in our nation; we have gone further and extended our democratic ideals not simply to all classes of our own nation, but to those of other nations of our blood and lineage—to what we call 'European' civilization. If we want real peace and lasting culture, however, we must go further. We must extend the democratic ideal to the yellow, brown, and black peoples.

To say this, is to evoke on the faces of modern men a look of blank hopelessness. Impossible! we are told, and for so many reasons,—scientific, social, and what not,—that argument is useless. But let us not conclude too quickly. Suppose we have to choose between this unspeakably inhuman outrage on decency and intelligence and religion which we call the World War and the attempt to treat black men as human, sentient, responsible beings? We have sold them as cattle. We are working them as beasts of burden. We shall not drive war from this world until we treat them as free and equal citizens in a world-democracy of all races and nations. Impossible? Democracy is a method of doing the impossible. It is the only method yet discovered of making the education and development of all men a matter of all men's desperate desire. It is putting firearms in the hands of a child with the object of compelling the child's neighbors to teach him, not only the real and legitimate uses of a dangerous tool but the uses of himself in all things. Are there other and less costly ways of accomplishing this? There may be in some better world. But for a world just emerging from the rough chains of an almost universal poverty, and faced by the temptation of luxury and indulgence through the enslaving of defenseless men, there is but one adequate method of salvation—the giving of democratic weapons of self-defense to the defenseless.

Nor need we quibble over those ideas,—wealth, education and political power,—soil which we have so forested with claim and counter-claim that we see nothing for the woods.

What the primitive peoples of Africa and the world need and must have if war is to be abolished is perfectly clear:—

First: land. To-day Africa is being enslaved by the theft of her land and natural resources. A century ago black men owned all but a morsel of South Africa. The Dutch and English came, and to-day 1,250,000 whites own 264,000,000 acres, leaving only 21,000,000 acres for 4,500,000 natives. Finally, to make assurance doubly sure, the Union of South Africa has refused natives even the right to *buy* land. This is a deliberate attempt to force the Negroes to work on farms and in mines and kitchens for low wages. All over Africa has gone this shameless monopolizing of land and natural resources to force poverty on the masses and reduce them to the 'dumb-driven-cattle' stage of labor activity.

Secondly: we must train native races in modern civilization. This can be done. Modern methods of educating children, honestly and effectively applied, would make modern, civilized nations out of the vast majority of human beings on earth to-day. This we have seldom tried. For the most part Europe is straining every nerve to make over yellow, brown, and black men into docile beasts of burden, and only an irrepressible few are allowed to escape and seek (usually abroad) the education of modern men.

Lastly, the principle of home rule must extend to groups, nations, and races. The ruling of one people for another people's whim or gain must stop. This kind of despotism has been in later days more and more skillfully disguised. But the brute fact remains: the white man is ruling black Africa for the white man's gain, and just as far as possible he is doing the same to colored races elsewhere. Can such a situation bring peace? Will any amount of European concord or disarmament settle this injustice?

Political power to-day is but the weapon to force economic power. Tomorrow, it may give us spiritual vision and artistic sensibility. To-day, it gives us or tries to give us bread and butter, and those classes or nations or races who are without it starve, and starvation is the weapon of the white world to reduce them to slavery.

We are calling for European concord to-day; but at the utmost European concord will mean satisfaction with, or acquiescence in, a given division of the spoils of world-dominion. After all, European disarmament cannot go below the necessity of defending the aggressions of the whites against the blacks and browns and yellows. From this will arise three perpetual dangers of war. First, renewed jealousy at any division of colonies or spheres of influence agreed upon, if at any future time the present division comes to seem unfair. Who cared for Africa in the early nineteenth century? Let England have the scraps left from the golden feast of the slave trade. But in the twentieth century? The end was war. These scraps looked too tempting to Germany. Secondly: war will come from the revolutionary revolt of the lowest workers. The greater the international jealousies, the greater the corresponding costs of armament and the more difficult to fulfill the promises of industrial democracy in advanced countries. Finally, the colored peoples will not always submit passively to foreign domination. To some this is a lightly tossed truism. When a people deserve liberty they fight for it and get it, say such philosophers; thus making war a regular, necessary step to liberty. Colored people are familiar with this complacent judgment. They endure the contemptuous treatment meted out by whites to those not 'strong' enough to be free. These nations and races, composing as they do a vast majority of humanity, are going to endure this treatment just as long as they must and not a moment longer. Then they are going to fight and the War of the Color Line will outdo in savage inhumanity any war this world has yet seen. For colored folk have much to remember and they will not forget.

But is this inevitable? Must we sit helpless before this awful prospect? While we are planning, as a result of the present holocaust, the disarmament of Europe and a European international world-police, must the rest of the world be left naked to the inevitable horror of war, especially when we know that it is directly in this outer circle of races, and not in the inner European household, that the real causes of present European fighting are to be found?

Our duty is clear. Racial slander must go. Racial prejudice will follow. Steadfast faith in humanity must come. The domination of one people by another without the other's consent, be the subject people black or white, must stop. The doctrine of forcible economic expansion over subject peoples must go. Religious hypocrisy must stop. 'Blood-thirsty' Mwanga of Uganda killed an English bishop because he feared that his coming meant English domination. It did mean English domination, and the world and the bishop knew it, and yet the world was 'horrified'! Such missionary hypocrisy must go. With clean hands and honest hearts we must front high Heaven and beg peace in our time.

In this great work who can help us? In the Orient, the awakened Japanese and the awakening leaders of New China; in India and Egypt, the young men trained in Europe and European ideals, who now form the stuff that Revolution is born of. But in Africa? Who better than the twenty-five million grandchildren of the European slave trade, spread through the Americas and now writhing desperately for freedom and a place in the world? And of these millions first of all the ten million black folk of the United States, now a problem, then a world-salvation.

Twenty centuries before the Christ a great cloud swept over sea and settled on Africa, darkening and wellnigh blotting out the culture of the land of Egypt. For half a thousand years it rested there until a black woman, Queen Nefertari, 'the most venerated figure in Egyptian history,' rose to the throne of the Pharaohs and redeemed the world and her people. Twenty centuries after Christ, black Africa, prostrate, raped, and shamed, lies at the feet of the conquering Philistines of Europe. Beyond the awful sea a black woman is weeping and waiting with her sons on her breast. What shall the end be? The world-old and fearful things, War and Wealth, Murder and Luxury? Or shall it be a new thing—a new peace and new democracy of all races: a great humanity of equal men? 'Semper novi quid ex Africa!'

Letter from W. E. B. Du Bois and the NAACP to President Woodrow Wilson (October 10, 1916)

To the President of the United States
Sir:

As an organization representing the Negro race and thousands of their friends we are deeply interested in the presidential election.

During the last campaign, believing firmly that the Republican Party and its leaders had systematically betrayed the interests of colored people, many of our members did what they could to turn the colored vote toward you. We received from you a promise of justice and sincere endeavor to forward their interests. We need scarcely to say that you have grievously disappointed us.

We find ourselves again facing a presidential campaign with but indifferent choice. We have waited for some time to gather from your writings and speeches something of your present attitude toward the colored people. We have thought that perhaps you had some statement or explanation which would account for the dismissal of colored public officials, segregation in the civil service, and other things which have taken place during your administration. You must surely realize that if Negroes were Americans—if they had a reasonable degree of rights and privileges, they need ask for no especial statement from a candidate for the high office of President; but being as they are, members of a segregated class and struggling against tremendous prejudices, disabilities and odds, we must for their own salvation and the salvation of our country ask for more than such treatment as is today fair for other races. We must continually demand such positive action as will do away with their disabilities. Lynching is a national evil of which Negroes are the chief victims. It is perhaps the greatest disgrace

from which this country suffers, and yet we find you and other men of influence silent in the matter. A republic must be based upon universal suffrage or it is not a republic; and yet, while you seem anxious to do justice toward women, we hear scarcely a word concerning those disfranchised masses of the South whose stolen votes are used to make Rotten Boroughs of a third of the nation and thus distort and ruin the just distribution of political power. Caste restrictions, fatal to Christian civilization and modern conceptions of decency, are slowly but forcibly entering this land and making black folk the chief victims. There should be outspoken protest against segregation by race in the civil service, caste in public travel and in other public accommodations.

As Negroes and as their friends; as Americans; as persons whose fathers have striven for the good of this land and who ourselves have tried unselfishly to make America the land of just ideals, we write to ask if you do not think it possible to make to the colored and white people of America some further statement of your attitude toward this grievous problem such as will allow us at least to vote with intelligence.

We trust, Sir, that you will not regard this statement and request as beyond the courtesy due you or as adding too much to the burdens of a public man.

We beg to remain, Sir,
Very respectfully yours,
National Association for the
Advancement of Colored People
W. E. Burghardt Du Bois
Director of Publications and
Research

A letter from W. E. B. Du Bois and fellow NAACP board members to President Woodrow Wilson shortly before Wilson's reelection in 1916. A similar letter was sent to the Republican candidate, Charles Evans Hughes.

Source: Du Bois, W. E. B. *The Correspondence of W. E. B. Du Bois: Selections 1877–1934.* Vol. 1. Edited by Herbert Aptheker. Amherst: University of Massachusetts Press, 1973. Reprinted with permission from the University of Massachusetts Press.

Albert Einstein

1879–1955
Physicist and Pacifist

The greatest scientist of the twentieth century, Albert Einstein was also one of its great public personalities and moral anchors.

Einstein was born to middle-class Jewish parents in Ulm, in southern Germany, on March 14, 1879; the family moved to Munich when he was young. His father ran a struggling electrical firm, and his mother encouraged Einstein to study music (the violin became a lifetime passion). As a child Einstein was something of a slow learner and also quite a free and unconventional thinker. As a result his attitude toward school was ambivalent at best. When his family moved to Milan, Italy, when Einstein was 15, his parents left him to stay on in Munich until he graduated from the strictly regimented high school he had been attending there. Instead, Einstein contrived to leave: he may have quit, faked a nervous breakdown, or been expelled. He finished high school at a small institution in Switzerland and then entered a Swiss technical university.

By 1900 Einstein had graduated and was struggling to make a living through temporary high school teaching jobs. He met a Serb physics student, Mileva Marić, who shared his interests and participated to a still-debated degree in the great discoveries that were soon to come. Einstein finally found a stable paycheck when he was hired by the Swiss government patent office in Berne in 1902, and he and Marić married the following year. It was thus as an obscure patents clerk that Einstein first formulated his so-called theory of relativity, parts of which emerged in a group of groundbreaking papers published in 1905. Essentially, his theory begins with the ideas that all things are in motion and that the speed of light is both constant and a maximum velocity of all things. In classical physics, properties of things and events in the physical world such as time, mass, and dimension seemed to be distorted when observers were in motion; Einstein showed that these properties themselves depended on the "relative" motion of observer and observed. The

From the collections of the Library of Congress.

mass of an object, for example, was not a constant but depended on its velocity. An extension of this idea, namely that the mass and energy of an object had a fixed relationship, was summarized in Einstein's famous equation $E=mc^2$, where E equals energy, m equals mass, and c equals the speed of light.

The papers of 1905 gained Einstein belated academic recognition, and he lectured at various European universities over the next several years. In 1914 he became a member of the faculty at the prestigious University of Berlin, remaining there until he fled the country before the rising tide of Nazism in 1933. During these years, Einstein worked to apply the theory of relativity to the phenomenon of gravity. The solution he reached during the war years involved the ideas that space itself is curved and that objects, because of their mass, actually affect the shape of the spaces around them. These ideas, like many others of Einstein's, seemed to defy common sense, but now Einstein suggested that they were susceptible to public proof or disproof through a series of tests. Einstein's most widely publicized contention was that the light from a star that passed near the Sun would be bent slightly because of the Sun's mass. This effect would be pronounced enough to be measurable only for stars that seemed to lie very near the Sun's edge, and these stars would be visible only during an eclipse of the Sun. The general public might not have understood much about Einstein's theories themselves, but the certainty of a unique test seized the imagination of the educated general observer. With several years of advance publicity, the confirmation of his prediction during the solar eclipse of 1919 resulted in considerable celebrity for Einstein.

During World War I Einstein and a small group of other scientists signed an antiwar petition at considerable personal risk. Einstein had been uncomfortable with the militaristic streak in the German character since his school days, and he became more and more interested in the philosophy of pacifism and in the cause of Zionism—the establishment of a new Jewish state in the Middle East. Einstein used his newfound celebrity to campaign on behalf of these beliefs; he traveled around the world, visiting the United States for the first time in 1921. The scientist's disheveled but luxuriant head of white hair became instantly recognizable. Einstein's fame increased when he was awarded the Nobel Prize for Physics in 1921—for his "services to Theoretical Physics, and especially for his discovery of the law of the photoelectric effect"—but not for his theory of relativity, which was still considered controversial.

To a large degree it was the revolutionary quality of Einstein's teachings that fascinated the public, their way of making people feel that the unshakable bases of their perceptions had been called into question. Absolutists of various kinds condemned Einstein, but many ordinary people found him intellectually stimulating. He often gave lectures about his continually evolving theories and worked tirelessly to convince his audiences of the folly of war, specifically urging the young to reject military service. The main purpose of many of Einstein's trips was to raise money for the Zionist cause; he first came to the United States with future president of Israel Chaim Weizmann. Some of his travels were motivated by the necessity of sidestepping ugly outbreaks of German anti-Semitism. As part of the growing anti-intellectualism of their nationalist campaigns, the Nazis in Germany condemned "Jewish physics" and Einstein's situation worsened.

Einstein believed in a supreme being, sometimes speaking of God as "der Alte" or "the old man." When the quantum mechanics theorists of the 1920s extended his ideas to a point where they seemed to indicate a fundamental randomness in what we can know of the physical world, he retorted with his famous remark that "God does not play dice with the universe." Nevertheless, some conservative religious organizations shared the dislike that political authoritarians felt for Einstein, sensing the overturning of seemingly immutable laws that his ideas entailed. Einstein traveled extensively in the United States in the early 1930s, and in advance of one trip the women's arm of a conservative organization called the National Patriotic Union protested, on the grounds of Einstein's pacifist activities, the issuance of an entrance visa. Einstein breezily told reporters that "never before have I been spurned so vigorously by the fair sex, or if this did ever happen, then not by so many at a time."

The visa was issued, however, and as the Nazis rose to power in Germany, Einstein settled in Pasadena, California. Einstein was prescient about Germany's future; the previous fall he had told his wife to take a good look around their summer home in Germany as they closed it up, because she would never see it again. Einstein remained in the United States and never went back to Germany. (Nazi storm troopers did indeed raid his summer home.) He accepted a position at Princeton University's Institute for Advanced Study in New Jersey, continuing to speak out on world issues and becoming a citizen of the United States in 1940. His pacifism, however, was put aside in response to the menace of Hitler's armies, and he wrote to President Franklin D. Roosevelt urging the establishment of what became the Manhattan Project, the research effort that created the first atomic bomb. Fully aware that his own discoveries about the relationship of mass and energy had paved the way for atomic weaponry, Einstein campaigned for nuclear disarmament after the war. With the outbreak of the Korean War in 1950, Einstein resumed his advocacy of conscientious objection to the military draft. In 1952 he was offered but did not accept the presidency of the young state of Israel. Einstein died in Princeton on April 18, 1955.

Einstein's revolutionary discoveries overturned scientific certainties that had lasted for centuries. For some years after he made these discoveries, few people understood them; they seemed to call into question some of the most basic assumptions of human knowledge of the physical world. Yet if Einstein seemed preoccupied with mysterious and abstract scientific priciples, he nevertheless cared deeply about the world around him. In an age when technological advances in science began to transform society, its greatest scientist of all spoke out about the potential power of human peacemaking.

James M. Manheim

For Further Reading
Clark, Ronald W. *Einstein: The Life and Times.* New York: H. N. Abrams, 1984.
Fölsing, Albrecht. *Albert Einstein: A Biography.* New York: Viking Press, 1997.
Hoffmann, Banesh. *Albert Einstein: Creator and Rebel.* Collaboration with Helen Dukas. New York: Viking Press, 1972.

ALBERT EINSTEIN AND CHAIM WEIZMANN (1921)

Einstein first came to the United States in 1921 to raise money for the establishment of a Jewish state in Palestine. He made the trip at the behest of future president of Israel Chaim Weizmann (second from right).

Source: ©Bettmann/ Corbis

ALBERT EINSTEIN'S LETTER TO MAX PLANCK (July 5, 1922) [EXCERPT]

In this excerpt from a July 5, 1922, letter to Max Planck, a German theoretical physicist, Einstein cancels his lecture at the annual meeting of the Congress of German Scientists and Physicians in Berlin. As the political situation in Germany worsened and nationalism increased, Einstein's pacifist and Zionist ideals generated much resentment against him in right-wing circles.

Source: Hoffmann, Banesh. *Albert Einstein: Creator and Rebel.* Collaboration with Helen Dukas. New York: Viking Press, 1972. Reprinted with permission from Viking Penguin, a division of Penguin Putnam, Inc.

. . . A number of people who deserve to be taken seriously have independently warned me not to stay in Berlin for the time being, and especially to avoid all public appearances in Germany. I am assumed to be among those whom the nationalists have marked for assassination. Of course, I have no definite proof but in the prevailing situation it seems quite plausible. If a really important cause were involved, I would not let myself be deterred by such reasons. But the present case involves only a simple formality, and someone (e.g., Laue) can easily take my place. The trouble is that the newspapers have mentioned my name too often, thus mobilizing the rabble against me. I have no alternative but to be patient—and to leave the city. I do urge you to take this little incident calmly, as I do myself. . . .

"Try to Make Out My Theory and Your Income Tax Work Will Look Simple!" Political Cartoon (1929)

In this cartoon, Albert Einstein shows his theory of relativity to a man working frantically on his 1928 income tax forms. By this time Einstein's fame had spread into the realm of popular culture; he had become an icon of the scientific advances that at once epitomized progress and baffled ordinary individuals.

Source: From the collections of the Library of Congress.

Albert Einstein Teaching (1931)

Einstein writing a complicated equation on the blackboard in the classroom at the California Institute of Technology, in Pasadena, California.

Source: ©Bettmann/ Corbis.

"My Credo" by Albert Einstein (1932)

In 1932, Einstein delivered this speech discussing his personal philosophy to the German League of Human Rights in Berlin.

Source: Gribbin, John, and Michael White. *Einstein*. New York: Penguin Books USA, 1994.

Our situation on this earth seems strange. Every one of us appears here involuntarily and uninvited for a short stay, without knowing the whys and the wherefore. In our daily lives we only feel that man is here for the sake of others, for those whom we love and for many other beings whose fate is connected with our own. I am often worried at the thought that my life is based to such a large extent on the work of my fellow human beings and I am aware of my great indebtedness to them. I do not believe in freedom of the will. Schopenhauer's words: 'Man can do what he wants, but he cannot will what he wills' accompany me in all situations throughout my life and reconcile me with the actions of others even if they are rather painful to me. This awareness of the lack of freedom of will preserves me from taking too seriously myself and my fellow men as acting and deciding individuals and from losing my temper. I never coveted affluence and luxury and even despise them a good deal. My passion for social justice has often brought me into conflict with people, as did my aversion to any obligation and dependence I do not regard as absolutely necessary. I always have a high regard for the individual and have an insuperable distaste for violence and clubmanship. All these motives made me into a passionate pacifist and anti-militarist. I am against any nationalism, even in the guise of mere patriotism. Privileges based on position and property have always seemed to me unjust and pernicious, as did any exaggerated personality cult. I am an adherent of the ideal of democracy, although I well know the weaknesses of the democratic form of government. Social equality and economic protection of the individual appeared to me always as the important communal aims of the state. Although I am a typical loner in daily life, my consciousness of belonging to the invisible community of those who strive for truth, beauty, and justice has preserved me from feeling isolated. The most beautiful and deepest experience a man can have is the sense of the mysterious. It is the underlying principle of religion as well as all serious endeavour in art and science. He who never had this experience seems to me, if not dead, then at least blind. To sense that behind anything that can be experienced there is a something that our mind cannot grasp and whose beauty and sublimity reaches us only indirectly and as a feeble reflection, this is religiousness. In this sense I am religious. To me it suffices to wonder at these secrets and to attempt humbly to grasp with my mind a mere image of the lofty structure of all that there is.

Duke Ellington

Duke Ellington was an African-American composer, band-leader, and pianist who crafted new musical styles and arrangements. His sophisticated artistry established his preeminent and lasting presence in jazz.

Born Edward Kennedy Ellington in Washington, D.C., on April 29, 1899, he grew up in a cultivated, middle-class family that instilled a strong sense of confidence and racial pride. With his privileged upbringing, polite manners, and fashionable dress, he earned the nickname "Duke" at Armstrong Technical High School. During these years, Ellington studied commercial art and pursued his interest in music. He began listening to local ragtime pianists and imitating their style on his piano at home. His first instrumental song, "Soda Fountain Rag" and his first song with lyrics, "What You Gonna Do When the Bed Breaks Down?" became popular hits at local teenage parties and dances. In 1916, Ellington won a poster contest sponsored by the National Association for the Advancement of Colored People (NAACP) and a scholarship to the Pratt Institute of Applied Arts in Brooklyn. Torn between continuing his studies in art or following his passion for music, Ellington declined the scholarship.

©Underwood and Underwood/Corbis.

Ellington left high school in his senior year to focus on a professional music career. He painted signs and posters during the day and played the piano at night. After working with Washington bandleaders like Louis Thomas, Russell Wooding, and Oliver "Doc" Perry, Ellington formed the Duke's Serenaders in 1917. The group started with small gigs at the True Reformer's Hall, but advanced to high society functions once they advertised in the telephone directory. As manager and band member, Ellington booked a variety of engagements for both blacks and whites at a time of heightened interracial conflict in the United States. The "Red Summer" of 1919 witnessed bloody violence with 76 lynchings of blacks and approximately 25 race riots, the worst incidents occurring in Chicago. Ellington, however, attempted to use his music to rise above categories of skin color and class status.

Resisting societal limitations and seeking career opportunities, Ellington entered the glamorous entertainment world of New York City in 1923. Manhattan alone offered almost 250 dance halls that answered the public's enthusiasm for latest steps like the Charleston. The booming dance craze coincided with the emerging jazz scene. Ellington joined former band member Elmer Snowden's the Washingtonians at the humble Hollywood Club. The next year he replaced Snowden as bandleader and received his first credit as a composer. Although the Washingtonians gradually expanded from a five-piece to a 10-piece combo, Ellington developed a sensibility for showcasing individual talent and creating an original sound. The band balanced composition with improvisation, classicism with exoticism, and images with emotions. Along with bandleader Fletcher Henderson and arranger Don Redman, Ellington was defining a new genre known as big-band jazz.

In 1927, Ellington's orchestra left the Kentucky Club (former Hollywood Club) in April and arrived at the luxurious Cotton Club in December. The Cotton Club was Harlem's chief nightspot; its elaborate and eclectic floor shows mingled music, dancing, and theater. Here, Ellington capitalized on a style that owed most of its distinctive edge to the plunger-muted growl techniques of trumpeter Bubber Miley and trombonist Tricky Sam Nanton. Their sonorous brass effects appear on Ellington's first major recordings: *East St. Louis Toodle-O* (1926), *Black and Tan Fantasy* (1927), and *Creole Love Call* (1927). The "jungle music" of their ensemble suited the Southern and African décor of the Cotton Club that, together, evoked a mood of exotic and romantic escape.

Like many clubs of the era, the Cotton Club hired black performers but admitted only white patrons. Ellington worked within this segregated system to advance his own artistic and technical skills as a composer. He performed six or seven nights a week and assembled a new show every six months. This demanding schedule allowed him to better connect with his players and perfect his creations. The more experience Ellington gained, the greater he experimented with tonal colors, harmonies, and unusual instrumental groupings. Now called Duke Ellington and His Cotton Club Orchestra, the band received national acclaim for its revues and radio broadcasts. Through radio, which transformed American culture in the 1920s by uniting diverse regions with a common experience, Ellington transported jazz from the Cotton Club into homes across the country, typically airing a sweeter syncopation in the evening and a racier one at midnight. In 1929, his orchestra also was starring on stage in the Broadway production, *Show Girl*. The "Duke" had made a name for himself in the Jazz Age not only because of his music but also because of his image, charming audiences with a self-assured manner and polished appearance.

Through the Cotton Club, radio, and Broadway, Ellington became a pivotal figure in jazz. He recorded his most famous composition, "Mood Indigo," in 1930 and departed from the Cotton Club to tour the United States in 1931. His brilliance scaled from popular tunes like "It Don't Mean a Thing" (1932) and "Sophisticated Lady" (1932) to longer masterpieces like *Reminiscing in Tempo* (1935) and *Black, Brown, and Beige* (1943). Ellington premiered *Black, Brown, and Beige*, a musical exploration of African-American history and culture, at the 1943 opening of an annual concert series at Carnegie Hall. Throughout his career he continuously broadened the scope of his composi-

tions, writing for symphonies, ballets, musicals, movies, and even religious concerts. Some of his honors include the NAACP Spingarn Medal (1959), the Presidential Medal of Freedom (1969), the Emperor's Star from Ethiopia (1973), and the Legion of Honor from France (1973). In 1971, the Royal Swedish Academy of Music elected him to membership, making him the first jazz composer to be inducted in its 200-year history. Ellington published his autobiography, *Music Is My Mistress*, in 1973 and died of lung cancer on May 24, 1974, in New York City.

Considered to be one of the most important composers in jazz history, Ellington intimately understood his orchestra. He designed compositions that illuminated the personal strengths of the band members and created a tapestry of rich tonal color and emotional depth. His orchestra concentrated less on rendering the latest jazz tunes and more on representing a palette of moods and emotions. Ellington's unique ensemble was an extension of his own style—the elegance, charisma, and debonair manner of the "Duke."

Renée Miller

For Further Reading

Ellington, Duke. *Music Is My Mistress*. Garden City, N.Y.: Doubleday, 1973.

Hasse, John Edward. *Beyond Category: The Life and Genius of Duke Ellington*. Foreword by Wynton Marsalis. New York: Simon & Schuster, 1993.

Lawrence, A. H. *Duke Ellington and His World: A Biography*. New York: Routledge, 2001.

Nicholson, Stuart. *Reminiscing In Tempo: A Portrait of Duke Ellington*. Boston: Northeastern University Press, 1999.

Tucker, Mark. *Ellington: The Early Years*. Urbana: University of Illinois Press, 1991.

CRITICISM IN THE *PHONOGRAPH MONTHLY REVIEW* by R. D. Darrell (1927–29) [EXCERPTS]

In the late 1920s, Ellington's career skyrocketed. These pieces, written by R. D. Darrell for the Phonograph Monthly Review, *chart his progress as a recording artist during this period. One of the earliest admirers of Ellington, Darrell provides insightful and thoughtful comments on the music of this up-and-coming luminary.*

Source: Duke Ellington: The Reader. Edited by Mark Tucker. New York: Oxford University Press, 1993.

July 1927

Two unusually interesting records lead the Brunswick list, indeed are right in the forefront of the releases from all companies. *The Black and Tan Fantasy* (coupled with *Soliloquy* on Brunswick 3526) deserves perhaps the first prize; in it The Washingtonians combine sonority and fine tonal qualities with some amazing eccentric instrumental effects. This record differs from similar ones by avoiding extremes, for while the "stunts" are exceptionally original and striking, they are performed musically, even artistically. A piece no one should miss! The snatch of the Chopin Funeral March at the end deserves special mention as a stroke of genius.

June 1928

If last month's dance releases seldom rose above the mediocre, the disks this month offer full atonement. From the smoothest symphonic dance pieces to the most highly seasoned jazzical eccentricities runs the range; there is a spiced variety of good things for every taste. Victor leads the field with the strongest stable in many months, although the individual prize goes to Duke Ellington with his Okeh coupling of *Jubilee*

Stomp and *Take It Easy* (41013). The former piece has a most arresting beginning and a development that sustains its first promise; it can be ranked very nearly with his great *Parlor Social Stomp* (and by the way, when will one of the major companies record that masterpiece?). *Take It Easy* is in the style of the memorable *Black and Tan Fantasy*; hardly as good, it is still miles above the best imitative efforts of any other orchestra.

July 1928

July brings us more worthy candidates for the jazzical Hall of Fame than any single month in the last year and a quarter. I find eight truly first class dance disks, records of originality and distinction, and of those eight no less than six bear the Victor label. Profound salaams are in order. I hesitate to assign a definite ranking to the leaders, so various and so contrasted are their characteristics, but there can be no possibility of error in leading off with Duke Ellington's first Victor Race Series release (21284), coupling a furious *Washington Wabble* and a *Harlem River Quiver* of sinewy construction and abundant pace and momentum. Both feature some pianny playing "as is," as well as all the throaty sonority and symphonic ingenuity which have made Ellington the most significant—if not the best known—figure in hot jazz.

August 1928

Leadership this month is divided (as it so often used to be) between the best of white and colored orchestras specializing in hot jazz, Red Nichols' Five Pennies and Duke Ellington's Cotton Club Orchestra. . . .Ellington's Vocalion disk of *Doin' the Frog* and *Red Hot Band* is characteristic of his best work, particularly in the former piece; the latter contains several remarkable effects, notably the furious banjo solo, but is a trifle too noisy. *Doin' the Frog*, however, is altogether admirable, with special mention going to the arresting beginning—a not uncommon feature of Ellington's arrangements, the first few bars of which are usually worth several complete pieces by less inspired directors.

September 1928

Again Ellington and Nichols contest honors in the realm of hot jazz, while Coon-Sanders and Waring's Pennsylvanians lead the field of smoother dance disks. . . .

Ellington quite surpasses himself on Vocalion 15704 in *Black Beauty* and *Take It Easy*, both his own compositions. Both rank with his finest efforts: the curiously twisted and wry trumpet passages, the amazing piano solo in *Black Beauty*, the splendid melodic urge that animates even the most eccentric measures, are all characteristic of his unique genius for the expression of an over-whelming nostalgia and bitterness in a new idiom, and one entirely his own. *Take It Easy* is superior in this version to those recorded for Victor and Perfect.

May 1929

Turning to the hot records, among which Victor releases have lately begun to figure prominently, we have no less than three magnificent disks from Duke Ellington of Cotton Club fame. On V-38036 he plays *High Life* and *Saturday Night Function,* both of which live fully up to their titles; on V-38035 he has a jaunty *Doin' the Voom Voom* (with a brief pianny interlude of his own) and a more songful *Flaming Youth*. And on V-38034 he has one side devoted to his famous *The Mooche*, while on the other King Oliver plays the *West End Blues*. All Ellington's pieces are of his own composition and all are in his characteristic vein. None of these—good as they are—quite manage to rank with his superb master disks, however. But one of the latter has just come to my attention. It was issued some time ago, but was never reviewed in these pages: Victor 21137, whereon Duke plays a *Creole Love Call* and the never-to-be-forgotten *Black and Tan Fantasy* that first won him phonographic renown. The performance of the fantasy here is perhaps a shade below that on the Okeh record, on account of the regular beat receiving somewhat undue prominence, but the *Creole Love Call* is a veritable masterpiece of its genre! Now may Ellington re-record some of his early successes, such as the *Parlor Social Stomp, New Orleans Low-Down,* and *Birmingham Breakdown.*

THE COTTON CLUB (1929)

The Cotton Club was "The Aristocrat of Harlem," the nightspot that presented talented black performers for an affluent, white, after-the-ater crowd. It was a must-see for New York tourists and residents with its two distinct night shows, 50 beautiful chorus girls, and the famous Duke Ellington orchestra.

Source: ©Underwood and Underwood/Corbis.

"BLACK AND TAN" POSTER FOR DUKE ELLINGTON AND HIS COTTON CLUB ORCHESTRA (1929)

Duke Ellington and His Cotton Club Orchestra played regularly at the Cotton Club in Harlem from 1927 to 1930 and received much praise for their shows, which were broadcast live from the club. This poster advertises a performance of "Black and Tan."

Source: Driggs Collection, Archive Photos.

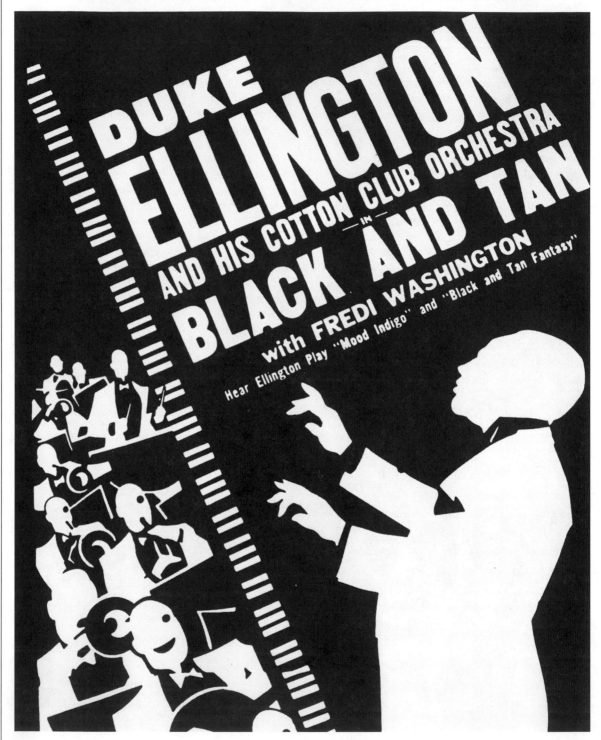

"BLACK AND TAN" POSTER FOR DUKE ELLINGTON AND HIS COTTON CLUB ORCHESTRA (1929)

F. Scott Fitzgerald

1896–1940
Author

F. Scott Fitzgerald, author of *The Great Gatsby*, was only 23 when he became famous as a chronicler of the Jazz Age (a term he coined) through his first novel and later his popular short stories. Scott and his beautiful, eccentric wife Zelda embodied the energies and frivolities of the Roaring Twenties.

Francis Scott Key Fitzgerald, born in St. Paul, Minnesota, on September 24, 1896, was named for a distant Maryland ancestor who wrote the words to "The Star-Spangled Banner." He entered Princeton in 1913 and wrote for the *Nassau Lit* magazine and cowrote two musical comedies produced by the Triangle Club. He withdrew from Princeton briefly on account of poor health and low grades, then returned as a member of the class of 1918. World War I intervened, however, and he never graduated.

Commissioned an infantry second lieutenant, Fitzgerald was assigned to Camp Sheridan near Montgomery, Alabama, in June 1918. In his spare time at training camp he wrote a novel, "The Romantic Egotist," the manuscript

for which he submitted several times to a New York publisher. In the summer of 1918 in Montgomery he met Zelda Sayre, the beautiful, vivacious daughter of a justice of the Alabama Supreme Court, and fell deeply in love. To his lifelong regret, the war ended before he could be sent overseas. Upon his discharge from the army in early 1919, he worked in New York City at an advertising agency, revised his novel, and tried to publish short stories. He visited Zelda in Montgomery repeatedly in the spring and summer of 1919, trying to convince her to marry him, but she hesitated to marry a young man with dim financial prospects.

He sold a short story to **H. L. Mencken**'s magazine *Smart Set* in June of 1919, and in September he was notified by Maxwell Perkins, an influential editor at Scribner's, that the revised novel, now titled *This Side of Paradise,* had been accepted for publication. The novel was published in late March 1920; Scott and Zelda married a week later in New York City.

This Side of Paradise, a coming-of-age story of a young Princeton man's education in love and modern manners, was an instant success. Although the novel seems mild today, in 1920 it was shocking in its casual depiction of young people kissing, petting, and partying with abandon; it showed what critic Edmund Wilson called "a gesture of indefinite revolt," affronting the upright Victorian morals that prevailed before World War I.

"Scott and Zelda" quickly became celebrities in New York City: young and beautiful, exuding charm, vitality, and wit, they made lively copy for the tabloid newspapers. The gossip columns reported their wild public behavior: riding atop a taxicab down Fifth Avenue, doing handstands in the Biltmore Hotel lobby, dancing in the fountain outside the Plaza Hotel, seemingly in perpetual motion from one party to another. They burned through their money at an alarming rate. The $18,000 earned from *Paradise* was gone in three months.

Fitzgerald maintained a high income by writing short stories for *The Saturday Evening Post* and other popular magazines, as well as another novel, *The Beautiful and Damned* (1922). He soon became one of the best-paid authors of his time. In May 1924 the Fitzgeralds went to Europe, staying mostly in Paris and in a villa on the Riviera. In France they became acquainted with many expatriate Americans—**Gertrude Stein** and **Ernest Hemingway** among them—and European artists of the Modernist period. Fitzgerald is associated more with the Jazz Age than with the Lost Generation (with which Hemingway is more closely linked), though the terms are essentially two aspects of the same phenomenon: on the one side, a rebellion from the constraints of Victorian morality combined with an ambition to succeed and acquire, and on the other side a turning away from the old verities of valor, honor, courage, fortitude, duty.

It was in France in 1924 that Fitzgerald wrote his masterpiece, *The Great Gatsby* (1925), about a man's quest to win back the love of his youth by illegally earning a fortune, naively believing it possible to recapture the past, and never quite understanding that "his dream was already behind him." Much has been written about the book's evocation of the dark underside of the American dream: Fitzgerald chronicled the Jazz Age—which he called "the greatest, gaudiest spree in history"—but he was a serious moralist who distrusted the rich as much as he admired wealth and its privileges.

Gatsby is considered to be Fitzgerald's finest work—beautiful, tragic, brief and intense, with rich prose and tight construction. Compared with his previous books, however, it was a commercial failure. Since his death, *The Great Gatsby* has become probably the most widely read and admired American novel of the twentieth century, and now sells more copies each month than it sold in his lifetime.

Nine years elapsed between the publication of *Gatsby* and his next novel, *Tender Is the Night* (1934), about a young psychiatrist who marries a wealthy patient, and then is dismissed by her family once she's cured. In 1930 Zelda suffered her first nervous breakdown and was institutionalized in a series of sanitariums. *Tender Is the Night* did not sell well, and fewer magazines wanted his short stories; in 1937, Fitzgerald went to Hollywood to work as a scriptwriter. He managed to pay off many of his debts, and was halfway through a novel when he died of a heart attack in 1940, at the age of 44. The unfinished novel, set in Hollywood, was published posthumously as *The Last Tycoon* (1941). Zelda Fitzgerald died in 1948 when the sanitarium where she was living near Asheville, North Carolina, caught fire.

In his brief life F. Scott Fitzgerald wrote five novels and some 160 short stories. Although his public largely neglected him in the 1930s, soon after his death his reputation began to rise. Frequent articles about Fitzgerald in periodicals like *Vanity Fair, The New Yorker,* and *The New York Review of Books* unvaryingly use the word "fresh" in describing his prose, his characters, and the enduring accuracy of his critical yet sympathetic view of American society: admiring glamour, yet distrusting it, and standing, like his narrator Nick Carraway in *The Great Gatsby,* "within and without, simultaneously enchanted and repelled by the inexhaustible variety of life."

Mark LaFlaur

For Further Reading

Bruccoli, Matthew. *Some Sort of Epic Grandeur: The Life of F. Scott Fitzgerald.* Rev. ed. New York: Harcourt Brace Jovanovich, 1991.

Kazin, Alfred, ed. *F. Scott Fitzgerald: The Man and His Work.* Rev. ed. New York: Collier Books, 1962.

Mizener, Arthur. *The Far Side of Paradise: A Biography of F. Scott Fitzgerald.* Rev. ed. Boston: Houghton Mifflin, 1965.

Turnbull, Andrew. *Scott Fitzgerald.* New York: Charles Scribner's Sons, 1962.

THIS SIDE OF PARADISE by F. Scott Fitzgerald (1920) [EXCERPT]

Published in 1920, Fitzgerald's first novel, This Side of Paradise, *was a coming-of-age story about a young man at Princeton University. This excerpt from the conclusion of the novel reflects the new morality and disillusionment of the post–World War I generation.*

Source: Fitzgerald, F. Scott. *This Side of Paradise.* New York: Charles Scribner's Sons, 1920.

Eight hours from Princeton Amory sat down by the Jersey roadside and looked at the frost-bitten country. Nature as a rather coarse phenomenon composed largely of flowers that, when closely inspected, appeared moth-eaten, and of ants that endlessly traversed blades of grass, was always disillusioning; nature represented by skies and waters and far horizons was more likable. Frost and the promise of winter thrilled him now, made him think of a wild battle between St. Regis and Groton, ages ago, seven years ago—and of an autumn day in France twelve months before when he had lain in tall grass, his platoon flattened down close around him, waiting to tap the shoulders of a Lewis gunner. He saw the two pictures together with somewhat the same primitive exaltation—two games he had played, differing in quality of acerbity, linked in a way that differed them from Rosalind or the subject of labyrinths which were, after all, the business of life.

"I am selfish," he thought.

"This is not a quality that will change when I 'see human suffering' or 'lose my parents' or 'help others.'

"This selfishness is not only part of me. It is the most living part.

"It is by somehow transcending rather than by avoiding that selfishness that I can bring poise and balance into my life.

"There is no virtue of unselfishness that I cannot use. I can make sacrifices, be charitable, give to a friend, endure for a friend, lay down my life for a friend—all because these things may be the best possible expression of myself; yet I have not one drop of the milk of human kindness."

The problem of evil had solidified for Amory into the problem of sex. He was beginning to identify evil with the strong phallic worship in Brooke and the early Wells. Inseparably linked with evil was beauty—beauty, still a constant rising tumult; soft in Eleanor's voice, in an old song at night, rioting deliriously through life like superimposed waterfalls, half rhythm, half darkness. Amory knew that every time he had reached toward it longingly it had leered out at him with the grotesque face of evil. Beauty of great art, beauty of all joy, most of all the beauty of women.

After all, it had too many associations with license and indulgence. Weak things were often beautiful, weak things were never good. And in this new loneness of his that had been selected for what greatness he might achieve, beauty must be relative or, itself a harmony, it would make only a discord.

In a sense this gradual renunciation of beauty was the second step after his disillusion had been made complete. He felt that he was leaving behind him his chance of being a certain type of artist. It seemed so much more important to be a certain sort of man.

His mind turned a corner suddenly and he found himself thinking of the Catholic Church. The idea was strong in him that there was a certain intrinsic lack in those to whom orthodox religion was necessary, and religion to Amory meant the Church of Rome. Quite conceivably it was an empty ritual but it was seemingly the only assimilative, traditionary bulwark against the decay of morals. Until the great mobs could be educated into a moral sense some one must cry: "Thou shalt not!" Yet any acceptance was, for the present, impossible. He wanted time and the absence of ulterior pressure. He wanted to keep the tree without ornaments, realize fully the direction and momentum of this new start.

The afternoon waned from the purging good of three o'clock to the golden beauty of four. Afterward he walked through the dull ache of a setting sun when even the clouds seemed bleeding and at twilight he came to a graveyard. There was a dusky, dreamy smell of flowers and the ghost of a new moon in the sky and shadows everywhere. . . .

Long after midnight the towers and spires of Princeton were visible, with here and there a late-burning light—and suddenly out of the clear darkness the sound of bells. As an endless dream it went on; the spirit of the past brooding over a new generation, the chosen youth from the muddled, unchastened world, still fed romantically on the mistakes and half-forgotten dreams of dead statesmen and poets. Here was a new generation, shouting the old cries, learning the old creeds, through a revery of long days and nights; destined finally to go out into that dirty gray turmoil to follow love and pride; a new generation dedicated more than the last to the fear of poverty and the worship of success; grown up to find all Gods dead, all wars fought, all faiths in man shaken. . . .

Amory, sorry for them, was still not sorry for himself—art, politics, religion, whatever his medium should be, he knew he was safe now, free from all hysteria—he could accept what was acceptable, roam, grow, rebel, sleep deep through many nights. . . .

There was no God in his heart, he knew; his ideas were still in riot; there was ever the pain of memory; the regret for his lost youth—yet the waters of disillusion had left a deposit on his soul, responsibility and a love of life, the faint stirring of old ambitions and unrealized dreams. But—oh, Rosalind! Rosalind! . . .

"It's all a poor substitute at best," he said sadly.

And he could not tell why the struggle was worth while, why he had determined to use to the utmost himself and his heritage from the personalities he had passed. . . .

He stretched out his arms to the crystalline, radiant sky.

"I know myself," he cried, "but that is all."

LETTER FROM F. SCOTT FITZGERALD TO H. L. MENCKEN (May 4, 1925) [EXCERPT]

TO: H. L. Mencken

14 Rue de Tilsitt
Paris, France
May 4th, 1925

Dear Menk—

Your letter was the first outside word that reached me about my book I was tremendously moved both by the fact that you liked it and by your kindness in writing me about it. By the next mail came a letter from Edmund Wilson and a clipping from Stallings, both bulging with interest and approval, but as you know I'd rather have you like a book of mine than anyone in America.

There is a tremendous fault in the book—the lack of an emotional presentment of Daisy's attitude toward Gatsby after their reunion (and the consequent lack of logic or importance in her throwing him over). Everyone has felt this but no one has spotted it because its concealed beneath elaborate and overlapping blankets of prose. Wilson complained: "The characters are so uniformly unpleasant," Stallings: "a sheaf of gorgeous notes for a novel" and you say: "The story is fundamentally trivial." I think the smooth, almost unbroken pattern makes you feel that. Despite your admiration for Conrad you have lately—perhaps in reaction against the merely well-made novels of James' imitators—become used to the formless. It is in protest against my own formless two novels, and Lewis' and Dos Passos' that this was written. I admit that in comparison to My Antonia and The Lost Lady it is a failure in what it tries to do but I think in comparison to Cytherea or Linda Condon it is a success. At any rate I have learned a lot from writing it and the influence on it has been the masculine one of The Brothers Karamazov, a thing of incomparable form, rather than the feminine one of The Portrait of a Lady. If it seems trivial or "anecdotal" (sp) it is because of an aesthetic fault, a failure in one every important episode and not a frailty in the theme—at least I don't think so. Did you ever know a writer to calmly take a just critisism and shut up?

Incidently, I had hoped it would amuse the Mencken who wrote the essay on New York in the last book of Prejudices—tho I know nothing in the new Paris streets that I like better than Park Avenue at twilight.

I think the book is so far a commercial failure—at least it was two weeks after publication—hadn't reached 20,000 yet. So I rather regret (but not violently) the fact that I turned down $15,000.00 for the serial rights. However I have all the money I need and was growing rather tired of being a popular author. My trash for the Post grows worse and worse as there is less and less heart in it—strange to say my whole heart was in my first trash. . . .

However I won't bore you any longer. I expect to spend about two years on my next novel and it ought to be more successful critically. Its about myself—not what I thought of myself in This Side of Paradise. Moreover it will have the most amazing form ever invented.

With many, many thanks
F. Scott Fitzg——

P.S. This is simply an acknowledgment and expects no answer.

In a letter from Paris dated May 4, 1925, to his friend H. L. Mencken, Fitzgerald acknowledges a significant flaw in The Great Gatsby, and laments its failure to sell as well as his first two novels. Mencken published some of Fitzgerald's short stories in The American Mercury.

Source: F. Scott Fitzgerald: A Life in Letters. New York: Charles Scribner's Sons, 1994. Excerpted with permission of Scribner, a division of Simon & Schuster, Inc. ©1994 by the Trustees under Agreement Dated July 3, 1975, created by Frances Scott Fitzgerald Smith.

COVER OF *LIFE* MAGAZINE (1926)

This 1926 cover of Life *magazine by John Held, Jr. depicts a flapper dancing the Charleston with an older well-dressed man. Held's illustrations captured the exuberant spirit of the period; he also illustrated the dust jacket for Fitzgerald's collection of short stories,* Tales of the Jazz Age *(1922).*

Source: From the collections of the Library of Congress.

"LOOKING BACK EIGHT YEARS" by F. Scott and Zelda Fitzgerald (1928)

F. Scott and Zelda co-wrote several articles for College Humor magazine. In "Looking Back Eight Years," published in June 1928, they review the decade they helped define.

Source: Bruccoli, Matthew J., Scottie Fitzgerald Smith, and Joan P. Kerr, eds. *The Romantic Egoists: A Pictorial Autobiography from the Scrapbooks and Albums of Scott and Zelda Fitzgerald.* New York: Scribner, 1974.

In those years of panic during and immediately after the war age became a sort of caste system, so that all people of the same number of years were automatically antagonistic to all others. Perhaps it was the civil effect of draft laws and perhaps it was because the days were so full around that time that each additional year of age seemed like an added century of emotional experience. Even the knitting of gray wool socks and the packing of Red Cross boxes was regulated by ages. The lowest of all these strata, the boys and girls who were just too young to go to France, blossomed out shortly afterwards as the Younger Generation. Even so late as a year ago people's attitudes and animosities toward a generation prematurely forced to maturity, furnished an astounding amount of newspaper copy.

The jazz and the petting parties with which that generation "tapered off" have become the custom of the country and the world has become interested in more mature crimes. Now that we have recovered our equilibrium we see again the superior attraction of the ax murder as opposed to the mythical checked corset, and the newest generation of young people is being born full-grown, parroting forth the ideas of President Coolidge or of H. L. Mencken in the rhythmic meters of Lloyd Mayer.

What has become of the youth which for so many years bore the blame for everything except the Prohibition Amendment, now that they are turning thirty and receiving the portions of responsibility doled out as we pass that landmark? For by that time one has either earned the right to take chances or established himself as indispensable in some routine.

As a matter of fact, the increasing importance of the youngest war generation is a constant surprise. If this, in some measure, is due to the inevitable vacancies left as others move on, it is also the result of a sort of debonair desperation—a necessity for forcing the moments of life into an adequacy to the emotions of ten years ago. The men who at twenty-one led companies of two hundred must, it seems to us, feel an eternal let-down from a time when necessity and idealism were one single thing and no compromise was ever necessary. That willingness to face issues, a relic of ten years ago, is perhaps the explanation of some of the unrest and dissatisfaction of today. With millions of young people ready to "face things" with so much personal feeling I can think of nothing short of another national crisis which would furnish strong enough material to unify and direct such valiant insistence upon essentials.

Success was the goal for this generation and to a startling extent they have attained it, and now we venture to say that, if intimately approached, nine in ten would confess that success is only a decoration they wished to wear; what they really wanted is something deeper and richer than that. An habituation to enormous effort during the years of the war left a necessity for trials and tests on them.

It was not only the war. The war was merely a heightening and hurrying forward of the inevitable reaction against the false premises doled out to their children by the florid and for the most fatuous mothers of the 'nineties and the early nineteen hundreds, parents who didn't experience the struggles and upheavals of the 'sixties and 'seventies and had no inkling of the cataclysmic changes the next decade would bring. Children were safe in the world and producing them apparently ended the mother's responsibility. With the streets free from automobiles and morals free from movies and, in a large portion of America, corners already free from saloons, what did it matter what these children thought as they lay awake on warm summer nights straining to catch the cries of newsboys about the attempted assassination of Roosevelt and the victory of Johnson at Reno? It was a romantic time to be a child, to be old enough to feel the excitement being stored up around them and to be young enough to feel safe. Formed in such a period of pregnant placidity, left free to wonder and dream in a changing age with little or no pressure exerted upon them by life, it is not amazing that when time, having brought everything else out of the hat, produced his *pièce de résistance*, the war, these children realized too soon that they had seen the magician's whole repertoire. This was the last piece of wizardry they believed in, and now, nearing middle age and the period when they are to be the important people of the world, they still hope wistfully that things will again have the magic of the theater. The teapot dome, and Mrs. Snyder and the unspeakable Forbes do not quite fill the gap.

It is not altogether the prosperity of the country and the consequent softness of life which have made them unstable, for almost invariably they are tremendously energetic; there has never been a time when so many positions of importance have been occupied by such young men or when the pages of newspapers and anthologies have borne the names of so many people under thirty. It is a great emotional disappointment resulting from the fact that life moved in poetic gestures when they were younger and has now settled back into buffoonery. And with the current insistence upon youth as the finest and richest time in the life of man it is small wonder that sensitive young people are haunted and harassed by a sense of unfilled destiny and grope about between the ages of twenty-five and forty with a baffled feeling of frustration. The philosophy with which most of the adolescents were equipped implied that life was a truncated affair ceasing abruptly with the twenty-first birthday, and it is hardly of enough stamina to serve an age in which so many have tasted the essence of life—which is death—just as a balloon is biggest when it bursts. From those inflated years to being concerned over whether the most oil or gold was stolen from the Government is a difficult adjustment but perhaps the cynicism with which the war generation approaches general affairs will eventual lead to a more intelligent attitude—even in the dim future to actual social interest.

Perhaps it is that we are still feeling the relaxation of the post-war years, but surely some of this irony and dissatisfaction with things supposedly solid and secure proceeds from the fact that more young people in this era were intense enough or clever enough or sensitive or shrewd enough to get what they wanted before they were mature enough to want the thing they acquired as an end and not merely as a proof of themselves. Perhaps we worked too much over man as the individual, so that his capabilities are far superior to the problems of life, and now we have endless youth of a responsible age floundering about in a morass of unused powers and feeling very bitter and mock heroic like all people who think the element of chance in their lives should have been on a bigger scale. Outside of war men of the hour haven't had a romantic opportunity near home since the last gold rush and a great proportion of young men feel that their mental agility or physical prowess can never be really measured in situations of their own making. This has perhaps been true of all times but it is more pronounced now that emergencies have, faced with the tremendous superiority of modern youth, lost their dignity as acts of God and been definitely relegated to the category of human inefficiency, if they are recognized at all.

We wonder if that is because a whole generation accustomed itself to a basic feeling that there are two ways to be; dead and alive, preferably alive and probably dead. So that now the nuances and gradations of society in general seem of the same importance as the overtones of society in particular; sauce and trimmings make better eating than the meat. And we predict a frightful pandemonium to eat it in unless indeed every generation has gone through the same difficulties of adjustment. It may be that this one is simply more expressive. Oddly enough we have but one set of contemporaries. It has always surprised us that whether there is a war or not we will always be of the war generation and we will always have unclarified ways of reacting, privy only to ourselves.

Henry Ford

1863–1947

Automobile Manufacturer

Henry Ford, the nation's most celebrated industrialist in the first decades of the twentieth century, launched the automobile industry by making sturdy, affordable cars for average-income Americans.

Ford was born on a farm in Wayne County, Michigan, on July 30, 1863. He received his formal education in rural schools between 1871 and 1879. Growing up, he was interested in machines of all kinds; by the age of 15, he was an expert in watch repair. He moved to Detroit in 1879 at age 16 and worked in a series of jobs and apprenticeships in machine shops, engine shops, and power plants. In his spare time he experimented with steam and gas engines. In 1888 he married Clara Bryant; they had one son.

In the late 1800s automobiles were being developed by French and German engineers; Americans, too, were working on early "horseless carriages." While employed as a night engineer by the Edison Illuminating Company in Detroit, Ford built his first vehicle, a 500-pound, all-wood "quadricycle" that made its initial run in June 1896. By mid-1899 he had made a second, two-passenger motorcar that impressed Detroit engineers and attracted investors.

Automobiles began as luxury items for the wealthy, but Ford conceived of a reliable utility vehicle that the middle class could afford. He and several partners founded the Ford Motor Company in 1903; as general manager, Ford was in charge of design, engineering, and production. That year the company issued its first car, the Model A. About 1,700 were sold in the first 15 months. In 1906 Ford introduced the Model N; with this model, Ford became the leading automaker in the United States. The company acquired a 60-acre tract in Highland Park and in 1908 began construction of the largest industrial plant in Michigan.

With the introduction of the Model T in 1908, Ford Motor surged far ahead of all competitors. Originally selling for $850 to $1,000, the Model T had a four-cylinder, 20-horsepower water-cooled engine, and weighed 1,200 pounds. Efficient, durable, and economical to operate, the "Tin Lizzie," or "flivver," as it was known, was designed for the rough roads

From the collections of the Library of Congress.

and small towns of rural America. (Its engine could also be hooked up to used to run farm machinery, such as saws and grinders.) By 1913 about 7,000 auto dealers were operating in the United States. As a result of increasing efficiencies in production, Ford was able to lower the price from $950 in 1910 to $325 in 1916, and down to $290 in 1924. By the time the Model T was phased out in 1927, almost one out of every two cars around the world was a Ford.

Ford was an innovator in his conception of an affordable "people's car" and in his systematic methods of streamlining production and controlling costs. Whereas most car manufacturers were simply assembling components produced by others, Ford made his company largely independent of outside suppliers and therefore able to reduce its expenses. Careful studies of production processes and worker movement resulted in the installation of continuous conveyor belts "to bring the work to the man," at waist level, to avoid unnecessary bending or reaching. Motors, transmissions, and other components were put together in subassembly lines, then moved on to the next phase. This innovation in 1913–14 reduced the assembly time for a chassis (automobile frame) from 728 minutes to 93 minutes. Production rose from 248,307 cars in 1913–14 to 472,350 in 1915–16, and kept rising, but at a cost: many workers found the grinding monotony of accelerating mass production intolerable. Nonetheless, Ford's introduction of moving assembly line production completely changed the way large industries operated.

Ford Motor quickly grew into a multinational corporation, establishing production facilities in Canada (1904) and England (1911); by 1928 Ford was making cars in 21 countries on six continents. The company further reduced its dependence on other suppliers by buying coal mines in Kentucky, glass plants in Pennsylvania, rubber plantations in Brazil, and a fleet of ships to transport these resources.

Ford stunned fellow industrialists when, on January 5, 1914, he announced that he was raising his workers' minimum daily wage from $2.30 to $5 and shortening the workday by two hours. At about the same time, Ford was fighting efforts to unionize his workers by the Industrial Workers of the World. The pay hike, a response to excessive employee turnover, not only improved his workers' standard of living but also enabled them to purchase Fords of their own.

However, the $5.00-a-day came with a catch. The rate was actually broken down into an hourly rate of about 62 cents, of which 28.5 cents was paid to the worker only if he met certain conditions. Besides satisfactory work on the assembly line, the worker had to abide by Ford's moral standards, such as showing proof of marriage, making sure the wife stayed at home to take care of the children, refraining from excessive drinking or smoking, and practicing good citizenship. To check on his workers, Ford established a "Sociological Department" with 200 investigators who visited homes and questioned neighbors and friends.

Ford's methodical increase in production, a powerful symbol (if not the very essence) of America's burgeoning industrial power, was matched by expansions in his sales and advertising forces—both early signs of the consumer-oriented business boom of the 1920s. Not only did he increase wages and decrease production costs, Ford also had sales departments offer credit plans to encourage purchases through modest down payments and easy monthly installments.

As World War I broke out in Europe in 1914, Ford spoke out against militarism and declared his willingness to spend half his fortune if it would shorten the war by one day. He joined the American Peace Society and sponsored an ocean liner, dubbed the "Peace Ship," which sailed to Norway with delegates and reporters on a 14-day antiwar publicity campaign. "Ford's folly" was ridiculed by the press for its naïveté, and he abandoned the mission early. Once the United States declared war on Germany, however, he pledged that he would place his factory "at the disposal of the United States government and will operate without one cent of profit." He cut back production on Model T's and built tractors, ambulances, aircraft motors, shells, steel helmets, submarine detectors and torpedo tubes, among other matériel.

Despite his aid to the war effort, Ford damaged his reputation further by publishing in his weekly *Dearborn Independent* a series of articles, including one titled "The International Jew: The World's Problem," blaming "international bankers" for World War I and blaming his loss in the 1918 Senate race on Wall Street "interests" and "the Jews." After an embarrassing lawsuit, Ford apologized and issued a formal retraction of his anti-Semitic views. His writings had spread to Europe, however, and won the admiration of Adolf Hitler, who in 1938 awarded Ford the Grand Cross of the Supreme Order of the German Eagle.

By about 1919, Ford had gained complete control of the company and had driven out many of his more independent-minded subordinates. He rejected suggestions for improvements on the Model T even as other carmakers were building more stylish cars with roomier interiors, more advanced engineering, and color options (Ford famously remarked that customers could have a Model T in any color they like, as long as that color was black). Most of his talented executives and engineers had been forced out, which hindered Ford's attempts to respond to General Motors and Chrysler, which were introducing new models about every three years. After losing market share to Chevrolet at an alarming rate—the Model T outsold Chevrolet by 13-to-1 in 1921, but by only two-to-one in 1926—Ford shut down the Model T plant from May to December 1927 to retool for production of the Model A.

Ford's difficulties were compounded by the start of the Great Depression in 1929 and the resulting demands for labor unions to defend workers' welfare. He resisted compliance with the National Automobile Chamber of Commerce and the National Labor Relations Board. In 1936 and 1937 the newly formed United Automobile Workers of America (UAW) engaged in sit-down strikes at General Motors and Chrysler, and Ford's Service Department thugs brutalized UAW organizers at the River Rouge, Michigan, plant in 1937. Ford held out against the union until forced to capitulate during a walkout by workers in May 1941. On April 7, 1947, Henry Ford died of a massive cerebral hemorrhage.

The automobile's most fundamental effects on daily life in America include an unprecedented mobility for all classes and an exodus from the city to a new place called suburbia. To get there—to get anywhere—a vast network of federally funded roads was built in the 1920s, and along every road sprouted traffic lights, road signs, gas stations, restaurants, and motels. As cars and trucks became more numerous, transportation of passengers by railroad and streetcar declined significantly.

Ford's cars forever altered American society, transforming the nation's landscape and lifestyle. Although in the 1920s Ford increasingly lost market share to more innovative and stylish competitors, that decade's burgeoning consumer economy was largely modeled on production and sales methods pioneered by Henry Ford and his many imitators. Yet while Ford may be praised for stimulating the American economy and making cars more widely available, he must also be remembered for a labor policy that on the surface sounded enlightened, but that was paternalistic and damaging to his relations with his workers.

Mark LaFlaur

For Further Reading

Folsom, Richard B. "Henry Ford." In *The Automobile Industry, 1896–1920*. Edited by George S. May. New York: Facts on File, 1990.

Ford, Henry, in collaboration with Samuel Crowther. *My Life and Work*. Garden City, N.Y.: Doubleday, Page, 1922; Reprint, Salem, N.H.: Ayer, 1987.

Hooker, Clarence. *Life in the Shadows of the Crystal Palace, 1910–1927: Ford*

Workers in the Model T Era. Bowling Green, Ohio: Bowling Green State University Popular Press, 1997.

Jackson, Kenneth T. *Crabgrass Frontier: The Suburbanization of the United States*. New York: Oxford University Press, 1985.

Lewis, David L. *The Public Image of Henry Ford: An American Folk Hero and His Company*. Detroit, Mich.: Wayne State University Press, 1976.

HENRY FORD BOARDING THE "PEACE SHIP" (1915)

As World War I erupted in Europe, Ford publicly spoke out against militarism; in 1915, he sponsored an ocean liner, dubbed the "Peace Ship," which sailed to Norway with delegates and reporters on a 14-day antiwar publicity campaign. In this photo, Ford is shown with Captain Hempel (right) and colleagues as he boards the ship.

Source: ©Bettmann/ Corbis.

"AN AMERICAN LADY" FORD ADVERTISEMENT (1924)

In this Ford car advertisement titled "An American Lady," published in Good Housekeeping *magazine in 1924, a businesswoman is shown in her office with her Ford sedan car parked outside.*

Source: Hulton/ Archive.

Her habit of measuring time in terms of dollars gives the woman in business keen insight into the true value of a Ford closed car for her personal use.

This car enables her to conserve minutes, to expedite her affairs, to widen the scope of her activities. Its low

first cost, long life and inexpensive operation and upkeep convince her that it is a sound investment value.

And it is such a pleasant car to drive that it transforms the business call which might be an interruption into an enjoyable episode of her busy day.

TUDOR SEDAN, $590   FORDOR SEDAN, $685   COUPE, $525   (All prices f. o. b. Detroit)

Ford
CLOSED CARS

"MASS PRODUCTION" by Henry Ford (c. 1926) [EXCERPT]

MASS PRODUCTION.— The term mass production is used to describe the modern method by which great quantities of a single standardized commodity are manufactured. As commonly employed it is made to refer to the quantity produced, but its primary reference is to method. In several particulars the term is unsatisfactory. Mass production is not merely quantity production, for this may be had with none of the requisites of mass production. Nor is it merely machine production, which also may exist without any resemblance to mass production. Mass production is the focussing upon a manufacturing project of the principles of power, accuracy, economy, system, continuity and speed. The interpretation of these principles, through studies of operation and machine development and their co-ordination, is the conspicuous task of management. And the normal result is a productive organisation that delivers in quantities a useful commodity of standard material, workmanship and design at minimum cost. The necessary, precedent condition of mass production is a capacity, latent or developed, or *mass consumption*, the ability to absorb large production. The two go together, and in the latter may be traced the reasons for the former.

I. THE ORIGINS OF MASS PRODUCTION

In origin mass production is American and recent; its earliest notable appearance falls within the first decade of the 20th century. The mere massing of men and materials is a procedure as old as the pyramids. Basic industries, like weaving, domestic baking, house construction and wooden ship building, are carried on, with only superficial changes, much as they were in ancient Egypt. Cottage manufactures and handicrafts moulded the practices of industry until the invention of the steam-engine. With the coming of power machines the seat of industry was removed from the homes of the people and a new work centre, the factory, was established. Much harsh criticism has been uttered against "the factory system," but it is perhaps fair to say that its first effect was to emancipate the home from being a mere adjunct to the loom or bench, and its later effect was to provide the home with means to develop the dignified status which it has now attained. . . .

The Motor Industry Leads the Way.—To the motor industry is given the credit of bringing mass production to experimental success, and by general consent the Ford Motor Co. is regarded as having pioneered in the largest development of the method under a single management and for a single purpose. It may, therefore, simplify the history of mass production and the description of its principles if the experience of this company is taken as a basis. It has been already suggested that mass production is possible only through the ability of the public to absorb large quantities of the commodity thus produced. These commodities are necessarily limited to necessities and conveniences. The greatest development of mass production methods has occurred in the production of conveniences. The automobile represents a basic and continuous convenience-transportation.

Mass production begins, then, in the conception of a public need of which the public may not as yet be conscious and proceeds on the principle that use-convenience must be matched by price-convenience. Under this principle the element of service remains uppermost; profit and expansion are trusted to emerge as consequences. As to which precedes the other, consumption or production, experiences will differ. But granted that the vision of the public need is correct, and the commodity adapted to meet it, the impulse to increased production may come in anticipation of demand, or in response to demand, but the resulting consumption is always utilised to obtain such increase of quality, or such decrease of cost, or both, as shall secure still greater use-convenience and price-convenience. As these increase, consumption increases, making possible still greater production advantages, and so on to a fulfillment that is not yet in view.

The commodities that conduce to civilised living are thus far enjoyed by only a small fraction of the world's inhabitants. The experience of the Ford Motor Co. has been that mass production precedes mass consumption and makes it possible, by reducing costs and thus permitting both greater use-convenience and price-convenience. If the production is increased, costs can be reduced. If production is increased 500%, costs may be cut 50%, and this decrease in cost, with its accompanying decrease in selling price, will probably multiply by 10 the number of people who can conveniently buy the product. This is a conservative illustration of production serving as the cause of demand instead of the effect.

II. THE PRINCIPLES OF MASS PRODUCTION

As to shop detail, the keyword to mass production is simplicity. Three plain principles underlie it: (a) the planned orderly progression of the commodity through the shop; (b) the delivery of work instead of leaving it to the workman's initiative to find it; (c) an analysis of operations into their constituent parts. These are distinct but not separate steps; all are involved in the first one. To plan the progress of material from the initial manufacturing operation until its emergence as a finished product involves shop planning on a large scale and the manufacture and delivery of material, tools and parts at various points along the line. To do this successfully with a progressing piece of work means a careful breaking up of the work into its "operations" in sequence. All three fundamentals are involved in the original act of planning a moving line of production.

This system is practised, not only on the final assembly line, but throughout the various arts and trades involved in the completed product. The automobile assembly line offers an impressive spectacle of hundreds of parts being quickly put together into a going vehicle, but flowing into that are other assembly lines on which each of the hundreds of parts have been fashioned. It may be far down the final assembly line that the springs, for example, appear, and they may seem to be a negligible part of the whole operation. Formerly one artisan would cut, harden, bend and build a spring. To-day the making of one leaf of a spring is an operation of apparent complexity, yet is really the ultimate reduction to simplicity of operation. . . .

III. THE EFFECTS OF MASS PRODUCTION

But it is not the history and principle of mass production which provoke the widest discussions; the *effects* of it have been placed under scrutiny. What have been the effects of mass production on society?

In this entry on "Mass Production" from The Encyclopaedia Britannica, *Ford writes about the origins, principles, and effects of mass production. Note: This entry was signed by Henry Ford but is believed actually to have been written by his personal publicist.*

Source: Encyclopaedia Britannica, 13th ed., Vol. 2. New York: The Encyclopaedia Britannica, 1926. Reprinted with permission. ©1926 by Encyclopaedia Britannica, Inc.

(1) Beginning with management, where unquestionably mass production methods take their rise, there is a notable increase in industrial control, as distinguished from financial control. The engineer's point of view has gained the ascendancy and this trend will undoubtedly continue until finance becomes the handmaid instead of the mistress of productive industry. Industrial control has been marked by a continuous refinement of standardisation, which means the instant adoption of the better method to the exclusion of the old, in the interests of production. Financial control was not, in its heyday, marked by the tendency to make costly changes in the interests of the product. The economy of scrapping the old equipment immediately upon the invention of the better equipment was not so well understood. It was engineering control, entrenched in mass production methods, that brought in this new readiness to advance. In this way management has been kept close to the shop and has reduced the office to a clearing house for the shop. Managers and men have been brought into closer contact and understanding. Manufacturing has been reduced to greater singleness of purpose.

(2) The effect of mass production on the product has been to give it the highest standard of quality ever attained in output of great quantities. Conditions of mass production require material of the best quality to pass successfully through the operations. The utmost accuracy must control all these operations. Every part must be produced to fit at once into the design for which it is made. In mass production there are no fitters. The presence of fitters indicates that the parts have been produced unfit for immediate placement in the design. In works of art and luxury this accuracy is achieved at the cost of careful handiwork. To introduce hand methods of obtaining accuracy into mass production would render mass production impossible with any reference to price-convenience. The standard quality of the product is guaranteed by the fact that machines are so constructed that a piece of work cannot go through them unless it exactly accords with specifications. If the work goes through the tools, it must be right. It will thus be seen that the burden of creation is on management in designing and selecting the material which is to be produced by the multiple processes utilized in mass production.

(3) The effect of mass production on mechanical science has been to create a wide variety of single-purpose machines which not only group similar operations and perform them in quantity, but also reproduce skill of hand to a marvellous degree. It is not so much the discovery of new principles as the new combination and application of old ones that mark this development. Under mass production the industry of machine making has increased out of all comparison with its previous history, and the constant designing of new machines is a part of the productive work of every great manufacturing institution.

(4) The effect of mass production on employees has been variously appraised. Whether the modern corporation is the destruction or salvation of arts and crafts, whether it narrows or broadens opportunity, whether it assists or retards the personal development of the worker, must be determined by observable facts. A cardinal principle of mass production is that hard work, in the old physical sense of laborious burden-bearing, is wasteful. The physical load is lifted off men and placed on machines. The recurrent mental load is shifted from men in production to men in designing. As to the contention that machines thus become the masters of men, it may be said the machines have increased men's mastery of their environment, and that a generation which is ceaselessly scrapping its machines exhibits few indications of mechanical subjection.

The need for skilled artisans and creative genius is greater under mass production than without it. In entering the shops of the Ford Motor Co., for example, one passes through great departments of skilled mechanics who are not engaged in production, but in the construction and maintenance of the machinery of production. Details of from 5,000 to 10,000 highly skilled artisans at strategic points throughout the shops were not commonly witnessed in the days preceding mass production. It has been debated whether there is less or more skill as a consequence of mass production. The present writer's opinion is that there is more. The common work of the world has always been done by unskilled labour, but the common work of the world in modern times is not as common as it was formerly. In almost every field of labour more knowledge and responsibility are required than a generation or two ago.

Some Criticisms Answered.—Mass production has also been studied with reference to what has been called the monotony of repetitive work. This monotony does not exist as much in the shops as in the minds of theorists and bookish reformers. There is no form of work without its hardness; but needless hardship has no place in the modern industrial scheme. Mass production lightens work, but increases its repetitive quality. In this it is the opposite of the mediaeval ideal of craftsmanship where the artisan performed every operation, from the preparation of the material to its final form. It is doubtful, however, if the mass of mediaeval toil was as devoid of monotony as has sometimes been pictured, but it is absolutely certain that it was less satisfactory in its results to the worker. In well-managed modern factories the tendency to monotony is combated by frequent changes of task.

The criticism of mass production as a means of reducing employment has long since been out of court. The experience of the Ford Motor Co. is that wherever the number of men has been reduced on manufacturing operations, more jobs have been created. A continuous programme of labour reduction has been paralleled by a continuous increase in employment. As to the effect of mass production on wages and the relations between managers and men, there is little need to speak. It is perhaps the most widely understood fact about mass production that it has resulted in higher wages than any other method of industry. The reason is at hand. The methods of mass production enable the worker to earn more and thus to have more. Moreover, the methods of mass production have thrown so much responsibility on the craftsmanship of management, that the old method of financial adjustment by reduction of wages has been abandoned by scientific manufacturers. A business that must finance by drafts out of the wage envelopes of its employees is not scientifically based. It is the problem of management so to organise production that it will pay the public, the workmen and the concern itself. Management that fails in any of these is poor management. Disturbed labour conditions, poor wages, uncertain profits indicate lapses in management. The craftsmanship of management absorbs the energies of many thousands of men who, without mass production methods, would have no creative opportunity. Here the modern method broadens instead of narrows individual opportunity.

(5) As to the effects of mass production on society, the increasing supply of human needs and the development of new standards of living are the elements to be estimated. The enlargement of leisure, the increase of human contacts, the extension of individual range, are all the result of mass production in various fields.

HENRY FORD'S RETRACTION (1927)

For some time past I have given consideration to the series of articles concerning Jews which since 1920 have appeared in the *Dearborn Independent*. Some of them have been reprinted in pamphlet form under the title *The International Jew*. Although public publications are my property, it goes without saying that in the multitude of my activities it has been impossible for me to devote personal attention to their management or to keep informed as to their contents. It has therefore inevitably followed that the conduct and policies of [my] publications had to be delegated to men whom I placed in charge of them and upon whom I relied implicitly.

To my great regret I have learned that Jews generally, and particularly those of this country, not only resent these publications as promoting anti-Semitism, but regard me as their enemy. Trusted friends with whom I have conferred recently have assured me in all sincerity that in their opinion the character of the charges and insinuations made against the Jews, both individually and collectively, contained in many of the articles which have been circulated periodically in the *Dearborn Independent,* and have been reprinted in the pamphlets mentioned, justifies the righteous and indignation entertained by Jews everywhere toward me because of the mental anguish occasioned by the unprovoked reflections made upon them.

This has led me to direct my personal attention on the subject, in order to ascertain the exact nature of these articles. As a result of this survey I confess I am deeply mortified that this journal, which is intended to be constructive and not destructive, has been made the medium for resurrecting exploded fictions, for giving currency to the so-called *Protocols of the Wise Men of Zion*, which have been demonstrated, as I learn, to be gross forgeries, and for contending that the Jews have been engaged in a conspiracy to control the capital and the industries of the world, besides laying at their door many offenses against decency, public order, and good morals.

Had I appreciated even the general nature, to say nothing of the details, of these utterances, I would have forbidden their circulation without a moment's hesitation. . . . I deem it my duty as an honorable man to make amends for the wrong done to the Jews as fellow-men and brothers, by asking their forgiveness for the harm that I have unintentionally committed, by retracting so far as lies within my power the offensive charges laid at their door by these publications, and by giving them the unqualified assurance that henceforth they may look to me for friendship and good will.

In this formal retraction, which was published in every major newspaper in the nation, Ford apologized for the anti-Semitic comments made in his Dearborn Independent *series of articles, including one titled "The International Jew: The World's Problem."*

Source: Lee, Albert. *Henry Ford and the Jews*. New York: Stein and Day Publishers, 1980.

FORD MOTOR COMPANY FACTORY (1928)

In this photo at the Ford Motor Company factory in Dearborn, Michigan, employees construct cars on a moving assembly line.

Source: Hulton/Archive.

Marcus Garvey

Marcus Garvey's Universal Negro Improvement Association became a mass movement after World War I, inspiring African Americans with visions of self-sufficiency and nationalism that helped counter the demoralizing effects of institutionalized discrimination and racist violence.

The youngest of 11 children, Marcus Moziah Garvey was born in St. Ann's Bay, Jamaica, on August 17, 1887. His parents were of pure African descent, which put the family at a disadvantage in a Jamaican social hierarchy that accorded higher status to blacks with some European ancestry. Nevertheless, Garvey received a solid primary education. When he was 14 he apprenticed himself to a printer to help pay his family's bills; already a gifted writer, he thereby gained a working knowledge of publishing and mass communications. Garvey's political consciousness was raised by his participation in a printers' strike in 1907 and honed by his observations of the plight of African and West Indian workers around the Caribbean and Central America in the early 1910s. Making his way to England, Garvey attended law lectures, met African intellectuals who exposed him to the glories of African civilization and culture, and warmed to the writings of the African-American leader Booker T. Washington, who emphasized economic self-sufficiency for blacks.

Garvey returned to Jamaica in July 1914 and founded the Universal Negro Improvement Association and African Communities League, commonly known as the Universal Negro Improvement Association (UNIA). Inspired by Washington's Tuskegee Institute in Alabama, the UNIA aimed to establish black educational institutions around the world. But the Africanist side of Garvey's London experience was equally important: with its slogan "One God! One Aim! One Destiny!" the group promoted the idea that a common bond existed among all Africans and African-descended people. Garvey exhorted his followers to work toward economic development, but he also worked to foster a sense of black pride and power at a time when the European countries were consolidating their hold over

From the collections of the Library of Congress.

their African colonies and when white racism in the West had reached new levels of virulence. Garvey called for the establishment of a black history and literature, and asked Africans and African Americans to worship a black God.

In 1916 Garvey moved to New York City, establishing branches of the UNIA there and in other U.S. cities with large black populations. Spreading his message through street speeches, he at first achieved little success. But by the end of the decade Garvey began to find fertile ground for his ideas among the new urban black populations that had migrated North with dreams of opportunity and found only chilly disillusionment. His crusade was also fueled in part by the anger of black soldiers who had helped the United States win the war in Europe, but who returned home to discrimination and, in 1919, violent race riots. Garvey established a newspaper, *Negro World*, and by 1920 he claimed four million followers. An accurate count was difficult, but even Garvey's critics conceded him many hundreds of thousands of admirers.

Garvey's most visible black-oriented business venture was a shipping company, the Black Star Line, for which he raised money by selling stock at the price of $5 a share. The Black Star Line launched its first ship in 1919, and for several years its three vessels circulated among the ports of the African diaspora and Africa. Garvey hoped the Black Star Line would stimulate pan-African trade, but its ships were in poor repair and the whole venture was inadequately capitalized. The line suffered as well from investigative pressure from the U.S. State Department and the Federal Bureau of Investigation. They failed to uncover evidence of the mail fraud they alleged but continued to harass Garvey, denying him reentry to the country for several months in 1921. Garvey also established numerous small businesses: factories, stores, laundries, restaurants, and publishing operations.

The most spectacular display of Garvey's influence came at the UNIA's month-long 1920 convention in New York City, attended by organization delegates from 25 countries. Garvey, wearing flashy paramilitary attire, led a parade of 50,000 followers through the streets of Harlem and was proclaimed president of a planned pan-African state. Such acts startled white residents and galvanized Garvey's black critics, of which he had many. But Garvey's African nationalist efforts, in fact, ran parallel to other attempts to establish home rule for persecuted and disenfranchised ethnic groups; Irish home rule and the Zionist movement in what would become the state of Israel were two examples. At the 1920 convention the colors of red, black, and green were used to symbolize African unity, a practice that has persisted to the present. Garvey later sought to move the UNIA's headquarters to Monrovia, Liberia.

In the early and middle 1920s Garvey's popularity slowly declined, dented by attacks from both within and outside the African-American community. In 1922 he was indicted on mail fraud charges in connection with the financing of the Black Star Line. That year, Garvey also addressed a meeting of the white racist Ku Klux Klan in New Orleans, expressing sympathy for its doctrine of racial separatism. Mainstream black publications such as the *Chicago Defender,* which had been wary of Garvey all along but had been unsure of how to deal with his considerable street charisma, now began to gain the upper hand. Garvey tangled with the prominent black intellectual **W. E. B. Du Bois**, and antagonized black labor leaders who were working to improve the situation of black workers within existing industrial formations. In 1925 Garvey was convicted on mail fraud charges and sent to prison. Partly as a result of widespread protests from within the African-American community, even from quarters formerly hostile to Garvey, his sentence was commuted by President **Calvin Coolidge** in 1927. Garvey was, however, deported to Jamaica. Garvey ran for political office there but failed to generate a significant revival of the UNIA's fortunes. He moved to England in 1935 and died in London on June 10, 1940. The UNIA, however, remained a significant force in several U.S. cities through the 1950s, and its general structure influenced later black mass movements profoundly.

In the years after World War I, Marcus Garvey responded to the profound oppression of African peoples with a fundamental message of pride that continues to reverberate. Before there was any coherent concept of "black power," Garvey articulated a comprehensive vision of African-centered economic and spiritual values. Successful at communicating those values at a grassroots level, Garvey showed African Americans a new path—one that did not depend upon the distant promise of integration into the racist society in which they lived.

James M. Manheim

For Further Reading

Cronin, Edmund David. *Black Moses: The Story of Marcus Garvey and the Universal Negro Improvement Association.* Madison: University of Wisconsin Press, 1981.

Fax, Elton C. *Garvey: The Story of a Pioneer Black Nationalist.* New York: Dodd, Mead, 1972.

Lewis, Rupert. *Marcus Garvey: Anti-Colonial Champion.* Trenton, N. J.: Africa World Press, 1988.

BLACK STAR LINE SHARE OF STOCK (1919)

Garvey's most ambitious step to realize his dream of African-American economic self-sufficiency was the Black Star Line, for which the UNIA sold 100,000 shares of stock at the price of $5 a share.

Source: Reproduced from Tony Sewell, Garvey's Children: The Legacy of Marcus Garvey. Trenton, N.J.: Africa World Press, 1990.

MARCUS GARVEY GIVING UNIA CONVENTION ADDRESS (1920)

In 1920, the UNIA held a month-long convention in New York City. In this photo, Garvey gives the convention address delivering the constitution for African-American rights.

Source: From the collections of the Library of Congress.

PHILOSOPHY AND OPINIONS OF MARCUS GARVEY (1923) [EXCERPT]

Garvey was an indefatigable speaker, letter writer, and pamphleteer. The Philosophy and Opinions of Marcus Garvey, a collection of Garvey's writings edited by his second wife Amy Jacques-Garvey, gained wide distribution.

Source: Garvey, Marcus. *Philosophy and Opinions of Marcus Garvey*. Edited by Amy Jacques-Garvey. Reprint ed. New York: Atheneum, 1992. Reprinted with the permission of Scribner, a division of Simon & Schuster. ©1923, 1925 Amy Jacques-Garvey.

THE IMAGE OF GOD

If the white man has the idea of a white God, let him worship his God as he desires. If a yellow man's God is of his race let him worship his God as he sees fit. We, as Negroes, have found a new ideal. Whilst our God has no color, yet it is human to see everything through one's own spectacles, and since the white people have seen their God through white spectacles, we have only now started out (late though it be) to see our God through our own spectacles. The God of Isaac and the God of Jacob let Him exist for the race that believes in the God of Isaac and the God of Jacob. We Negroes believe in the God of Ethiopia, the everlasting God—God the Father, God the Son and God the Holy Ghost, the One God of all ages. That is the God in whom we believe, but we shall worship Him through the spectacles of Ethiopia.

SHALL THE NEGRO BE EXTERMINATED?

The Negro now stands at the cross roads of human destiny. He is at the place where he must either step forward or backward. If he goes backward he dies; if he goes forward it will be with the hope of a greater life. Those of us who have developed our minds scientifically are compelled, by duty, to step out among the millions of the unthinking masses and convince them of the seriousness of the age in which we live.

From Adam and Eve

We are either on the way to a higher racial existence or racial extermination. This much is known and realized by every thoughtful race and nation; hence, we have the death struggle of the different races of Europe and Asia in the scramble of the survival of the fittest race.

As we look at things we see that the great world in which we live has undergone much change since the time of the creation. When God created the world, and all therein, He handed His authority over to the two beings He created in His own image; namely, Adam and Eve. From the time of Adam and Eve the human race has multiplied by leaps and bounds. Where we once had two persons to exercise authority over the world, we today have one billion five hundred millions claiming authority and possession of the same world that was once the property of the two.

The Tragedy of Race Extinction

When the Colonists of America desired possession of the land they saw that a weak aboriginal race was in their way. What did they do? They got hold of them, killed them, and buried them underground. This is a fair indication of what will happen to the weaker peoples of the world in another two or three hundred years when the stronger races will have developed themselves to the position of complete mastery of all things material. They will not then as they have not in the past, allow a weak and defenseless race to stand in their way, especially if in their doing so they will endanger their happiness, their comfort and their pleasures. These are the things that strike the thoughtful Negro as being dangerous, and these are the things that cause us who make up the Universal Negro Improvement Association to be fighting tenaciously for the purpose of building up a strong Negro race, so as to make it impossible for us to be exterminated in the future to make room for the stronger races, even as the North American Indian has been exterminated to make room for the great white man on this North American continent.

The illiterate and shallow-minded Negro who can see no farther than his nose is now the greatest stumbling block in the way of the race. He tells us that we must be satisfied with our condition; that we must not think of building up a nation of our own, that we must not seek to organize ourselves racially, but that we must depend upon the good feeling of the other fellow for the solution of the problem that now confronts us. This is a dangerous policy and it is my duty to warn the four hundred million Negroes of the world against this kind of a leadership—a leadership that will try to make Negroes believe that all will be well without their taking upon themselves the task of bettering their condition politically, industrially, educationally and otherwise.

The time has come for those of us who have the vision of the future to inspire our people to a closer kinship, to a closer love of self, because it is only through this appreciation of self will we be able to rise to that higher life that will make us not an extinct race in the future, but a race of men fit to survive.

The Price of leadership

Those of us who are blazing the way in this new propaganda of the Universal Negro Improvement Association to enlighten our people everywhere are at times very much annoyed and discouraged by the acts of our own people in that consciously or unconsciously they do so many things to hurt our deeper feeling of loyalty and love for the race. But what can we do? Can we forsake them because they hurt our feelings? Surely not. Painful though it may be to be interfered with and handicapped in the performance of the higher sense of duty, yet we must, martyr-like, make up our minds and our hearts to pay the price of leadership. We must be sympathetic, we must be forgiving, we must really have forbearance, so that when the ignorant and illiterate fellow who happens to be a member of your own race stands up to block the passage of some cause that you believe would be to his benefit and to yours as a people you will be able to overlook him, even though he fosters his opposition with the greatest amount of insult to your intelligence and to your dignity.

The excuse that some of our most brilliant men give for not identifying themselves with race movements is, that they cannot tolerate the interference of the illiterate Negro, who, being a member of the same organization will attempt to dictate what you should do in the interest of the race, when his act is based upon no deeper judgment than his like or dislike for the person he is opposing, or the satisfaction it would give him to embarrass the person he feels like opposing. Many an able leader is lost to his race because of this fear, and sometimes we must admit the reasonableness of this argument; but as I have said leadership means martyrdom, leadership means sacrifice, leadership means giving up one's personality, giving up of everything for the cause that is worth while. It is only because of that feeling that I personally continue to lead the Universal Negro Improvement Association, because like every other leader, I have had to encounter the opposition, the jealousy, the plotting of men who take advantage of the situation, simply because they happen to be members of the organization, and that we may have to depend upon their vote one way or the other for the good of the cause. Not that some of us care one row of pins what the other fellow thinks, but when it is considered that we can only achieve success through harmony and unity, then it can be realized how much one has to sacrifice as a leader for getting that harmony that is necessary to bring about the results that are desired.

The White Race

We desire harmony and unity to-day more than ever, because it is only through the bringing together of the four hundred million Negroes into one mighty bond that we can successfully pilot our way through the avenues of opposition and the oceans of difficulties that seem to confront us. When it is considered that the great white race is making a Herculean struggle to become the only surviving race of the centuries, and when it is further considered that the great yellow race under the leadership of Japan is making a like struggle, then more than ever the seriousness of the situation can be realized as far as our race is concerned. If we sit supinely by and allow the great white race to lift itself in numbers and in power, it will mean that in another five hundred years this full grown race of white men will in turn exterminate the weaker race of black men for the purpose of finding enough room on this limited mundane sphere to accommodate that race which will have numerically multiplied itself into many billions. This is the danger point. What will become of the Negro in another five hundred years if he does not organize now to develop and to protect himself? The answer is that he will be exterminated for the purpose of making room for the other races that will be strong enough to hold their own against the opposition of all and sundry.

An appeal to the Intelligentsia

The leadership of the Negro of to-day must be able to locate the race, and not only for to-day but for all times. It is in the desire to locate the Negro in a position of prosperity and happiness in the future that the Universal Negro Improvement Association is making this great fight for the race's emancipation everywhere and the founding of a great African government. Every sober-minded Negro will see immediately the reason why we should support a movement of this kind. If we will survive then it must be done through our own effort, through our own energy. No race of weaklings can survive in the days of tomorrow, because they will be hard and strenuous days fraught with many difficulties.

I appeal to the higher intelligence as well as to the illiterate groups of our race. We must work together. Those of us who are better positioned intellectually must exercise forbearance with the illiterate and help them to see the right. If we happen to be members of the same organization, and the illiterate man tries to embarras you, do not become disgusted, but remember that he does it because he does not know better, and it is your duty to forbear and forgive because the ends that we serve are not of self, but for the higher development of the entire race. It is on this score, it is on this belief, that I make the sacrifice of self to help this downtrodden race of mine. Nevertheless, I say there is a limit to human patience, and we should not continue to provoke the other fellow against his human feelings for in doing so we may be but bringing down upon our own heads the pillars of the temple.

MARCUS GARVEY IN PARAMILITARY ATTIRE (1926)

Garvey made speeches and led parades clothed in paramilitary attire. His image scandalized the established African-American leadership of the day, which strove to cultivate a more conventionally respectable ethos, but it resonated with ordinary African Americans, and later with the leaders of independence movements in Africa who were inspired by Garvey's example.

Source: From the collections of the Library of Congress.

George **Gershwin**

1898–1937

Broadway Composer

One of the composers who brought the Broadway musical and the American popular song to new heights of sophistication, George Gershwin might serve as a musical icon of the ambitious, overachieving 1920s.

George Gershwin was born Jacob Gershvin in Brooklyn, New York, on September 26, 1898. His parents were Russian Jews who had arrived in New York in 1895; they cobbled together a living, moving more than 20 times between 1895 and 1917. Little in his background suggested that Gershwin would embark upon a musical career, but when the family bought a piano in 1910, he took to it readily and learned classical music from his piano teacher. Gershwin dropped out of school in 1914 to work as a "song plugger"—a salesman and song demonstrator—for the Remick music publishing firm in New York. The job let Gershwin rub elbows with songwriters and Broadway entrepreneurs.

He began writing songs, and in 1918 the Harms publishing company recognized his talent, offering him a payment of $35 a week in return for the rights to his future compositions. The company's judgment was soon vindicated; Gershwin had his first hit in 1920 when star vocalist Al Jolson recorded "Swanee." That piece netted royalty payments of some $10,000 for the young composer, who set to work energetically. He scored five annual variety revues, entitled *George White's Scandals,* between 1920 and 1924. Gershwin's songwriting career would flourish during the heyday of the stage musical and would stretch into the era when film dominated, but it began in the hothouse musical assembly line of New York's Tin Pan Alley.

Gershwin began to collaborate with his lyricist brother, Ira, who succeeded in creating lyrics that matched George's rhythmic flexibility, musical wit, and subtle shades of emotion. By 1924 the pair had achieved a genuine Broadway hit with the musical *Lady, Be Good,* from which the title track and the song "Fascinating Rhythm" have endured as masterpieces. Even after he gained recognition for his classical compositions, Gershwin continued to

From the collections of the Library of Congress.

write for the stage. Among his successful musicals of the period was *Oh, Kay!* (1926), another collaboration with Ira; it featured the song "Someone To Watch Over Me."

In the realm of popular song Gershwin is especially notable for having created a rhythmic idiom that bore clear evidence of his encounter with the African-American jazz and blues that were beginning to alter the pop musical landscape. "Someone to Watch Over Me" and Gershwin's other romantic ballads offered rhythmically-free melody lines that challenged performers' interpretive skills, and a song such as "I Got Rhythm" had rhythmic complexities that showed a real appreciation of jazz. Jazz musicians later made the song the basis for numerous improvisations of their own. In an age that casually classified almost any popular music as jazz, Gershwin came closer to the real thing than did his contemporaries.

What propelled him to national fame, however, was not a popular song but rather a composition for the classical concert hall: *Rhapsody in Blue.* This 1924 work for piano and small orchestra arose as part of an "Experiment in Modern Music," an evening of jazz with ambitions toward respectability organized by the dance bandleader Paul Whiteman. *Rhapsody* had the outward trappings of a classical concerto, but incorporated jazz elements; its unfailing melodic inspiration instantly endeared it to concert audiences, while also providing fuel to the growing understanding that the jazz form was much more than just another fad.

After *Rhapsody in Blue* came other orchestral works; the Piano Concerto in F represented Gershwin's nearest approach to pure classical ideals, and *An American in Paris* (1928) communicated Gershwin's own impressions of the "City of Light." In Paris, Gershwin socialized with the best of the European avant-garde. His admirers included Arnold Schoenberg, who later became Gershwin's tennis partner in Hollywood.

The Gershwins continued to write for the musical stage; *Girl Crazy* (1930), which included "I Got Rhythm," was among their most successful shows. Gershwin's 1935 opera *Porgy and Bess*, which portrayed the unique language and culture of the Gullah people (derived from their West African heritage) in an African-American neighborhood in Charleston, South Carolina, is perhaps his masterpiece. The Gershwins moved to Hollywood in 1936, and amid the fast pace of his new life, the symptoms of George Gershwin's growing brain tumor were attributed to stress. He died on July 11, 1937.

Gershwin was one of a group of remarkable composers—others included Irving Berlin, Jerome Kern, and Richard Rodgers—who defined the post–World War I era as a golden age of song in the United States. What set Gershwin apart from this group was the broad reach of his

genius: his music ranged from romantic ballads of the Broadway stage, to songs that crackled with the energy of jazz, to instrumental compositions that aspired to the aesthetic altitude of the European classics. As it was with Gershwin, so it was with a nation coming into its own as a world power—nothing was beyond reach and all things seemed possible. George Gershwin was a symbol of a nation whose ambition was fully reflected in its music.

James M. Manheim

For Further Reading

Jablonski, Edward. *Gershwin*. New York: Doubleday, 1987.

Peyser, Joan. *The Memory of All That: The Life of George Gershwin*. New York: Simon & Schuster, 1993.

Rosenberg, Deena. *Fascinating Rhythm: The Collaboration of George and Ira Gershwin*. Ann Arbor: University of Michigan Press, 1997.

TIN PAN ALLEY (c. 1905)

The dense concentration of Manhattan music publishers known as Tin Pan Alley was the scene of Gershwin's education in popular music. Pictured here are the offices of the Remick publishing firm, where Gershwin worked as a song demonstrator while still in his mid-teens.

Source: Hulton/Archive.

New York Herald Tribune Article Announcing the "Experiment in Modern Music" (January 4, 1924)

Among the members of the committee of judges who will pass on "What Is American Music?" at the Paul Whiteman concert to be given at Aeolian Hall, Tuesday afternoon, February 12, will be Serge Rachmaninoff, Jascha Heifetz, Efrem Zimbalist and Alma Gluck.

Leonard Leibling, editor of "The Musical Courier," will be chairman of the critics' committee, which is to be composed of the leading musical critics of the United States.

This question of "just what is American music?" has aroused a tremendous interest in music circles and Mr. Whiteman is receiving every phase of manuscript, from blues to symphonies.

George Gershwin is at work on a jazz concerto, Irving Berlin is writing a syncopated tone poem and Victor Herbert is working on an American suite.

Gershwin's Rhapsody in Blue *was composed for a 1924 concert organized by bandleader Paul Whiteman. Gershwin had informally discussed the project with Whiteman, but forgot about it in the constant rush of his other work and learned of the commission only when he read this* New York Herald Tribune *article.*

Rhapsody in Blue Manuscript by George Gershwin (1924)

The beginning of Gershwin's manuscript of Rhapsody in Blue.

MANUSCRIPT FOR *SECOND RHAPSODY FOR ORCHESTRA AND PIANO* by George Gershwin (1931)

The sequel to Gershwin's Rhapsody in Blue, *the* Second Rhapsody for Orchestra and Piano *was first performed by the Boston Symphony orchestra in 1932 with Gershwin as pianist. Here is the first page of the original manuscript, completed by Gershwin in 1931.*

Source: Hulton/Archive.

Emma Goldman

Emma Goldman was a passionate advocate of anarchism, birth control, free speech, and free love, and was finally deported at the height of the 1919 Red Scare for having encouraged resistance to the draft during World War I.

Goldman was born on June 27, 1869, in Kovno (now Kaunas), Lithuania, in the Russian empire, and later moved to St. Petersburg, Russia. In St. Petersburg she read widely and became associated with a radical student group. In December 1885, she and a sister left Russia and settled in Rochester, New York, where they were soon joined by the rest of their family.

Goldman was briefly married in 1887 to a fellow immigrant, Jacob Kersner, and worked in a garment sweatshop whose drudgery was a depressing contrast with the American paradise she had expected. She began attending meetings of German socialists and developed an increasing interest in anarchism, that is, the abolition of the state and the promotion of individual liberty over laws that protected the property of the ruling class. She moved to New York City in 1889, where she became close friends with Alexander Berkman, another Russian Jewish immigrant from Lithuania. In 1890 she began speaking publicly on anarchist themes. Between 1896 and 1917, she would travel coast-to-coast on lecture tours about anarchism, workers' rights, birth control, free speech, and other controversial subjects.

In 1893, Goldman was arrested for "inciting to riot" with a fiery speech during a demonstration in Union Square in New York City, and was sentenced to a year in Blackwell's Island Penitentiary. Upon her release, she went to Vienna for a year of medical training at the Vienna General Hospital (1895–96), where she heard lectures by Sigmund Freud, then returned to New York to work as a nurse and midwife in the tenements of the Lower East Side.

Like her friend **Margaret Sanger**, Goldman believed that access to some form of birth control was necessary

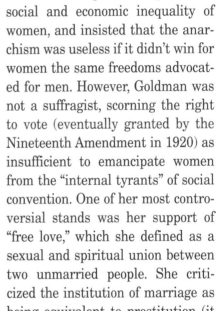

From the collections of the Library of Congress.

and in her lectures she promoted Sanger's radical feminist monthly, *The Woman Rebel*. After Sanger and her husband were arrested for distributing birth control information, Goldman began speaking more forcefully for birth control and encouraging her listeners to buy Sanger's *Family Limitation* pamphlet. In 1916 after a lecture on birth control she was arrested and imprisoned for two weeks for having violated a law prohibiting the sale or advertisement of contraceptives.

Goldman spoke out against the social and economic inequality of women, and insisted that the anarchism was useless if it didn't win for women the same freedoms advocated for men. However, Goldman was not a suffragist, scorning the right to vote (eventually granted by the Nineteenth Amendment in 1920) as insufficient to emancipate women from the "internal tyrants" of social convention. One of her most controversial stands was her support of "free love," which she defined as a sexual and spiritual union between two unmarried people. She criticized the institution of marriage as being equivalent to prostitution (it was "merely a question of degree," she said, "whether [a woman] sells herself to one man, in or out of marriage, or to many men"). She also regarded the women's rights movement as too middle class and dismissive of the social and economic needs of workers and the poor.

When Alexander Berkman was released from prison in 1906 (for an assassination attempt on industrialist Henry Clay Frick in 1892), they founded the monthly anarchist magazine, *Mother Earth*, which they published until 1917. In 1911 she published her first book, *Anarchism and Other Essays*. As the United States was preparing to enter World War I, Goldman founded the No Conscription League. She and Berkman were arrested in 1917 on charges of conspiring against the draft, fined $10,000 each, and sentenced to two years in prison; the judge recommended deportation after time served.

The wartime crackdown on antiwar activists through the Espionage Act of 1917 and the Sedition Act of 1918 led to a climate of terror and suspicion that came to be known as the Red Scare. An epidemic of labor strikes across the nation was suppressed, often brutally, and foreign-born anarchists were blamed for any civil disorder, such as a series of sensational anarchist bombings in 1919 targeting (but not injuring), among others, Attorney General **A. Mitchell Palmer** and Supreme Court Justice **Oliver Wendell Holmes, Jr.** Politicians and newspaper headlines screamed that anarchists and "Reds" must be deported to restore order. The Justice Department responded with a mass roundup of alien radicals—the Palmer Raids of 1919–20.

Immediately upon their release from prison in October 1919, Goldman and Berkman, dubbed by journalists the "Red Queen" and the "Red King," were sent as "trophy deportees" to the Soviet Union. Goldman had appealed to the Supreme Court, claiming that she was a United States citizen by marriage, but her citizenship claims were denied. Deported along with 247 radicals seized in the Palmer Raids on a ship known in the newspapers as the "Soviet Ark," this incident publicly demonstrated that the government would not tolerate disruptions by foreign "extremists."

Although in the United States Goldman had defended the Bolshevik Revolution, in Russia she was appalled by the new Soviet government's repression of dissidents. She left the Soviet Union in December 1921 for Western Europe, where she denounced the Bolsheviks' betrayal of the masses and imprisonment of political enemies. A collection of her articles was published under the title *My Disillusionment in Russia* (1923). In the 1920s and 1930s she continued writing—her autobiography, *Living My Life*, was published in 1931—and lecturing in Europe and Canada. Goldman was in Toronto, Canada, on a speaking tour when she died on May 14, 1940.

In her energetic advocacy of the freedom of speech, equality of the sexes, tolerance for homosexuals, and birth control and reproductive freedom, Emma Goldman was ahead of her time, and yet she was also very much of her time. Many liberties she advocated would be taken for granted by the jazz-age flappers in the 1920s, but that decade's excessive pursuit of material wealth would almost entirely ignore the plight of workers and the poor on whose behalf Goldman struggled.

Mark LaFlaur

For Further Reading
Drinnon, Richard. *Rebel in Paradise: A Biography of Emma Goldman*. Chicago: University of Chicago Press, 1982.
Goldman, Emma. *Red Emma Speaks: An Emma Goldman Reader*. 3rd ed. Compiled and edited by Alix Kates Shulman. Atlantic Highlands, N.J.: Humanities Press, 1996.
Murray, Robert K. *Red Scare: A Study of National Hysteria, 1919–1920*. New York: McGraw-Hill, 1962.
Solomon, Martha. *Emma Goldman*. Boston: Twayne/G. K. Hall, 1987.
Stansell, Christine. *American Moderns: Bohemian New York and the Creation of a New Century*. New York: Metropolitan Books/Henry Holt, 2000.

"WOMAN SUFFRAGE" by Emma Goldman (1910) [EXCERPT]

In her essay "Woman Suffrage," first published in Anarchism and Other Essays, *Goldman criticizes suffragists' contention that the right to vote will by itself liberate women from oppressive conditions.*

Source: Goldman, Emma. Anarchism and Other Essays. *New York: Mother Earth Publishing Association, 1910.*

We boast of the age of advancement, of science, and progress. Is it not strange, then, that we still believe in fetich worship? True, our fetiches have different form and substance, yet in their power over the human mind they are still as disastrous as were those of old.

Our modern fetich is universal suffrage. Those who have not yet achieved that goal fight bloody revolutions to obtain it, and those who have enjoyed its reign bring heavy sacrifice to the altar of this omnipotent deity. Woe to the heretic who dare question that divinity!

Woman, even more than man, is a fetich worshiper, and though her idols may change, she is ever on her knees, ever holding up her hands, ever blind to the fact that her god has feet of clay. Thus woman has been the greatest supporter of all deities from time immemorial. Thus, too, she has had to pay the price that only gods can exact—her freedom, her heart's blood, her very life.

Nietzsche's memorable maxim, "When you go to woman, take the whip along," is considered very brutal, yet Nietzsche expressed in one sentence the attitude of woman towards her gods.

Religion, especially the Christian religion, has condemned woman to the life of an inferior, a slave. It has thwarted her nature and fettered her soul, yet the Christian religion has no greater supporter, none more devout, than woman. Indeed, it is safe to say that religion would have long ceased to be a factor in the lives of the people, if it were not for the support it receives from woman. The most ardent churchworkers, the most tireless missionaries the world over, are women, always sacrificing on the altar of the gods that have chained her spirit and enslaved her body.

The insatiable monster, war, robs woman of all that is dear and precious to her. It exacts her brothers, lovers, sons, and in return gives her a life of loneliness and despair. Yet the greatest supporter and worshiper of war is woman. She it is who instills the love of conquest and power into her children; she it is who whispers the glories of war into the ears of her little ones, and who rocks her baby to sleep with the tunes of trumpets and the noise of guns. It is woman, too, who crowns the victor on his return from the battlefield. Yes, it is woman who pays the highest price to that insatiable monster, war.

Then there is the home. What a terrible fetich it is! How it saps the very life-energy of woman—this modern prison with golden bars. Its shining aspect blinds woman to the price she would have to pay as wife, mother, and housekeeper. Yet woman clings tenaciously to the home, to the power that holds her in bondage.

It may be said that because woman recognizes the awful toll she is made to pay to the Church, State, and the home, she wants suffrage to set herself free. That may be true of the few; the majority of suffragists repudiate utterly such blasphemy. On the contrary, they insist always that it is woman suffrage which will make her a better Christian and homekeeper, a staunch citizen of the State. Thus suffrage is only a means of strengthening the omnipotence of the very gods that woman has served from time immemorial.

What wonder, then, that she should be just as devout, just as zealous, just as prostrate before the new idol, woman suffrage. As of old, she endures persecution, imprisonment, torture, and all forms of condemnation, with a smile on her face. As of old, the most enlightened, even, hope for a miracle from the twentieth-century deity—suffrage. Life, happiness, joy, freedom, independence—all that, and more, is to spring from suffrage. In her blind devotion woman does not see what people of intellect perceived fifty years ago: that suffrage is an evil, that it has only helped to enslave people, that it has but closed their eyes that they may not see how craftily they were made to submit.

Woman's demand for equal suffrage is based largely on the contention that woman must have the equal right in all affairs of society. No one could, possibly, refute that, if suffrage were a right. Alas, for the ignorance of the human mind, which can see a right in an imposition. Or is it not the most brutal imposition for one set of people to make laws that another set is coerced by force to obey? Yet woman clamors for that "golden opportunity" that has wrought so much misery in the world, and robbed man of his integrity and self-reliance; an imposition which has thoroughly corrupted the people, and made them absolute prey in the hands of unscrupulous politicians.

The poor, stupid, free American citizen! Free to starve, free to tramp the highways of this great country, he enjoys universal suffrage, and, by that right, he has forged chains about his limbs. The reward that he receives is stringent labor laws prohibiting the right of boycott, of picketing, in fact, of everything, except the right to be robbed of the fruits of his labor. Yet all these disastrous results of the twentieth-century fetich have taught woman nothing. But, then, woman will purify politics, we are assured.

Needless to say, I am not opposed to woman suffrage on the conventional ground that she is not equal to it. I see neither physical, psychological, nor mental reasons why woman should not have the equal right to vote with man. But that can not possibly blind me to the absurd notion that woman will accomplish that wherein man has failed. If she would not make things worse, she certainly could not make them better. To assume, therefore, that she would succeed in purifying something which is not susceptible of purification, is to credit her with supernatural powers. Since woman's greatest misfortune has been that she was looked upon as either angel or devil, her true salvation lies in being placed on earth; namely, in being considered human, and therefore subject to all human follies and mistakes. Are we, then, to believe that two errors will make a right? Are we to assume that the poison already inherent in politics will be decreased, if women were to enter the political arena? The most ardent suffragists would hardly maintain such a folly. . . .

The misfortune of woman is not that she is unable to do the work of man, but that she is wasting her life force to outdo him, with a tradition of centuries which has left her physically incapable of keeping pace with him. Oh, I know some have succeeded, but at what cost, at what terrific cost! The import is not the kind of work woman does, but rather the quality of the work she furnishes. She can give suffrage or the ballot no new quality, nor can she receive anything from it that will enhance her own quality. Her development, her freedom, her independence, must come from and through herself. First, by asserting herself as a personality, and not as a sex commodity. Second, by refusing the right to anyone over her body; by refusing to bear children, unless she wants them; by refusing to be a servant to God, the State, society, the husband, the family, etc.; by making her life simpler, but deeper and richer. That is, by trying to learn the meaning and substance of life in all its complexities, by freeing herself from the fear of public opinion and public condemnation. Only that, and not the ballot, will set woman free, will make her a force hitherto unknown in the world, a force for real love, for peace, for harmony; a force of divine fire, of life giving; a creator of free men and women.

EMMA GOLDMAN AT BIRTH CONTROL RALLY (1916)

Goldman was an out-spoken supporter of women's reproductive rights. At this 1916 rally in Union Square, New York City, Goldman delivers a speech on birth control.

Source: ©Bettmann/ Corbis.

"WE DON'T BELIEVE IN CONSCRIPTION" SPEECH by Emma Goldman (May 18, 1917)

Goldman delivered this speech at the Harlem River Casino in New York City on May 18, 1917. It was later introduced in the June–July 1917 anti-conscription trial of Goldman and Alexander Berkman.

Source: Goldman, Emma. "We Don't Believe in Conscription." Emma Goldman Papers. Document maintained at: sunsite.berkeley.edu /Goldman/Writings/ Speeches/170518.html (September 20, 2001).

9:45 P.M., May 18, 1917

We don't believe in conscription, this meeting tonight being a living proof. This meeting was arranged with limited means. So, friends, we who have arranged the meeting are well satisfied if we can only urge the people of entire New York City and America, there would be no war in the United States—there would be no conscription in the United States—[applause]—if the people are not given an opportunity to have their say. Therefore, we hope at least that a small portion of the population of New York City tonight is having its say.

Friends, what I have to tell you tonight I want to impress upon your minds with all the intensity of my being, that we have with us people who came to break up this meeting, and therefore, friends, I ask you, friends, in the name of peace, in the name of freedom, and all that is dear to you, to be perfectly quiet, and when the meeting is over to leave the hall quietly, for that is a better argument than by the provocators who came here tonight to break up the meeting. Therefore, friends, I repeat once more, that after our speakers will be through, I hope you will leave the hall quietly, and, if there is the slightest trouble, we will hold the troublemakers, the provocators and the police responsible for the trouble. [applause]

Friends, I know perfectly well that tomorrow morning the daily papers will say that the German Kaiser paid for this meeting. I know that they will say that those employed in the German service have arranged this meeting. But there is all of us, friends, who have something serious at hand—those of us to whom liberty is not a mere shadow—and found to be celebrated on the 4th of July, and to be celebrated with fire crackers—that we will not only speak for it, but die for it if necessary. [applause]

We are concerned in our own conscience, and we know that the meeting tonight has been arranged by working men and working women, who probably gave their last cent from their wages which the capitalistic regime is granting them.

And so, friends, we do not care what people will say about us, we only care for one thing, and that is to demonstrate tonight and to demonstrate as long as we can be able to speak, that when America went into war, ostensibly for the purpose of fighting for democracy—because it is a dastardly lie—it never went into war for democracy. If it is true that America went into war in order to fight for democracy—why not begin at home? We need democracy. [applause] We need democracy even more than Germany, and I will tell you why. The German people were never brought up with the belief that they lived in democracy. The German people were nursed from their mothers' breasts that they were living in liberty and that they had all the freedom they desired. Therefore, the German people are not disappointed in the Kaiser. They have a Kaiser, the kind of a Kaiser they want and are going to stand for.

We in America have been brought up, we have been told that this is a free Republic. We have been told that free speech and free press and free assembly are guaranteed by the Constitution. Incidentally, friends, the only people who still believe in the Constitution are you poor fools for the other fellows [applause]. We are rather disappointed. When suddenly, out of the clear sky, a few months after we have been told he kept us out of war—we are now told he drew us into war. [applause]

We, who came from Europe, came here looking to America as the promised land. I came believing that liberty was a fact. And when we today resent war and resent conscription, it is not that we are foreigners and don't care, it is precisely because we love America and we are opposed to war. [applause]

My friends, when I say we love America, I wish you to remember that we don't love the American Wall Street, that we don't love the American Morgan, that we don't love the American Rockefeller, we don't love the American Washington, we don't love the American ammunition manufacturers, we don't love the American National Security League—for that America is Russia transferred to America. [applause]

We mean the America of Wendell Phillips, we mean Emerson, we mean America of great pioneers of liberty. We mean writers, and great men and women, who have fought for years to maintain the standard of effort. I, for one, am quite willing to stand up face to face with patriots every night—patriots blind to the injustice committed in this country—patriots who didn't care a hang. We are willing to stand up and to say to them: "Keep your dirty hands off America." You have no right to tell the people to give their lives in behalf of democracy, when democracy is the laughing stock before all Europe. And therefore, friends, we stand here and we tell you that the war which is now declared by America in the last six weeks is not a war of democracy and is not a war of the urging of the people. It is not a war of economic independence. It is a war for conquest. It is a war for military power. It is a war for money. It is a war for the purpose of trampling under foot every vestige of liberty that you

people have worked for, for the last forty or thirty or twenty-five years and, therefore, we refuse to support such a war—[Hurray—applause].

We are told, friends, that the people want war. If it is true that the American people want war, why not give the American people a chance to say whether they want war. Friends, we were told that the American people have a chance to say whether they want war through Congress and through the Senate. Congress is in the hands of those who pull the string. It is a jumping jack. [applause]

Friends, in Congress there are a few men in the Senate [mentioning some names] who wanted to keep America out of war. They have been hounded and persecuted and abused and insulted and degraded because they stood up for a principle. And so it was not true that the people of America have a chance to express its views. It was impossible, because each Congressman and each Senator is taken into a private room where spiritualistic mediums are being used, and they are mesmerized and massaged until every revolutionary fibre is out of them, and then they come out and do as they're told by the administration in Washington.

The same is true about conscription. What chance have you men, to say, if you men are to be conscripted. It took England eighteen months—a monarchy—to decide whether she shall have conscription. Upon the people born under a free sky—conscription has been imposed upon you. You cannot have democracy and have compulsory military training. You have become Russia. [applause]

Friends, I suggest that Wall Street and the military powers invite the Russian Czar to America—he belongs here,—and tell them how to deal with the revolution, with the anti-militarists—the Czar ought to know, he handled them. He used every method in his power in order to subdue all human beings. But he succeeded—I should say not. He is now sitting in his palace, that the revolution may go a little further. [applause] Americans evidently are working for the Czar. We already have the beginning of the Czar, who wants to employ all of the liberties of the American people.

Now, friends, do you suppose for one minute that this Government is big enough and strong enough and powerful enough to stop men who will not engage in the war because they don't want the war, because they don't believe in the war, because they are not going to fight a war for Mr. Morgan? What is the Government going to do with them? They're going to lock them up—You haven't prisons enough to lock up all the people. [applause]

We believe in violence and we will use violence. Remember, friends, that the very Government which worships at the altar of the Christian religion, that this very Government knows perfectly well, that they attempted to silence them. And so, if it is their intention to make us quiet, they may prepare the noose, they may prepare the gallows, they may build more prisons—for the spread of revolt and conscience. [applause] How many people are going to refuse to conscript, and I say there are enough. I would count at

Reprinted by courtesy of the Emma Goldman Papers Project at the University of California, Berkeley.

least 50,000, and there are enough to be more, and they're not going to when only they're conscripted. They will not register. [applause]

I realize perfectly, that it is possible to gather up 50 and 100 and 500 people—and what are you going to do if you have 500,000 people? It will not be such an easy job, and it will compel the Government to sit up and take notice and, therefore, we are going to support, with all the means at our support with money and publicity—we are going to support all the men who will refuse to register and who will refuse to fight. [applause]

We want you to fill out these slips and as you go out drop them into the baskets at the door. We want to know how many men and women of conscriptive age—and they're going to take women and not soldiers. It is the same thing as if you fight in the war. Don't let them tell you that they will send you to the farm. Every stroke of what you do you are supporting the war, and the only reply that you can make against the war is that you are making men—that you are busy fighting your internal enemy, which is the capitalistic class. [applause]

I hope that this meeting is not going to be the first and last. As a matter of fact, we are planning something else.

Friends, listen, think of it. Not only are you going to be compelled—coerced—to wear the soldier's uniform, but on the day when you leave to be educated to the monster war, on the day when it will be decided that you shall be driven into the trenches and battlefield, on that day we are going to have a demonstration [applause], but be careful whom [applause]—you might bury yourself and not the working class [applause]. We will have a demonstration of all the people who will not be conscripted and who will not register. We are going to have the largest demonstration this city has ever seen, and no power on earth will stop us.

I will say, in conclusion, that I, for one, am quite willing to take the consequences of every word I said and am going to say on the stand I am taking. I am not afraid of prison—I have been there often. It isn't quite so bad. I am not afraid of the authorities—I have dealt with them before—and rather, they have dealt with me, and am still living and stand here before you. I am not afraid of death. I would rather die the death of a lion than live the life of a dog. [applause]

For the cause of human liberty, for the cause of the working class, for the cause of men and women who live and till the soil—if I am to die for them, I could not wish a more glorious death ever in my wildest dreams. And so, patriots, and police, and gentlemen, who represent wealth and power, help yourself—you cannot stop the revolutionary spirit. It may take as long as one year or two. You cannot do it, because the spirit of revolution has a marvelous power of liberty. It can break through bars—it can go through safely. It can come out stronger and braver. If there is any man in this hall that despairs—let's look across Russia—let's look across. [applause] Als—who was tortured by the Russian soldiers, who never believed that she would see Russia and see her people alive, and yet see the wonderful thing that revolution has done. It has thrown the Czar and his clique and his ever staunch henchmen into prison. It has opened Siberia and all the dungeons, and the men and women are going to be free. They are not going to be free according to American democracy. [applause]

Friends, I insist it is a good place for them in Russia. Let's go back home tomorrow. So, friends, don't be afraid. Take this marvelous meeting, take this wonderful spirit, and remember that you are not alone—that tonight, in every city, in every hamlet and in every village and town, there are hearts beating that they don't want war, that they don't want conscription—that they are not going to be conscripted.

The ruling classes fight a losing game. The Wall Street men are fighting a losing game. They represented the past and we represent the future. [applause]

The future belongs to the young men, who are barely of age and barely realizing their freedom. The future belongs to the young girls and young boys. They must be free from militarism. They must be free from the military yoke. If you want war, help yourself. Fight your own battle. We are not going to fight it for you. [applause]

So, friends, it is our decision tonight. We are going to fight for you, we are going to assist you and co-operate with you, and have the grandest demonstration this country has ever seen against militarism and war. What's your answer? Your answer to war must be a general strike, and then the governing class will have something on its hands.

So, friends, before I close, I want to make an appeal to you. I want to make you know that this meeting sprang simultaneously from a group of people. It cost money and therefore I ask you to contribute as much as you can. I wish to say that Mother Earth is opening pledges with $50. I hope that those who can do so will do so. We want to have money, we want to have more literature, we want to have a demonstration, and we want to prove that with little money, no public support, with no militia, with no soldiers, we can support the point of real freedom and liberty and brotherhood.

Samuel Gompers

1850–1924
U.S. Labor Leader

Samuel Gompers, a leader of American organized labor for nearly half a century, used his diplomatic skills to unify workers behind the war effort during World War I.

Samuel Gompers was born in a working-class neighborhood in London on January 27, 1850, the son of Dutch Jewish immigrants. His father was a cigar maker, a skilled occupation in the days before machine rolling. His family moved to the United States in 1863 and settled in New York City.

During Gompers's early life, industrialism was reshaping the American economy and the worker's place within it. Machines were putting former skilled tradesmen out of work, and increasing immigration brought in large numbers of unskilled workers who spoke different languages and could not easily be organized by craft, occupation, or any other unifying factor.

In the late 1860s Gompers became active in the Cigarmakers International Union (CMIU). He and his friend Adolph Strasser reorganized the union and introduced benefits that would be imitated by other unions: they charged higher dues, but provided unemployment compensation, sick relief funds, and travel money so that unemployed members could search for new jobs.

In 1881 Gompers helped organize the Federation of Organized Trades and Labor Unions, an association of skilled craft workers, which was reorganized in 1886 as the American Federation of Labor (AFL) with about 50,000 members. He was elected the federation's first president. The AFL was a federation of autonomous trade unions whose two main principles were voluntarism and trade union autonomy. Gompers opposed the formation of a single big union, believing instead that skilled tradesmen would be better served by autonomous unions within each trade, coordinated by a national umbrella organization.

Gompers's exclusive focus on skilled tradesmen made possible the rise of the radical **William "Big Bill" Haywood** and the Industrial Workers of the World (I.W.W.), or "Wobblies." The I.W.W., which welcomed the unskilled and immigrant masses (as Gompers did not), was filling a gap left by the AFL. The AFL did not include the millions employed in such mass production industries as steel, meatpacking, agricultural machinery, and automobiles. The entire American labor movement would have been much stronger—and certainly more populous—if the AFL had recruited the unskilled and industrial workers in addition to the skilled craft workers.

From the collections of the Library of Congress.

Although he would often be criticized for being too accommodating to business, Gompers kept a strict focus on the federation's aims: he refused to engage with radical or socialistic programs, instead pushing for realization of a limited but consistent set of goals—higher wages, shorter hours, and increased freedom for workers to bargain for improved conditions. He urged negotiation in labor disputes and approved of striking only when good-faith efforts at bargaining had failed. He opposed the formation of a national labor party and opposed alliances between unions and political parties, insisting that the federation remain nonpartisan; it was not until 1912 that he publicly endorsed a presidential candidate, Democrat **Woodrow Wilson**.

During Wilson's administration, which was unusually supportive of labor's right to organize and bargain collectively, the U.S. Department of Labor was founded in March 1913. Organized labor's votes for Wilson were quickly rewarded by the administration's support of the Clayton Antitrust Act (1914), which legalized peaceful strikes, picketing, and boycotts. Although it would be somewhat weakened by subsequent court decisions, Gompers praised the Clayton Act as "Labor's Magna Carta."

Gompers, formerly a pacifist, was an invaluable ally to the Wilson administration during World War I. He rallied the support of industrial workers in preparation for war and drove out or marginalized labor's antiwar elements, arguing that advocacy of peace efforts could strengthen Germany. Appointed by President Wilson to serve on the Council of National Defense, Gompers mediated between labor and employers and the government, calling on the workers not to strike and urging the employers and Congress not to pass legislation that would compel the workers to forfeit their right to strike. He repeatedly advised the War Labor Board that the best way to ensure uninterrupted production would be to trust the workers to labor without compulsion; meanwhile he urged unions to honor a no-strike policy, for if they went on strike, Congress would certainly pass laws to force them to work.

His success in guiding organized labor toward preparedness, and then through wartime production with relatively few disturbances, was briefly rewarded by an all-time high in AFL membership: in 1920, the union's membership peaked at more than four million. He was further honored by Wilson with an appointment as a member of the Commission on International Labor Legislation at the Paris Peace Conference in 1919.

The fortunes of both Gompers and the AFL turned after the war, however. The 1917 Bolshevik Revolution in Russia and a wave of violent anarchist bombings across the United States in 1919 provoked an antiforeigner hysteria known as the Red Scare of 1919–20. Mainstream organized labor tended to have little or no interest in socialism, communism, or anarchism, but conservatives attributed 1919's rash of labor strikes to Bolshevik "revolutionists." Labor was also weakened by the illness of President Wilson, who suffered a stroke in September 1919 and never recovered. The election of Republican **Warren G. Harding** in 1920 (succeeded after his death in 1923 by **Calvin Coolidge**) made conditions even worse, as Harding and Coolidge were far more sympathetic to business than to employees.

From 1919 to 1923 Gompers wrote his autobiography, *Seventy Years of Life and Labor* (1925). In 1924 he endorsed the Progressive Party candidate Wisconsin Senator **Robert Marion La Follette** (rather than the Democratic candidate) in an effort to revive labor's political potency, but La Follette lost by a large margin. Gompers died in December 1924, about a month after Coolidge's sweeping victory.

By the time of Samuel Gompers's death, many of labor's hard-won accomplishments were being weakened by court reversals and a relaxation of federal control. Nonetheless, this persuasive and diplomatic organizer led the way in battles for an eight-hour workday, child labor laws, and the right of labor to organize, all of which would gain increasing importance in the following decade during the Great Depression.

Mark LaFlaur

For Further Reading

Chasan, Will. *Samuel Gompers: Leader of American Labor.* New York: Praeger, 1971.

Livesay, Harold C. *Samuel Gompers and Organized Labor in America.* Boston: Little, Brown, 1978.

Mandel, Bernard. *Samuel Gompers.* Yellow Springs, Ohio: The Antioch Press, 1963.

Stearn, Gerald Emanuel. *Gompers.* Englewood Cliffs, N.J.: Prentice-Hall, 1971.

"Labor's Service to Freedom" Speech by Samuel Gompers (c. 1917–18)

In this speech, Gompers acknowledges the wartime demands placed on American labor and reassures the nation that the U.S. work force is fully prepared and willing to support the nation's war efforts.

Source: Samuel Gompers, *American Leaders Speak: Recordings from World War I and the 1920 Election.* American Memory, Library of Congress, analog sound disk.

Fellow countrymen, our republic, our people, are at war. Whatever individuals may have thought upon the European situation before the Congress of the United States declared war against the Imperial German and Austrian governments, that must now be laid aside. War means victory for our cause or danger to the very existence of our nation.

The World War in which we are engaged in is on such a tremendous scale that we must readjust practically the whole nation's social and economic structure from a peace to a war basis. It devolves upon liberty-loving citizens, and particularly the workers of this country, to see to it that the spirit and the methods of democracy are maintained within our own country while we are engaged in a war to establish them in international relations. The fighting and the concrete issues of the war are so removed from our country that not all of our citizens have a full understanding of the principles of autocratic force which the Central Powers desire to substitute for the real principles of freedom.

In addition to the fundamental principles at issue, labor has a further interest in the war. This war is a people's war—labor's war. The final outcome will be determined in the factories, the mills, the shops, the mines, the farms, the industries, and the transportation agencies of the various countries. That group of countries which can most successfully organize its agencies of production and transportation, and which can furnish the most adequate and effective agencies with which to conduct the war, will win.

The workers have a part in this war equal with the soldiers and sailors on the ships and in the trenches. America's workers understand the gravity of the situation and the responsibility that devolves upon them. They are loyal to the republic. They have done and are doing their part.

There was struggle for freedom and for a better life—gives them a keen appreciation of the opportunities and privileges of free, the free government has given them. They are demonstrating their appreciation and loyalty by war work, by loaning their savings, and by the supreme sacrifice. Labor will do its part in every demand the war makes. Our republic, the freedom of the world, progress, and civilization hang in the balance. We dare not fail. We will win.

"LABOR: A RABBIT KEEPER" from *Time* (October 1, 1923) [EXCERPT]

A rabbit with a cork leg, wobbly ears and a false eye, its bodily structure fabricated of brown cotton, is paying a visit to Portland, Ore. The reason for this animal's visit is the opening of the annual Convention of the American Federation of Labor on Oct. 1. The rabbit is there as the mascot of the greatest cigar-maker in the world's history — Samuel Gompers. . . .

[H]is vigourous personality was competent to handle the difficult situations of labor politics. His power of persuasion is only equaled by his fighting power, and it is rarely that one or the other is not triumphant.

In 1881 he helped to organize the Federation of Organized Trades and Labor Unions, reorganized five years later into the American Federation of Labor. He might have been its first President, but he declined and was made Vice President. The following year he was President. He has held that position ever since, except in 1894–95, when he was barely defeated by John McBride, leader of the coal miners. For practically 43 years he has dominated the greatest labor organization in America.

Br'er Rabbit, of whom the brown cotton bunny is a representation, was suggested years ago by Mr. Gompers' secretary, who detected a decided likeness between Uncle Remus' Br'er Rabbit and her chief. It was the play of wits between Br'er Rabbit and the enemies that sought to corner him that made the secretary think of the mental adroitness of Samuel Gompers in a similar situation. She found the rabbit "human looking, with a glint of knowingness in his eye, an all-pervading air of good-will, an absence of bitterness in his make-up." So she purchased the cotton rabbit and presented it to Mr. Gompers. And "Br'er" has sat ever since as mascot on the labor leader's desk, has accompanied him on his travels.

HIS TENETS:

As labor leaders go, Samuel Gompers is a conservative.

Organized labor is one of Mr. Gompers' ideals. "I can explain my position," he has said, "by a story. You see a boy whistling mightily as he approaches a yellow dog. He kicks the dog into the gutter and goes on whistling loudly. Then he comes to a bulldog. He looks at him but he doesn't touch him." Unorganized labor is the yellow dog; organized labor the bulldog.

One big union is an idea to which Mr. Gompers has always been vigorously opposed. He believes in autonomous unions within each trade, co-ordinated and assisted by the Federation of which he is leader.

A labor party is contrary to his principles. He fears it might split union ranks. Nevertheless his organization makes a practice of disseminating political information in regard to records of candidates for public offices and their attitude toward labor.

Government ownership he vigorously opposes, and one of his few great defeats was when the A.F. of L. Convention of 1920 voted for Government ownership of the railroads.

Woman Suffrage had his approval.

Socialism and Communism have always been anathema to him. He fought the propaganda of the Socialist Berger and still fights the radicalism of William Z. Foster and the "Soviet invasion" of the U.S. He has said in his speeches: "I pity the Socialists. . . . I have read all their books. I know all their arguments. . . . I do not regard them as rational beings. . . . If the lesser and immediate demands of labor could not be obtained from society as it is, it would be mere dreaming to preach and pursue the will-o'-the-wisp, a new society constructed from rainbow materials. . . ."

Capitalism is not a Gompers fetish, as his opposition to Socialism indicates. He declared: "There is no necessity to worry about how labor and capital can be reconciled, for they are one and the same."

Life is no pathway of roses in Mr. Gompers' view. "Happiness cannot be granted to man below," he philosophized. "Life is but a strife. . . . I have almost had my very soul burned in the trials of life. . . ."

HIS ROPE:

The A.F. of L. has been called "a rope of sand" because it is a federation of autonomous unions, not a union of dependent bodies. It was originally formed in opposition to the contrary ideal of the Knights of Labor. The fact that the rope of sand has become a powerful organization may be attributed largely to the personal energy of the man at its head.

But the fact that the A.F. of L. is a loosely knit body means that Mr. Gompers still has to fight the battles he has waged from the very beginning. He will be faced at Portland by demands for one big union, for recognition of Soviet Russia and other radical measure. There will be two days for the presentation of resolutions, and the remainder of a two weeks' session will be devoted to committee hearings and the passage of resolutions. Among the questions to be dealt with will be restriction of immigration, labor schools, labor injunctions, compulsory arbitration, child and female labor legislation, labor banks.

About 500 delegates will be in attendance who will cast about 3,500 votes, one vote for each 1,000 members in the entire organization of about 3,500,000. Theoretically the functions of the Federation extend little beyond this annual passage of resolutions. Actually the Federation settles jurisdictional disputes between unions, issues charters and assists in the formation of local unions and trade unions which become its members. Over its member unions, especially the smaller ones, it exercises an effective, if unrecognized, general discipline.

Mr. Gompers may proudly survey his work — an organization with 3,500,000 members, which he helped to found with less than 50,000; an organization with a budget of over half a million dollars as compared to less than $200 43 years ago; a power in labor; a power in politics.

This excerpt from a Time *article (October 1, 1923) summarizes Gompers's views on labor, woman suffrage, capitalism, and socialism. The AFL's membership had peaked at about four million in 1920; by the fall of 1923 the rolls were down to about 3.75 million members.*

Source: "Labor: A Rabbit Keeper." *Time,* October 1, 1923. ©1923 Time Inc. Reprinted by permission.

POLITICAL CARTOON ON AMERICAN LABOR STRATEGIES (Undated)

"SAMUEL GOMPERS" by Emma Goldman (1925)

Anarchist Emma Goldman published this essay in 1925, about a year after Gompers's death, criticizing the former president of the American Federation of Labor for his inability to challenge existing class divisions within labor.

Source: Goldman, Emma, "Samuel Gompers" in The Road to Freedom 1, March 1925. Emma Goldman Papers. Document maintained at: sunsite.berkeley.edu/Gol dman/Writings/Essays/g ompers.html (September 23, 2001). Reprinted by courtesy of the Emma Golman Papers Project at the University of California, Berkeley.

The numerous tributes paid to the late President of the American Federation of Labor, emphasized his great leadership. "Gompers was a leader of men," they said. One would have expected that the disaster brought upon the world by leadership would have proven that to be a leader of men is far from a virtue. Rather is it a vice for which those who are being led are usually made to pay very heavily.

The last fifteen years are replete with examples of what the leaders of men have done to the peoples of the world. The Lenins, Clemenceaus, the Lloyd Georges and Wilson, have all posed as great leaders. Yet they have brought misery, destruction and death. They have led the masses away from the promised goal.

Pious Communists will no doubt consider it heresy to speak of Lenin in the same breath with the other statesmen, diplomats and generals who have led the people to slaughter and half of the world to ruin. To be sure, Lenin was the greatest of them all. He at least had a new vision, he had daring, he faced fire and death, which is more than can be said for the others. Yet it remains a tragic fact that even Lenin brought havoc to Russia. It was his leadership which emasculated the Russian revolution and stifled the aspirations of the Russian people.

Gompers was far from being a Lenin, but in his small way his leadership has done a great harm to the American workers. One has but to examine into the nature of the American Federation of Labor, over which Mr. Gompers lorded for so many years, to see the evil results of leadership. It cannot be denied that the late President raised the organization to some power and material improvement, but at the same time, he prevented the growth and development of the membership towards a higher aim or purpose. In all these years of its existence the A. F. of L. has not gone beyond its craft interests. Neither has it grasped the social abyss which separates labor from its masters, an abyss which can never be bridged by the struggle for mere immediate material gains. That does not mean, however, that I am opposed to the fight labor is waging for a higher standard of living and saner conditions of work. But I do mean to stress that without an ultimate goal of complete industrial and social emancipation, labor will achieve only as much as is in keeping with the interests of the privileged class, hence remain dependent always upon that class.

Samuel Gompers was no fool, he knew the causes underlying the social struggle, yet he set his face sternly against them. He was content to create an aristocracy of labor, a trade union trust, as it were, indifferent to the needs of the rest of the workers outside of the organization. Above all, Gompers would have none of a liberating social idea. The result is that after forty years of Gompers' leadership the A. F. of L. has really remained stationary, without feeling for, or understanding of the changing factors surrounding it.

The workers who have developed a proletarian consciousness and fighting spirit are not in the A. F. of

L. They are in the organization of the Industrial Workers of the World. The bitterest opponent of this heroic band of American proletarians was Samuel Gompers. But then, Mr. Gompers was inherently reactionary. This tendency asserted itself on more than one occasion in his career. Most flagrantly did his reactionary leanings come to the fore in the MacNamara case, the War and the Russian Revolution.

The story of the MacNamara case is very little known in Europe. Yet their story has played a significant part in the industrial warfare of the United States, the warfare between the Steel Trust, the Merchants' Manufacturers' Association, and the infamous Labor baiter, the *Los Angeles Times*, arrayed against the Iron Structural Union. The savage methods of the unholy trinity expressed themselves in a system of espionage, the employment of thugs for the purpose of slugging strikers with violence of every form, besides the use of the entire machinery of the American Government, which is always at the beck and call of American capitalism. This formidable conspiracy against labor, the Iron Structural Union, in defence of its existence fought desperately for a period of years.

J. J. and Jim MacNamara, being among the most ardent and unflinching members of the Union, consecrated their lives and took the most active part in the war against the forces of American industrialism and high finance until they were trapped by the despicable spies employed in the organization of William J. Burns, the infamous man hunter. With the MacNamaras were two other victims, Matthew A. Schmidt, one of the finest types of American proletarians, and David Caplan.

Samuel Gompers, as the President of the A. F. of L. could not have been unaware of the things these poor men were charged with. He stood by them as long as they were considered innocent. But when the two brothers, led by their desire to shield "the higher ups" admitted their acts, it was Gompers who turned from them and left them to their doom. The whitewash of the organization was more to him than his comrades, who had carried out the work in constant danger to their own lives, while Mr. Samuel Gompers enjoyed the safety and the glory as President of the A. F. of L. The four men were sacrificed. Jim MacNamara and Matthew A. Schmidt sent to life imprisonment, while J. J. MacNamara and David Caplan received fifteen and ten years respectively. The latter two have since been released, while the former are continuing a living death in St. Quentin Prison, California. And Samuel Gompers was buried with the highest honors by the class which hounded his comrades to their doom.

In the War, the late President of the A. F. of L., turned the entire organization over to those he had ostensibly fought all his life. Some of his friends insist that Gompers became obsessed by the War mania because the German Social Democrats had betrayed the spirit of Internationalism. As if two wrongs ever made a right! The fact is, that Gompers was never able to swim against the tide. Hence he made common cause with the war lords and delivered the membership of the A. F. of L., to be slaughtered in the War, which is now being recognized by many erstwhile ardent patriots, to have been a war not for democracy, but for conquest and power. The attitude of Samuel Gompers to the Russian Revolution, more than anything else, showed his dominant reactionary leanings. It is claimed for him that he had the "goods" on the Bolsheviki. Therefore he supported the blockade and intervention. That is absurd for two reasons: First, when Gompers began his campaign against Russia, he could not possibly have had any knowledge of the evil doings of Bolshevism. Russia was then cut off from the rest of the world. And no one knew exactly what was happening there. Secondly, the blockade and intervention struck down the Russian people, at the same time strengthening the power of the Communist State.

No, it was not his knowledge of the Bolsheviki which made Gompers go with the slayers of Russian women and children. It was his fear for and his hatred of, the Revolution itself. He was too steeped in the old ideas to grasp the gigantic events that had swept over Russia, the burning idealism of the people who had made the Revolution. He never took the slightest pains to differentiate between the Revolution and the machine set up to sidetrack its course. Most of us who now must stand out against the present rulers of Russia do so because we have learned to see the abyss between the Russian Revolution, the ideals of the people and the crushing dictatorship now in power. Gompers never realized that.

Well, Samuel Gompers is dead. It is to be hoped that his soul will not be marching on in the ranks of the A. F. of L. More and more the conditions in the United States are drawing the line rigidly between the classes. More and more it is becoming imperative for the workers to prepare themselves for the fundamental changes that are before them. They will have to acquire the knowledge and the will as well as the ability to reconstruct society along such economic and social lines that will prevent the repetition of the tragic debacle of the Russian Revolution. The masses everywhere will have to realize that leadership, whether by one man or a political group, must inevitably lead to disaster.

Not leadership, but the combined efforts of the workers and the cultural elements in society can successfully pave the way for new forms of life which shall guarantee freedom and well-being for all.

D. W. Griffith

1875–1948

Cinematic Pioneer

D. W. Griffith developed many of the techniques that define cinema as an art form over a career that stretched from the early days of film until after the advent of the "talkies." That career exemplified some of the contradictions of American culture from the Great War to the Great Depression, for Griffith was at once a leading-edge technical genius and a backward-looking sentimentalist whose most famous film, *The Birth of a Nation*, glorified the racist Ku Klux Klan.

Born in rural La Grange, Kentucky, on January 22, 1875, David Lewelyn Wark Griffith was the son of a Confederate Civil War officer and slaveholding landowner. The family fell on hard times during the Reconstruction era; Griffith was raised in Louisville, where he began appearing in plays at age 20. He toured as an actor and began to write plays, short stories, and poetry. Only occasionally successful, Griffith was drawn to the film industry that was emerging in New York in the first years of the twentieth century. He landed a starring role in a short 1907 film, *Rescued from an Eagle's Nest,* and directed his first film, *The Adventures of Dollie,* a year later. Over the next five years he directed some 450 films for New York's Biograph studios—most of them one reel long. In these films, slight as they were, Griffith transformed the young art of cinema into something distinct from filmed stage action: he developed and popularized such fundamentals as the long shot, the close-up, creative use of camera angles and lighting, intercutting of story lines, and many other techniques.

Griffith's final film for Biograph, *Judith of Bethulia* (1914), gave signs of the broad scope of his ambitions. A then-unheard-of four reels in length (it runs for slightly more than one hour), the film was a full-fledged biblical epic far removed from the slapstick comedy, miniature melodramas, and moralistic fables that had been the stuff of the movies until then. Griffith had already left Biograph for the Reliance-Majestic studio to gain more creative control over his career, thus anticipating the long struggles

From the collections of the Library of Congress.

between creative and administrative talent that have characterized the film industry ever since.

Griffith's quantum leap forward came in 1915 with *The Birth of a Nation,* which ran for nearly three hours in its original release and dwarfed all previous productions, not only in size but also in range of technique and visual imagination. In another sign of things to come, it ran far over budget and several times sent Griffith's producers scurrying for additional funding. The melodramatic film followed the life of a Southern Civil War soldier through the end of the war and into Reconstruction. It featured several elaborate and precisely choreographed battle scenes. Based on a novel called *The Clansman*, by Southern author and minister Thomas Dixon, *The Birth of a Nation* vividly depicted the night riders of the terrorist Ku Klux Klan as they moved along moonlit roads and attacked groups of newly freed slaves. The film's portrayals of Reconstruction-era African-American legislators were tinged with ridicule and prejudice. Tellingly, at the premiere Dixon remarked that he would not have allowed anyone but the son of a Confederate soldier to direct a film version of his story.

In terms of sheer technique, *The Birth of a Nation* is widely considered one of the most important and influential films in the history of the art. Its realistic portrayal of war and of the arising of a massive social movement were closely studied, not only in America but also abroad. The groundbreaking social epics of post–Revolutionary Soviet Russia owed much to Griffith's cinematic approach, an idea that might have horrified the courtly Southerner had he ever really become aware of it. The general public, too, was awed by the scope of Griffith's accomplishment, and the film amply repaid its backers' investment despite its unprecedented two-dollar ticket price. One estimate held that 825,000 people viewed *The Birth of a Nation* in New York City alone—close to a quarter of the city's population.

The civil rights movement was still decades away, and African Americans in 1915 had few avenues of legal or moral persuasion that they could follow in attempting to counter the power of Griffith's racist vision. Nevertheless, the volume of protest that accompanied the film's distribution is notable; the newly formed National Association for the Advancement of Colored People (NAACP) called for a ban on showings of the film, and it found allies in such prominent white progressives as the social worker Jane Addams. Even the cautious *New York Times* characterized the film as "inflammatory" while praising its visual inventiveness. The protests had some effect; Griffith was pressured to cut some of the film's most offensive scenes, although he initially resisted on anticensorship grounds. "Whatever happened during Reconstruction," argued an NAACP pamphlet, "this film is aggressively vicious and defamatory. It is spiritual assassination. It degrades the censors that passed it and the white race that endures it." In some cities the film was picketed by NAACP demonstrators, but in others Klansmen rode into town on horses to promote showings.

Indeed, many historians attribute the resurgence of the Klan in the 1920s in part to the film's popularity. The new Ku Klux Klan gained in strength in rural areas of the South and Midwest, and the group claimed between 4.5 and 6 million members at its height. In addition to its prejudiced views of African Americans, Roman Catholics, Jews, and immigrants, the Klan also supported Prohibition (which made the manufacture, sale, and distribution of alcohol illegal) and fundamentalism, and criticized Darwinism, birth control, and internationalism.

Perhaps in response to the widespread criticism of *Birth of a Nation*, Griffith planned for his next major project an ultra-ambitious exploration of the theme of intolerance throughout history. The resulting 1916 film, *Intolerance*, dwarfed even *The Birth of a Nation* in scope. Fifteen reels and close to four hours long, with gargantuan sets and backdrops and pulsing crowd scenes, *Intolerance* told four separate stories from different historical eras, joining them together at the end. It might be regarded as the film industry's first "blockbuster," and even by modern standards its effect is spectacular. *Intolerance* is regarded by film historians as equal in significance to *The Birth of a Nation,* but audiences of the day were put off by its complex structure; it failed to match the strong financial performance of its predecessor and left its creator deeply in debt.

Toward the end of World War I, Griffith filmed two war stories, *The Great Love* (now lost) and *Hearts of the World,* which partially restored his reputation as a moneymaker. Both these dramas drew on footage that Griffith shot on location in England and France, some of it in the war zone. The sweeping battle scenes of *Hearts of the World,* however, failed to capture the contest of attrition that World had become; Griffith even complained to a journalist "viewed as a drama, the war is in some ways disappoint

In 1919 Griffith, together with actors Dou Fairbanks, **Charlie Chaplin**, and Mary Pickford, for the United Artists Corporation. This business vent enabled them to work independently of the ma Hollywood studios, whose rigid production system and fa tory-like atmosphere was incompatible with their workir methods and desire for creative freedom. Around 1920 Griffith turned to smaller subjects and produced a series o finely wrought sentimental melodramas whose romanti mood did much to define the image that silent film vould have for succeeding generations. The first and most artisti-cally successful of these was *Broken Blossoms* (1919), it starred the actress who would dominate Griffith's later productions, Lillian Gish. The mawkish romance *Way Down East* (1920), based on a popular play from before the war, became Griffith's second-biggest box office hit.

Griffith returned to the epic scale with *Orphans of the Storm* (1922), starring both Lillian Gish and her sister Dorothy. A sweeping tale of the French Revolution, the film offered detailed sets replicating eighteenth-century Paris, all constructed on a 14-acre set in the New York City suburb of Mamaroneck. *America* (1924) was another vast historical drama, this time taking the Revolutionary War as its subject. Griffith moved to Paramount in 1924 and made two films starring comedian **W. C. Fields**, *Sally of the Sawdust* (1925) and *That Royle Girl* (1925). In general, though, his high-minded melodramatic style was falling out of favor by the late 1920s, and his films of that period—such as *The Sorrows of Satan* (1926), *Drums of Love* (1927), and *The Battle of the Sexes* (1928)—are generally regarded as lacking a personal stamp. Griffith found the new Hollywood film industry alien, and, most important, he had little use for the great technical innovation that rocked the film world at the end of the 1920s: the introduction of sound. "Give us back our beauty," he is reported to have said in response to the rise of sound films; indeed, the utterance might have served as an epitaph for the career of this supreme visual craftsman who so often seemed caught in the aesthetic and moral past.

Griffith made two sound films. The first, *Abraham Lincoln* (1930), brought about a temporary revival of his career. With a subject that matched Griffith's heroic style, script contributions by author Stephen Vincent Benét, and a strong performance by a young Walter Huston in the title role, it enjoyed critical and box office success. But an antialcohol weeper called *The Struggle,* released a year later toward the end of Prohibition, elicited groans from

diences and critics by then accustomed to more realistic
re. Griffith moved back to Kentucky and lived in semire-
rement. He lasted long enough to see historians begin to
ppreciate his contributions; a retrospective of his work
as assembled by New York's Museum of Modern Art in
940. D. W. Griffith died after suffering a stroke in a
Hollywood hotel room on July 23, 1948.

With his at once progressive and reactionary art,
Griffith was perhaps the quintessential creator of World
War I-era films in the United States. He nurtured the infant
art of cinema, defined its vocabulary, and brought it to a
central position in the nation's cultural life. Yet he was also
the white South's foremost mythmaker, and as such he set
in motion forces that would, for years to come, exacerbate
the country's violent racial divide.

James M. Manheim

For Further Reading
Gunning, Tom. *D. W. Griffith and the Origins of American Narrative Film: The Early Years at Biograph.* Urbana: University of Illinois Press, 1994.
Henderson, Robert M. *D. W. Griffith: His Life and Work.* New York: Garland, 1985.
Schickel, Richard. *D. W. Griffith: An American Life.* New York: Simon & Schuster, 1984.
Williams, Martin T. *Griffith, First Artist of the Movies.* New York: Oxford University Press, 1980.

Audiences and promoters were well aware of the magnitude of Griffith's technical achievement; the poster reads in part, "The Expression of Genius in a New Realm of Art." The film's top ticket price of two dollars was unprecedented; Griffith and his associates settled on it only with extreme trepidation.

Source: From the collections of the Library of Congress.

MOVIE POSTER FOR *THE BIRTH OF A NATION* (1915)

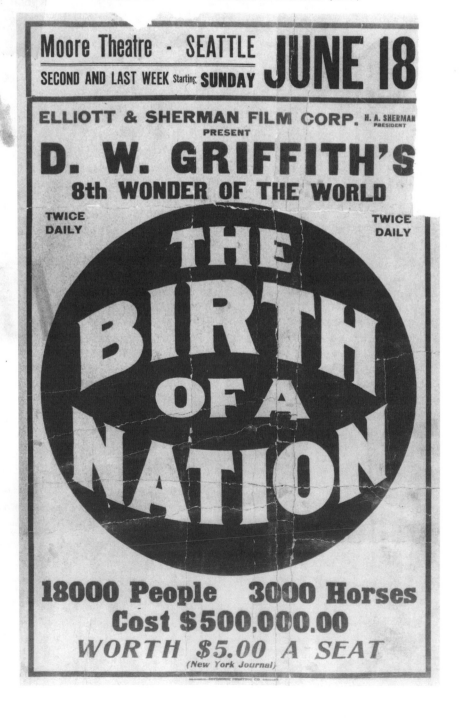

ANALYSIS BY FRANCIS HACKETT FROM THE NAACP'S *FIGHTING A VICIOUS FILM: PROTEST AGAINST THE BIRTH OF A NATION* (1915) [EXCERPT]

If history bore no relation to life, this motion picture drama could well be reviewed and applauded as a spectacle. As a spectacle it is stupendous. It lasts three hours, represents a staggering investment of time and money, reproduces entire battle scenes and complex historic events; amazes even when it wearies by its attempt to encompass the Civil War. But since history does bear on social behavior, *The Birth of a Nation* cannot be reviewed simply as a spectacle. It is more than a spectacle. It is an interpretation, the Rev. Thomas Dixon's interpretation, of the relations of the North and South and their bearing on the Negro. . . .

In *The Birth of a Nation* Mr. Dixon protests sanctimoniously that his drama "is not mean to reflect in any way on any race or people of today." And then he proceeds to give to the Negro a kind of malignity that is really a revelation of his own malignity.

Passing over the initial gibe at the Negro's smell, we early come to a negrophile senator whose mistress is a mulatto. As conceived by Mr. Dixon and as acted in the film, this mulatto is not only a minister to the senator's lust but a woman of inordinate passion, pride and savagery. Gloating as she does over the promise of "Negro equality," she is soon partnered by a male mulatto of similar brute characteristics. Having established this triple alliance between the "uncrowned king," his diabolic colored mistress and his diabolic colored ally, Mr. Dixon shows the revolting processes by which the white South is crushed "under the heel of the black South." "Sowing the wind," he calls it. On the one hand we have "the poor bruised heart" of the white South, on the other "the new citizens inflamed by the growing sense of power." We see Negroes shoving white men off the sidewalk, Negroes quitting work to dance, Negroes beating a crippled old white patriarch, Negroes slinging up "faithful colored servants" and flogging them till they drop, Negro courtesans guzzling champagne with the would-be head of the Black Empire, Negroes "drunk with wine and power," Negroes mocking their white master in chains, Negroes "crazy with joy" and terrorizing all the whites in South Carolina.

We see the blacks flaunting placards demanding "equal marriage." We see the black leader demanding a "forced marriage" with an imprisoned and gagged white girl. And we see continually in the background the white Southerner in "agony of soul over the degradation and ruin of his people."

Encouraged by the black leader, we see Gus the renegade hover about another young white girl's home. To hoochy-coochy music we see the long pursuit of the innocent white girl by this lust-maddened Negro, and we see her fling herself to death from a precipice, carrying her honor through "the opal gates of death."

Having painted this insanely apprehensive picture of an unbridled, bestial, horrible race, relieved by only a few touches of low comedy, "the grim reaping begins." We see the operations of the Ku Klux Klan, "the organization that saved the South from the anarchy of black rule." We see Federals and Confederates uniting in a Holy War "in defence of their Aryan birthright," whatever that is. We see the Negroes driven back, beaten, killed. The drama winds up with a suggestion of "Lincoln's solution"—back to Liberia—and then, if you please, with a film representing Jesus Christ in "the halls of brotherly love."

My objection to this drama is based partly on the tendency of the pictures but mainly on the animus of the printed lines I have quoted. The effect of these lines, reinforced by adroit quotations from Woodrow Wilson and repeated assurances of impartiality and goodwill, is to arouse in the audience a strong sense of the evil possibilities of the Negro and the extreme propriety and godliness of the Ku Klux Klan. So strong is this impression that an audience invariably applauds the refusal of the white hero to shake hands with a Negro, and under the circumstances it cannot be blamed. Mr. Dixon has identified the Negro with cruelty, superstition, insolence and lust. . . .

Whatever happened during Reconstruction, this film is aggressively vicious and defamatory. It is spiritual assassination. It degrades the censors that passed it and the white race that endures it.

One of the first campaigns of the then-young NAACP was to try to prevent Birth of a Nation *from being shown, or, failing that, to have some of its most objectionable scenes trimmed. In the latter effort the organization was partly successful. The NAACP's Boston chapter published a pamphlet entitled* Fighting a Vicious Film: Protest Against The Birth of a Nation; *it included statements of support from various prominent Bostonians, including* The New Republic's *first literary editor, Francis Hackett.*

Source: *Fighting a Vicious Film: Protest Against* The Birth of a Nation. Boston: Boston Branch of the National Association for the Advancement of Colored People, 1915.

STILL FROM *THE BIRTH OF A NATION* (1915)

The Civil War scenes in Birth of a Nation *were elaborately choreographed and enhanced by a variety of cinematic techniques. The cumulative effect was a sense of realism that audiences had never before experienced. The film, however, was fatally marred by crude racism that was losing its acceptability even in Griffith's own day.*

Source: From the collections of the Library of Congress.

STILL FROM *INTOLERANCE* (1916)

Intolerance, *Griffith's next film after* Birth of a Nation, *was gargantuan not only in length (it runs for over four hours), but also in its sets, which were major construction projects. Pictured here is the set for the film's Babylon sequence, one of four interlocking stories from different historical eras.*

Source: From the collections of the Library of Congress.

FOUNDING OF UNITED ARTISTS ANNOUNCEMENT (1919)

Mary Pickford
Charlie Chaplin
Douglas Fairbanks
D.W. Griffith

More enduring than tablets of bronze is the hold that these master-artists have on the minds and affections of the millions. To them has come the supreme tribute of the seekers of happiness and the better things of life—men, women and children alike—who have enshrined them in their hearts for all time.

And that they may give to the full as their art grows in its maturing richness, they have dedicated themselves to making the motion picture screen free—an unfettered medium, for all that is best in life's play hours.

To make the pictures of Mary Pickford, Charlie Chaplin, Douglas Fairbanks and D.W. Griffith available to the entire film world without the restrictions and obligations and limitations of the program and star series systems of film rental, United Artists Corporation has been created.

Each production—as nearly perfect as human skill and genius and art can make it—will be rented on its own individual merits.

United Artists Corporation thus guarantees to Exhibitors their full freedom in the booking and exploiting of the screen's supreme productions. It gives to them the opportunity to reap the full benefits of their own ability as showmen.

First Release September 1st, 1919
A Douglas Fairbanks Picture
Bookings now being made

United Artists Corporation
729 Seventh Avenue, New York

Oscar A. Price, President
Hiram Abrams, General Manager

Griffith was not only a creative pioneer of film, but also helped to establish the modern film industry. In 1919 he became one of four founders of the United Artists Corporation, still a dominant force in U.S. cinema. In the 1920s, however, he tangled with his partners over the budgets his elaborate spectacles required.

Source: Hart, James, ed. *The Autobiography of D. W. Griffith*. Louisville, Ken.: Touchstone, 1972.

FOUNDING OF UNITED ARTISTS (1919)

In this photo documenting the founding of United Artists in 1919, Griffith (far right) is shown with his partners (from left to right) Douglas Fairbanks, Mary Pickford, and Charlie Chaplin.

Source: Culver Pictures.

Warren G. Harding

Warren G. Harding, a compromise "dark horse" candidate picked by Republican Party bosses in 1920, is widely regarded as not only the least competent chief executive in U.S. history but also the too-trusting appointer of one of the most unscrupulous Administrations ever to scandalize Washington.

Warren Gamaliel Harding was born on a farm near Blooming Grove (now Corsica), Ohio, on November 2, 1865. He graduated from Ohio Central College in 1882, and then worked as a teacher, journalist, and printer's helper. He purchased a struggling newspaper, the Marion *Star*, in 1884, and worked tirelessly to revive it. In 1891 he married Florence Mabel Kling DeWolfe, a widow five years his senior. She and Harding did not have any children, but together they made the *Star* a success.

Harding failed in his first try for elected office, that of county auditor, in 1892. In 1899 he was elected to the Ohio State Senate and was reelected in 1901. Two years later, with the help of former state representative Harry M. Daugherty, Harding was elected lieutenant governor. He was denied the nomination for governor in 1905 and returned to the *Star*. In 1914, again managed by Daugherty, Harding won a seat in the U.S. Senate. He would serve one term (1915–21) in the Senate, which he described as "a very pleasant place."

As a U.S. senator, Harding backed most of President **Woodrow Wilson**'s war initiatives: he voted for the declaration of war against Germany, the Espionage Act of 1917, and the Selective Service Act of 1917, although he opposed high taxes on war profits in the belief that they would harm business. In May 1919, he was named to the Senate Foreign Relations Committee, from which platform he attacked Wilson's League of Nations as "a surrender of national sovereignty."

At the 1920 Republican National Convention, delegates were unable to choose among the party's main presidential contenders. Although Harding was little known outside Washington, he emerged as an acceptable compro-

From the collections of the Library of Congress.

mise because of his party loyalty, likability, conservatism, and his talent for conciliating opposing factions. On the night of June 11, 1920, in a room in Chicago's Blackstone Hotel, Republican bosses decided Harding was their man— or at least, in the words of Senator Frank Brandegee, "the best of the second-raters"—and Massachusetts governor **Calvin Coolidge** was chosen as his running mate.

Harding conducted a "front porch" campaign, receiving visitors and occasionally issuing politically "safe" statements expressing vague support for "an association of nations," stricter immigration standards, and lower taxes. Most famously, Harding called for "a return to normalcy," which appealed to Americans who were disillusioned by World War I and Wilson's internationalist idealism. His Democratic opponent, Ohio Governor James M. Cox (running with Franklin D. Roosevelt), campaigned energetically in support of the League of Nations and Wilson's foreign policies. Harding, promising to put "America first," won 61 percent of the popular vote, and 404 electoral votes to Cox's 127; he carried every state outside the South (then heavily Democratic) except Tennessee.

Harding partly fulfilled his pledge to appoint the "best minds" to his administration by recruiting financier Andrew Mellon to head the Treasury Dept., Herbert Hoover to serve as secretary of commerce, and Charles Evans Hughes to serve as secretary of state. But his other choices showed poor character judgment and proved disastrous for his Administration. Harry Daugherty, the "Ohio Gang" lobbyist, was named attorney general; and "Colonel" Charles R. Forbes, a deserter from the army, as head of the Veterans' Bureau. The most regrettable choice turned out to be his appointment of New Mexico Senator Albert B. Fall as secretary of the interior.

In domestic affairs, Harding was true to the pro-business interests who backed his candidacy. He raised tariffs, lowered taxes on high incomes and business profits, and restricted immigration. He also backed certain progressive, reformist policies, advocated by Hoover and

Agriculture Secretary Henry C. Wallace, that alleviated farm and labor troubles, and he supported Hoover's attempts to force the steel industry to shorten the workday from 12 hours to eight. The Administration's greatest foreign policy achievement, thanks to Hughes, was the Washington Naval Disarmament Conference (1921–22), which set limits to naval expansion among the United States, Britain, Japan, and other powers.

In 1923, a number of scandals involving Harding's "Ohio Gang" appointees began to surface. Charles R. Forbes of the Veterans' Bureau was convicted of defrauding the government and was sentenced to jail. Meanwhile, Attorney General Daugherty had caused the Justice Department to be nicknamed "the Department of Easy Virtue" by loosely granting pardons, immunities, and selling bootleggers' permits; in 1924, he resigned in disgrace.

On August 2, 1923, Harding died suddenly of either a heart attack or a stroke while in San Francisco. Following his death, the worst scandal of his Administration erupted— the Teapot Dome affair. A Senate investigating committee found that Interior Secretary Fall had deceived Harding into signing a transfer of leases for naval oil reserves at Teapot Dome, Wyoming, and Elk Hills, California, from the jurisdiction of the navy (with Navy Secretary Edwin M. Denby's knowledge) to the Interior Department. Fall then secretly leased the petroleum reserves to oilmen Harry F. Sinclair and Edward L. Doheny in exchange for personal gifts and payments exceeding $400,000. Secretaries Fall and Denby were forced to resign, and Fall and Sinclair served short prison terms. More damaging to Harding's personal reputation was the publication in 1927 of *The President's Daughter,* a book by a former mistress about an illegitimate daughter conceived while he was a senator.

Harding himself was not personally involved in the deals of his appointees, but he did little to prevent their schemes. As a result, his good qualities were largely forgotten as the sordid dealings of his Administration were revealed. The Harding scandals unsettled public confidence in government, but the sober demeanor of his successor, Coolidge, and the excitement of the 1920s business boom soon caused people to forget Harding and his failures.

Mark LaFlaur

For Further Reading
Allen, Frederick Lewis. *Only Yesterday: An Informal History of the 1920's.* New York: Wiley, 1997.
Downes, Randolph C. *The Rise of Warren G. Harding, 1865–1920.* Columbus: Ohio State University Press, 1970.
Murray, Robert K. *The Harding Era: Warren G. Harding and His Administration.* Minneapolis: University of Minnesota Press, 1969.
Russell, Francis. *The Shadow of Blooming Grove: Warren G. Harding and His Times.* New York: McGraw-Hill, 1968.
Trani, Eugene P., and David L. Wilson. *The Presidency of Warren G. Harding.* Lawrence: University Press of Kansas, 1977.

"A Free People: Speech on the Wilson League of Nations" by Warren G. Harding (August 28, 1920) [Excerpt]

I greet you in a spirit of rejoicing; not a rejoicing in the narrow personal or partisan sense, not in the gratifying prospects of party triumph; not in the contemplation of abundance in the harvest fields and ripening corn fields and maturing orchards; not in the reassuring approach of stability after a period of wiggling and wobbling which magnified our uncertainty—though all of these are ample of our wide rejoicing—but I rejoice that America is still free and independent and in a position of self-reliance and holds to the right of self-determination, which are priceless possessions in the present turbulence of the world. . . .

One can have no quarrel with those who have convinced themselves that our underlying purpose in entering the great conflict was to create a league of nations. The fact remains however, that no such intent was officially acclaimed, no allusion, nor even a suggestion to that effect appeared in the joint resolution of Congress which declared the existence of a state of war between this country and Germany. For myself I left no room for doubt of the motives which led me to cast my vote in favor of that resolution. It so happened that I made the concluding speech upon the war resolution, from my place in the Senate, on the night of April 4, 1917. These were my own words at the time:

"I want it known to the people of my state and to the nation that I am voting for war tonight for the maintenance of just American rights, which is the first essential to the preservation of the soul of this Republic.

"I vote for this joint resolution to make war, not a war thrust upon us, if I could choose the language of the resolution, but a war declared in response to affronts: a war that will at least put a soul into our American life; a war not for the cause of the allies of Europe; a war not for France, beautiful as the sentiment may be in reviving at least our gratitude to the French people; not precisely a war for civilization, worthy and inspiring as that would be; but a war that speaks for the majesty of a people properly governed, who finally are brought to the crucial test where they are resolved to get together and wage a conflict for the maintenance of their rights and the preservation of the covenant inherited from their fathers.

"We have given to the world the spectacle of a great nation that could make war without selfish intent. We unsheathed the sword some eighteen years ago for the first time in the history of the world, in the name of humanity, and we gave proof to the world at that time of an unselfish nation. Now, whether it is the fate or fortune, or travail of destiny, it has come to us to unsheathe the sword again, not alone for humanity's sake—though that splendid inspiration will be involved—but to unsheathe the sword against a great power in the maintenance of the rights of the Republic, in the maintenance which will give to us a new guaranty of nationality. That's the great

A campaign speech delivered by Harding on August 28, 1920, from his front porch at home in Marion, Ohio, outlining his objections to the ratification of U.S. membership in the League of Nations and his views on international cooperation.

Source: Harding, Warren G. A Free People: Speech on the Wilson League of Nations. New York: Republican National Committee, 1920.

thing, and I want it known, Mr. President and Senators, that this is the impelling thought with me for one, when I cast my vote." ...

We know now that the league constituted at Versailles is utterly impotent as a preventive of wars. It is so obviously impotent that it has not even been tried. It could not survive a single test. The original League, mistakenly conceived and unreasonably insisted upon, has undoubtedly passed beyond the possibility of restoration. The maturer judgment of the world will be that it deserved to pass for the very simple reason that, contrary to all of the tendencies developed by the civilizing processes of the world, it rested upon the power of might, not of right. ...

The difference between a court of international justice and the council created by the League Covenant is simple but profound.

The one is a judicial tribunal to be governed by fixed and definite principles of law administered without passion or prejudice. The other is an association of diplomats and politicians whose determinations are sure to be influenced by considerations of expediency and national selfishness. The difference is one with which Americans are familiar, the old and fundamental difference between a government of laws and a government of men.

I do not mean to say, nor do I mean to permit any such construction, that I would decline to cooperate with other nations in an honest endeavor to prevent wars. Nobody living would take that position. The only question is one of method or of practicability within the bounds prescribed by fundamental principles. ...

I want America to be the rock of security at home, resolute in righteousness and unalterable in security and supremacy of the law. Let us be done with wiggling and wobbling. Steady, America! Let us assure good fortune to all. We may maintain our eminence as a great people at home and resume our high place in the estimate of the world. Our moral leadership was lost when "Ambition" sought to superimpose a reactionary theory of discredited autocracy upon the progressive principle of living, glowing democracy. My chief aspiration, my countrymen, if clothed with power, will be to regain that lost leadership, not for myself, not even for my party, though honoring and trusting it as I do, but for my country, the country that I love from the bottom of my heart, and with every fibre of my being, above all else in the world.

This cartoon by Clifford Berryman contrasts the campaign approaches of Republican candidate Harding and Democratic candidate Ohio Governor James M. Cox during the 1920 presidential election. Instead of engaging in a speaking tour around the country, Harding conducted a "front porch" campaign, during which he read speeches to visitors at his home.

Source: From the collections of the Library of Congress.

"Presidential Fishing" Political Cartoon (1920)

TEAPOT DOME SCANDAL POLITICAL CARTOON (1923)

"TEXT OF THE PRESIDENT'S PROCLAMATION OF A NATIONAL DAY OF MOURNING" by Calvin Coolidge (August 5, 1923)

A Proclamation

To the People of the United States

In the inscrutable wisdom of Divine Providence, Warren Gamaliel Harding, twenty-ninth President of the United States, has been taken from us. The nation has lost a wise and enlightened statesman and the American people a true friend and counselor, whose whole public life was inspired with the desire to promote the best interests of the United States and the welfare of all its citizens. His private life was marked by gentleness and brotherly sympathy and by the charm of his personality he made friends of all who came in contact with him.

It is meet that the deep grief which fills the hearts of the American people should find fitting expression.

Now therefore, I, Calvin Coolidge, President of the United States of America, do appoint Friday next, Aug. 10, the day on which the body of the dead President will be laid in its last earthly resting place, as a day of mourning and prayer throughout the United States. I earnestly recommend the people to assemble on that day in their respective places of Divine worship, there to bow down in submission to the will of Almighty God, and to pay out of full heart the homage and love and reverence to the memory of the great and good President whose death has so sorely smitten the nation.

In witness, I have hereunto set my hand and cause the seal of the United States to be affixed.

Done at the City of Washington, the fourth day of August, in the year of our Lord, one thousand nine hundred and twenty-three, and of the Independence of the Untied States the one hundred and forty-eighth.

CALVIN COOLIDGE

By the President.

Charles E. Hughes, Secretary of State.

The White House, Washington, Aug. 4, 1923.

William "Big Bill" Haywood

1869–1928
Labor Organizer

William "Big Bill" Haywood, demonized by conservatives as "the most dangerous man in America," was a cofounder and leader of the Industrial Workers of the World, a radical labor union of unskilled workers.

Born William Richard Haywood in Salt Lake City, Utah, on February 4, 1869, Haywood was three when his father died. He lost the use of his right eye in an accident when he was nine; it was around this time that he changed his middle name to Dudley. He received only a few years of schooling and began working in a mining camp at age nine. In his teens he worked as a miner in Nevada and Utah, and from 1895 to 1900 Haywood worked in a mine in Silver City, Idaho. He joined the Western Federation of Miners (WFM) and rose quickly through its ranks, becoming president of his local union in 1900, and soon became a member of the WFM's national executive board. The powerfully built, charismatic Haywood collected the dues of a thousand members, administered a medical plan, and oversaw the construction of a hospital for union members.

From the collections of the Library of Congress.

In the early days of industrialization, workers had few means of negotiating for better working conditions. Attempts at collective bargaining were discouraged and often brutally suppressed by company owners, whose antiunion actions were usually backed up by the courts. Workers tended to be recent immigrants separated by language, religion, and ethnicity or race, and often cautious in asserting their rights to unionize. Recessions and depressions in 1893–97, 1907–09, and 1913–15 made socialism and radicalism increasingly attractive, both of which demanded social, economic, and political change.

Haywood was an advocate of radical industrial unionism, which he defined as socialism with its working clothes on. When necessary, Haywood believed, workers should not rely on mere voting or protest, but should actually fight their employers. Gunfights and violence between radical workers and management were common in this era; companies hired strikebreakers, while rebellious miners often sabotaged company property and murdered managers and executives. Haywood opposed the "craft unionism" espoused by **Samuel Gompers** and the American Federation of Labor (AFL), which concentrated on skilled workers such as printers, carpenters, and bricklayers, and was unwelcoming to immigrants.

In June 1905 Haywood presided over a convention in Chicago that, with the help of **Eugene V. Debs** and Daniel DeLeon, founded the Industrial Workers of the World (IWW), which Haywood described as "the continental congress of the working class." The IWW (incorporating the Western Federation of Miners— WFM), whose members were nicknamed "Wobblies," invited membership by all workers regardless of skill, nationality, race, or sex, and aimed to take control of industry away from corporations and put it in the hands of the workers. In the long term, the IWW sought to abolish capitalism and destroy the power of the state.

In December 1905 former Idaho Governor Frank R. Steunenberg was assassinated, and the killer identified Haywood and two other WFM officials as the planners. The accused were taken to Idaho to stand trial, where they were defended by the labor-friendly Chicago attorney **Clarence Darrow**. On July 28, 1907, Haywood was acquitted, leaving the trial a celebrity.

Following his acquittal, Haywood campaigned for the Socialist Party and for the IWW In 1912 Haywood led the IWW to prominence through a textile strike in Lawrence, Massachusetts, and a strike the following year of silk workers in Paterson, New Jersey. He was elected national secretary-treasurer of the IWW in 1914, and under his administration the union's membership grew among loggers, migratory farm workers, copper miners, and others. Intellectuals and bohemians hailed him as a hero and invited him to their parties. The union had no more than 150,000 workers at its peak in 1917, but about three million workers passed through its ranks, and it influenced many more.

When World War I broke out in Europe in 1914, Haywood and the IWW condemned the conflict as a war for the benefit of the rich at the cost of workingmen's lives.

In an effort to protect the union from patriotic backlash and government crackdown, however, Haywood warned against any agitations likely to antagonize the government. Whereas Samuel Gompers urged his AFL members not to strike at all during the war, Haywood supported strikes for better working conditions, writing to Wobblies in Detroit, "Keep cool [regarding antiwar protests] and confine our agitation to job control." Wobbly strikes in such vital war industries as copper production in the western states provoked a harsh response by the companies and the federal government, which regarded the IWW as a threat to the coordinated mobilization of workers in the war effort (an effort Gompers was leading).

On September 5, 1917, federal agents stormed the IWW's national headquarters in Chicago and the offices of smaller locals and hauled away five tons of files, literature, and furniture. The agents returned for a second sweep on September 28 and arrested some 200 Wobbly leaders, including Haywood, charging them with various violations of the 1917 Espionage Act, such as conspiracy to obstruct the draft. The trial, from April to August 1918, foreshadowed the Red Scare—a fear that communism had spread from Russia to the United States—that would grip the nation from 1919 to 1920. After four months of testimony, the jury took only a few hours to find all the defendants guilty. Haywood's sentence was a $20,000 fine and 20 years in jail.

He was released pending an appeal and slipped out of the United States in disguise on March 31, 1921, on a ship bound for Russia. He was warmly welcomed by the Soviets, but he was not given any position of authority in the new government. In Russia, he made several speaking tours and worked on his autobiography *Bill Haywood's Book* (1929). He suffered a paralytic stroke in March 1928 and died two months later. Soviet officials buried a portion of his ashes in the Kremlin Wall.

Haywood missed the Roaring Twenties in the United States, where he might well have felt useless and out of place, as union membership dropped during that decade. But the "Coolidge prosperity" left many workers behind. Although he was hated and feared by business and government, Haywood laid much of the groundwork for the collective bargaining that would defend and expand workers' rights and inspire millions who felt ignored by the mainstream labor unions.

Mark LaFlaur

For Further Reading
Carlson, Peter. *Roughneck: The Life and Times of Big Bill Haywood.* New York: W. W. Norton, 1983.
Dubofsky, Melvyn. *"Big Bill" Haywood.* New York: St. Martin's Press, 1987.
Haywood, William D. *Bill Haywood's Book: The Autobiography of William D. Haywood.* 1929. Reprint, Westport, Conn.: Greenwood Press, 1983.

"Is Colorado In America?" (c. 1900s)

A union poster designed by Haywood in the early 1900s, protesting the violations of federal law by government officials and others seeking to crush the workers' unions in Colorado.

Note: Original image has been cropped.

Source: Idaho State Historical Society.

PREAMBLE TO THE 1908 CONSTITUTION OF THE IWW (1908)

The Preamble to the 1908 Constitution of the Industrial Workers of the World was printed in the Industral Union Bulletin—the organizational bulletin of the IWW—on November 7, 1908.

Source: Dubofsky, Melvyn. *"Big Bill" Haywood.* New York: St. Martin's Press, 1987.

The working class and the employing class have nothing in common. There can be no peace as long as hunger and want are found among millions of working people and the few, who make up the employing class, have all the good things in life.

Between these two classes a struggle must go on until the workers of the world organize as a class, take possession of the earth and the machinery of production, and abolish the wage system.

We find that the centering of the management of industries into fewer and fewer hands makes the trade unions unable to cope with the ever growing power of the employing class. The trade unions foster a state of affairs which allows one set of workers to be pitted against another set of workers in the same industry, thereby helping to defeat one another in wage wars. Moreover, the trade unions aid the employing class to mislead the workers into the belief that the working class have interests in common with their employers.

These conditions can be changed and the interest of the working class upheld only by an organization formed in such a way that all its members in any one industry, or in all industries if necessary, cease work whenever a strike or lockout is on in any department thereof, thus making an injury to one an injury to all.

Instead of the conservative motto, "A fair day's wage for a fair day's work", we must inscribe on our banner the revolutionary watchword, "Abolition of the wage system".

It is the historic mission of the working class to do away with capitalism. The army of production must be organized, not only for the every-day struggle with capitalists, but also to carry on production when capitalism shall have been overthrown. By organizing industrially we are forming the structure of the new society within the shell of the old.

POSTER FOR THE PAGEANT OF THE PATERSON STRIKE (1913)

A poster for the Paterson Strike Pageant, a reenactment of scenes from the violent confrontation between mill owners and factory workers in Paterson, New Jersey, in 1913. The Pageant was the idea of Greenwich Village writers and artists sympathetic to the workers and friendly with Haywood.

Source: Robert Wagner Labor Archives, New York University, New York.

OPENING STATEMENT AT THE TRIAL OF HAYWOOD AND OTHERS by George Vanderveer (1918) [EXCERPT]

This case is unusual. It is supposed to be a case against William D. Haywood, James P. Thompson, John Foss, and a great number of other men whom you never heard of before, but—it is a charge of "conspiracy" wherein the prosecution claims these defendants have conspired to violate certain laws of the United States and for which alleged crime the prosecution here purposes to send these defendants to prison. Yet in reality, it is the purpose of the prosecution to destroy the organization with which these men are connected and to break the ideal for which their organization stands.

You are told that this case is of great importance to the nation; yet it involves more than the nation—it involves the whole social order. There are five counts in the indictment which recites numerous "overt acts" supposedly committed in furtherance of the "conspiracy"; one of these acts is the circulation of the Preamble of the I.W.W. Constitution; and an editorial stating that "the present industrial system is useless and we mean to destroy it." It is the function of the defense to explain this to you. We want you to notice especially that the purpose of this organization is not to destroy government but to control industry—two things which ought to be separated.

It is manifestly impossible for me, gentlemen, within the limit of time allotted to me to attempt it—to tell you all that these hundred or more defendants have said or done, and all that they have had in their minds.

They classify themselves, however, into two classes. Some have had something to do with strikes—not unlawful as such—and which become unlawful only when accompanied by a certain sinister, unlawful purpose which is attributed to them in these various counts of the indictment.

Some of these men, again, have had no direct connection with any strike, but they have engaged during the period of supposed conspiracy in organizing men on various jobs—or have gone out as lecturers, or have carried the gospel of the organization in whatever manner to the workers.

I am not clear, in my own mind, upon what theory counsel seeks to hold here men who have had nothing to do with strikes, men who have had nothing to do with war activities. It may be counsel's contention that their activities as members became unlawful by reason of the unlawful character of the organization. Again the question whether or not it is lawful or unlawful in its character must be determined by its purpose.

Now, in every issue of *Solidarity*, about which you have heard a great deal here—on top of the front page you will find these words: "Education—Organization—Emancipation." What do they mean? What do they mean standing alone or taken in connection with other things which you will find stated as part of the philosophy of the organization?

For instance, what do they mean in connection with the statement that the two classes in our society have nothing in common, the working class and the employing class?

I want to state to you what these men have said, what they have done, and what their intention has been in doing these things.

His Honor has struck out my reference to the Industrial Relations Commission Report. I do not want to repeat. You will remember—how the vast majority of our common laborers in the basic industries from which this organization recruits its membership, are unable to earn the barest living for themselves and their families. It has been the function of these men to tell these facts to the working people, in order that, understanding their conditions, and the causes of their conditions, they may more intelligently and efficiently go out and find and apply the remedy. It is a sad commentary on our system that 79 per cent of the heads of our working class families are utterly unable to support their families and educate their children on a plane of civic decency. Nobody can right the wrongs of the past. All we can do is to concern ourselves with the future and prevent, if possible, further development and growth of a system which brings these things about. . . .Why political action? This thing was not reared by law. It grew because some men by combining in trusts and corporations within industry got power to exploit labor. And it will quit growing just as soon as labor organizes and gets the power to stop its being exploited. "But you use sabotage," says counsel. Yet out of the thousands of lumber mills in Washington, he brings only two which had saws broken by something not proven and a few threshing machines out of hundreds testified about here by witnesses. We will bring witnesses—not the kind you have seen here, I hope—but reputable farmers, who have been dealing with the I.W.W. for years in the places best organized by it, who will tell you they never had better workers than the I.W.W. . . .

An excerpt from the opening statement by chief defense attorney George Vanderveer at the 1918 trial of Haywood and a large number of other Wobblies arrested on charges of violating the 1917 Espionage Act—in particular, conspiring to obstruct the draft. All defendants would be found guilty. Rather than serving time in a federal penitentiary, Haywood would jump bail and immigrate to the Soviet Union.

Source: Haywood, William D. *Bill Haywood's Book: The Autobiography of William D. Haywood.* 1929. Reprint, Westport, Conn.: Greenwood Press, 1983.

William Randolph Hearst

1863–1951
Newspaper Publisher
and Politician

William Randolph Hearst was by far the most powerful—and most hated—newspaper publisher of the early twentieth century. During World War I he was vilified as a "spokesman for the Kaiser" because of his anti-British stance and calls for nonintervention. Hearst was born in San Francisco on April 29, 1863, the son of George Hearst, a wealthy mine developer (and later a U.S. senator), and Phoebe Apperson Hearst, one of the greatest philanthropists in California history. He briefly attended St. Paul's School in New Hampshire and Harvard College (1882–85), but was expelled from both for mischievous behavior.

After Harvard, Hearst briefly served an internship on Joseph Pulitzer's *New York World*, which he greatly admired, and there he learned the ins and outs of publicity and sensation journalism. Only 23 when he took charge of his father's San Francisco *Examiner*, he quickly made it a commercial success. With millions to spend, he moved to New York City in 1895 and acquired the *New York Morning Journal*. He reduced its price to a penny per copy, forcing Pulitzer to follow suit, and hired away Pulitzer's talent by offering doubled salaries. The term "yellow journalism" came to describe the papers' jostling, screaming approach to increasing circulation (and was also a reference to publishers' tug-of-war over the cartoonist who invented the comic strip character the *Yellow Kid)*. The Hearst papers, explained one of their editors, sought to arouse "the gee-whiz emotion" with their lurid headlines ("Nailed Her Father's Head to the Front Door"), breathless copy, liberal use of illustrations, and casual disregard for accuracy. The papers were also liberal politically: in the early decades of his career, despite his family's wealth, Hearst sympathized with the poor, with laborers, the woman suffrage movement, and other progressive causes.

In the late 1890s, when Cuba was struggling for independence from Spain, Hearst sent reporters and artists to document alleged Spanish atrocities against Cuban revolutionaries. When artist Frederic Remington cabled his boss that Cuba was quiet and requested permission to return,

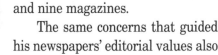

From the collections of the Library of Congress.

Hearst cabled back, PLEASE REMAIN. YOU FURNISH THE PICTURES AND I'LL FURNISH THE WAR. He exploited the explosion of the USS *Maine* in Havana harbor in 1898 to goad the nation into war with Spain. During the height of the Spanish-American War, Hearst sold more than a million copies of the *Journal* per day.

Hearst's publishing empire expanded rapidly, and he was the "Chief" (as he liked to be called) of a far-reaching media empire even before World War I. Already owning newspapers in San Francisco, New York, and Chicago, he bought papers in Boston, Los Angeles, Atlanta, and San Francisco. He expanded into magazine publishing, purchasing *Motor, Cosmopolitan, Good Housekeeping,* and *Harper's Bazaar.* He founded the highly profitable King Features Syndicate and the International News Service in 1910, and started a newsreel company in 1913. By 1919 he owned 13 newspapers and six magazines; at its height the Hearst empire comprised 18 newspapers in 12 cities and nine magazines.

The same concerns that guided his newspapers' editorial values also drove Hearst to seek political office: sympathy for labor and support of woman suffrage, the income tax, and government regulation of railroads and other major corporations. In 1902 he was elected to the first of two terms as U.S. representative from New York City, but he failed in his bids for mayor (1905, 1909) and governor of New York (1906), losses that quashed his hopes for the presidency.

Already shunned by polite society and detested by civic leaders (*Harper's Weekly* ridiculed him as the "Wizard of Ooze"), Hearst became the most detested public figure in America during World War I because of his papers' many articles critical of Great Britain and sympathetic to Germany. Once the United States declared war, however, Hearst gradually tempered his papers' anti-British tone and began printing little American flags atop every front page.

In 1919, with an inheritance estimated at about $20 million following the death of his mother, Hearst plunged enthusiastically into the burgeoning movie business, motivated by his burning ambition that his mistress, Marion Cecilia Davies, should become America's greatest movie star. When they met in 1917, Davies, at least 30 years his junior, was a showgirl in the Ziegfeld Follies in New York, and he was a married father of five. Hearst began producing a series of films in which Miss Davies could star, such as *Cecilia of the Pink Roses* (1918) and *When Knighthood Was in Flower* (1922). Hearst spared no expense: in 1922, when an "expensive" film cost about $100,000 to make, production costs for *Knighthood* were around $1.5 million. The *Journal* and other Hearst papers built up Davies's films with elaborate advertisements and praised her performances with gushing reviews. The *Journal's* critic wrote of *Knighthood*, "Nothing previously done in motion pictures can compare with this perfect photoplay. . . ." The public, however, was not deceived. Though she was attractive, she was not a great talent.

While Hearst was expanding his involvement in the motion picture business in the 1920s, he hired architect Julia Morgan to design a palace, La Casa Grande, at San Simeon, his 375-acre family estate on the California coast. La Casa Grande became one of the repositories of Hearst's always-expanding collection of art and antiquities, and served as the model for Xanadu in *Citizen Kane* (1941), Orson Welles's famous film based on the life of Hearst. The Chief's reaction to the film was fury—his papers pretended the film did not exist, and fearful movie magnates would not let their theater chains run it: Paramount, Loew's, and Warner theaters refused the film. Although *Citizen Kane* was a box office flop, it is now regarded by many as the best film ever made.

In 1947, Hearst suffered a heart seizure at the age of 83, and abandoned San Simeon to live with Davies in Los Angeles, increasingly an invalid. He died in 1951 at the age of 88. Hearst pushed American journalism toward sensationalism, but he treated his employees well and was not afraid to take an unpopular position even if it caused a drop in revenue. The growth of tabloid journalism in the late 1910s and 1920s was a natural extension of the brash, pushy style he pioneered, while woman suffrage and other social changes were helped along by his papers' promotion.

Mark LaFlaur

For Further Reading

Nasaw, David. *The Chief: The Life of William Randolph Hearst.* Boston: Houghton Mifflin, 2000.
Robinson, Judith. *The Hearsts: An American Dynasty.* New York: Avon Books, 1992.
Swanberg, W. A. *Citizen Hearst.* New York: Galahad Books, 1996.

"THE BIG TYPE WAR OF THE YELLOW KIDS" POLITICAL CARTOON (1898)

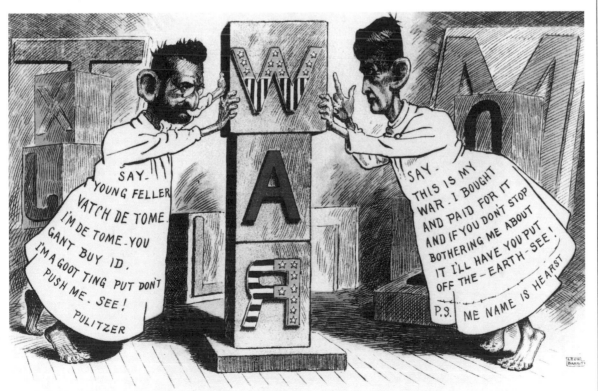

In this 1898 political cartoon by Leon Barritt, Hearst and Joseph Pulitzer are dressed as the comic strip character the Yellow Kid. In part, it was the two publishers' tug-of-war over the cartoonist who created the character that led to the term "yellow journalism."

Source: From the collections of the Library of Congress.

THE BIG TYPE WAR OF THE YELLOW KIDS.

This telegram, wired in February 1917 to Bradford Merrill, editor of the New York American, *included instructions on projecting a pro-American impression (and erasing the public's view of Hearst as pro-German) as the United States approached intervention in World War I.*

Source: Coblentz, Edmond D., ed. *William Randolph Hearst: A Portrait in His Own Words.* New York: Simon & Schuster, 1952.

TELEGRAM FROM WILLIAM RANDOLPH HEARST TO BRADFORD MERRILL (1917)

"For future guidance yourself and Francis, I offer following comment on editorial congratulating Senate on peace endorsement.

"First, there is too little congratulation of Senate and too much partisan anti-Ally statement. The matter is discussed from a foreign viewpoint and not from an American viewpoint.

"Second, the editorial will help Lodge, because New England is violently pro-Ally, and will approve the anti-German pro-Ally attitude of which we accuse him.

"My opinion emphatically is that no editorial taking partisan stand in European conflict should be printed.

"Peace and such questions discussed from purely American viewpoint have united American support, but discussed from a pro-Ally or pro-German standpoint have but small and divided support.

"The attack on Lodge which I suggested for opposing wise and humanitarian peace move of President for party opposition reasons would have been effective. An attack accusing him of pro-Ally sentiment is not effective.

"The vast majority of American people are pro-Ally.

"Print NOTHING BUT PRO-AMERICAN EDITORIALS."

Hearst produced a series of films starring his mistress, actress Marion Davies. In When Knighthood Was in Flower, *Davies (center) stars as Mary Tudor opposite Lyn Harding as King Henry VIII.*

Source: Hulton/ Archive.

STILL FROM *WHEN KNIGHTHOOD WAS IN FLOWER* (1922)

MEMO TO WILLIAM RANDOLPH HEARST'S EDITORS REGARDING EDITORIAL GUIDELINES (1933)

Have a good exclusive news feature as often as possible.

PAY LIBERALLY for big exclusive stuff and encourage tipsters. Get reporters with acquaintance.

When a big story must get in all the papers, try to have notably the best account in your paper.

Try to get scoops in pictures. They are frequently almost as important as news. I don't mean pictures of chorus girls, but pictures of important events.

Make the paper thorough. Print all the news. Get all the news into your office and see that it gets into the paper. Condense it if necessary. Frequently it is better when intelligently condensed BUT GET IT IN.

Get your best news on your first page and get as much as possible on that page. Don't use up your whole first page with a few long stories, but try to get a large number of interesting items in addition to your picture page and your two or three top head stories.

Of course, if your feature is big enough it must get display regardless of everything, but mere display does not make a feature. When you have two features it is frequently better to put one on the first page and one on the third, so as not to overcrowd the first page.

Get important items and personal news about well-known people on the first page, and sometimes condense a big news story to go on the first page rather than make it run longer inside. Make your departments complete and reliable so that the reader will know that he can find a thing in your paper and that he can find it right.

Make a paper for the NICEST KIND OF PEOPLE—for the great middle class. Don't print a lot of dull stuff that they are supposed to like and don't.

Omit things that will offend nice people. Avoid coarseness and slang and a low tone. The most sensational news can be told if it is written properly.

Make the paper helpful and kindly. Don't scold and forever complain and attack in your news columns. Leave that to the editorial page.

Be fair and impartial. Don't make a paper for Democrats or Republicans, or Independent Leaguers. Make a paper for all the people and give unbiased news of ALL CREEDS AND PARTIES. Try to do this in such a conspicuous manner that it will be noticed and commented upon.

PLEASE BE ACCURATE. Compare statements in our paper with those in other papers, and find out which are correct. Discharge reporters and copy readers who are consistently inaccurate.

Don't allow exaggeration. It is a cheap and ineffective substitute for real interest. Reward reporters who can make THE TRUTH interesting, and weed out those who cannot.

Make your headlines clear and concise statements of interesting facts. The headlines of a newspaper should answer the question, "WHAT IS THE NEWS?" Don't allow copy readers to write headlines that are too smart to be intelligible.

Don't' allow long introduction to stories, or involved sentences. Don't repeat unnecessarily. Don't serve up the story in the headlines and then in the introduction and then in the box. Plunge immediately into the interesting part of the story.

Run pretty pictures and interesting layouts, but don't run pictures just to "illuminate the text." If a picture occupies a column of space it should be as interesting as a column of type. Pictures of pretty women and babies are interesting. Photographs of interesting events with explanatory diagrams are valuable. They tell more than the text can, and when carefully and accurately drawn people will study them. . . . Make every picture worth its space.

Please sum up your paper every day and find wherein it is distinctly better than the other papers. If it isn't distinctly better you have missed that day. Lay out plans to make it distinctly better the next day.

If you cannot show conclusively your own paper's superiority, you may be sure the public will never discover it.

A succession of superior papers will surely tell.

When you beat your rivals one day try harder to beat them the next, for success depends upon a complete victory.

This 1933 memo from Hearst to his editors shows the editorial principles on which Hearst had based his publishing empire—in particular, the attention to eye-catching illustrations, appeal to "the great middle class," and generosity of payment for exclusive features.

Source: Grunwald, Lisa, and Stephen J. Adler. *Letters of the Century.* New York: Dial Press, 1999.

Ernest Hemingway

1899–1961
Author

Ernest Hemingway, a larger-than-life adventurer who was one of the most influential writers in the twentieth century, popularized the Lost Generation in the 1920s.

Ernest Miller Hemingway was born in the Chicago suburb of Oak Park, Illinois, on July 21, 1899. He grew up in a prosperous middle class family, the second of six children, and spent pleasant summers at a lakeside camp near Petoskey, Michigan, where he developed a lifelong love for the outdoors. His childhood hero was Theodore Roosevelt, the robust, game-hunting adventurer-president. After high school in 1917 Hemingway became a reporter for the Kansas City *Star*. Poor eyesight made him ineligible for the army, so in World War I he volunteered to drive ambulances for the Red Cross on the Italian front. In July 1918 he was severely wounded in the legs and feet by an Austrian trench mortar, but though he was hurt, he carried a dying comrade to the rear. He was awarded the Silver Medal for Military Valor by the Italian government, and for a half year he was bedridden in hospitals in Italy recovering from injuries. He returned to the United States in January 1919 and began writing serious fiction and feature articles for the Toronto *Star*, but yearned to go back to Italy. In Chicago in 1921 he met Elizabeth Hadley Richardson, his first wife. There he also met the author Sherwood Anderson, who advised him to go to Paris, not Italy. Hemingway and Hadley (as she was known) married in September 1921 and several months later they sailed for Europe.

Following World War I many American writers and artists settled in Paris, long a cosmopolitan gathering place for artists from all over Europe. Although France was terribly scarred by the war, the exchange rate was good (inflation in the United States reduced the value of the dollar) and the cultural atmosphere in Paris was an easygoing contrast to that of the more puritanical United States. Having discovered European culture, many former servicemen found America provincial; further, the Eighteenth Amendment's prohibition of alcohol and the repression of

From the collections of the Library of Congress.

political dissidents that culminated in the Red Scare of 1919–20—caused by the government's fear that communism had spread from Russia to the United States—made many veterans disillusioned with the homeland whose ideals of liberty and democracy they had fought to defend.

During a 20-month period between 1922 and 1923, Hemingway filed some 88 stories as a foreign correspondent for the Toronto *Star*. He was sent to Italy to cover the Genoa Economic Conference in April 1922 and to Constantinople (now Istanbul) to cover the Greco-Turkish War (Sept.–Oct. 1922). He attended the Lausanne Peace Conference (Nov.–Dec. 1922), and in early 1923 he covered the French military occupation of Germany's Ruhr valley.

Hemingway's work as a reporter constituted a sort of crash course in politics, as he was called upon to write articles about fascists, anarchists, anti-Semitism, disarmament, and German inflation. He saw at close range many of the political leaders of the time, including Georges Clemenceau of France and Great Britain's David Lloyd George, and went to Milan to interview the fascist dictator Benito Mussolini, "the biggest bluff in Europe." Between assignments, he wrote short stories, including "Up in Michigan" and "My Old Man," and enjoyed vacations with Hadley in Switzerland and a walking tour with Ezra Pound in Italy.

Around 1924 Pound urged him to help the British novelist Ford Madox Ford with the editing of Ford's new *Transatlantic Review*. Through this position as a columnist and unpaid assistant to Ford, Hemingway got to know practically every expatriate writer in Paris, and also saw a few of his stories published in the *Transatlantic*. While attending **Gertrude Stein**'s salon and visiting Sylvia Beach's bookshop, Shakespeare and Co., he became acquainted with James Joyce, André Gide, and most of the writers and artists in Paris. He became friends with **F. Scott Fitzgerald**; in 1924 Fitzgerald wrote to his editor at Scribner's, Maxwell Perkins, recommending Hemingway as "the real thing," a writer with a "brilliant future."

A collection of his stories, *In Our Time*, was published in Paris in 1924 and in the United States in 1925, but Hemingway's breakthrough came with Scribner's publication of his first novel, *The Sun Also Rises*, in 1926. *The Sun Also Rises* concerns a circle of cynical, aimless friends in Paris, focusing primarily on the unconsummated love between a jaded young American named Jake Barnes and Lady Brett Ashley, an Englishwoman. Jake had expected the war to transform him from youth to manhood, but instead he was made impotent by a wound in his groin—not a very subtle symbol, but typical of Hemingway's life-long concern with virility and masculinity. Readers were thrilled not only by the novel's evocative scenes—featuring bullfights in Spain—but by the terse, no-nonsense style and the unsentimental, hard-boiled dialogue: no flowery prose or unnecessary adjectives, as though the novel were a newspaperman's cablegram.

It was in *The Sun Also Rises* that Hemingway used as one of his epigraphs a sentence spoken to him by Gertrude Stein, "You are all a lost generation." In *Exile's Return*, critic Malcolm Cowley explains that the generation—those born around 1900—was "lost because its training had prepared it for another world than existed after the war. . . . they were seceding from the old and yet could adhere to nothing new."

Hemingway's first marriage ended in divorce in 1927; in the settlement he gave Hadley lifelong rights to all income from *The Sun Also Rises*. That year he married Pauline Pfeiffer in Paris. Their first child was born in Key West, Florida, where Hemingway finished his second novel, *A Farewell to Arms* (1929), about a love affair between a wounded soldier and a nurse during World War I in Italy. In this novel, as well as in *The Sun Also Rises*, the Hemingway hero bears his wounds with a stoic's fortitude, aided by savoring life's passing pleasures. "If people bring so much courage to this world," says *Farewell*'s narrator Frederic Henry, "the world has to kill them to break them, so of course it kills them. . . . It kills the very good and the very gentle and the very brave impartially."

Hemingway's depictions of the war and his narrator's expressions of disgust and weariness are among twentieth-century literature's finest accounts of human suffering and endurance. A passage from *A Farewell to Arms* makes clear why Hemingway wrote in a spare style, and why his language appealed to readers: "[In the war] I had seen nothing sacred, and the things that were glorious had no glory and the sacrifices were like the stockyards at Chicago if nothing was done with the meat except to bury it. . . . Abstract words such as glory, honor, courage, or hallow were obscene beside the concrete names of villages, the numbers of roads, the names of rivers. . . ." His bare-knuckled style satisfied the appetite of readers, disillusioned by the contrast between noble-sounding slogans and the grim realities of war, for straight writing about tangible things.

Hemingway returned to the United States in 1930, living mostly in Key West, but over the next 30 years he also lived in Cuba and in Idaho. He wrote many novels and stories over the next several decades, often concerning characters engaged (like the author) in bullfighting in Spain and hunting big game in Africa, and many of which, such as *To Have and Have Not* (1937), were made into popular movies. Ever eager to grab hold of life and prove his strength, he worked as a war correspondent during the Spanish Civil War in 1936, which was the source of his 1940 novel *For Whom the Bell Tolls*. During World War II he reported on the D-Day landing at Normandy and was among the first to enter Paris with Allied troops in 1944; he claimed to have "liberated the Ritz" hotel, whose bar was a favorite Lost Generation watering hole. Although in the 1940s and 1950s many critics claimed that Hemingway was "written out," in 1952 he published one of his finest and most popular books, *The Old Man and the Sea*. The following year he won a Pulitzer Prize, and in 1954 he was awarded the Nobel Prize for Literature "for his powerful, style-forming mastery of the art of modern narration." Plagued by depression in his later years, Hemingway committed suicide in Ketchum, Idaho, on July 2, 1961.

When he died, writers around the world praised him as one of the most influential writers of the century, to be ranked with Joyce, William Butler Yeats, and Marcel Proust. Dramatist Tennessee Williams observed that Hemingway "knew that an artist's work, the heart of it, is finally himself and his life, and he accomplished . . . the embodiment of what his work meant on its highest and most honest level." While his friend and competitor F. Scott Fitzgerald evoked the glamour and the turbulence of the Jazz Age, Ernest Hemingway depicted the numbed nihilists of the Lost Generation, the "walking wounded" survivors of the modern age.

Mark LaFlaur

For Further Reading
Baker, Carlos. *Ernest Hemingway: A Life Story*. New York: Bantam Books, 1970.
Cowley, Malcolm. *Exile's Return: A Literary Odyssey of the 1920s*. New York: Viking Press, 1973.
———. *A Second Flowering: Works and Days of the Lost Generation*. New York: Penguin Books, 1980.
Hemingway, Ernest. *A Moveable Feast*. New York: Scribner Classics, 1996.
Reynolds, Michael. *Hemingway: The Paris Years*. New York: W. W. Norton, 1999.

ERNEST HEMINGWAY'S PASSPORT PHOTO (1923)

The photograph used by Hemingway in his 1923 passport. Though he soon grew a mustache, this is how he looked while he was working as a European correspondent for the Toronto Star *and writing the short stories "Up in Michigan" and "My Old Man."*

Source: John Fitzgerald Kennedy Library, Boston, Massachusetts.

THE SUN ALSO RISES (1926) by Ernest Hemingway [EXCERPT]

A passage from The Sun Also Rises *in which the narrator, Jake Barnes, grieves over his war wound before and after a visit from his friend Lady Brett Ashley.*

Source: Hemingway, Ernest. *The Sun Also Rises*. New York: Scribner's Sons, 1926.

. . .I lit the lamp beside the bed, turned off the gas, and opened the wide windows. The bed was far back from the windows, and I sat with the windows open and undressed by the bed. Outside a night train, running on the street-car tracks, went by carrying vegetables to the markets. They were noisy at night when you could not sleep. Undressing, I looked at myself in the mirror of the big armoire beside the bed. That was a typically French way to furnish a room. Practical, too, I suppose. Of all the ways to be wounded. I supposed it was funny. I put on my pajamas and got into bed. I had the two bull-fight papers, and I took their wrappers off. One was orange. The other yellow. They would both have the same news, so whichever I read first would spoil the other. *Le Toril* was the better paper, so I started to read it. I read it all the way through, including the Petite Correspondance and the Cornigrams. I blew out the lamp. Perhaps I would be able to sleep.

My head started to work. The old grievance. Well, it was a rotten way to be wounded and flying on a joke front like the Italian. In the Italian hospital we were going to form a society. It had a funny name in Italian. I wonder what became of the others, the Italians. That was in the Ospedale Maggiore in Milano, Padiglione Ponte. The next building was the Padiglione Zonda. There was a statue of Ponte, or maybe it was Zonda. That was where the liaison colonel came to visit me. That was funny. That was about the first funny thing. I was all bandaged up. But they had told him about it. Then he made that wonderful speech: "You, a foreigner,

an Englishman" (any foreigner was an Englishman) "have given more than your life." What a speech! I would like to have it illuminated to hang in the office. He never laughed. He was putting himself in my place, I guess. "Che mala fortuna! Che mala fortuna!"

I never used to realize it, I guess. I try and play it along and just not make trouble for people. Probably I never would have had any trouble if I hadn't run into Brett when they shipped me to England. I suppose she only wanted what she couldn't have. Well, people were that way. To hell with people. The Catholic Church had an awfully good way of handling all that. Good advice, anyway. Not to think about it. Oh, it was swell advice. Try and take it sometime. Try and take it.

I lay awake thinking and my mind jumping around. Then I couldn't keep away from it, and I started to think about Brett and all the rest of it went away. I was thinking about Brett and my mind stopped jumping around and started to go in sort of smooth waves. Then all of a sudden I started to cry. Then after a while it was better and I lay in bed and listened to the heavy trams go by and way down the street, and then I went to sleep.

I woke up. There was a row going on outside. I listened and I thought I recognized a voice. I put on a dressing gown and went to the door. The concierge was talking down-stairs. She was very angry. I heard my name and called down the stairs.

"Is that you, Monsieur Barnes?" the concierge called.

"Yes. It's me."

"There's a species of woman here who's waked the whole street up. What kind of a dirty business at this time of night! She says she must see you. I've told her you're asleep."

Then I heard Brett's voice. Half asleep I had been sure it was Georgette. I don't know why. She could not have known my address.

"Will you send her up, please?"

Brett came up the stairs. I saw she was quite drunk. "Silly thing to do," she said. "Make an awful row. I say, you weren't asleep, were you?"

"What did you think I was doing?"

"Don't know. What time is it?"

I looked at the clock. It was half-past four. "Had no idea what hour it was," Brett said. "I say, can a chap sit down? Don't be cross, darling. Just left the count. He brought me here."...

"I'd better go now."

"Why?"

"Just wanted to see you. Damned silly idea. Want to get dressed and come down? He's got the car just up the street."

"The count?"

"Himself. And a chauffeur in livery. Going to drive me around and have breakfast in the Bois. Hampers. Got it all at Zelli's. Dozen bottles of Mumms. Tempt you?"

"I have to work in the morning," I said. "I'm too far behind you now to catch up and be any fun."

" Don't be an ass."

"Can't do it."

"Right. Send him a tender message?"

"Anything. Absolutely."

" Good night, darling."

"Don't be sentimental."

"You make me ill."

We kissed good night and Brett shivered. "I'd better go," she said. "Good night, darling."

"You don't have to go."

"Yes."

We kissed again on the stairs and as I called for the cordon the concierge muttered something behind her door. I went back upstairs and from the open window watched Brett walking up the street to the big limousine drawn up to the curb under the arc-light. She got in and it started off. I turned around. On the table was an empty glass and a glass half-full of brandy and soda. I took them both out to the kitchen and poured the half-full glass down the sink. I turned off the gas in the dining-room, kicked off my slippers sitting on the bed, and got into bed. This was Brett, that I had felt like crying about. Then I thought of her walking up the street and stepping into the car, as I had last seen her, and of course in a little while I felt like hell again. It is awfully easy to be hard-boiled about everything in the daytime, but at night it is another thing. . . .

"A BOOK OF GREAT SHORT STORIES (*MEN WITHOUT WOMEN* BY ERNEST HEMINGWAY)" by Dorothy Parker (October 29, 1927)

Ernest Hemingway wrote a novel called *The Sun Also Rises*. Promptly upon its publication, Ernest Hemingway was discovered, the Stars and Stripes were reverentially raised over him, eight hundred and forty-seven book reviewers formed themselves into the word "welcome," and the band played "Hail to the Chief" in three concurrent keys. All of which, I should think, might have made Ernest Hemingway pretty reasonably sick.

For, a year or so before *The Sun Also Rises*, he had published *In Our Time*, a collection of short pieces. The book caused about as much stir in literary circles as an incompleted dogfight on upper Riverside Drive. True, there were a few that went about quick and stirred with admiration for this clean, exciting prose, but most of the reviewers dismissed the volume with a tolerant smile and the word "stark." It was Mr. Mencken who slapped it down with "sketches in the bold, bad manner of the Café du Dôme," and the smaller boys, in their manner, took similar pokes at it. Well, you see, Ernest Hemingway was a young American living on the left back of the Seine in Paris, France; he had been seen at the Dôme and the Rotonde and the Select and the Closerie des Lilas. He knew Pound, Joyce, and Gertrude Stein. There is something a little — well, a little *you-know* — in all of those things. You wouldn't catch Bruce Barton or Mary Roberts Rinehart doing them. No, sir.

And besides, *In Our Time* was a book of short stories. That's no way to start off. People don't like that;

they feel cheated. Any bookseller will be glad to tell you, in his interesting *argot*, that "short stories don't go." People take up a book of short stories and say, "Oh, what's this? Just a lot of these short things?" and put it right down again. Only yesterday afternoon, at four o'clock sharp, I saw and heard a woman do that to Ernest Hemingway's new book, *Men Without Women*. She had been one of those most excited about his novel.

Literature, it appears, is here measured by a yard-stick. As soon as *The Sun Also Rises* came out, Ernest Hemingway was the white-haired boy. He was praised, adored, analyzed, best-sold, argued about, and banned in Boston; all the trimmings were accorded him. People got into feuds about whether or not his story was worth the telling. (You see this silver scar left by a bullet, right up here under my hair? I got that the night I said that any well-told story was worth the telling. An eighth of an inch nearer the temple, and I wouldn't be sitting here doing this sort of tripe.) They affirmed, and passionately, that the dissolute expatriates in this novel of "a lost generation" were not worth bothering about; and then they devoted most of their time to discussing them. There was a time, and it went on for weeks, when you could go nowhere without hearing of *The Sun Also Rises*. Some thought it without excuse; and some, they of the cool, tall foreheads, called it the greatest American novel, tossing *Huckleberry Finn* and *The Scarlet Letter* lightly out

Dorothy Parker, The New Yorker's *anonymous book critic who signed her reviews "The Constant Reader," praised Hemingway's new short story collection* Men Without Women *when it appeared in 1927. In this review she explains why she greatly preferred Hemingway's short stories to his novels.*

Source: Parker, Dorothy. *The Portable Dorothy Parker.* Introduction by Brendan Gill. New York: Viking Press, 1980.

the window. They hated it or they revered it. I may say, with due respect to Mr. Hemingway, that I was never so sick of a book in my life.

Now *The Sun Also Rises* was as "starkly" written as Mr. Hemingway's short stories; it dealt with subjects as "unpleasant." Why it should have been taken to the slightly damp bosom of the public while the (as it seems to me) superb *In Our Time* should have been disregarded will always be a puzzle to me. As I see it — I knew this conversation would get back to me sooner or later, preferably sooner — Mr. Hemingway's style, this prose stripped to its firm young bones, is far more effective, far more moving, in the short story than in the novel. He is, to me, the greatest living writer of short stories; he is, also to me, not the greatest living novelist.

After all the high screaming about *The Sun Also Rises*, I feared for Mr. Hemingway's next book. You know how it is — as soon as they all start acclaiming a writer, that writer is just about to slip downward. The littler critics circle like literary buzzards above only the sick lions.

So it is a warm gratification to find the new Hemingway book, *Men Without Women,* a truly magnificent work. It is composed of thirteen short stories, most of which have been published before. They are sad and terrible stories; the author's enormous appetite for life seems to have been somehow appeased. You find here little of that peaceful ecstasy that marked the camping

trip in *The Sun Also Rises* and the lone fisherman's days in "Big Two-Hearted River" in *In Our Time*. The stories include "The Killers," which seems to me one of the four great American short stories. (All you have to do is drop the nearest hat, and I'll tell you what I think the others are. They are Wilbur Daniel Steele's "Blue Murder," Sherwood Anderson's "I'm a Fool," and Ring Lardner's "Some Like Them Cold," that story which seems to me as shrewd a picture of every woman at some time as is Chekhov's "The Darling." Now what do *you* like best?) The book also includes "Fifty Grand," "In Another Country," and the delicate and tragic "Hills like White Elephants." I do not know where a greater collection of stories can be found.

Ford Madox Ford has said of this author, "Hemingway writes like an angel." I take issue (there is nothing better for that morning headache than taking a little issue.) Hemingway writes like a human being. I think it is impossible for him to write of any event at which he has not been present; his is, then, a reportorial talent, just as Sinclair Lewis's is. But, or so I think, Lewis remains a reporter and Hemingway stands a genius because Hemingway has an unerring sense of selection. He discards details with a magnificent lavishness; he keeps his words to their short path. His is, as any reader knows, a dangerous influence. The simple thing he does looks so easy to do. But look at the boys who try to do it.

Dust jacket of the ninth edition of The Sun Also Rises, *published by Scribner's in 1929.*

Source: Culver Pictures.

DUST JACKET OF *THE SUN ALSO RISES* (1929)

Oliver Wendell, Jr. Holmes

Supreme Court Justice Oliver Wendell Holmes, Jr., known as "the Great Dissenter" for his forceful and eloquent defenses of judicial restraint and freedom of speech, was the most influential (and most often quoted) justice of the twentieth century.

The son of the famous physician, poet, and essayist Oliver Wendell Holmes, Sr., Holmes, Jr., was born in Boston on March 8, 1841. He attended private schools and Harvard College (1857–61), then served three years in the Twentieth Massachusetts Volunteer Infantry in the Civil War. He attended Harvard Law School (1864–66), traveled extensively in Britain and Europe, and returned to Boston in 1867 to begin a career in law. He wrote articles, edited the *American Law Review* (1870–73), and lectured at Harvard and the Lowell Institute in Boston. In 1872 he married Fanny Bowditch Dixwell.

Holmes had a penetrating intellect that he used to address legal matters such as the extent to which the practice of law and judicial decisions arise from reason or from the unconscious. He systematized his ideas into "a connected treatise" he published as *The Common Law* (1881), which became a classic in the field. "The life of the law," he wrote, "has not been logic: it has been experience.... The law embodies the story of a nation's development through many centuries, and it cannot be dealt with as if it contained only the axioms and corollaries of a book of mathematics."

Through the efforts of **Louis Brandeis**, a future fellow justice, a chair was established for Holmes at the Harvard Law School in January 1882. At the end of the year he was appointed to the Supreme Judicial Court of Massachusetts. In the 20 years he served on the state supreme court, Holmes wrote some 1,300 opinions. He became chief justice in 1899.

Holmes was 61 in 1902 when President Theodore Roosevelt appointed him to the United States Supreme Court. He served nearly 30 years on the Supreme Court, under four chief justices, and wrote 873 opinions, more than

From the collections of the Library of Congress.

any other justice in the Court's history. Although he came to be known as the Great Dissenter, it was not because he was always disagreeing with his fellow justices; in fact, he wrote fewer dissents than many other justices. Rather, Holmes's reputation as a dissenter was based on the blunt and forceful language of his opinions and the fact that many of his dissents, particularly in constitutional cases, became the core arguments for majority opinions in later generations.

Holmes often dissented in favor of anarchists, socialists, and other defendants with unpopular views when he believed they had been prosecuted not for their actions but for their ideas. His most controversial and historically significant opinions concerned the First Amendment's guarantee of freedom of speech. After the United States declared war on Germany in April 1917, Congress enacted a series of laws to limit antiwar protests, such as the Espionage Act of 1917, which made it a federal offense to obstruct recruitment or enlistment or otherwise advocate resistance to the war effort. The Sedition Act of 1918 was designed to silence anarchists, pacifists, and other "trouble-makers." As a result, thousands of people were prosecuted and imprisoned for opposing mobilization or for interfering with war production.

In the 1919 case *Schenck* v. *United States*, a high official in the Socialist Party of America was prosecuted under the Espionage Act for having urged resistance to the draft. Holmes upheld the conviction, and rejected Schenck's claims of protection under the First Amendment:

> ... the character of every act depends upon the circumstances in which it is done. The most stringent protection of free speech would not protect a man in falsely shouting fire in a theatre and causing a panic.... The question in every case is whether the words used are used in such circumstances and are of such a nature as to create a clear and present danger that they will bring about the substantive evils that Congress has a right to prevent.

Holmes made this first articulation of the "clear and present danger" test in a context in which the speech itself was not illegal; rather, Schenck's leaflet advocated the commission of an illegal act: the refusal to obey federal draft laws. In the *Schenck* decision the court was unanimous. Insisting that the freedom of speech was not absolute, Holmes wrote: "When a nation is at war, many things that might be said in time of peace are such a hindrance to its effort that their utterance will not be endured so long as men fight and that no Court could regard them as protected by any constitutional right." Holmes applied the same standard in upholding a series of such decisions, including the conviction of Socialist leader **Eugene V. Debs** for an antiwar speech that implicitly urged noncompliance with the draft.

The "clear and present danger" rule was used for many years by lower courts to uphold convictions, a trend that Holmes criticized as rigid and one-sided: he insisted that each case must be decided on its own merits, its own circumstances. It was one thing to prosecute draft resisters, but he particularly objected to the government's broadening of its prosecutorial powers to clamp down on political dissidents.

Nine months after *Schenck*, in *Abrams* v. *United States* (1919), the Court upheld an Espionage Act conviction in a similar case, but Holmes and Justice Brandeis dissented. Defendant Jacob Abrams and others had distributed leaflets urging workers in ammunition factories to strike to protest American intervention in the Russian revolution. The Espionage Act pertained to the war against Germany, not to an American expeditionary force's deployment to Siberia, thus Holmes saw no clear and present danger posed by Abrams's leaflets. Holmes went on to argue that free speech served a public good and that to restrict speech, however unpopular the ideas expressed, would be more harmful to the nation than allowing it to be heard: "the best test of truth is the power of the thought to get itself accepted in the competition of the market."

Although Holmes increasingly ruled, and dissented, in favor of individuals' rights and against the machinery of the state, he was a conservative justice. Rather than judi-

cial activism, or "legislating from the bench," Holmes preferred to exercise judicial restraint, whereby a justice (or judge) limits interpretation to the particular point of law in question and defers to the policy making power of the legislative or executive branches of government. He supported Prohibition and antitrust legislation, for example, even though he believed that "legislation to make people better" was futile. At the same time, Holmes did not believe in "delegislating" from the bench: the judicial attempts to undo legislation simply on the basis of political disagreement.

After nearly 30 years of service on the Supreme Court, Holmes retired from the Court in 1932, shortly before his ninety-first birthday. His fellow justices, whom he called his "brethren," wrote him a letter, which they all signed, reading in part: "Your profound learning and philosophic outlook have found expression in opinions which have become classic, enriching the literature of the law as well as its substance." He died on March 6, 1935, in Washington, D.C., and was buried two days later, on what would have been his ninety-fourth birthday.

In an era of the Red Scare and increasing police power, Holmes steadfastly argued for the protection of free speech and against the use of illegal methods by law enforcement agencies. As the power of corporations grew and workers' rights diminished in the 1920s, Holmes (at least in his dissenting opinions) was often a bulwark against judicial erosions of protections for labor. Chief Justice William H. Taft called Holmes the court's "most brilliant and learned member," and biographer and fellow Justice Felix Frankfurter has written that Justice Benjamin N. Cardozo "deemed [Holmes] probably the greatest legal intellect in the history of the English-speaking judiciary."

Mark LaFlaur

For Further Reading

Baker, Liva. *The Justice from Beacon Hill.* New York: HarperCollins, 1991.
Chafee, Zechariah. *Free Speech in the United States.* Cambridge, Mass.: Harvard University Press, 1967.
Frankfurter, Felix. *Mr. Justice Holmes and the Supreme Court.* 2d ed. Cambridge, Mass.: Harvard University Press, 1961.
Novick, Sheldon M. *Honorable Justice: The Life of Oliver Wendell Holmes.* Boston: Little, Brown, 1989.

COURT'S OPINION IN *SCHENCK* V. *UNITED STATES* (1919) [EXCERPT]

Justice Holmes wrote the Court's opinion in Schenck v. United States (1919), a freedom-of-speech case arising from alleged violations of the wartime Espionage Act. It was in this decision that Holmes articulated the concept of a "clear and

This is an indictment in three counts. The first charges a conspiracy to violate the Espionage Act of June 15, 1917... by causing and attempting to cause insubordination, etc., in the military and naval forces of the United States, and to obstruct the recruiting and enlistment service of the United States, when the United States was at war with the German Empire, to-wit, that the defendant wilfully conspired to have printed and circulated to men who had been called and accepted for military service under the Act of May 18, 1917... a document set forth and

alleged to be calculated to cause such insubordination and obstruction. The count alleges overt acts in pursuance of the conspiracy, ending in the distribution of the document set forth. The second count alleges a conspiracy to commit an offense against the United States, to-wit, to use the mails for the transmission of matter declared to be nonmailable by title 12, sec. 2, of the Act of June 15, 1917... to-wit, the above mentioned document, with an averment of the same overt acts. The third count charges an unlawful use of the mails for the transmission of the same matter and otherwise as above. The defendants were found guilty on all the counts. They set up the First Amendment to the Constitution forbidding Congress to make any law abridging the freedom of speech, or of the press, and bringing the case here on that ground have argued some other points also of which we must dispose. . .

[5] The document in question upon its first printed side recited the first section of the Thirteenth Amendment, said that the idea embodied in it was violated by the conscription act and that a conscript is little better than a convict. In impassioned language it intimated that conscription was despotism in its worst form and a monstrous wrong against humanity in the interest of Wall Street's chosen few. It said, "Do not submit to intimidation," but in form at least confined itself to peaceful measures such as a petition for the repeal of the act. The other and later printed side of the sheet was headed "Assert Your Rights." It stated reasons for alleging that any one violated the Constitution when he refused to recognize "your right to assert your opposition to the draft," and went on, "If you do not assert and support your rights, you are helping to deny or disparage rights which it is the solemn duty of all citizens and residents of the United States to retain." It described the arguments on the other side as coming from cunning politicians and a mercenary capitalist press, and even silent consent to the conscription law as helping to support an infamous conspiracy. It denied the power to send our citizens away to foreign shores to shoot up the people of other lands, and added that words could not express the condemnation such cold-blooded ruthlessness deserves, etc., etc., winding up, "You must do your share to maintain, support and uphold the rights of the people of this country." Of course the document would not have been sent unless it had been intended to have some effect, and we do not see what

effect it could be expected to have upon persons subject to the draft except to influence them to obstruct the carrying of it out. The defendants do not deny that the jury might find against them on this point. . . .

It well may be that the prohibition of laws abridging the freedom of speech is not confined to previous restraints, although to prevent them may have been the main purpose, as intimated in Patterson v. Colorado. . . . We admit that in many places and in ordinary times the defendants in saying all that was said in the circular would have been within their constitutional rights. But the character of every act depends upon the circumstances in which it is done. . . . The most stringent protection of free speech would not protect a man in falsely shouting fire in a theatre and causing a panic. It does not even protect a man from an injunction against uttering words that may have all the effect of force. . . . The question in every case is whether the words used are used in such circumstances and are of such a nature as to create a clear and present danger that they will bring about the substantive evils that Congress has a right to prevent. It is a question of proximity and degree. When a nation is at war many things that might be said in time of peace are such a hindrance to its effort that their utterance will not be endured so long as men fight and that no Court could regard them as protected by any constitutional right. It seems to be admitted that if an actual obstruction of the recruiting service were proved, liability for words that produced that effect might be enforced. The statute of 1917 in section 4 . . . punishes conspiracies to obstruct as well as actual obstruction. If the act, (speaking, or circulating a paper,) its tendency and the intent with which it is done are the same, we perceive no ground for saying that success alone warrants making the act a crime. . . .

present danger" to the public interest.

Source: *Schenck v. United States,* 249 U.S. 47 (1918).

THE TAFT COURT (c. 1920s)

Group portrait of the U.S. Supreme Court with previous U.S. President William Howard Taft as Chief Justice (Taft served on the court from 1921–30). Seated left to right are: Willis Van Devanter, Joseph McKenna, Taft, Oliver Wendell Holmes, Jr., James C. McReynolds. Standing left to right are: Pierce Butler, Louis Brandeis, George Sutherland, and Edward T. Sanford.

Source: ©Underwood & Underwood/Corbis.

"Mr. Justice Holmes" by H. L. Mencken (1929)

The Dissenting Opinions of Mr. Justice Holmes *was arranged by Alfred Lief and included a forward by George W. Kirchwey. This review of the book was written by H. L. Mencken and appeared in* The American Mercury *in May 1930. Evaluating the dissenting opinions of Holmes, Mencken criticizes Holmes for upholding the "rights of lawmakers" rather than protecting the voice of the people.*

Source: Mencken, H. L. "Mr. Justice Holmes." *The American Mercury,* May 1930. Published in H. L. Mencken, *A Mencken Chrestomathy.* ©1929 by Alfred A. Knopf, a division of Random House, Inc. and renewed 1954 by H. L. Mencken. Used by permission of Alfred A. Knopf, a division of Random House, Inc.

Mr. Justice Holmes's dissenting opinions have got so much fawning praise from liberals that it is somewhat surprising to discover that Mr. Lief is able to muster but fifty-five of them, and even more surprising to hear from Dr. Kirchwey that in only one case did the learned justice stand quite alone, and that the cases "in which he has given expression to the judgement of the court, [sic] or in which he has concurred in its judgement, far outnumber, in the ratio of eight or ten to one, those in which he felt it necessary to dissent."

There is even more surprising stuff in the opinions themselves. In three Espionage Act cases, including the *Debs* case, one finds a clear statement of the doctrine that, in war time, the rights guaranteed by the First Amendment cease to have any substance, and may be set aside by any jury that has been sufficiently alarmed by a district attorney itching for higher office. In *Fox v. the State of Washington,* we learn that any conduct "which shall tend to encourage or advocate disrespect for the law" may be made a crime, and that the protest of a man who believes that he has been jailed unjustly, and threatens to boycott his persecutors, may be treated as such a crime. In *Moyer v. Peabody,* it appears that the Governor of a state, "without sufficient reason but in good faith," may call out the militia, declare martial law, and jail anyone he happens to suspect or dislike, without laying himself open "to an action after he is out of office on the ground that he had no reasonable ground for his belief." And, in *Weaver v. Palmer Bros. Co.* there is the plain inference that in order to punish a theoretical man, A, who is suspected of wrong-doing, a State Legislature may lay heavy and intolerable burdens upon a real man, B, who has admittedly done no wrong at all.

I find it hard to reconcile such notions with any plausible concept of Liberalism. They may be good law, but it is impossible to see how they can conceivably promote liberty. My suspicion is that the hopeful Liberals of the 20s, frantically eager to find at least one judge who was not violently and implacably against them, seized upon certain of Mr. Justice Holmes's opinions without examining the rest, and read into them an attitude that was actually as foreign to his ways of thinking as it was to those of Mr. Chief Justice Hughes. Finding him, now and then, defending eloquently a new and uplifting law which his colleagues proposed to strike off the books, they concluded that he was a sworn advocate of the rights of man. But all the while, if I do not misread his plain words, he was actually no more than an advocate of the rights of lawmakers. There, indeed, is the clue to his whole jurisprudence. He believed that the law-making bodies should be free to experiment almost *ad libitum,* that the courts should not call a halt upon them until they clearly passed the uttermost bounds of reason, that everything should be sacrificed to their autonomy, including apparently, even the Bill of Rights. If this is liberalism, then all I can say is that Liberalism is not what it was when I was young.

In those remote days, sucking wisdom from the primeval springs, I was taught that the very aim of the Constitution was to keep law-makers from running amok, and that it was the highest duty of the Supreme Court, following *Marbury v. Madison,* to safeguard it against their forays. It was not sufficient, so my instructors maintained, for Congress or a State Legislature to give assurance that its intentions were noble; noble or not, it had to keep squarely within the limits of the Bill of Rights, and the moment it went beyond them its most virtuous acts were null and void. But Mr. Justice Holmes apparently thought otherwise. He held, it would seem, that violating the Bill of Rights is a rare and deliberate malice, and that it is the chief business of the Supreme Court to keep the Constitution loose and elastic, so that blasting holes through it may not be too onerous. Bear this doctrine in mind, and you will have an adequate explanation, on the one hand, of those forward-looking opinions which console the Liberals—for example in *Lochner v. New York* (the bakery case), in the child labor case, and in the Virginia case involving the compulsory sterilization for imbeciles—and on the other hand, of the reactionary opinions which they so politely overlook—for example in the *Debs* case, in *Bartels v. Iowa* (a war-time case, involving the prohibition of foreign-language teaching), in the Mann Act case (in which Dr. Holmes concurred with the majority of the court, [sic] and thereby helped pave the way for the wholesale blackmail which Mr. Justice McKenna, who dissented, warned against), and finally in the long line of Volstead Act cases.

Like any other man, of course, a judge sometimes permits himself the luxury of inconsistency. Mr. Justice Holmes, it seems to me, did so in the wiretapping case and again in the *Abrams* case, in which his dissenting opinion was clearly at variance with the prevailing opinion in the *Debs* case, written by him. But I think it is quite fair to say that his fundamental attitude was precisely as I have stated it. Over and over again, in these opinions, he advocated giving the legislature full headroom, and over and over again he protested against using the Fourteenth Amendment to upset novel and oppressive laws, aimed frankly at helpless minorities. If what he said in some of those opinions were accepted literally, there would be scarcely any brake at all upon lawmaking, and the Bill of Rights would have no more significance than the Code of Manu.

The weak spot in his reasoning, if I may presume to suggest such a thing, was his tacit assumption that the voice of the legislature was the voice of the people. There is, in fact, no reason for confusing the people and the legislature: the two, in these later years, are quite distinct. The legislature, like the executive, has ceased, save indirectly, to be even the creature of the people: it is the creature, in the main, of pressure groups, and most of them, it must be manifest, are of dubious wisdom and even more dubious honesty. Laws are no longer made by a rational process of public discussion; they are made by a process of blackmail and intimidation, and they are executed in the same manner. The typical lawmaker of today is a man wholly devoid of principle—a mere counter in a grotesque and knavish game. If the right pressure could be applied to him he would be cheerfully in favor of polygamy, astrology or cannibalism.

It is the aim of the Bill of Rights, if it has any remaining aim at all, to curb such prehensile gentry. Its function is to set a limitation upon their power to harry and oppress us to their own private profit. The Fathers, in framing it, did not have the powerful minorities in mind; what they sought to hobble was simply the majority. But that is a detail. The important thing is that the Bill of Rights sets forth, in the plainest of plain language, the limits beyond which even the legislature may not go. The Supreme Court, in *Marbury* v. *Madison*, decided that it was bound to execute that intent, and for a hundred years that doctrine remained the cornerstone of American constitutional law. But in late years the court has taken the opposite line, and the public opinion seems to support it. Certainly, Dr. Holmes did not go as far in that direction as some of his brother judges, but equally certainly he went far enough. To call him Liberal is to make the word meaningless. . . .

LETTER TO OLIVER WENDELL HOLMES, JR. FROM FELLOW JUSTICES (January 13, 1932)

Supreme Court of the United States
Washington, D.C.

January 12, 1932.

Dear Justice Holmes:

We cannot permit your long association in the work of the Court to end without expressing our keen sense of loss and our warm affection. Your judicial service of over forty-nine years – twenty years in the Supreme Judicial Court of Massachusetts and twenty-nine years upon this bench – has a unique distinction in uninterrupted effectiveness and exceptional quality. Your profound learning and philosophic outlook have found expression in opinions which have become classic, enriching the literature of the law as well as its substance. With a most conscientious exactness in the performance of every duty, you have brought to our collaboration in difficult tasks a personal charm and a freedom and independence of spirit which have been a constant refreshment. While we are losing the privilege of daily companionship, the most precious memories of your unfailing kindliness and generous nature abide with us, and these memories will ever be one of the choicest traditions of the Court.

Deeply regretting the necessity for your retire-

Supreme Court of the United States
Washington, D.C.

ment, we trust that – relieved of the burden which had become too heavy – you may have a renewal of vigor and that you may find satisfaction in your abundant resources of intellectual enjoyment.

Affectionately yours,

Charles E. Hughes
Willis Van Devanter
J. C. McReynolds
Louis D. Brandeis
Geo. Sutherland
Pierce Butler
Harlan F. Stone
Owen J. Roberts

Upon his retirement from the Supreme Court in 1932, Holmes received this letter from his fellow Supreme Court justices.

Source: From the collections of the Library of Congress.

Langston Hughes

1902–1967
African-American Writer

Langston Hughes was an African-American writer most remembered for his blues and jazz poems of the 1920s that depicted the common realities of the black community.

Born into a prominent black family on February 1, 1902, in Joplin, Missouri, James Mercer Langston Hughes spent most of his childhood living with his maternal grandmother in Lawrence, Kansas. A lonely child, Hughes found solace in reading and developed a reverence for the written word. He was elected Class Poet at 13 and wrote his first poem for his grammar school graduation ceremony. A year after his grandmother's death, Hughes moved with his mother and stepfather to Cleveland, Ohio, where he attended Central High School. Many of his classmates were European immigrants who introduced him to the writings of Guy de Maupassant and Friedrich Nietzsche. Hughes also studied American poets such as Walt Whitman and Carl Sandburg, emulating their free verse in his own works, some of which appeared in the Central High literary magazine, *The Belfry Owl*.

In the summer after graduating from high school in 1920, Hughes wrote the poem "The Negro Speaks of Rivers" and published it the next year in **W. E. B. Du Bois**'s *The Crisis,* the official journal of the National Association for the Advancement of Colored People (NAACP). Hughes deeply respected Du Bois, whose 1903 novel *The Souls of Black Folk* profoundly influenced his thoughts on racism. "The Negro Speaks of Rivers" pays tribute to the black race and their struggle using the expressive language of their spirituals. For the next few years, Hughes continued to contribute to *The Crisis* and traveled the world. He explored the culture of Harlem as a resident working odd jobs (1922–23); the ports of West Africa as a mess boy on the steamship USS *Malone* (1923); and the music of Paris as a dishwasher and cook at the cabaret Le Grand Duc (1924). While in Paris, Hughes heard leading black musicians and saw blues and jazz respected as art forms.

In 1925, Hughes settled in Washington, D.C., and won first prize for "The Weary Blues," a poem about a piano

From the collections of the Library of Congress.

player from Harlem, in an *Opportunity* magazine contest sponsored by the National Urban League. Hughes further promoted his career that year while working as a busboy at the Wardman Park Hotel. Spotting the famous white poet Vachel Lindsay, Hughes set three of his poems beside Lindsay's dinner plate. Lindsay later declared at his poetry reading that he had discovered a busboy poet and the story soon appeared in the nation's leading newspapers.

Following this publicity, Hughes was awarded a scholarship to Lincoln University in Pennsylvania. He met the demands of college while publishing his first two books of poetry, *The Weary Blues* (1926) and *Fine Clothes to the Jew* (1927). Both collections contain blues- and jazz-inspired poems that use pathos to evoke compassion for those who suffer from racial injustice, and humor to describe the hardships of the ordinary black person. While *The Weary Blues* was well reviewed, *Fine Clothes to the Jew* received disapproval from white and black critics who perceived its starker portraits to be racial stereotypes.

In the 1920s, Hughes and other black writers represented the New Negro literary movement, which departed from the conventional literature of white society in order to describe African-American culture in the voice and vision of its people. They promoted racial pride by portraying a realistic picture of black culture and life. The New Negro movement was a period of artistic growth among black Americans and centered on the community of Harlem; hence, it is commonly called the Harlem Renaissance. "The Negro Artist and the Racial Mountain," an essay published by Hughes in a 1926 edition of the *Nation*, eloquently expresses the values of this movement and urges blacks to create from their own experiences rather than assimilate into the dominant white culture. By writing in the rhythms of the blues and using the idiomatic expressions of Harlem, Hughes became a leading figure of the Harlem Renaissance.

Shortly after graduating from Lincoln University in 1929, Hughes branched beyond poetry with the publication of his first novel, *Not Without Laughter* (1930). Even though the Great Depression in the 1930s put an end to the prosperity of the Harlem Renaissance, Hughes broke from his former patron Charlotte Mason to regain control over his artistic endeavors. Much of his work began to reflect leftist politics, particularly his essays and poems for the communist magazine *New Masses*. He delved deeper into these ideas during his travels to the Soviet Union, Haiti, and Spain. After a stint as a newspaper correspondent in the Spanish Civil War (1936–39), Hughes returned to the United States to found the radical Harlem Suitcase Theater in 1937. He also wrote children's literature, character sketches, short stories, lyrics, plays, and the autobiographies *The Big Sea* (1940) and *I Wonder As I Wander* (1956). Hughes died on May 22, 1967, in New York City, leaving behind a substantial and varied body of work.

In response to his poems about prostitutes, drunkards, betrayers, and beggars, some critics dubbed Hughes as a "sewer dweller" and the "poet lowrate of Harlem." Hughes, however, claimed that he wrote from the root of his personal experience: "I knew only the people I had grown up with, and they weren't people whose shoes were always shined, who had been to Harvard, or who had heard of Bach." Hughes embraced the real and human aspects of his heritage and expressed disdain for black intellectuals' lofty and flowery imitations of white literature. Hughes found inspiration in the unique dialect, music, and spirit of the black community. Even though much of his work stimulated controversy, it also won praise for its creativity and originality.

Renée Miller

For Further Reading
Berry, Faith. *Langston Hughes: Before and Beyond Harlem.* New York: Wings Books, 1995.
Hughes, Langston. *The Big Sea: an Autobiography.* 2d ed. New York: Hill and Wang, 1993.
———. *The Collected Poems of Langston Hughes.* New York: Random House, 1994.
Rampersad, Arnold. *The Life of Langston Hughes.* 2 vols. New York: Oxford University Press, 1986–88.

"THE NEGRO SPEAKS OF RIVERS" by Langston Hughes (1921)

I've known rivers:
I've known rivers ancient as the world and older than the
　　flow of human blood in human veins.

My soul has grown deep like the rivers.

I bathed in the Euphrates when dawns were young.
I built my hut near the Congo and it lulled me to sleep.
I looked upon the Nile and raised the pyramids above it.

I heard the singing of the Mississippi when Abe Lincoln went down to New Orleans, and I've seen its muddy bosom turn all golden in the sunset.

I've known rivers:
Ancient, dusky rivers.

My soul has grown deep like the rivers.

Appearing in W. E. B. Du Bois's The Crisis, *Hughes's first major poem remains one of his most famous.*

Source: Hughes, Langston. The Collected Poems of Langston Hughes. *New York: Random House, 1994. ©1994 by the Estate of Langston Hughes. Used by permission of Alfred A. Knopf, a division of Random House, Inc.*

"THE WEARY BLUES" by Langston Hughes (1925)

Droning a drowsy syncopated tune,
Rocking back and forth to a mellow croon,
　　I heard a Negro play,
Down on Lenox Avenue the other night
By the pale dull pallor of an old gas light
　　He did a lazy sway. . . .
　　He did a lazy sway. . . .
To the tune o' those Weary Blues.
With his ebony hands on each ivory key
He made that poor piano moan with melody.
　　O Blues!
Swaying to and fro on his rickety stool
He played that sad raggy tune like a musical fool.
　　Sweet Blues!
Coming from a black man's soul.
　　O Blues!
In a deep song voice with a melancholy tone
I heard that Negro sing, that old piano moan—

"Ain't got nobody in all this world,
　　Ain't got nobody but ma self.
　　I's gwine to quit ma frownin'
　　And put ma troubles on the shelf."

Thump, thump, thump, went his foot on the floor.
He played a few chords then he sang some more—
　　"I got the Weary Blues
　　　and I can't be satisfied.
　　Got the Weary Blues
　　And can't be satisfied—
　　I ain't happy no mo'
　　And I wish that I had died."
And far into the night he crooned that tune.
The stars went out and so did the moon.
The singer stopped playing and went to bed
While the Weary Blues echoed through his head.
He slept like a rock or a man that's dead.

"The Weary Blues" won first prize in a 1925 Opportunity *magazine contest. Hughes later called this his "lucky poem" and used its title for his first book of poetry, published in 1926. The poem reflects the influence of the rhythms of the blues and tells the story of a tired Harlem piano player.*

Source: Hughes, Langston. The Collected Poems of Langston Hughes. *New York: Random House, 1994. ©1994 by the Estate of Langston Hughes. Used by permission of Alfred A. Knopf, a division of Random House, Inc.*

"THE NEGRO ARTIST AND THE RACIAL MOUNTAIN" by Langston Hughes (June 23, 1926)

"The Negro Artist and the Racial Mountain," published by Hughes in the June 23, 1926, edition of The Nation, *became a manifesto for the New Negro movement. This essay declares the importance of racial pride and the need for black artists to create from the traditions of their culture, rather than trying to meet the standards set for them by white society.*

Source: Hughes, Langston. "The Negro Artist and the Racial Mountain." *The Nation* 122, no. 318, June 23, 1926. Reprinted with permission from *The Nation*.

One of the most promising of the young Negro poets said to me once, "I want to be a poet—not a Negro poet," meaning, I believe, "I want to write like a white poet"; meaning subconsciously, "I would like to be a white poet"; meaning behind that, "I would like to be white." And I was sorry the young man said that, for no great poet has ever been afraid of being himself. And I doubted then that, with his desire to run away spiritually from his race, this boy would ever be a great poet. But this is the mountain standing in the way of any true Negro art in America—this urge within the race toward whiteness, the desire to pour racial individuality into the mold of American standardization, and to be as little Negro and as much American as possible.

But let us look at the immediate background of this young poet. His family is of what I suppose one would call the Negro middle class: people who are by no means rich yet never uncomfortable nor hungry—smug, contented, respectable folk, members of the Baptist church. The father goes to work every morning. He is a chief steward at a large white club. The mother sometimes does fancy sewing or supervises parties for the rich families of the town. The children go to a mixed school. In the home they read white papers and magazines. And the mother often says, "Don't be like niggers" when the children are bad. A frequent phrase from the father is, "Look how well a white man does things." And so the word white comes to be unconsciously a symbol of all the virtues. It holds for the children beauty, morality, and money. The whisper of "I want to be white" runs silently through their minds. This young poet's home is, I believe, a fairly typical home of the colored middle class. One sees immediately how difficult it would be for an artist born in such a home to interest himself in interpreting the beauty of his own people. He is never taught to see that beauty. He is taught rather not to see it, or if he does, to be ashamed of it when it is not according to Caucasian patterns.

For racial culture the home of a self-styled "high-class" Negro has nothing better to offer. Instead there will perhaps be more aping of things white than in a less cultured or less wealthy home. The father is perhaps a doctor, lawyer, landowner, or politician. The mother may be a social worker, or a teacher, or she may do nothing and have a maid. Father is often dark but he has usually married the lightest woman he could find. The family attend a fashionable church where few really colored faces are to be found. And they themselves draw a color line. In the North they go to white theaters and white movies. And in the South they have at least two cars and a house "like white folks." Nordic manners, Nordic faces, Nordic hair, Nordic art (if any), and an Episcopal heaven. A very high mountain indeed for the would-be racial artist to climb in order to discover himself and his people.

But then there are the low-down folks, the so-called common element, and they are the majority—may the Lord be praised! The people who have their nip of gin on Saturday nights and are not too important to themselves or the community, or too well fed, or too learned to watch the lazy world go round. They live on Seventh Street in Washington or State Street in Chicago and they do not particularly care whether they are like white folks or anybody else. Their joy runs, bang! into ecstasy. Their religion soars to a shout. Work maybe a little today, rest a little tomorrow. Play awhile. Sing awhile. O, let's dance! These common people are not afraid of spirituals, as for a long time their more intellectual brethren were, and jazz is their child. They furnish a wealth of colorful, distinctive material for any artist because they still hold their own individuality in the face of American standardization. And perhaps these common people will give to the world its truly great Negro artist, the one who is not afraid to be himself. Whereas the better-class Negro would tell the artist what to do, the people at least let him alone when he does appear. And they are not ashamed of him—if they know he exists at all. And they accept what beauty is their own without question.

Certainly there is, for the American Negro artist who can escape the restrictions the more advanced among his own group would put upon him, a great field of unused material ready for his art. Without going outside his race, and even among the better classes with their "white" culture and conscious American manners, but still Negro enough to be different, there is sufficient matter to furnish a black artist with a lifetime of creative work. And when he chooses to touch on the relations between Negroes and whites in this country with their innumerable overtones and undertones, surely, and especially for literature and the drama, there is an inexhaustible supply of themes at hand. To these the Negro artist can give his racial individuality, his heritage of rhythm and warmth, and his incongruous humor that so often, as in the Blues, becomes ironic laughter mixed with tears. But let us look again at the mountain.

A prominent Negro clubwoman in Philadelphia paid eleven dollars to hear Raquel Meller sing Andalusian popular songs. But she told me a few weeks before she would not think of going to hear "that woman," Clara Smith, a great black artist, sing Negro folksongs. And many an upper-class Negro church, even now, would not dream of employing a spiritual in its services. The drab melodies in white folks' hymnbooks are much to be preferred. "We want to worship the Lord correctly and quietly. We don't believe in 'shouting.' Let's be dull like the Nordics," they say, in effect.

The road for the serious black artist, then, who would produce a racial art is most certainly rocky and the mountain is high. Until recently he received almost no encouragement for his work from either white or colored people. The fine novels of Chestnutt go out of print with neither race noticing their passing. The quaint charm and humor of Dunbar's dialect verse brought to him, in his day, largely the same kind of encouragement one would give a sideshow freak (A colored man writing poetry! How odd!) or a clown (How amusing!).

The present vogue in things Negro, although it may do as much harm as good for the budding colored artist, has at least done this: it has brought him forcibly to the attention of his own people among whom for so long, unless the other race had noticed him beforehand, he was a prophet with little honor. I understand that Charles Gilpin acted for years in Negro theaters without any special acclaim from his own, but when Broadway gave him eight curtain calls, Negroes, too, began to beat a tin pan in his honor. I know a young colored writer, a manual worker by day, who had been writing well for the colored magazines for some years, but it was not until he recently broke into the white publications and his first book was accepted by a prominent New York publisher that the "best" Negroes in his city took the trouble to discover that he lived there. Then almost immediately they decided to give a grand dinner for him. But the society ladies were careful to whisper to his mother that perhaps she'd better not come. They were not sure she would have an evening gown.

The Negro artist works against an undertow of sharp criticism and misunderstanding from his own group and unintentional bribes from the whites. "O, be respectable, write about nice people, show how good we are," say the Negroes. "Be stereotyped, don't go too far, don't shatter our illusions about you, don't amuse us too seriously. We will pay you," say the whites. Both would have told Jean Toomer not to write "Cane." The colored people did not praise it. The white people did not buy it. Most of the colored people who did read "Cane" hate it. They are afraid of it. Although the critics gave it good reviews the public remained indifferent. Yet (excepting the work of Du Bois) "Cane" contains the finest prose written by a Negro in America. And like the singing of Robeson, it is truly racial.

But in spite of the Nordicized Negro intelligentsia and the desires of some white editors we have an honest American Negro literature already with us. Now I await the rise of the Negro theater. Our folk music, having achieved world-wide fame, offers itself to the genius of the great individual American Negro composer who is to come. And within the next decade I expect to see the work of a growing school of colored artists who paint and model the beauty of dark faces and create with new technique the expressions of their own soul-world. And the Negro dancers who will dance like flame and the singers who will continue to carry our songs to all who listen—they will be with us in even greater numbers tomorrow.

Most of my own poems are racial in theme and treatment, derived from the life I know. In many of them I try to grasp and hold some of the meanings and rhythms of jazz. I am sincere as I know how to be in these poems and yet after every reading I answer questions like these from my own people: Do you think Negroes should always write about Negroes? I wish you wouldn't read some of your poems to white folks. How do you find anything interesting in a place like a cabaret? Why do you write about black people? You aren't black. What makes you do so many jazz poems?

But jazz to me is one of the inherent expressions of Negro life in America: the eternal tom-tom beating in the Negro soul—the tom-tom of revolt against weariness in a white world, a world of subway trains, and work, work, work; the tom-tom of joy and laughter, and pain swallowed in a smile. Yet the Philadelphia club-woman is ashamed to say that her race created it and she does not like me to write about it. The old subconscious "white is best" runs through her mind. Years of study under white teachers, a lifetime of white books, pictures, and papers, and white manners, morals, and Puritan standards made her dislike the spirituals. And now she turns up her nose at jazz and all its manifestations—likewise almost everything else distinctly racial. She doesn't care for the Winold Reiss portraits of Negroes because they are "too Negro." She does not want a true picture of herself from anybody. She wants the artist to flatter her, to make the white world believe that all Negroes are as smug and as near white in soul as she wants to be. But, to my mind, it is the duty of the younger Negro artist, if he accepts any duties at all from outsiders, to change through the force of his art that old whispering "I want to be white," hidden in the aspirations of his people, to "Why should I want to be white? I am a Negro—and beautiful!"

So I am ashamed for the black poet who says, "I want to be a poet, not a Negro poet," as though his own racial world were not as interesting as any other world. I am ashamed, too, for the colored artist who runs from the painting of Negro faces to the painting of sunsets after the manner of the academicians because he fears the strange un-whiteness of his own features. An artist must be free to choose what he does, certainly, but he must also never be afraid to do what he might choose.

Let the blare of Negro jazz bands and the bellowing voice of Bessie Smith singing Blues penetrate the closed ears of the colored near-intellectuals until they listen and perhaps understand. Let Paul Robeson singing Water Boy, and Rudolph Fisher writing about the streets of Harlem, and Jean Toomer holding the heart of Georgia in his hands, and Aaron Douglas drawing strange black fantasies cause the smug Negro middle class to turn from their white, respectable, ordinary books and papers to catch a glimmer of their own beauty. We younger Negro artists who create now intend to express our individual dark-skinned selves without fear or shame. If white people are pleased we are glad. If they are not, it doesn't matter. We know we are beautiful. And ugly too. The tom-tom cries and the tom-tom laughs. If colored people are pleased we are glad. If they are not, their displeasure doesn't matter either. We build our temples for tomorrow, strong as we know how, and we stand on top of the mountain, free within ourselves.

"REVIEW OF *FINE CLOTHES TO THE JEW*" by J. A. Rogers (1927) [EXCERPT]

A controversial Harlem Renaissance poet, Hughes often received criticism for his verses that included ghetto idioms and humble subjects. In this 1927 review from the Pittsburgh Courier, *J. A. Rogers condemns Hughes's* Fine Clothes to the Jew *as "a collection of piffling trash" and concludes that the collection lacks sophistication and promotes social degradation.*

Source: Mullen, Edward J., ed. *Critical Essays on Langston Hughes.* Boston: G. K. Hall, 1986.

The fittest compliment I can pay this latest work by Langston Hughes is to say that it is, on the whole, about as fine a collection of piffling trash as is to be found under the covers of any book. If *The Weary Blues* made readers of a loftier turn of mind weary, this will make them positively sick. . . .

And the pity of it is that Mr. Hughes is capable of producing other than such degenerate stuff as this. He is capable of finer, loftier expression. The fact that he writes of Negroes in the humbler walks of life has nothing to do with it. With Mr. Hughes, it is indeed a case of "Fine Clothes to the Jew"; of selling his best clothes to the ragman.

Nor must the blame for this prostitution of talent be laid wholly on Mr. Hughes. The Negro group is even more to blame in that it has made absolutely no provision for its writers, expecting the Nordic to do it. Poets, like ladies, must live, and if they are to get along they must put their feet under the white man's kitchen table or starve. And when one sits to another's table he can't very well dictate the dishes.

What is aimed at in America is the social degradation of the Negro to a stage where his labor can be had in the cheapest market. The rage over books like this and the vogue of the spirituals among white people is but a red herring drawn across the trail. When it comes to books or articles that vitally affect the question then these same folk will be found, generally, to be the rankest kind of conservatives. Recently George S. Schuyler sent some of his Southern snapshots to the New Masses, a Communist paper, and after the editor had finished trimming it, it looked as if the Imperial Wizard, bitterest foe of the Communists, had been through it, instead.

This book, while it has some modicum of truth and beauty, is plainly an attempt to exploit the jazzy, degenerate, infantile and silly vogue inspired by the success of such plays as "Lulu Belle." It has 89 pages, and it is safe to say that the matter in the whole could be held in sixteen pages.

Fine Clothes to the Jew is unworthy both of Mr. Hughes and Messrs. Knopf, the publishers. I would very much rather have said a good word for both, especially as Knopf is publisher of *The Fire in the Flint*. But a reviewer owes a duty both to himself and his readers, for, in proportion as one praises the bad he detracts from the good. We have had enough of Mr. Hughes in this vein,—too much in fact—and the Negro public, if it will not help Mr. Hughes to publish his worthy poems, can do at least this, it can discourage the marketing of such books, books that help but to tighten the chains of social degradation.

"REVIEW OF *FINE CLOTHES TO THE JEW*" by Lewis Alexander (1927) [EXCERPT]

This review of Fine Clothes to the Jew, *published in 1927 by Lewis Alexander in the* Carolina Magazine, *praises Hughes's poetic candor and originality. The review suggests that, writing on his personal experiences and observations, Hughes neither censored reality nor shied away from disturbing topics.*

Source: Mullen, Edward J., ed. *Critical Essays on Langston Hughes.* Boston: G. K. Hall, 1986. Reprinted with permission from the University of North Carolina at Chapel Hill.

Fine Clothes to the Jew, reveals the fact that Mr. Hughes understands completely the lives of the more primitive types of Negro. No one who knows intimately the Negro crap shooters, gamblers, typical gin Mary's, bootblacks, bell boys, cabaret girls, piano plunkers, makers of folk songs, street walkers, and old rounders can deny this. This poet enters into the spirit of the lives of these people and paints them with a sympathy and understanding not matched in contemporary literature. It is true that there is much sordidness and ugliness in the lives of the more primitive types of the Negro, but yet the same is true of the more primitive types of any racial group. The sordidness and ugliness present in the lives of these folks do not constitute a reason why they are not fit subjects for literary treatment. In real life we find ugliness right along side of beauty; hence in literature which is true to life we must expect to find the same conditions existing and without a shadow of doubt. Mr. Hughes has not failed to portray the life of which he treats with all its terrible reality.

Nowhere does he attempt to cover up; therefore his work has that fine sincerity which is the essence of all true poetry. We may select from his work at random but at all times we feel that the author knows whereof he speaks. He has actually lived with and knows well the people and conditions of which he writes. No vain pretensions or fanciful imagination here—only reality.

In addition to his sincerity, Mr. Hughes possesses an originality in his writing which is quite refreshing. He goes directly to the source for his material and reports his findings as he sees them. The result is quite delightful. . . .

Mr. Hughes will continue in his good work. He is a real poet and at the rate he is going will develop into a genuine folk poet worthy of being called the spokesman of the black masses of American. He is a real poet despite the fact that he does not adhere strictly to the conventional subject matter and conventional poetic patterns, but those who understand anything about the matter at all will concede that the essence of real poetry certainly does not lie in conventionality.

Zora Neale Hurston

c. 1891–1960
African-American
Writer and Folklorist

Zora Neale Hurston was an African-American writer and folklorist who used her talents to celebrate and preserve the black culture of the rural South.

Hurston was born on January 3, 1891 (some sources give 1901 or 1903), in Eatonville, Florida, the first incorporated all-black township in the United States. Still a child when her mother died, Hurston followed her advice to "jump at the sun." She worked her way through high school and early years of college as a manicurist, waitress, and maid. Between 1919 and 1924, Hurston intermittently attended Howard University in Washington, D.C., publishing her first short story "John Redding Goes to Sea" (1921) and poem "O Night" (1921) in the school's literary magazine *Stylus*.

Hurston's writing blossomed after moving to New York City in January 1925. After World War I, many Southern blacks migrated to the North in search of social and economic opportunities—described by historians as the Great Migration. Hurston took second prize in an *Opportunity* magazine contest sponsored by the National Urban League

From the collections of the Library of Congress.

for her play *Color Struck* and short story "Spunk," which was also included in Alain Locke's landmark anthology, *The New Negro* (1925). Along with poets such as **Langston Hughes**, Countee Cullen, and Claude McKay, whose work was also featured in the anthology, Hurston became part of a cultural movement called the Harlem Renaissance, a period of black artistic prosperity in the 1920s also known as the New Negro movement. Harlem, the capital of African-American culture, was one of many places that hosted a new generation of black talent dedicated to authentic cultural expression. This awakening of racial pride celebrated black heritage in literature, art, and music.

In the fall of 1925, Hurston secured a scholarship to Barnard College in New York City, where she became its first black student and graduated with a bachelor of arts degree in 1928. Studying under famed anthropologist Franz Boas, she developed an interest in African-American folklore that enriched her intuitive fiction with an intellectual perspective. Her 1926 short works "Sweat," featured in the single issue of the radical quarterly *Fire!!*, and "The Eatonville Anthology," released in three installments in the *Messenger*, signal her literary maturation. Set in her hometown, *The Eatonville Anthology* combines folklore with fiction through 14 sketches ranging from a begging woman to a village liar.

In the 1928 essay "How It Feels to Be Colored Me," published in the *World Tomorrow*, Hurston rejoices in her racial identity by refusing to be "tragically colored"; she wrote, "I do not belong to the sobbing school of Negrohood who hold that nature somehow has given them a lowdown dirty deal and whose feelings are all hurt about it." Hurston preferred artistic prose to social protest, utilizing the rural dialect, daily experiences, and folklore of Eatonville and other Southern black communities throughout her literary career. Black intellectuals like **W. E. B. Du Bois** criticized her for being politically naive and for dismissing the exploitation of blacks.

In 1927, Hurston traveled to the South to collect her first African-American folklore as an anthropologist. She had obtained a $1,400 research fellowship from Columbia University to record songs, customs, tales, superstitions, jokes, dances, and games. Her mentor Boas felt that her background would strengthen her rapport with the examined African-American communities; however, Hurston's social scientist role and what she later called her "carefully accented Barnardese" alienated her from the residents. Learning from her initial failings, Hurston resumed her fieldwork the next year on a $200 monthly stipend from her white patron Charlotte Osgood Mason. This time Hurston earned the trust of the communities and gathered invaluable materials such as folktales, work songs, proverbs, sermons, and children's rhymes. As her study evolved, Hurston traveled to the West Indies to compare and contrast African-American and Afro-Caribbean folklore.

The cultural traditions Hurston began preserving in the 1920s filled her literature in the 1930s. Her classic folklore collection *Mules and Men* (1935) intimately documents the South, while her novel *Tell My Horse* (1938) explores voodoo in Haiti and Jamaica. In 1937, Hurston published her masterpiece *Their Eyes Were Watching God*, which describes a black woman's soul-search for awareness and fulfillment. Other prominent publications include her autobiography *Dust Tracks on a Road* (1942) and novels *Jonah's Gourd Vine* (1934) and *Seraph on the Suwanee* (1948). Hurston's tremendous literary output established her as a leading black writer, but she was plagued by failing health, financial problems, and harsh criticism. Black intellectuals resented her avoidance of race issues and indifference toward injustice. By the 1950s, she barely earned a living between freelance writing and odd jobs, dying penniless and forgotten in Fort Pierce, Florida, on January 28, 1960.

After decades of obscurity, Hurston's writing gained renewed interest and respect. Black female writers like Alice Walker and June Jordan call her "Queen of the Renaissance," a woman who honored and explored her heritage. Hurston searched within herself and the rural black South to uncover imaginative stories and invaluable folklore. Her fiery spirit lives on through her humorous anecdotes, metaphoric language, and cultural surveys.

Renée Miller

For Further Reading

Hemenway, Robert E. *Zora Neale Hurston: A Literary Biography*. Urbana: University of Illinois Press, 1980.
Howard, Lillie P. *Zora Neale Hurston*. Boston: Twayne Publishers, 1980.
Hurston, Zora Neale. *I Love Myself When I Am Laughing. . .and Then Again When I Am Looking Mean and Impressive: A Zora Neale Hurston Reader*. Edited by Alice Walker. New York: The Feminist Press, 1979.

THE EATONVILLE ANTHOLOGY by Zora Neale Hurston (1926) [EXCERPT]

Hurston's hometown of Eatonville provided the tone and setting for many of her stories. Released in three installments in the Messenger in 1926, The Eatonville Anthology contains 14 tragicomic sketches that combine folklore with fiction.

Source: Hurston, Zora Neale. I Love Myself When I Am Laughing . . . and Then Again When I Am Looking Mean and Impressive: A Zora Neale Hurston Reader. Edited by Alice Walker. New York: The Feminist Press, 1979.

I. THE PLEADING WOMAN

Mrs. Tony Roberts is the pleading woman. She just loves to ask for things. Her husband gives her all he can rake and scrape, which is considerably more than most wives get for their housekeeping, but she goes from door to door begging for things.

She starts at the store. "Mist' Clarke," she sing-songs in a high keening voice, "gimme lil' piece uh meat tuh boil a pot uh greens wid. Lawd knows me an' mah chillen is SO hungry! Hits uh SHAME! Tony don't fee-ee-eee-ed me!"

Mr. Clarke knows that she has money and that her larder is well stocked, for Tony Roberts is the best provider on his list. But her keening annoys him and he rises heavily. The pleader at his elbow shows all the joy of a starving man being seated at a feast.

"Thass right Mist' Clarke. De Lawd loveth de cheerful giver. Gimme jes' a lil' piece 'bout dis big (indicating the width of her hand) an' de Lawd'll bless yuh."

She follows this angel-on-earth to his meat tub and superintends the cutting, crying out in pain when he refuses to move the knife over just a teeny bit mo'.

Finally, meat in hand, she departs, remarking on the meanness of some people who give a piece of salt meat only two-fingers wide when they were plainly asked for a hand-wide piece. Clarke puts it down to Tony's account and resumes his reading.

With a slab of salt pork as a foundation, she visits various homes until she has collected all she wants for the day. At the Piersons, for instance: "Sister Pierson, plee-ee-ease gimme uh han'ful u collard greens fuh me an' mah po' chillen! 'Deed, me an' mah chillen is SO hungry. Tony doan' fee-ee-eeed me!"

Mrs. Pierson picks a bunch of greens for her, but she springs away from them as if they were poison. "Lawd a mussy, Mis' Person, you ain't gonna gimme dat lil' eye-full uh greens fuh me an' mah chillen, is you? Don't be so graspin'; Gawd won't bless yuh. Gimme uh han'full mo'. Lawd, some folks is got everything, an' theys jes' as gripin' an stingy!"

Mrs. Pierson raises the ante, and the pleading woman moves on to the next place, and on and on. The next day, it commences all over.

II. TURPENTINE LOVE

Jim Merchant is always in a good humor—even with his wife. He says he fell in love with her at first sight. That was some years ago. She has had all her teeth pulled out, but they still get along splendidly.

He says the first time he called on her he found out that she was subject to fits. That didn't cool his love, however. She had several in his presence.

One Sunday, while he was there, she had one, and her mother tried to give her a dose of turpentine to stop it. Accidentally, she spilled it in her eye and it cured her. She never had another fit, so they got married and have kept each other in good humor ever since.

III.

Becky Moore has eleven children of assorted colors and sizes. She has never been married, but that is not her fault. She has never stopped any of the fathers of her children from proposing, so if she has no father for her children it's not her fault. The men round about are entirely to blame.

The other mothers of the town are afraid that it is catching. They won't let their children play with hers.

IV. TIPPY

Sykes Jones' family all shoot craps. The most interesting member of the family—also fond of bones, but of another kind—is Tippy, the Jones' dog. He is so thin, that it amazes one that he lives at all. He sneaks into village kitchens if the housewives are careless about the doors and steals meats, even off the stoves. He also sucks eggs.

For these offenses he has been sentenced to death dozens of times, and the sentences executed upon him, only they didn't work. He has been fed bluestone, strychnine, nux vomica, even an entire Peruna bottle beaten up. It didn't fatten him, but it didn't kill him. So Eatonville has resigned itself to the plague of Tippy, reflecting that it has erred in certain matters and is being chastened.

In spite of all attempts upon his life, Tippy is still willing to be friendly with anyone who will let him.

V. THE WAY OF A MAN WITH A TRAIN

Old Man Anderson lived seven or eight miles out in the country from Eatonville. Over by Lake Apopka. He raised feed-corn and cassava and went to market with it two or three times a year. He bought all of his victuals wholesale so he wouldn't have to come to town for several months more.

He was different from citybred folks. He had never seen a train. Everybody laughed at him for even the smallest child in Eatonville had either been to Maitland or Orlando and watched a train go by. On Sunday afternoons all of the young people of the village would go over to Maitland, a mile away, to see Number 35 whizz southward on its way to Tampa and wave at the passengers. So we looked down on him a little. Even we children felt superior in the presence of a person so lacking in worldly knowledge.

The grown-ups kept telling him he ought to go see a train. He always said he didn't have time to wait so long. Only two trains a day passed through Maitland. But patronage and ridicule finally had its effect and Old Man Anderson drove in one morning early. Number 78 went north to Jacksoville at 10:20. He drove his light wagon over in the woods beside the railroad below Maitland, and sat down to wait. He began to fear that his horse would get frightened and run away with the wagon. So he took him out and led him deeper into the grove and tied him securely. Then he returned to his wagon and waited some more. Then he remembered that some of the train-wise villagers had said the engine belched fire and smoke. He had better move his wagon out of danger. It might catch fire. He climbed down from the seat and placed himself between the shafts to draw it away. Just then 78 came thundering over the trestle spouting smoke, and suddenly began blowing for Maitland. Old Man Anderson became so frightened he ran away with the wagon through the woods and tore it up worse than the horse ever could have done. He doesn't yet know what a train looks like, and says he doesn't care.

"How It Feels to Be Colored Me" by Zora Neale Hurston (1928) [Excerpt]

Sometimes, I feel discriminated against, but it does not make me angry. It merely astonishes me. How *can* any deny themselves the pleasure of my company? It's beyond me.

But in the main, I feel like a brown bag of miscellany propped against a wall. Against a wall in company with other bags, white, red and yellow. Pour out the contents, and there is discovered a jumble of small things priceless and worthless. . . . In your hand is the brown bag. On the ground before you is the jumble it held—so much like the jumble in the bags, could they be emptied, that all might be dumped in a single heap and the bags refilled without altering the content of any greatly. A bit of colored glass more or less would not matter. Perhaps that is how the Great Stuffer of Bags filled them in the first place—who knows?

In this small excerpt from the end of the 1928 essay "How It Feels to Be Colored Me," published in the World Tomorrow, *Hurston refuses to be ashamed of her racial identity. Much to the disappointment of black critics, she preferred to appreciate cultural beauty rather than lament social inequality. The full essay discusses her attitudes toward her racial identity.*

Source: Hurston, Zora Neale. *I Love Myself When I am Laughing . . . and Then Again When I Am Looking Mean and Impressive: A Zora Neale Hurston Reader.* Edited by Alice Walker. New York: The Feminist Press, 1979.

Review of *Jonah's Gourd Vine* by Andrew Burris (1934)

As the author of "Spunk," one of the best short stories in *The New Negro* (edited by Alan Locke, New York, 1925), Zora Neale Hurston was in the vanguard of the movement which took its name from that book. Some of us have had the pleasure of hearing Miss Hurston tell, in her inimitable way, stories about the people in her native village, Eatonville in Florida, or have read and enjoyed the lusty humor, the rich folkways and authentic speech of the characters in her (as yet unproduced) play "Mulebone," done in collaboration with Langston Hughes, or have seen the interesting folk sketches resulting from her anthropological studies that were produced for a brief run at the John Golden Theatre in New York City two years ago; and we have felt that a

From her literary emergence in the 1920s, Hurston was both criticized and applauded by sponsors of the New Negro movement. In this 1934 review from The Crisis, *the journal of the*

National Association for the Advancement of Colored People (NAACP), Andrew Burris criticizes her first novel Jonah's Gourd Vine *for its oversimplified characters and underdeveloped story line.*

Source: Bloom, Harold, ed. *Zora Neale Hurston.* New York: Chelsea House Publishers, 1986. We wish to thank The Crisis Publishing Co., Inc., the publisher of the magazine of the National Association for the Advancement of Colored People, for the use of this work.

great delight lay in store for us when finally Miss Hurston committed herself to a book.

We have believed that Zora Hurston was not interested in writing a book merely to jump on the bandwagon of the New Negro movement, as some quite evidently were; but we felt that she was taking her time, mastering her craft, and would, as a result, produce a really significant book.

Now Miss Hurston has written a book, and despite the enthusiastic praise on the jacket by such eminent literary connoisseurs as Carl Van Vechten, Fannie Hust, and Blanche Colton Williams, all sponsors for the *New Negro,* this reviewer is compelled to report that *Jonah's Gourd Vine* is quite disappointing and a failure as a novel.

One must judge Miss Hurston's success by the tasks she has set herself—to write a novel about a backward Negro people, using their peculiar speech and manners to express their lives. What she has done is just the opposite. She has used her characters and the various situations created for them as mere pegs upon which to hang their dialect and their folkways. She has become so absorbed with these phases of her craft that that she has almost completely lost sight of the equally essential elements of plot and construction, characterization and motivation. John Buddy emerges from the story through his mere presence on every page, and not from an integrated life with the numerous others who wander in and out and do things often without rhyme or reason. It is disappointing when one considers what Miss Hurston might have done with John Buddy, illegitimate offspring of a white man and a Negro woman, who at an early age leaves the thankless toil and hovel of a home provided by a shiftless,

jealous stepfather and a protecting mother, and loves, prays, preaches, and sings his way up to the eminent position of moderator in the Baptist church. In John Buddy she had the possibility of developing a character that might have stamped himself upon American life more indelibly than either John Henry or Black Ulysses. But like the chroniclers of these two adventurers she has been unequal to the demands of her conception.

The defects of Miss Hurston's novel become the more glaring when her work is placed beside that of contemporary white authors of similar books about their own people—such as the first half of Fielding Burke's novel of North Carolina hillbillies, *Call Home the Heart,* or two novels of Arkansas mountaineers, *Mountain Born* by Emmett Gowen and *Woods Colt* by T. R Williamson. The first two names are, like Miss Hurston's, first novels, and we feel that it is not asking too much of her to expect that in writing novels about her own people she gives us work of equal merit to these.

Lest this criticism of *Jonah's Gourd Vine* seem too severe, let us add that there is much about the book that is fine and distinctive, and enjoyable. Zora Hurston has assembled between the pages of this book a rich store of folklore. She has captured the lusciousness and beauty of the Negro dialect as have few others. John Buddy's sermon on the creation is the most poetic rendition of this familiar theme that we have yet encountered in print. These factors give the book an earthiness, a distinctly racial flavor, a somewhat primitive beauty which makes its defects the more regrettable. We can but hope that with time and further experience in the craft of writing, Zora Hurston will develop the ability to fuse her abundant material into a fine literary work.

ZORA NEALE HURSTON INTERVIEWING EATONVILLE RESIDENTS (1935)

Hurston had a great interest in African-American folklore. As part of the Works Progress Administration Writers and Music projects of the 1930s, Hurston traveled to Georgia, Florida, and the Bahamas to document music, religion, and folktales of the communities. In this photo, Hurston (left) interviews two residents in Eatonville, Florida.

Source: From the collections of the Library of Congress.

"MULE ON DE MOUNT" from *Mules and Men* (1935)

Cap'n got a mule, mule on the mount called Jerry
Cap'n got a mule, mule on the mount called Jerry
    I can ride, Lawd, Lawd, I can ride.

I don't want no cold corn bread and molasses,
I don't want no cold corn bread and molasses,
    Gimme beans, Lawd, Lawd, gimme beans.

I don't want no coal-black woman for my regular,
I don't want no coal-black woman for my regular,
    She's too low-down, Lawd, Lawd, she's too low-down.

I got a woman, she's got money 'cumulated,
I got a woman, she's got money 'cumulated,
    In de bank, Lawd, Lawd, in de bank.

I got a woman she's pretty but she's too bulldozing,
I got a woman she's pretty but she's too bulldozing,
    She won't live long, Lawd, Lawd, she won't live long.
Every pay day, pay day I gits a letter,
Every pay day, pay day I gits a letter,
    Son come home, Lawd, Lawd, son come home.

If I can just make June, July and August,
If I can just make June, July and August,
    I'm going home, Lawd, Lawd, I'm going home.

Don't you hear them, coo-coo birds keep a'hollering,
Didn't you hear them, coo-coo birds keep a'hollering,
    It's sign of rain, Lawd, Lawd, it's sign of rain.

I got a rainbow wrapped and tied around my shoulder,
I got a rainbow wrapped and tied around my shoulder,
    It ain't goin' rain, Lawd, Lawd, it ain't goin' rain.

Hurston made several trips to the South and collected invaluable African-American folklore. This famous work song "Mule on De Mount" appeared in the appendix of her classic folklore collection Mules and Men *(1935).*

Source: Hurston, Zora Neale. *Zora Neale Hurston: Folklore, Memoirs, and Other Writings.* Edited by Cheryl A. Wall. New York: The Library of America, 1995.

Shoeless Joe Jackson

1887–1951
Professional Baseball Player

Shoeless Joe Jackson was a professional baseball player and one of the eight members of the Chicago White Sox who conspired to throw the 1919 World Series, a scandal that disenchanted the nation and led to his banishment from baseball.

Joseph Jefferson Jackson was born on July 16, 1887, in Pickens County, South Carolina. Growing up poor, he worked in a cotton mill instead of attending school and remained illiterate throughout his life. Jackson quit his factory job in 1908 when he joined the minor league baseball team, the Greenville Spinners. According to Jackson, the nickname "Shoeless Joe" originated when, after getting blisters from new shoes, he played outfield the next day in his stocking feet. This incident amused spectators but his baseball skills attracted even more attention, and by 1910, he had earned a position in the major leagues with the Cleveland Indians. During his first full season, Jackson ranked second only to Ty Cobb in the American League batting title and set the highest batting average ever for a rookie. Traded to the Chicago White Sox in 1915, he

Courtesy of National Baseball Hall of Fame, Cooperstown, New York.

became the top hitter and left fielder for the team that went on to beat the New York Giants in the 1917 World Series.

The White Sox entered another World Series against the Cincinnati Reds in 1919, but they lost five games to three in a best-of-nine contest. In the months following, rumors of a conspiracy circulated among the public. Fans were reluctant to believe that their favorites like Shoeless Joe would mix baseball with gambling; at the same time, it seemed unlikely that the White Sox, a superior team with five to one odds, would lose to the underdog. On September 28, 1920, the ugly rumors proved true. Eight players were accused of conspiring to throw the World Series: Chick Gandil, Eddie Cicotte, Swede Risberg, Fred McMullin, Lefty Williams, Buck Weaver, Happy Felsch, and Jackson. During the grand jury investigation into the event known as the "Black Sox" Scandal, Jackson testified that he accepted a bribe to participate in the Series fix, and Cicotte, Williams, and Felsh likewise confessed their

involvement. They were motivated by greed and also by their contempt for their closefisted owner, Charles Comiskey. Jackson had batted an impressive .375 for the season yet made a mere $6,000—almost half as much as Cincinnati's lead hitter, Ed Roush. His frustration with his low pay lured him into the scheme, which dishonored not only his name but also America's most treasured sport.

The grand jury indicted all eight players, and Comiskey had no choice but to suspend seven of them despite the upcoming American League pennant. (Gandil was already on suspension over a wage dispute.) News of the scandal, particularly the incrimination of Jackson, shocked the public and disillusioned countless young fans. The scandal came to symbolize the moral decline of the new era.

In the Black Sox trial of 1921, the eight players were acquitted because of lack of evidence—their original testimonies mysteriously disappearing from the court files. However, Judge Kenesaw Mountain Landis, the commissioner of baseball, intended to ensure they never played again and banned them from professional baseball in an attempt to restore integrity to the game. Jackson, wanting to separate himself from the scandal, always contended that he still played his best in the championship. He supported this claim with his postseason statistics: .375 batting average, six runs, and 12 hits that set a Series record. However, Jackson's involvement inevitably stained his reputation, exiling him from the White Sox and forever linking him to the scandal.

Leaving Chicago soon after, Jackson settled in Savannah, Georgia. By 1929, he had returned to his roots in Greenville, South Carolina, where he lived quietly. He pursued his passion for baseball by playing in the minor leagues under assumed names, and he maintained admirers who fought to clear his name. On December 5, 1951, Jackson died of a heart attack.

As one of the greatest hitters of the game and an idol of young baseball fans, Jackson's connection with the Black Sox scandal deeply saddened and disappointed the public.

Americans prided themselves on their love for baseball and the scandal was a blow to the national ego and to its innocence. As **Babe Ruth** said: "It was like hearing that my church had sold out." The event not only ended eight careers but also foreshadowed the corruption to come in the new decade.

Renée Miller

For Further Reading

Asinof, Eliot. *Eight Men Out: The Black Sox and the 1919 World Series.* New York: Henry Holt, 2000.

Frommer, Harvey. *Shoeless Joe and Ragtime Baseball.* Dallas, Tex.: Taylor Publishing, 1992.

Gropman, Donald. *Say It Ain't So, Joe!: The True Story of Shoeless Joe Jackson.* Adapted by Alan M. Dershowitz. Rev. ed. Secaucus, N.J.: Carol Publishing, 1999.

PLAYER STATISTICS OF SHOELESS JOE JACKSON (1910–20)

Year	Team	League	Games	At Bats	Runs	Hits	Doubles	Triples	Home Runs	Runs Batted In (RBI)	Bases On Balls (Walks)	Strike Outs	Batting Average
1908	Philadelphia	American	5	23	0	3	0	0	0	3	0		.130
1909	Philadelphia	American	5	17	3	3	0	0	0	3	1		.176
1910	Cleveland	American	20	75	15	29	2	5	1	11	8		.387
1911	Cleveland	American	147	571	126	233	45	19	7	83	56		.408
1912	Cleveland	American	154	572	121	226	44	26	3	90	54		.395
1913	Cleveland	American	148	528	109	197	39	17	7	71	80	26	.373
1914	Cleveland	American	122	453	61	153	22	13	3	53	41	34	.338
1915	Cleveland	American	83	303	42	99	16	9	3	45	28	11	.327
	Chicago	American	45	158	21	43	4	5	2	36	24	12	.272
	Yr*		128	461	63	142	20	14	5	81	52	23	.308
1916	Chicago	American	155	592	91	202	40	21	3	78	46	25	.341
1917	Chicago	American	146	538	91	162	20	17	5	75	57	25	.301
1918	Chicago	American	17	65	9	23	2	2	1	20	8	1	.354
1919	Chicago	American	139	516	79	181	31	14	7	96	60	10	.351
1920	Chicago	American	146	570	105	218	42	20	12	121	56	14	.382
Total			1332	4981	873	1772	307	168	54	785	519	158	.356

* Year's total for play with two or more clubs in same league; denotes combined total.

Jackson's player statistics contain his central batting and baserunning averages for his major league career with the Philadelphia Athletics, Cleveland Indians, and Chicago White Sox. It includes his 1911 batting average of .408 that set the highest record ever for a rookie and his all-time batting average of .356 that remains the third highest in history.

Source: Record adapted from John Thorn, Pete Palmer, Michael Gershman, and David Pietrusza, eds., Total Baseball: The Official Encyclopedia of Major League Baseball. 6th ed. Kingston, N.Y.: Total Sports Publishing, 1999.

THE GRAND JURY TESTIMONY OF SHOELESS JOE JACKSON (September 28, 1920) [EXCERPT]

(as recorded by E.A. Eulass & Co., Court and General Stenographic Reporters)

BASEBALL INQUIRY   Tuesday, September 28, 1920
GRAND JURY   3:00 P.M.

JOE JACKSON,
called as a witness, having been first duly sworn, testified as follows:

EXAMINATION BY
Mr. Replogle

...**Q** You played in the World Series between the Chicago American Baseball Club and the Cincinnati Baseball Club, did you?

A I did.

Q What position did you play in that series?

A Left Field.

Q Were you present at a meeting at the Ansonia Hotel in New York about two or three weeks before—a conference there with a number of ball players?

A I was not, no, sir.

Q Did anybody pay you any money to help throw that series in favor of Cincinnati?

A They did.

Q How much did they pay?

A They promised me $20,000, and paid me five.

Q Who promised you the twenty thousand?

A "Chick" Gandil.

Q Who is Chick Gandil?

A He was their first baseman on the White Sox Club.

Q Who paid you the $5,000?

A Lefty Williams brought it in my room and threw it down.

Q Who is Lefty Williams?

A The pitcher on the White Sox Club. . . .

Q At the end of the first game you didn't get any money, did you?

A No, I did not, no, sir.

Q What did you do then?

A I asked Gandil what is the trouble? He says, "Everything is all right," he had it.

Q Then you went ahead and threw the second game, thinking you would get it then, is that right?

A We went ahead and threw the second game, we went after him again. I said to him, "What are you going to do?" "Everything is all right," he says, "What the hell is the matter?"

In this testimony from September 28, 1920, Jackson reveals that he never directly dealt with any gamblers but did receive $5,000 of the $20,000 promised him to throw the series. This confession severely tainted his image as an idol and disillusioned baseball lovers.

Source: Frommer, Harvey. Shoeless Joe and Ragtime Baseball. Dallas, Tex.: Taylor Publishing, 1992.

Q After the third game what did you say to him?

A After the third game I says, "Somebody is getting a nice little jazz, everybody is crossed." He said, "well, Abe Attel and Bill Burns had crossed him, that is what he said to me.

Q He said Abe Attel and Bill Burns had crossed him?

A Yes, sir. . . .

Q Do you know who was the first man that the gamblers approached, that Burns and Attel approached on your team?

A Well, I don't know who the first man was.

Q Who do you think was the man they approached?

A Why, Gandil.

Q What makes you think Gandil?

A Well, he was the whole works of it, the instigator of it, the fellow that mentioned it to me. He told me that I could take it or let it go, they were going through with it.

Q Didn't you think it was the right thing for you to go and tell Comiskey about it?

A I did tell them once, "I am not going to be in it." I will just get out of that altogether.

Q Who did you tell that to?

A Chick Gandil.

Q What did he say?

A He said I was into it already and I might as well stay in. I said, "I can go to the boss and have every damn one of you pulled out of the lime-light." He said it wouldn't be well for me if I did that.

Q Gandil said to you?

A Yes, sir.

Q What did you say?

A Well, I told him any time they wanted to have me knocked off, to have me knocked off.

Q What did he say?

A Just laughed.

Q When did that conversation take place, that you said any time they wanted to have you knocked off, to have you knocked off?

A That was the fourth game, the fifth night going back to Cincinnati. I met Chick Gandil and his wife going to the 12th Street Station. They got out of the cab there. I was standing on the corner.

Q Do you recall the fourth game that Cicotte pitched?

A Yes, sir.

Q Did you see any fake plays made by yourself or anybody on that game, that would help throw the game?

A Only the wildness of Cicotte.

Q What was that?

A Hitting the batter, that is the only thing that told me they were going through with it.

Q Did you make any intentional errors yourself that day?

A No, sir, not during the whole series.

Q Did you bat to win?

A Yes.

Q And run the bases to win?

A Yes, sir.

Q And fielded the balls at the outfield to win?

A I did.

Q Did you ever hear anyone accusing Cicotte of crossing the signals that were given to him by Schalk.

A No, sir, I did not.

Q Do you know whether or not any of those signals were crossed by Cicotte?

A No, sir, I couldn't say.

Q But you didn't hear any of the boys talking about that, did you?

A No. . . .

Q In the second game, did you see any plays made by any of those fellows that would lead you to believe that they were trying to throw the game, that is the game that Claude Williams pitched with Cincinnati?

A There was wildness, too, that cost that game. Two walks, I think, and a triple by this fellow, two or three men out.

Q Was there any other moves that would lead you to believe they were throwing the game?

A No, sir, I didn't see any plays that I thought was throwing the game.

Q In the third game Kerr pitched there, 1 to nothing. Did you see anything there that would lead you to believe anyone was trying to throw the game?

A No, sir, I think if you would look that record up, I drove in two and hit one.

Q You made a home run, didn't you?

A That was in the last game here.

Q The fourth game Cicotte pitched again? It was played out here in Chicago and Chicago lost it 2 to nothing? Do you remember that?

A Yes, sir.

Q Did you see anything wrong about that game that would lead you to believe there was an intentional fixing?

A The only thing I was sore about that game, the throw I made to the plate, Cicotte tried to intercept it.

Q It would have gone to the first base if he had not intercepted it?

A Yes.

Q Did you do anything to throw these games?

A No, sir.

Q Any game in the Series?
A Not a one. I didn't have an error or make no misplay.

Q Supposing the White Sox would have won this Series, the World's Series, what would you have done then with the $5,000?
A I guess I would have kept it, that was all I could do. I tried to win all the time.

Q To keep on with these games, the fifth game, did you see anything wrong with that or any of the games, did you see any plays that you would say might have been made to throw that particular game?

A Well, I only saw one play in the whole series, I don't remember what game it was in, either, it was in Cincinnati.

Q Who made it?
A Charlie Risberg.

Q What was that?
A It looked like a perfect double play. And he only gets one, gets the ball and runs over to the bag with it in place of throwing it in front of the bag. . . .

TELEGRAM FROM CHARLES COMISKEY (1920)

You and each of you are hereby notified of your indefinite suspension of the Chicago American League Baseball Club. your suspension is brought about by information which has just come to me, directly involving you (and each of you) in the baseball scandal now being investigated by the (present) grand jury of Cook County, resulting from the World Series of 1919.

If you are innocent of any wrongdoing, you and each of you will be reinstated; if you are guilty, you will be retired from organized baseball for the rest of your lives if I can accomplish it.

Until there is a finality to this investigation, it is due to the public that I take this action even though it costs Chicago the pennant.

Although the Chicago White Sox faced an upcoming pennant, owner Charles Comiskey felt compelled to send this telegram suspending the eight players recently indicted by the Cook County Grand Jury. (Chick Gandil, though already on suspension, also received the wire.)
Source: Frommer, Harvey. Shoeless Joe and Ragtime Baseball. Dallas, Tex.: Taylor Publishing, 1992.

HUGH FULLERTON'S COMMENTARY from *New York Evening World* (1920) [EXCERPT]

From out of the hills of North Carolina years ago, there came a raw-boned, strong, active youth. His shoulders were broad and his body lithe and active. Some scout for the teams of organized baseball had discovered him up in the hills playing baseball. In two years he had risen from a poor mill boy to the rank of a player in the major leagues.

The rumor went around the country that he had been found playing ball in his bare feet, and that it was with difficulty that the scout who hired him to play with a minor league club was forced to hog-tie him to get shoes on him, and that he had wailed that he couldn't hit unless he could get toe-holds.

The story, perhaps, was untrue, but it survived, and its fame grew as the youth commenced to hit. In his first year in the big leagues as a member of the Cleveland club, he became one of the famous figures of the national sport. Of all the players in America, this boy had become one of the greatest. Each season, he and Ty Cobb battled for the honors of hitting and "Shoeless Joe" Jackson, the unknown, the rough, uncouth mill boy from the mountains, became one of the famous men of the United States. . . .He could not

read nor write. . . .There came a day when a crook spread money before this ignorant idol, and he fell. For a few dollars, which perhaps seemed a fortune to him, he sold his honor. And when the inevitable came, when the truth stood revealed, Joe Jackson went before a body of men and told the story of his own infamy.

While he related the sordid details to the stern-faced, shocked men, there gathered outside the big stone building a group of boys. Their faces were serious—more serious than those who listened inside to the shame of the nation's sport. There was no shouting, no scuffling. They did not talk of baseball or of anything else. A great fear and a great hope fought for mastery within each kid's heart. It couldn't be true.

After an hour, a man, guarded like a felon by other men, emerged from the door. He did not swagger. He slunk along between his guardians, and the kids with wide eyes and tightening throats watched. And one, bolder than the others, pressed forward and said:

"It ain't so Joe, is it?"

Jackson gulped back a sob. The shame of utter shame flushed his brown face. He choked an instant.

"Yes, kid, I'm afraid it is."

Jackson was a romanticized figure—mythic tales told of a country boy called "Shoeless Joe" who rose to fame after a scout forced him to stop playing barefoot. Hugh Fullerton's commentary from the New York Evening World mocks such stories as well as glorifies his own account of Jackson. Its power lies in the quote "It ain't so Joe, is it?" This remark, reported various ways, contained a central message: Americans desperately wanted to hold onto their wholesome picture of baseball and its heroes.
Source: Frommer, Harvey. Shoeless Joe and Ragtime Baseball. Dallas, Tex.: Taylor Publishing, 1992.

Joseph P. Kennedy

1888–1969

Ambassador and Businessman

Joseph P. Kennedy, the founder of the "Kennedy dynasty," exemplified the self-made man by his energetic ascent to wealth and power as a stock market manipulator and movie producer in the 1920s.

Joseph Patrick Kennedy was born in East Boston on September 6, 1888, the son of a successful Massachusetts politician and businessman. He was educated at the prestigious Boston Latin School, where he was captain of the baseball team and president of his class, and at Harvard, graduating in the class of 1912. From an early age, he was intensely ambitious and determined to be a millionaire by the age of 35. At 25, he became president of the Columbia Trust Company in East Boston, making him the youngest bank president in the United States. Less than a year later, on October 7, 1914, he married the belle of Boston's Irish society, Rose Fitzgerald, the daughter of Boston mayor John F. "Honey Fitz" Fitzgerald. They settled in Brookline, Massachusetts, and had nine children.

In October 1917, not long after the United States began mobilizing to enter World War I, Kennedy became assistant general manager of Bethlehem Steel's Fore River shipyard in Quincy, Massachusetts, and supervised the company's wartime production. From 1919 to 1924 he managed the stock department in the Boston office of Hayden, Stone & Co., where, privy to inside information, he learned how to manipulate stock prices (before such practices were outlawed by the Securities and Exchange Commission in 1934). Kennedy was one of the most successful and secretive speculators (one who buys and sells goods in the hope of profiting from fluctuations in price) in the stock market during the boom of the 1920s, when the U.S. economy, bolstered by huge reserves of investment capital, grew by an average of 6 percent a year.

One of his better-known manipulations was to thwart efforts by raiders to diminish the value of the Yellow Cab Company's stock. In the spring of 1924 Kennedy holed up for a month in a room in New York's Waldorf-Astoria hotel

From the collections of the Library of Congress.

and, with $5 million in spending money and a bank of telephones, manipulated Yellow Cab's stock price through purchases by associates until the raiders were driven off.

About 1927 he became deeply involved in the emerging motion picture industry. Like the new medium of radio, the popularity of movies exploded in the 1920s, and elaborately decorated theaters were built in big cities and small towns across the nation. Even before "talkies" began replacing silent films in 1927, audiences longed to escape into the movies' world of fantasy and glamour, as projected by Theda Bara, **Clara Bow**, and Rudolph Valentino. With some fellow Boston investors, Kennedy bought a chain of 31 cinemas in New England. In 1928 he helped arrange the merger that formed RKO Pictures and profited handsomely.

In the late 1920s, after about four profitable years in Hollywood, he returned to Wall Street. In his dealings Kennedy showed impeccable timing; he had converted most of his investments into cash by the time of the stock market crash in October 1929. After the crash, he made further millions by buying cheap the stocks dumped by ruined investors.

One of the biggest businesses in the Roaring Twenties was the illegal distribution of "intoxicating liquors," prohibited by the Eighteenth Amendment and enforced by the Volstead Act of 1919. Between 1920 and 1933, when the failed amendment was repealed, the "noble experiment" resulted in more drinking—and more violence when gangsters such as **Al Capone** took over the bootlegging trade. According to legend, much of Joe Kennedy's wealth derived from bootlegging during Prohibition, but such stories are impossible to substantiate (he once advised his children to never put in writing anything they wouldn't want printed on the front page of the *New York Times*). It is a fact, however, that not long before the repeal of the ammendment—thanks to connections made through James Roosevelt, Franklin D. Roosevelt's son—Kennedy secured franchise licenses to distribute premium brands of scotch, gin, and rum from British manufacturers "for medicinal purposes." By the time Prohibition was repealed in late 1933, his warehouses were stocked and ready for business.

Kennedy hoped that his business success would open the way to an illustrious career in politics, but he would be greatly disappointed. President Franklin D. Roosevelt, astutely reasoning that it takes a thief to catch one, named Kennedy chairman (1934–35) of the new Securities and Exchange Commission, established to regulate Wall Street. In 1937 he was appointed ambassador to Great Britain, but instead of elevating his political career he ruined it through his vocal support of British Prime Minister Neville Chamberlain's strategy of appeasing Adolf Hitler and the Nazis.

His proudest moment came in January 1961 as he watched his son John Fitzgerald Kennedy being sworn in as the thirty-fifth president of the United States. Soon afterward his son Robert Francis Kennedy was named attorney general, and Edward Moore "Teddy" Kennedy was elected to the U.S. Senate. In December 1961 Joe Kennedy suffered a massive stroke that left him paralyzed on one side and unable to speak. He would live for another eight years, confined to bed and wheelchair, a mute witness to the assassinations of John and Robert. Joseph Kennedy died at Hyannis Port, Massachusetts, on November 18, 1969.

Decades before he became known as the founding father of a political dynasty, Joseph Kennedy was one of the most astute businessmen of his era, blessed with charm, timing, the right connections, and public relations savvy. Through his investments in the stock market, the movie business, and the liquor trade, Kennedy was one of the wheeler-dealers who made the twenties roar—and one of the few who came out of the decade a richer man.

Mark LaFlaur

Further Reading

Kessler, Ronald. *The Sins of the Father: Joseph P. Kennedy and the Dynasty He Founded.* New York: Warner Books, 1996.

Koskoff, David E. *Joseph P. Kennedy: A Life and Times.* Englewood Cliffs, N.J.: Prentice-Hall, 1974.

Smith, Amanda. *Hostage to Fortune: The Letters of Joseph P. Kennedy.* New York: Viking Press, 2001.

Whalen, Richard J. *The Founding Father: The Story of Joseph P. Kennedy.* Toronto: New American Library of Canada, 1966.

JOSEPH P. KENNEDY (1914)

In 1914, at the age of 25, Kennedy became the president of Columbia Trust Co. in East Boston, making him the youngest bank president in the United States. He is shown here in his office at Columbia Trust, a company founded by his father to serve the financial needs of the immigrant community in East Boston.

Source: John Fitzgerald Kennedy Library, Boston, Massachusetts.

LETTERS FROM JOSEPH P. KENNEDY TO ALBERT GARCEAU (1921) AND MATTHEW BRUSH (1922)

Among the few existing documents that link Kennedy with the alcohol trade are these two letters, dated 1921 and 1922, to a Boston attorney and to a Harvard classmate, respectively.

Source: Smith, Amanda, ed. *Hostage to Fortune: The Letters of Joseph P. Kennedy.* New York: Viking Press, 2001. ©2001 by the Trustees of the John F. Kennedy Library Foundation. Used by permission of Viking Penguin, a division of Penguin Putnam Inc.

Boston, June 14, 1921
My Dear Mr. Garceau:

The following account has probably missed your attention, due to the many mistakes made in the original bill. As I am very anxious to get the matter cleaned up and out of the way, I would appreciate your sending me a check as soon as you conveniently can.

7 – 16 oz Bots.	Charteau	$ 15.05
22 – 24 " "	Pommerner	36.00
12 – 24 " "	Chat. Gircour	20.00
8 – 24 " "	" Carmeil	11.20
7 – 24 " "	" Macon	20.42
5 – 12 " "	" Giscours	10.34
14 – 24 " "	" Ruat	14.00
4 –12 " "	" "	8.00
3 – 24 " "	" Olivier	3.44
100 – 12 " "	" Perrier	14.50
50 – 24 " "	" "	10.50
		$163.45

Yours very truly,

June 26, 1922
Dear Matt:

Eddie Moor spoke to me about some gin you would like to get hold of. Before selling it to you I would like you to get the whole story on it.

The committee on our Decennial at Harvard bought 190 proof alcohol, and had it blended and fixed up by a Mr. Dehan, who formerly worked for my father, and who really is one of the best men on this in this part of the country. The stuff turned out very well indeed, and was perfectly satisfactory to all the fellows in the class who are, of course, used to the best—and the worst. Twenty-five dollars is the actual cost of the stuff, and I would be very happy for you to have it, if you think it would be satisfactory.

I would appreciate it if you would let me know at once, because the committee itself will take all of it that is not used.

With best regards.
Sincerely yours,

LETTERS FROM JOSEPH P. KENNEDY TO GRENVILLE MACFARLAND (1921) AND LOUIS B. MAYER (1928)

Letters from Kennedy to attorney Grenville MacFarland, general counsel to the Hearst papers and editor of Hearst's Boston American, *and to Louis B. Mayer, head of MGM. These letters, on a proposed corporate reorganization and about Kennedy's efforts on a film for Gloria Swanson, show his influence and the variety of his ventures in the film industry in the 1920s.*

Source: Smith, Amanda, ed. *Hostage to Fortune: The Letters of Joseph P. Kennedy.* New York: Viking Press, 2001. ©2001 by the Trustees of the John F. Kennedy Library Foundation. Used by permission of Viking Penguin, a division of Penguin Putnam Inc.

Boston, June 18, 1921
Dear Grenville:

Confirming my conversation with you over the telephone this morning, I have been representing the Grahams of London, one of the biggest trading houses in England and India, and Cox's Bank of London, who have an investment in the Robertson-Cole Company of over $5,000,000. I have just reorganized the company and we are going to go on. My own notion is, however, that all these smaller companies are on their way to the poorhouse and nothing can stop them unless a consolidation goes through.

I have talked with some people at Goldwyn's, and I feel sure that if we could make some deal with Mr. Hearst he could get hold of an organization that would consist of Goldwyn, Metro, Robertson-Cole, and Selznick, and would, to my mind, make a really worth while proposition. He is turning over enough product and of calibre sufficient enough to warrant his own organization, and sooner or later, when Paramount gets control, if they do, they will take all the cream he has made for himself.

What I would like to do is to have a talk with Mr. Hearst personally, not with one of his lieutenants, to find out whether he would be interested and whether we could get something started. My present plan is to be in New York next Wednesday and Thursday, and I would like to see Mr. Hearst sometime Thursday morning, if possible, or Wednesday morning if more convenient for him. Will you first see whether he would be interested and, if so, if you can make an appointment?

Sincerely yours,

May 25, 1928
Dear Mr. Mayer:

As you may or may not know, I have taken unto myself the responsibility of financing and producing the next Swanson picture. I have arranged to get von Stronheim to direct, and I can already hear you saying: "You have had no troubles in the picture business yet—they have just started." However, we shall try to do the best we can under the circumstances.

As both of these people expressed a desire to borrow Ollie Marsh from you (your cameraman), they have asked me if I would write you to see whether it would be possible. I realize you are very busy, but if it would be possible for us to use him in about nine weeks from now for the shooting of the Swanson picture, I would regard it as a personal favor.

As you probably know, not feeling that there was enough excitement in the picture business, I have gone into the vaudeville game—God knows what will happen there.

With kindest regards, believe me
Cordially yours,

"JOE KENNEDY HAS NEVER LIKED ANY JOB HE'S TACKLED" by John B. Kennedy (May 1928) [EXCERPT]

". . . I knew the time had arrived for me to do at thirty-four what I had been determined to do at twenty-four—be my own master in my own business.

"So I took a bold step and announced that I had launched my own private banking business. The day he received the notice, the managing editor of a Boston newspaper came to see me. He had a friend, an important figure in industry, whose business was threatened by a combination of brokers. They were depressing his concern's stock, and to offset this aggression a delicate and far-reaching campaign, involving vast resources, was needed.

"I was told that five million dollars in cash would be at my disposal to finance operations. If ever I was scared, it was then. After two days' discussion with my wife I took the assignment. For four solid months I lived in a New York office, watching every tick of the stock tape, buying stock at strategic moments, scouring the country for blocks of it, until, finally, enough was bought to defeat the onslaught on my client.

"Several of us emerged wealthy men. At thirty-five I found myself with a competence, six children, something of a reputation; but no real job. Canvassing the field I discerned one promising opening, which to me was not attractive—motion pictures.

"As a banker, several motion picture men had approached me for loans, never with success. I held the business suspect. Yet I knew one concern that had a tempting market which had been practically lost through bad management. I investigated, and found that this business was controlled by English capital. English pounds sterling to a value of seven million dollars had been sunk in it, with no prospect of ever rising to the surface.

"Again Mrs. Kennedy and I discussed the matter.

"I feel sure I can take this thing and make a go of it," I told her.

"Why not?" she said.

"I don't like the business. Motion pictures are not my idea of a sound and progressive career."

"All the more reason," said she, "that you should get into them."

"That settled it. Three days later I was on my way to England, after an exchange of cables. There I met the board of directors of the Film Booking Offices and made them a flat offer of $1,000,000 for the business. After an extensive palaver they declined, and I returned to the United States relieved, if anything, that somebody had decided for me that I should not enter the motion picture business.

"There I was mistaken, for within a month Lord Inverforth walked into my Boston office, where I was busy doing nothing, and announced, in that quiet but decisive way English business men have, that his company had decided to reconsider my offer. Before he left Boston I had control of one of the largest and most profitable motion picture concerns in the world." . . .

"But I soon found that the picture business, attuned to an extravagant note, was amenable to ordinary business arithmetic. The trouble with many concerns, like my own, was that employees occupying positions parallel to positions in other lines were vastly overpaid. It was no uncommon thing for accountants to receive $20,000 a year, when in other business they graded from $5,000 to $10,000.

"My first problem was to change that, which was easy. My second was to find an exclusive field in a rush of high-powered competition, which was not so easy. But I remembered the passengers on our sightseeing buses from Faneuil Hall to Lexington. Producers were fighting to get their pictures on Broadway, New York, and State Street, Chicago. I concentrated on getting and keeping Film Booking Offices' pictures on Main Street." . . .

"It took a long time for my distaste for this job to wear off," said Kennedy. "But what helped most was the fact that I could make my family partners. From the beginning I determined that Film Booking Offices would produce only clean pictures. One director, a high-priced man, put in what is known as the sex punch. One of his pictures went before my first board of review—Mrs. Kennedy and the seven Kennedys. They didn't like it. The director objected to the veto; but he was given the alternative of changing the picture or his job. He accepted the revision.

"Another time, when Red Grange's services were offered to me, I had doubts. I went home and asked my sons whether or not they'd like to see Red Grange in a picture. Their vote was unanimously yes. We engaged Grange." . . .

In this article written by John B. Kennedy and published in The American Magazine *in May 1928, Joseph P. Kennedy narrates the story of his successes in banking and motion pictures.*

Source: Kennedy, John B. "Joe Kennedy Has Never Liked Any Job He's Tackled." *The American Magazine,* May 1928.

Robert Marion La Follette

1855–1925
U.S. Senator and Reformer

Robert Marion La Follette was an impassioned senator and presidential candidate who championed progressive causes aimed at economic, social, and political reform.

La Follette was born into a family of farmers in Dane County, Wisconsin, on June 14, 1855. Graduating from the University of Wisconsin in 1879, he began his political career a year later as a Dane County district attorney. La Follette then went on to serve three terms as a Republican representative between 1884 and 1890; he lost his reelection bid in the Democratic landslide of 1890 and returned to practicing law. In 1900, La Follette reemerged as the governor of Wisconsin and a spokesman for the common people, attacking corrupt politics and big business, and improving living and working conditions in his state. His reputation as a reformer spread throughout the nation, and in 1906, his popularity earned him a seat in the U.S. Senate. Opposing the conservative policies of President William Howard Taft, he led the way for progressive Republicans. In 1912, La Follette contended for the Republican presidential nomina-

From the collections of the Library of Congress.

tion, as did the incumbent Taft and former President Theodore Roosevelt, which resulted in a sharply divided Republican Party and, ultimately, the election of Democrat **Woodrow Wilson**.

Over the course of Wilson's presidency (1913–21), Senator La Follette successfully shepherded progressive legislation through Congress. He advocated the 1913 adoption of the Seventeenth Amendment to the Constitution, which provided for the direct election of senators by state voters, and sponsored the 1915 Seaman's Bill, which improved the working conditions of sailors and the safety of passengers. This legislation, commonly known as the "La Follette Seaman's law," was one of his greatest victories and one of the federal government's first efforts to assist laborers. La Follette dedicated himself to the welfare of workers by helping to establish the Department of Labor and the Federal Trade Commission, and fought for the equality of all citizens by supporting

voting rights for women and civil rights for ethnic and racial minorities.

As the United States approached entry into World War I in 1917, though, relations between La Follette and President Wilson dissolved into bitter tensions. La Follette adamantly protested American intervention, believing that international battles benefited only wealthy corporations; he claimed that "War is the money changer's opportunity and the social reformer's doom." After a German submarine torpedoed the British liner *Laconia*, President Wilson submitted the Armed Ship Bill to Congress in March 1917. La Follette and five antiwar colleagues banded together to stop its passage in Congress by holding a filibuster—debating the measure at length and intentionally holding the floor until the session adjourned in order to prevent a vote. Outraged, President Wilson decided to arm U.S. merchant ships without congressional approval, and he publicly denounced those who had thwarted the bill: "A little group of willful men, representing no opinion but their own, have rendered the great Government of the United States helpless and contemptible."

As the leader of this "little group," La Follette received the most criticism for his antiwar stance, as well as the most admiration for his steadfast convictions. On April 4, 1917, in a special session of the sixty-fifth Congress, he was one of six senators to vote against the declaration of war on Germany. During World War I, he also opposed the draft, protected the civil liberties of war objectors, and promoted a tax system to keep individuals and corporations from profiting from the war. La Follette's bold actions in the face of patriotic fervor prompted the media, political cartoonists, pro-war organizations, and fellow constituents to condemn him as a traitor. The Senate Committee on Elections and Privileges even considered expelling him from Congress and conducted an investigation. La Follette, eventually exonerated by the committee, continued his crusades.

Following the war, La Follette contested the Versailles Treaty and the League of Nations, arguing that both peace measures preserved the status quo of powerful nations. Loathing the inequities between the laboring and wealthy classes, he focused on helping ordinary citizens by exposing industrial crimes. His most significant achievement was spearheading the investigation of the Teapot Dome scandal during President **Warren G. Harding**'s administration. The Teapot Dome scandal concerned the secret leasing of naval oil reserves to private oil companies. In 1921 and 1922, Secretary of the Interior Albert B. Fall supplied these leases in exchange for cash gifts and interest-free "loans." La Follette furiously declared that this exploitation of natural resources enabled private interests to gain further control over farmers, businessmen, and anyone who used petroleum for automobiles and other types of machinery. This scandal, made public in 1924, came to symbolize the political corruption characteristic of this era.

For many Americans searching for social and political change, La Follette was the natural presidential candidate for the new Progressive Party. Formed at a 1924 Conference for Progressive Political Action, party supporters included farm and labor groups, church and women's organizations, socialists, and progressive Republicans and Democrats. Accepting their nomination, La Follette ran independently against Republican **Calvin Coolidge** and Democrat John Davis. His platform called for a national referendum on declarations of war, elimination of child labor, nationalized railroads, decreased power of the Supreme Court, increased taxes on the wealthy, and the relief of farmers burdened by high tariffs. He stressed that "the supreme issue" was "the encroachment of the powerful few upon the rights of many." In November 1924, La Follette lost the election to Coolidge, but he carried his home state of Wisconsin and polled almost 5,000,000 votes, or 16.6 percent of the popular vote. Less than a year later, he died in Washington, D.C., on June 18, 1925.

Known as "Battling Bob," La Follette protested World War I and proposed reform measures in an atmosphere of national patriotism and political conservatism. The public viewed him both as a radical who generated chaos and a reformer who symbolized freedom. For farmers, laborers, minorities, and everyday Americans, La Follette fought to rectify the corruption of the privileged classes and represent the causes of the common people.

Renée Miller

For Further Reading

Burgchardt, Carl R. *Robert M. La Follette, Sr.: the Voice of Conscience.* New York: Greenwood Press, 1992.

La Follette, Belle Case and Fola. *Robert M. La Follette, June 14, 1855–June 18, 1925.* New York: Hafner Publishing, 1971.

Thelen, David P. *Robert M. La Follette and the Insurgent Spirit.* Madison: University of Wisconsin Press, 1985.

Unger, Nancy C. *Fighting Bob La Follette: The Righteous Performer.* Chapel Hill: University of North Carolina Press, 2000.

"THE ONLY ADEQUATE AWARD" POLITICAL CARTOON (March 7, 1917)

THE ONLY ADEQUATE REWARD.

In the tide of national patriotism, supporters of World War I condemned La Follette as a traitor. Appearing in the New York World *in 1917, this political cartoon by Rollin Kirby shows the hand of Germany honoring La Follette with the Iron Cross, the country's award for heroic wartime service. Pictured behind him are other antiwar politicians: William J. Stone, James A. O'Gorman, Moses E. Clapp, James K. Vardaman, and George W. Norris—who also objected to Wilson's decision to act against German aggression.*

Source: From the collections of the Library of Congress.

WRITTEN MESSAGE FROM ROBERT MARION LA FOLLETTE (1924) [EXCERPT]

La Follette hoped that the 1924 presidential election would unite the country's diverse progressive elements into a major political organization. This message, written by him and delivered by his son Robert La Follette, Jr., addresses a variety of delegates at that year's eventful Conference for Progressive Political Action, where La Follette received the nomination as the presidential candidate from the new Progressive Party.

Source: La Follette, Belle Case and Fola. *Robert M. La Follette, June 14, 1855–June 18, 1925.* New York: Hafner Publishing, 1971.

"I stand for an honest realignment in American politics, confident that the people in November will take such action as will insure the creation of a new party in which all Progressives may unite. I would not, however, accept a nomination or an election to the Presidency if doing so meant for Progressive Senators and Representatives and Progressive state governments, the defeat which would inevitably result from the placing of complete third party tickets in the field at the present time. . . . Permanent political parties have been born in this country after, and not before national campaigns, and they have come from the people, not from the proclamations of individual leaders. . . . If the hour is at hand for the birth of a new political party, the American people next November will register their will and their united purpose by a vote of such magnitude that a new political party will be inevitable. . . . I shall submit my name as an Independent Progressive candidate for President, together with the names of duly qualified candidates for electors, for filing on the ballots in every state in the Union. My appeal will be addressed to every class of the people in every section of the country. I am a candidate upon the basis of my public record as a member of the House of Representatives, as Governor of Wisconsin, and as a member of the United States Senate. I shall stand upon that record exactly as it is written, and shall give my support only to such progressive principles as are in harmony with it."

ROBERT MARION LA FOLLETTE GIVING RADIO SPEECH (1924)

La Follette gained a reputation as an independent, persistent, and impassioned leader of progressive politics. This photo of La Follette giving a speech over the radio captures his famous fighting image.

Source: From the collections of the Library of Congress.

"LA FOLLETTE" from *The Outlook* (July 1, 1925)

Though a Mid-Westerner by birth and breeding, Mr. La Follette, particularly in the later years of his life, seemed to think of America with a European mind.

It was because he thought in a European rather than American way that he became progressively more and more incapable of understanding his own country. As his life drew to a close his spirit seemed to become increasingly bitter. His illusions, rising out of his misunderstanding of his fellow-countrymen, brought him disappointment that culminated in the defeat of his plans to become President. The wonder is, not that such a man should have met with so many rebuffs, but that he should have found in his own country so large a following. The reason for his leadership is to be found in the fact that in America there is an enormous number of people who have brought with them from other lands or have inherited or imbibed from those who brought them here prejudices, assumptions, modes of thought, that belong to a hard and rigid class system characteristic of Europe and have missed the freedom of spirit, the resentment against paternalism, the self-reliance, and the social sense of natural equality that are the products of the fluid society which has developed here in America.

If to be Americanized means to conform to the outward fashion of manner, speech, customs, ways of living, prevalent in America, hundreds of thousands of those who followed La Follette were completely Americanized, as was Mr. La Follette himself. But if to be Americanized means to have the sort of a spirit that established this country and made it great, many of those who wear American collars and shoes and the clothes that come between and who live in American towns or villages after the fashion of other Americans, attend Chautauqua assemblies, and belong to lodges after the most orthodox American fashion, are really not American at all. It is easier to illustrate than to define the American spirit. It is the spirit that is common in John Hancock and Patrick Henry and John Paul Jones and Andrew Jackson and Abraham Lincoln. It shows itself in the plebeian Ben Franklin and the aristocratic George Washington. You cannot think of any of these men as dividing Americans up into permanent classes with conflicting interests, to be used as material for political maneuvering and agitation. Not only in our big cities but in large portions of the Northwest there are masses of people who have no liking for that which these names represent, for they have little understanding of it. These various elements are diverse in politics; but they have one thing in common—their antipathy to the American tradition.

It was of these that Mr. La Follette became spokesman. He thought as they thought. He has been called a demagogue; but he was not a demagogue if by that word is meant one who insincerely appeals to the passions and prejudices of the people he seeks to control. Mr. La Follette shared the prejudices and the passions of those whom he led. His colleagues who differed from him most decidedly were generally ready to recognize his honesty of purpose. It was inevitable that he

should not only oppose but attempt to obstruct the entrance of America into the World War. He thought of that war in purely European terms, as did most of his constituents. He could not conceive of it as an issue involving the soul of America, for the simple reason that he did not understand America's soul. It was not that he consciously wished to weaken his country. On the contrary, after America entered the war he voted to provide the Nation with the resources necessary to prosecute it. His isolation at that time was really symbolic of the isolation of his spirit from the spirit of his country not only at that time but throughout the larger part of his public career.

Of course such a man, representing the antagonism of the hyphenate and the un-Americanized to the American spirit, incurred the active hostility of those who felt themselves particularly the heirs of that spirit. Such a one, for instance, was the late Barrett Wendell, of Harvard. With varying phrase he reiterated his opinion "that no one can be of any nation who feels bound to any other;" and, believing this, he distrusted the Americanism of any who had retained "a particle of direct personal traditions not native to this country." Naturally, such a man was wholly out of patience with La Follette—"a distorted fool-fire, a begrimed Will-o'-the-Wisp," as he called him,; and he further characterized him as "fantastic, to me, man and name alike; mistily, freakishly untrue to the vagrant nature of the soul of him." More discerning, because more discriminating, is the comment of one who, though not a native American, now understands and shares the spirit of America. John Spargo, an Englishman by birth and for many years a member and leader of the Socialist Party in the United States, characterized Mr. La Follette's leadership in an article in The Outlook last October. Expressing great admiration for him personally, Mr. Spargo said of Mr. La Follette: "His social philosophy I hold to be antiquated, his political programme to be alien in conception and inimical to the orderly evolution of our life, and his foreign policy to be pregnant with possibility of disaster, not to this Nation alone, but to mankind." And of La Follette's proposal for nationalization, Mr. Spargo said: "In essence it is a proposal to check arbitrarily the natural evolution of American economic life along lines prescribed by its own needs and experience, and to force it into channels prescribed by European needs and experience."

Can any leader take Mr. La Follette's place as the head of those diverse elements whose only common bond is their antipathy to the American tradition? No such leader seems to be in sight. Mr. La Follette was called a radical by some and a progressive by others. There are radical leaders and progressive leaders who may develop conspicuously; but Mr. La Follette's peculiar position in this country was not his by virtue of being a radical or progressive. In no sense did he succeed to the progressive leadership laid down by Mr. Roosevelt. Indeed, he was the advocate of the very

During his lifetime, La Follette was viewed both as a radical and a reformer. Appearing in The Outlook *on July 1, 1925, this obituary reflects on the varying elements of La Follette's Midwestern background, European mind-set, and rebellion against American traditions.*

Source: "La Follette." *The Outlook*, July 1, 1925.

things that Mr. Roosevelt most strenuously and successfully fought.

Politically Senator Ladd, whose death has quickly followed that of Senator La Follette, might in one sense have been a successor of Mr. La Follette. But Mr. Ladd was a native of Maine, where he received his university education, and had a New England background. His radicalism was that engendered by his fight against special interests, and his association with Mr. La Follette was not such as to make him the leader of the hyphenates. On the other hand, no mere hyphenate could take Mr. La Follette's place; for he would at once be under the suspicion of those whose hyphens pointed in different directions from his

Senator La Follette's greatest service was undoubtedly rendered to his own State. He upset there a political regime composed of alliances between politics and moneyed interests that were as obnoxious as those existing in any State of the Union. In its place he built up a political machine of which he remained the engineer. In the process he produced laws the benefit of which have extended to other States through imitation. In particular Wisconsin under his leadership pointed the way toward the public control of public service corporations and the modification of the system of more or less oligarchical nominating conventions for which the direct primary is not yet fully a satisfactory substitute. To rehearse even briefly the achievements in Wisconsin since La Follette's rise to control would require space not here available.

In the Senate La Follette's record has been one of contradiction, as elsewhere in his life. It has been marked by constructive achievement. An outstanding instance is the Seamen's Law, which has aroused and still arouses diversity of opinion, but which seems firmly established. During his Senatorial career no one challenged his pre-eminence as a filibusterer. His capacity for speech-making killed legislation even when it was employed only as a threat.

To the casual visitor Mr. La Follette's home life was obviously that which has characterized the sound and wholesome communities of the Middle West. His devotion to his family has been more than once exemplified, but never more poignantly than when he nursed one of his sons back to health while he himself was practically ostracized, or, rather, had virtually ostracized himself. In his career his wife has been his partner, and is expected now that his career is over to carry on.

Mr. La Follette represented an epoch in American political life, or, rather, one aspect of that epoch. He was in a sense a survival of a period when the real struggle in America was between the Government in State or Nation and its creature the corporation. He survived the close of that epoch without recognizing that the epoch had closed. In spite of his claims to the title progressive, he had failed to progress with the times. He will be remembered for what he did; but he will also be remembered for what he tried to do after the need of doing it had passed. He was a rebel. He tried to carry on his revolt after the essentials for which he had been fighting had virtually been won. He had a habit of rebelling and became in the end the captain of that minority whose only ground for rebellion was a lack of understanding in their own country. When the historian of the future comes to write of the first quarter of the twentieth century in America, one of the figures which it will be necessary for him to paint, in however gloomy colors, will be that of Robert Marion La Follette.

Albert Lasker

1880–1952

Influential Advertising Executive

Albert Lasker, often considered the founder of modern advertising, restructured the advertising industry and recognized its power to reshape society. Grasping how advertising could actually create needs where none had existed previously, Lasker was nothing less than an architect of consumerism.

Albert Davis Lasker, born in Freiburg, Germany, on May 1, 1880, was the son of American parents of German-Jewish background who were traveling in Germany. Soon the family returned home to Galveston, Texas, where Lasker grew up. He showed a flair for writing early on, starting his own weekly newspaper before he had entered his teens. As a high school student Lasker edited a school magazine and worked for the *Galveston Morning News*. He seemed set on a career in journalism, but his father, a wealthy businessman, insisted that he try advertising instead, arranging for his son an entry-level job at Chicago's Lord & Thomas agency in 1898. Initially planning to stay at Lord & Thomas only long enough to placate his father, Lasker remained at the firm for 44 years.

Ascending rapidly through the company's hierarchy, Lasker became a partner in 1903 and the owner of the agency in 1912. By that time a new concept of advertising had already taken shape in his mind, and he had hired a stable of copywriters who were well along the way to putting it into practice. A print advertisement, Lasker believed, should persuade potential buyers that a product was superior to its competitors, irresistibly inexpensive, or desirable in itself in a way that the reader might not have realized. During the late nineteenth century, most advertisements did little more than state the existence and excellence of the products they represented; the primary function of an advertising agency at the time was simply to place advertisements in various publications. Lasker, partly inspired by Canadian-born copywriter John E. Kennedy and by other writers that he snared for Lord & Thomas, came to believe that advertising copy should imaginatively promote products rather than just politely

inform readers of their presence on the market. To implement these ideas, Lasker reorganized his agency, creating the position of account executive as a liaison between the client and his creative staff. Lord & Thomas grew rapidly under Lasker's leadership; one of his most successful campaigns, mounted on behalf of the California Fruit Growers Exchange (later Sunkist, Inc.), promoted drinking orange juice as part of a healthful daily routine.

Between 1918 and 1923 Lasker relinquished day-to-day control over Lord & Thomas, becoming involved in two new arenas of modern image-making that served to deepen his thinking about the power of the media in modern society. Those arenas were politics and sports. In 1918 Lasker became publicity chief for the Republican National Committee for the midterm congressional election; two years later he became one of the party's top operatives, directing the advertising campaign for the successful Republican presidential candidate, **Warren G. Harding**. Harding rewarded Lasker with the chairmanship of the U.S. Shipping Board. (Although he supported the isolationism espoused by the Republicans, Lasker later became a supporter of Democratic Presidents Franklin D. Roosevelt and Harry S. Truman.) After World War I Lasker had become the majority stockholder in the Chicago Cubs baseball team. Like other baseball bigwigs he saw his investment threatened by the "Black Sox" scandal in which gambling cartels conspired with Chicago White Sox players, including **Shoeless Joe Jackson**, to fix the 1919 World Series. At a time when the game's future was uncertain, Lasker understood the public appeal of yielding some jurisdiction over the game to an outside authority; he was instrumental in the appointment of Judge Kenesaw Mountain Landis as the first Commissioner of Baseball. In 1925 Lasker sold his Cubs stock to the Chicago chewing gum magnate William Wrigley; the renaming of Cubs Park as Wrigley Field is said to have been a Lasker suggestion.

In Lasker's absence Lord & Thomas had lost its preeminent position in the advertising industry, and in 1923 he returned to the helm determined to regain the top spot. The campaigns he directed in the 1920s brought his ideas to their highest expression. Lord & Thomas's campaign for the American Tobacco Company's Lucky Strike cigarette brand involved an effort to fundamentally alter one of the norms of U.S. society: the taboo against female cigarette smoking. Lasker adopted a two-pronged approach. He appealed to the glamour that Americans perceived in European high culture by recruiting stars from New York's Metropolitan Opera to represent the brand—"I protect my precious voice with Lucky Strikes," said one. As movies exploded in popularity following the introduction of sound, movie stars were brought in to give endorsements as well. Lasker also noticed changes in the conception of the ideal female body and of a new emphasis on weight control—advertisements advised women to "Reach for a Lucky Instead of a Sweet." The campaign's success was phenomenal: Lasker increased sales of Lucky Strikes by 312 percent within a year and made the brand the nation's top seller. Although image was the underlying factor in such campaigns, Lasker was a believer in the power of text over image in advertisements. He consistently argued that advertising copy should give the consumer a "reason why" he or she should choose to purchase the product featured in the ad, and he paid copywriters large bonuses for successful slogans.

Although he rarely wrote copy himself, Lasker oversaw every aspect of the advertising process from recruiting the client to the selection of media; such was his reach that he might be considered an actual creator of several familiar products that emerged during this period, Kleenex facial tissues and Kotex sanitary napkins among them. In part his expanded success in the 1920s came from his successful adaptation of his print-advertising ideas to the new medium of radio, and he cemented the ties between advertising and the programming of that new mass medium. The *Amos 'n' Andy* radio program owed its existence to the massive campaign Lord & Thomas undertook to promote Pepsodent toothpaste, a sponsor of the show. By the early 1930s Lord & Thomas had regained its position atop the advertising industry.

Advertising under Lasker became the quintessential high-pressure industry, and Lasker himself suffered three psychiatric episodes, or "nervous breakdowns." He eventually entered a psychoanalyst's care. The individual who had done so much to homogenize the tastes of the American public became dismayed by advances in market research in the 1930s, and he tangled with several companies that tried to apply quantitative methods to measure the success of his campaigns. Shaken by the refusal of his son Edward to enter the advertising business, Lasker once again cut back his activities, retiring as Lord & Thomas's president in 1938 and cutting his ties with the company altogether four years later; the agency was reorganized under Lasker's three top lieutenants as Foote, Cone, and Belding.

In retirement Lasker became a noted art collector, but he found an outlet for his still considerable persuasive abilities in philanthropic activity related to medical research. With his third wife, the former Mary Woodard Reinhardt, he established the Albert and Mary Lasker Foundation to provide financial support for medical research projects, and in 1944 he led a fund-raising campaign for cancer research that almost doubled annual spending on the disease in the United States. He used his influence to promote public-private partnerships in the medical research field; one of the final accomplishments of his immensely influential career was the establishment of the National Institutes of Health in the years following World War II. He also was a key U.S. supporter of the new state of Israel. Lasker died in New York on May 30, 1952.

The extent of Albert Lasker's impact on U.S. society during the interwar period and beyond may be measured in the estimated $750 million of advertising that his agency placed while he was director, in the familiar consumer products that he introduced to the marketplace, and, most of all, in the changes he wrought in the psyche of American consumers, in whom he divined needs of which they themselves had hardly been aware.

James M. Manheim

For Further Reading

Gunther, John. *Taken at the Flood: The Story of Albert D. Lasker.* New York: Harper, 1960.

Morello, John A. *Selling the President, 1920: Albert D. Lasker, Advertising, and the Election of Warren G. Harding.* Westport, Conn.: Praeger Publishers, 2001.

Ogilvy, David. *Ogilvy on Advertising.* New York: Vintage Books, 1985.

BUSINESS CREED FROM LORD & THOMAS (1917)

PSYCHOLOGY
This is the twenty-first of a series of
business creeds by
Lord & Thomas

Unguided by psychology, salesmanship is crude. Good advertising must recognize facts like these:

People are dilatory. Without some incentive to prompt action or decision they will usually delay and forget.

It is natural to follow others. Impress folks with the crowd that goes your way.

It is natural to obey. A direct command is more effective than request.

People don't like problems. Present them only the worked-out solutions.

Too evident desire to sell puts men on guard against you.

Curiosity incites men more than fact. Half-told tales have an interest which completed tales have not.

Men covet an advantage. Things they can get which others can't are things they want the most.

Folks are not impressed by boasting.

When you quote others to confirm your statements you indict your own veracity.

Evident bias kills influence. Praise of an article is made doubly effective by a touch of criticism.

One's honesty can never be impressed save by some evident self-denial.

Masterful advertising has to consider a thousand such basic axioms.

That's one reason for its rarity.

CALIFORNIA SUNKIST ORANGES ADVERTISEMENT (1924)

"It is natural to follow others. Impress folks with the crowd that goes your way." Lasker's methods were not unique in the advertising world, but he often far outpaced his competitors because he was unafraid to think big—to try to modify public behavior on a large scale through his advertising campaigns.

Source: Gunther, John. *Taken at the Flood: The Story of Albert D. Lasker.* New York: Harper, 1960.

A 1924 advertisement for California Sunkist (originally the California Fruit Growers Exchange). Advertising, Lasker believed, should give customers a "reason why" they should choose a particular product; in this campaign, he stressed the nutritional value of drinking orange juice.

Source: From the collections of the Library of Congress.

"Is Advertising Read?" from Lord & Thomas (1927)

Three examples that bring out the answer.

The word *halitosis* lay buried in the widely "read" dictionary of the English language scores of years until set in ordinary type in an advertisement it became a byword of the millions.

As a result, a product 40 years on the market with moderate sale became a world leader. Bad breath became almost a fashion.

On the other hand, yeast was something merely to make bread with—until Fleischmann advertisements said otherwise.

Now we gain fair skins, robust health, cure ourselves of many of the common ills of mankind, and even look forward hopefully to Eternal Youth because of it.

For centuries women used makeshift hygienic pads. The subject itself was admittedly a forbidden one. A subject no one spoke about, much less wrote about, except in medical practice.

Then came Kotex. A sanitary pad. A product no woman had ever heard about. A product that admitted no definitely descriptive words in headlines to describe it.

Thus to learn what Kotex was intended for, the reader had to go *deep into the text* of the ads. Kotex headlines perforce had to be more or less indirect. No person could get the import of a Kotex ad *without reading virtually every word of the ad itself.*

That women did, everyone who follows advertising knows. Over 80% of the better class of women in America today employ Kotex. The makers of this product would be quick to answer whether or not advertising is read.

Thus Listerine, Fleischmann's Yeast and Kotex—at least three of the most notably successful products of the day—must be regarded as Simon Pure Advertising successes.

All had their basic selling stories, not in the headlines, but in the text of their ads. And readers had to read that text to be "sold." All stand as indisputable answers to the question, "Is Advertising Read?"

If people didn't read ads as carefully as news or feature matter, most of the successful concerns whose names are household words would be virtually unknown to the reading millions.

Men who have made money through advertising know how true that it.

Number 37 of a series . . . from Foote, Cone & Belding's file of Lord & Thomas originals.
Published April 21, 1927.

Lucky Strike Cigarettes Advertisement (1929)

Charles Lindbergh

1902–1974
Aviation Pioneer

Charles Lindbergh was an American aviator who became a national hero after making the first nonstop solo flight across the Atlantic Ocean in 1927.

Charles Augustus Lindbergh was born in Detroit, Michigan, on February 4, 1902. He inherited a tenacious spirit and respect for nature from his father and a reserved manner and love for science from his mother. In 1907, when his father was elected a U.S. representative to Congress, Lindbergh began spending half the year in Washington, D.C., and the rest of the year on the family farm in Minnesota. He enjoyed Washington, D.C.'s culture, visiting historic sites and exhibitions, and appreciated Minnesota's landscape, hunting and fishing on the west banks of the Mississippi River. After watching an air show at age 10, he became fascinated with airplanes and intent on flying.

Never fond of traditional schooling, Lindbergh attended the University of Wisconsin for only three semesters before pursuing the study of flight at Nebraska Aircraft Corporation. He flew for the first time in 1922 and left school shortly thereafter with just eight hours of instruction to travel through the South and Midwest and perform flying tricks. He entertained spectators with piloting and parachuting stunts, and offered five-minute plane rides for $5.00. In an age attracted to spectacles, small-town America marveled at these wild feats exhibiting modern technology.

In 1924, Lindbergh enlisted for formal training in the Army Air Service Cadet Program in San Antonio, Texas, and graduated the next year at the top of his class as a second lieutenant. Appointed as an airmail pilot in 1926, Lindbergh flew the dangerous route from Chicago to St. Louis fearlessly. He performed four emergency parachute jumps, and survived a two-plane, in-air collision. Lindbergh elevated the term "daring youth"—the barnstormers and adventurers who were the new heroes of the Roaring Twenties—to new levels. This success, however, seemed minor compared to his quest to make the first nonstop solo flight from New York to Paris. The successful pilot would win $25,000 from philan-

From the collections of the Library of Congress.

thropist Raymond B. Orteig. Backed by St. Louis businessmen, Lindbergh bought a single-engine plane called the *Spirit of St. Louis* and prepared to complete the trip that was attracting attention on both sides of the Atlantic.

On May 20, 1927, Lindbergh left New York City in his monoplane as a young daredevil and landed 33½ hours later at Le Bourget Field, Paris, as an international hero. His historic flight exhilarated Americans—from schoolchildren to political leaders. People longed for a pure and noble idol in an era known for its bootlegging and gambling. President Calvin Coolidge, while awarding him with the Distinguished Flying Cross and the Congressional Medal of Honor, called Lindbergh "a boy representing the best traditions of this country." The press described Lindbergh as a modern pioneer exploring the open sky instead of the wild frontier, and a newspaper cartoon juxtaposed the *Spirit of St. Louis* leaving from Paris in 1927 with a covered wagon heading for California in 1849. Seen as a demigod on both sides of the Atlantic, he went on to promote aviation on a goodwill tour through Europe and America and plot air routes for Pan American and Trans World Airlines.

In 1932, tragedy followed triumph when Lindbergh's two-year-old son was kidnapped and later found dead. A crime highly sensationalized by the press and public, its investigation in court was called the "Trial of the Century." In 1935 he and his wife sought refuge in Europe from the hounding of the media. Lindbergh toured throughout Europe studying aviation centers in various countries; after praising the Germany's air force, he recieved an honorary medal from Nazi Germany in 1938. He returned to the United States in 1939 and traveled the country promoting American neutrality in World War II. When the United States entered the war, his "treasonable" conduct lead to his rejection from the Army Air Corps in 1941. Instead, the civilian Lindbergh served by consulting for aircraft companies and flying secretly in 50 combat missions. He eventually was restored to his position in the Air

Force, contributed to advancements in fields such as aeronautics and cryogenics, and wrote several books. In 1954, his book, The *Spirit of St. Louis*, won the Pulitzer Prize for autobiography. Living his final years in Maui, Hawaii, Lindbergh died there on August 26, 1974.

A single achievement made Lindbergh, perhaps, the greatest hero of the 1920s. His nonstop solo flight across the Atlantic showed that pioneering was still possible even in the midst of an urban and industrial society. Whereas the legendary Daniel Boone and Davy Crockett explored land, Lindbergh ventured into the sky, infusing Americans with pride. Lindbergh's bravery, honor, and modesty fit the archetype of the chivalrous hero, yet, at the same time, his bold adventures marked him as a leader among the decade's daring youth.

Renée Miller

For Further Reading

Berg, A. Scott. *Lindbergh*. New York: G. P. Putnam's Sons, 1998.

Hixson, Walter L. *Charles A. Lindbergh: Lone Eagle*. New York: HarperCollins, 1996.

Lindbergh, Charles A. *The Spirit of St. Louis*. New York: Charles Scribner's Sons, 1953.

REPORT BY CHARLES LINDBERGH (1925)

As one of the decade's daring youth, Lindbergh set his first aviation record in 1925 when he survived a two-plane collision on his airmail route from Chicago to St. Louis. Here, he relays the chaotic events of his emergency parachute jump with clarity and calm. Both Aviation *magazine and the New York Evening World posted this report.*

Source: Gill, Brendan. Lindbergh Alone. New York: Harcourt Brace Jovanovich, 1977. Reprinted with permission from Aviation Week and Space Technology.

Report by Cadet C.A Lindbergh on the collision in air between S.E. 5.E. No.50 piloted by Lt. McAllister and S.E. 5.E. No. 55 piloted by Cadet C.A. Lindbergh at about 8:50 A.M. March 6th, 1925, approximately ten miles north of Kelly Field.

A nine-ship SE-5 formation, commanded by Lieutenant Blackburn, was attacking a DH4B, flown by Lieutenant Maughan at about a 5,000 foot altitude and several hundred feet above the clouds. I was flying on the left of the top unit, Lieut. McAllister on my right, and Cadet Love leading. When we nosed down on the DH, I attacked from the left and Lieut. McAllister from the right. After Cadet Love pulled up, I continued to dive on the DH for a short time before pulling up to the left. I saw no other ship nearby. I passed above the DH and a moment later felt a slight jolt followed by the crash. My head was thrown forward against the cowling and my plane seemed to turn around and hang nearly motionless for an instant. I closed the throttle and saw an SE-5 with Lieut. McAllister in the cockpit, a few feet on my left. He was apparently unhurt and getting ready to jump.

Our ships were locked together with the fuselages approximately parallel. My right wing was damaged and had folded back slightly, covering the forward right-hand corner of the cockpit. Then the ships started to mill around and the wires began whistling. The right wing commenced vibrating and striking my head at the bottom of each oscillation. I removed the rubber band safetying the belt, unbuckled it, climbed out past the trailing edge of the damaged wing, and with my feet on the cowling on the right side of the cockpit, which was then in a nearly vertical position, I jumped backwards as far from the ship as possible. I had no difficulty in locating the pullring and experienced no sensation of falling. The wreckage was falling nearly straight down and for some time I fell in line with its path and only slightly to one side. Fearing the wreckage might fall on me, I did not pull the rip-cord until I dropped several hundred feet and into the clouds. During this time I had turned one-half revolution and was falling flat and face downward. The parachute functioned perfectly; almost as soon as I pulled the rip-cord the risers jerked on my shoulders, the leg straps tightened, my head went down, and the chute fully opened.

I saw Lieut. McAllister floating above me and the wrecked ships pass about 100 yards to one side, continuing to spin to the right and leaving a trail of lighter fragments along their path. I watched them until, still locked together, they crashed in the mesquite about 2000 feet below and burst into flames several seconds after impact.

Next I turned my attention to locating a landing place. I was over mesquite and drifting in the general direction of a plowed field which I reached by slipping the chute. Shortly before striking the ground, I was drifting backwards, but was able to swing around in the harness just as I landed on the side of a ditch 100 feet from the edge of the mesquite. Although the impact of the landing was too great for me to remain standing, I was not injured in any way. The parachute was still held open by the wind and did not collapse until I pulled in one group of shroud lines.

During my descent I lost my goggles, a vest-pocket camera which fitted tightly in my hip pocket, and the rip-cord of the parachute.

Lieut. Maughan landed his DH in the field and took our chutes back to Kelly. Twenty minutes later Captain Guidera brot [sic] a DH and a chute over for me and I returned to Kelly Field with him.

An hour after the crash we were flying in another nine-ship S.E. 5 formation with two new S.E.5's.

CHARLES LINDBERGH'S MEDAL (1927)

Shown here is Lindbergh's medal for being the first aviator to fly nonstop between New York and Paris.

Source: From the collections of the Library of Congress.

LE BOURGET AIRFIELD BEFORE CHARLES LINDBERGH'S LANDING (1927)

The world watched the Spirit of St. Louis *with anticipation on its first transatlantic journey, mapping its progress over Ireland and Great Britain into France. In this photo, the bright searchlights direct Lindbergh in his landing on the airfield. Lindbergh best described the crowd's greeting: "It was like drowning in a human sea."*

Source: ©Bettmann/ Corbis

CHARLES LINDBERGH AND *SPIRIT OF ST. LOUIS* (1927)

In this photo, taken on May 31, 1927, Lindbergh appears in front of the Spirit of St. Louis. *After completing his unprecedented feat, Lindbergh and his monoplane became inseparable images in the minds of the public.*

Source: From the collections of the Library of Congress.

"LINDBERGH—EAGLE OF THE USA" by the High Hatters (1927)

For Lindbergh
Oh what a flying fool was he
Lindbergh
His name will live in history
Over the ocean, he flew all alone
Gambling with fate and with dangers unknown
Others may take that trip across the sea
Upon some future day
But take your hats off to Lucky Lucky Lindbergh
The Eagle of the USA

The High Hatters, a popular jazz band from the 1920s, wrote this song celebrating Lindbergh's nonstop solo flight. Reflective of the frenzy following Lindbergh's feat, the patriotic lyrics express spirited admiration for his daring achievement.

Source: The Jazz Age Page. "Calvin Coolidge Welcomes Charles Lindbergh Home!" 1999. *www.btinternet.com/~dreklind/coollind.htm* (Aug. 28, 2001).

Henry Cabot Lodge

1850–1924

Statesman

Henry Cabot Lodge, chairman of the Senate Foreign Relations Committee at the end of World War I, thwarted President **Woodrow Wilson** by leading Congress's rejection of the Treaty of Versailles and the entry of the United States into the League of Nations.

Lodge was born on May 12, 1850, in Boston, the son of a wealthy merchant and shipowner. He graduated from Harvard in 1871 and married his cousin, Anna Cabot "Nannie" Davis, on graduation day. After earning his degree from the Harvard Law School (1872–74), he studied political science at Harvard and in 1876 was awarded the college's first doctorate in that subject.

He was elected to the Massachusetts House of Representatives in 1879 and became increasingly involved in the Republican Party. Lodge served from 1887 until 1893 in the U.S. House of Representatives, where he quickly earned a reputation as a hard worker, a party loyalist, and a compelling speaker. In January 1893 he was chosen by the legislature of Massachusetts to replace a retiring senator; he would serve in the U.S. Senate until his death in 1924. Representative Lodge was one of the authors of the Sherman Anti-Trust Law (1890), designed to weaken the power of monopolies, and as senator he helped draft the Pure Food and Drug Act (1906). International relations was his primary interest, however, and he hoped to become chairman of the Foreign Relations Committee.

As a senator, Lodge was a conservative, party-line Republican, but he supported some of the reform measures of President Theodore Roosevelt, and advised Roosevelt on foreign relations from 1901–09. He was a consistent protectionist of U.S. trade and industry, as shown in his support of high tariffs. He also advocated a strong navy to defend U.S. interests and was suspicious of international agreements that would subject the United States to international arbitration or disarmament.

Even before Wilson was elected president in 1912, Lodge distrusted him, suspecting that Wilson was a con-

From the collections of the Library of Congress.

servative at heart who had adopted progressive policies only to win votes. "I think he would sacrifice any opinion at any moment for his own benefit," he wrote to a colleague, and Lodge was not alone in distrusting the sincerity of the president's convictions. When World War I began in Europe in August 1914, Lodge supported Wilson's declaration of United States neutrality, but as German submarines repeatedly sank American ships, he began to consider Wilson's reluctance to strengthen American armed forces to be a sign of weakness. Lodge praised the president, however, when Wilson asked Congress in April 1917 for a declaration of war against Germany, and he supported most of the Administration's war legislation.

When Republicans won a majority in the midterm congressional elections of 1918, Lodge was named chairman of the Senate's Foreign Relations Committee, which was his dream come true. He attained this position at a time when United States involvement in world affairs was more extensive than ever. American leadership in the Allied victory and in the subsequent peace talks required international peacekeeping responsibilities that isolationists found excessive, though a majority of the population was willing to accept U.S. membership in the League of Nations.

After the armistice in November 1918, Lodge approved many of the terms reached at the Paris Peace Conference, and even agreed with the general idea of an international organization to provide for peace and stability, but he regarded the League of Nations as "loose, involved, and full of dangers." He objected in particular to Article 10 of the League's covenant, which, in providing for the protection of member states' territorial integrity, could potentially drag the United States into any number of foreign disputes. Lodge declared to the Senate, "We are asked [to] subject our own will to the will of other nations. . . . That guarantee we must maintain at any cost when our word is once given."

Chairman Lodge led the fight against U.S. membership in the League of Nations. He drafted 14 "reservations" to the League's covenant, the most important of which was that Article 10 would not be binding on the United States "unless in any particular case the Congress . . . shall by act or joint resolution so provide." A two-thirds majority was required for ratification of the Treaty of Versailles, and more than one-third of the Senate agreed with enough of Lodge's reservations to prevent ratification. A compromise might have been possible, but Wilson insisted that the covenant be part of the treaty and refused to yield in the slightest: "Let Lodge compromise," he said to one of his aides. On November 19, 1919, almost exactly a year after the armistice was signed, the Treaty of Versailles was rejected by the Senate by a vote of 55 to 35. A second vote early the next year brought a majority in favor of the League with Lodge's reservations, but fell short of the required two-thirds majority.

Lodge's opposition to the League of Nations hurt him in the election of 1920, though he managed to win reelection by 7,000 votes out of about 900,000 votes cast. He was one of the senators who backed the nomination of **Warren G. Harding** as the Republican presidential candidate that year, and early in Harding's Administration he served as a delegate to the Washington Disarmament Conference, intended to end the naval competition between the United States, Great Britain, and Japan. Lodge helped win the passage of the disarmament treaty in early 1922. He died in Boston on November 9, 1924.

As the United States became a world power, Henry Cabot Lodge was admired as a strong defender of the national interest, particularly in his efforts to ensure that United States sovereignty would not be sacrificed "to the will of other nations." His combative nature and stubbornly partisan views, however, have caused him to be remembered more for what he opposed than for what he stood for.

Mark LaFlaur

For Further Reading

Garraty, John A. *Henry Cabot Lodge.* New York: Knopf, 1965.

Lodge, Henry Cabot. *The Senate and the League of Nations.* New York: Scribner's, 1925.

Schriftgiesser, Karl. *The Gentleman from Massachusetts: Henry Cabot Lodge.* Boston: Little, Brown, 1944.

Widenor, William C. *Henry Cabot Lodge and the Search for an American Foreign Policy.* Berkeley: University of California Press, 1980.

LETTER FROM WOODROW WILSON TO HENRY CABOT LODGE (August 15, 1919)

In this 1919 letter, President Woodrow Wilson requests a meeting with Henry Cabot Lodge and the Senate Committee on Foreign Relations to discuss the Treaty of Versailles.

Source: National Archives.

THE WHITE HOUSE
WASHINGTON

15 August, 1919.

My dear Mr. Chairman:

I have received your letter of yesterday, and in reply hasten to express the hope that the Senate Committee on Foreign Relations will give me the pleasure of seeing them at the White House on Tuesday morning next, the 19th, at ten o'clock.

I also welcome the suggestion of the committee that nothing said at the conference shall be regarded as confidential. In order that the committee may have a full and trustworthy record of what is said, I shall have a stenographer present, and take the liberty of suggesting that if you should wish to bring one of the committee's stenographers with you, that would be entirely agreeable to me. The presence of the two stenographers would lighten the work.

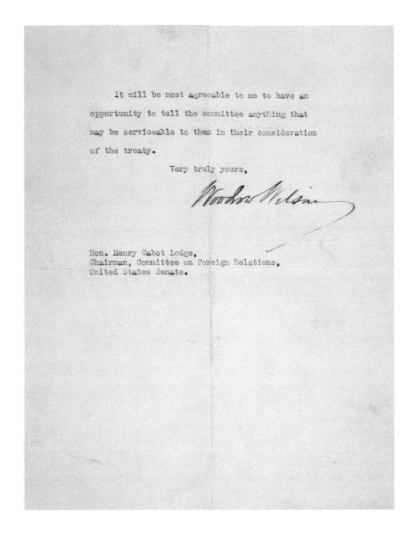

It will be most agreeable to me to have an opportunity to tell the committee anything that may be serviceable to them in their consideration of the treaty.

Very truly yours,

Woodrow Wilson

Hon. Henry Cabot Lodge,
Chairman, Committee on Foreign Relations,
United States Senate.

The Fourteen Reservations by Henry Cabot Lodge (1919)

Resolved (two-thirds of the Senators present concurring therein), That the Senate advise and consent to the ratification of the treaty of peace with Germany concluded at Versailles on the 28th day of June, 1919, subject to the following reservations and understandings, which are hereby made a part and condition of this resolution of ratification, which ratification is not to take effect or bind the United States until the said reservations and understandings adopted by the Senate have been accepted by an exchange of notes as a part and a condition of this resolution of ratification by at least three of the four principal allied and associated powers, to wit, Great Britain, France, Italy, and Japan:

1. The United States so understands and construes article 1 that in case of notice of withdrawal from the league of nations, as provided in said article, the United States shall be the sole judge as to whether all its international obligations and all its obligations under the said covenant have been fulfilled, and notice of withdrawal by the United States may be given by concurrent resolution of the Congress of the United States.

2. The United States assumes no obligation to preserve the territorial integrity or political independence of any other country or to interfere in controversies between nations—whether members of the league or not—under the provisions of article 10, or to employ the military or naval forces of the United States under any article of the treaty for any purpose, unless in any particular case the Congress, which, under the Constitution has the sole power to declare war or to authorize the employment of the military or naval forces of the United States, shall by act or joint resolution so provide.

3. No mandate shall be adopted by the United States under article 22, part 1, or any other provision of the treaty of peace with Germany, except by action of the Congress of the United States.

4. The United States reserves to itself exclusively the right to decide what questions are within its domestic jurisdiction and declares that all domestic and political questions relating wholly or in part to its internal affairs, including immigration, labor, coastwise traffic, the tariff, commerce, the suppression of traffic in women and children, and in opium and other dangerous drugs, and all other domestic questions, are solely within the jurisdiction of the United States and are not under this treaty to be submitted in any way either to arbitration or to the consideration of the council or of

Senate Foreign Relations Committee Chairman Lodge drafted this list of 14 reservations—an allusion to Wilson's Fourteen Points—to the League of Nations Covenant. The most important reservation was his objection to Covenant article X, which Lodge asserted would have required the United States Congress to surrender its constitutional power to declare war.

Source: Bailey, Thomas A. *Woodrow Wilson and the Great Betrayal*. New York: Macmillan, 1945.

the assembly of the league of nations, or any agency thereof, or to the decision or recommendation of any other power.

5. The United States will not submit to arbitration or to inquiry by the assembly or council of the league of nations, provided for in said treaty of peace, any questions which in the judgment of the United States depend upon or relate to its long-established policy, commonly known as the Monroe Doctrine; said doctrine is to be interpreted by the United States alone and is hereby declared to be wholly outside the jurisdiction of said league of nations and entirely unaffected by any provision contained in said treaty of peace with Germany.

6. The United States withholds its assent to articles 156, 157, and 158, and reserves full liberty of action with respect to any controversy which may arise under said articles between the Republic of China and the Empire of Japan.

7. The Congress of the United States will provide by law for the appointment of the representatives of the United States in the assembly and the council of the league of nations, and may in its discretion provide for the participation of the United States in any commission, tribunal, court, council, or conference, or in the selection of any members thereof and for the appointment of members of said commissions, committees, tribunals, courts, councils, or conferences, or any other representatives under the treaty of peace, or in carrying out its provisions, and until such participation and appointment have been so provided for and the powers and duties of such representatives have been defined by law, no person shall represent the United States under either said league of nations or the treaty of peace with Germany or be authorized to perform any act for or on behalf of the United States thereunder, and no citizen of the United States shall be selected or appointed as a member of said commissions, committees, tribunals, courts, councils, or conferences except with the approval of the Senate of the United States.

8. The United States understands that the reparation commission will regulate or interfere with exports from the United States to Germany, or from Germany to the United States, only when the United States by act or joint resolution of Congress approves such regulation or interference.

9. The United States shall not be obligated to contribute to any expenses of the league of nations, or of the secretariat, or of any commission, or committee, or conference, or other agency, organized under the league of nations or under the treaty or for the purpose of carrying out the treaty provisions, unless and until an appropriation of funds available for such expenses shall have been made by the Congress of the United States.

10. If the United States shall at any time adopt any plan for limitation of armaments proposed by the council of the league of nations under the provisions of article 8, it reserves the right to increase such armaments without the consent of the council whenever the United States is threatened with invasion or engaged in war.

11. The United States reserves the right to permit, in its discretion, the nationals of a covenant-breaking State, as defined in article 16 of the covenant of the league of nations, residing within the United States or in countries other than that violating said article 16, to continue their commercial, financial, and personal relations with the nationals of the United States.

12. Nothing in articles 296, 297, or in any of the annexes thereto or in any other article, section, or annex of the treaty of peace with Germany shall, as against citizens of the United States, be taken to mean any confirmation, ratification, or approval of any act otherwise illegal or in contravention of the rights of citizens of the United States.

13. The United States withholds its assent to Part XIII (articles 387 to 427, inclusive) unless Congress by act or joint resolution shall hereafter make provision for representation in the organization established by said Part XIII, and in such event the participation of the United States will be governed and conditioned by the provisions of such act or joint resolution.

14. The United States assumes no obligation to be bound by any election, decision, report, or finding of the council or assembly in which any member of the league and its self-governing dominions, colonies, or parts of empire, in the aggregate have cast more than one vote, and assumes no obligation to be bound by any decision, report, or finding of the council or assembly arising out of any dispute between the United States and any member of the league if such member, or any self-governing dominion, colony, empire, or part of empire united with politically has voted.

"Refusing to Give the Lady a Seat" Political Cartoon (c. 1919)

Four-Power Pacific Treaty (December 13, 1921)

The four-Power treaty relating to the Pacific, one of the fruits of the Washington Conference of 1921–22, was signed at Washington on December 13, 1921. Appended to the treaty is a declaration reciting the understanding of the signatory Powers (1) "that the treaty shall apply to the Mandated Islands in the Pacific Ocean; provided, however, that the making of the treaty shall not be deemed to be an assent on the part of the United States of America to the mandates and shall not preclude agreements between the United States of America and the Mandatory Powers respectively in relation to the mandated islands"; and (2) "that the controversies to which the second paragraph of Article I refers shall not be taken to embrace questions which according to principles of international law lie exclusively within the domestic jurisdiction of the respective Powers." The deposit of ratifications at Washington on August 17, 1923, was accompanied by the further "reservation and understanding" on the part of the United States "that under the statement in the preamble of under the terms of this treaty there is no commitment to armed force, no alliance, no obligation to join in any defense." On August 21 the treaty was proclaimed. A supplementary treaty of February 6, 1922, further defined the term "insular possessions and insular dominions" in its application to Japan.

References — *Text*, English and French, in *U.S. Stat. at Large*, XLIII, Part II, 1646–1649. The text of the supplementary treaty is in *ibid.*, 1652–1654.

I.

The High Contracting Parties agree as between themselves to respect their rights in relation to their insular possessions and insular dominions in the region of the Pacific Ocean.

If there should develp between any of the High Contracting Parties a controversy arising out of any Pacific question and involving their said rights which is not satisfactorily settled by diplomacy and is likely to affect the harmonious accord now happily subsisting between them, they shall invite the other High Contracting Parties to a joint conference to which the whole subject will be referred for consideration and adjustment.

II.

If the said rights are threatened by the aggressive action of any other Power, the High Contracting Powers shall communicate with one another fully and frankly in order to arrive at an understanding as to the most efficient measures to be taken, jointly or separately, to meet the exigencies of the particular situation.

III.

This Treaty shall remain in force for ten years from the time it shall take effect, and after the expiration of said period it shall continue to be in force subject to the right of any of the High Contracting Parties to terminate it upon twelve months' notice.

Louis B. Mayer

1885–1957

Head of Metro-Goldwyn-Mayer

Louis B. Mayer was the most prominent motion picture executive of Hollywood during the 1920s, producing glamorous stars and spectacular films that appealed to a new generation of moviegoers.

Born Eliezer Mayer in Minsk, Russia, of Jewish descent in 1885, Mayer immigrated with his family to New York City in the late 1880s; they settled in St. John, New Brunswick, Canada, in 1892. (Mayer's exact birthday remains unknown, but in the spirit of patriotism and public relations, he claimed to be born on July 4.) At age 19, he moved to Boston just before the nickelodeon boom swept through the country, providing the public with motion pictures for the cost of five cents. Nickelodeons started out as converted storefronts with wooden chairs, piano accompaniment, and a projection screen displaying short films. Over time, they evolved into the "movies" with better amenities, longer pictures, and higher prices. Mayer developed an interest in this emerging enterprise, and, in 1907, he opened his first nickelodeon in Haverhill, Massachusetts. Less than a decade later, Mayer owned the largest movie theater chain in New England and the region's sole distribution rights to **D. W. Griffith**'s 1915 masterpiece *The Birth of a Nation*.

Leaving the East Coast for the West Coast in 1918, he entered the Hollywood film world as an independent producer with the formation of the Louis B. Mayer Company. This production house primarily released romantic melodramas, a number of which featured Anita Stewart, Mayer's first star, and Mildred Harris, **Charlie Chaplin**'s estranged wife. Following World War I, Mayer was one of many producers hoping to profit from Hollywood's growing film industry, which rapidly expanded as studios began promoting feature-length films. As the country entered a period of prosperity in the 1920s, the growing middle class made up the majority of moviegoers and grander theaters replaced the modest nickelodeons.

To capitalize on America's love of motion pictures, Mayer merged his company with film executive Marcus

©*Hulton-Deutsch Collection / Corbis.*

Loew's Metro Pictures Corporation and Goldwyn Pictures Corporation for a combined net worth of $65,000,000. On April 26, 1924, the consolidated Metro-Goldwyn-Mayer (MGM) celebrated its founding at its studio headquarters in Culver City, California. (The official company name was Metro-Goldwyn until 1926.) Appointed vice president and general manager of all productions, Mayer emerged as a powerful studio chief who ruled MGM with parental authority, rewarding the compliant and punishing those who dared to defy him.

Through the "studio system," which gave film companies full power over production, distribution, and exhibition, businessmen like Mayer could govern the careers of the industry's artists. MGM exploited actors on and off the set by holding them to demanding contracts and controlling their personal lives. Mayer's business and marketing skills helped MGM land the era's finest stars, including Greta Garbo and Joan Crawford. Mayer teamed with associate Irving Thalberg to transform MGM into a colossal enterprise, turning out more than 200 films within the first five years of operation.

MGM pictures captured the public's imagination through three characteristic features: glamorous stars, ornate costumes, and elaborate sets. With its "Golden Age" of movie stars and Hollywood allure, MGM created escapist films geared toward mainstream values and advertised through the "star system," which promoted a film's lead actors and encouraged the adoration of screen personalities. Mayer achieved success early with the 1925 blockbuster hits *The Big Parade, The Merry Widow*, and *Ben-Hur: A Tale of the Christ*. One of MGM's greatest triumphs, *Ben-Hur* remains a striking religious and antiracist film based on the biblical story of Jesus Christ. Critics and audiences praised its dramatic action, showcasing a suspenseful nine-minute chariot race, and visual artistry, contrasting the opulent Roman Empire with the natural landscape.

As a rule, Mayer avoided controversial material in pictures such as overt sexuality, heavy drinking, or other possibly offensive subjects. Unlike Paramount Pictures, whose popular star **Clara Bow** epitomized the sexually carefree flapper who defied social conventions, MGM refrained from risqué portrayals of the Jazz Age's "flaming youth." In 1927, Mayer even delivered a speech on immoral topics that should be censored at the Motion Picture Trade Conference in New York. That same year he also co-founded the Academy of Motion Picture Arts and Sciences.

Throughout the 1930s and early 1940s, Mayer reigned as the leading Hollywood mogul. He received an annual salary of more than $1,000,000, the highest earnings of any individual in the nation. Under his control, MGM made a smooth transition into talking pictures and maintained their initial level of excellence with films like the 1933 comedy *Dinner at Eight* and the 1944 musical *Meet Me in St. Louis.* Mayer also exercised much political clout in the conservative establishment; he helped derail Democratic candidate Upton Sinclair's gubernatorial campaign in California when Sinclair proposed a special tax on the movie industry. After World War II, Mayer experienced a downfall when the studio suffered financial strain. Forced to resign in 1951, he died six years later in Los Angeles on October 29, 1957.

Mayer rose to power at MGM in a decade captivated by material wealth and decadent lifestyles. Entertaining audiences with extravagant sets and ravishing stars, he built a movie empire that was both respected and envied in Hollywood. Although his vision and work distinctly reflected the times, they continue to live on through MGM's success and lasting trademark—the famous roaring lion.

Renée Miller

For Further Reading

Altman, Diana. *Hollywood East: Louis B. Mayer and the Origins of the Studio System.* New York: Carol Publishing, 1992.

Crowther, Bosley. *Hollywood Rajah: The Life and Times of Louis B. Mayer.* New York: Holt, 1960.

Higham, Charles. *Merchant of Dreams: Louis B. Mayer, M.G.M., and the Secret Hollywood.* New York: D. I. Fine, 1993.

Marx, Samuel. *Mayer and Thalberg: The Make-Believe Saints.* New York: Random House, 1975.

"$65,000,000 MOVIE MERGER COMPLETED" from the *New York Times* (April 18, 1924)

One of the largest mergers in the history of the motion picture industry was consummated yesterday by Marcus Loew, who heads the consolidated interests which will be operated under the name of the Metro-Goldwyn Corporation. The corporations included in the merger are Metro Pictures, Goldwyn Pictures and the Louis B. Mayer Company. Their combined authorized capital stock is approximately $65,000,000. Distribution of Cosmopolitan Productions is included in the merger.

Mr. Loew, as President of Metro Pictures, heads the new combine. The Board of Directors of the new corporation includes F. J. Godsol, President of Goldwyn Pictures, which was developed largely by Samuel Goldwyn, and Edwin Bowes, Vice President of Goldwyn.

Another member of the board is Messmore Kendall, President of the Moredall Realty Corporation, owning a half interest in the Capitol Theatre, Fifty-first Street and Broadway, the largest motion picture house in New York City. The assessment rolls for 1924 fixed its value at $2,500,000. William Braden, a director of the Moredall Realty Corporation, becomes a director of the new corporation.

The Capitol Theatre is only one of many theatres formerly controlled by Goldwyn Pictures, which are brought into the fold of the Metro-Goldwyn Corporation.

MAYER TO SUPERVISE PRODUCTIONS

Mr. Mayer will be Vice President in charge of all production activities of the Metro-Goldwyn Corporation.

The announcement of the merger discloses that the "negotiations, which have been in progress for some time, were initiated by F. J. Godsol." It further says that the consolidation "in no way will submerge Goldwyn pictures, reports to the contrary notwithstanding."

"Godwyn executives and the Goldwyn organization will be retained throughout," says the announcement. "Abraham Lehr, Vice President of Goldwyn, in charge of its studios, has not yet indicated whether he will remain with the merged company.

"The amalgamation brings to the support of the Metro-Goldwyn Company the immense Loew chain of theatres and the large number of houses which Goldwyn at present controls throughout the country, the most important being the Capitol Theatre, New York. The policy and personnel of the Capitol will remain absolutely unchanged. Also included in the deal are two theatres in Los Angeles, the California and Miller's; theaters in Seattle and Tacoma, Wash., and Portland, Ore., of which one-half are owned by Goldwyn and one-half by W. R. Hearst; also the Ascher Circuit of houses in Chicago and adjacent territory, comprising more than twenty theatres in which the Goldwyn Company owns a one-half interest."

MR. LOEW'S STATEMENT

Mr. Loew, in commenting on the amalgamation and explaining the status of the four companies in the merger, said:

"The motion picture business is going through a stabilizing process and is working itself out on sane, economic principles. Through combining our forces in the best interest of all parties to the merger, Metro, Goldwyn, Cosmopolitan and the Louis B. Mayer Company are going a long way in the right direction. In order to obtain the greatest efficiency and economy in production such a step was inevitable.

"Every other business has experienced the same difficulties in its beginnings and has come to realize the economic necessity of centralization. In the railroad busi-

The formation of MGM profoundly influenced the film industry's operation methods and production standards. This article discusses the historic merger that made Mayer the most prominent motion picture executive in Hollywood.

Source: "$65,000,000 Movie Merger Completed." New York Times, April 18, 1924.

ness, for instance, this was brought about by the Union Pacific, the Southern Pacific, the Central Pacific and the Illinois Central, who gradually achieved the amalgamation of all the Western roads. They were centralized, as they are today, yet all retain their individuality.

"The merger will accomplish mutual savings that will react to the benefit of the exhibitor, and through the exhibitor to the public, which is what we wish to bring about."

The Goldwyn Studios at Culver City, Cal., which are included in the merger, cover forty acres, and are reported to represent an investment of $14,000,000. It will be the producing centre of the combined corporations, according to the announcement.

TO TAKE OVER SEVERAL BIG FILMS

The consolidated organization will take over for release in the approaching season several large films which are being produced abroad. These include "Ben-Hur," now being filmed in Italy by arrangement with A. L. Erlanger; Rex Ingram's "The Arab," recently filmed in North Africa; Marshall Neilan's "Tess of D'Urbervilles,"

now being completed, and Eric Von Stroheim's "Greed," which has been a year in the making..

Directors for the new corporation will include Clarence Badger, Reginald Barker, Frank Borzage, Charles Brabin, Edward Cline, Alan Crosiand, Scott Dunlap, Emmett Flynn, Hobart Henley, E. Mason Hopper, Rupert Hughes, Robert E. Leonard, Fred Niblo, Harry Rapf, J. Parker Read Jr., Victor Schertzinger, Victor Seastrom, King Vidor, Robert Vignola and others.

T. Coleman du Pont is one of the heavy investors in and a director of the Moredall Realty Corporation, owners of the Capitol. Frank H. Hitchcock and Robert W. Chambers also are members of that corporation's directorate.

According to the directories of the merged companies, Goldwyn Pictures was capitalized at $20,000,000 and Metro Pictures at $31,000,000. The stock of Loew's, Inc. is shown to be $26,000,000. Louis B. Mayer is entered as a corporation with a capitol stock of $300,000. Loew's, Inc. controls or is affiliated with fifty theatre companies and 500 theatres in the United States. Its interests also reach into Canada.

STILL FROM CHARIOT RACE IN *BEN-HUR* (1925)

Lauded by critics and audiences for its visual artistry and dramatic action, Ben-Hur's suspense scenes placed before the backdrop of the Roman Empire created breathtaking cinematography. This 1925 photo is a still from the film's nine-minute chariot race.

Source: Kobal Collection/MGM.

REVIEW OF *BEN-HUR* from *Variety* (January 6, 1926)

The 1925 blockbuster hit Ben-Hur *cemented MGM's reputation as the top Hollywood film studio. In the following*

"Ben Hur" in film form has been years in coming to the screen; millions have been spent on it; one large film corporation as a result of its production was compelled to merge with another; actors and directors lost their reputations as a result of it; likewise others, also actors

and directors, have made theirs. And it was well worth waiting all these years for!

Those who saw "Ben Hur" on the stage are the only ones that will realize what a really tremendous work has been accomplished through the screen production of the novel and play. Those who have through the years the play was an outstanding attraction on the road have been in the towns and smaller cities where it played, saw the mobs that gathered hours and hours prior to the opening of the doors to the gallery to get the cheaper seats that were unreserved, brought their own dinner in the form of sandwiches, so as to wait, will be the ones qualified to gather the tremendous sphere the present production of "Ben Hur" will have.

There will be no further reason for a future production of "Ben Hur" for the screen, unless there is some tremendous change in the art of visualization of the dramatic that is as yet unrealized. Then and only then, providing that there is some tremendous advancement in the art of direction and photography, will another "Ben Hur" be necessary. As the industry today stands, so does "Ben Hur" stand: the greatest achievement that has been accomplished on the screen for not only the screen itself, but for all modern picturedom.

The word "epic" has been applied to pictures time and again, but at the time that it was utilized there was no "Ben Hur," therefore you can scrap all the "epics" that have been shown prior to the arrival of "Ben Hur" and start a new book. This is the "epic" of motion picture achievement to date and don't let anybody tell you otherwise.

It isn't a picture! It's the Bible! And as does all literature as to fundamental plot come from the Bible, so does this picture above all pictures come from the same source.

"Ben Hur" is a picture that rises above spectacle, even though it is spectacle. When produced as a play the great Chariot Race scene was relied on to carry the play. On the screen it isn't the Chariot Race or the great battle scenes between the fleet of Rome and the pirate galleys of Golthar, which after all are the most tremendous scenes of this ilk that have ever been portrayed, that carry the great thrills. It is the tremendous heart throbs that one experiences leading to those scenes that make them great. It is the heart interest that has been inculcated into the silent presentation of Gen. Lew Wallace's tremendous play that make these scenes greater than any that have heretofore been photographed for projection.

It is the story of the oppression of the Jews, the birth of the Saviour, the progression of the Christus to the time of his crucifixion, the enslavement of the race from which Jesus himself sprang, and withal the tremendous love tale of the bond slave and a Prince of Jerusalem that holds an audience spell bound.

There is the kick, and with it all a clutch at the throat that will bring tears to the eyes of the most blasé and hardened, no matter be he Christian, Jew or Atheist. And the latter will possibly get the greatest kick of all out of this presentation. Surely there are none, no matter what their faith, creed or religious belief who can stand forth and say that there is a single motif in this picture that gives offense.

In "Ben Hur" for all time the motion picture industry has an answer to the so-called reformer who cries that the industry is in the hands of the Jews. For never

has the subject of the Christus been handled with greater delicacy, with greater reverence or with greater splendor than in the handling of the scenes in which Jesus and the Virgin Mary are included. No matter whether it was in oils painted by those now immortal whose works now grace the greatest cathedrals of the world, or by sculptors whose works are the images at which we worship in our churches, those of us that are of the Faith, all that one will have to point to when accusations are made against the picture industry is the production of "Ben Hur" and say that those in control made it mattering not what their religion.

Their's was the money that financed this picture. Their's was the faith that placed more than $5,000,000 into its production. Their's was the faith that this story in which Christ, the Almighty, was so tremendous a figure that there was none other that could overshadow Him.

But aside from the biggest question of the picture, which naturally is the religious side, to return to the production itself: "Ben Hur" is the picture of pictures today. That isn't excepting "The Big Parade" or any other of the tremendous productions that have come forth in the entire life of the picture industry.

"Ben Hur" is a picture for all times. No matter what happens to others, "Ben Hur" will remain, as the Bible remains. There is a doubt in the writer's mind if "Ben Hur" will ever get to be shown in the picture theatres. It is a subject to remain in the legitimate theatre, the colleges, the schools and that ilk of community gatherings, but if it does eventually get to the picture houses, the prediction is made herewith that it will be more than three years before it does so. Those calendar periods of 1926, 1927, 1928 will have long rolled past before the regular picture theatres will get the production and that is something that one can have the greatest faith in that they ever had in anything.

"Ben Hur" will go down the ages of the picture industry to mark an epoch in its progress. An event that swung the tidal wave of humanity to the screen. The miracle picture that will convert the most skeptical.

In trying to describe the screen play itself one approaches a task that far more worthy fingers should try to pound out on a typewriter. To say that it is colossal, tremendous, terrific, magnificent, awe-inspiring, all means nothing. "Ben Hur" on the screen must be seen.

It immediately places Fred Niblo, who is given credit for the entire direction, in the class of the immortals among the directors of the screen. There always has been a question heretofore when a tremendous picture was turned out whether or not it equalled the things that D. W. Griffith has done in the past. This surpasses anything that Griffith ever did. Of course Niblo had the assistance of colors and the natural advance in technique, but when all is said and done, Fred Niblo today, after "Ben Hur," stands supreme among the modern directors.

The opening of the picture has scenes in old Jerusalem at the time of the exodus into Egypt, the passing of Joseph with Mary to his home, the appearance of the Star of Bethlehem and its guidance of the

film review from January 6, 1926, Variety *applauds* Ben-Hur's *religious and antiracist themes and describes the film as a masterpiece, "the 'epic' of motion picture achievement to date."*

Source: Variety, *January 6, 1926. Reprinted with permission from* Variety Magazine.

Three Wise Men to the scene of the Birth of the Saviour, and then with the passing of a score of years, a new era. The House of Hur, which has borne a long line of the Princes of the Blood, and Ben Hur, the youthful Prince, meets with his chum of years agone. The chum, Messala, has become a Roman officer, and would shun his companion of boyhood because the latter is a Jew. Yet he goes to his house and while there informs Ben Hur that he should forget he is a Jew. To that Ben Hur replies: "Forget that you are a Roman."

Thus starts the feud that finally culminates in the great chariot race at Antioch. But not before Ben Hur has suffered as a galley slave, with his mother and sister imprisoned beneath Jerusalem. Through all of the story the picturization carries a sustained interest that none can escape.

In detail there is too much in the picture to be conveyed in words. Suffice to say that there have been cheers at every performance since the day that the picture opened at the Cohan theatre in New York.

As to individual performance: first the Mary of Betty Bronson. It is without doubt the most tremendous individual score that any actress has ever made with but a single scene with a couple of close-ups. And in the color scenes she appears simply superb.

Then as to Ramon Novarro: he may never have appealed in former productions, but anyone who sees him in this picture will have to admit that he is without doubt a man's man and 100 per cent of that. Novarro is made for all time by his performance here.

Francis X. Bushman does a comeback in the role of the heavy (Messala) that makes him stand alone.

Don't let Bushy ever go back to the heroic stuff. He can land in that but if he will stick to heavies there is no doubt but with this background he will be the heavy of all times.

Nigel de Brulier gives a character performance as Simonides that is worthy of the greatest of artists, especially in the latter scenes of the picture. While as to Frank Currier as Arrius, all that it is necessary to say is "great," and he is all of that. If there ever was a true screen Roman, here is one. Mitchell Lewis as the great Sheik Ilderim carries himself well and scores to greatest advantage while watching the race scene.

As to the women, following Miss Bronson, May McAvoy in blond tresses as Esther deserves a full measure of credit for her performance. While Claire McDowell, as the Mother of Hur, and Kathleen Key, as his sister, both scored tremendously. But Carmel Myers, as the vampire Iras, looked a million dollars worth of woman and it is hard to understand how Ben Hur, even in the picture, could finally resist her.

There must have been considerable cutting in the final effort to get the picture down to the 12 reels as it is now at present, judging from the illustrations that appear in the booklet dispensed in the lobby. Both scenes and titles are missing. In some places the scenes are retained and other titles utilized, while in others the titles remained but are fitted to other scenes.

But in all it is a picture of pictures and certain to compel as widespread interest in the theatre as did the play in its time, only today the masses are greater and surely if there ever were a picture for the masses and classes alike, the young and the old, "Ben Hur" is it.

LEO THE LION (1928)

In this photo from 1928, two men are shown recording Leo, the roaring lion, who would become the lasting trademark of Metro-Goldwyn-Mayer.

Source: From the collections of the Library of Congress.

Aimee Semple McPherson

1890–1944
Controversial
American Evangelist

Aimee Semple McPherson was a controversial American evangelist whose magnetic personality and religious spectacles attracted a mass following to her Church of the Foursquare Gospel.

Born Aimee Elizabeth Kennedy on October 9, 1890, near Ingersoll, Ontario, Canada, McPherson was raised by her mother in the Christian and humanitarian teachings of the Salvation Army. In 1907, McPherson converted to Pentecostalism under the guidance of evangelist Robert J. Semple, whom she married a year later and worked with as a missionary in China. After his death in 1910, she returned to the United States and married Harold S. McPherson in 1912. Their marriage eventually ended due to her devotion to itinerant evangelism—a traveling preaching circuit. She delivered her first sermon at Mount Forest, Ontario, in August 1915, and she toured the East Coast the following summer in her "Gospel Car" painted with Bible verses and evangelical slogans. When she embarked on a transcontinental tour, her dynamic lectures attracted crowds of enthusiastic supporters. In 1918, McPherson established her headquarters in Los Angeles, where she gathered a large following who donated time and $1.5 million to help her build the Angelus Temple.

On January 1, 1923, McPherson dedicated the Angelus Temple as the Church of the Foursquare Gospel. The church seated more than 5,000 and offered everything from members' and converts' meetings to healing services and preaching. McPherson emphasized the call to salvation and the need for spiritual restoration, a creed reflective of fundamentalists and Pentecostals. Fundamentalism, a Protestant movement based upon the literal interpretation of the Bible, grew in opposition to the increasing liberalism at the end of World War I. It particularly rejected the theory of evolution, which made headlines in the 1920s during the Scopes trial, when a high school teacher was charged with violating a state law prohibiting the teaching of evolution. Although ordained Pentecostal, McPherson simply

©Bettmann/Corbis.

described herself as a Bible Christian who professed the "old-fashioned gospel" and promoted a nondenominational ministry for people of varied beliefs and backgrounds. McPherson interwove the sacred and the secular to deliver her message with crafted pageantry. A religious celebrity, she enthralled thousands with her orchestra, choir, brass band, costumes, stage sets, and illustrated sermons. Crowds waited for hours on Sunday nights in hopes of witnessing one of these elaborate performances, and many followers added to the everyday drama through their participation in faith healing and adult baptism by immersion. At a time when women had just started to gain independence, McPherson challenged theological and social conventions.

McPherson reached millions more beyond Angelus Temple through a variety of media, including radio, a new technology in the 1920s. Americans by the thousands bought radio receivers or built their own, and radio stations blossomed across the country; even farms and schools set up their own transmitters in a deluge of "going on the air." A Schenectady, New York, station manager pointed out that the "the power to say something loud enough to be heard by thousands" would result in more voices promoting more ideas. One of those voices belonged to McPherson.

McPherson took full advantage of the radio mania, becoming the first American woman to obtain a broadcast license and the first American ever to own a full-time religious radio station. McPherson carefully coordinated the opening of her station KFSG (Kall Four-Square Gospel) on February 6, 1924, with Los Angeles's second annual Radio and Electrical Exposition. A forerunner in religious broadcasting, her motto was "Help convert the world by radio!" At about the same time, she published weekly and monthly magazines and the books *This Is That* (1923) and *In the Service of the King* (1927).

Whether in the pulpit or on the radio, McPherson attracted the spotlight. In 1926, she received much publicity after disappearing while swimming at the beach in

Venice, California. She surfaced a month later in Agua Prieta, Mexico, claiming to have been kidnapped—a story that her followers believed but that the general public doubted. Los Angeles District Attorney Asa Keyes suggested that she escaped to a Carmel, California, bungalow for a love affair with Angelus Temple's radio operator Kenneth G. Ormiston; journalists sensationalized this suggestion with incriminating articles. The event resulted in a grand jury investigation and perjury charges against McPherson, but the case was ultimately dropped for lack of evidence. Despite the scandal, many of McPherson's devotees remained loyal; McPherson even extended her ministry, founding the International Church of the Foursquare Gospel in 1927.

She increased her global following on a tour of the Holy Land in 1930 and Asia in 1931; meanwhile, graduates of her Bible College, Lighthouse of International Foursquare Evangelism, founded new congregations at home and abroad. During the Depression (1929–39), the Angelus Temple Commissary also assisted the poverty-stricken with food, clothing, shelter, and employment. This charitable work, however, resulted in an accumulation of debt for the Angelus Temple. Between 1935 and 1937,

McPherson faced financial difficulties and leadership conflicts within her ministry that led to lawsuits between her family and associate pastor, Rheba Crawford. The Angelus Temple prevailed and prospered in the 1940s. Her son, Rolf McPherson, took over the movement after McPherson died on September 27, 1944, from an overdose of sleeping pills that was declared accidental.

In "the age of ballyhoo," McPherson used her pulpit as a stage to entertain her audience of worshipers, making her church appear less like a religion and more like a form of theater. Her Sunday revivals were compared to vaudeville shows, appealing to a public that craved the characteristic flamboyance of the 1920s, but without the debauchery. Calling herself "Everybody's Sister," McPherson fascinated many and frequently sparked controversy for both her colorful evangelism and scandalous life.

Renée Miller

For Further Reading
Blumhofer, Edith L. *Aimee Semple McPherson: Everybody's Sister.* Grand Rapids, Mich.: William B. Eerdmans, 1993.
Epstein, Daniel Mark. *Sister Aimee.* New York: Harcourt Brace Jovanovich, 1993.
McPherson, Aimee Semple. *The Story of My Life: Aimee Semple McPherson.* Edited by Raymond W. Becker. Hollywood, Calif.: International Correspondence Publishers, 1951.

LETTER TO AIMEE SEMPLE MCPHERSON (1923)

Beginning in 1916, McPherson traveled the East Coast as an itinerant evangelist in her Gospel Car painted with Bible verses and evangelistic slogans. The author of this letter, excerpted from McPherson's 1923 book This Is That, *explains that the Gospel Car's phrase "Where Will You Spend Eternity?" saved her brother's life as well as restored his faith.*

*Source: Blumhofer, Edith L. *Aimee Semple McPherson: Everybody's Sister.* Grand Rapids, Mich.: William B. Eerdmans, 1993.*

Sister McPherson:
Praise God for sending you and your Gospel Car to our town; if you had not come here, my brother, his wife and sister-in-law would probably have been blown into hell, as my brother had resolved to shoot both of them and himself; but while he was on the piazza he saw God's car go by, and he read: 'Where will y-o-u spend eternity?' It held and gripped him. He went in and told his wife (a very wicked woman—a saloon-keeper's daughter). She 'Poo-poohed!' and hardened her heart, although she knew him to be desperate. Only a very short time before they found him in the cellar basement, gas turned on at two o'clock in the morning, unconscious; in five minutes more would have been past all early help, the doctor said.

My brother was wonderfully convicted and has since been saved, and is now seeking the baptism of the Holy Spirit. It pays to pray. After fifty-five years of prayer by Mother, he has at last yielded to God. Bless His Name!

C.A.S

DEFENSE STATEMENT OF AIMEE SEMPLE MCPHERSON (1926)

McPherson's kidnapping story in 1926 led to skepticism, scandal, and a grand jury investigation. In this defense

I have tried to confine myself just to the questions, but I have had it on my heart all day that I would like to speak a word. I didn't know whether I would have the privilege to speak again, and I want to say that I realize that this story may sound strange to many of you,

may be difficult for some of you to believe. It is difficult for me, sometimes, to believe; sometimes it seems that it must be just a dream. I would to God that it was; that I could wake up and pinch myself and know that it was not true. I realize that, and whether that was a part of the plan of it all, I want to say in my own behalf—I want to say if character counts a little and if a person's past life counts a little, then I want you to look back. Our family has a family of ministers on both sides. My mother gave me to God before I was born. My earliest training has been in Bible and religious work. As a little child I lined the chairs up and preached to them as early as five years of age, and gave my testimony. I was converted at 17, married an evangelist, preached the gospel in my humble way at home and then sailed for China, never expecting to come back to this land, but willing to give up my life for Jesus. They buried my precious husband there. I came back with my little baby in my arms, born a month after her father died. I took up the Lord's work again as soon as I was able to go on. I have had no great denominations back of me, but have been inspired only by my love for God and my love of the work, and of this precious Word, but I began very humbly.

Now, until this crushing thing that none of us can explain why even God would permit, although we cannot question like that—it would be wrong to do that—before that came I was on the pinnacle of success as far as my work for God was concerned, but I have not always been there. I began preaching to farmers, ranchers, under the trees to farmers in their blue overalls sitting on the grass and using the piazza as a mourner's bench. From there, with the $60 that came in the collection, I bought a little tent, a poor little tent very full of holes, and from that I saved my money and bought a bigger one, and that has been the history.

I have never put my money in oil wells or ranches or even clothes or luxuries. My great thought has been always—and this can be absolutely proven—for the service of the Lord and my dear people. I am not saying this in any unkindness, but I would rather never have been born than to have caused this blow to God's Word and to his work. I had rather I had never been born or have seen the light of day than that the name of Jesus Christ, whose name I love, should be crucified and people would say, "There is Sister; she has been preaching, and if her story is wrong"—that is the sad part to me, not only my children should go through life and people say, "See what her mother did," but the blow to my work is the greatest thing.

The turn in my career came at the International Camp given at Philadelphia. I could bring to you, I believe, hundreds of thousands of letters and telegrams over the route from friends in different cities, and during all those years no one has ever said that they saw me out with a man, nor never has my name been linked in any way with anyone like that. I don't believe that I have told lies or cheated or done anything that people could put their finger on.

I traveled for two years with a tent. I drove my own stakes, patched the tent and tied the guy ropes almost like a man. And then came the time when we began to get bigger buildings and theatres and buildings costing sometimes as much as $100 a day in buildings where I have preached to as many as 16,000 in a day.

Then came the building of Angelus Temple. I came here to a neighborhood that had no special buildings in it, got a piece of land and hired horses and scrapers and bossed the men myself and went out to build the foundation myself with a little capital. I told people my dream to preach the gospel as God had given it to me, and they came to me to help me, not here, but from other cities through the "Bridal Call," my magazine. I have been here for years. I have visited the jails. We have workers in the penitentiary. We have appeared at almost every bedside we could reach in the county hospital, and at the county farm we journey each week to gather the old folks and preach for them. We preach at the shops and factories to men at noon. We have never turned anyone away but give free food and clothes. And my life, I feel, has been lived in a broad spotlight.

Naturally, I have preached a gospel which made some enmity. I have gone unmercifully after the dope ring, gambling, liquor, tobacco, dancing, and made the statement that I would rather see my children dead than in a public dance hall. I have perhaps laid myself open to enmity in those lines about evils in the schools, et cetera, but in everything, I have tried to live as a lady and as a Christian, and I just want one more thought—it is so kind of you to grant me this opportunity. It does mean so much. I will feel happier for having said it. The thought is that one should doubt my story. Perhaps you are skeptical; I don't blame anyone, because it does sound absurd, but it did happen, ladies and gentlemen.

Suppose one should doubt it; a trained investigator, it would seem to me, would need but look for a month, so would I get by? As one said who was here at this moment, they couldn't think of any other reason than that I might be insane. I would not work with one hand for seventeen years, and just as I saw my dearest dreams coming true, sweep it over, and not only that, but attempt to heal little babies in Christ who were too weak to stand.

Motive? If I were sick—someone said, "Maybe she went away to rest"—but it was not that; I had just passed an examination for life insurance a while ago and they said I passed 100 percent.

Amnesia? It could not be that. I am willing to have my mind examined or any test that could be put on that.

And as for falling in love, I am in love with the work I do.

There might be a baser motive. I almost blush to mention it in the jury room, but some might think of it. They say the waters of the mind are like the waters of the sea, that cast up strange things, and that I might be in trouble of some sort, and had to go away and come back. I would like to say, although I apologize for having to mention such a thing, that I had a thorough examination upon coming home, although that was not necessary, as the history of my case for twelve years back would show that such a thing would be absolutely out of the question.

statement, McPherson uses artful argument to demonstrate her innocence and discredit her accusers, who believed she had faked her abduction. She begins with her humble background and dedication to her work, and ends by dismissing the motives suggested by the prosecutors, such as that she had terminated a pregnancy.

Source: Epstein, Daniel Mark. *Sister Aimee.* New York: Harcourt Brace Jovanovich, 1993.

"An Evangelist Drowns" by Upton Sinclair (1926)

"An Evangelist Drowns," written by Upton Sinclair and published in The New Republic, satirizes McPherson's disappearance after swimming in the Pacific Ocean. Sinclair employs the persona of McPherson in the first two stanzas to mock her ministry and he uses his own voice for the last two stanzas to describe her devoted followers.

Source: Sinclair, Upton. "An Evangelist Drowns." The New Republic, June 30, 1926. Reprinted by courtesy of The New Republic.

Through green-white breakers swift I leap,
Sun-sparkled seas by body keep;
Bearer of Gospel-Glory I
With singing angels in my sky,
And earthly chorus at command,
The trumpets of my silver band!
The cripples to my temple crowd,
I heal them, and they shout aloud.
A thousand miles my raptures go
Upon my magic radio.
Time, space and flesh I rise above,
I turn them into singing love . . .

What's this? A terror-spasm grips
My heart-strings, and my reason slips.
Oh, God, it cannot be that I,
The bearer of Thy Word, should die!
My letters waiting in the tent!
The loving messenger I sent!
My daughter's voice, my mother's kiss!

My pulpit-notes on Genesis!
Oh, count the souls I saved for Thee,
My Savior-wilt Thou not save me?
Ten thousand to my aid would run,
Bring me my magic microphone!
Send me an angel, or a boat . . .

The senseless waters fill her throat.
Ten million tons of water hide
A woman's form, her Faith deride;
While thousands weep upon the shore,
And searchlights seek . . . and breakers roar . . .

Oh, gallant souls that grope for light
Through matter's blind and lonely night!
Oh, pity our minds that seek to know
That which is so—
And piteously have forgot
That which is not!

"Vaudeville at Angelus Temple" by Sheldon Bissell (May 23, 1928) [Excerpt]

McPherson's charismatic preaching made her an American phenomenon of the 1920s. "Vaudeville at Angelus Temple," written by Sheldon Bissell and published in The Outlook on May 23, 1928, wryly describes the eclectic atmosphere and religious spectacle of the Angelus Temple. Praising McPherson as "a superb actress," he compares her church services to "a sensuous debauch served up in the name of religion."

Source: Bissell, Sheldon. "Vaudeville at Angelus Temple." The Outlook, May 23, 1928.

Take the Edendale car out of Los Angeles some Sunday afternoon toward five o' clock. Ride for a bit less than a half-hour and alight at Echo Park. Here are much shade, cool green water, pleasant grassy glades, and, beyond and above it all, looming stark, ugly, bloated, a huge gray concrete excrescence on this delightful bit of nature. It is Angelus Temple, citadel of Aimee Semple McPherson and the Four-Square Gospel.

At 6:15 the doors swing open. The Temple holds 5,300, and probably one-fourth that number are in line at this time. Within fifteen minutes the huge auditorium with its two flaring balconies is completely filled. The interior is plain, the stained-glass windows garish, but the lighting is adequate, the opera chairs restful after your long stand in line, and the ventilation through scores of doors and transoms is satisfactory. The platform is arranged for an orchestra of fifty, and the "throne" of "Sister" McPherson on a dais just below the high organ loft, softly bathed in creamy light from overhead electrics. Behind the "throne" is a shell of flowers and greenery. The musicians, mostly young and all volunteers, come in at 6:30. . . .

Now, at five minutes to seven, the vested choir, half a hundred strong, enters from either side. There is a moment of tension and hushed expectancy. All is in readiness. The dramatic has surely not been neglected by this super-dramatist. Audience, workers, band, choir, even microphones—all are here. But the throne is still empty, bathed in its soft light. Suddenly through a door far up on the wall, opening out on her private grounds, appears Mrs. McPherson. She is clad in white, with a dark cloak thrown loosely around her shoulders; her rich auburn hair, with its flowing permanent wave, is heaped high on her head. In her left arm she carries a bouquet of roses and lilies of the valley, artfully planned to illustrate a point in her sermon (Canticles ii. 1), a description ignorantly applied by her to Jesus; on her face is the characteristic expansive, radiant McPherson smile. She is a beautiful woman, seen from the auditorium, with the soft spotlight shining upon her. Let no man venture to deny it. And, in fact, no man will. The writer has seen screen beauties in his day, and confesses to a slight clutch of the heart as he watched her superb entrance. Assisted to her "throne," she gracefully seats herself, turns to her audience—and her microphone—and is ready to begin. . . .

"Open all windows, all the doors," commands "Sister." "We have a rule in the Temple that no one shall leave during the sermon, under any circumstance. I become utterly helpless if there is any motion before me. No one must stir. The ushers will enforce this, please."

Smilingly said, but the tone is that of Napoleon before battle. All settle down as the lights are lowered, and the sermon, the climax of this astonishing religious vaudeville, begins.

Aimee preaches with a beautiful white-leather Bible in her right hand. The book is open, and the leaves of her sermon are within it. She is rather closely bound to her notes, yet so deftly does she handle them that it almost seems as though she were preaching extempore. The sermon, from the theme "What Think Ye of Christ?" is crude, rambling, now and then artfully self-laudatory, a handful of proof-texts loosely strung together with commonplace illustrations. Summoning fanciful figures to her side with a vigorous hand-clap, she conducts a court of inquisition. Builder, banker, jeweler, architect, politician, schoolboy—on they come in fancy, with many others, and each is asked the question, "What Think Ye of Christ?" to be answered with an ecstatically uttered text of Scripture. "He is the door," said the builder. "The pearl of great price," said the banker. "The Prince of Peace," said the statesman. "The rose of Sharon and the lily of the valley," said the florist—it was here that Aimee's bouquet made effective entrance. Even the grocer had to bear his testimony, for Jesus was to him "the fuller's soap." With illustrations, almost all of them more or less improbable, these gentlemen with their testimonies were homiletically strung together. But it was reserved to the schoolboy to make the hit of the evening.

"Schoolboy," shouted Aimee, summoning him with a clap of her hand from the aisles of memory, "what think YE of Christ?"

"Oh, he is the elder brother!"

"Yes," shouts "Sister," "he is. See the poor little schoolboy going home from school. Behind that tree lurks a big, blustering bully. He pounces on the little boy and pummels him. But down the road comes the elder brother on a bicycle. He leaps on the bully, and has him down; he rubs his face in the dirt." The action is graphically illustrated by Aimee, and greeted by the excited laughter of the thousands. "He saves the schoolboy. Amen." "Amen" is echoed by all. "Oh, how often have I been like that schoolboy," she goes on, a note of pathos creeping into her voice. "No husband, no father, no brother—all alone in the world. The big bully, the devil, has me down. He is pummeling poor Sister. But suddenly down the road, on his bicycle of love and grace, comes the Lord Jesus Christ. Praise the Lord! He rescues me." Fervent ejaculations from her auditors.

It was hopeless as a sermon, but it was consummate preaching. She knew her audience. She knew what she was after, and she got it. She is a superb actress. Her rather harsh and unmelodious voice has yet a modulation of pitch which redeems it from utter disagreeableness. To her carefully manicured and polished finger-tips she is dramatic. In her pose, her gesture, her facial expression, her lifted eyebrows, her scintillating smile, her pathetic frown, Aimee is a perfect exponent of the art of how to say a platitude and delude her hearers into thinking that it is a brand-new truth, just minted by her. She sweeps her audience as easily as the harpist close beside her sweeps the wires in soft broken chords while she preaches. And not for one instant of time is Mrs. McPherson unmindful of that great unseen listening multitude "on the air." She moves the microphone from time to time. She rests her hand lovingly upon it. She never shifts her position one step away from it. All her climaxes are enhanced to the listening thousands throughout Southern California and near-by states who regularly "tune-in" on Sunday nights. Radio KFSG is as dear to her as the five thousand and more in Angelus Temple. . . .

What shall be said? Aimee is Aimee, and there is none like her. A religious message utterly devoid of sound thinking, loose and insubstantial in its construction, preposterously inadequate in its social implications, but amazingly successful after five years of running, and still going strong, judging from statistics, the infallible appeal of churchmen. No American evangelist of large enough caliber to be termed National has ever sailed with such insufficient mental ballast. The power of McPhersonism resides in the personality of Mrs. McPherson. The woman is everything; the evangel nothing. There is no way to understand how a jejune and arid pulpit output has become a dynamic of literally National proportions but to hear and see the woman. To visit Angelus Temple, the home of the Four-Square Gospel, is to go on a sensuous debauch served up in the name of religion.

AIMEE SEMPLE McPHERSON'S 25TH ANNIVERSARY PAGEANT (1935)

McPherson celebrated her 25th year as an evangelist with a theatrical pageant, "Cavalcade of Christianity" at the Shrine Auditorium in Los Angeles. McPherson is shown in this photo (standing) with a few of the 1,000 participants. *Source*: ©Bettmann/Corbis.

H.L. Mencken

H. L. Mencken, the irreverent, iconoclastic columnist and editor of the *Baltimore Sun*, the *Smart Set*, and the *American Mercury*, was a vigorous attacker of intolerance and complacency, and the most influential opinion maker in the 1920s. As a writer he offended just about everyone at one time or another, and as an editor he championed **F. Scott Fitzgerald**, James Joyce, and Eugene O'Neill, among others.

The son of a cigar manufacturer, Henry Louis Mencken was born into an affluent German-American family in Baltimore, Maryland, on September 12, 1880. From an early age he read widely— he called his discovery of *The Adventures of Huckleberry Finn* "the most stupendous of my whole life"— and graduated as the valedictorian of his high school class in 1896. He did not go to college, but, after several years in the family cigar factory, joined the *Baltimore Morning Herald* in 1899; after covering the police and city hall beats he became city editor, managing editor, and in 1906, at the age of 25, editor in chief of the *Herald*. That same year he became editor of the Sunday edition of the *Baltimore Sun*; he would write for

Hulton/Archive.

the *Sun* until 1948. All the while he was also trying his hand at poetry, contributing articles to other publications, and writing books on the dramas of George Bernard Shaw (1905) and the philosophy of Friedrich Nietzsche (1908).

In 1908 Mencken became the literary editor of the *Smart Set,* a New York monthly he would serve for 15 years, the last nine (1914–23) as coeditor with critic George Jean Nathan. He was still writing for the *Baltimore Sun*, but his work on the *Smart Set* gained him a national audience. "Our policy," he wrote to a fellow magazine editor, "is to be lively without being nasty. On the one hand no smut, and on the other, nothing uplifting. A magazine for civilized adults in their lighter moods."

In his book reviews and in the fiction published in the *Smart Set,* Mencken and Nathan introduced American readers to the works of James Joyce, Aldous Huxley, and W. Somerset Maugham, and championed the writers Willa Cather, Theodore Dreiser, and Sherwood Anderson.

Blessed with uncommon energy and a wide range of interests, Mencken was amazingly productive; it has been estimated that for 40 years he wrote an average of 5,000 words daily. He developed a trademark style of outrageous irreverence, never leaving his readers in doubt about his opinion. He skewered reformers, moralists, progressives, business boosters, and patriotism and chauvinism; ridiculed Anglo-Saxon puritanism ("the haunting fear that someone, somewhere, may be happy") and its deadening moralism, which he believed sapped American culture of its vitality; and lashed out at stupidity in general and folly in government ("Democracy is the art of running the circus from the monkey cage").

In the early years of World War I, most Americans wanted nothing to do with "the Great European War," and many, including publisher **William Randolph Hearst**, sympathized more with the Germans than with the British. Mencken defended Germany, but when the United States entered the war he was quickly silenced by his newspapers and magazines; no matter how well respected or influential a writer was, during the war the government policy was that only one voice should be heard: pro-intervention, pro-Ally. Congress passed a Trading with the Enemies Act (1917) authorizing the establishment of a Censorship Board to control the content of mail and foreign-language newspapers in the United States, and the Sedition Act (1918) to silence antiwar protesters, pacifists, anarchists, and others who would distract the public from a unified war effort. Mencken turned his attention to less volatile subjects: he published *In Defense of Women* (1918), not a "defense" but a suffragist-maddening lampoon of the relations between the sexes. In 1919 he released the first edition of *The American Language*, a serious, though often humorous, examination of the differences between American and British English; subsequent editions of this long-term project would occupy him for the rest of his life. Not only did he study the English language, but also he contributed to it by coining the words "Bible Belt" (certain regions in the United States characterized by a fundamentalist, literal interpretation of the Bible) and "booboisie" (from *boob* + *bourgeoisie*, referring to average middle-class Americans), among others.

After the armistice (1918), having held his tongue for two years, Mencken unleashed the first of a six-volume series of collected essays titled *Prejudices* (1919–27), in which no aspect of American life—and no region of the country—escaped his ridicule. In "The Sahara of the Bozart," (*beaux arts* = fine arts) he scorned the South, formerly "a civilization of manifold excellences," as a "stupendous region of worn-out farms, shoddy cities, and paralyzed cerebrums." New England and California fared little better. He abused "the Archangel **Woodrow**" **Wilson** for his moral rectitude, and in later volumes of *Prejudices* he was nearly as harsh toward Presidents **Warren G. Harding**, **Calvin Coolidge**, and Herbert Hoover. Appalled by the speeches of Harding, he wrote that the president's English "reminds me of a string of wet sponges; it is so bad that a sort of grandeur creeps into it."

The Scopes "Monkey" trial in Dayton, Tennessee, in 1925, in which a public school science teacher was tried for having violated a state law prohibiting the teaching of evolution, would seem to have been tailor-made for Mencken. This struggle between small-town tradition and the secular (nonreligious) modern world was a perfect target for Mencken's attacks on narrowmindedness. Accordingly, he traveled to Tennessee and wrote dispatches for the *Sun* in which he portrayed the locals as "gaping primates of the Cumberland slopes." Soon after the trial, following the death of **William Jennings Bryan**, who had served as prosecuting attorney, Mencken wrote a nasty denunciation of the former presidential candidate and secretary of state as "ignorant, bigoted, . . . deluded by a childish theology."

With its boundless energy and abundant capital for investment, the 1920s were a boom time not only for business in general but also for the founding of magazines. In addition to *Time, Reader's Digest*, and *The New Yorker*, the 1920s saw the founding of a new magazine called *The American Mercury*, established by Mencken and former *Smart Set* coeditor Nathan and backed by the eminent book publisher Alfred A. Knopf. Edited by Mencken between 1924 and 1933, *The American Mercury* published work by the very best writers of the time, including Sinclair Lewis, F. Scott Fitzgerald, and Sherwood Anderson. In the quality of its writing, its elegant design, and the intelligent (as well as ironic and sarcastic) tone it maintained in appealing to the "civilized minority" with a wide range of opinions, the *American Mercury* was one of the most remarkable journals of its time, indeed, of the century. It reached its peak circulation of 77,000 in 1927.

The objects of Mencken's scorn did not take their public thrashings lying down, though compared to Mencken's harsh criticism, their words of retaliation appeared weak. The Ku Klux Klan of Arkansas condemned "in the strongest possible language the vile mouthings of this writer," and his agnostic views prompted the Rev. S. Parkes Cadman of Brooklyn to urge that students "be saved from the beliefs preached by H. L. Mencken."

By the late 1920s, Mencken was shifting from editing literature and damning the public to being more of a language scholar, memoirist, and political reporter. He attended the Democratic and Republican national conventions in each presidential election year—which he enjoyed like a child at the circus—and stayed busy denouncing President Franklin D. "Roosevelt Minor," whom he regarded as a fraud. He worked energetically on supplements to *The American Language*, and wrote a series of autobiographical works, including *Happy Days* (1940), *Newspaper Days* (1941), and *Heathen Days* (1943). He suffered a stroke in 1948 that took away his ability to read and write; he died in 1956.

People who knew Mencken have reported that although in print he was forceful with his sharp opinions, in person he was an attentive listener and enjoyed hearing others voice opposing views. He also had a warm place in his heart for the underdog. In "Epitaph" (1921) he wrote, "If, after I depart this vale, you ever remember me and have thought to please my ghost, forgive some sinner and wink your eye at some homely girl."

H. L. Mencken's writings on politics, culture, literature, and American life and language remain lively and in many ways just as pertinent as when they were first published. In the bold and satirical tradition of Jonathan Swift, Voltaire, and Mark Twain, he held the mirror up to his time and was admired by many who sought relief from the falsehoods of advertising and boosterism, who were not amused by the Roaring Twenties' commercial joyride, and wanted someone to speak out against the stupidity of the Red Scare of 1919–20, the folly of Prohibition, and the poisonous intolerance of the Ku Klux Klan. Journalist Walter Lippmann expressed the view of many when he praised Mencken as "the most powerful personal influence on this whole generation of educated people" in the 1920s.

Mark LaFlaur

For Further Reading

Hobson, Fred. *Mencken: A Life*. New York: Random House, 1994.

Manchester, William. *H. L. Mencken: Disturber of the Peace*. New York: Collier Books, 1962. (First published as *Disturber of the Peace: The Life of H. L. Mencken*. New York: Harper, 1950.)

Mencken, H. L. *The American Scene: A Reader*. Selected and edited by Huntington Cairns. New York: Knopf, 1965.

Mencken, H. L. *The Vintage Mencken*. Gathered by Alistair Cooke. New York: Vintage Books, 1990.

"The Woman Voter" by H. L. Mencken (1922)

An excerpt from "The Woman Voter," published in Mencken's satirical collection In Defense of Women, in which he poked fun at the relations between the sexes.

Source: Mencken, H. L. In Defense of Women. New York: Knopf, 1922.

Thus there is not the slightest chance that the enfranchised women of Protestantdom, once they become at ease in the use of the ballot, will give, any heed to the ex-suffragettes who now presume to lead and instruct them in politics. Years ago I predicted that these suffragettes, tired out by victory, would turn out to be idiots. They are now hard at work proving it. Half of them devote themselves to advocating reforms, chiefly of a sexual character, so utterly preposterous that even male politicians and newspaper editors laugh at them; the other half succumb absurdly to the blandishments of the old-time male politicians, and so enroll themselves in the great political parties. A woman who joins one of these parties simply becomes an imitation man, which is to say, a donkey. Thereafter she is nothing but an obscure cog in an ancient and creaking machine, the sole intelligible purpose of which is to maintain a horde of scoundrels in public office. Her vote is instantly set off by the vote of some sister who joins the other camorra. Parenthetically, I may add that all of the ladies to take to this political immolation seem to me to be frightfully plain. I know those of England, Germany and Scandinavia only by their portraits in the illustrated papers, but those of the United States I have studied at close range at various large political gatherings, including the two national conventions first following the extension of the suffrage. I am surely no fastidious fellow—in fact, I prefer a certain melancholy decay in women to the loud, circus-wagon brilliance of youth—but I give you my word that there were not five women at either national convention who could have embraced me in camera without first giving me chloral. Some of the chief stateswomen on show, in fact, were so downright hideous that I felt faint every time I had to look at them.

The reform-mongering suffragists seem to be equally devoid of the more caressing gifts. They may be filled with altruistic passion, but they certainly have bad complexions, and not many of them know how to dress their hair. Nine-tenths of them advocate reforms aimed at the alleged lubricity of the male—the single standard, medical certificates for bridegrooms, birth-control, and so on. The motive here, I believe, is mere rage and jealousy. The woman who is not pursued sets up the doctrine that pursuit is offensive to her sex, and wants to make it a felony. No genuinely attractive woman has any such desire. She likes masculine admiration, however violently expressed, and is quite able to take care of herself. More, she is well aware that very few men are bold enough to offer it without a plain invitation, and this awareness makes her extremely cynical of all women who complain of being harassed, beset, storied, and seduced. All the more intelligent women that I know, indeed, are unanimously of the opinion that no girl in her right senses has ever been actually seduced since the world began; whenever they hear of a case, they sympathize with the man. Yet more, the normal woman of lively charms, roving about among men, always tries to draw the admiration of those who have previously admired elsewhere; she prefers the professional to the amateur, and estimates her skill by the attractiveness of the huntresses who have hitherto stalked it. The iron-faced suffragist propagandist, if she gets a man at all, must get one wholly without sentimental experience. If he has any, her crude manoeuvres make him laugh and he is repelled by her lack of pulchritude and amiability. All such suffragists (save a few miraculous beauties) marry ninth-rate men when they marry at all. They have to put up with the sort of castoffs who are almost ready to fall in love with lady physicists, embryologists, and embalmers.

Fortunately for the human race, the campaigns of these indignant viragoes will come to naught. Men will keep on pursuing women until hell freezes over, and women will keep luring them on. If the latter enterprise were abandoned, in fact, the whole game of love would play out, for not many men take any notice of women spontaneously. Nine men out of ten would be quite happy, I believe, if there were no women in the world, once they had grown accustomed to the quiet. Practically all men are their happiest when they are engaged upon activities—for example, drinking, gambling, hunting, business, adventure—to which women are not ordinarily admitted. It is women who seduce them from such celibate doings. The hare postures and gyrates in front of the hound. The way to put an end to the gaudy crimes that the suffragist alarmists talk about is to shave the heads of all the pretty girls in the world, and pluck out their eyebrows, and pull their teeth, and put them in khaki, and forbid them to wriggle on dance-floors, or to wear scents, or to use lipsticks, or to roll their eyes. Reform, as usual, mistakes the fish for the fly.

"On Being an American" by H. L. Mencken (1922) [Excerpt]

An excerpt from "On Being an American," published in Prejudices: Third Series, shows Mencken's intense dissatisfaction with American culture.

Source: Mencken, H. L. Prejudices: Third Series. New York: Knopf, 1922.

. . .Nowhere else in the world is superiority more easily attained or more eagerly admitted. The chief business of the nation, as a nation, is the setting up of heroes, mainly bogus. It admired the literary style of the late Woodrow; it respects the theological passion of Bryan; it venerates J. Pierpont Morgan; it takes Congress seriously; it would be unutterably shocked by the proposition (with proof) that a majority of its judges are ignoramuses, and that a respectable minority of them are scoundrels. . . .

The chief national heroes—Lincoln, Lee and so on—cannot remain mere men. The mysticism of the medieval peasantry gets into the communal view of them, and they begin to sprout haloes and wings. As I say, no intrinsic merit—at least, none commensurate with the mob estimate—is needed to come to such august dignities. Everything American is a bit amateurish and childish, even the national gods. The most conspicuous and respected American in nearly every field of endeavor, saving only the purely commercial (I exclude even the financial) is a man who would attract little attention in any other country. . . .

[T]he United States is essentially a commonwealth of third-rate men—that distinction is easy here because the general level of culture, of information, of taste and judgment, of ordinary competence is so low. . . .

Third-rate men, of course, exist in all countries, but it is only here that they are in full control of the state, and with it of all the national standards. The land was peopled, not by the hardy adventurers of legend, but simply by incompetents who could not get on at home, and the lavishness of nature that they found here, the vast ease with which they could get livings, confirmed and augmented their native incompetence. . . .

The old notion that the United States is people by the offspring of brave, idealistic and liberty-loving minorities, who revolted against injustice, bigotry and medievalism at home—this notion is fast succumbing to the alarmed study that has been given of late to the immigration of recent years. . . .

Nor is there much soundness in the common assumption, so beloved of professional idealists and wind-machines, that the people of America constitute "the youngest of the great peoples." The phrase turns up endlessly; the average newspaper editorial writer would be hamstrung if the post office suddenly interdicted it, as it interdicted "the right to rebel" during the war. What gives it a certain specious plausibility is the fact that the American Republic, compared to a few other existing governments, is relatively young. But the American Republic is not necessarily identical with the American people; they might overturn it tomorrow and set up a monarchy, and still remain the same people. The truth is that, as a distinct nation, they go back fully three hundred years, and that even their government is older than that of most other nations, e.g., France, Italy, Germany, Russia. Moreover, it is absurd to say that there is anything properly describable as youthfulness in the American outlook. It is not that of young men, but that of old men. All the characteristics of senescence are in it: a great distrust of ideas, an habitual timorousness, a harsh fidelity to a few fixed beliefs, a touch of mysticism. The average American is a prude and a Methodist under his skin, and the fact is never more evident than when he is trying to disprove it. His vices are not those of a healthy boy, but those of an ancient paralytic escaped from the *Greisenheim*. . . .

From such exhausted men the American stock has sprung. It was easier for them to survive here than it was where they came from, but that ease, though it made them feel stronger, did not actually strengthen them. It left them what they were when they came: weary peasants, eager only for the comfortable security of a pig in a sty. Out of that eagerness has issued many of the noblest manifestations of American *Kultur*: the national hatred of war, the pervasive suspicion of the aims and intents of all other nations, the short way with heretics and disturbers of the peace, the unshakable belief in devils, the implacable hostility to every novel idea and point of view. . . .

"H. L. MENCKEN: A REVIEW OF HIS NOTES ON DEMOCRACY" by Walter Lippmann (1926) [EXCERPT]

. . .The democratic phase which began in the eighteenth century has about run its course. Its assumptions no longer explain the facts of the modern world and its ideals are no longer congenial to modern men. There is now taking place a radical change of attitude not merely toward parliamentary government but toward the whole conception of popular sovereignty and majority rule. This change is as radical in its way as that which took place, say between 1776 and 1848.

In the United States Mr. Mencken's is the most powerful voice announcing the change. The effect of his tremendous polemic is to destroy, by rendering it ridiculous and unfashionable, the democratic tradition of the American pioneers. This attack on the divine right of demos is an almost exact equivalent of the earlier attacks on the kings, the nobles, and the priests. He strikes at the sovereign power, which in America to-day consists of the evangelical churches in the small communities, the proletarian masses in the cities, and the organized smaller business men everywhere. The Baptist and Methodist sects, the city mobs, and the Chamber of Commerce are in power. They are the villains of the piece. Mr. Mencken does not argue with them. He lays violent hands upon them in the conviction, probably correct, that you accomplish results quicker by making your opponent's back teeth rattle than by laboriously addressing his reason. Mr.

Mencken, moreover, being an old newspaper man, has rather strong notions about the capacity of mankind to reason. He knows that the established scheme is not supported by reason but by prejudice, prestige, and reverence, and that a good joke is more devastating than a sound argument. He is an eminently practical journalist, and so he devotes himself to dogmatic and explosive vituperation. The effect is a massacre of sacred cows, a holocaust of idols, and the poor boobs are no longer on their knees.

Mr. Mencken is so effective just because his appeal is not from mind to mind but from viscera to viscera. If you analyze his arguments you destroy their effect. You cannot take them in detail and examine their implications. You have to judge him totally, roughly, approximately, without definition, as you would a barrage of artillery, for the general destruction rather than for the accuracy of the individual shots. He presents an experience, and if he gets you, he gets you not by reasoned conviction, but by a conversion which you may or may not be able to dress up later as a philosophy. If he succeeds with you, he implants in you a sense of sin, and then he revives you with grace, and disposes you to a new and somewhat fierce pride in a non-gregarious excellence.

One example will show what happens if you pause to analyze his ideas. The thesis of this whole book is that we must cease to be governed by "the inferior four-

In this review of Mencken's Notes on Democracy, *the eminent journalist Walter Lippmann describes Mencken's role as a critic and his influence among the public.*

Source: Lippmann, Walter. *Men of Destiny.* New York: Macmillan, 1927. Reprinted with the permission of Scribner, a division of Simon & Schuster, Inc., from *Men of Destiny* by Walter Lippmann. ©1927 by the Macmillan Company, copyright renewed ©1955 by Walter Lippmann.

fifths of mankind." Here surely is a concept which a thinker would have paused to define. Mr. Mencken never does define it, and, what is more, he quite evidently has no clear idea of what he means. Sometimes he seems to think that the difference between the inferior four-fifths and the superior one-fifth is the difference between the "haves" and the "have nots." At other times he seems to think it is the difference between the swells and the nobodies, between the well born and those who come "out of the gutter." At other times he abandons these worldly distinctions and talks and thinks about "free spirits," a spiritual elite, who have no relation either to income or to a family tree. This vagueness as to whether the superior one-fifth are the Prussian Junkers or the Pittsburgh millionaires, or the people who can appreciate Bach and Beethoven, persists throughout the book.

This confusion is due, I think, to the fact that he is an outraged sentimentalist. Fate and his own curiosity have made him a connoisseur of human ignorance. Most educated men are so preoccupied with what they conceive to be the best thought in the field of their interest, that they ignore the follies of uneducated men. . . . But Mr. Mencken is overwhelmingly preoccupied with popular culture. He collects examples of it. He goes into a rage about it. He cares so much about it that he cannot detach himself from it. And he measures it not by relative standards, but by the standards which most educated men reserve for a culture of the first order. . . .

When he measures the popular culture by the standards of the elite, the humor is all on the surface. The undertone is earnest and intensely sincere. One feels that Mr. Mencken is deeply outraged because he does not live in a world where all men love truth and excellence and honor. I feel it because I detect in this book many signs of yearning for the good old days. When Mr. Mencken refers to feudalism, to kings, to the Prussian aristocracy, to any ordered society of the ancient regime, he adopts a different tone of voice. I don't mean to say that he talks like an *émigré* or like a writer for the *Action Francaise*, but it is evident to me that his revolt against modern democratic society exhausts his realism, and that the historic alternatives are touched for him with a romantic glamour. The older aristocratic societies exist only in his imagination; they are idealized sufficiently to inhibit that drastic plainness of perception which he applies to the democratic society all about him.

The chief weakness of the book, as a book of ideas, arises out of this naïve contrast in Mr. Mencken's mind between the sordid reality he knows and the splendid society he imagines. He never seems to have grasped the truth that the thing he hates is the direct result of the thing he most admires. This modern democracy meddling in great affairs could not be what it is but for that freedom of thought which Mr. Mencken, to his everlasting credit, cares more about than about anything else. It is freedom of speech and freedom of thought which have made all questions popular questions. What sense is there then in shouting on one page for a party of "liberty," and on another bewailing the hideous consequences? The old aristocracies which Mr. Mencken admires did not delude themselves with any nonsense about liberty. They reserved what liberty there was for a privileged elite, knowing perfectly well that if you granted liberty to everyone you would have sooner or later everything that Mr. Mencken deplores. But he seems to think that you can have a privileged, ordered, aristocratic society with complete liberty of speech. That is as thoroughgoing a piece of utopian sentimentalism as anything could be. You might as well proclaim yourself as a Roman Catholic and then ask that excerpts from *The American Mercury* and the works of Charles Darwin be read from the altar on the first Sunday of each month. If Mr. Mencken really wishes an aristocracy he will have to give up liberty as he understands it; and if he wishes liberty he will have to resign himself to hearing *homo boobiens* speak his mind.

What Mr. Mencken desires is in substance the distinction, the sense of honor, the chivalry, and the competence of an ideal aristocracy combined with the liberty of an ideal democracy. This is an excellent wish, but like most attempts to make the best of both worlds, it results in an evasion of the problem. The main difficulty in democratic society arises out of the increasing practice of liberty. The destruction of authority, of moral values, of cultural standards is the result of using the liberty which has been won during the last three or four centuries. Mr. Mencken is foremost among those who cry for more liberty, and who use that liberty to destroy what is left of the older tradition. I do not quarrel with him for that. But I am amazed that he does not see how fundamentally the spiritual disorder he fights against is the effect of that regime of liberty he fights for. Because he fails to see that, I think he claims too much when he says that he is engaged in a diagnosis of the democratic disease. He has merely described with great emphasis the awful pain it gives him.

In the net result these confusions of thought are a small matter. It is no crime not to be a philosopher. What Mr. Mencken has created is a personal force in American life which has an extraordinarily cleansing and vitalizing effect. How else can you explain the paradox of his popularity, and the certainty that before he dies he will find himself, like Bernard Shaw to-day, one of the grand old men, one of the beloved patriarchs of his time? How in this land where all politicians, pedagogues, peasants, etc., etc., are preposterous, has Henry L. Mencken, not yet aged fifty, become the pope of popes? The answer is that he has the gift of life. His humor is so full of animal well-being that he acts upon his public like an elixir. The wounds he inflicts heal quickly. His blows have the clean brutality of a natural phenomenon. They are directed by a warm and violent but an unusually healthy mind which is not divided, as most minds are, by envy and fear and ambition and anxiety. When you can explain the heightening effect of a spirited horse, of a swift athlete, of a dancer really in control of his own body, when you can explain why watching them you feel more alive yourself, you can explain the quality of his influence.

For this reason the Mencken manner can be parodied, but the effect is ludicrous when it is imitated. The same prejudices and the same tricks of phrase employed by others are usually cheap and often nasty. I never feel that in Mr. Mencken himself even when he calls quite harmless people cockroaches and lice. I do not care greatly for phrases like that. They seem to me like spitting on the carpet to emphasize an argument. They are signs that Mr. Mencken writes too much and has occasionally to reach for the effect without working for it. I think he is sometimes lazy, and when he is lazy he is often unfair, not in the grand manner but in the small manner. And yet his wounds are clean wounds and they do not fester. I know, because I have fragments of his shellfire in my own skin. The man is admirable. He writes terribly unjust tirades, and yet I know of nobody who writes for his living who will stay up so late or get up so early to untangle an injustice. He often violates not merely good taste according to the genteel tradition, but that superior kind of good taste according to which a man refuses to hurt those who cannot defend themselves.

Nevertheless I feel certain that in so far as he has influenced the tone of public controversy he has elevated it. The Mencken attack is always a frontal attack. It is always explicit. The charge is all there. He does not leave the worst unsaid. He says it. And when you have encountered him, you do not have to wonder whether you are going to be stabbed in the back when you start to leave and are thinking of something else.

I have not written this as a eulogy, but as an explanation which to me at least answers the question why Henry L. Mencken is as popular as he is in a country in which he professes to dislike most of the population. I lay it to the subtle but none the less sure sense of those who read him that here is nothing sinister that smells of decay, but that on the contrary this holy terror from Baltimore is splendidly and exultantly and contagiously alive. He calls you a swine and an imbecile, and he increases your will to live.

"MENCKEN SEES TRANQUILITY ARISE IN U.S. FROM ASHES OF PROHIBITION" by Sheilah Graham (November 12, 1933)

Baltimore, Nov. 11. [1933] – I wanted to know what repeal of Prohibition will do to the way of life of the average American, whether it will restore temperance to the home, end the "wild party," make connoisseurs out of drunkards, bring back a taste for good food along with good drink and, in short, launch an era in which the "art of living" will flourish as they say it used to in the dear old days.

And so I came down to pleasant Baltimore to see that American who has been described to me as the one "best liver" among his fellow countrymen—that is to say, one whom despite his fulminations against the American character, appreciates most keenly the color and glamour of life in the United States and who, despite American laws and conventions, has managed—they told me—to live his own life pleasantly and well.

WHAT MENCKEN SAYS

Meet H. L. Mencken, author, critic and editor, as he seats himself before his great desk in the library of his home, where he has retired from the direction of the *American Mercury* to read, study, write books and enjoy the years in manners and pastimes becoming—to borrow one of his own phrases—to the "civilized man." And hear what Mencken has to say about America and repeal.

By your leave, Mr. Mencken, I shall present the interview in the dialogue form which you and your friend, Mr. Nathan, once made so popular in the Smart Set.

Miss Graham: What are you going to do about the decease of the Eighteenth Amendment, Mr. Mencken? I am sure an era of tranquility will arise from its dead ashes. They have drawn your teeth of attack, I am afraid.

Mr. Mencken: Don't worry, Miss Graham. Repeal itself will have a soothing effect, but the American people face a host of curses and pestilences, and so they will probably enjoy very little tranquility for years to come.

WON'T BANISH DRUNKS

Miss Graham: That is a big relief. But aren't you afraid it will mean the end of drunkenness?

Mr. Mencken: Not a bit. People who have been afflicted by God with the inclination to drunkenness will go on getting drunk. The only change there will be is that those who have no desire to get drunk will not be forced into it. That necessity has lain very heavily upon them during all the years of Prohibition.

Miss Graham: Have you been forced to drink against your own inclinations, Mr. Mencken?

Mr. Mencken: Not exactly, but others have. My pastor, for example, is a broad churchman who likes to go into society. He told me the other day that during the 13 black years he had got down at least 15,000 drinks of hard liquor unwillingly—perhaps half of them as mere gestures against Prohibition, and the rest as indications of his confidence in the bootleggers of his parishioners. Now he is on beer again and a happy man.

Miss Graham: I'm hoping the re-appearance of wine in restaurants will improve the food in this country. Americans pour scorn on the food they eat in England, but I think their own is worse. I have suffered indigestion ever since I came to this country five months ago. Do you think America is in for some kitchen reform?

Mr. Mencken: I doubt it. Americans, talking one with another, have a congenital antipathy to decent food. They eat bad stuff by choice and heave it in as fast as possible. This despite the fact their cooks have the best raw materials in the world. Nowhere else is there better meat or a wider range of good vegetables. But American cookery still grounds itself on English cookery and is thus but once removed from cannibalism.

ACTUALLY LAZY

Miss Graham: Perhaps you are right. But here is something Americans could copy with advantage from the English. A quieter method of living. The American rushes round, is very difficult to reach in his office, always looks busy, thinks he's important, and in actual fact accomplishes much less than the Englishman, who works and lives quietly.

Shortly before the repeal of Prohibition (by adoption of the Twenty-First Amendment to the Constitution on December 5, 1933), British journalist Sheilah Graham interviewed H. L. Mencken on the likely consequences of repeal. The interview was published as "Mencken Sees Tranquility Arise in U.S. from Ashes of Prohibition." (Graham later moved to Hollywood, where for several years she was the companion of F. Scott Fitzgerald until his death in 1940.)

Source: Mencken, H. L. "Mencken Sees Tranquility Arise in U.S. from Ashes of Prohibition," interview by Sheilah Graham, *Detroit Sunday Times,* November 12, 1933. Reprinted with permission from the *Detroit News.*

Mr. Mencken: The American thinks he's a busy important man, but that is a figment of his imagination. He is actually a lazy fellow. No other man works shorter hours or takes longer holidays. The appearance of rushing is mainly due to the fact that every American tries to do his day's work in half a day. Naturally he usually does it badly. Very few Americans are competent at their trades.

Take any example you choose. Consider our policemen. Our novelists. Our bankers. Or if you want to descend to humor, the brain trust. The United States is the utopia of quacks. It is difficult in this country, Miss Graham, for a man who really knows his business to make a living. The most a genuinely learned and honest lawyer can hope for is the patronage of some rich shyster.

A really good medical man is outrun by flashy quacks and must live on their leavings. If Shakespeare came back to earth tomorrow, even under some such grand old American name as Ginsberg or O'Brien, he'd have a hard time getting his plays produced on Broadway. I know a banker who in the palmy days of three or four years ago, guarded his depositors' money very carefully, never speculated with it and was ready when the crash came to pay them 100 cents on the dollar. He is a relatively poor man today. He had to face the competition of hordes of swindlers, many of whom are now rich and in receipt of high public honors.

Miss Graham: What I cannot understand, Mr. Mencken, is why Americans moan about depression and starvation when the meanest pauper feeds better than the British workingman. I expected to find women in rags, instead they are wearing furs. I expected to find men shabby and without adequate homes. I found them living very comfortably?

CHARITY MONGERS

Mr. Mencken: The Americans have always lived comfortably—that is, according to their lights. There is seldom any actual want in the country, even in the midst of depressions. All the gaudy talk you hear about starvation comes from professional charity-mongers. They have got their hooves into the public trough and are determined to stay there.

Their figures are laughable. I haven't the slightest doubt that if they were forced to publish lists of the people actually starving they would put down my name. Yet, I eat regularly, have five suits of clothes and the last time I saw the figure of the banking auditor, I had nearly $300 to my credit.

Miss Graham: Yes, you look very well fed, and I can see why you live very comfortably. I envy you. I can't think of any greater reward in a future life than to be another Mr. Mencken. Can you?

Mr. Mencken (rather testily): Yes, I can. I'd like to be a hermit [and] live in a place where bores and nuisances couldn't reach me. I'd then be as happy as the boy who killed his father. Please don't think I mean you, Miss Graham, when I talk of bores. I'm delighted that you came to see me. I'm talking of the pest who devotes himself to demanding the attention of strangers. It's a kind of puerile egotism. No doubt Freud has it on his list of complexes. Write a book, and swarms of such insects will be down on you.

A. Mitchell Palmer

A. Mitchell Palmer, attorney general of the United States from 1919 to 1921 under President **Woodrow Wilson**, is remembered for the infamous Palmer Raids during the Red Scare of 1919–20.

Alexander Mitchell Palmer was born in Moosehead, Pennsylvania, on May 4, 1872. He grew up in a Quaker household and attended Swarthmore College, where he was class president and, at the age of 19, graduated first in his class in 1891. He was admitted to the Pennsylvania bar in 1893, practiced law in Stroudsburg, Pennsylvania, and became active in the Democratic Party. In 1898 he married Roberta Bartlett Dixon; they had one child. He was elected to the U.S. House of Representatives in 1908, serving as a congressman from 1909 to 1915.

Palmer rose rapidly in Congress. He served on the powerful House Committee on Ways and Means, which deals with taxation and government finance, and introduced progressive reform legislation that included a woman suffrage bill and a child labor bill described as "the most momentous of the progressive era"; it passed in the House but was defeated in the Senate. Palmer was also highly commended by the American Federation of Labor (AFL) for his voting record on labor issues. As Wilson's floor leader at the 1912 Democratic National Convention, Palmer helped assure Wilson's nomination by delivering Pennsylvania's large block of delegates. Wilson later appointed him to a judgeship on the U.S. Court of Claims and in October 1917, named him Alien Property Custodian.

Palmer was appointed attorney general on March 5, 1919, at a time of national turmoil. While the president was occupied with international concerns, such as the Versailles Peace Treaty and the League of Nations, the United States was rocked by inflation, riots, strikes, and bombings. The cost of living had risen 100 percent since 1914; in 1919 alone there were 3,600 labor strikes involving more than four million workers. A tight labor market, compounded by the return from France of two million war veterans, bred

From the collections of the Library of Congress.

intense xenophobia, or hatred of foreigners. The Russian (Bolshevik) revolution of October 1917 worsened the nativist contempt for immigrants; about 90 percent of all socialists, anarchists, and communists in America were foreign-born, and editorial writers and politicians demanded the deportation of "alien radicals" to prevent a Bolshevik-style overthrow of the U.S. government.

As attorney general, Palmer had hesitated to intervene in labor disputes but was under intense pressure from business owners and the press to get tough with the unions. In October 1919 he used a court injunction to stop a threatened United Mine Workers walkout, which infuriated the unions but won Palmer praise in the newspapers. When the Big Four railroad brotherhoods struck in April 1920, he accused them of being radicals and charged that a walkout would prove they were Bolsheviks.

At the same time, the nation was alarmed by a series of anarchist bombings and sensational press accounts of clashes between police and socialists, anarchists, and communists. In April 1919, authorities intercepted most of a series of 36 mail bombs addressed to some of the most prominent men in America, including John D. Rockefeller and Palmer. On the night of June 2, a bomb exploded outside Palmer's house in Washington, D.C. At the same hour in eight other cities, bombs exploded at public buildings and the homes of high government officials. Palmer and his family were unhurt, but the assassination attempt turned the attorney general into a red-hunter with a vengeance.

Palmer asked Congress for a budget increase and began laying the groundwork for a mass roundup and deportation of alien radicals that would become known as the Palmer Raids. On August 1, 1919, he created the General Intelligence Division (GID) of the Justice Department to collect information about radicals and coordinate with the Bureau of Investigation and other agencies. He appointed as director of the GID, or Anti-Radical division, an industrious 24-year-old named J. Edgar Hoover.

The Palmer Raids began on November 7, 1919, when Justice Department agents in 12 U.S. cities raided meeting places of the Union of Russian Workers (URW), a social and educational club. In New York City approximately 650 people were arrested, 43 of whom were eventually deported. About 250 members of the URW were arrested in the other 11 cities. Many of the men and women were roughed up, jailed without being charged, and held without bail. Palmer was hailed as a hero when, in December, a deportation ship dubbed the "Soviet Ark" left New York with 249 alien radicals on board, including America's most famous anarchists, **Emma Goldman** and Alexander Berkman. On January 2, 1920, a Justice Department sweep of the Communist and Communist Labor Parties in dozens of American cities netted about 3,000 radicals. Some were held for a few hours, others for several months.

By the middle of 1920 the nation's mania for deportation had subsided, and most of the prisoners were released. Some of the nation's most respected attorneys and law professors denounced the raids as lawless violations of civil liberties, and Palmer began to lose credibility with the public. Further, he had damaged himself politi-cally by "red-smearing" the striking workers, and many prominent Democrats protected their own standing with labor by declining to support Palmer in his quest for the presidency. He failed to secure the 1920 Democratic nomination, and retired from government to practice law. He was later asked by his friend Franklin D. Roosevelt to help in crafting the 1932 Democratic Party platform. Palmer suffered a fatal heart attack on May 11, 1936.

A. Mitchell Palmer was one of the most promising politicians of his time, with a meteoric 12-year rise and fall, but his use of the Red Scare for political gain damaged his reputation beyond repair. Although his contributions in public service were mostly benevolent, he is remembered primarily for his tenure as the United States' chief law enforcement officer presiding over a time of such gross violations of civil liberties as were not seen again until Senator Joseph McCarthy's Red Scare in the 1950s.

Mark LaFlaur

For Further Reading

Coben, Stanley. *A. Mitchell Palmer: Politician.* New York: Da Capo Press, 1972.

Link, Arthur S. *Wilson: The New Freedom.* Princeton, N.J.: Princeton University Press, 1956.

Murray, Robert K. *Red Scare: A Study of National Hysteria, 1919–1920.* New York: McGraw-Hill, 1964.

A. MITCHELL PALMER'S HOUSE AFTER BOMB EXPLOSION (1919)

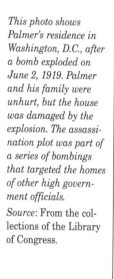

This photo shows Palmer's residence in Washington, D.C., after a bomb exploded on June 2, 1919. Palmer and his family were unhurt, but the house was damaged by the explosion. The assassination plot was part of a series of bombings that targeted the homes of other high government officials.

Source: From the collections of the Library of Congress.

"THE CASE AGAINST THE 'REDS'" by A. Mitchell Palmer (1920) [EXCERPT]

In this brief review of the work which the Department of Justice has undertaken, to tear out the radical seeds that have entangled American ideas in their poisonous theories, I desire not merely to explain what the real menace of communism is, but also to tell how we have been compelled to clean up the country almost unaided by any virile legislation. Though I have not been embarrassed by political opposition, I have been materially delayed because the present sweeping processes of arrests and deportation of seditious aliens should have been vigorously pushed by Congress last spring. The failure of this is a matter of record in the Congressional files.

The anxiety of that period in our responsibility when Congress, ignoring the seriousness of these vast organizations that were plotting to overthrow the Government, failed to act, has passed. The time came when it was obviously hopeless to expect the hearty cooperation of Congress in the only way to stamp out these seditious societies in their open defiance of law by various forms of propaganda.

Like a prairie-fire, the blaze of revolution was sweeping over every American institution of law and order a year ago. It was eating its way into the homes of the American workmen, its sharp tongues of revolutionary heat were licking the altars of the churches, leaping into the belfry of the school bell, crawling into the sacred corners of American homes, seeking to replace marriage vows with libertine laws, burning up the foundations of society.

Robbery, not war, is the ideal of communism. This has been demonstrated in Russia, Germany, and in America. As a foe, the anarchist is fearless of his own life, for his creed is a fanaticism that admits no respect of any other creed. Obviously it is the creed of any criminal mind, which reasons always from motives impossible to clean thought. Crime is the degenerate factor in society.

Upon these two basic certainties, first that the "Reds" were criminal aliens and secondly that the American Government must prevent crime, it was decided that there could be no nice distinctions drawn between the theoretical ideals of the radicals and their actual violations of our national laws. An assassin may have brilliant intellectuality, he may be able to excuse his murder or robbery with fine oratory, but any theory which excuses crime is not wanted in America. This is no place for the criminal to flourish, nor will he do so so long as the rights of common citizenship can be exerted to prevent him.

OUR GOVERNMENT IN JEOPARDY

It has always been plain to me that when American citizens unite upon any national issue they are generally right, but it is sometimes difficult to make the issue clear to them. If the Department of Justice could succeed in attracting the attention of our optimistic citizens to the issue of internal revolution in this country, we felt sure there would be no revolution. The Government was in jeopardy; our private information of what was being done by the organization known as the Communist Party of America, with headquarters in Chicago, of what was being done by the Communist Internationale under their manifesto planned at Moscow last March by Trotzky,

Lenin and others addressed "To the Proletariats of All Countries," of what strides the Communist Labor Party was making, removed all doubt. In this conclusion we did not ignore the definite standards of personal liberty, of free speech, which is the very temperament and heart of the people. The evidence was examined with the utmost care, with a personal leaning toward freedom of thought and word on all questions.

The whole mass of evidence, accumulated from all parts of the country, was scrupulously scanned, not merely for the written or spoken differences of viewpoint as to the Government of the United States, but, in spite of these things, to see if the hostile declarations might not be sincere in their announced motive to improve our social order. There was no hope of such a thing.

By stealing, murder and lies, Bolshevism has looted Russia not only of its material strength but of its moral force. A small clique of outcasts from the East Side of New York has attempted this, with what success we all know. Because a disreputable alien—Leon Bronstein, the man who now calls himself Trotzky—can inaugurate a reign of terror from his throne room in the Kremlin, because this lowest of all types known to New York can sleep in the Czar's bed, while hundreds of thousands in Russia are without food or shelter, should Americans be swayed by such doctrines?

Such a question, it would seem, should receive but one answer from America.

My information showed that communism in this country was an organization of thousands of aliens who were direct allies of Trotzky. Aliens of the same misshapen caste of mind and indecencies of character, and it showed that they were making the same glittering promises of lawlessness, of criminal autocracy to Americans, that they had made to the Russian peasants. How the Department of Justice discovered upwards of 60,000 of these organized agitators of the Trotzky doctrine in the United States is the confidential information upon which the Government is now sweeping the nation clean of such alien filth. . . .

WILL DEPORTATION CHECK BOLSHEVISM?

Behind, and underneath, my own determination to drive from our midst the agents of Bolshevism with increasing vigor and with greater speed, until there are no more of them left among us, so long as I have the responsible duty of that task, I have discovered the hysterical methods of these revolutionary humans with increasing amazement and suspicion. In the confused information that sometimes reaches the people they are compelled to ask questions which involve the reasons for my acts against the "Reds." I have been asked, for instance, to what extent deportation will check radicalism in this country. Why not ask what will become of the United States Government if these alien radicals are permitted to carry out the principles of the Communist Party as embodied in its so-called laws, aims and regulations?

There wouldn't be any such thing left. In place of the United States Government we should have the horror and terrorism of bolsheviki tyranny such as is destroying

In this Forum article, published in 1920, Attorney General A. Mitchell Palmer defends the actions of the U.S. Justice Department during the raids and summarizes his plan for removing the "menace of Bolshevism."

Source: Palmer, A. Mitchell. "The Case Against the 'Reds.'" Forum 63, 1920.

Russia now. Every scrap of radical literature demands the overthrow of our existing government. All of it demands obedience to the instincts of criminal minds, that is, to the lower appetites, material and moral. The whole purpose of communism appears to be a mass formation of the criminals of the world to overthrow the decencies of private life, to usurp property that they have not earned, to disrupt the present order of life regardless of health, sex or religious rights. By a literature that promises the wildest dreams of such low aspirations, that can occur to only the criminal minds, communism distorts our social law. . . .

It has been inferred by the "Reds" that the United States Government, by arresting and deporting them, is returning to the autocracy of Czardom, adopting the system that created the severity of Siberian banishment. My reply to such charges is that in our determination to maintain our government we are treating our alien enemies with extreme consideration. To deny them the privilege of remaining in a country which they have openly deplored as an unenlightened community, unfit for those who prefer the privileges of Bolshevism, should be no hardship. It

strikes me as an odd form of reasoning that these Russian Bolsheviks who extol the Bolshevik rule should be so unwilling to return to Russia. The nationality of most of the alien "Reds" is Russian and German. There is almost no other nationality represented among them.

It has been impossible in so short a space to review the entire menace of the internal revolution in this country as I know it, but this may serve to arouse the American citizen to its reality, its danger, and the great need of united effort to stamp it out, under our feet, if needs be. It is being done. The Department of Justice will pursue the attack of these "Reds" upon the Government of the United States with vigilance, and no alien, advocating the overthrow of existing law and order in this country, shall escape arrest and prompt deportation.

It is my belief that while they have stirred discontent in our midst, while they have caused irritating strikes, and while they have infected our social ideas with the disease of their own minds and their unclean morals we can get rid of them! and not until we have done so shall we have removed the menace of Bolshevism for good.

Introduction of *To the American People* from the National Popular Government League (1920) [Excerpt]

To the American People: Report Upon the Illegal Practices of the United States Department of Justice, a 67-page booklet compiled and published in May 1920 by the National Popular Government League with help from members of the National Civil Liberties Bureau, consisted of affidavits from aliens who had been arrested illegally and mistreated during the Palmer Raids It also included testimony and documents presented as evidence in Colyer et al. v. Skiffington, a federal trial in Boston involving 18 aliens arrested in the January 1920 raids.

Source: Brown, R.G., Zechanah Chafee, Jr., Felix Frankfurter, et al. To the American People: Report upon the Illegal Practices of the United States Department of Justice. New York: Call Printing Co., 1920.

For more than six months we, the undersigned lawyers, whose sworn duty it is to uphold the Constitution and Laws of the United States, have seen with growing apprehension the continued violation of the Constitution and breaking of those Laws by the Department of Justice of the United States government.

Under the guise of a campaign for the suppression of radical activities, the office of the Attorney General, acting by its local agents throughout the country, and giving express instructions from Washington, has committed continual illegal acts. Wholesale arrests both of aliens and citizens have been made without warrant or any process of law; men and women have been jailed and held *incommunicado* without access of friends or counsel; homes have been entered without search-warrant and property seized and removed; other property has been wantonly destroyed; workingmen and workingwomen suspected of radical views have been shamefully abused and maltreated. Agents of the Department of Justice have been introduced into radical organizations for the purpose of informing upon their members or inciting them to activities; these agents have even been instructed from Washington to arrange meetings on certain dates for the express purpose of facilitating wholesale raids and arrests. In support of these illegal acts, and to create sentiment in its favor, the Department of Justice has also constituted itself a propaganda bureau, and has sent to newspapers and magazines of this country quantities of material designed to excite public opinion against radicals, all at the expense of the government and outside the scope of the Attorney General's duties.

We make no argument in favor of any radical doctrine as such, whether Socialist, Communist, or Anarchist. No one of us belongs to any of these schools of thought. Nor do we now raise any question as to the Constitutional protection of free speech and a free press.

We are concerned solely with bringing to the attention of the American people the utterly illegal acts which have been committed by those charged with the highest duty of enforcing the laws—acts which have caused widespread suffering and unrest, have struck at the foundation of American free institutions, and have brought the name of our country into disrepute. . . .

Since these illegal acts have been committed by the highest powers in the United States, there is no final appeal from them except to the conscience and condemnation of the American people. American institutions have not in fact been protected by the Attorney General's ruthless suppression. On the contrary, those institutions have been seriously undermined, and revolutionary unrest has been vastly intensified. No organization of radicals acting through propaganda over the last six months could have created as much revolutionary sentiment in America as has been created by the acts of the Department of Justice itself.

Even were one to admit that there existed any serious "Red menace" before the Attorney General started his "unflinching war" against it, his campaign has been singularly fruitless. Out of the many thousands suspected by the Attorney General (he had already listed 60,000 by name and history on November 14, 1919, aliens and citizens) what do the figures show of the net results? Prior to January 1, 1920, there were actually deported 263 persons. Since January 1 there have actually been deported 18 persons. Since January 1 there have been ordered deported an additional 529 persons, and warrants for 1,547 have been cancelled (after full hearings and consideration of the evidence) by Assistant Secretary of Labor Louis F. Post, to whose courageous re-establishment of American Constitutional Law in deportation proceedings (see Exhibit 16) are due the attacks that have been made upon him. The Attorney General has consequently got rid of 810 alien suspects, which, on his own showing, leaves him at least 59,160 persons (aliens and citizens) still to cope with.

It has always been the proud boast of America that this is a government of laws and not of men. Our Constitution and laws have been based on the simple elements of human nature. Free men cannot be driven and repressed; they must be led. Free men respect justice and follow truth, but arbitrary power they will oppose until the end of time. There is no danger of revolution so great as that created by suppression, by ruthlessness, and by deliberate violation of the simple rules of American law and American decency.

It is a fallacy to suppose that, any more than in the past, any servant of the people can safely arrogate to himself unlimited authority. To proceed upon such a supposition is to deny the fundamental American theory of the consent of the governed. Here is no question of a vague and threatened menace, but a present assault upon the most sacred principles of our Constitutional liberty.

EXHIBIT 12, "INSTRUCTIONS TO AGENTS," from *To the American People* (1920)

1. Each person named in the warrant to be taken into custody.
2. Upon taking person into custody *try to obtain all documentary evidence possible* to establish membership in the COMMUNIST PARTY, including membership cards, books, correspondence etc.
3. Also *try to secure charters, meeting minutes, membership books, due books, membership correspondence, etc., in possession of such person,* which may lead to further investigations of members not yet known.
4. All such evidence secured, as above, to be properly marked and sealed as belonging to such person, with name of arrestee, place where secured, date secured, and by whom secured marked plainly on same.
5. *Person or persons taken into custody not to be permitted to communicate with any outside person until after examination by this office and until permission is given by this office.*
6. Upon making arrest, *person in custody to be brought to the place designated by this office for a preliminary examination.*
7. *Preliminary examination to be made by Agent making arrest on forms provided for that purpose by this office.* This form to be followed closely and filled out in detail. The form then to be read to person in custody for him to sign and swear to same. If he refuses to swear and sign to same, then Agent, in presence of one witness to examination, to sign and swear to same and to have witness do the same.
8. *If a person claims American citizenship, he must produce documentary evidence of same.* If native born, through birth records. If naturalized, through producing for Agent copy of naturalization papers. Be sure that these papers are final papers, containing words "and is hereby admitted to become a citizen of the United States."
9. In case of any uncertainty as to citizenship or non-citizenship of person taken into custody, or for any other reason, consult the office.
10. Absolutely no publicity or information to be given by an agent. All such requests for information to be referred to Division Superintendent. Also request observances above by assisting officers.

1. At the time of apprehension, every effort must be made to establish definitely the fact that one arrested is a member of either the Communist Party of America or Communist Labor Party.
2. It is of utmost importance to make every effort to ascertain location of all books and records of these organizations, and that same be secured at time of arrest.
3. Upon making arrests, *endeavor to secure admissions* as to membership in Communist and Communist Labor Parties, together with any possible documentary proof.
4. *Endeavor apprehend officers of either party of aliens, searching residences for literature, membership cards, records and correspondence.*
5. Search meeting rooms and endeavor to locate charters of Communist or Communist Labor Parties, as well as membership and financial records, which, however, may be found at homes of Recording and Financial Secretaries. *Literature, books, papers and anything on the walls should be gathered up,* and ceilings and partitions sounded for biding places. Wrap anything taken and mark the location of place, names of persons obtaining evidence, and contents of each.
6. *Upon apprehension, aliens should be searched thoroughly; if found in groups in meeting rooms, line them up against the wall and there search them.* Take anything which tends to establish connection with either Communist or Communist Labor Parties, in other words, only such materials referring to these parties, and nothing distinctly personal such as money and other valuables. Mark envelopes showing contents; whether found in possession of alien or in his room, with address, as well as names of those obtaining evidence. Duplicate record of all this should be kept; original evidence obtained in the cases to be turned over to the Immigration Officers.
7. *Only aliens should be arrested; if American citizens are taken by mistake, their cases should be immediately referred to the local authorities.*
8. Arrest of members covered by warrants to be made Friday, at 9 P.M. Only aliens, and connected with Communist and Communist Labor Parties; make preliminary examination as per office memorandum.

Exhibit 12 in To the American People *included two sets of confidential instructions to Department of Justice agents in New England who were to conduct the raids of January 2, 1920.*
Source: Brown, R.G., Zechanah Chafee, Jr., Felix Frankfurter, et al. *To the American People: Report upon the Illegal Practices of the United States Department of Justice.* New York: Call Printing Co., 1920.

NOTE: These instructions are extremely confidential; are issued only for the guidance of authorized agents of this office; are charged to such agents and must be returned to this office upon completion of assignment.

Dorothy Parker

1893–1967

Fiction Writer and Humorist

Dorothy Parker, a founding member of the Algonquin "Round Table" and among *The New Yorker*'s original writers, was famous for her caustic wit, biting drama reviews, and her poetry and short stories that portrayed the "dark side" of the Roaring Twenties.

Dorothy Rothschild was born in West End, New Jersey, on August 22, 1893. Her Scots mother died shortly after she was born, her Jewish father remarried, and Dorothy was raised by a stern Christian step-mother. After graduating from a private finishing school in 1911, Dorothy took a room in a boarding-house—an unusual step for a young unmarried woman in those days—and supported herself by playing piano for a dancing school in New York City. She wrote light verse, and a poem was accepted for publication in *Vanity Fair* in 1913. She was hired as a writer of captions for fashion illustrations in *Vogue*. In 1917 she married Edwin Pond Parker II, a Wall Street stockbroker. The marriage did not survive long after he returned from service in World War I, but she kept his surname, which she preferred to her maiden name.

©*Bettmann/Corbis*

In 1916 she was transferred to *Vanity Fair*, where she wrote verse, satirical sketches, essays, and drama reviews, and befriended fellow writers Robert Benchley and Robert E. Sherwood. In 1920 she was fired for writing harsh drama reviews; Benchley and Sherwood resigned in sympathy. Parker and Benchley then worked as freelance writers and shared a tiny office where space was so tight that, according to Parker, "If it had been any smaller it would have been adultery."

Parker, Benchley, and Sherwood often ate lunch at the Algonquin Hotel in Manhattan, where they were joined by critic Alexander Woollcott, columnist Franklin P. Adams (F.P.A.), and editor Harold Ross. Soon a large circle of literary and theatrical talents began gathering and gossiping around a table at the Algonquin—the Round Table—skewering one another with clever puns and barbs that they often published in their newspaper and magazine columns. Among the regulars at the Algonquin were the

dramatist George S. Kaufman, Pulitzer Prize–winning novelist and dramatist Edna Ferber, and occasionally performers Harpo Marx, Paul Robeson, Tallulah Bankhead, and Ethel Barrymore. The group also came to be known as the Vicious Circle, and any especially witty or cutting remark was ascribed—often erroneously—to Mrs. Parker. (Upon hearing that the famously tight-lipped, buttoned-down President **Calvin Coolidge** had just died, she asked, "How could they tell?")

With its vibrant energy and abundance of capital, the 1920s was a propitious time for founding magazines—some of which, such as *Time* (1923) and *Reader's Digest* (1922), have since become American institutions. When Harold Ross founded a sophisticated new magazine, *The New Yorker*, in 1925, Parker was one of the six founding editors. She wrote book reviews under the pen name "Constant Reader" (1927–33) and contributed short stories and satirical verse.

Her writings explored the themes of deception, class snobbery, and racism. Perhaps her sensitivity to the plight of outsiders derived from her own ambiguous identity—not fully Jewish, but not *not* Jewish, either. In 1929 her powerful, autobiographical short story "Big Blonde" won the O. Henry Award for the year's best short story by an American. Her humor was often self-deprecating. She would later comment, "The Round Table thing was *greatly* overrated. It was full of people looking for a free lunch and asking, 'Did you hear the funny thing I said yesterday?'"

To her admirers, Parker's cynical verse and caustic comments conveyed the adventurous, reckless spirit of the time when young women were smoking, drinking, bobbing their hair scandalously short, and exploring casual sexual relationships. The witticisms fired around the Round Table bespoke the restless energy of a time of extravagance and irresponsibility. To prudish and disapproving elders, the freedoms taken for granted by the new "anything goes" generation seemed to threaten the boundaries of civilized behavior. Young ladies were supposed to be well mannered and to believe in romantic love. Instead, sassy, wisecracking young Mrs. Parker was writing about faithless men, lying and self-deluded women, and, repeatedly, about suicide, as in these lines from "Résumé": "Guns aren't lawful; / Nooses give; / Gas smells awful; / You might as well live." Suffering from manic depression and disappointments in love, she developed a reputation for heavy drinking, suicide attempts, missed deadlines, and burned bridges.

In her writings and actions, however, Parker showed a social conscience during an age not noted for political activism: she wrote "Arrangement in Black and White" after witnessing the black performer Paul Robeson treated condescendingly at a bohemian party, and she was arrested in a march in Boston protesting the execution of Italian anarchists **Nicola Sacco and Bartolomeo Vanzetti** in 1927. Parker helped organize the Screen Actors Guild in 1934 and the Anti-Nazi League in 1936; the following year she went to Spain to report on the Loyalist cause in the Spanish Civil War for the *New Masses*, a communist magazine. (She was blacklisted for "un-American activities" in 1949 and was called before the House Un-American Activities Committee in 1951.)

Parker married (then divorced and remarried) Alan Campbell, an actor and writer 11 years her junior (and also half-Jewish and half-Scots) with whom she went to Hollywood as a screenwriting team. Her many screenplays included the Academy Award–winning *A Star Is Born* (1937). The money was good, but she detested the film industry.

Although she seemed to envy those who die young, Mrs. Parker outlived most of her Round Table companions. She died in New York City in 1967, having willed her estate to the Rev. Dr. Martin Luther King, Jr., or, in the event of his death (he died the next year), to the National Association for the Advancement of Colored People (NAACP).

While the 1920s are often associated with frivolity, Dorothy Parker didn't flinch from the dark side. She is famous for being clever, but her terse, epigrammatic poetry and lean, sympathetic fiction still stand up well among the best works written in that decade crowded with ambitious, talented writers.

Mark LaFlaur

For Further Reading

Parker, Dorothy. "Dorothy Parker," interview by Marion Capon, in *Writers at Work: The Paris Review Interviews*, Vol. 1. ed. Malcolm Cowley. New York: Viking, 1958.

Keats, John. *You Might as Well Live: The Life and Times of Dorothy Parker*. New York: Paragon House, 1986.

Meade, Marion. *Dorothy Parker: What Fresh Hell Is This?* New York: Penguin, 1989.

Parker, Dorothy. *The Portable Dorothy Parker*. Introduction by Brendan Gill. New York: Viking Press, 1980.

"A WELL-WORN STORY" by Dorothy Parker (1927)

In April, in April,
My one love came along,
And I ran the slope of my high hill
To follow a thread of song.

His eyes were hard as porphyry
With looking on cruel lands;
His voice went slipping over me
Like terrible silver hands.

Together we trod the secret lane
And walked the muttering town.
I wore my heart like a wet, red stain
On the breast of a velvet gown.

In April, in April,
My love went whistling by,
And I stumbled here to my high hill
Along the way of a lie.

Now what should I do in this place
But sit and count the chimes,
And splash cold water on my face
And spoil a page with rhymes?

In "A Well-Worn Story," included in her 1927 collection Enough Rope, *Parker distills yet another disappointment into poetry—art that outlives a broken heart.*

Source: Parker, Dorothy. *Enough Rope*. New York: Boni & Liveright, 1927.

REVIEW OF *ENOUGH ROPE* by Edmund Wilson (1927)

Edmund Wilson, one of the greatest literary critics of the 1920s—and the twentieth century—reviews Parker's 1927 collection Enough Rope *and praises her "edged and acrid style" and her poetry's "peculiar intensity and frankness."*

Source: Wilson, Edmund. *The New Republic* 49, no. 633, January 19, 1927. Reprinted by courtesy of *The New Republic*.

Mrs. Dorothy Parker began her poetic career as a writer of humorous verse of the school of Franklin P. Adams. There are specimens of her early vein in this book: a comic roundel, a roundeau redoublé "(and scarcely worth the trouble at that)" and a parody of some verses of Gilbert. Mrs. Parker's special invention (aside from her vers libre "hymns of hate," unrepresented here), was a kind of burlesque sentimental lyric which gave the effect, till you came to the end, of a typical magazine filler, perhaps a little more authentically felt and a little better written than the average: the last line, however, punctuated the rest with incredible ferocity. Thus, to quote only a comparatively mild example included in this book, the old, old gate wreathed with lilacs where the lady waits with yearning in the gloaming turns out, at the end of the poem, to be "the gate her true love gave her."

Mrs. Parker has had scarcely a rival in the contrivance of these loaded cigars, these squirting boutonnieres and these pigs-in-clover puzzles of literature; and she could have put together a most amusing book of them. Her present book is, however, quite different. During the last two or three years, Dorothy Parker—though still in the pages of *Life* and the *New Yorker*—has emerged as a distinguished and interesting poet. It is true that, in America just now, we do not lack distinguished women poets: there are so many women who write creditable lyrics that we have come to take them more or less for granted and are no longer very much excited over the appearance of another promising apprentice of the school of Elinor Wylie or Edna Millay. But Mrs. Parker seems somehow to stand a little apart from this group. It is true that she sometimes echoes Mrs. Wylie and, more frequently, Miss Millay; yet on the whole, her poems give the impression of differing from those of many of her sisters in being a good deal less "literary"—that is, they have the appearance of proceeding, not merely from the competent exercise of an attractive literary gift, but from a genuine necessity to write. We may be conscious that there are at least thirty women in the country who would have been incapable of spoiling an excellent epigram with such a final couplet as this,

> Inertia rides and riddles me;
> The which is called Philosophy

or who would never have commenced another as follows,

> Oh, both my shoes are shiny new
> And pristine is my hat

—we may be conscious, I say, that there are perhaps thirty expert poets who would have known why "pristine" and "the which" were impossible. But we feel, also, that a sound instinct for style has here merely been betrayed by the bad habits of humorous versifying. And, in a similar way, we are convinced that her addiction to the idiom of Miss Millay is less an evidence of imitative weakness than an accidental and possible passing phase, due to the fact that Mrs. Parker has only just begun to attempt serious poetry and that, of all the poets who are read just now, Miss Millay's temperament, in certain of its aspects, has most affinity with her own. It is on the side of bareness and sharpness that Mrs. Parker most resembles Miss Millay; but the edged and acrid style which emerges in her book is unmistakably individual.

And the personality which reveals itself in Mrs. Parker's poems is quite different from that of Miss Millay: Mrs. Parker has her own complex of emotions, her own philosophy of love. Take the sonnet of which the octet begins as follows,

> If you should sail for Trebizond, or die,
> Or cry another name in your first sleep,
> Or see me board a train, and fail to sigh,
> Appropriately, I'd clutch my breast and weep.

Here she has caught precisely the idiom of Edna Millay; yet Miss Millay would never have drawn the same moral:

> Therefore the mooning world is gratified,
> Quoting how prettily we sigh and swear;
> And you and I, correctly side by side,
> Shall live as lovers when our bones are bare;
> And though we lie forever as enemies,
> Shall rank with Abélard and Héloïse.

This is not one of Mrs. Parker's most satisfactory poems: it is, on the contrary, one of her most derivative; yet, at the same time, it is interesting precisely because of a certain originality of accent and of point of view. Perhaps few poems in this book are completely successful: they tend, on the one hand, as I have already suggested, to become a little cheapened in the direction of ordinary humorous verse and, on the other, to become too deeply saturated with the jargon of ordinary feminine poetry, to go in too much for plaintive Aprils, for red stains on velvet gowns and for "pretty maids" and "likely lads." But her best work is extraordinarily vivid: it has a peculiar intensity and frankness which, when they appear in poetry, seem to justify any style or method, no matter how strange to literary convention. Dorothy Parker's unprecedented feat has been to raise to the dignity of poetry the "wise-cracking" humor of New York: she has thus almost invented a new kind of epigram: she has made the comic anti-climax tragic. With the publication of this volume, her figure becomes distinct and her voice unmistakable: in her satires, in her short stories, in her play, we had long been aware of her as somebody and something in particular; and from now on, she must command our attention. We have never before had anything quite like:

> Oh, life is a glorious song,
> A medley of extemporanea,
> And love is a thing that can never go wrong;
> And I am Marie of Roumania.

any more than anything like:

> That a heart falls tinkling down,
> Never think it ceases.
> Every likely lad in town
> Gathers up the pieces.
> If there's one gone whistling by
> Would I let it grieve me?
> Let him wonder if I lie;
> Let him half believe me.

We have nothing quite like the dark hard crystals of Dorothy Parker's irony: they do not spark with prismatic colors and a great many of them are imperfect, but they are beginning to become valuable.

"Big Blonde" by Dorothy Parker (1929) [Excerpt]

. . . She was completely bewildered by what happened to their marriage. First they were lovers; and then, it seemed without transition, they were enemies. She never understood it.

There were longer and longer intervals between his leaving his office and his arrival at the apartment. She went through agonies of picturing him run over and bleeding, dead and covered with a sheet. Then she lost her fears for his safety and grew sullen and wounded. When a person wanted to be with a person, he came as soon as possible. She desperately wanted him to want to be with her; her own hours only marked the time till he would come. It was often nearly nine o'clock before he came home to dinner. Always he had had many drinks, and their effect would die in him, leaving him loud and querulous and bristling for affronts.

He was too nervous, he said, to sit and do nothing for an evening. He boasted, probably not in all truth, that he had never read a book in his life.

"What am I expected to do — sit around this dump on my tail all night?" he would ask, rhetorically. And again he would slam out.

She did not know what to do. She could not manage him. She could not meet him.

She fought him furiously. A terrific domesticity had come upon her, and she would bite and scratch to guard it. She wanted what she called "a nice home." She wanted a sober, tender husband, prompt at dinner, punctual at work. She wanted sweet, comforting evenings. The idea of intimacy with other men was terrible to her; the thought that Herbie might be seeking entertainment in other women set her frantic.

It seemed to her that almost everything she read — novels from the drug-store lending library, magazine stories, women's pages in the papers — dealt with wives who lost their husbands' love. She could bear those, at that, better than accounts of neat, companionable marriage and living happily ever after.

She was frightened. Several times when Herbie came home in the evening, he found her determinedly dressed—she had had to alter those of her clothes that were not new, to make them fasten—and rouged.

"Let's go wild tonight, what do you say?" she would hail him. "A person's got lots of time to hang around and do nothing when they're dead."

So they would go out, to chop houses and the less expensive cabarets. But it turned out badly. She could no longer find amusement in watching Herbie drink. She could not laugh at his whimsicalities, she was so tensely counting his indulgences. And she was unable to keep back her remonstrances—"Ah, come on, Herb, you've had enough, haven't you? You'll feel something terrible in the morning."

He would be immediately enraged. All right, crab; crab, crab, crab, crab, that was all she ever did. What a lousy sport *she* was! There would be scenes, and one or the other of them would rise and stalk out in fury.

She could not recall the definite day that she started drinking, herself. There was nothing separate about her days. Like drops upon a window-pane, they ran together and trickled away. She had been married six months; then a year; then three years.

She had never needed to drink, formerly. She could sit for most of a night at a table where the others were imbibing earnestly and never droop in looks or spirits, nor be bored by the doings of those about her. If she took a cocktail, it was so unusual as to cause twenty minutes or so of jocular comment. But now anguish was in her. Frequently, after a quarrel, Herbie would stay out for the night, and she could not learn from him where the time had been spent. Her heart felt tight and sore in her breast, and her mind turned like an electric fan.

She hated the taste of liquor. Gin, plain or in mixtures, made her promptly sick. After experiment, she found that Scotch whisky was best for her. She took it without water, because that was the quickest way to its effect.

Herbie pressed it on her. He was glad to see her drink. They both felt it might restore her high spirits, and their good times together might again be possible.

" 'Atta girl," he would approve her. "Let's see you get boiled, baby." . . .

With "Big Blonde," Dorothy Parker won the O. Henry Prize for the best short story published in 1929 and captured at once a fictional portrait of her own life and that of her generation.

Source: Parker, Dorothy. *The Portable Dorothy Parker.* Introduction by Brendan Gill. New York: Viking Press, 1980.

Alice **Paul**

1885–1977
Radical Suffragist Leader

The militant Alice Paul galvanized the suffragist movement during the final push to the Nineteenth Amendment and led a new generation of feminist leaders.

On January 11, 1885, Paul was born in Moorestown, New Jersey, into a Quaker family. She graduated from Swarthmore College in 1905 and did postgraduate work at the New York School of Philanthropy (1906), the University of Pennsylvania, from which she earned a master's degree in 1907 and a doctorate in 1912. She also attended a Quaker training school in Woodbridge, England. From 1907 to 1910, while in England, Paul worked as a caseworker and as an activist for the radical suffragists Emmeline and Christabel Pankhurst. During their activities, Paul underwent a series of arrests, imprisonments, and hunger strikes, and she returned home promoting the use of militant tactics in the U.S. suffragist struggle.

In 1912, she chaired the congressional committee of the National American Woman Suffrage Association (NAWSA) but soon came to oppose their conservative policies. Paul left a year later and co-founded the Congressional Union for Woman Suffrage, which in 1916 became the National Woman's Party (NWP). Their sole mission was to campaign for passage of the Nineteenth Amendment, which gave women the right to vote.

As head of the NWP, Paul employed aggressive strategies of nonviolent civil disobedience. The NWP symbolized a new generation of enthusiastic and determined suffragists. They perceived the previous generation as feeble women who compromised their rights, whereas they fought as ardent feminists ready to take risks for their cause. In January of 1917, the NWP became the first group to picket the White House. These picket lines, which even many other feminists found shocking, lasted for 18 months and involved thousands of women volunteers beyond NWP membership. Paul, one of the many imprisoned during these protests, waged a hunger strike to establish her rights as a political prisoner and was subjected to forced feedings. Her

From the collections of the Library of Congress.

protests—on the picket lines and in prison—stemmed from her guiding principle that women should be self-governed.

In 1920, the Nineteenth Amendment was finally ratified, a giant victory for American women at the beginning of an era that would continue to witness their growing independence. During World War I, labor shortages had enabled many women to work outside of the home. Once the war had ended, many of these women wanted to retain the social and economic freedoms they had gained. The modern emancipated woman, most extraordinarily represented by the image of the flapper, sought out gender equality and rebelled against the social conventions of the previous generations. Intellectual feminists, like Paul, shared with flappers a willingness to reject old ideas in search of a better, more equitable future.

Winning the vote, however, brought new challenges; once united by a common goal, suffragists now found themselves divided by diverging objectives and special interests. On February 15, 1921, the NWP held a ceremony in Washington, D.C., that was attended by over 100 women's organizations with differing concerns. A three-day convention followed where Paul presented the next step toward emancipation: constitutional equality between the sexes. Many suffragists, particularly social reformer Florence Kelley, opposed Paul's position. Kelley felt that equal rights would eliminate protective labor laws for women in the workplace, whereas Paul believed that protective legislation hindered rather than helped women's economic status. Paul was also criticized for promoting equality while ignoring the African-American delegates and their concern—racial discrimination in the South.

Although Paul resigned at the 1921 convention, she continued to be a pivotal force for the NWP in her campaign for equal rights. At Seneca Falls, New York, in 1923, on the seventy-fifth anniversary of the first Seneca Falls Convention, Paul presented the first Equal Rights Amendment (ERA): "Men and women shall have equal rights throughout the United States and every place subject to its jurisdiction." She first had this amendment introduced into Congress that year in December, and it was repeatedly introduced and rejected throughout the 1920s.

Paul pursued her campaign for equal rights the remainder of her life both locally and internationally. In 1938, she founded and administered in Geneva the World Party for Equal Rights, known as the World Women's Party. Returning to the United States three years later, Paul was elected chairperson of the NWP in 1942 and submitted her second version of the ERA to the Senate Judiciary Committee in 1943. She fought for including references to gender equality in the preamble to the United Nations Charter and in the 1964 Civil Rights Act. When Paul died in her hometown on July 9, 1977, the ERA required just three more states for ratification. Today the amendment still has not passed.

By drinking and smoking in public and cutting her hair short, the flapper resisted the moral restrictions imposed upon her by society; however, at the same time more serious women shaped this social rebellion into an intensified fight for women's rights—as exemplified by the introduction of the Equal Rights Amendment into Congress in 1923. At the core of Paul's convictions was the belief that women should be in charge of their own lives rather than regulated by the government as a specialized group. She understood that winning the vote for women was only one victory in a long battle toward equality; thus, she forcefully campaigned for the passage of the ERA, which she felt would enable women to choose freely their own path in life.

Renée Miller

For Further Reading

Ford, Linda G. *Iron-Jawed Angels: The Suffrage Militancy of the National Woman's Party, 1912–1920.* Lanham, Md.: University Press of America, 1991.

Irwin, Inez Hayes. *The Story of Alice Paul and the National Woman's Party.* Fairfax, Va.: Denlinger's Publishers, 1977.

Lunardini, Christine A. *From Equal Suffrage to Equal Rights: Alice Paul and the National Woman's Party, 1910–1928.* New York: New York University Press, 1986.

"Colby Proclaims Woman Suffrage" from the *New York Times* (August 27, 1920) [Excerpt]

WASHINGTON, Aug. 26 – The half-century struggle for woman suffrage in the United States reached its climax at 8 o'clock this morning, when Bainbridge Colby, as Secretary of State, issued his proclamation announcing that the Nineteenth Amendment had become a part of the Constitution of the United States.

The signing of the proclamation took place at that hour at Secretary Colby's residence, 1507 K Street Northwest, without ceremony of any kind, and the issuance of the proclamation was unaccompanied by the taking of movies or other pictures, despite the fact that the National Woman's Party, or militant branch of the general suffrage movement, had been anxious to be represented by a delegation of women and to have the historic event filmed for public display and permanent record.

Secretary Colby did not act with undue haste in signing the proclamation, but only after he had given careful study to the packet which arrived by mail during the early morning hours containing the certificate of the Governor of Tennessee that that State's Legislature had ratified the Congressional resolution submitting the amendment to the States for action.

NO SUFFRAGE LEADERS SEE SIGNING.

None of the leaders of the woman suffrage movement was present when the proclamation was signed.

"It was quite tragic," declared Mrs. Abby Scott Baker of the National Woman's Party. "This was the final culmination of the women's fight, and, women, irrespective of factions, should have been allowed to be present when the proclamation was signed. However, the women of America have fought a big fight and nothing can take from them their triumph."

Leaders of both branches of the woman's movement—the militants, headed by Miss Alice Paul, and the conservatives, led by Mrs. Carrie Chapman Catt—some of whom had been on watch nearly all night for the arrival of the Tennessee Governor's certification, visited the State Department, and the militants sought to have Secretary Colby go through a duplication of the signing scene in the presence of movie cameras. This Mr. Colby declined to do, on the ground that it was not necessary to detract from the dignity and importance of the signing of the proclamation by staging a scene in imitation of the actual signing of the proclamation. . . .

FACTIONS DISPUTE OVER CEREMONY.

Differences between the rival organizations of suffragists as to who should be present at the signing of the proclamation developed yesterday, and as no agreement could be brought about between them, it is believed that Secretary Colby decided to sign the proclamation in his own home to avoid a clash at his offices.

"It was decided," said the Secretary in a statement this afternoon, "not to accompany this simple ministerial action on my part with any ceremony or setting. This secondary aspect of the subject has regretfully been the source of considerable contention as to who shall participate in it and who shall not. Inasmuch as I am not interested in the aftermath of any of the friction or collisions which may have been developed in the long struggle for the ratification of the amendment, I have contented myself with the performance in the simplest manner of the duty devolving upon me under the law."

Representatives of both factions visited the State Department this morning. Mrs. Catt and members of her party were photographed by movie operators as they left the State Department. Miss Alice Paul and her associates of the militant wing of the suffragists waited in the corridor of the State Department to be seen by the Secretary of State, who sent word he would receive them, but at this moment the Spanish Ambassador arrived and

On August 26, 1920, Secretary of State Bainbridge Colby ratified the Nineteenth Amendment at his residence. However, due to disagreements between rival suffragist organizations, including Paul's National Women's Party, women suffragist leaders were not present to view Colby's signing of the proclamation, as reported in this article from the New York Times *published the following day.*

Source: New York Times, August 27, 1920.

took precedence over the delegation of militants.

As time wore on the militant delegation thinned and finally left the department without having an audience with the Secretary of State.

Secretary Colby late this afternoon was asked by newspaper men to picture the scene that took place at his home when the final chapter of the story of ratification was reached. . . .

PHOTO OF ALICE PAUL (1920)

After ratification of the Nineteenth Amendment in 1920, Paul celebrates by saluting a toast at a feminist rally.

Source: From the collections of the Library of Congress.

TEXTS OF THE EQUAL RIGHTS AMENDMENT (1923 and 1943)

VERSION I
Men and women shall have equal rights throughout the United States and every place subject to its jurisdiction.

VERSION II
Equality of rights under the law shall not be denied or abridged by the United States or by any State on account of sex.

Paul insisted that the true enfranchisement of women depended upon legalized equality between the sexes. Here are Paul's two versions of the Equal Rights Amendment: the first introduced to Congress in 1923 and the second submitted to the Senate Judiciary Committee in 1943.

Source: Lunardini, Christine A. *From Equal Suffrage to Equal Rights: Alice Paul and the National Woman's Party, 1910–1928.* New York: New York University Press, 1986.

"How New Jersey Laws Discriminate Against Women" (1926)

How New Jersey Laws Discriminate Against Women

Married women are discriminated against in the collection of their wages for work performed in the home for third persons.

Married women are discriminated against in the distribution of damages for personal injuries.

Married women are discriminated against as to the power to contract.

Married women are discriminated against in the control of their real estate.

Mothers are discriminated against as to rights over their children.

Unmarried mothers are discriminated against as to the burden of illegitimate parenthood.

Women in industry are discriminated against by special restrictions and regulations.

Women are discriminated against in jury service.

NATIONAL WOMAN'S PARTY, New Jersey
National Headquarters, Capitol Hill, Washington, D. C.
State Headquarters, 822 DeGraw Avenue, Newark, N. J.

TWENTY-FIVE CENTS A COPY
Copyright 1926, by National Woman's Party

In this 1926 flyer, Paul and the National Woman's Party address "How New Jersey Laws Discriminate Against Women" in marriage, motherhood, industry, and politics. Distributed by their New Jersey branch, it lays out the legalized oppression Paul and the NWP fought in the 1920s. Paul's principal conviction was that women should choose for themselves in both their personal and professional lives.

Source: Special Collections/University Archives, Rutgers University Libraries/Jack Abraham.

"The Liberty Belle—She's Cracked" Political Cartoon (1926)

DOWN WITH INHIBITIONS

LIBERATE THE LIBIDO!

The political cartoon, published in Judge on February 6, 1926, portrays the public perception of the modern emancipated woman—shown here advocating free love. Representations like this one made a mockery of the goals and protests of ardent feminists such as Paul and the National Woman's Party.

Source: From the collections of the Library of Congress.

John J. Pershing

General John J. Pershing commanded the two-million-man American Expeditionary Force (AEF) in Europe in World War I, and in 1919 he received the highest military ranking of any United States general since George Washington.

John Joseph Pershing was born on September 13, 1860, in Laclede, Missouri. He graduated from the Missouri State Normal School in Kirksville and became a teacher before deciding to enroll at the U.S. Military Academy. He entered West Point in 1882 and in 1886 he was named first captain of the Corps of Cadets, an honor accorded the student most respected by students and faculty. He studied law in **William Jennings Bryan**'s library while an instructor of military science at the University of Nebraska (1891–93), and was awarded a law degree in 1893.

Pershing pursued a wide and varied military career, first leading cavalry units in the Apache campaign in 1886 and the Sioux campaign in 1890–91, teaching at West Point in 1897–98, and serving in the Spanish-American War in Cuba in 1898 and in the Philippines as a brigadier general and administrator from 1906 to 1913. He acquired the nickname "Black Jack" while leading a cavalry regiment of African-American soldiers in Montana and in Cuba, though the name also referred to his firm discipline—over himself as well as his troops and students. In 1905 he married Frances Warren, the daughter of a Wyoming senator. They had three daughters and one son.

Between 1914 and 1917, while war was being fought in Europe, the United States was bedeviled by a chaotic power struggle in the Mexican Revolution. After the revolutionary Pancho Villa and his *villistas* murdered 17 American miners and engineers on a Mexican train in early 1916, then sacked the town of Columbus, New Mexico, President **Woodrow Wilson** sent Pershing with a force of some 11,000 men in pursuit of Villa and his followers. Although the punitive expedition penetrated some 300 miles into Mexico and lasted almost a year, Pershing never did catch Villa, although the rebel's ability to make trouble was diminished.

From the collections of the Library of Congress.

When the U.S. Congress declared war on Germany in 1917, Wilson appointed Pershing as head of the American Expeditionary Force. Although the general, at age 56, was junior to five other major generals, he was favored by Wilson (as he had been by Theodore Roosevelt) for his organizational skills and his discipline. Pershing had urged preparations for intervention in Europe and was dismayed by the army's weakness: at the beginning of 1917, the U.S. Army, with fewer than 110,000 men, ranked seventeenth in the world. In his "General Organization Report" of June 1917 he recommended an army of one million men by 1918 and three million by 1919.

After three years of stalemate in the trenches, the French and British forces were exhausted and demoralized, and facing a strengthened enemy. The abdication of Russia's Czar Nicholas in March 1917 and the Bolsheviks' separate peace with Germany in March 1918 allowed Germany to pull back 50 divisions from the eastern front and reinforce their comrades on the western front.

Pershing fought two campaigns: one was the rapid assembly and training of a large fighting force, and the other was a struggle with the supreme Allied commander, France's Marshal Ferdinand Foch, and with Britain's Field Marshal Sir Douglas Haig, who wanted the fresh Americans to replenish their own thinned ranks. Wilson's orders were that the AEF would remain "a separate and distinct component of the combined forces." When German troops threatened Paris in the spring of 1918, however, Pershing allowed Marshal Foch to borrow some of his "doughboys," or "Yanks," as the American soldiers were known.

American troops began arriving in France in mid-1917, but did not join in active fighting until May 1918 at Cantigny, and in June at the battles of Château-Thierry and Belleau Wood. By August, 1.3 million Americans of an eventual two million, had been deployed in France. The AEF was involved in heavy fighting for 110 days, particularly in two large assaults: on September 12–16 at the St.-

Mihiel salient south of Verdun (from which the Germans were already beginning to withdraw), and the Meuse-Argonne offensive of September–November, a joint Allied operation that broke down the German resistance in early October and led to Germany's request for an armistice. Pershing halted, though he would have preferred to drive the enemy back to Berlin.

Hailed as a hero by the victorious Allies, the French in particular, on September 3, 1919, Pershing was named general of the armies, an almost unprecedented honor: among American generals, only George Washington had been granted this distinction. (Pershing had been made major general in September 1916 and general in October 1917.) On September 10, Pershing and 25,000 of his First Division troops in full combat dress were given a massive victory parade in New York City amid cheering crowds.

When he was named chief of staff on July 1, 1921, Pershing became the senior officer in the U.S. Army, subordinate only to the war secretary and the commander in chief (the president). Predicting a resurgence of trouble from Germany, he urged Congress not to reduce peacetime forces too radically, but his warning went unheeded. Pershing also headed a committee that developed a map of strategically important roads across the United States. Published in 1922, the "Pershing Map" indirectly laid the foundation of the interstate highway system. He retired on September 13, 1924, his sixty-fourth birthday, and subsequently headed several commissions, including the American Battle Monuments Commission dedicated to honoring the memory of his "boys." In 1931 he published *My Experiences in the World War,* for which he was awarded the Pulitzer Prize for History (1932). Pershing died of natural causes at the Walter Reed Army Hospital in Washington, D.C., on July 15, 1948, and was buried at Arlington National Cemetery.

John J. Pershing excelled not only as a field commander but also as an administrator of an international military coalition, and is widely regarded as the first of the modern generals. His success as the first leader of United States troops in a European war reflected his nation's growing influence in world events and foreshadowed the vitality of the United States in the 1920s.

Mark LaFlaur

For Further Reading

Pershing, John J. *My Experiences in the World War.* 2 vols. New York: Frederick A. Stokes, 1931.

Smythe, Donald. *Guerrilla Warrior: The Early Life of John J. Pershing.* New York, Charles Scribner's Sons, 1973.

———. *Pershing: General of the Armies.* Bloomington: Indiana University Press, 1986.

Vandiver, Frank E. *Black Jack: The Life and Times of John J. Pershing.* 2 vols. College Station: Texas A&M University Press, 1977.

"THE ANNOUNCEMENT" POLITICAL CARTOON (1915)

The sinking by a German submarine of the Lusitania *on May 7, 1915, was one of the crises that edged the United States closer to intervention in World War I. This drawing by William A. Rogers was reproduced in the* New York Herald *(May 8, 1915); the skull is wearing a German-style helmet and the sign in the background features an ominous message warning* Lusitania *passengers that they would be traveling through perilous waters at their own risk.*

Source: From the collections of the Library of Congress.

The Zimmermann telegram, intercepted by the British Naval Intelligence Service and relayed to the U.S. State Department, shocked the public and prompted Wilson to break off diplomatic relations with Germany.

Source: Grunwald, Lisa, and Stephen J. Adler, eds. *Letters of the Century: America, 1900-1999.* New York: Dial Press, 1999.

ZIMMERMANN TELEGRAM (January 19, 1917)

Berlin, January 19, 1917

On the first of February we intend to begin submarine warfare unrestricted. In spite of this it is our intention to keep neutral the United States of America.

If this attempt is not successful we propose an alliance on the following basis with Mexico: That we shall make war together and together make peace. We shall give general financial support, and it is understood that Mexico is to reconquer the lost territory in New Mexico, Texas, and Arizona. The details are left for your settlement.

You are instructed to inform the President of Mexico of the above in the greatest confidence as soon as it is certain there will be an outbreak of war with the United States, and we suggest that the President of Mexico on his own initiative should communicate with Japan suggesting adherence at once to this plan; at the same time offer to mediate between Germany and Japan.

Please call to the attention of the President of Mexico that the employment of ruthless submarine warfare now promises to compel England to make peace in a few months.

Zimmermann.

U.S. FOOD ADMINISTRATION WAR POSTER (1918)

At the outbreak of war, the U.S. government established a food-control program that regulated food production and distribution. This poster, created by George John Illian for the U.S. Food Administration Headquarters, encourages U.S. citizens to ration their food and cut back on consumption.

Source: National Archives.

KEEP *it* COMING

"We must not only feed our Soldiers at the front but the millions of women & children behind our lines"
Gen. John J. Pershing

WASTE NOTHING

UNITED   STATES   FOOD   ADMINISTRATION

ARTICLE DESCRIBING PERSHING'S VICTORY PARADE from the *New York Times* (September 11, 1919) [EXCERPT]

TROOPS USE MACHINE GUN ON BOSTON MOB;
5,000 GUARDING CITY AS RIOTS CONTINUE;
CITY ACCLAIMS PARADE OF FIGHTING FIRST

New York lived yesterday probably the last chapter in its history of great military spectacles growing out of the war.

Devoted to honoring General John J. Pershing, Commander in Chief of the American Expeditionary Forces, and to paying tribute to the final array of veteran fighting men to parade down Fifth Avenue, it was a fitting chapter. For the city proved that, though it is ten months since Armistice Day, it has not forgotten either the hosts who fought in France or the man who led them to Victory.

It was the town's first opportunity to greet the men of the 1st Division, and to let them know it remembered their glorious part in the American Army's smashing drives at Toul, at Cantigny, at Soissons, at St. Mihiel, and at the Meuse and the Argonne. Likewise, it was the first appearance here of "Pershing's Own," that regiment of stalwart veterans picked from the first six regular army divisions in France, which paraded as Pershing's escort in Paris and in London, as it did here. Altogether, more than 25,000 fighting men were in line.

A vast throng turned out, which stood in places many deep, all along Fifth Avenue from 107th Street to Washington Square. More than that, it was an enthusiastic crowd, as prone to applause and acclaim as any that a spectacle of the war has called forth.

If the cheers swelled into real outbursts of greeting only at those spots where there were dense masses of spectators, such as at the reviewing stand and the seats which flanked it from Eighty-fifth to Seventy-fourth Street, they were never absent. The applause was continuous, hearty and manifestly genuine.

PERSHING'S NAME RISES ABOVE THE DIN

Pershing's name resounded over the general din countless thousands of times. Three cheers were given for him over and over again, and every one within hearing joined each time they started. Here and there the chimes of church bells put an edge of sweetness on the noise. Again, bells less musical, wooden "crickets," and improvised instruments of discord converted the plaudits into outbursts of great popular demonstration. Now and then, in areas of great office buildings, showers of confetti, long, trailing paper streamers and clouds of paper snow helped on the gayety.

They did more than cheer Pershing, more than call his name over and over, more than shout unintelligible phrases of thanksgiving for victory and appreciation for the Commander in Chief's share in the victory. Here and there some club or some business house had provided a band of its own—a particularly fortunate contribution to the day, for in the parade itself music was disappointingly scarce.

A group of army airplanes from Hazelhurst Field at Mineola, L.I., were sent to Manhattan when the parade started, as a special aerial escort. They flew low over the Park and up and down the Avenue, at times disappearing from the ken of the watchers, only to come roaring back a few minutes later over their heads. One carried a photographer, who made a record of the event as it appeared from the air for the War Department archives.

The whole route was gay and colorful with flags and bunting. Most colorful, most picturesque of all was the way Pershing, the members of his staff, officers and men of lesser rank, all the long line of marchers, were pelted with flowers. At times Pershing rode over stretches of asphalt carpeted with laurel. At others roses and simpler flowers rained about him. Again some enthusiast, high above him, would toss a single blossom, perhaps to fall almost at his feet, perhaps to drop far behind him.

Even where the crowds were least dense, Pershing was kept at almost continual salute by the tributes volleyed at him from both sides of the avenue. Once he had reached the stands, and again when he was below Fifty-ninth Street, from which points the crowds were increased, it was impossible for him to acknowledge a tithe of the applause. . . .

This article from the New York Times describes the victory parade held for General Pershing and 25,000 veterans of the First Division in New York City on September 10, 1919.

Source: New York Times, September 11, 1919.

FINAL REPORT OF GEN. JOHN J. PERSHING (1920) [EXCERPT]

GENERAL HEADQUARTERS AMERICAN EXPEDITIONARY FORCES
September 1, 1919

To the SECRETARY OF WAR.

SIR: I have the honor to submit herewith my final report as Commander-in-Chief of the American Expeditionary Forces in Europe.

... In the five months ending June 30 [1917], German submarines had accomplished the destruction of more than three and one-quarter million tons of Allied shipping. During three years Germany had seen practically all her offensives except Verdun crowned with success. Her battle lines were held on foreign soil and she had withstood every Allied attack since the Marne. The German general staff could now foresee the complete elimination of Russia, the possibility of defeating Italy before the end of the year and, finally, the campaign of 1918 against the French and British on the western front which might terminate the war.

It can not be said that German hopes of final victory were extravagant, either as viewed at that time or as viewed in the light of history. Financial problems of the Allies were difficult, supplies were becoming exhausted and their armies had suffered tremendous losses. Discouragement existed not only among the civil population but throughout the armies as well. Such was the Allied morale that, although their superiority on the western front during the last half of 1916 and during 1917 amounted to 20 per cent, only local attacks could be undertaken and their effect proved wholly insufficient against the German defense. Allied resources

In his Final Report on the American Expeditionary Forces' role in World War I, General Pershing outlined the military situation prior to the entry of the United States into the war and the forces that he determined would be necessary to defeat Germany.

Source: Final Report of Gen. John J. Pershing: Commander-in-Chief, American Expeditionary Forces. Washington, D.C.: Government Printing Office, 1920.

in man power at home were low and there was little prospect of materially increasing their armed strength, even in the face of the probability of having practically the whole military strength of the Central Powers against them in the spring of 1918.

8. This was the state of affairs that existed when we entered the war. While our action gave the Allies much encouragement yet this was temporary, and a review of conditions made it apparent that America must make a supreme material effort as soon as possible. After duly considering the tonnage possibilities I cabled the following to Washington on July 6, 1917:

> Plans should contemplate sending over at least 1,000,000 men by next May.

ORGANIZATION PROJECTS

9. A general organization project, covering as far as possible the personnel of all combat, staff, and administrative units, was forwarded to Washington on July 11. This was prepared by the Operations Section of my staff and adopted in joint conference with the War Department Committee then in France. It embodied my conclusions on the military organization and effort required of America after a careful study of French and British experience. In forwarding this project I stated:

> It is evident that a force of about 1,000,000 is the smallest unit which in modern war will be a complete, well-balanced, and independent fighting organization. However, it must be equally clear that the adoption of this size force as a basis of study should not be construed as representing the maximum force which

should be sent to or which will be needed in France. It is taken as the force which may be expected to reach France in time for an offensive in 1918, and as a unit and basis of organization. Plans for the future should be based, especially in reference to the manufacture of artillery, aviation, and other material, on three times this force—i.e., at least 3,000,000 men.

The original project for organized combat units and its state of completion on November 11, 1918, are shown in the charts appended to this report. With a few minor changes, this project remained our guide until the end.

10. While this general organization project provided certain Services of Supply troops, which were an integral part of the larger combat units, it did not include the great body of troops and services required to maintain an army overseas. To disembark 2,000,000 men, move them to their training areas, shelter them, handle and store the quantities of supplies and equipment they required called for an extraordinary and immediate effort in construction. To provide the organization for this purpose, a project for engineer services of the rear, including railways, was cabled to Washington August 5, 1917, followed on September 18, 1917, by a complete service of the rear project, which listed item by item the troops considered necessary for the Services of Supply. Particular attention is invited to the charts herewith, which show the extent to which this project had developed by November 11, 1918, and the varied units required, many of which did not exist in our Army prior to this war. . . .

Jeannette Rankin

1880–1973

First United States Congresswoman

The first woman elected to the U.S. Congress, Jeannette Rankin used her political office and organizations to advocate peace, social reform, and feminist causes.

Rankin was born into a prominent family of ranchers near Missoula, Montana, on June 11, 1880. She graduated from Montana University in 1902 and attended the New York School of Philanthropy (later the Columbia University School of Social Work) between 1908 and 1909. During further study at the University of Washington in Seattle, Rankin broadened her focus from social to political issues, participating in the 1910 campaign for woman suffrage. Before the passage of the Nineteenth Amendment, woman suffrage was a state-by-state decision, and many of the Western states had granted women the right to vote before the Eastern states. After Washington state passed its suffrage amendment in November of 1910, Rankin organized the Equal Franchise Society in Montana. In 1911, she became the first woman to address the Montana legislature in a speech on women's voting rights. Rankin then crusaded in several states for the New York Woman Suffrage Party (NYWSP), and in 1913, she served as field secretary for the National American Woman Suffrage Association (NAWSA).

At the beginning of 1914, when the suffrage amendment neared submission to Montana voters, Rankin resigned her position with NAWSA to preside over the campaign in her home state. Her strategy involved direct interaction with the community. In the cities, Montana suffragists delivered speeches from wagons, automobiles, storefronts, and movie theaters. In rural areas, they often held rallies followed by a Saturday night dance. These personal touches and persuasive tactics endeared Rankin to the working class in urban and rural areas. At a fall parade organized by Rankin, suffragist leader Rev. Anna Howard Shaw, and physician Dr. Maria Dean, thousands gathered in Helena to celebrate the suffrage movement. On November 3, 1914, Montana women gained the right to vote. Soon after, Rankin arrived at NAWSA's annual con-

From the collections of the Library of Congress.

ference in Nashville, Tennessee, where she received thunderous applause.

In 1916, four years before ratification of the Nineteenth Amendment, Rankin not only cast her ballot but also won a seat in the U.S. House of Representatives. As a progressive Republican, she ran on a platform advocating national woman suffrage, child welfare, labor protection laws, Prohibition (which made the manufacture, sale, and distribution of alcohol illegal), and a general commitment to social justice. News of her official victory, on November 7, astonished the public, both in the United States and abroad. Rankin was the first woman to hold a seat in Congress and one of the first women in the world to serve in a major legislature. Her colleagues assumed that she would be either an austere suffragist or a naïve country girl, but her femininity and sophistication refuted their biased judgments. Rankin was installed as a House member at a special session of the 65th Congress in Washington, D.C., on April 2, 1917.

Rankin, a self-identified pacifist, immediately faced political pressure and heightened publicity when, following Germany's decision to resume unrestricted submarine warfare in January 1917 and its attack on three U.S. merchant ships in March, President **Woodrow Wilson** called for a declaration of war. Even though most predicted that the majority of Congress would support war, the nation anticipated the final vote of the first congresswoman. Some, like NAWSA suffragist **Carrie Chapman Catt**, feared that an antiwar stance would undermine Rankin's authority and suffragist goals. Others, like her brother Wellington, feared that an unpopular position would destroy her political career. By the time the House met on April 5, 1917, the Senate had overwhelmingly voted in favor of war. Rankin rose before her fellow representatives on the second roll call and announced, "I want to stand by my country, but I cannot vote for war. I vote no." The House adjourned with 374 in favor, 50 against, and 9 not voting. Rankin was not the only one to resist the war resolution, but as a female legislator and therefore something of a public curiosity, her vote spoke the loudest.

Despite being denounced by the press, religious leaders, and even some fellow suffragists for her antiwar stance, Rankin remained true to her conscience and ideals of democracy. She voted against the Espionage Act of 1917, which was used to suppress opposition to the war, specifically among foreign residents in the United States. She also fought to expose illegal industry practices and improve labor conditions, particularly in the U.S. Bureau of Printing and Engraving, where women often worked 12 to 15 hours a day, and in Butte, Montana's, copper mines, where lax enforcement of safety regulations resulted in men injured and killed. In 1917, she cosponsored the Rankin-Shepard Bill, which would grant women citizenship independent from their husbands, and the Rankin-Robertson Bill, which would provide maternity, childcare, and birth control education to women. The 66th Congress passed both of these bills, but after Rankin's term had expired. In 1918, Rankin opened the debate to submit a federal suffrage amendment for ratification by the states.

Although she rejected the idea of United States involvement in international battles, Rankin backed most of President Wilson's war measures. She promoted Liberty Bonds, which were sold to support the war effort, and voted for a declaration of war on Austria-Hungary in 1917, stressing that her vote was "a mere technicality in the prosecution of a war already declared." Since she could not stop the war, Rankin voted for measures that she believed would help the United States win and quickly restore peace. Nonetheless, her first antiwar vote ruined her chances for reelection in 1918. Rankin lost the chance to run for the Senate in the Republican primary; running on the National Party ticket during the general elections, she lost the election.

Leaving Congress in 1919, Rankin dedicated herself to the promotion of peace and civil liberties. She helped found the Women's International League for Peace and Freedom (WILPF) and became vice president of the executive committee. Having established this organization in Europe, Rankin returned to the United States to serve as field secretary of Florence Kelley's National Consumers League. Rankin also served as field secretary for the WILPF in 1925, but inadequate staffing and funding caused her to quit her post that year. She settled in Georgia and, in 1928, founded the Georgia Peace Society.

Rankin guided this group and worked for the National Council for the Prevention of War for the following decade. Winning election to the House in 1940, she again stirred up controversy on Capitol Hill by casting the only vote against the declaration of war on Japan after the bombing of Pearl Harbor. Her term expired in 1943 but her pacifism never wavered. She traveled throughout the world to study various cultures, and particularly admired Mohandas Gandhi and his philosophy of nonviolent resistance. In 1968, at age 87, she protested the Vietnam War in Washington, D.C., leading a procession of 5,000 women known as the "Jeannette Rankin Brigade." She died in Carmel, California, on May 18, 1973.

Peace advocate, social reformer, and staunch feminist, Jeannette Rankin courageously acted upon her beliefs and principles. At a time when most women were still denied the vote, Rankin became the first female politician on the national stage and introduced legislation to protect civil liberties and promote social justice. However, the country was not ready to accept a woman in Congress—let alone an outspoken pacifist—and many fellow politicians and suffragists wanted Rankin to repress her personal convictions in order to comply with popular opinion.

Renée Miller

For Further Reading
Giles, Kevin S. *Flight of the Dove: The Story of Jeannette Rankin.* Beaverton, Ore.: Touchstone Press, 1980.
Josephson, Hannah. *Jeannette Rankin: First Lady in Congress.* Indianapolis, Ind.: Bobbs-Merrill, 1974.
Morin, Isobel V. *Women of the United States Congress.* Minneapolis, Minn.: Oliver Press, 1994.

"THE FIRST WOMAN ELECTED TO CONGRESS" from *The Outlook* (November 22, 1916)

Published in 1916, this article from The Outlook *presents a portrait of Rankin after she became the first woman elected to Congress and describes her Montana upbringing and suffragist goals.*

Source: "The First Woman Elected to Congress." *The Outlook*, 114, November 22, 1916.

On another page appears the portrait of Miss Jeannette Rankin, Republican, the first woman to be elected to Congress. Her victory is the more striking as Montana went Democratic on the Presidential issue.

Miss Rankin is reported to be about thirty four years of age, slender, and with light brown hair; of personal attractiveness and with unusual intellect. She is the daughter of one of the Montana pioneers. "She is this sort of girl," reports one of her friends.

> Her father was trying to rent one of his houses in Missoula, Montana, and there wasn't any sidewalk in front of it. A prospective tenant was found, but the tenant said he wouldn't take the house unless it had a side-

walk. Jeannette called up some carpenters and found them too busy to lay the sidewalk. And so she bought the lumber, borrowed a hammer and saw, and laid the sidewalk herself.

Miss Rankin is a graduate of the University of Montana and of the School of Philanthropy. She has been an ardent worker for woman suffrage, going to the farms and into the mines to argue the question. She is credited with having been more than any other woman the means of obtaining the suffrage in Montana. She wanted to carry the fight into the National Legislature, and made a hard fight against several men aspirants for the nomination as Republican candidate-at-large for Congress. It is reported that she did much of her campaigning on horseback. After her election she said, as reported:

I knew the women would stand by me. The women worked splendidly, and I am sure they feel that the results have been worth the work. I am deeply conscious of the responsibility, and it is wonderful to have the opportunity to be the first woman to sit in Congress. I will not only represent the women of Montana, but also the women of the country, and I have plenty of work cut out for me.

Of course I know I'll be the first woman Member of Congress, but I believe I'll be received with courtesy and as an equal by those Eastern Congressmen, even though they are enemies of suffrage. While working for suffrage in the East I found that, no matter how strenuously our opponents fought us, they were always ready to hear our side.

JEANNETTE RANKIN AND CARRIE CHAPMAN CATT (1917)

In this photo taken moments before her first session in Congress on April 2, 1917, Rankin greets women from the balcony of the National American Woman Suffrage Association headquarters in Washington, D.C. President of the association, Carrie Chapman Catt, stands behind her on this day of celebration.

Source: Montana Historical Society.

"WHAT WE WOMEN SHOULD DO" by Jeannette Rankin (1917)

With the outbreak of war the cry for economy has gone out to every woman in every kitchen in the country. But when all is said and done, the greatest and most effective instruments of economy are modern industry and modern machinery. The economies which were practiced by our grandmothers are not those which will be practiced by our granddaughters nor will they greatly avail us in the forthcoming years of scarcity. Clearly what we need to-day is to reach out for forward-looking and not backward-looking methods. The whole tendency of the present time is toward large-scale production and the effect of war will be to accelerate that tendency.

Women need to hold fast to this essential fact in the long campaign of conservation upon which we are now entering. With modern methods of production the individual housewife can not hope to compete. It is a doubtful service when we advise her to return to primitive housekeeping customs as a means of economy. For instance, it has been seriously suggested that home grinding of grains should be revived. This would be to turn the hands of the kitchen clock backward and spoil the works. Milling has gone out of the home for economic reasons which are stronger to-day than ever before—reasons which the conditions of wartime have prodigiously enhanced.

The outstanding effects of the war in Europe have not been to revive soap making, candle making and home grinding in the individual household, but rather to do away with many domestic occupations of a much less primitive character. Overwhelming changes have taken place in the homes of French, German and English women. The first revolution to follow upon the war might even be said to have broken out in the woman's world rather than in the Russian Empire.

No small part in the "New World" of Europe's women has been played by the establishment of community feeding on an unprecedented scale. Public food kitchens, under government control, have long been established in France and Germany and are now under way in England. Undoubtedly, as time goes on and the need for economy grows more stringent, in this country also we shall be forced to adopt, in our congested cities and industrial centers, the greater economy of cooperation instead of the lesser economy of saving.

Women should, therefore, prepare themselves not only for a thrifty administration within their own kitchens, but also for professional and paid work, which must be done in connection with public food kitchens, free school lunches and other forms of community feeding. Such food measures will have a double value in that they conserve the food supply and also the strength and energy of our women.

Our program of frugality needs to be conceived in a constructive and not merely negative spirit. Thrift must be intelligent; it must not degenerate into mere "skimp-

A peace advocate and social reformer, Rankin realized that the sorrows of war extended far beyond battlefield casualties. This 1917 article, published in the Ladies' Home Journal, *emphasizes warfare's debilitating effects on women and children and proposes practical solutions to amend these problems.*

Source: Rankin, Jeanette. "What We Women Should Do." *Ladies' Home Journal,* August 1917.

ing" and "going without." What is needed is not wholesale self-denial, but right utilization. Petty economies which cramp the soul should be avoided. This is the time to be generous with useful things, but frugal with the useless "accessories." Wholesome food, suitable clothing and uninterrupted education for the children—these are things in which we cannot afford to economize, or we shall pay the penalty in the lowered vitality and decreased earning power of the citizens of to-morrow.

We must have national frugality on a large scale if waste is to be prevented in such proportions as will really count in the conservation of our food supply. Such economies as the housekeepers of the country have it in their power to effect fall far short of the real and imperative need. Let us by all means urge the housewives not to waste a single slice of bread or an ounce of meat; but let us also assure them that they, in turn, shall be protected against the far more wanton waste of the food speculator.

The disheartened housekeeper should know that, while she is conscientiously measuring the food for her children, the apple harvest is not going to waste in the fields for lack of transportation facilities. She should know that it is possible to prevent the price of bread from soaring and that it will be done.

The mothers of the country should be assured that the grain which they save will not be made into alcoholic drinks, but into bread for the hungry children beyond the seas. Only the other day the Bishop of London protested in a great public gathering against the "solemn hypocrisy" of exhorting every poor housewife to save every crumb of bread and allowing hundreds of thousands of tons of foods to be turned into beer and spirits.

Carried along on the waves of a misguided patriotism have come subtle attempts to destroy the industrial standards of this country—standards which have been wrought with so much toil and strife and suffering during the last half century. Perhaps the most threatening of these attempts was that made by the Brown bills in the New York Legislature, proposing to abrogate the labor laws for the protection of women and children and to suspend the compulsory education laws.

The action of Governor Whitman in exercising his veto and the storm of commendation which greeted his action are significant, coming as they do at this time of emotional stress, and should be a warning to the false patriots who understand the laws of conservation as little as they understand the laws of psychology. Recent events in Russia should be a warning to America that those who begin by forcing the workers to accept ten-hour and twelve-hour standards may, by so doing, finally be faced by the necessity of granting the six-hour day.

Of grave import, also, is the threatened unemployment among women. In England the outbreak of war reduced the amount of unemployment of men, but vastly increased the unemployment of women. At best there will be a dislocation of industry in this country, a widespread change of occupation, in which women familiar with one sort of work will be forced to take up unfamiliar work, perhaps in a strange environment. Salesgirls, discharged from the department stores, will not be eager to go into the munitions factories; the fear and the real dangers of migration will stand between many girls and the only available jobs. In this interim of unemployment much suffering may be endured and the great abyss of prostitution may receive unhoped-for victims, unless intelligent measures are adopted to prevent the well-known evils of unemployment.

Economies in public education, such as are now being threatened in many parts of the country, are spendthrift policies in disguise. We cannot afford to let the schools do less in wartime, for they must give us the trained minds and skilled workers who will be needed to cope with the problems of reconstruction and to insure the nation against decline in the critical period after the war. At present only seventy-five per cent of our children are actually in school. All of them should be there, especially those who will be destitute by the absense of fathers who are fighting at the front. To accept public or private financial aid is more patriotic than to take a child out of school. The country needs trained minds more than it needs the money that must be paid in separation allowances and widows' pensions.

A timely suggestion has come from the Department of Education that our kindergartens, elementary and high schools should run to their fullest capacity throughout the entire year. As the fathers are withdrawn from the home and the mothers enter the industrial field home life must be inevitably disturbed and home care dangerously relaxed. To keep the schools open all year would be one of the most effective methods of counteracting the effects of much unavoidable domestic neglect.

It is easy to estimate the casualties of the battlefield, but the casualties of the home in wartime remain uncounted and unreported. We know that the war abroad has resulted in a heavily increased mortality of the very old and the very young. Life is sweet even to the oldest men and women, and that the hardships of war conditions may shorten their days is a prospect ineffably sad. But against the possibility of an increase of infant mortality we should not even seek to muster our philosophy.

The only mood in which women can or should face the years of conflict is one which declares that any increase in infant mortality must and shall be prevented. We must remember that the cost in child life is still not fully paid by the appalling number of babies who perish in wartime. Those who survive must continue to pay with their unfulfilled and uncompleted lives. Stamped in body and mind by long years of privation, they bear through later life the physical and mental scars of premature and long-persisting hardships. We should reflect that ten years of underfeeding for children who have not reached their teens or rounded out their physical development is far more disastrous in its consequences than for full-grown adults.

Similarly, a decade of mental stress and strain, the signs of which are already visible in the faces of those we pass in the street, must fall heaviest upon the developing minds and characters of our adolescent boys and girls. The spirit of youth, that fragile and priceless heritage of humanity—what will be its fate in wartime? There are many still living who can recall the sad experience of a soul's awakening under the shadow of a great war.

But buoyancy, and not resignation, is the law of youth. Vital impulses will not down. In both England and

Germany there have been vast increases in juvenile delinquency and crime since the war began. Ominous statistics from these foreign countries warn us of dangers which confront the boys and girls of our land. Must this tragedy be repeated in a country which has millions of organized women to prevent it? It is for the collective motherhood of America to say.

Other casualties will occur within the home—the sacrifice of women's lives in the service of maternity—for which we have no public roll of honor. Yet it is not a roll of honor for dead mothers which we need, but protection and security for the living. We are told by the Children's Bureau of the Department of Labor that "maternal deaths are largely preventable by proper care and skilled attendance." Is it not, then, a staggering indictment of public indifference that 15,000 deaths from maternal causes take place every year in this country?

Since 1900, the death rate from typhoid has been cut in half and the death rate from tuberculosis has been greatly reduced, while the death rate from childbirth and its consequences has remained stationary. During this period alone 250,000 mothers—a quarter of a million—have died from causes connected with childbirth. The total number of soldiers of both sides slain on the battlefields of the Civil War was not so great. And yet this terrible waste of maternal life is largely preventable. To let it go on is to acquiesce in the unnecessary sacrifice of thousands upon thousands of the mothers of to-morrow.

In England the effect of the war has been to focus public attention on the welfare of mothers and babies. The Notification of Births Act, of 1915, made birth registration uniform and obligatory throughout the country. This is the first and indispensable step in a program of maternity and infant protection. Every child should be registered, as well as both of its parents, whether they are married or unmarried. The next step should be the provision of maternity aid, similar to that already established in England. But certain mistakes of the English should be recalled in order that they may be avoided. In its first form the English maternity aid provided a cash benefit, to be paid to the husband, and it said nothing at all about nursing and medical attention.

The first mistake, that of paying the benefit to the husband instead of the wife, was soon corrected, mainly owing to the efforts of one of the large women's organizations known as the Women's Cooperative Guild. The second mistake, that of failing to supplement the cash benefit by nursing and medical attention, was not rectified until the hardships induced by the great war spurred the local Government Board to action. Public money has been appropriated for the purpose of establishing maternity clinics and child-welfare centers all over the country, where mothers may go for free examination and advice.

While it is generally true that the welfare of the mother and that of the child are inseparable, the conditions which contribute to maternal and infant mortality are not always the same. Exhaustive studies have been made in England during the war years, which show that, while the death rate of infants tends to run highest in congested city districts, the death rate of the mothers mounts alarmingly in such rural and mining districts as are found in Wales. The explanation is not far to seek. It lies in the lack of obstetrical aid for the women in the farming and mining districts.

If such fatal conditions exist in Wales, what must they be like when magnified, as they are, to the scale of one of our own great Western states? The vastness of the distance between the mother and the nearest doctor calls for the establishment of maternity hospitals in every county seat, combined with a rural nursing service as broadcast as the rural postal service.

There are many stories, too harrowing to tell and too inhumane for belief, of the dire need of these American mothers. But one unforgettable picture I must recall. It is that of a dry-land farm and a solitary cabin in the darkness. The cabin door stands open and within the doctor is at work by the light of a lantern held by the hired man. And over the doorsill there trickles a thin, dark stream. It is the sacrificial blood of the life bringer within; symbol of the blood of all the mothers, poured out that human life might be—that children might laugh in the world, that youth might hope and that men and women might live to seek courage and happiness, wisdom and love.

To the woman who had just driven up after a long night in the company of the worried husband dispatched for help, that picture will always say more than the most inspired words could say of the terrible need for maternity protection in this country; of the struggle to make existence possible; and of the precautions we must take to make impossible in the future the tragic futility of giving life only to be destroyed.

War Speech by Jeannette Rankin (1917)

Mr. Chairman, I still believe that war is a stupid and futile way of attempting to settle international disputes. I believe that war can be avoided and will be avoided when the people, the men and women in America, as well as in Germany, have the controlling voice in their government. Today special commercial interests are controlling the world. When we declared war on Germany we virtually declared war on Germany's allies. The vote we are to cast is not a vote on a declaration of war. This is a vote on a mere technicality in the prosecution of a war already declared. I shall vote for this, as I voted for money and men.

After voting against U.S. entry into World War I, Rankin voted for a declaration of war on Austria-Hungary. In this speech from April 1917, she explains her decision.

Source: Josephson, Hannah. *Jeannette Rankin: First Lady in Congress*. Indianapolis, Ind.: Bobbs-Merrill, 1974.

Knute Rockne

1888–1931

Notre Dame Football Coach

Knute Rockne was a football coach who developed the University of Notre Dame into a college football powerhouse during the 1920s, captivating the public imagination with his successful teams and colorful personality.

Knute Kenneth Rockne was born in Vass, Norway, on March 4, 1888, and immigrated with his family to the north side of Chicago in 1893. At 22, he enrolled at the University of Notre Dame in South Bend, Indiana. Both a scholar and an athlete, Rockne majored in chemistry while running track and playing end on the football team. In 1913, the undefeated Army team at West Point invited the unrenowned Notre Dame to fill an opening on its football schedule. The experimental forward passes of quarterback Charles "Gus" Dorais to captain Rockne stunned opponents and spectators, from the first Notre Dame touchdown to their 35–13 upset over Army. The dynamic teamwork of Dorais and Rockne forever modified the game.

After graduating magna cum laude in 1914, Rockne worked as a chemistry instructor, head track coach, and assistant football coach at Notre Dame. He became head football coach and athletic director in 1918; however, the majority of varsity men enlisted in the military to fight in World War I, thus making college sports a secondary concern.

The prosperous decade following the war was the "Golden Age" of American sports and the glory years of Notre Dame football—the "Fighting Irish." New stadiums and vibrant marching bands created a carnival setting for the boom in college football. Rockne's coaching was in tune with the times, producing rousing plays and spirited players. His first and greatest football star was halfback George Gipp, a rebel who followed his own rules yet still excelled under pressure. Scoring 83 touchdowns in 32 games (1917–20), Gipp's success on the field ended when he died of pneumonia in his senior year. During Rockne's toughest season in 1928, he motivated his players with the famous half-time speech, "Win One for the Gipper." Notre Dame came from behind in the second half for a 12–6 victory over Army, resurrecting

From the collections of the Library of Congress.

Gipp as a football legend. It was in these compelling moments that Rockne's persistent and triumphant attitude enabled his team to persevere and prevail.

Rockne next molded the 1922–24 backfield force known as the "Four Horsemen," a reference to the Apocalyptic allegory in the Book of Revelation. This adept unit, composed of fullback Elmer Layden, left halfback Jim Crowley, right halfback Don Miller, and quarterback Harry Stuhldreher, perfected Rockne's "shift" and benefited from his "shock troops." The "shift" involved fast and resourceful movements that deceived the opposing defense when the ball snapped and made it difficult to discern the position of the ball carrier. Although college and high school coaches tried to use this tactic, no one could execute the formation. Rockne also outsmarted rivals with his offensive "shock troops." These second string substitutes opened the game, allowing the first string regulars time to observe the strength and weaknesses of their challengers. Under the "Rockne System," psychological acuteness and physical prowess created crowd-thrilling plays and touchdowns.

Training the Fighting Irish to use wits and speed over pure brawn, Rockne cemented his reputation as an outstanding mentor and leader of college football. He believed that Notre Dame could match any team in the country and became the first to popularize intersectional rivalries, competing from the East Coast to the West Coast. He directed five undefeated squads (1919, 1920, 1924, 1929, and 1930) and claimed three national championships (1924, 1929, and 1930). In his 13-year career as head coach, Rockne totaled 105 wins, 12 losses, and five ties. His .881 winning record still ranks highest among Division 1-A coaches.

Aside from these achievements, Rockne inspired people with his charismatic and ambitious personality. He bolstered the confidence of his team with zealous and humorous pep talks that empowered the image of the Fighting Irish, a superior team with energy, drive, and talent. His optimism and courage and intolerance of pessimism and fear made him an authority on success. He published the books *Coaching—The Way of the Winner* (1925) and *The Four Winners* (1925), wrote two weekly syndicated newspaper columns, marketed his own sports equipment, and gave inspirational presentations for the Studebaker Corporation. Throughout the 1920s, the influence of Rockne was everywhere.

On March 31, 1931, Rockne boarded an airplane bound for Los Angeles that crashed near Bazaar, Kansas. All eight passengers died. Many eulogized the life of Rockne, but humorist **Will Rogers** best expressed the effect of his death: "It takes a mighty big calamity to shock this country all at once, but Knute, you did it! You died one of our national heroes. Notre Dame was your address, but every gridiron in America was your home."

Rockne commanded the Fighting Irish of Notre Dame with inventive strategies and inspiring speeches. His life history, in the eyes of many, reaffirmed the American dream; this Norwegian immigrant—who made a name for himself through hard work and a positive outlook—proved that anything was possible. He symbolized victory, virility, and virtue. In the "Golden Age" of sports, Rockne emerged as the golden coach of college football.

Renée Miller

For Further Reading

Brondfield, Jerry. *Rockne: The Coach, The Man, The Legend.* New York: Random House, 1976.

Rockne, Knute. *The Autobiography of Knute Rockne.* Bonnie Skiles Rockne, ed. Indianapolis, Ind.: Bobbs-Merrill, 1931.

Robinson, Ray H. *Rockne of Notre Dame: The Making of a Football Legend.* New York: Oxford University Press, 1999.

Wallace, Francis. *Knute Rockne.* Garden City, N.Y.: Doubleday, 1960.

KNUTE ROCKNE'S GAME RECORD AS HEAD COACH OF NOTRE DAME (1918–30)

1918

Notre Dame	26	Case	6
Notre Dame	66	Wabash	7
Notre Dame	7	Great Lakes N.T.S.	7
Notre Dame	7	Michigan Aggies	13
Notre Dame	26	Purdue	6
Notre Dame	0	Nebraska	0

1919

Notre Dame	14	Kalamazoo	0
Notre Dame	60	Mt. Union	7
Notre Dame	14	Nebraska	9
Notre Dame	53	West. Normal	0
Notre Dame	16	Indiana	3
Notre Dame	12	Army	9
Notre Dame	13	Michigan Aggies	0
Notre Dame	33	Purdue	13
Notre Dame	14	Morningside	6

1920

Notre Dame	39	Kalamazoo	0
Notre Dame	42	West. State N.	0
Notre Dame	16	Nebraska	7
Notre Dame	28	Valparaiso	3
Notre Dame	27	Army	17
Notre Dame	28	Purdue	0
Notre Dame	13	Indiana	10
Notre Dame	33	Northwestern	7
Notre Dame	25	Michigan Aggies	0

1921

Notre Dame	56	Kalamazoo	0
Notre Dame	57	De Pauw	0
Notre Dame	7	Iowa	10
Notre Dame	33	Purdue	0
Notre Dame	7	Nebraska	0
Notre Dame	28	Indiana	7
Notre Dame	28	Army	0
Notre Dame	48	Rutgers	0
Notre Dame	42	Haskell	7
Notre Dame	21	Marquette	7
Notre Dame	48	Michigan Aggies	9

1922

Notre Dame	46	Kalamazoo	0
Notre Dame	46	St. Louis	0
Notre Dame	20	Purdue	7
Notre Dame	34	De Pauw	7
Notre Dame	13	Georgia Tech.	3
Notre Dame	27	Indiana	0
Notre Dame	0	Army	0
Notre Dame	38	Butler	3
Notre Dame	19	Carnegie Tech.	0
Notre Dame	6	Nebraska	14

1923

Notre Dame	74	Kalamazoo	0
Notre Dame	14	Lombard	0
Notre Dame	13	Army	0
Notre Dame	25	Princeton	2
Notre Dame	35	Georgia Tech.	7
Notre Dame	34	Purdue	7
Notre Dame	7	Nebraska	14
Notre Dame	34	Butler	7
Notre Dame	26	Carnegie Tech.	0
Notre Dame	13	St. Louis U	0

1924

Notre Dame	40	Lombard	0
Notre Dame	34	Wabash	0
Notre Dame	13	Army	7
Notre Dame	12	Princeton	0
Notre Dame	34	Georgia Tech.	3
Notre Dame	38	Wisconsin	3
Notre Dame	34	Nebraska	6
Notre Dame	13	Northwestern	6
Notre Dame	40	Carnegie Tech.	19
Notre Dame	27	Stanford	10

1925

Notre Dame	41	Baylor	0
Notre Dame	69	Lombard	0
Notre Dame	19	Beloit	3
Notre Dame	0	Army	27
Notre Dame	19	Minnesota	7
Notre Dame	13	Georgia Tech.	0
Notre Dame	0	Penn State	0
Notre Dame	26	Carnegie Tech.	0
Notre Dame	13	Northwestern	10
Notre Dame	0	Nebraska	17

1926

Notre Dame	77	Beloit	0
Notre Dame	20	Minnesota	7
Notre Dame	28	Penn State	0
Notre Dame	6	Northwestern	0
Notre Dame	12	Georgia Tech.	0
Notre Dame	26	Indiana	0
Notre Dame	7	Army	0
Notre Dame	21	Drake	0
Notre Dame	0	Carnegie Tech.	19
Notre Dame	13	So. California	12

The Fighting Irish of Notre Dame became a powerhouse in college football under Rockne. This record shows his game history as head coach from 1918 to 1930, tallying an amazing 105 wins, 12 losses, and five ties in 13 seasons.

Source: Record adapted from Delos W. Lovelace, Rockne of Notre Dame. New York: G. P. Putnam's Sons, 1931.

1927			
Notre Dame	38	Coe	7
Notre Dame	20	Detroit	0
Notre Dame	19	Navy	6
Notre Dame	19	Indiana	6
Notre Dame	26	Georgia Tech.	7
Notre Dame	7	Minnesota	7
Notre Dame	0	Army	18
Notre Dame	32	Drake	0
Notre Dame	7	So. California	6

1928			
Notre Dame	12	Loyola (La.)	6
Notre Dame	6	Wisconsin	22
Notre Dame	7	Navy	0
Notre Dame	0	Georgia Tech.	13
Notre Dame	32	Drake	6
Notre Dame	9	Penn State	0
Notre Dame	12	Army	6
Notre Dame	7	Carnegie Tech.	27
Notre Dame	14	So. California	12

1929			
Notre Dame	14	Indiana	0
Notre Dame	14	Navy	7
Notre Dame	19	Wisconsin	0
Notre Dame	26	Georgia Tech.	6
Notre Dame	7	Carnegie Tech.	0
Notre Dame	19	Drake	7
Notre Dame	13	So. California	12
Notre Dame	26	Northwestern	6
Notre Dame	7	Army	0

1930			
Notre Dame	20	So. Methodist	14
Notre Dame	26	Navy	2
Notre Dame	21	Carnegie Tech.	6
Notre Dame	35	Pittsburgh	19
Notre Dame	27	Indiana	0
Notre Dame	60	Pennsylvania	20
Notre Dame	28	Drake	0
Notre Dame	14	Northwestern	0
Notre Dame	7	Army	6
Notre Dame	27	So. California	0

Summary	W.	L.	T.
1918	3	1	2
1919	9	0	0
1920	9	0	0
1921	10	1	0
1922	8	1	1
1923	9	1	0
1924	10	0	0
1925	7	2	1
1926	9	1	0
1927	7	1	1
1928	5	4	0
1929	9	0	0
1930	10	0	0
Total	105	12	5

THE "FOUR HORSEMEN" (1924)

The "Four Horsemen" earned their title from sportswriter Grantland Rice after winning the Notre Dame–Army game on October 18, 1924. In this publicity photo (starting from left), Don Miller, Elmer Layden, Jim Crowley, and Harry Stuhldreher pose on the backs of four horses in their uniforms with footballs. Like the legendary George Gipp, they remain part of the football lore of Rockne and Notre Dame.

Source: ©Bettmann/ Corbis.

LETTER FROM KNUTE ROCKNE TO JEROME J. CROWLEY (1928)

Mr. Jerome J. Crowley
742 Junior Terrace
Chicago, Illinois

Dear Crowley:

You may perhaps have felt discouraged a little as a freshman center out there, with so many veterans but I just want to say that as a freshman your center play was not bad at all and that you are real varsity timber.

I liked your spirit and I liked the improvement you showed—I feel very sincere in saying that with another year's experience you will be right in there with the best of them.

I want you to come back here for the opening practice, all ready to go. The Reserves are playing a great schedule this year—perhaps 10 in all—and I hope you will get in some of these games and get experience for the year following.

Trust you have had a good Summer and I will see you the first thing in the Fall when I get back from Europe.

Kindest regards,
Your Sincerely,
K. K. Rockne
Director of Athletics

P. S. Please remember me to your good Dad.

Rockne served as a dedicated football coach and athletic director to the Notre Dame star players as well as the unknowns. This 1928 letter written by him to Jerome J. Crowley, a member of the 1927 freshman team, illustrates Rockne's personal touch. With fatherly warmth, Rockne compliments Crowley's past performance and encourages him to return for another season.

Source: McCallum, John D., and Paul Castner. *We Remember Rockne.* Huntington, Ind.: Our Sunday Visitor, 1975.

SPEECH TO STUDEBAKER CORPORATION by Knute Rockne (1931) [EXCERPT]

. . . I don't know anything about selling automobiles, I never sold a car in my life. Perhaps a few remarks here on the psychology that is necessary for success in a football organization might not be out of place, because the same psychology that makes for success in a football organization will make for success in any organization, particularly in a *selling* organization.

Now, in the Fall when we issue our first call for the team to report to practice, about 350 of them assemble in a large room in the library, and it is my idea to talk to them on the correct psychology before I take them out on the field. I talk to them about ambition and I tell them that most of what I read about ambition is bunk. There is not plenty of room at the top. There is very little room at the top only for the few who have the ability and imagination and the daring and the personality and the energy that makes them stand out from among their fellow men. But there is success for any man in his own job if he does it as well as it can be done. As far as I am able to observe, the greatest satisfaction I can get on this earth is to do the particular job I am doing as well as it can be done, and I think that holds good for anyone. There may be other things that are easier, but they generally leave a headache or a heartache the day after.

I tell the lads there are five types of athlete I do not want. And I say that the first type I have in mind is the swellhead. The man who was a success a year ago and who is content to rest on his laurels, who wants to play on his rep-

utation. Dry rot sets in and he ceases to make an effort. To that kind of boy there will come quite a shock, because the chances are there will be someone playing in his place today.

The second type of lad I don't want is the chronic complainer. He crabs at everyone but himself. I say no organization can afford to have that type because his discontent becomes infectious. And I say he is in for quite a shock, too, because as soon as I find out who he is, why, some evening when he comes out for practice there will be no suit in his locker.

The third type is the quitter. The quitter is the fellow who wishes he could play, but who is not willing to pay the price, and I tell the boys if any of that type is here he might just as well quit now and not wear out the equipment.

I don't want boys to dissipate physically or emotionally. I tell them that I have no brief against playing pool long hours in the afternoon, dancing half the night, or learning to drive an automobile with one hand, but I tell them that we have no time for it. If we are going to compete with organizations who do not do that sort of thing and who are saving all their energy for the contest, I say, do not dissipate any energy emotionally; and by that I mean they should not give way to emotions such as jealousy, hatred or anything of that sort. I say that this sort of thing destroys any organization, and then I tell them that we should look upon one another in a friendly way. Look for the good in one another and be inspired by the fine qualities in those around us and forget about their

In 1928, the Studebaker Corporation hired Rockne to inspire their company members to the same excellence demonstrated by his Notre Dame teams. This 1931 speech delivered for a Studebaker convention at the Detroit-Leland Hotel contains numerous Fighting Irish anecdotes and analogies. In a confident and conversational manner, Rockne relays the attitudes and characteristics needed to overcome obstacles and achieve success.

Source: McCallum, John D., and Paul Castner. *We Remember Rockne.* Huntington, Ind.: Our Sunday Visitor, 1975.

faults. I tell them that the chances are that I will notice them—and won't stutter when I mention them to the particular individual who has them.

There is a sixth type of man who suffers from an inferiority complex. He generally comes from a small community and he says to himself: "What chances have I got to get on the first string of 33 men here when there are 350 boys trying out for it. I don't believe I've got a chance and I don't believe I can make it." If there are any among you who feel that way, forget about it and get a *superiority* complex. I say to the lads: "You are just as good as any man out here, and by getting a superiority complex you can show the coach you belong at the top of the 33 men where you think you would like to be."

About four years ago I divided the men on the field in groups—the ends, the tackles, the guards, the centers, the quarterbacks, and so forth. I walked over to the group of guards. Now, a guard is a position demanding a certain amount of physical ruggedness. There were fifteen good-sized boys in the group and one little chap whose name was Metzger. I said to him, "Aren't you a little slight and small to be playing guard?" And he replied, "Yes, but I'm also a little rough." In spite of the fact that he only weighed 149 pounds, that same confidence enabled him last season to hold his own against any opponent on our schedule, even against the 240-pounders.

In two weeks, I call them together again and I will tell them that there are certain among them who have great potential but that they have not shown any improvement. I will tell them that there are certain among them that I do not want unless their attitudes change.

The first is the chap who alibis, one who tries to justify his own failure, and I will tell the whole team that a boy who does this had better watch out or he will get into a second class, that of feeling sorry for himself, in which case the bony part of his spine turns into a soft colloidal substance known as "soap" and he is absolutely worthless.

The second class of lad—I generally have very few of them—is the slicker, the mucker, who tries to get by with unfair football tactics. I tell that type of boy that we cannot afford to have him on the team, for he will bring discredit on the school and our organization. I try to impress upon him that slugging and unfairness does not pay either in a game or in life after leaving school.

Then, third, is the boy who lacks courage, who is afraid. What is courage? Courage means to be afraid to do something and still going ahead and doing it. If a man has character, the right kind of energy, mental ability, he will learn that fear is something to overcome and not to run away from.

Before the first game of the year I talk to the players again along the same lines on ambition. I say ambition—the *right* kind of ambition—means that you must have the ability to cooperate with the men around you, men who are working with you; and it is my observation that ability to cooperate is more essential than individual technique. In this day and age of ours no individual stands alone anymore; he must be able to cooperate in every sense of the word, and that is not a very easy thing

to do in football, because I know at Notre Dame we often get boys who have been spoiled by the local press in their high school days. They kick the ball well and pass pretty well and once in a while they run with it. Teaching cooperation is not always the easiest thing in the world to do, especially to a group of boys. . . .

In any organization no one man can enjoy the spotlight all the time while the rest of the boys are doing the chores. Each one has to take a turn doing the chores.

After that, I began the practice of putting up signs in the locker room where the boys could see them. I put up a half-dozen signs, figuring that would impress certain things on their minds. One sign which applied in this particular case read: "Success Is Based On What The *Team* Does, Not On How *You* Look." I have not had much trouble along that line since, although, of course, now and then I may have to hang up that sign in an individual locker, and when I do the boy will bring it back to me and say, "You got me all wrong, Coach." And I say, "Was that hanging in your locker? Oh, I beg your pardon." But it has its effect just the same.

Now, I want to impress the necessity for cooperation on the minds of you distributors, dealers, sellers of trucks and automobiles. Unless you understand the problems of production, engineering, bookkeeping, service, advertising, and all the departments which go to make up your organization, you cannot succeed. The failure of any one of them may cause your business to fail.

Each football season, after a game or two, particularly after a game where I have sensed that the lads gave up, I have gathered them together and lectured to them about ambition. I tell them that there can be no ambition without perseverance. By perseverance I mean the ability to stick in there and keep giving your best at all times; the ability to stay in there and keep trying when the going is tough and you are behind and everything seems hopeless. There can be no success, no reward, unless every man has the ability to stay in there until the last whistle blows.

I was in New York a few years ago (1926), and in the company of Lawrence Perry, the author. He took me to the Players' Club. He was showing me through the Club and was telling me about its being founded by the famous Shakespearean actor, Booth. He explained that Booth was the first president of the Club and under his guidance it had always maintained a very fine standard of membership. We then came to a room featuring a certain table and chair, and Perry told me that Booth was wont to come there when he was tired to read and study. One afternoon, while sitting and reading there, he died. The table and chair were left in the same place in memory of Booth, and the book he was reading has been left open at the very place he had reached when he passed away. Out of curiosity, I stepped up to find out what he had been reading at that moment his heart stopped beating. It was Pope's "Essay on Man." You all remember it. The first line reads: "Hope springs eternal in the human breast." Glancing quickly down the page I read the last line: "But if hope eludes you, all is lost."

When I returned to Notre Dame I carried this message to my players. I talked to them about it until I felt that each of them was thoroughly imbued with that psychology. That year, we had played the first eight games of a nine-game schedule, and the last game was against Southern California out in Los Angeles. With but seven or eight minutes remaining in the game, we were ahead, 7 to 6. Of course, I thought the game was pretty well over and felt that the one-point lead was sufficient to win, but just then the Southern Cal boys began to collect themselves and started smashing their way downfield. I changed my guards, tackles, and still they drove on, three and four yards at a clip—until they were over our goal line. They missed the try-for-point but now they were ahead, 12 to 7, with only about three minutes to play. "Well," I said, half to myself, "I guess it's all over but the shouting."

We elected to receive the kickoff and brought the ball back to the 20-yard line. There we tried three plays without making an inch and were forced to punt. Much to my very pleasant surprise, USC punted the ball right back as if to say: "There it is—what are you going to do with it?" We had 70 yards to go for a touchdown. In the previous three plays back on our 20-yard line I had seen something I hoped I wouldn't see. I saw 10 men still doggedly trying for all they were worth, but the 11th lad, a little third-string quarterback, was through for the day. As far as he was concerned, the game was over. Hope had eluded him. I don't blame him, for he was just a normal 19-year-old lad. I turned around to a little chap sitting behind me on the bench who had been injured earlier in the season and hadn't seen much action—little Art Parisien—and I said, "Art, how do you feel? Do you think if I put you in there you can pull old 83 and 84, those left-handed passes of yours, and maybe still pull the game out of the fire?" Before I had finished the last sentence he had his headgear on and was already out on the field. As he was leaving, he turned around and hollered back at me, "Coach, it's a cinch!"

That might sound like egotism, but it wasn't. A man once defined egotism to me as, "The anesthetic that deadens the pain of one's stupidity." Rest assured that that was not the case with this lad. He felt he could do the job because he had done it just a short time previously against Northwestern in Chicago, and he felt he could do it because he was filled with hope. On the first play he pulled a play good for nine yards straight through the line, after which he called time out. Then he called his 10 teammates around him (for according to the rules he could not talk to them until after the first play) and you could see him imbuing them with his optimism. He lifted those teammates of his, and to my very happy surprise, they lined up and did pull old 83, that left-handed pass, which was good for a gain of 23 yards. I thought that was fine, great, but I still didn't see how we could possibly have a chance. At least, I thought to myself, it would sound good to all our alumni listening to the game over their radios. Only two minutes remained in the game. Next, Parisien called for a side-end run to the right for field position, and suddenly there was less than a minute to play. Then he pulled old 84, that left-hand pass to a lad named Niemiec, who caught the ball and fell into the end zone with the winning touchdown. Now, winning that game wasn't the most important thing. The most important thing to me was the fact that this team wouldn't be beaten and proved to me that the team or the individual who wouldn't be beaten couldn't be beaten.

This also applies to you men out there on the firing line. You men are facing keen competition this year, perhaps facing more opposition than you ever faced in your lives, but I say to you that this is the sort of challenge you should thrill to. I think your organization—the Studebaker organization—has demonstrated that you can go better when the going is tougher, and I say to you that this year you should thrill to this challenge.

Now, I remember last Fall (1930) when we went out to play the University of Southern California again. Earl Carpenter, Paul Hoffman's partner in Los Angeles, wrote a letter to Mr. Hoffman shortly before the game and told him to advise me not to go out to the Coast because I would surely suffer a relapse after the beating we would get from Southern California. Mr. Carpenter warned that the Trojans had the strongest team in Pacific Coast Conference history and that there was no way we could win. On the way out to Los Angeles on the train, I read his letter to our lads during a stop at Tucson, Arizona, and they thrilled to the challenge. I remember very well the pregame dressing-room scene.

The boys were unusually quiet, and from out in the stadium we could hear the USC band playing. Gradually the music faded away as the band marched off the field. I then turned to the team and said, "Boys, you are today going up against a great football team; how great we don't know, but I don't think they are a bit better than you are. In fact, I think you're just as good as they are." I said, "I know what shape you are in physically, and I know how much football you know mentally—but there's one thing I don't know and that's *what's in your hearts*. What *is* in your hearts? You're going out there this afternoon and show more than 70,000 people what's in your hearts! Now, if we win the toss and kick off, I want you to go down that field with everything you have—hit 'em hard right at the start—and take the heart out of them. And I want you men in the backfield to be alert, play heads-up football—watch for forward passes—and when that ball is in the air—go and get it! And when we get that ball, that's when we go—that's when we lift our knees high and go inside of 'em and outside of 'em—inside of 'em and outside of 'em— that's when we charge down the field—that's when we GO! GO! GO!"

P.S. Final Score—Notre Dame 27, USC 0.

Will **Rogers**

Will Rogers was a humorist and actor who endeared himself to audiences during the first decades of the twentieth century with his wry wisdom, affable nature, and downhome comedy.

Born William Penn Adair Rogers on November 4, 1879, near Oologah, Indian Territory, now part of Oklahoma, Rogers was proud of his Cherokee ancestry and ranch upbringing. By the age of five, he rode horses, went on roundups, and learned his first rope tricks. Life on the open range prepared him for a later career in show business. After performing with Texas Jack's Wild West Show and the Wirth Brothers Circus, Rogers made his 1905 vaudeville debut at Hammerstein's Victoria Theatre in New York City, featuring his signature trick in which he threw two ropes at once to separately lasso his pony, Teddy, and assistant, Buck McKee. Although Rogers's stunts pleased audiences, more than a decade would pass before he achieved stardom.

Combining political commentary with his cowboy persona, Rogers became the premier headliner for the *Ziegfeld Follies* beginning in 1916. His gags combined rope tricks with a monologue on current events. Using hyperbole, wit, and improvisation, Rogers offered his own colorful take on the era's news, cracking jokes on the policies of President **Woodrow Wilson**, the tensions of World War I, and the hypocrisy of Prohibition, which made the manufacture, sale, and distribution of alcohol illegal. Rogers could turn nearly any topical subject into playful banter, and he often introduced his material with the remark, "Well, all I know is what I read in the papers." Playing up his image as a naïve hick, he criticized greedy business tycoons, crooked politicians, and societal shortcomings in a chatty, nonchalant manner. He further enhanced his satire through two trademarks—speaking with a mouth full of chewing gum and a pronounced Southwestern drawl. Rogers's performance in the *Follies* provided a sharp contrast to the show's glamorous dancers, and Americans from prominent leaders to average citizens fell in love with his gregarious personality and homespun humor.

©*Underwood and Underwood/Corbis.*

Following the *Follies* tour of 1918, Rogers released his first major publications and entered into a two-year movie contract with Goldwyn Pictures in Los Angeles. His books, *The Cowboy Philosopher on the Peace Conference* (1919), which parodied the diplomatic discussions of the Versailles Treaty following World War I, and *The Cowboy Philosopher on Prohibition* (1919), which examined the contradictions of the Volstead Act (passed by Congress to enforce the 18th Amendment), were based on his *Follies* skits. His films, on the other hand, placed him in cowboy roles but eliminated his comedy routines. Rogers's humor relied on words more than action, and in the era of the silent film, the physical comedy of actors like **Charlie Chaplin** was more effective for this medium. Rogers typically played an unsophisticated Westerner who eventually gains confidence, good fortune, and the affection of the leading lady. His pictures included *Jubilo* (1919), *Water, Water Everywhere* (1919), *Cupid, the Cowpuncher* (1920), and *Doubling for Romeo* (1921). In May 1921, when his contract expired, Rogers began writing and acting in films for his own production company.

Unsuccessful in this new endeavor, Rogers returned to New York in 1922 and gained success as a mass media entertainer. He starred in the *Follies*, made speeches, broadcast on radio, performed in plays, and wrote a series of syndicated newspaper columns (McNaught Syndicate, 1922–1935). In 1924, Rogers published a collection of these articles in *The Illiterate Digest,* a book highlighting his pithy wisecracks: "We have had six months of Prohibition and the casualty list from drinking wood alcohol reads like the war." Known for this type of terse, metaphorical wit, he simplified complex issues in a humorous way that appealed to the general public.

Rogers possessed a honed sense of irony similar to humorists Mark Twain and **H. L. Mencken**, but unlike these men, he projected a more congenial demeanor and positive outlook on humanity. In the last half of the 1920s, Rogers also extended his comedy into international affairs, traveling abroad and publishing *Letters of a Self-Made Diplomat to His President* (1926) and *There's Not a Bathing Suit in Russia* (1927).

By the 1930s, with the advances in radio and the advent of talkies, Rogers hosted a weekly radio show and became a box office sensation for Fox Film. Broadcasting allowed him to reach the largest number of people, and sound movies proved a perfect medium for his colloquial speech and earthy style. Rogers entertained until his untimely death; he was killed in an airplane crash near Point Barrow, Alaska, on August 15, 1935.

All of America seemed to mourn his loss. For two decades, Rogers had amused audiences with his quirky personality and shrewd observations. Simple yet savvy, Rogers was the country's treasured cowboy philosopher and prototypical American humorist.

Renée Miller

For Further Reading

Carter, Joseph H. *Never Met a Man I Didn't Like: The Life and Writings of Will Rogers.* Introduction by Jim Rogers. New York: Avon Books, 1991.

Ketchum, Richard M. *Will Rogers: His Life and Times.* New York: American Heritage Publishing, 1973.

Maturi, Richard J. and Mary Buckingham Maturi. *Will Rogers, Performer: An Illustrated Biography with a Filmography.* Forewords by Jim Rogers and Joseph H. Carter. Jefferson, N.C.: McFarland, 1999.

Robinson, Ray. *American Original: A Life of Will Rogers.* New York: Oxford University Press, 1996.

Yagoda, Ben. *Will Rogers: A Biography.* Norman: University of Oklahoma Press, 2000.

PUBLICITY PHOTO OF WILL ROGERS (Undated)

Amid the glamorous showgirls of the Ziegfeld Follies, *Rogers presented a striking contrast with his Western wear and down-home comedy. In this publicity photo, the grinning Rogers poses in his fringed chaps and cowboy boots while holding his prized lasso and cowboy hat.*
Source: ©Bettmann/Corbis

"DUCK, AL! HERE'S ANOTHER OPEN LETTER" by Will Rogers (OCTOBER 29, 1927) [EXCERPT]

This is another one of those open letters that always litter up Al Smith's mail. Al has got so many open letters that it looks like everybody that writes to him has run out of saliva for the tongue. . . .

Now you want the nomination—that's no more than human—and if you get it you will split your party, because unfortunately they are not composed entirely of the brains of our commonwealth. They think that if they elected a wet that the Constitution would be changed the next day and the country would be wet. They don't know that, as a matter of fact, the President never gets what he wants. Pres. Wilson wanted the League of Nations; every President has wanted something that he did'ent get but Mr. Coolidge, and he was smart enough not let anybody know what he wanted so they would never know what he had been disappointed over.

Now here is what I am getting at: It's not that you ain't strong all over the Country, Al, for you are; you are the strongest one they got—that is, for a Democrat—and if you was running against Democrats you would beat 'em. But unfortunately in the finals of this somebody has to meet a Republican, and when a Democrat meets him next year it's just too bad. Everybody talks about what's wrong with the Democratic Party. Well, if they will be honest with themselves they will admit there is just one thing wrong with it. They havent got enough voters.

Now why go into a race when you can't win? Politics is the only sporting events in the world where they don't

In response to Charles C. Marshall's "An Open Letter to the Honorable Alfred E. Smith," Rogers published this 1927 article in The Saturday Evening Post *entitled "Duck, Al! Here's Another Open Letter." Using puns, wit, and lighthearted commentary, Rogers addresses the political issues surrounding Governor Smith's*

Democratic presidential nomination and anti-Prohibition stance. Note: Language and spelling from original document has been retained.

Source: Rogers, Will. "Duck, Al! Here's Another Open Letter." The Saturday Evening Post, October 29, 1927.

pay off for second money; a man to run second in any other event in the world it's an honor. But any time he runs second for president it's not an honor; it's a pity.

Now, Al, don't let them kid you; you can't beat this Guy Coolidge. There has been too much prosperity among big capital to allow a change to be made at this time. As for farmers, there is not enough of them to get anything. The minute they get some bill to want to raise the price of what they raise, they make mad the millions of others that have to buy what they raise. You see, you won't ever remedy that, because there is more people eating than there is raising things to eat....

You got the chance of making yourself the biggest man the Democratic Party has housed in many a day. Just frame up a statement something like this—get all the boys in, print it on a slip of paper and just hand it out and don't say a word:

I, Al Smith, of my own free will and accord, do this day relinquish any claim or promise that I might have of any support or Deligates at the next Democratic Convention. I don't want to hinder what little harmony there is left in the party. I not only do not choose to run, but I refuse to run. But will give all my time and talents to work faithfully for whoever is nominated by the party.

Alfred E. Smith

Now, Al, you do that and you will knock 'em for a majority in 1932. You will be the second Thomas Jefferson. You will be so much bigger than the Democratic nominee that it will be embarrassing to both of you. Here is the slick part about it—the mob will think you have done the big generous thing and sacrificed your own welfare to the good of the party. "Gee, that fellow Smith is a real fellow! He is the only real Democrat we have had in years." But in reality you won't be giving up a thing; you will just be saving yourself. Then look where you will be sitting in 1932! Why, they won't even hold a convention; they will nominate you by radio. There would be no way in the world to keep you out; the party would owe it to you.

Now let's just look at the thing and see what four years could do. You know that your Prohibition stand wouldent be any the worse off in four years. It's not going to be an issue this election. Both sides are afraid of it. You watch those platforms and you will see both parties walk around prohibition like a skunk in the road. If you think this Country ain't dry, you just watch 'em vote; and if you think this Country ain't wet, you just watch 'em drink. You

see, when they vote, it's counted; but when they drink, it ain't. So that's why the drys will win. If you could register the man's breath that cast the ballots, that would be great. But the voting strength of this country is dry....

Now next year is another Republican year. You got no platform. What are the Democrats going to run on? You can't get people to throw another man out just because you all want the job. You got to promise the people something, even if you don't ever expect to give it to them. In four years prohibition might be much more of an issue than it is today—that is, it might be an issue by popular demand, and then you would be sitting pretty.

Besides, you making this move for party harmony might shame some of the rest of the party into doing something to get together and in the next four years be all united. You might round up the West to go in with the South, and then you come in with your Gang from the East, and I tell you the party would be in shape to make a race instead of a sacrifice. And in the meantime you distribute yourself all around the country and let people see what kind of a Guy you are.

A lot of them think you got stripes and drag a long curly tail. Speak to 'em in person; that's where you shine. The old farmers would fall for you just like the Pants pressers on the East Side. The Radio is all right but it's only good for ones with a Tenor voice. They don't get your personality and that's your long suit.

You see, here is something you never hear about, but it's just what would happen if you were nominated. It would split the ticket. These rabid ones would nominate a dry Protestant in less than forty-eight hours. Now the Democrats ain't hardly got enough to split. But if you give up to them now, they wouldent hardly feel like being so ungrateful to you as to split it in '32....

I will meet you in three or four years from now and I believe you will admit that this was the best plan. If they get you into this, they have kidded you into it, and a New Yorker is supposed to be a wise Guy. A smart Prize fight Manager or a smart race-horse trainer make great prize fighters and great race horses simply by knowing what race to put 'em in or who to fight, and what race to keep 'em out of, and what fighters not to let 'em meet.

I am telling you how you might be President—not just Candidate. And remember, Al, get around and let 'em know you. I have often said you could go into the strongest Clan town, meet all of them and get acquainted, and by the end of the week by elected Honorary Grand Kleagle Dragon.

"How To Be Funny" by Will Rogers (1929) [Excerpt]

Americans of all ages and backgrounds fell in love with Rogers's homespun humor. In this 1929 article "How To Be Funny," published in American Magazine, Rogers relays the questions addressed to him by a Nebraska college student and provides his

I have been interviewed in every Town in the United States, by serious-looking young College Boys, with horn-rimmed glasses and no hat, on the subject, "How would you advise a beginner to be funny?" ...

Some of these Boys when they come to interview me had their questions written out. About the best and most complete one was handed to me at Lincoln, Nebraska, where their State University is. I was playing there that night, and back stage come just about as dejected a looking Senior as I had ever seen. He was just about to finish school and was about to have to meet the world head on,

and he wanted to be fortified with a profession. So he picked out humor, and he had from then to June to "Major" in it. He was matriculating in laughter at Bryans old stronghold. But he lost all confidence in me as a funny man when I couldent answer right off the reel the few little simple questions that he had written down and handed me. So I got him to let me take the paper and send him back the answers later.

Now, here is his exact questions in the exact order he had them, and my answers:

"Is the field of Humor crowded?"

Only when Congress is in session.

"What talent is necessary? Must one be born with a funnybone in his head?"

Its not a talent, its an affliction. If a funnybone is nessasary I would say that in the head is the place to have it. That's the least used of a humorists equipment.

"Which offers the best field, the Essayist or the Humorist Feature Writer?"

Now, I don't know what an "Essayist" is. But if its one of those fellows that write what we used to call "Essays" at school, one of those recitations that you get up and speak, I am agin em. And as to the Humorous Feature Writer, just change the H to N and there you have it.

"What field of Humor offers the best field now and which is most liable to develop?"

Well, I think the "Nut" or "Cuckoo" field is best bet now, and from what I see of modern America, I think "Nuttier Still" or "Super Cuckoo" will be more apt to develop.

"In training what should one aim for?"

Aim for Mark Twain, even if you land with Mutt and Jeff.

"Whats the best way to start being a Humorist?"

Recovery from a Mule kick is one way that's used a lot. Being dropped head downward on a pavement in youth, has been responsible for a lot. And discharge from an Asylum for mental cases is almost sure fire.

"How should one practice for it after starting it?"

By reading Editorials in Tabloid Magazines and three pages of the Congressional Record before retiring every night.

"Should one jot down ideas?"

No! there will be so few that you can remember them.

"Should one read other Humorists?"

If you are a Humorist, there is no other Humorist.

"Is it profitable to read other Humorists?"

Profitable but terribly discouraging.

"Do you think it does any good to play the Fool and wit at social gatherings?"

Not if they will feed you without it. But if you feel that you need the practice and just cant remain normal any longer, why go ahead. Everybody will perhaps want to kill you, and may. As for Social gatherings, I never knew of a Humorist getting into one if it had any social standing.

"Does College training add to your chances?"

Yes, nothing enhances a mans humor more than College. Colleges and Ford cars have been indespensible to humor.

"Should one specialize in any particular subject?"

Everything but English.

"What College would you suggest in preperation for a Humorous career?"

Harvard, if its present football continues.

"Must one have a heterogenous background of experience?"

You got me with that hetegenerous. But I will say "yes" to that question and take a chance. I want to answer these 100%.

"What's the best place to study human nature?"

At the source.

"Does a budding Humorist have to wait till he has acquired a philosophy?"

No, just a "Carona" typewriter is all.

"What is the procedure in submitting jokes or skits to Papers or Magazines?"

A return envelope stamped.

"Whats the best Magazine for Amateurs?"

Ladies Home Journal.

"How do you get into Syndicate work?"

Lose all other jobs on a newspaper, or knock 50 home runs, or work 12 years with the Follies, and dodge all Literacy tests.

"Any advantage in Illustrating your own work?"

Yes, it's the only way you can get it done right. Inferior Illustrators are spoiling our work.

"Do you think cartooning has a future?"

I certainly do. Its never had a boom, just a steady growth. The more we raise that cant read the more will look at Pictures.

"Any demand for 'slangy' short stories on the style of Lardner and H. L. Mencken?"

Yes, Lardners must sell. I saw him in Florida last winter with a stack of all Blue chips in front of him. Mencken has his own magazine where he uses what he cant sell.

"What Magazine would you send your first stories too?"

The nearest one.

"What's the oppurtunities of a good Gag man in the Movies?"

The oppurtunities are great, but the chances of getting in are small.

"Is there such a thing as running stale or getting out of material?"

I have heard of that happening, but in very rare cases. Every article seems better than the preceeding one, and continues so right up to the execution.

"Is it hard to get into Vaudeville for a summer or a year?"

No, with all the different grades and classes of Vaudeville they have nowadays, its almost impossible to have an act so poor that somebody hasent got a Circuit that will fit you.

"This thing you do around the Country where you do a whole evenings entertainment yourself, just what is it?"

Son, I couldent tell you. With the old-timers they called it a Lecture. With Politicians they call it a "Message." But with me its just a Graft.

"Is there any demand for Chalk talks?"

Not unless you are a Football coach.

"Is summer a bad time to start anything"

If you want to make up your mind to start to be a Humorist, I believe I would wait till spring, if you can afford to lay off that long. Then if you should get disappointed, why you have a summer coming on instead of a winter.

"Mr. Rogers, could you tell me where I could be apt to sell this interview with you?"

No! But if you ever see it in print, I can give you a pretty good idea what Magazine might have used it.

witty replies on the art of comedy.
Note: Language and spelling from original document has been retained.

Source: Rogers, Will. "How To Be Funny." *American Magazine,* September 1929.

Babe Ruth

1895–1948

Popular American Baseball Player

One of the all-time greats of professional baseball, Babe Ruth's spectacular performances exhilarated Americans in the 1920s and revitalized their national pastime.

Born George Herman Ruth in Baltimore, Maryland, on February 6, 1895, he grew up a deprived and troubled youth. At age seven, his parents committed him to St. Mary's Industrial School for Boys, a reformatory and orphanage run by the Catholic Order of Xaverian Brothers. His strongest influences during these years were Brother Matthias and baseball. Brother Matthias taught him to read and write as well as hit, field, and pitch. Ruth became the school's best baseball player and, by 1914, the young star of the minor league team the Baltimore Orioles. In the first days of spring training, Orioles manager Jack Dunn doted on the promising Ruth, leading the elder players to call him Dunn's "babe."

Ruth soon rose as the "Babe" of baseball with a stellar rookie season. Starting in the minors in the spring, his pitching skills advanced him to the majors that summer with the Boston Red Sox. He quickly progressed as the leading left-handed pitcher of the American League. In the 1916 and 1918 World Series, Ruth pitched 29⅔ consecutive scoreless innings, a record that lasted for more than 40 years. He also proved himself as a left-handed hitter by tying Philadelphia Athletics outfielder Tilly Walker for the most home runs in 1918. The next season Ruth left the mound for the outfield and broke the major league home run record.

In January 1920, Red Sox owner Harry Frazee, needing money desperately, traded Ruth to the New York Yankees for $125,000. Up to the 1919 season, the Red Sox had won five of 16 World Series and the Yankees had never won a pennant. All of this changed after Ruth joined the Yankees, which came to be known as the Red Sox's "Curse of the Bambino." The reputation of the Red Sox plummeted (they won their last World Series in 1918) while that of the Yankees skyrocketed in the 1920s and following decades.

Upon Ruth's arrival, the Yankees overshadowed the Giants as New York's favorite team. Ruth was the greatest drawing card in baseball. He enlivened the game by interacting with the crowd and altering the game's style from shorter to longer plays, replacing bunts and sacrifices with home runs and high-scoring innings. His soaring hits and personal panache doubled attendance at Yankee games in 1920, drawing nearly 1,300,000 fans. With Americans working fewer hours after World War I, people had more leisure time to focus on baseball and their baseball heroes.

Courtesy of National Baseball Hall of Fame, Cooperstown, New York.

Ruth's image sold everything from his "Home Run" candy bar and "Bambino" tobacco to Wheaties cereal and Barbasol shaving cream, products eagerly purchased in an age that welcomed mass consumerism and glorified sports figures. This enthusiasm, however, diminished late in the 1920 season when the public discovered that eight Chicago White Sox players had accepted a bribe to throw the 1919 World Series to the Cincinnati Reds. Although the "Black Sox Scandal" disenchanted baseball fans, the "Babe" continued to inspire their appreciation of the game.

Standing 6 feet 2 inches and weighing more than 200 pounds, Ruth swung the bat with confidence and power. He set major league home run records three years in a row: 29 in 1919, 54 in 1920, and 59 in 1921. Six seasons later he topped his score with 60 home runs in a 154-game schedule, a major league record that stood until 1961 (although his record was broken during a 162-game schedule). He also set a record with his lifetime total of 714 home runs, which was not surpassed until 1974 by Hank Aaron. He is the only player to twice claim three home runs in a World Series game (1926 and 1928) and, until 2001, he retained the record for bases on balls (walks) with 2,062. Supporting his team with his prodigious swing, Ruth inspired crowds and helped the Yankees win pennants (1921–23, 1926–28, and 1932) and world championships (1923, 1927–28, and 1932). On opening day in 1923, Yankee Stadium was dubbed "The House That Ruth Built."

Despite his records, Ruth was not the golden boy of baseball. He had a defiant streak, an explosive temper, and a foul tongue. In 1922, he was suspended five times for professional misconduct, including incidents such as throwing dirt in an umpire's face and hurdling the grandstand to chase a heckling fan. His excessive drinking and carousing off the field resulted in another suspension and a $5,000 fine in 1925. Despite Ruth's rash and irresponsible side, fans and sportswriters ignored his unbecoming behavior and praised his superb ball playing and flamboyant personality. Ruth was their ultimate sportsman and showman.

While Ruth fueled the excitement of the Roaring Twenties, he provided a diversion from the Great Depression of the 1930s. Proof of his steadfast appeal and value as a player was his two-year contract for an annual salary of $80,000, earning him $5,000 more a year than President Herbert Hoover. After signing the contract in 1931, he went on to hit his most famous home run. In game three of the 1932 World Series, down two balls and two strikes, Ruth allegedly pointed to center field and then unleashed a homer in that direction. The legendary "Called Shot" remains debatable, but the play indisputably ranks among the classic moments in baseball history. Ruth ended his final season with the Yankees in 1934 and his career with the Boston Braves in 1935. One of the five charter members elected to the Baseball Hall of Fame (1936), Ruth died an American hero in New York on August 16, 1948.

No sports idol of the era reached his stature: Babe Ruth was indelible and colossal. To many in the 1920s, Ruth's performances on the field transformed him into a mythic figure. Ruth's presence not only established the Yankees as an elite sports power but his popularity also benefited every major league club. In his heyday, baseball attendance increased more rapidly than the country's population. Although Ruth could be brash and boorish on and off the diamond, his heroic feats enabled the public to overlook any misconduct. Baseball fans admired Ruth for his generosity and affection, his high spirits and home runs.

Renée Miller

For Further Reading

Creamer, Robert W. *Babe: The Legend Comes to Life.* New York: Simon & Schuster, 1992.

Smelser, Marshall. *The Life That Ruth Built.* Lincoln: University of Nebraska Press, 1993.

Wagenheim, Kal. *Babe Ruth: His Life and Legend.* Maplewood, N.J.: Waterfront Press, 1990.

BABE RUTH'S BASEBALL RECORD (1914–35)

BATTING

Year	Team	League	Games	At Bats	Strike Outs	Bases On Balls (Walks)	Hits	Doubles	Triples	Runs	Home Runs	Runs Batted In (RBI)	Batting Average
1914	Boston	American	5	10	4	0	2	1	0	1	0	2	.200
1915	Boston	American	42	92	23	9	29	10	1	16	4	21	.315
1916	Boston	American	67	136	23	10	37	5	3	18	3	15	.272
1917	Boston	American	52	123	18	12	40	6	3	14	2	12	.325
1918	Boston	American	95	317	58	58	95	26	11	50	11	66	.300
1919	Boston	American	130	432	58	101	139	34	12	103	29	114	.322
1920	New York	American	142	458	80	150	172	36	9	158	54	137	.376
1921	New York	American	152	540	81	145	204	44	16	177	59	171	.378
1922	New York	American	110	406	80	84	128	24	8	94	35	99	.315
1923	New York	American	152	522	93	170	205	45	13	151	41	131	.393
1924	New York	American	153	529	81	142	200	39	7	143	46	121	.378
1925	New York	American	98	359	68	59	104	12	2	61	25	66	.290
1926	New York	American	152	495	76	144	184	30	5	139	47	146	.372
1927	New York	American	151	540	89	137	192	29	8	158	60	164	.356
1928	New York	American	154	536	87	137	173	29	8	163	54	142	.323
1929	New York	American	135	499	60	72	172	26	6	121	46	154	.345
1930	New York	American	145	518	61	136	186	28	9	150	49	153	.359
1931	New York	American	145	534	51	128	199	31	3	149	46	163	.373
1932	New York	American	133	457	62	130	156	13	5	120	41	137	.341
1933	New York	American	137	459	90	114	138	21	3	97	34	103	.301
1934	New York	American	125	365	63	104	105	17	4	78	22	84	.288
1935	Boston	National	28	72	24	20	13	0	0	13	6	12	.181
Major League Totals			2,503	8,399	1,330	2,062	2,873	506	136	2,174	714	2,213	.342

BATTING/ WORLD SERIES

Year	Team	League	Games	At Bats	Strike Outs	Bases On Balls (Walks)	Hits	Doubles	Triples	Runs	Home Runs	Runs Batted In (RBI)	Batting Average
1915	Boston	American	1	1	0	0	0	0	0	0	0	0	.000
1916	Boston	American	1	5	2	0	0	0	0	0	0	1	.000
1918	Boston	American	3	5	2	0	1	0	1	0	0	2	.200
1921	New York	American	6	16	8	5	5	0	0	3	1	4	.313

A strong pitcher and a superb batter, Ruth continuously made baseball history, from his record-breaking scoreless World Series innings (1916 and 1918) to his 714th and final home run (1935). The following record lists his batting and pitching statistics in the major leagues, World Series, and All-Star Games.

Source: Record adapted from Lawrence S. Ritter and Mark Rucker, *The Babe: A Life in Pictures.* New York: Ticknor & Fields, 1988 and The Official Site of Major League Baseball. 2001. www.mlb.com (September 21, 2001).

BATTING/ WORLD SERIES (cont)

Year	Team	League	Games	At Bats	Strike Outs	Bases On Balls (Walks)	Hits	Doubles	Triples	Runs	Home Runs	Runs Batted In (RBI)	Batting Average
1922	New York	American	5	17	3	2	2	1	0	1	0	1	.118
1923	New York	American	6	19	6	8	7	1	1	8	3	3	.368
1926	New York	American	7	20	2	11	6	0	0	6	4	5	.300
1927	New York	American	4	15	2	2	6	0	0	4	2	7	.400
1928	New York	American	4	16	2	1	10	3	0	9	3	4	.625
1932	New York	American	4	15	3	4	5	0	0	6	2	6	.333
World Series Totals			41	129	30	33	42	5	2	37	15	33	.326

PITCHING

Year	Team	League	Games	Innings Pitched	Wins	Losses	Hits	Strike Outs	Bases On Balls (Walks)	Earned Run Average
1914	Boston	American	4	24	2	1	21	3	7	3.91
1915	Boston	American	32	218	18	8	166	112	85	2.44
1916	Boston	American	44	324	23	12	230	170	118	1.75
1917	Boston	American	41	326	24	13	244	128	108	2.02
1918	Boston	American	20	166	13	7	125	40	49	2.22
1919	Boston	American	17	133	9	5	148	30	58	2.97
1920	New York	American	1	4	1	0	3	0	2	4.50
1921	New York	American	2	9	2	0	14	2	9	9.00
1930	New York	American	1	9	1	0	11	3	2	3.00
1933	New York	American	1	9	1	0	12	0	3	5.00
Major League Totals			163	1,221	94	46	974	488	441	2.28

PITCHING/WORLD SERIES

Year	Team	League	Games	Innings Pitched	Wins	Losses	Hits	Strike Outs	Bases On Balls (Walks)	Earned Run Average
1916	Boston	American	1	14	1	0	6	4	3	0.64
1918	Boston	American	2	17	2	0	13	4	7	1.06
World Series Totals			3	31	3	0	19	8	10	0.87

BOSTON RED SOX AND NEW YORK YANKEES AGREEMENT (December 26, 1919)

The trade of Ruth became known as the "Curse of the Bambino" for the Boston Red Sox and turned into the deal of the decade for the New York Yankees. Yankee owner Colonel Jacob Ruppert agreed to pay Red Sox owner Harry Frazee $125,000 for the greatest player of the era. This contract, dated December 26, 1919, is for partial payment ($25,000) of the agreed amount. Eleven days later the trade was made public.

Source: Courtesy of National Baseball Hall of Fame, Cooperstown, New York.

RADIO TRANSCRIPT FROM WORLD SERIES (1926)

The Babe is up. Two home runs today. One ball, far outside. Babe's shoulders look as if there is murder in them down there, the way he is swinging that bat down there. A high foul into the left-field stands. That great big bat of Babe's looks like a toothpick down there, he is so big himself. Here it is. Babe shot a bad one and fouled it. Two strikes and one ball. The outfield have all moved very far towards right. It is coming up now. A little too close. Two strikes and two balls. He has got two home runs and a base on balls so far today. Here it is, and a ball. Three and two. The Babe is waving that wand of his over the plate. Bell is loosening up his arm. The Babe is hit clear into the center-field bleachers for a home run! For a home run! Did you hear what I said? Where is that fellow who told me not to talk about Ruth anymore? Send him up here.

Oh, what a shot! Directly over second. The boys are all over him over there. One of the boys is riding on Ruth's back. Oh, what a shot! Directly over second base far into the bleachers out in center field, and almost on a line and then that dumbbell, where is he, who told me not to talk about Ruth! Oh, boy! Not that I love Ruth, but oh, how I love to see a shot like that! Wow! That is a world's series record, three home runs in one world's series game and what a home run! That was probably the longest hit ever made in Sportsman's Park. They tell me this is the first ball ever hit in the center-field stand. That is a mile and a half from here. You know what I mean.

Baseball fans of both the New York Yankees and the St. Louis Cardinals cheered for Ruth when he hit his third home run in game four of the 1926 World Series. In this verbatim radio transcript, the announcer colorfully describes the progression of the play that set yet another record for Ruth and again awed the sports world.

Source: Smelser, Marshall. *The Life That Ruth Built.* Lincoln: University of Nebraska Press, 1993. Reprinted with permission of the University of Nebraska Press. ©1975 by Marshall Smelser.

*N.B. Smelser notes the unnamed announcer as either Graham McNamee or Phillips Carlin. Both gave accounts of the game that appeared in the *Times*.

THE "CALLED SHOT" HOME RUN (October 1, 1932)

On October 1, 1932, during game three of the 1932 World Series, Ruth allegedly pointed to center field and then hit a home run in that direction in what became known as the "Called Shot." Here, Ruth crosses home plate and is congratulated by teammate Lou Gehrig.

Source: National Baseball Hall of Fame, Cooperstown, New York.

Nicola Sacco and Bartolomeo Vanzetti

1891–1927; 1888–1927

Anarchists and Alleged Murderers

Italian immigrants Nicola Sacco and Bartolomeo Vanzetti were anarchists, convicted of murder in highly questionable trials at the height of the Red Scare (1919–20). Despite repeated appeals for retrial and worldwide protests, they were put to death in 1927.

Nicola Sacco was born in Torre Maggiore, Italy, on April 22, 1891. He immigrated to the United States in 1908 and worked in shoe factories in Milford and Stoughton, Massachusetts. Bartolomeo Vanzetti was born on June 11, 1888, in Villafalletto, Italy. Vanzetti, too, came to America in 1908. He worked in New York as a dishwasher and farmer, and moved to Plymouth, Massachusetts, around 1915.

Both men developed an interest in anarchism (the theory that all government is oppressive and should be destroyed), and became followers of Luigi Galleani, a radi-

From the collections of the Library of Congress.

cal Italian-born anarchist who advocated the abolition of private property, called for violent revolution against the capitalist ruling class, and urged his followers, known as *Galleanisti*, not to submit to the "slavery" of conscription for World War I. When in 1917 the United States began raising troops for the war, Sacco and Vanzetti fled to Mexico with about 60 other Galleanisti, waiting to join an Italian revolution that they believed would soon follow the Russian revolution of March 1917. When Italy did not revolt, Sacco and Vanzetti returned to Massachusetts, where Sacco found work in a Stoughton shoe factory and Vanzetti sold fish in Plymouth. On June 24, 1919, the United States deported Galleani and eight followers for antiwar activities, but many Galleanisti remained. They waged a terror campaign that included the attempted bombing of the home of Attorney General **A. Mitchell Palmer** in Washington, D.C., on June 2, 1919, and the horrific Wall Street explosion on September 16, 1920, that killed 38 and wounded 300. These attacks prompted a government crackdown, the infamous Palmer Raids, by Justice Department officials on anarchists, communists, and others who were considered subversive.

On April 15, 1920, the paymaster and security guard of a South Braintree, Massachusetts, shoe factory were murdered and the nearly $16,000 payroll stolen. About three weeks later, on the night of May 5, Sacco, Vanzetti, and fellow anarchist Riccardo Orciani were arrested on suspicion of connection with the South Braintree robbery and murders, as well as an attempted robbery of a Bridgewater, Massachusetts, shoe factory's payroll truck the previous Christmas Eve.

Sacco and Vanzetti were already on file at the Justice Department's Boston office as "radicals to be watched," and were known associates of the Palmer bomber. When arrested, Sacco and Vanzetti were both carrying pistols and ammunition; under interrogation both lied and gave contradictory statements to the police. However, despite their suspicious behavior upon arrest, neither man had a prior police record, neither had possessed any of the stolen payroll money, and neither had attempted to hide from authorities in the weeks following the April 15 robbery.

Orciani was released eventually because he had been at work on the days of the robberies, but Sacco and Vanzetti could not provide believable alibis for either day, although Sacco's was good enough to free him from suspicion for the December 24 robbery. Sacco was charged only with the South Braintree robbery and murders, while Vanzetti was charged with both crimes.

Vanzetti's trial for the attempted Christmas Eve heist in Bridgewater was held in Plymouth, Massachussetts, from June 22 to July 1, 1920, under Judge Webster Thayer. After shoddy work by the prosecution and defense attorneys, Vanzetti was found guilty and sentenced to 12 to 15 years in prison. For the South Braintree robbery and murders, Sacco and Vanzetti stood trial together, again before Judge Thayer, in Dedham, Massachusetts, from May 31 to July 14, 1921. Thayer, known to be biased against immigrants and intolerant of anarchists, allowed the prosecutor to introduce extraneous information about the accused that could only heighten the jury's prejudices against the defendants—such as the fact that they were atheists and anarchists. The judge showed contempt for the Italian witnesses for the defense, implying that they lied to help their countrymen. Although the prosecution's ballistics testimony never directly tied Sacco and Vanzetti's weapons to the South Braintree murders, the jury found both men guilty on July 14, 1921, and sentenced them to death.

Many observers decried the trial as a sham, and six years of international protest and appeals for a retrial followed the guilty verdict. From 1919 to 1920 the nation had been shaken by a Red Scare—a fear, inflamed by politicians and journalists, that the Bolshevik Revolution was spreading communism from Russia to the United States—resulting in the Palmer Raids against suspected subversives and mass deportations of politically suspect foreigners. But the public soon recovered from its fever, and the guilty verdict in the Sacco and Vanzetti trial appeared to many as an ugly, unjust continuation of the political repression and xenophobia (fear of foreigners) exemplified by sharp cutbacks in immigration and a rise in membership in the Ku Klux Klan.

The requests for appeals introduced evidence of perjured testimony by prosecution witnesses and of collusion between police and the Justice Department. Eight motions for a new trial were submitted to Judge Thayer and each was denied. (One appeal called for a retrial based on comments Thayer made after denying a previous motion: "Did you see what I did with those anarchistic bastards the other day? I guess that will hold them for a while.") In 1925, convicted bank robber Celestino F. Madieros confessed that he and the criminal Morelli gang had committed the South Braintree holdup and murders, but this confession did not bring a retrial. The Massachusetts Supreme Court ruled that the trial had been fair, and Judge Thayer set a date for execution. Pressured by widespread protests, Governor Alvan T. Fuller appointed a committee, headed by Harvard president A. Lawrence Lowell, to review the case. The Lowell committee, too, validated the trial and counseled against clemency. On August 23, 1927, Sacco and Vanzetti were electrocuted in the Charlestown State Prison near Boston.

Many sympathizers believe Nicola Sacco and Bartolomeo Vanzetti were guilty of nothing more than being foreigners—and atheist anarchists at that—during the Red Scare. They were executed during a time of increasing political conservatism and a turning inward that marked America's desire for stability in the 1920s.

Mark LaFlaur

For Further Reading

Avrich, Paul. *Sacco and Vanzetti: The Anarchist Background.* Princeton, N.J.: Princeton University Press, 1991.

Ehrmann, Herbert B. *The Case That Will Not Die: Commonwealth vs. Sacco and Vanzetti.* Boston: Little, Brown, 1969.

Frankfurter, Felix. *The Case of Sacco and Vanzetti: A Critical Analysis for Lawyers and Laymen.* New York: Grosset & Dunlap, 1967.

Murray, Robert K. *Red Scare: A Study of National Hysteria, 1919–1920.* Westport, Conn.: Greenwood Press, 1980.

Speech of Nicola Sacco to Judge Webster Thayer (April 9, 1927)

CLERK WORTHINGTON: Nicola Sacco, have you anything to say why sentence of death should not be passed upon you?

NICOLA SACCO: Yes, sir. I am no orator. It is not very familiar with me the English language, and as I know, as my friend has told me, my comrade Vanzetti will speak more long, so I thought to give him the chance.

I never knew, never heard, even read in history anything so cruel as this Court. After seven years prosecuting they still consider us guilty. And these gentle people here are arrayed with us in this court today.

I know the sentence will be between two classes, the oppressed class and the rich class, and there will be always collision between one and the other. We fraternize the people with the books, with the literature. You persecute the people, tyrannize them and kill them. We try the education of people always. You try to put a

path between us and some other nationality that hates each other. That is why I am here today on this bench, for having been of the oppressed class. Well, you are the oppressor.

You know it, Judge Thayer—you know all my life, you know why I have been here, and after seven years that you have been persecuting me and my poor wife, and you still today sentence us to death. I would like to tell all my life, but what is the use? You know all about what I say before, that is, my comrade, will be talking, because he is more familiar with the language, and I will give him a chance. My comrade, the kind man to all the children, you sentenced him two times, in the Bridgewater case and the Dedham case, connected with me, and you know he is innocent.

You forget all this population that has been with us for seven years, to sympathize and give us all their

The following court statement from Nicola Sacco was addressed to Judge Webster Thayer on April 9, 1927. Sacco, as well as Vanzetti, was asked, "Have you anything to say why sentence of death should not be passed upon you?"

Source: Frankfurter, Marion Denman, and Gardner Jackson, eds. *The Letters of Sacco and Vanzetti.* New York: Viking Press, 1928.

energy and all their kindness. You do not care for them. Among that peoples and the comrades and the working class there is a big legion of intellectual people which have been with us for seven years, to not commit the iniquitous sentence, but still the Court goes ahead. And I want to thank you all, you peoples, my comrades who have been with me for seven years, with the Sacco-Vanzetti case, and I will give my friend a chance.

I forget one thing which my comrade remember me. As I said before, Judge Thayer know all my life, and he know that I am never guilty, never—not yesterday, nor today, nor forever.

"Justice Underfoot" by Oswald Garrison Villard (August 17, 1927) [Excerpt]

An editorial in the August 17, 1927, issue of The Nation by editor Oswald Garrison Villard, like thousands of protests over the preceding several years, was not enough to stay the execution of Sacco and Vanzetti. They were executed a week later on August 23, 1927.

Source: Villard, Oswald Garrison. "Justice Underfoot." The Nation, August 17, 1927 in The Nation, 1865–1990: Selections from the Independent Magazine of Politics and Culture, edited by Katrina Vanden Heuvel. New York: Thunder's Mouth Press, 1990. Reprinted with permission from The Nation.

One of the most momentous decisions in the history of American jurisprudence has been rendered—and Sacco and Vanzetti are condemned to death. Around the earth the news has winged its way as fast as light and wherever the tidings have reached millions of workers now believe that justice does not exist in America, that two innocent men are going to their doom in order that a social system may be upheld, a tottering social order may triumph. As we write no one can foretell the consequences of Governor Fuller's astounding decision, but from remote quarters there already comes the news of protest meetings, of protest strikes, of the windows of the American Consulate in Buenos Aires smashed, of a sense of horror-struck outrage in one country after another. Talk about the solidarity of the human race! When has there been a more striking example of the solidarity of great masses of people than this? Ten years ago people were reading of thirty thousand, forty thousand, fifty thousand men done to death in a single day in the war that statesmen, with horrible sacrilege, had falsely dedicated to democracy and to civilization. Those useless massacres nowhere stirred the neutral world as has the fate of these two Italian workers, who have dared to say that they were anarchists, but innocent of the murder with which they are charged. Wherever the American flag flies in foreign lands today, it has to be guarded; it appears the symbol of a monstrous wrong. Men may yet die by the dozen because of Governor Fuller's decision. Rightly or wrongly, we repeat, uncountable multitudes today believe that in America justice is dead.

For ourselves, we are shaken to the core. We had not believed such a decision possible. We do not retract one word from our praise of the industry Governor Fuller has shown, his painstaking examination of the topography of the scene of the crime, of witnesses and jurors, judge and prisoners. We recognize again his honesty of purpose; we acquit him of any charge of political maneuvering; we admit the superficial ability of his opinion. Yet we cannot for one instant accept this verdict in the face of facts known to us for years as they have been known to multitudes of others. It seems to us that he has missed all the important points in the case and that his decision reveals his complete inability to rise above the point of view of his surroundings, his class, and the setting in which great wealth has placed him. Nor are we convinced by the facile report of the Governor's committee of three eminent and conventional gentlemen, two chosen from the highest Boston social circles, all of one type of mind and not one of them representing the vast groups that have felt from the first that they had a vital stake in the fate of these men. After a brief investigation, partaking of the nature of a star-chamber in hearing Judge Thayer and his attorney without attendance of the defense's counsel, they have upheld the court. . . .

[H]ere is an instance of a headlong collision of certain viewpoints which are and must be hopelessly antagonistic. The liberals and the workers who are championing the cause of these men may also have their blind eyes. The truth remains that the question of the guilt of these men has been subordinated to the clash of these two vital currents of human thought, and the world at large knows that Sacco and Vanzetti have been judged and will have been executed by the representatives of one of these viewpoints alone. And still another fact, a great and unanswerable fact, stands out that in its essence the guilt or innocence of these men has been passed upon by only one judge; that what is forbidden in New York and is impossible in other States of the Union has come to pass in Massachusetts: the *evidence*—not the technical legal procedure—has been ruled upon only by the trial judge, he who, if a tithe of the charges against him by reputable witnesses is true, ought to be impeached and disgraced—even the Lowell committee admits what it kindly calls his "indiscretion."

Is it any wonder that M. Herriot, who has repeatedly, as Prime Minister of France and as the present Minister of Education, given proof of his friendship for America, has cried out in protest, against not only this final act of barbarity but what has gone on before. "To the depths of my soul," he declares, "I am against this punishment that has lasted seven years. I am sorry to be unable to make my voice heard, but I belong to the Government and my words might pledge the whole cabinet. Personally I never varied my opinion. Sacco and Vanzetti ought to be released. They have earned such a measure of clemency." This is what affects the European opinion more than Americans can possibly realize—that these men have been in jeopardy of their lives for seven long years. We are informed on high authority that a group of the foremost London jurists, after devoting an entire evening to a discission of the Sacco and Vanzetti trial, was unanimously of the opinion that they ought to be freed now, *whether guilty or innocent*, since even the crime of murder does not merit the cruel and unusual punishment of keeping men in such torture for seven years. Governor Fuller smugly condemns the defense for the delay—would he be as quick to denounce Messrs. Sinclair and Doheny and Fall and Daugherty for dragging out their trials for five years?—but the hideous circumstance is there. It is impossible in any other civilized country for men to be tortured as have been these. . . . Even if Governor Fuller felt that he must uphold the decision, could not justice have been tempered with mercy?

Yield to foriegn or American threats of course he could not. But the hands of millions have been outstretched to him for pardon or commutation of sentence. A great executive would justly have taken note of that, would have strengthened justice by recognizing an unparalleled demand for clemency; might even have weighed the cost to his country of making martyrs of these men; could have upheld the majesty of the law far, far better by exercising forbearance than by a brutal insistence upon an eye for an eye, a tooth for a tooth, a life for a life.

As for Governor Fuller's opinion, he sweeps away the testimony as to the bias of Judge Thayer by affirming that the judge had a right to be biased after the testimony was in, whereas the affidavits of reputable men and women affirm that that bias was evident from the earliest stages of the trial. We pass over aghast his tribute to the "clear-eyed" and "courageous" witnesses—some of whom are of doubtful reputation, contradicted themselves, and testified to the impossible. Nor would we stress today the old question of the identifications or the fact that the deadly bullet was never proved to have been from Sacco's revolver; nor dwell upon the Governor's describing in one hundred words the Bridgewater hold-up which had nothing to do with the question of a fair trial in the Braintree case. As for the latter, the Governor is quite satisfied that Judge Thayer was right in denying all the seven motions for a new trial. He is not willing that the men should be given the benefit of a doubt, nor will he appeal to the legislature to start the machinery for a new trial in a different atmosphere under a different judge. Would that have rocked the foundations of Massachusetts justice? It might have inflamed the Back Bay clubs, but it would have meant joy and satisfaction wherever newspapers appear.

And not merely to radicals. It is *not* the radicals alone who fought for Sacco and Vanzetti. Noble souls have given years of their lives and their money to this cause who are neither Reds nor foreign-born Americans; nor have they belonged to those holding the anarchist views of the condemned. If there are finer types of our citizenship, or men and women of older American lineage, we should like to have them pointed out to us. They, too, have read every word of the testimony; they have examined the new witnesses; they, too, have studied the motions for a new trial and perused Judge Thayer's denials of them; they have read the affidavits against the judge and they are as good lawyers as the Governor himself. They are as eager as he for the good repute of Massachusetts and its courts, yet they are unconvinced. To them an incredible tragedy is being finished before their eyes; a judicial murder is being committed. Does not the passionate belief of these unselfish supporters of the right merit consideration, if not assent?

As for Sacco and Vanzetti, sometimes we have asked ourselves whether it was not intended that they should die, and whether it is not best for the cause of human progress that they should perish. In his wonderful address to the court—made to Judge Thayer, who did not once dare to look at the prisoners as he condemned them to the chair—Vanzetti voiced this in amazing exaltation of spirit:

> If it had not been for these thing, I might have live out my life, talking at street corners to scorning men. I might have die, unmarked, unknown, a failure. Now we are not a failure. This is our career and our triumph. Never in our full life can we hope to do such work for tolerance, for joostice, for man's onderstanding of man, as now we do by an accident. Our words—our lives— our pains—nothing! The taking of our live—lives of a good shoemaker and a poor fish-peddler—all! That last moment belong to us—that agony is our triumph!

This, we believe will be the verdict of history. Certain it is that if the precedents of history hold true, monuments are likely to be erected to Sacco and Vanzetti and the names of their prosecutors will fade out of history. . . .

LETTER FROM BARTOLOMEO VANZETTI TO DANTE SACCO (August 21, 1927) [EXCERPT]

My Dear Dante:

I still hope, and we will fight until the last moment, to revindicate our right to live and to be free, but all the forces of the State and of the money and reaction are deadly against us because we are libertarians or anarchists.

I write little of this because you are now and yet too young to understand these things and other things of which I would like to reason with you.

But, if you do well, you will grow and understand your father's and my case and your father's and my principles, for which we will soon be put to death.

I tell you now that all that I know of your father, he is not a criminal, but one of the bravest men I ever knew. Some day you will understand what I am about to tell you. That your father has sacrificed everything dear and sacred to the human heart and soul for his fate in liberty and justice for all. That day you will be proud of your father, and if you come brave enough, you will take his place in the struggle between tyranny and liberty and you will vindicate his (our) names and our blood.

If we have to die now, you shall know, when you will be able to understand this tragedy in its fullest, how good and brave your father has been with you, your father and I, during these eight years of struggle, sorrow, passion, anguish and agony.

Even from now you shall be good, brave with your mother, with Ines, and with Susie—brave, good Susie— and do all you can to console and help them.

I would like you to also remember me as a comrade and friend to your father, your mother and Ines, Susie and you, and I assure you that neither have I been a criminal, that I have committed no robbery and no murder, but only fought modestly to abolish crimes from among mankind and for the liberty of all.

Remember Dante, each one who will say otherwise of your father and I, is a liar, insulting innocent dead men who have been brave in their life. Remember and know also, Dante, that if your father and I would have

Excerpt from Bartolomeo Vanzetti's letter to Dante, son of Nicola Sacco, written August 21, 1927, from the death house of the Massachusetts State Prison at Charlestown, two days before execution. Note: Language and spelling from original document has been retained.

Source: Frankfurter, Marion Denman, and Gardner Jackson, eds. *The Letters of Sacco and Vanzetti.* New York: Viking Press, 1928. Renewed ©1955 by The Viking Press, Inc. Used by permission of Viking Penguin, a division of Penguin, Putnam, Inc.

been cowards and hypocrits and rinnegetors of our faith, we would not have been put to death. They would not even have convicted a lebbrous dog; not even executed a deadly poisoned scorpion on such evidence as that they framed against us. They would have given a new trial to a matricide and abitual felon on the evidence we presented for a new trial.

Remember, Dante, remember always these things; we are not criminals; they convicted us on a frame-up; they denied us a new trial; and if we will be executed after seven years, four months and seventeen days of unspeakable tortures and wrong, it is for what I have already told you; because we were for the poor and against the exploitation and oppression of the man by the man.

The documents of our case, which you and other ones will collect and preserve, will prove to you that your father, your mother, Ines, my family and I have sacrificed by and to a State Reason of the American Plutocratic reaction.

The day will come when you will understand the atrocious cause of the above written words, in all its fullness. Then you will honor us.

Now Dante, be brave and good always. I embrace you.

P.S. I left the copy of *An American Bible* to your mother now, for she will like to read it, and she will give it to you when you will be bigger and able to understand it. Keep it for remembrance. It will also testify to you how good and generous Mrs. Gertrude Winslow has been with us all. Good-bye Dante.

BARTOLOMEO

DEMONSTRATION IN NEW YORK CITY (1927)

A crowd of 12,000 radicals and other sympathizers gathered in New York City to protest the execution of Sacco and Vanzetti.

Source: ©Bettmann/Corbis.

Margaret Sanger

Margaret Sanger founded the American birth control movement to advance women's sexual and reproductive freedom. Despite many challenges and arrests, Sanger tirelessly promoted the education and practice of safe and effective contraception through her publications, lectures, and clinics.

Sanger was born Margaret Louise Higgins in Corning, New York, on September 14, 1879, and grew up the sixth of 11 children in an Irish working-class family. After witnessing her mother's failing health from numerous pregnancies and her premature death from tuberculosis, Sanger became interested in health care and enrolled in nursing school at White Plains Hospital. In 1902, upon completing her second year of practical nursing, she married William Sanger, an architect and also a socialist. In 1910, they and their three children moved from a suburban home to a Manhattan apartment. That year Sanger began working as a maternity nurse on the Lower East Side, where she observed the links between poverty, ill health, venereal diseases, unplanned pregnancies, and deaths from illegal abortions. These encounters with powerless women inspired her to abandon nursing in 1912 for a career advocating birth control and sexual reform.

From the collections of the Library of Congress.

In the United States at the turn of the nineteenth century, contraception was met with strong antipathy, especially from Protestants and Roman Catholics who considered it immoral to engage in sexual intercourse without the possibility of conception. Additionally, Victorian-era opponents of birth control feared that the use of contraception would interfere with a woman's primary duty—to give birth and raise children. Under pressure from these societal forces, as well as state and federal laws, physicians refrained from discussing birth control with their patients. For her part, Sanger believed that women could enjoy personal freedom only after they gained power over procreation. Her 1914 monthly newsletter, *Woman Rebel*, addressed this topic and opposed female servitude, releasing the first issue with the masthead slogan "No Gods. No Masters." Even though Sanger did not discuss specific methods to prevent pregnancy, the mere mention of birth control incited a scandal. She was indicted for violating a postal code called the Comstock law, antiobscenity legislation that classified the paper's subject matter as "obscene" and prohibited the delivery of several editions. Before fleeing to Europe to avoid prosecution, Sanger began circulating the pamphlet *Family Limitation*, which contained information and diagrams on contraceptive devices such as condoms, sponges, and diaphragms. She returned to the United States a year later, and, in the beginning of 1916, the charges were dropped.

Sanger and her sister Ethel Bryne launched America's first birth control clinic in a destitute section of Brooklyn. Sanger attempted to provide the poor with contraceptive information familiar to the rich by dispelling common myths and offering reliable methods. On October 16, 1916, the clinic welcomed more than 140 women on opening day. The following week, more women with similar complaints of low income, high fertility, and physical and emotional strain journeyed to the clinic from out of state. On the tenth day of business, every staff member was arrested under Section 1142 of the New York State Penal Code, which forbade access to contraceptive information; both Sanger and Bryne received a 30-day jail sentence in the Blackwell Island workhouse in New York City. Their willingness to sacrifice their liberty drew attention to their cause around the country. Although Appeals Court Judge Frederick Crane sustained Sanger's conviction in 1918, he also granted New York physicians the right to provide birth control advice for the treatment and prevention of disease. Sanger's minor defeat turned into a major victory for reproductive rights.

Sanger founded the American Birth Control League and organized the first American Birth Control Conference in 1921. The final meeting in New York City's Town Hall dealt with the question, "Birth Control: Is It Moral?" but before the meeting even began, the police intervened at the persuasion of Archbishop Patrick Joseph Hayes. This shutdown enraged free speech activists and increased the turnout for the rescheduled meeting. Despite opposition from antivice and religious organizations, in 1923 Sanger established the Birth Control Clinical Research Bureau, the first physician-staffed birth control clinic in the United States. Used as a model for a national chain of birth control clinics, the facility provided contraceptive instruction for married women and trained doctors to prescribe safe and effective contraception, served as a progressive health and research center, and marked one of Sanger's most significant achievements.

Sanger's work gathered support from prominent and wealthy patrons. One of her greatest financial backers, president of the Three-In-One Oil Company, J. Noah Slee, became her second husband. In 1922, two years after divorcing her first husband, Sanger agreed to marry Slee under unique provisions: she would live in her own apartment, entertain guests separately, pursue her career actively, and retain her first and famous married name. Shortly after the Nineteenth Amendment gave women the vote in 1920, Sanger came to symbolize the liberated woman who exercised autonomy in her personal and professional life. Radical by even today's standards, Sanger defied conventional views of matrimony and motherhood.

Recognition of Sanger's work further strengthened after police raided her Research Bureau in 1929. The arrest of doctors and nurses as well as the confiscation of confidential medical files led to much public outrage and the eventual expansion of her clinics. Resigning as president of the American Birth Control League in 1928, Sanger headed the National Commission for Federal Legislation for Birth Control until 1937, when a United States Circuit Court of Appeals legalized the practice of birth control under medical supervision. Her promotion of birth control in the United States, Europe, and the Far East led to the establishment of clinics and teaching centers worldwide. She formed the Planned Parenthood Federation of America in 1942 and the International Planned Parenthood Federation in 1953. At the time of her death on September 6, 1966, in Tucson, Arizona, birth control education had earned respect and family planning had become an international concern.

Sanger helped women around the world gain control over their own bodies by elevating birth control from a forbidden word to a common practice. Her belief that every birth should be made by choice instead of chance remains controversial. A feminist before her time, Sanger rebelled against the church, law, and public opinion to improve the lives of women and children.

Renée Miller

For Further Reading

Chesler, Ellen. *Woman of Valor: Margaret Sanger and the Birth Control Movement in America.* New York: Anchor Books, 1993.

Gray, Madeline. *Margaret Sanger: A Biography of the Champion of Birth Control.* New York: Richard Marek, 1979.

Kennedy, David M. *Birth Control in America: The Career of Margaret Sanger.* New Haven, Conn.: Yale University Press, 1970.

Sanger, Margaret. *Margaret Sanger: An Autobiography.* 1938. Reprint, with an introduction by Kathryn Cullen-DuPont. New York: Cooper Square Press, 1999.

Sanger, Margaret. *My Fight for Birth Control.* 1931. Reprint, New York: Maxwell Reprint, 1969.

LETTER FROM MARGARET SANGER TO *WOMAN REBEL* SUBSCRIBERS (1914)

Under the Comstock law, several issues of Sanger's Woman Rebel *were considered "obscene" and censored from the mail. This October 1914 letter informs subscribers that oppressive postal codes will not suppress her work to increase birth control awareness.*

Source: Sanger, Margaret. My Fight for Birth Control. *New York: Farrar and Rinehart, 1931.*

Comrades and Friends,—

Every paper published should have a message for its readers. It should deliver it and be done. *The Woman Rebel* had for its aim the imparting of information for the prevention of conception. (None of the suppressed issues contained such information.) It was not the intention to labor for years advocating the idea, but to give the information directly to those who desired it. The March, May, July, August, September and October issues have been suppressed and confiscated by the Post Office. They have been mailed regularly to all subscribers. If you have not received your copies, it has been because the U. S. Post Office has refused to carry them on to you.

My work in the nursing field for the past fourteen years has convinced me that the workers desire the knowledge of prevention of conception. My work among women of the working class proved to me sufficiently that it is they who are suffering because of the law which forbids the imparting of the information. To wait for this law to be repealed would be years and years hence. Thousands of unwanted children may be brought into the world in the meantime, thousands of women made miserable and unhappy.

Why should we wait?

Shall we who have heard the cries and seen the agony of dying women respect the law which has caused their deaths?

Shall we watch in patience the murdering of 25,000 women each year in the United States from criminal abortions?

Shall we fold our hands and wait until a body of sleek and well fed politicians get ready to abolish the cause of such slaughter?

Shall we look upon a piece of parchment as greater than human happiness, greater than human life?

Shall we let it destroy our womanhood, or hold millions of workers in bondage and slavery? Shall we who respond to the throbbing pulse of human needs concern ourselves with indictments, courts, and judges, or shall we do our work first and settle with these evils after?

This law has caused the perpetuation of quackery. It has created the fake and quack who benefit by its existence.

Jail has not been my goal. There is special work to be done and I shall do it first. If jail comes after, I shall call upon all to assist me. In the meantime, I shall attempt to nullify the law by direct action and attend to the consequences afterward.

Over 100,000 working men and women in the United States shall hear from me.

The Boston Tea Party was a defiant and revolutionary act in the eyes of the British Government, but to the American Revolutionist it was but an act of courage and justice.

Yours fraternally,
Margaret Sanger

HANDBILL FOR FIRST BIRTH CONTROL CLINIC (1916)

MOTHERS!

Can you afford to have a large family?
Do you want any more children?
If not, why do you have them?
DO NOT KILL, DO NOT TAKE LIFE, BUT PREVENT
Safe, Harmless Information can be obtained of trained
Nurses at

46 AMBOY STREET
NEAR PITKIN AVE. — BROOKLYN.

Tell Your Friends and Neighbors.   All Mothers Welcome
A registration fee of 10 cents entitles any mother to this information.

מוטערס!

ווים איהר פערמעגליך צו האבען א גרויסע פאמיליע?
וולט איהר האבען נאך קינדער?
אויב ניט, וואָרום האָט איהר זיי?

מערדערט ניט, נעהממט ניט קיין לעבען, נור פערהים זיך.
זיכערע, אונשעדליכע אויסקינפטע קענט איהר בעקומען פֿן ערפֿארענע נירסעס אין

46 אמבאי סטריט ניער פיטקין עוועניו **ברוקלין**

מאכם דאָס בעקאנם צו אייערע פריינד און שכנות.   יעדער מומער איז ווילקאמען
פֿיר 10 סענט אינשרייב-געלד קענט איהר בעקעמענ צו דיעזע אינפֿאָרמיישאן.

MADRI!

Potete permettervi il lusso d'avere altri bambini?
Ne volete ancora?
Se non ne volete piu', perche' continuate a metterli al mondo?
NON UCCIDETE MA PREVENITE!
Informazioni sicure ed innocue saranno fornite da infermiere autorizzate a
46 AMBOY STREET   Near Pitkin Ave. Brooklyn
a cominciare dal 12 Ottobre. Avvertite le vostre amiche e vicine.
Tutte le madri sono ben accette. La tassa d'iscrizione di 10 cents da diritto
a qualunque madre di ricevere consigli ed informazioni gratis.

On October 16, 1916, Sanger and her sister Ethel Bryne opened America's first birth control clinic in Brooklyn, welcoming all women. Five thousand copies of this handbill, printed in English, Yiddish, and Italian, were distributed in the surrounding neighborhoods.

Source: Reproduced from Margaret Sanger, *My Fight for Birth Control.* New York: Farrar and Rinehart, 1931.

MARGARET SANGER'S TRIAL (1917) [EXCERPT]

THE COURT: If Mrs. Sanger will state publicly and openly that she will be a law-abiding citizen without any qualifications whatsoever, this court is prepared to exercise the highest degree of leniency.

MARGARET SANGER: I'd like to have it understood by the gentlemen of the court that the offer of leniency is very kind and I appreciate it very much. It is with me not a question of personal imprisonment or personal disadvantage. I am today and always have been more concerned with changing the law regardless of what I have to undergo to have it done.

THE COURT: Then I take it you are indifferent about this matter entirely.

MARGARET SANGER: No, I am not indifferent. I am indifferent as to the personal consequences to myself, but I am not indifferent to the cause and the influence which can be attained for the cause.

THE COURT: Since you are of that mind, am I to infer that you intend to go on in this matter, violating the law, irrespective of the consequences?

MARGARET SANGER: I haven't said that. I said I am perfectly willing not to violate Section 1142—pending the appeal.

JUSTICE HERRMANN: The appeal has nothing to do with it. Either you do or you don't.

THE COURT (to Mr. Goldstein): What is the use of beating around the bush? You have communicated to me in my chambers the physical condition of your client, and you told me that this woman would respect the law. This law was not made by us. We are simply here to judge the case. We harbor no feeling against Mrs. Sanger. We have nothing to do with her beliefs, except in so far as she carries those beliefs into practice and violates the law. But in view of your statement that you intend to prosecute this

Sanger consistently proved her willingness to make sacrifices in order to promote birth control awareness. In 1917, Sanger went to trial after being arrested for opening her first Brooklyn clinic. Refusing to compromise her beliefs for a lighter penalty, Sanger received a 30-day sentence in the Blackwell Island workhouse.

Source: Coigney, Virginia. *Margaret Sanger: Rebel with a Cause.* Garden City, N.Y.: Doubleday, 1969.

appeal and make a test case out of this and in view of the fact that we are to regard her as a first offender, surely we want to temper justice with mercy and that's all we are trying to do. And we ask her, openly and aboveboard, "Will you publicly declare that you will respect the law and not violate it?" and then we get an answer with a qualification. Now, what can the prisoner at the bar for sentence expect? I don't know that a prisoner under such circumstances is entitled to very much consideration after all.

THE COURT (to the defendant): We don't want you to do impossible things, Mrs. Sanger, only the reasonable thing and that is to comply with this law as long as it remains the law. It is the law for you, it is the law for me, it is the law for all of us until it is changed; and you know what means and avenues are open to you to have it changed, and they are lawful ways. You may prosecute these methods, and no one can find fault with you. If you succeed in changing the law, well and good. If you fail, then you have to bow in submission to the majority rule.

MARGARET SANGER: It is just the chance, the opportunity to test it.

THE COURT: Very good. You have had your day in court; you advocated a cause, you were brought to the bar, you wanted to be tried here, you were judged, you didn't go on the stand and commit perjury in any sense, you took the facts and accepted them as true, and you are ready for judgment, even the worst. Now, we are prepared, however, under all the circumstances of this case, to be extremely lenient with you if you will tell us that you will respect this law and not violate it again.

MARGARET SANGER: I have given you my answer.

THE COURT: We don't want any qualifications. We are not concerned with the appeal.

MR. GOLDSTEIN: Just one other statement, your Honor, one final statement on my part. Your Honor did well say that you didn't want anything unreasonable. With all due deference to your Honor, to ask a person what her frame of mind will be with so many exigencies in future, that is, if the commission did nothing or the legislature did nothing—

THE COURT: All we are concerned about is this statute, and as long as it remains the law will this woman promise here and now unqualifiedly to respect it and obey it? Now, it is yes or no. What is your answer, Mrs. Sanger? Is it yes or no?

MARGARET SANGER: I can't respect the law as it stands today.

THE COURT: Margaret Sanger, there is evidence that you established and maintained a birth control clinic where you kept for sale and exhibition to various women articles which purported to be for the prevention of conception, and that there you made a determined effort to disseminate birth control information and advice. You have challenged the constitutionality of the law under consideration and the jurisdiction of this court. When this is done in an orderly way no one can find fault. It is your right as a citizen. . . . Refusal to obey the law becomes an open defiance of the rule of the majority. While the law is in its present form, defiance provokes anything but reasonable consideration. The judgment of the court is that you be confined to the workhouse for the period of thirty days.

DEBATE ON BIRTH CONTROL BETWEEN WINTER RUSSELL AND MARGARET SANGER (1921) [EXCERPT]

In this excerpt from a 1921 debate with Margaret Sanger, New York lawyer Winter Russell defends his anti–birth control stance. Instead of presenting arguments based on religion or the law, he describes the importance of sexual restraint in marriage and condemns the use of birth control as "race suicide."

Source: Debate on Birth Control: Mrs. Sanger and W. Russell and Shaw vs. Roosevelt on Birth Control. Edited by E. Haldeman-Julius. Girard, Kansas: Haldeman-Julius, 1921.

MR. RUSSELL: Ladies and gentlemen. I am very glad to have the opportunity of speaking to you this afternoon, and I may say at the outset that it is obvious that my adversary and I agree upon one thing, and that is that we are discussing what is absolutely the most vital question before the American people today. (Applause.) We are absolutely in accord on that, and we are just as far opposed in our method of approach as it is possible to be. . . .

I am not concerned with Scripture or authorities. I am going to deal with this question from what I believe are the cold, inevitable facts of life as we know them, and meet them every day.

Now I am going to admit in the first place that there are many families with too many children. It would be foolish to gainsay that. They are a burden to the mother. They are a hardship to the father who tries to provide for them. They make conditions unfair and unjust for the other children. The fact is, and I hope that she will admit it also, that there are thousands of homes in the United States of America that are too lacking in children—although I think she has once stated that the most immoral thing a person can do is to bring a large family into the world. Here we have the problem and the question is, how are we going to meet it?

I propose that we should meet this problem by the measure of self-control. I believe by this means we can solve it, and at the same time gain one of the greatest advantages you can possibly win on the face of the earth. Sex control is the best path to self-control and to self-discipline. It is the key to wisdom. It is the key to power. It is the key to intellectual and mental development; indeed, she has once stated that only those people who are mentally developed are capable of self-control and I want to say that they got a large measure of their mental development by self-control. She is looking through the wrong end of the telescope.

And so we come to this method. I want to say, as another part of the platform upon which I am to stand, that I conceive and hold marriage to be more than physical. It is not a purely sensual relationship. It borders on the aesthetic, spiritual, mental, and modern aspects of life, and when you try to take the physical by itself you find a condition of naked sensuality which is disastrous in the extreme.

My contentions are these: In the first place, fundamentally, universally, infinitely from every point of view, it is vicious. It is false from every scientific construction that you can possibly conceive of; it is one of the most vitiating things from every point of philosophy, physiology and psychology.

I believe it is disastrous intellectually, mentally, and spiritually. It is disastrous and perpetrates a great wrong upon the unborn millions who are waiting for entrance upon this great amphitheatre of life. It is disastrous physically, mentally, and spiritually upon the future. It is disastrous to the same degree upon the people who practice it—husbands and wives who resort to these measures. I hold that it perpetrates the greatest crime of all the ages, namely, race suicide. . . .

"THE CASE FOR BIRTH CONTROL" by Margaret Sanger (February 23, 1924)

Everywhere we look, we see poverty and large families going hand in hand. We see hordes of children whose parents cannot feed, clothe or educate even one-half of the number born to them. We see sick, harassed, broken mothers whose health and nerves cannot bear the strain of further childbearing. We see fathers growing despondent and desperate, because their labor cannot bring the necessary wage to keep their growing families. We see that those parents who are least fit to reproduce the race are having the largest number of children; while people of wealth, leisure and education are having small families.

It is generally concluded by sociologists and scientists that a nation cannot go on indefinitely multiplying without eventually reaching the point when population presses upon means of subsistence. While in this country there is perhaps no need for immediate alarm on this account, there are many other reasons for demanding Birth Control. At present, for the poor mother, there is only one alternative to the necessity of bearing children year after year, regardless of her health, of the welfare of the children she already has, and of the income of the family. This is alternative is abortion, which is so common as to be almost universal, especially where there are rigid laws against imparting information for the prevention of conception. It has been estimated that there are about one million abortions in the United States each year.

To force poor mothers to resort to this dangerous and health-destroying method of curtailing their families is cruel, wicked and heartless, and it is often the mothers who care most about the welfare of their children who are willing to undergo any pain or risk to prevent the coming of infants for whom they cannot properly care.

There are definite reasons when and why parents should not have children, which will conceded by most thoughtful people.

First.—Children should not be born when either parent has an inheritable disease, such as insanity, feeble-mindedness, epilepsy or syphilis.

Second.—When the mother is suffering from tuberculosis, kidney disease, heart disease or pelvic deformity.

Third.—When either parent has gonorrhea. This disease in the mother is the cause of ninety per cent of blindness in newborn babies.

Fourth.—When children already born are not normal, even though both parents are in good physical and mental condition.

Fifth.—Not until the woman is twenty-three years old and the man twenty-five.

Sixth.—Not until the previous baby is at least three years old. This gives a year to recover from the physical ordeal of the birth of the baby, a year to rest, be normal and enjoy her motherhood, and another year to prepare for the coming of the next.

We want mothers to be fit. We want them to conceive in joy and gladness. We want them to carry their babies during the nine months in a sound and healthy body and with a happy, joyous, hopeful mind. It is almost impossible to imagine the suffering caused to women, the mental agony they endure, when their days and nights are haunted by the fear of undesired pregnancy.

Seventh.—Children should not be born to parents whose economic circumstances do not guarantee enough to provide the children with the necessities of life.

A couple who can take care of two children and bring them up decently in health and comfort, give them an education and start them fairly in life, do more for their country and for mankind than the couple who recklessly reproduce ten or twelve children, some of them to die in infancy, others to survive but to enter the mill or factory at an early age, and all to sink to that level of degradation where charity, either state or private, is necessary to keep them alive. The man who cannot support three children should not have ten, notwithstanding all pleas of the militarists for numbers.

Eighth.—A woman should not bear children when exhausted from labor. This especially applies to women who marry after spending several years in industrial or commercial life. Conception should not take place until she is in good health and has overcome her fatigue.

Ninth.—Not for two years after marriage should a couple undertake the great responsibility of becoming parents. Thousands of young people enter marriage without the faintest idea of what marriage involves. They do not know its spiritual responsibilities. If children are born quickly and plentifully, people consider that the marriage is justified. I claim that this is barbaric and wrong. It is wrong for the wife, for the man, for the children.

It is impossible for two young people to really know each other until they have lived together in marriage. After the closeness and intimacy of that relation there often comes to the woman a rude awakening; the devoted lover becomes careless and dissatisfied. If she becomes pregnant immediately she becomes physically disturbed, nervous and irritable. The girl has changed, and the boy who knew her as a happy smiling sweetheart finds her disagreeable and disgruntled. Of course thousands of people learn to adjust themselves. Nevertheless, I maintain that young people should marry early and wait at least two years to adjust their own lives, to play and read together and to build up a cultural and spiritual friendship. Then will come the intense desire to call into being a little child to share their love and happiness. When children are conceived in love and born into an atmosphere of happiness, then

Sanger believed that birth control could advance public health and family stability. Published in The Woman Citizen *on February 23, 1924, her article "The Case for Birth Control" discusses nine reasons to practice contraception, stressing the importance of eliminating botched abortions and unwanted pregnancies.*

Source: Sanger, Margaret. "The Case for Birth Control." *The Woman Citizen,* February 23, 1924.

will parenthood be a glorious privilege, and the children will grow to resemble gods. This can only be obtained through the knowledge and practice of Birth Control.

P. S.—The American Birth Control League desires that the instruction in Birth Control should be given by the medical profession. Only through individual care and treatment can a woman be given the best and safest means of controlling her offspring. We do not favor the indiscriminate diffusion of unreliable and unsafe Birth Control advice.

LETTER TO MARGARET SANGER (January 5, 1925)

Englishtown, N. J.
January 5, 1925

Dear Mrs. Sanger

I received your pamphlet on family limitation. . . . I am 30 years old have been married 14 years and have 11 children the oldest 13 and the youngest one year. I have kidney and heart disease, and every one of my children is defictived and we are very poor. Now Mrs. Sanger can you please help me. I have miss a few weeks and I don't know how to bring myself around. I am so worred and I have cryed my self sick and if I dont come around I know I will go like my poor sister she went insane and died. My Doctor said I will surely go insane if I keep this up but I cant help it and the Doctor wont do anything for me. Oh Mrs. Sanger if I could tell you all the terrible things that I have been through with my babys and children you would know why I would rather die then have another one. Please help me just this once and I will be all right. Oh please I beg you. Please no one will ever know and I will be so happy and I will do anything in this world for you and your good work. Please please just this time. Doctors are men and have not had a baby so they have no pitty for a poor sick Mother. You are a Mother and you know so please pitty me and help me. Please Please.

Sincerely yours
[J.M.]

p.s. Please tell me how to get the pessary rubber womb cap. Not even the Doctors here know about them that is what thay tell me.

Countless desperate and impoverished women begged Sanger to help them prevent another unwanted pregnancy. This letter from January 5, 1925, exemplifies the adverse circumstances Sanger fought to eliminate by educating both the public and physicians on the need as well as the benefits of birth control. Note: Language and spelling from original document has been retained.

Source: Asbell, Bernard. *The Pill: A Biography of the Drug that Changed the World*. New York: Random House, 1995.

Alfred E. Smith

1873–1944

Democratic Party Politician

Alfred E. Smith was a Democratic Party politician who became a champion of urban politics as a four-term governor of New York and the first Roman Catholic to run for the presidency of the United States.

Alfred Emanuel Smith was born on December 30, 1873, in New York City's Lower East Side. Raised in an Irish Catholic family, Smith attended St. James Parochial School until age 14, when he dropped out of the eighth grade to provide for his widowed mother and sister. In 1895, after a series of odd jobs, he started working for the commissioner of jurors at Tammany Hall, the infamous home base of New York's Democratic Party, remembered both for its corrupt and autocratic politics and for its charity to New York's immigrants. Smith worked his way up the ladder, winning election to the state assembly as a Democratic Party representative in 1903; by 1907, he had earned recognition as a strong debater. Thanks to his oratorical skills and dedication to the community he was promoted to speaker of the Assembly in 1913. In these early years, Smith emerged as both a Tammany loyalist and progressive reformer, protecting political interests while also supporting social causes.

From the collections of the Library of Congress.

Respected for his knowledge of state government, Smith began making powerful contacts and rising in the political ranks. He served as sheriff of New York County between 1915 and 1917 and president of the New York City Board of Aldermen in 1918. That same year Smith successfully ran his first of five gubernatorial campaigns, defeating the Republican incumbent Governor Charles S. Whitman by a narrow margin. To promote his platform, he had organized the Independent Citizens' Committee for Alfred E. Smith— made up of distinguished politicians, reformers, and professionals, among them women and minorities. Smith's own ethnic background and acceptance of other religions and races appealed to many urban New Yorkers who admired his humane policies and shared similar immigrant experiences.

Although he lost his bid for reelection to the governorship in the 1920 Republican landslide, Smith reclaimed the office for three consecutive terms from 1923 until 1928. As governor, he led an efficient, progressive administration, restructuring state departments, reducing state expenditures, developing affordable housing, expanding the parks and recreation system, and vastly increasing funding for public healthcare and education. Smith also fought to improve factory conditions by supporting workmen's compensation, safety regulations, and protective labor laws for women and children. His legislative record strengthened his popularity throughout New York and the nation. During the **Calvin Coolidge** era of sober conservatism, Smith invigorated politics by confronting social abuses and implementing reforms.

During his second term, Smith's ambitions turned to becoming the president of the United States. The 1924 election, though, divided the Democratic Party between supporters of William Gibbs McAdoo, the rural-wing candidate, and Smith, the urban-wing candidate. Prohibition forces from the South and West in favor of the Eighteenth Amendment, which outlawed alcohol in the United States, backed the "dry" McAdoo, while Roman Catholic anti-Prohibition forces from the Northeast sided with the "wet" Smith. At the Democratic National Convention in New York City, a deadlock resulted when neither candidate gained the required two-thirds majority needed for nomination. After no decision had been reached on the 102nd ballot, McAdoo and Smith retired from the race, leading to the nomination of John W. Davis on the 103rd ballot. The final poll results in 1924 gave slightly over 8,000,000 votes to Davis and well over 15,000,000 to Coolidge.

With Democrats wanting to avoid repeating the mistakes of 1924, Smith easily received the nomination for the presidency in 1928, becoming the first Roman Catholic to run for the highest office in the United States. His close political adviser, Jewish-American reformer Belle Moskowitz, became his campaign manager. In an atmosphere of prejudice and intolerance, the possibility of a Roman Catholic president incited passionate debate. With the help of Moskowitz, Smith projected himself as a self-made man of honesty and integrity and campaigned on a platform promoting federal aid to farmers and laborers, the creation of public power plants, and the revision of the Eighteenth Amendment. Known as "The Happy Warrior," he spoke to voters with frank enthusiasm and played his famous theme song "The Sidewalks of New York," a tune that endeared him to voters on the East Coast but alienated him from the rest of the country.

Not only was his religious faith and big-city image brought to the forefront but also his anti-Prohibition stance and Tammany connections. During his 1918 gubernatorial race Smith had endured slanderous cheers such as "Rum, Romanism, and Rebellion," but now he faced the intense bigotry of the Ku Klux Klan, the white supremacist group. In addition to its prejudiced views of African Americans, the Klan also disliked Jews, Catholics, and immigrants. The Klan demonstrated its opposition to Smith by setting up burning crosses along the railroad tracks as Smith campaigned through Oklahoma and Montana. Beyond these direct signs of hostility, his election chances further narrowed as the public sought to retain the prosperity experienced under Republican leadership and policies. On election day, Republican Herbert Hoover beat Smith by 21,400,000 to 15,000,000 votes. Despite the loss, Smith won the country's 12 largest cities and the most votes of any previous Democratic candidate.

Disillusioned by the bigotry of the 1928 presidential election, Smith rejected politics and entered the business community. He became president of the Empire State Building Corporation and director of the County Trust Company, both of which experienced financial difficulties after the 1929 stock market crash. In the ensuing Great Depression (1929–39), a hardened Smith condemned President Franklin D. Roosevelt's New Deal and joined the anti-Roosevelt American Liberty League. Smith's disapproval of Roosevelt subsided with his support of Roosevelt's Neutrality Act and Lend-Lease proposals during World War II, and, in 1942, the two of them met at the White House. On October 4, 1944, Smith died in New York City.

Overcoming poverty and combating prejudice, Smith's four-term governorship of New York proved that class status and ethnic background need not predetermine future prospects. At the same time, his 1928 presidential campaign indicated that the United States was not the land of liberty and justice for all. Smith, the "wet" Irish Catholic, became an icon to immigrants but could achieve his goals only in limited regions and hope for greater national acceptance of all religions, races, and creeds in the future.

Renée Miller

For Further Reading

Handlin, Oscar. *Al Smith and His America*. Boston: Northeastern University Press, 1987.
Josephson, Matthew, and Hannah Josephson. *Al Smith: Hero of the Cities*. Boston: Houghton Mifflin Company, 1969.
Smith, Alfred E. *Up to Now: An Autobiography*. New York: Viking Press, 1929.
Slayton, Robert A. *Empire Statesman: the Rise and Redemption of Al Smith*. New York: Free Press, 2001.

NEW YORK STATE DEMOCRATIC CONVENTION ADDRESS by Alfred E. Smith (1924)

Smith was proud of his political record that signified his dedication to the people of New York. In this 1924 address at a State Democratic Convention, after thanking his party members for their efforts and his presidential nomination, Smith stresses that his first priority remains his work as governor.

Source: Moskowitz, Henry. *Alfred E. Smith: An American Career*. New York: Thomas Seltzer, 1924.

I want to take this opportunity at the first Democratic gathering I have had a chance to speak at in a long while to thank very sincerely and from the bottom of my heart the Democratic members of both houses of the Legislature, the Democratic State officers elected in 1922 and the heads of the great department of the State government. They have so conducted their offices that when your delegates elected here today or selected in the Congressional districts at the primary, go to the national convention, they will be able to look every other Democrat in United States squarely in the eye.

There is a record there that you will have abundant reason to be proud of, spelling it out, from beginning to end, it constitutes a record of unselfish devotion to the best interests of this State and of our people. You will have imposed upon you the duty of representing this State in the make-up of the National platform. Whatever else you do, insist on plain talk. The people of this country are worn out with this Court of Appeals language. So, what you want to say, say in understandable terms, say it so that the man on the street, the plain, ordinary man, can know what you promise to do; because if you intend to carry out the promise you don't

have to be the least bit afraid of how explicit you make it. Make it definite. Make it concrete. And make it to the point; and get away from qualifications. That is a Democratic platform, the only kind that ought to come out from a Democratic convention.

I want to step out of my character as Governor and have a personal word with you. I heard the resolution that you passed. In fact, I read it, before it came up here.

It would be a difficult task for any man to stand before an audience of this kind and be able to adequately express the appreciation he would have to feel for the great compliment, the great honor and the great distinction that comes to him to be spoken of as the choice of his party in the greatest State in the Union for the highest office in all the world.

If I were to tell you that I haven't heard anything on this particular subject for the last year, you wouldn't believe it, because it wouldn't be true. I have heard a great deal about it; but in the frankness that ought to exist among friends and comrades, together, let me say this to you: I have done absolutely nothing about it, either inside or outside the of the State, and I do not intend to do anything about it. The man who would not have an ambition for that office would have a dead heart. But I stand exactly in the position that I stood in on the floor of the Constitutional Convention in 1915, when I said that the man who used one office and neglected it in order to climb to a higher one was not deserving of the one he had.

I am going to do nothing about it, because there is nothing I can do. In the first place, I haven't got the means to do it. In the second place, I haven't got the time to do it. For the next thirty days I will be just as busy as any man could possibly be in the consideration of the nine hundred odd bills left for my attention in the Legislature. Then, within a reasonably short time, after five solid months, without a vacation, I will have to turn my attention to the administrative details of some of the departments of government.

This work I propose to do, right up to the time the convention starts. If I fell down on this job, I would never forgive myself and I would not ask forgiveness from any one else. If the required number of delegates in the National Convention takes your view of it, I will be honored beyond the power of expression to lead the forces of my party in the next campaign.

In conclusion, I want to leave just one thought with you. If my nomination is brought about, and it results in a triumph for the party, you can say to every delegate that you meet at the convention in New York City, that I promised you in the Capital City of this State before God Almighty Himself that neither they nor you will have any cause to regret any confidence they or you see fit to repose in me.

"HAVE A HEART!" POLITICAL CARTOON (c. 1920s)

A political cartoon, probably published in the Washington Star *in the 1920s, commenting on Congress's ruling on Prohibition, which outlawed the sale of alcohol in the United States. Smith's anti-Prohibition stance would play a major role in his political career during the 1920s.*

Source: From the collections of the Library of Congress.

"AN OPEN LETTER TO THE HONORABLE ALFRED E. SMITH" by Charles C. Marshall (1927) [EXCERPT]

Sir:—

The American people take pride in viewing the process of an American citizen from the humble estate in which his life began toward the highest office within the gift of the nation. It is for this reason that your candidacy for the Presidential nomination has stirred the enthusiasm of a great body of your fellow citizens. They know and rejoice in the hardship and the struggle which have fashioned you as a leader of men. They know your fidelity to the morality you have advocated in public and private life and to the religion you have revered; your great record of public trusts successfully and honestly discharged; your spirit of fair play, and justice to even your political opponents. Partisanship bids fair to quail before the challenge of your personal-

ity, and men who vote habitually against your party are pondering your candidacy with sincere respect; and yet—through all this tribute there is a note of doubt, a sinister accent of interrogation, not as to intentional rectitude and moral purpose, but as to certain conceptions which your fellow citizens attribute to you as a loyal and conscientious Roman Catholic, which in their minds are irreconcilable with that Constitution which as President you must support and defend, and with the principles of civil and religious liberty on which American institutions are based.

To this consideration no word of yours, or on your behalf, has yet been addressed. Its discussion in the interests of the public weal is obviously necessary, and yet a strange reticence avoids it, often with the unjust and

In an atmosphere of prejudice and intolerance, Smith became the first Roman Catholic to run for the presidency of the United States. "An Open Letter to the Honorable Alfred E. Smith," published by Charles C. Marshall in the April 1927 issue of the Atlantic Monthly, *shows the biased attitudes of the time and questions Smith's ability to separate his religious beliefs from his political duties.*

Source: Marshall, Charles C. "An Open Letter to the Honorable Alfred E. Smith." *Atlantic Monthly*, April 1927.

withering attribution of bigotry or prejudice as the unworthy motive of its introduction. Undoubtedly a large portion of the public would gladly avoid a subject the discussion of which is so unhappily associated with rancor and malevolence, and yet to avoid the subject is to neglect the profoundest interests in our national welfare.

American life has developed into a variety of religious beliefs and ethical systems, religious and nonreligious, whose claims press more and more upon public attention. None of these presents a more definite philosophy or makes a more positive demand upon the attention and reason of mankind than your venerable Church, which recently at Chicago, in the greatest religious demonstration that the world has ever seen, declared her presence and her power in American life. Is not the time ripe and the occasion opportune for a declaration, if it can be made, that shall clear away all doubt as to the reconcilability of her status and her claims with American constitutional principles? With such a statement the only question as to your proud eligibility to the Presidential office would disappear, and the doubts of your fellow citizens not of the Roman Catholic Church would be instantly resolved in your favor.

The conceptions to which we refer are not superficial. They are of the very life and being of that Church, determining its status and its relation to the State, and to the great masses of men whose convictions deny them the privilege of membership in that Church. Surely the more conscientious the Roman Catholic, and the more loyal to his Church, the more sincere and unqualified should be his acceptance of such conceptions. . . .

Furthermore, the doctrine of the Two Powers, in effect and theory, inevitably makes the Roman Catholic Church at times sovereign and paramount over the State. It is true that in theory the doctrine assigns to the secular State jurisdiction over secular matters and to the Roman Catholic Church jurisdiction over matters of faith and morals, each jurisdiction being exclusive of the other within undisputed lines. But the universal experience of mankind has demonstrated, and reason teaches, that many questions must arise between the State and the Roman Catholic Church in respect to which it is impossible to determine to the satisfaction of both in which jurisdiction the matter at issue lies.

Here arises the irrepressible conflict. Shall the State or the Roman Catholic Church determine? The Constitution of the United States clearly ordains that the State shall determine the question. The Roman Catholic Church demands for itself the sole right to determine it, and holds that within the limits of that claim it is superior to and supreme over the State. The *Catholic Encyclopedia* clearly so declares: 'In case of direct contradiction, making it impossible for both jurisdictions to be exercised, the jurisdiction of the Church prevails and that of the State is excluded.' And Pope Pius IX in the Syllabus asserted: 'To say in the case of conflicting laws enacted by the Two Powers, the civil law prevails, is error.'

Extreme as such a conclusion may appear, it is inevitable in Roman Catholic philosophy. That Church by the very theory of her existence cannot yield, because what she claims as her right and her truth she claims is hers by the 'direct act of God'; in her theory, God himself directly forbids. The State cannot yield because of a great mass of citizens who are not Roman Catholics. By its constitutional law and in the very nature of things, practices of religion in its opinion inconsistent with its peace and safety are unlawful; the law of its being—the law of necessity—forbids. If we could all concede the 'divine and exclusive' claims of the Roman Catholic Church, conflict would be eliminated: but, as it is, there is a wide consensus of opinion that those claims are false in fact and in flat conflict with the very being and order of the State. . . .

We have no desire to impute to the Roman Catholic Church aught but high and sincere motives in the assertion of her claims as one of the Two Powers. Her members believe in those claims, and so believing, it is their conscientious duty to stand for them. We are satisfied if they will but concede that those claims, unless modified and historically redressed, precipitate an inevitable conflict between the Roman Catholic Church and the American State irreconcilable with domestic peace. . . .

Nothing will be of greater satisfaction to those of your fellow citizens who hesitate in their endorsement of your candidacy because of the religious issues involved than such a disclaimer by you of the convictions here imputed, or such an exposition by others of the questions here presented, as may justly turn public opinion in your favor.

Yours with great respect,
CHARLES C. MARSHALL

"CATHOLIC AND PATRIOT: GOVERNOR SMITH REPLIES" by Alfred E. Smith (1927) [EXCERPT]

Responding to Charles C. Marshall's accusations, Smith published an article in the May 1927 issue of the Atlantic Monthly entitled, "Catholic and Patriot: Governor Smith Replies." Here, Smith defends his Roman Catholic faith and affirms his allegiance to the U.S. Constitution.

Dear Sir: —

In your open letter to me in the April *Atlantic Monthly* you 'impute' to American Catholics views which, if held by them, would leave open to question the loyalty and devotion to this country of more than twenty million American Catholic citizens. I am grateful to you for defining this issue in the open and for your courteous expression of the satisfaction it will bring to my fellow citizens for me to give 'a disclaimer of the convictions' thus imputed. Without mental reservation I can and do make that disclaimer. These convictions are neither held by me nor by any other American Catholic, as far as I know. Before answering the argument of your letter, however, I must dispose of one of its implications. You put your questions to me in connection with my candidacy for the office of President of the United States. My attitude with respect to that candidacy was fully stated in my last inaugural address as Governor, when on January 1, 1927, I said:

'I have no idea what the future has in store for me. Everyone else in the United States has some notion about it except myself. No man could stand before this intelligent gathering and say that he was not receptive to the greatest position the world has to give anyone.

But I can say this, that I will do nothing to achieve it except to give to the people of the State the kind and character of service that will make me deserve it.'

I should be a poor American and a poor Catholic alike if I injected religious discussion into a political campaign. Therefore I would ask you to accept this answer from me not as a candidate for any public office but as an American citizen, honored with high elective office, meeting a challenge to his patriotism and his intellectual integrity. Moreover, I call your attention to the fact that I am only a layman. The *Atlantic Monthly* describes you as 'an experienced attorney' who 'has made himself an authority upon canon law.' I am neither a lawyer nor a theologian. What knowledge of law I have was gained in the course of my long experience in the Legislature and as Chief Executive of New York State. I had no such opportunity to study theology.

My first thought was to answer you with just the faith that is in me. But I knew instinctively that your conclusions could be logically proved false. It seemed right, therefore, to take counsel with someone schooled in the Church law, from whom I learned whatever is here set forth in definite answer to the theological questions you raise. I selected one whose patriotism neither you nor any other man will question. He wears upon his breast the Distinguished Service Cross of our country, its Distinguished Service Medal, the Ribbon of the Legion of Honor, and the Croix de Guerre with Palm of the French Republic. He was the Catholic Chaplain of the almost wholly Catholic 165th Regiment in the World War—Father Francis P. Duffy, now in the military service of my own State.

Taking your letter as a whole and reducing it to commonplace English, you imply that there is a conflict between religious loyalty to the Catholic faith and patriotic loyalty to the United States. Everything that has actually happened to me during my long public career leads me to know that no such thing as that is true. I have taken an oath of office in this state nineteen times. Each time I swore to defend and maintain the Constitution of the United States. All of this represents a period of public service in elective office almost continuous since 1903. I have never known any conflict between my official duties and my religious beliefs. No such conflict could exist. Certainly the people of this State recognize no such conflict. They have testified to my devotion to public duty be electing me to the highest office within their gift four times. You yourself do me the honor, in addressing me, to refer to 'your fidelity to the morality you have advocated in public and private life and to the religion you have revered; your great record of public trusts successfully and honestly discharged.' During the years I have discharged those trusts I have been a communicant of the Roman Catholic Church. If there were conflict, I, of all men, could not have escaped it, because I have not been a silent man, but a battler for political and social reform. These battles would in their very nature disclose this conflict if there were any.

I regard public education as one of the foremost functions of government and I have supported to the last degree the State Department of Education in every effort to promote our public school system. The largest single item of increased appropriations under my administration appears in the educational group for the support of common schools. Since 1919, when I first became Governor, this item has grown from $9,000,000 to $82,500,000. My aim—and I may say I have succeeded in achieving it—has been legislation for child welfare, the protection of working men, women, and children, the modernization of the State's institutions for the care of helpless or unfortunate wards, the preservation of freedom of speech and opinion against the attack of war-time hysteria, and the complete reorganization of the structure of government of the State.

I did not struggle for these things for any single element, but in the interest of all of the eleven million people who make up the State. In all of this work I had the support of churches of all denominations. I probably know as many ecclesiastics of my Church as any other layman. During my long and active public career I never received from any of them anything except cooperation and encouragement in full and complete discharge of my duty to the State. Moreover, I am unable to understand how anything that I was taught to believe as a Catholic could possibly be in conflict with what is good citizenship. The essence of my faith is built upon the Commandments of God. The law of the land is built upon the Commandments of God. There can be no conflict between them. . . .

I summarize my creed as an American Catholic. I believe in the worship of God according to the faith and practice of the Roman Catholic Church. I recognize no power in the institutions of my Church to interfere with the operations of the Constitution of the United States or the enforcement of the law of the land. I believe in absolute freedom of conscience for all men and in equality of all churches, all sects, and all beliefs before the law as a matter of right and not as a matter of favor. I believe in the absolute separation of Church and State and in the strict enforcement of the provisions of the Constitution that Congress shall make no law respecting an establishment of religion or preventing the free exercise thereof. I believe that no tribunal of any church has any power to make any decree of any force in the law of the land, other than to establish the status of its own communicants within its own church. I believe in the support of the public school as one of the corner stones of American liberty. I believe in the right of every parent to choose whether his child shall be educated in a public school or in a religious school supported by those of his own faith. I believe in the principle of noninterference by this country in the internal affairs of other nations and that we should stand steadfastly against any such interference by whomsoever it may be urged. And I believe in the common brotherhood of man under the common fatherhood of God.

In this spirit I join with my fellow Americans of all creeds in a fervent prayer that never again in this land will any public servant be challenged because of the faith in which he has tried to walk humbly with his God.

Very truly yours,
ALFRED E. SMITH

Source: Smith, Alfred E. "Catholic and Patriot: Governor Smith Replies." *Atlantic Monthly,* May 1927.

Bessie Smith

1894–1937
Blues Vocalist

Known as "The Empress of the Blues," Bessie Smith thrilled audiences of the 1920s with her commanding stage performances and recordings. A true star, one of the first to emerge in the field of African-American music, she influenced countless later performers.

Born Elizabeth Smith in Chattanooga, Tennessee, on April 15, 1894, Smith grew up poor. She worked her way up through the world of small-time minstrel and medicine shows, first as a dancer and then as a singer. She met Gertrude "Ma" Rainey, the pioneer of the female vaudeville blues, in the early 1910s and, like many other singers, was inspired by her. By the end of the decade Smith was regularly headlining shows on the vaudeville circuit for the TOBA (Theater Owners' Booking Association, or, as it was informally known, "Tough on Black Artists"). From very early on, Smith was a compelling performer on stage, captivating audiences with her charisma and vocal power. Often refusing to use a microphone, she could be heard all through a large auditorium.

From 1920 on, recordings of blues vocalists were made and marketed in the category of "race records," and these recordings broadened Smith's reach beyond the vaudeville circuit. Her first recording, 1923's "Down Hearted Blues," sold an estimated 780,000 copies; during this period Smith's popularity did much to revive the sagging fortunes of her record company, Columbia. Smith's recordings joined her with such leading jazz instrumentalists as pianist James P. Johnson (who played on her 1927 "Back Water Blues," her best-known recording in her own time) and, most famously of all, trumpeter Louis Armstrong. The recordings on which Smith and Armstrong worked included the famous 1925 "St. Louis Blues," which elevated that familiar set of blues verses into a masterpiece of dignified sadness. In her performances and recordings with jazz musicians, Smith showed technical control over her voice as well as sheer power.

Her popularity also stemmed not just from charisma but from vocal versatility, which was her way of infusing deep

From the collections of the Library of Congress.

emotion into whatever she sang and which provided inspiration for the many performers who followed her. Known best for slow, tragic blues, Smith also excelled with the Saturday-night spirit of "Gimme a Pigfoot," recorded in 1933; she likewise offered rhythmically sharp interpretations of popular songs of the day such as Irving Berlin's "Alexander's Ragtime Band," which she recorded in 1927.

Smith perhaps made as much of an impression with her flamboyant personal style as with her music. She purchased her own railroad car and traveled from city to city in it with her retinue; for African-American audiences this mode of transport suggested not only luxury but also an escape from the humiliating segregation of public accommodations that they had to endure daily. At the height of her career in the 1920s Smith's sold-out shows required major crowd-control efforts from city police departments. Smith was the first African-American woman who became a true big-city marquee headliner, and, as such, she had an immense impact in her own lifetime. Her peak weekly earnings of $2,000 transformed the blues, in the minds of African Americans and others, from an indigenous folk music to a powerful commercial force.

Smith made a short film, *St. Louis Blues,* in 1929, but the sudden popularity of sound movies along with the deepening Great Depression (1929–39) made it difficult for the record companies to sell records. A disastrous marriage and her abuse of alcohol made things worse. Several leading swing bandleaders and blues aficionados of the 1930s recognized Smith's talent, and she seemed on the verge of a comeback when she died in an auto crash in Clarksdale, Mississippi, on September 26, 1937. Legends sprang up around her: it was said that Ma Rainey had kidnapped her to mold her talents, and that she died because a whites-only Mississippi hospital refused her admittance after her fatal accident. Both tales are questionable, but they testify to the sheer power that Smith held in the imagination of the public that remembered her long after her death.

Bessie Smith helped bring the blues from the streets and tent shows of the South to theaters all over the country, making it into a vehicle for powerful artistry. In a prosperous era, she served notice that African Americans wanted their piece of the American Dream.

James M. Manheim

For Further Reading

Albertson, Chris. *Bessie Smith: Empress of the Blues.* New York: Schirmer, 1975.

Grimes, Sara. *Back Water Blues: In Search of Bessie Smith.* Amherst, Mass.: Rose Island Publishing, 2001.

Harrison, Daphne Duval. *Black Pearls: Blues Queens of the 1920s.* New Brunswick, N.J.: Rutgers University Press, 1988.

Kay, Jackie. *Bessie Smith.* New York: Absolute, 1997.

PUBLICITY PHOTO OF BESSIE SMITH (1923)

Over the course of her career, Smith's stage attire vacillated between a simpler look and an image of over-the-top luxury. This 1923 publicity shot captures something of the sense of humor that animated several of Smith's best songs.
Source: ©Bettmann/ Corbis.

"Singer Began at Seven Years Old" by Mabel Chew (March 27, 1926)

In the Baltimore Afro-American, *Mabel Chew presents a brief overview of Smith's early career performing in tent shows and cabarets and commends Smith on her hard work and humble demeanor.*

Source: Bessie Smith, "Singer Began at Seven Years Old," interview by Mabel Chew, *Baltimore Afro-American,* March 27, 1926. Reprinted by permission of GRM Associates, Inc., agents for the *Baltimore Afro-American.* ©1926 by the *Baltimore Afro-American.*

Bessie Smith, star of the Harlem Follies and nationally known Blues singer, playing at the Royal this week is a likeable person. She is not "upstage" in manner, nor has she forgotten her struggles before she became famous.

Miss Smith says her greatest ambition now is to carry her marvelous voice into the small towns and villages so that young people of our race may be inspired to use their talent and develop themselves.

BEGAN AT SEVEN

Since she was seven years old, Miss Smith has been singing. In tent shows, cabarets and small offerings, although her success seemed to come overnight. Miss Smith said it was really the culmination of years of gruelling work.

From the time when the now famous "Ma" Rainey, the oldest blues singer on the stage of a big amusement park in Chattanooga, Tenn., her home town, where she

proceded to cry all over the place, Miss Smith has travelled hard and far. She has known what it means to work for ten dollars a week and "find" yourself and now, she told me, her show grosses $2,500 a week.

ORGANIZES TENT SHOW

In order to realize her ambition to spread her wonderful success Miss Smith and her manager-husband, Jack Gee, plan to work the tent Circuit this summer. Miss Smith might best be described as buxom. Her clothes are made and fitted well, and together with her smooth brown skin, which is not rouged, she presents a very attractive appearance.

ARTIST IS LIKEABLE

She received me with true Southern hospitality and so pleasant was our chat that she asked me to come again, and talk to her. I certainly enjoyed our conversation and her approachability and kindly simplicity.

Columbia Records Poster Advertising "Race Records" (1928)

In the 1920s, recordings of blues vocalists were marketed in the category of "race records," as seen here in this 1928 Columbia Records poster. These recordings broadened Smith's (center photo) reach beyond the vaudeville circuit.

Source: Driggs Collection, Archive Photos.

Gertrude Stein

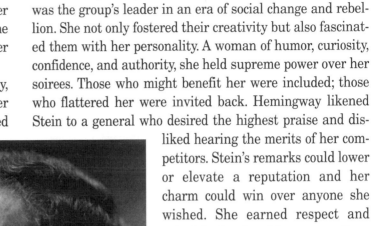

Gertrude Stein was an avant-garde American writer known for her eccentric personality and literary style, as well as her association with other experimental artists and writers. In the 1920s, her work pioneered new modes of expression and her image personified a new generation of thought and values.

Stein was born on February 3, 1874, in Allegheny, Pennsylvania, to German-Jewish immigrants. Although her first four years were spent in Vienna and Paris, she lived most of her childhood in Oakland, California. At 18 she entered Harvard Annex (now Radcliffe College) in Cambridge, where she studied under psychologist William James and developed an interest in philosophy and writing. In 1903, she settled at 27, rue de Fleurus in Paris with her brother Leo, a student of modern art, and started collecting contemporary paintings. Soon their apartment turned into a gathering place for avant-garde artists and intellectuals such as Henri Matisse, Juan Gris, and Pablo Picasso. Stein's relationship with revolutionary creators and thinkers strongly influenced her writing. Her first book, *Three Lives* (1909), reflected the psychological teachings of James, and her poetry collection, *Tender Buttons* (1914), simulated the techniques of abstract art.

During World War I, she continued to experiment with language and, with the help of her live-in companion, Alice B. Toklas, attempted to find publishers for her growing body of work. Toklas became key to Stein's development. She read, typed, and critiqued Stein's manuscripts as well as understood them and supported Stein's work. Together, they also aided the American Friends of the French Wounded, for which they received the Medal of French Recognition in 1918. After the war, they returned to the famous Paris apartment to host a new group of expatriate writers. Stein dubbed this literary circle, which included Sherwood Anderson, **F. Scott Fitzgerald**, and **Ernest Hemingway**, the Lost Generation due to their disillusionment with the war and rejection of mainstream culture. Moved by Stein's phrase, Hemingway quoted her in an epigraph to his first novel, *The Sun Also Rises* (1926): "You are all a lost generation."

From the collections of the Library of Congress.

In turn, Stein, considered the "Mother of Modernism," was the group's leader in an era of social change and rebellion. She not only fostered their creativity but also fascinated them with her personality. A woman of humor, curiosity, confidence, and authority, she held supreme power over her soirees. Those who might benefit her were included; those who flattered her were invited back. Hemingway likened Stein to a general who desired the highest praise and disliked hearing the merits of her competitors. Stein's remarks could lower or elevate a reputation and her charm could win over anyone she wished. She earned respect and notoriety by breaking conventions with her lifestyle and literature. Whether in her choice of a life partner or a writing style, Stein paved her own path, leaving behind the standards of the Victorian era.

Despite her admirers, Stein achieved little commercial success. Publishers and critics dismissed her experimental writings as ludicrous and incomprehensible, frequently comparing them to Cubism, a school of painting that favored abstract forms over realistic representation. In 1922, with the release of *Geography and Plays,* she reinforced her image as a radical and enigmatic literary figure of the interwar period. This collection of short pieces—filled with puns, repetitions, and rhythmic phrases—introduced her most memorable line in the poem "Sacred Emily": "Rose is a rose is a rose is a rose." In America and Paris, these words evolved as a catchphrase for her work and captured the essence of Modernism, a literary movement from the post–World War I period that rejected the optimism and realism of nineteenth-century authors and proposed alternative forms of expression, such as nonlinear narratives and fragmented language.

Stein's 1925 publication, *The Making of Americans,* marked a milestone in her career. Opening with her family history, over the course of 925 pages the novel develops into a history of the entire human race. Characteristic of her work, it contains minimal punctuation and no dialogue or action. Stein believed that narration could not convey the complexity of human nature and, therefore, she used description to create what she called "a continuous present." Stein as well as some contemporaries and critics perceived this book as a masterpiece moving profoundly beyond nineteenth-century fiction and characterizing distinctly modern literature. Once again, though, sales were poor and recognition was limited.

Some of the appreciation Stein longed for came after her 1926 lecture, "Composition as Explanation," delivered to the Oxford and Cambridge literary societies. For the first time, she attempted to publicly explain her writing. Her discussion focused on the importance of expressing "the modern composition" in the present and stressed that her Modernist process was a natural progression for the time period. Stein likewise commented that her art remained too peculiar for the majority to accept as classic and would gain significance only after her era had passed, an assertion illustrating her arrogance and confidence. This address, published that same year, had a deep impact on the literary world. Oxford and Cambridge professors began visiting her studio, and imitations of her style began appearing in literary magazines.

By the end of the 1920s, Stein was well known as a leader in modern literature, but monetary success arrived only after her 1933 bestseller *The Autobiography of Alice B. Toklas*. The witty title reflects Stein's departure from the traditional autobiography by presenting it from Toklas's point of view. Written in accessible language, the book details the art world following World War I and characterizes the people who gathered at the rue de Fleurus apartment. Its popularity led to a lecture tour in the United States, where Stein attended the New York performance of her opera *Four Saints in Three Acts*, for which she wrote the words. The 1937 sequel, *Everybody's Autobiography*, recounts this six-month visit.

Stein remained with Toklas in France and continued to write until her death. World War II forced them to move from Paris to Culoz, an unoccupied village in France where they escaped persecution as Jews. Following the liberation of Paris in 1944, they returned to the city. In 1946, Stein published *Brewsie and Willie*, a book honoring the American GIs, and finished the words for *The Mother of Us All*, an opera loosely based on Susan B. Anthony. The latter was her last completed work before dying of cancer on July 27, 1946.

Stein's emergence as a mentor of Modernism in the 1920s made her a legend in her own time. Her celebrity status equaled, even transcended, her literary reputation. The Lost Generation looked to her for guidance as she shaped modern literature with innovative sounds and rhythms and unconventional meaning and grammar. More important, she intrigued them with her individualism as she defied Victorian notions of female decorum and became a guiding light in a transformative era.

Renée Miller

For Further Reading

Hobhouse, Janet. *Everybody Who Was Anybody: A Biography of Gertrude Stein.* New York: G. P. Putnam's Sons, 1975.

Stein, Gertrude. *The Autobiography of Alice B. Toklas.* 1933. Reprint, New York: Modern Library, 1980.

———. *The Making of Americans: Being a History of a Family's Progress.* c. 1925. Reprint, Fort Washington, Penn.: Dalkey Archive Press, 1995.

———. *A Stein Reader.* Edited by Ulla E. Dydo. Evanston, Ill.: Northwestern University Press, 1993.

PORTRAIT OF GERTRUDE STEIN by Pablo Picasso (1906)

Pablo Picasso painted this portrait of Stein during the period of her first soirees at the rue de Fleurus salon, marking her emergence as a central figure among the Paris Modernists. In 1927, after she cut her hair like the Duchesse de Clermont-Tonnerre, Picasso felt that Stein's change in image would violate the timelessness of his portrait. The painting, however, remains one of his most famous. Today it hangs at the Metropolitan Museum of Art, bequeathed by Stein in 1946.

Source: ©2001 Estate of Pablo Picasso/Artists Rights Society (ARS), New York.

"Susie Asado" by Gertrude Stein (1922)

Sweet sweet sweet sweet sweet tea.
   Susie Asado.
Sweet sweet sweet sweet sweet tea.
Susie Asado.
Susie Asado which is a told tray sure.
A lean on the shoe this means slips slips hers.
When the ancient light grey is clean it is yellow, it
is a silver seller.
   This is a please this is a please there are the saids
to jelly. These are the wets these say the sets to leave
a crown to Incy.
   Incy is short for incubus.
   A pot. A pot is a beginning of a rare bit of trees.
Trees tremble, the old vats are in bobbles, bobbles which
shade and shove and render clean, render clean must.
         Drink pups.
   Drink pups drink pups lease a sash hold, see it shine
and a bobolink has pins. It shows a nail.
   What is a nail. A nail is unison,
Sweet sweet sweet sweet sweet tea.

Inspired by the flamenco dancer "La Argentina," who Stein and Toklas admired on a trip to Spain, this portrait-poem represents the richness of lyrical puns and repetitions in her 1922 Geography and Plays.

Source: Stein, Gertrude. *Geography and Plays.* With an introduction by Cyrena N. Pondrom. Madison: University of Wisconsin Press, 1993.

"Composition as Explanation" by Gertrude Stein (1926) [Excerpt]

. . . No one is ahead of his time, it is only that the particular variety of creating his time is the one that his contemporaries who also are creating their own time refuse to accept. And they refuse to accept it for a very simple reason and that is that they do not have to accept it for any reason. They themselves that is everybody in their entering the modern composition and they do enter it, if they do not enter it they are not so to speak in it they are out of it and so they do enter it. But in as you may say the non-competitive efforts where if you are not in it nothing is lost except nothing at all except what is not bad, there are naturally all the refusals, and the things refused are only important if unexpectedly somebody happens to need them. In the case of the arts it is very definite. Those who are creating the modern composition authentically are naturally only of importance when they are dead because by that time the modern composition having become past is classified and the description of it is classical. That is the reason why the creator of the new composition in the arts is an outlaw until he is a classic, there is hardly a moment in between and it is really too bad very much too bad naturally for the creator but also very much too bad for the enjoyer, they all really would enjoy the created so much better just after it has been made than when it is already a classic, but it is perfectly simple that there is no reason why the contemporaries should see, because it would not make any difference as they lead their lives in the new composition anyway, and as every one is naturally indolent why naturally they don't see. For this reason as in quoting Lord Grey it is quite certain that nations not actively threatened are at least several generations behind themselves and it is very much too bad, it is so very much more exciting and satisfactory for everybody if one can have contemporaries, if all one's contemporaries could be one's contemporaries.

There is almost not an interval.

For a very long time everybody refuses and then almost without a pause almost everybody accepts. In the history of the refused in the arts and literature the rapidity of the change is always startling. Now the only difficulty with the *volte-face* concerning the arts is this. When the acceptance comes, by that acceptance the thing created becomes a classic. It is a natural phenomena a rather extraordinary natural phenomena that a thing accepted becomes a classic. And what is the characteristic quality of a classic. The characteristic quality of a classic is that it is beautiful. Now of course it is perfectly true that a more or less first rate work of art is beautiful but the trouble is that when that first rate work of art becomes a classic because it is accepted the only thing that is important from then on to the majority of the acceptors the enormous majority, the most intelligent majority of the acceptors is that it is so wonderfully beautiful. Of course it is wonderfully beautiful, only when it is still a thing irritating annoying stimulating then all quality of beauty is denied to it.

Of course it is beautiful but first all beauty in it is denied and then all the beauty of it is accepted. If every one were not so indolent they would realise that beauty is beauty even when it is irritating and stimulating not only when it is accepted and classic. Of course it is extremely difficult nothing more so than to remember back to its not being beautiful once it has become beautiful. This makes it so much more difficult to realise its beauty when the work is being refused and prevents every one from realising that they were convinced that beauty was denied, once the work is accepted. Automatically with the acceptance of the time-sense comes the recognition of the beauty and once the beauty is accepted the beauty never fails any one. . . .

In 1926, at the Oxford and Cambridge literary societies, Stein delivered this lecture on her specific writing process and general thinking about contemporary art. In this excerpt, she discusses her theories on the role of the artist in society. Making a significant impression, she finally received some of the recognition she so desired with the publication of her speech that same year and an outpouring of admirers and imitators.

Source: Stein, Gertrude. *A Stein Reader.* Edited by Ulla E. Dydo. Evanston, Ill.: Northwestern University Press, 1993.

"EVERYBODY IS A REAL ONE" by Katherine Anne Porter (JANUARY 16, 1927) [EXCERPT]

"Everybody Is a Real One" by Katherine Anne Porter, originally published in the New York Herald Tribune *in 1927, was one of the first favorable reviews from the United States of* The Making of Americans. *In the opening, the essay notes Stein's legendary reputation and contribution to a new generation of writers who view her as "the combination of tribal wise woman and arch-priestess of aesthetic." From there, Porter commends the book and compares reading it to walking through a spiral—an effect Stein called "a continuous present."*

Source: Critical Essays on Gertrude Stein. Compiled by Michael J. Hoffman. Boston, Mass.: G. K. Hall, 1986. Originally published in the New York Herald Tribune, *January 16, 1927. ©1927 New York Herald Tribune Inc. All Rights Reserved. Reproduced by permission.*

All I know about Gertrude Stein is what I find in her first two books, *Three Lives* and *The Making of Americans*. Many persons know her, they tell amusing stories about her and festoon her with legends. Next to James Joyce she is the great influence on the younger literary generation, who see in her the combination of tribal wise woman and arch-priestess of aesthetic.

This is all very well; but I can go only by what I find in these pages. They form not so much a history of Americans as a full description and analysis of many human beings, including Gertrude Stein and the reader and all the reader's friends; they make a psychological source book and the diary of an aesthetic problem worked out momently under your eyes.

One of the many interesting things about *The Making of Americans* is its date. It was written twenty years ago (1906–1908), when Gertrude Stein was young. It precedes the war and cubism; it precedes *Ulysses* and *Remembrance of Things Past*. I doubt if all the people who should read it will read it for a great while yet, for it is in such a limited edition, and reading it is anyhow a sort of permanent occupation. Yet to shorten it would be to mutilate its vitals, and it is a very necessary book. In spite of all there is in it Gertrude Stein promises all the way through it to write another even longer and put in it all the things she left unfinished in this. She has not done it yet; at least it has not been published.

Twenty years ago, when she had been living in Paris only a few years, Gertrude Stein's memory of her American life was fresh, and I think both painful and happy in her. "The old people in a new world, the new people made out of the old, that is the story that I mean to tell, for that is what really is and what I really know." This is a deeply American book, and without "movies" or automobiles or radio or prohibition or any of the mechanical properties for making local color, it is a very up-to-date book. We feel in it the vitality and hope of the first generation, the hearty materialism of the second, the vagueness of the third. It is all realized and projected in these hundreds of portraits, the deathlike monotony in action, the blind diffusion of effort, "the spare American emotion," "the feeling of rich American living"—rich meaning money, of course—the billion times repeated effort of being born and breathing and eating and sleeping and working and feeling and dying to no particular end that makes American middle-class life. We have almost no other class as yet. "I say vital singularity is as yet an unknown product with us." So she observes the lack of it and concerns herself with the endless repetition of pattern in us only a little changed each time, but changed enough to make an endless mystery of each individual man and woman.

In beginning this book you walk into what seems to be a great spiral, a slow, ever-widening, unmeasured spiral unrolling itself horizontally. The people in this world appear to be motionless at every stage of their progress, each one is simultaneously being born, arriving at all ages and dying. You perceive that it is a world without mobility, everything takes place, has taken place, will take place; therefore nothing takes place, all at once. Yet the illusion of movement persists, the spiral unrolls, you follow; a closed spinning circle is even more hopeless than a universe that will not move. Then you discover it is not a circle, not machinelike repetition, the spiral does open and widen, it is repetition only in the sense that one wave follows upon another. The emotion progresses with the effort of a giant parturition. Gertrude Stein describes her function in terms of digestion, of childbirth: all these people, these fragments of digested knowledge, are in her, they must come out.

The progress of her family, then, this making of Americans, she has labored to record in a catalogue of human attributes, acts and emotions. Episodes are nothing, narrative is by the way, her interest lies in what she calls the bottom nature of men and women, all men, all women. "It is important to me, very important indeed to me, that I sometimes understand every one. . . . I am hoping some time to be right about every one, about everything."

In this intensity of preoccupation there is the microscopic observation of the near-sighted who must get so close to their object they depend not alone on vision but on touch and smell and the very warmth of bodies to give them the knowledge they seek. This nearness, this immediacy, she communicates also, there is no escaping into the future nor into the past. All time is in the present, these people are "being living," she makes you no gift of comfortable ripened events past and gone. "I am writing everything as I am learning everything," and so we have lists of qualities and defects, portraits of persons in scraps, with bits and pieces added again and again in every round of the spiral; they repeat and repeat themselves to you endlessly as living persons do, and always you feel you know them, and always they present a new bit of themselves.

Gertrude Stein reminds me of Jacob Boehme in the way she sees essentials in human beings. He knew them as salt, as mercury; as moist, as dry, as burning; as bitter, sweet or sour. She perceives them as attacking, as resisting, as dependent independent, as having a core of wood, of mud, as murky, engulfing; Boehme's chemical formulas are too abstract, she knows the substances of man are mixed with clay. Materials interest her, the moral content of man can often be nicely compared to homely workable stuff. Sometimes her examination is almost housewifely, she rolls a fabric under her fingers, tests it. It is thus and so. I find this very good, very interesting. "It will repay good using."

"In writing a word must be for me really an existing thing." Her efforts to get at the roots of existing life, to create fresh life from them, give her words a dark liquid flowingness, like the murmur of the blood. She does not strain words or invent them. Many words have retained their original meaning for her, she uses them simply. Good means good and bad means bad—next to the Jews the Americans are the most moralistic people, and Gertrude Stein is American Jew, a combination which by no means lessens the like quality in both. Good and bad are attributes to her, strength and weakness are real things that live inside people, she looks for these things, notes them in their likenesses and differences. She loves the difficult virtues, she is tender toward good people, she has faith in them.

An odd thing happens somewhere in the middle of the book. You will come upon it suddenly and it will surprise you. All along you have had a feeling of submergence in the hidden lives of a great many people, and unaccountably you will find yourself rolling up the surface, on the outer edge of the curve. A disconcerting break into narrative full of phrases that might have come out of any careless sentimental novel, alternates with scraps of the natural style. It is astounding, you

read on out of chagrin. Again without warning you submerge, and later Miss Stein explains she was copying an old piece of writing of which she is now ashamed, the words mean nothing: "I commence again with words that have meaning, " she says, and we leave this limp, dead spot in the middle of the book.

Gertrude Stein wrote once of Juan Gris that he was, somehow, saved. She is saved, too; she is free of pride and humility, she confesses to superhuman aspirations simply, she was badly frightened once and has recovered, she is honest in her uncertainties. There are only a few bits of absolute knowledge in the world, people can learn only one or two fundamental facts about each other, the rest is decoration and prejudice. She is very free from decoration and prejudice.

"Tests for Counterfeit in the Arts" by Wyndham Lewis (1927)

In the beginning was the Word should rather be, *in the beginning was Time*, according to Miss Stein (as also according to Bergson, Prof. Alexander, Einstein, Whitehead, Minkowski, etc. etc.) And she is one of the most eminent writers of what I have described as our *musical society*; that is our time-society, the highly-intellectualized High-Bohemia.

> In the beginning there was the time in the composition that naturally was in the composition but time in the composition comes now and this is what is now troubling every one the time in the composition is now a part of distribution and equilibration.

In Miss Stein's composition there is above all *time*, she tells us as best she can. As best she can, as you see; for she is not able to tell us this is or anything else clearly and simply; first of all because a time-obsession, it seems interferes, so we are given to understand. The other reason is that she is not simple at all, although she writes usually so like a child—like a confused, stammering, rather "soft" (bloated, acromegalic, squinting and spectacled, one can figure it as) child. Miss Stein, you might innocently suppose from her naïf stuttering to be, if not a child, simple, at least, in spite of maturity. But that is not so; though, strangely enough, she would like it to be thought that it is. That is only the old story of people wanting to be things they are not; or else, either as strategy or out of pure caprice, enjoying any disguise that reverses and contradicts the personality.

Composition as Explanation is a little pamphlet just published by the Hogarth Press. In it you have the announcement that "The time of the composition is the time of the composition." But simple as that sounds, it is only roguishness on the part of its authoress, all the while. That is her fun only. She is just pretending, with a face of solemn humbug, not to be able to get out the word; what this verbal inhibition results in is something *funny*, that will make you laugh. It is a form of clowning, in short; she will disarm and capture you by her absurdity.

But *Time*, you are told, is at the bottom of the matter; though that you could have guessed, since it has

been so for a very long time, from the beginning of the present period; from the birth of Bergson, shall we say? (Bergson was supposed by all of us to be dead, but Relativity, oddly enough at first sight, has recently resuscitated him; for the *time-spacer* has turned out to be the old-timer, or timist, after all.)

Miss Stein announces her time-doctrine in character, as it were. She gives you an "explanation," and illustrations, side by side; but the explanation is done in the same way as the examples that follow it. A further "explanation" would be required of the "explanation," and so on. And in that little, perhaps unregarded, fact, we have, I believe, one of the clues to this writer's mind. It tells us that her mind is a sham, to some extent.

In doing her "explanation" of her compositions in the same manner as her compositions (examples of which she gives), she is definitely making-believe that it is impossible for her to write in any other way. She is making a claim, in fact, that suggests a lack of candour on her part; and she is making it with an air of exaggerated candour. Supposing that the following line represented a typical composition of yours: –

FugfuggFFF-fewg:fugfug-Fug-fugue-fffffffuuuuuuG
Supposing, having become celebrated for that, you responded to a desire on the part of the public to know what you were driving at. Then the public would be justified in estimating your sincerity of a higher order if you sat down and tried to "explain" according to the canons of plain speech (no doubt employed by you in ordering your dinner, or telling the neighbouring newsagent to send you the *Herald, Tribune,* or *Daily Express* every morning), your verbal experiments, than if you affected to be unable to use that kind of speech at all.

Every painter who has experimented in abstract design, for example, has often been put into that situation; he must often have been asked the familiar question: "But do you really *see* things like that, Mr. So-and-So?" Were Miss Stein that painter, we know now what would happen. She would roll her eyes, squint, point in a frenzy at some object, and, of course, stammer hard. She would play up to the popular ignorance as to the

In the essay "Test for Counterfeit in the Arts," originally published in Time and Western Man *in 1927, Wyndham Lewis sarcastically critiques Stein's* Composition as Explanation *and* Three Lives *and denounces her work for feigning artistry and lacking vitality. His examination boldly concludes that "she is a sham." Even in the face of such contempt, Stein disregarded popular opinion in pursuit of her own ideas and expressions.*

Source: Lewis, Wyndham. *Time and Western Man.* Edited with afterword and notes by Paul Edwards. Santa Rosa, Calif.: Black Sparrow Press, 1993. ©1993 by the Estate of Mrs. G. A. Wyndham Lewis by permission of the Wyndham Lewis Memorial Trust and reprinted from *Time and Western Man* with the permission of Black Sparrow Press.

processes by which her picture had been arrived at, in short. She would answer "in character," implying that she was cut off from the rest of the world entirely by an exclusive and peculiar sensibility. Yet every one knows who engages in experiments of any sort, verbal or pictorial, that that is not at all the point of the matter. It is a *deliberate* adjustment of things to some formula which transforms what is treated into an organism, strange according to the human norm, though it might appear normal enough to the senses of some other animal. Normal speech, or normal vision, are not interfered with in the practitioner of these experiments, on the one hand; nor does what in the result has an abnormal appearance arise *literally* in an abnormal experience, or an experience without a normal, non-visionary, basis.

For these reasons Miss Stein's illustrations would have been much more impressive if she had not pretended, to start with, that, as to the explanation, she "could not do it in any other way." In this fact, that "explanation" and "composition" are both done in the same stuttering dialect, you have the proof that you are in the presence of a *faux-naïf*, not the real article. Miss Stein's merits elsewhere are not cancelled by this—people are often gifted without being able to lay any claim to being "sincere," as we say. But it is a little difficult to understand how she could be so stupid. Her assumption that any advantage was to be gained by this studied obscurity, where it was, after all, pointless, is that. Perhaps, however, it was only conceit.

Should my ensuing remarks sting Miss Stein into a rejoinder, then I think you would see something like the situation that would be created if some beggar shamming blindness observed a person about to disappear with his offertory box. The "blind" under such conditions would see at once, and rush after the robber. It is the classic test case in the everyday world of everyday sham. I am afraid, however, that Miss Stein is too cunning a stammerer to be so easily unmasked. Miss Stein's stutter in her *explanation* even of her other celebrated stutterings, is a proof, then, to my mind, that she is a homologue of the false-blind; that, in some measure, she is a sham.

Alfred Stieglitz

1864–1946
American Photographer
and Art Exhibitor

Alfred Stieglitz was a pioneering American photographer who used his galleries to advance the cause of modern art in the United States.

Stieglitz was born in Hoboken, New Jersey, on January 1, 1864. While in Berlin, Germany, at age 19, he began studying photography and espousing it as a valid mode of artistic expression. His photographic experiments earned him numerous awards worldwide, and during the 1890s, he produced the first successful photographs taken at night and in snow and rain, such as *Winter, Fifth Avenue* (1893), *A Wet Day on the Boulevard* (1894), and *The Savoy Hotel, New York* (1898). To protest conventional photography and promote abstract, pictorial photography, Stieglitz founded the organization Photo-Secession in 1902 and the magazine *Camera Work* in 1903. At the Little Galleries of the Photo-Secession in New York, formed in 1905 and later known by its street number "291," Stieglitz presented American and European pictorial photographs and eventually avant-garde artwork. Beginning in 1908, he introduced modern art to American audiences through showings of Henri Matisse, Henri Rousseau, Paul Cézanne, and Pablo Picasso. He also exhibited work by American artists such as painters John Marin, Mardsen Hartley, Arthur Dove, and Max Weber. These progressive exhibitions encouraged innovative and intuitive expression and challenged America's rational approach to art, which was based on conservative traditions and viewed by many as inferior to the European art world.

His radical gallery, "291," and magazine *Camera Work* profoundly influenced the 1913 Armory Show by the Association of American Painters and Sculptors (AAPS). Stieglitz did not directly organize this revolutionary exhibit of modern art, but he had laid the foundation for its success. However, Stieglitz disliked its commercial and sensational aspects. The hype surrounding the event strengthened his dedication to artistic honesty and idealism. He remained faithful to his vision, holding the first American

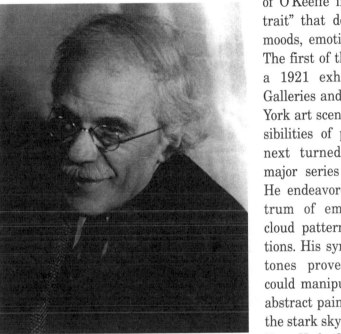

From the collections of the Library of Congress.

showings by sculptors Constantin Brancusi and Elie Nadelman and painters Francis Picabia, Gino Severini, Stanton Macdonald-Wright, and Georgia O'Keeffe.

In 1917, World War I brought the collapse of "291" and *Camera Work*. Stieglitz began focusing more on his own photography and developed a personal relationship with O'Keeffe, who became his wife in 1924 and the centerpiece of his life and work. Stieglitz created more than 400 prints of O'Keeffe in his "composite portrait" that documented her many moods, emotions, and experiences. The first of this series appeared in a 1921 exhibition at Anderson Galleries and reawakened the New York art scene to the aesthetic possibilities of photography. Stieglitz next turned toward his second major series called "Equivalents." He endeavored to portray a spectrum of emotion by presenting cloud patterns as abstract formations. His symmetry of shapes and tones proved that photography could manipulate reality and rival abstract painting. He also explored the stark skyline at his residence in New York City as well as other aspects of the natural landscape at his summer home in Lake George, New York. In 1924, the Royal Photographic Society of Great Britain awarded him the Progress Medal for his groundbreaking achievements.

While advancing his photography, Stieglitz continued to support modern art. He increasingly concentrated on sponsoring the artwork of Americans in an art world dominated by Europeans. Stieglitz's 1925 show "Seven Americans," including 159 works by Paul Strand, Charles Demuth, Marin, Hartley, Dove, O'Keeffe, and himself, provided a visual representation of the artistic integrity and originality that transcended American provincialism. After its considerable success, he opened the Intimate Gallery (1925–29) and An American Place (1929–46), both nonprofit organizations dedicated to the survey of American artists and exhibition of unique works. In the 1920s, Stieglitz helped foster in the United States an original artistic identity, distinct from European traditions. He became a cultural prophet to writers like Sherwood Anderson, Paul Rosenfeld, and Waldo Frank, inspiring a new generation that opposed complacent attitudes and traditions.

Stieglitz remained devoted to pictorial photography throughout the 1930s and early 1940s. From the windows of his apartment and An American Place, he recorded the architectural changes in New York during the early stages of the Great Depression (1929–39). Many of his photographs from this series are of buildings under construction that evoke the chaos of the times. Unable to maneuver his heavy cameras because of declining health, Stieglitz took his last photographs in 1937 but continued his gallery work until days before his death on July 13, 1946.

A seminal figure of the twentieth-century art world, Stieglitz established photography as a fine art and created an appreciation of American painting and sculpture around the world. He valued intuition over intellect, concept over technique, and self-expression over imitation. Through his exhibitions, Stieglitz transformed the American art scene; through his camera lens, he captured emotional beauty in a modern industrial society.

Renée Miller

For Further Reading

Bry, Doris. *Alfred Stieglitz: Photographer.* Boston: Museum of Fine Arts; Bullfinch Press/Little, Brown, 1996.
Norman, Dorothy. *Alfred Stieglitz: An American Seer.* New York: Aperture, 1990.
Seligmann, Herbert J. *Alfred Stieglitz Talking.* New Haven, Conn.: Yale University Library, 1966.

PORTRAIT OF GEORGIA O'KEEFFE by Alfred Stieglitz (1920)

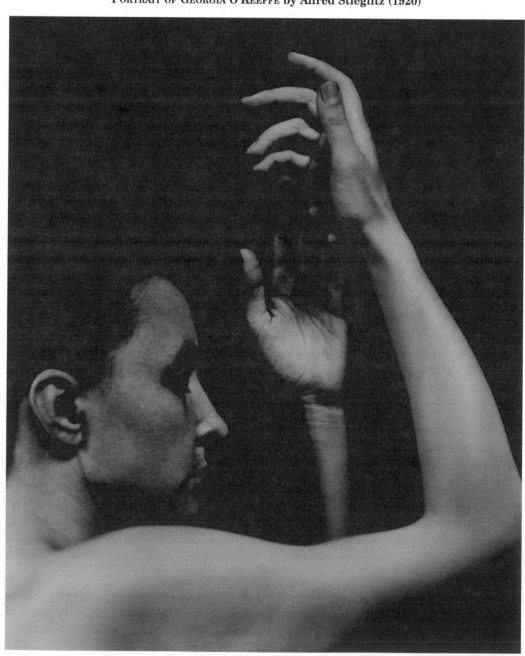

Georgia O'Keeffe served as Stieglitz's muse for his "composite portrait" series of over 400 prints. At a 1921 Anderson Gallery showing, the first print of this series awakened the New York art scene. Stieglitz photographed various angles of her face, hair, feet, torso, and hands to reveal the multiple facets of her individuality. Today this 1920 O'Keeffe portrait is part of the Stieglitz collection at the Museum of Fine Arts in Boston.

Source: Courtesy of the Museum of Fine Arts, Boston. Reproduced with permission. ©2000 Museum of Fine Arts, Boston. All Rights Reserved.

"A Photographer Challenges" by Herbert J. Seligmann (February 16, 1921)

A place without doors, it was called by a street car conductor who happened upon the top floor of 291 Fifth Avenue, New York. It was an expression of literal truth. In the thirteen years Alfred Stieglitz experimented there, holding exhibitions of Rodin, of Brancusi, of children's drawings, of Matisse, of Picasso and of Negro sculpture, of Marin and of other work, and receiving everyone who came, the place had not been locked or guarded nor its contents insured.

Their experience there made people ask: "What is 291?" It was obviously not merely a place. And the man who maintained it said it was not himself. Letters came even from Europe asking what was 291. So Stieglitz undertook to inquire what it did mean to people. He asked some thirty people what it made them feel and received more than twice as many replies, which were published in Number 47 of the magazine, *Camera Work*, dated July, 1914. He has now, after more than six years, undertaken again to question and to affirm, this time in an exhibition of 145 photographs at the Anderson Galleries, beginning February 7.

Stieglitz affirms photography. Its mechanical processes he has used to explore life and to record his exploration. Loving the visible world, the peace of harvest fields with people working in them, the glistening bodies of swimmers pearled with bubbles, the quite dignity of a child in a doorway, the shadow of a steep Italian street, he gave utterance to that love through a craftsmanship constantly formulating and solving new problems in the use of photographic machinery.

His work of experiment with his medium went on, always, and as time passed the utterance of the man took on new, more conscious insistence. Returning from Europe, an American, he photographed the steerage of an ocean liner, its human cargo cut off by a cruelly white bridge from the remainder of the ship. In terms of what could be seen he stated the unfulfilled promise of American life. Having returned to this country he became, of necessity, one of those lonely beings whose hope beats against the slagheap of an age of steel and fear and exploitation. It is not as a passerby merely that Stieglitz photographed the crenelated skyline of lower Manhattan, swept with swirls of steam; a Fifth Avenue stage coach enveloped in whirling snow; the steaming bodies of car horses in the New York of twenty-nine years ago. In the print of a darkening railroad yard, harboring no human being, only a locomotive belching smoke and the telegraph poles that link cities, it is as though the lines of gleaming steel rails had cut through the twilight into the soul of the man who saw and recorded them.

The photographer realized that men as they build express their age. Those prints of office buildings looming in daytime and by night over the dwelling places about which they have grown, are a photographer's record of what an American city gave to his eye. Just so, upon the rancid society of our time, with its diseases of fear and pretense, he turned that searching eye of the camera, seeking out men and women. For Stieglitz a portrait is not an acceptance of looking pleasant. The spirit of inquiry that made him ask people what 291 meant to them pursued him as he photographed people. What is this man, this woman? If he or she can look pleasant, then that pleasantness is only the gesture concealing something of which that human being is afraid. Very well. Move the camera closer Push farther the limits of chemistry, of developing and printing, of paper and mounting. Photograph every pore in that person's face at the extremes of looking pleasant and of terror. A Stieglitz portrait, then, becomes one, two, or three, or half a hundred photographs.

Hope, longing, drive this lonely spirit on. What is America, what are Americans? Love of the world leads him to the purest expression of it, to woman. It is from woman's hands, from her face, breasts, feet, that he evokes a terrible sense of the innocence and sensitiveness that have no home in America. This woman, who comes to be an embodied love of the world, a living, quivering being, that is flung up for a moment out of night, eloquent of death; this dying chestnut tree that thrusts its tripartite trunk into a darkening sky; these raindrops on the branches of a young tree in autumn—what place is there for them in this America? Is it not afraid of them? Do not Americans fear woman as they fear the plague? With reason, for woman is terrible, as terrible as life.

What is it that this despised box, fitted with lens and shutters and called a camera, has done in this man's hands? It has penetrated the fear which human beings have of themselves lest those selves be made known to others. So doing it has laid bare the raw material which life in America has not yet dared to look upon and absorb. When Americans are ready to undertake inquiry about themselves, their nation, the world, as the camera has been made to inquire, there may dawn a sense of common humanity. That inquiry cannot be undertaken by grotesque puppets gesturing in the mirror of what they conceive will be affluence and popular approbation and calling their gestures art, science, sociology, democracy, or any of the names with which civilization reeks. It can not be undertaken by people who think they will use other human beings for their own profit, while they proclaim freedom.

In a land where disinterest, inquiry, instinct with feeling, does not exist, photography has become an instrument of it. No human being can ever retrace the living and suffering that culminated in the moments out of which Alfred Stieglitz's photographs sprang. But his affirmation carries a challenge to men and women of the future. It is the challenge implicit in that question asked just before the war: "What is 291?" The spirit of 291 and of its gallery or "Place of Demonstration" was an attempt to make room for disinterested inquiry, for work and respect for workmanship irrespective of person. There the attempt was made to fight free of the use of one human being by another for profit, the subordination of creative impulses to personal advancement, all the tragedies which are the harvest of greed and jealousy. It was such a spirit that made possible the life recorded in Stieglitz's photographs. It is such a spirit that Randolph Bourne, dead protagonist of Youth and Life, gave voice to. Bourne foresaw in a trans-national America a concert of eager

Following the opening in 1921 of Stieglitz's exhibition at the Anderson Galleries in New York City, Herbert J. Seligmann published this piece in The Nation. *Seeking to uncover the spirit behind Stieglitz's work and his legendary gallery "291," which had closed in 1917, Seligmann praises the photographer's experimental work, critical and unflinching eye, and selfless promotion of his fellow artists.*

Source: Seligmann, Herbert J. "A Photographer Challenges." *The Nation,* 112, February 16, 1921.

spirit, conscious of one another, creating each in his own form a common heritage of expressiveness. The peoples in America Bourne conceived to be in a common enterprise. He saw, in a world that dreamed of internationalism, America as the first international nation built unawares. Was his dream a dream merely? Did the quality of Bourne's hope die with him? Will the passions of self-seeking and fear which masquerade as patriotism, will intolerance and race hatreds destroy the hope of this unique experiment in the world?

The answer is in the challenges of Stieglitz's work. It is achieved in the spirit in which trans-national America will be realized if that is to come to pass. Significant of that spirit is the fact that of the fifty numbers of *Camera Work*, the magazine which Sieglitz published with no thought of gain and at financial loss to himself, not one

contained his work after 1911, work which represents the maturity of the man and gives body to the exhibition at the Anderson Galleries. It is significant of Stieglitz's spirit that 291 was maintained to give workers opportunity to work, to exhibit, to see the work of others, even to sell their work, and that his own photography during those years was held in abeyance, so much so that among photographers the world over the impression had spread that Stieglitz had stopped photographing.

I once heard Stieglitz wonder aloud whether there were more such fools as he had been. That is the question which his exhibition asks. If there are young men and young women who will attempt to answer that question, in their lives and their work, with affirmation, then there is indeed hope of the fulfillment of the promise America made to Stieglitz and to us, a promise as yet unredeemed.

More than just a series on clouds, "Equivalents" proved that the beauty of Stieglitz's photography did not rest solely on subject matter. This "Equivalent" print from 1923, donated to the Art Institute of Chicago, illustrates his presentation of cloud patterns as abstract formations.

Source: The Art Institute of Chicago.

"Equivalent" by Alfred Stieglitz (1923)

Helen Wills 1905–1998
American Tennis Player

Helen Wills was an American tennis player celebrated for her strength, beauty, and skill. She transformed not only women's tennis but also the image of the female athlete.

Helen Newtington Wills was born on October 6, 1905, in Centerville, California. An only child, she had a close relationship with her parents, who encouraged academic study and athletic activity. Her father particularly spent time engaging her in outdoor sports. Wills first took up swimming and horseback riding, but she later found her niche playing tennis. She developed her skills and learned the fundamentals of the game while practicing with her father and other children on the public courts. At Live Oak Park in Berkeley, California, tennis coach William C. "Pops" Fuller spotted her natural talent. Wills impressed Fuller with her mental agility and physical stamina and became his star pupil in the junior program at the Berkeley Tennis Club. In 1919, the summer before her fourteenth birthday, she received recognition in the local papers after winning the title for her age group in the Bay Region Tournament.

From the collections of the Library of Congress.

Wills went on to become a notable figure in women's amateur tennis and to win the U.S. girls' singles championship in both 1921 and 1922. She achieved national attention in 1923 by earning her first women's singles title and international fame in 1924 by returning from the Summer Olympics in Paris with two gold medals. Admired for her penetrating serve and powerful ground strokes, Wills was known as a highly consistent backcourt player. Her intense focus and her poise led to the nicknames "Miss Poker Face" and "Queen Helen." Although often considered shy, reserved, or haughty, Wills's overall image appealed to many Americans. She represented the ambitious energy and democratic spirit of her country. In the minds of many observers at the time, Wills—the hard-working stoic—was a refreshing contrast to the more tawdry and self-indulgent flapper of the 1920s.

On February 16, 1926, Wills faced her first and only singles encounter against French rival Suzanne Lenglen in Cannes, France. Called "The Match of the Century," much of the media hype surrounding the event centered on their striking differences; Wills was the reserved and less experienced American champion chaperoned by her mother, while Lenglen was the flamboyant Wimbledon and French champion who sipped brandy on the sidelines. On the day of their match, fans and reporters packed the stands at the Carlton Club to witness a possible victory by Wills in Lenglen's home country. Although Wills aggressively challenged Lenglen, she lost the first set 6-3 and the second set 8-6. The public eagerly anticipated a rematch between the two best female players of the era, but Lenglen's decision to turn professional later that year excluded her from most major tournaments. (Unlike today, all tennis tournaments were strictly for amateurs until 1926 and remained traditionally for amateurs for the next 40 years.)

After the legendary Cannes match, Wills further improved her play and dominated women's tennis. Between 1927 and 1932, she won 180 singles matches in a row and also won every set within all 180 matches. Her illustrious singles career included four French championships (1928–30, and 1932), seven U.S. championships (1923–25, 1927–29, and 1931), and eight Wimbledon wins (1927–30, 1932–33, 1935, and 1938). In 1928, she became the first tennis player ever to claim the singles titles of the United States, France, and Great Britain within the same year, a feat she again accomplished in 1929. By setting these records, Wills demonstrated the evolution of the female athlete while destroying her competition. U.S. tennis player Helen Jacobs posed the strongest challenge to Wills, yet she repeatedly failed to dethrone Wills. In the shadow of "Queen Helen," Jacobs was dubbed "Helen the Second."

In 1933, Wills faced her one defeat by Jacobs when she defaulted from the finals of the U.S. Open because of severe back pain. Critics debated if Wills really left the game for fear of actually losing, and the press further speculated on what they referred to as the "Jacobs–Wills feud." However, Wills had indeed suffered a serious back injury and did not compete for 18 months. She permanently retired from tennis in 1939 and was inducted into the Tennis Hall of Fame in 1959. Remarkably, Wills was also a writer, an artist, and a graduate of the University of California at Berkeley. She published her autobiography *Fifteen-thirty: The Story of a Tennis Player* (1937) and, after retirement, focused on her lifelong interest in art. On January 1, 1998, she died at age 92 in Carmel, California.

Wills revolutionized women's tennis and shattered existing gender stereotypes. Gracing the court in her starched white cottons and her trademark white visor, she intrigued spectators with her combination of strength and beauty. As a fierce competitor, Wills proved to America and the world that women could be more than gentle nurturers. Rising to the status of a sports celebrity in the 1920s, Wills dazzled fans, made young men swoon, and, most important, excelled at the game she loved.

Renée Miller

For Further Reading

Cummings, Parke. *American Tennis: The Story of a Game and Its People.* Boston: Little, Brown, 1957.

Engelmann, Larry. *The Goddess and the American Girl: The Story of Suzanne Lenglen and Helen Wills.* New York: Oxford University Press, 1988.

King, Billie Jean, and Cynthia Starr. *We Have Come a Long Way: The Story of Women's Tennis.* New York: McGraw-Hill, 1988.

Wills, Helen. *Fifteen-thirty: The Story of a Tennis Player.* New York: C. Scribner & Sons, 1937.

Wills's backcourt playing power earned her an astonishing number of victories and virtually eliminated her challengers. This tennis record shows her wins in singles, doubles, and mixed competitions in the 1920s and 1930s.

Source: International Tennis Hall of Fame, *www.tennisfame.com*

TENNIS RECORD OF HELEN WILLS (1922–38)

Grand Slam Record

French Open	Singles	1928–30, 32
	Doubles	1930, 32
	Mixed finalist	1928, 29, 32
Wimbledon	Singles	1927–30, 32–33, 35, 38
	Singles finalist	1924
	Doubles	1924, 27, 30
	Mixed	1929
U.S. Open	Singles	1923–25, 27–29, 31
	Singles finalist	1922
	Doubles	1922, 24–25, 28
	Doubles finalist	1933
	Mixed	1924, 28
	Mixed finalist	1922

Tournament Record

Olympic	Singles	1924
	Doubles	1924
Wightman Cup		1923–25, 1927–32, 1938

SUZANNE LENGLEN AND HELEN WILLS (1926)

Suzanne Lenglen and Wills (right) shake hands after their 1926 legendary Cannes match, which Wills lost.

Source: ©Bettmann/Corbis.

"LITTLE MISS POKER FACE" by John B. Kennedy (September 18, 1926) [EXCERPT]

Eight years ago, at a sunny country club in Berkeley, Cal., Dr. C. A. Wills placed a tennis racket in the hands of his little daughter. Helen had just skipped into her thirteenth year, a prankless youngster principally marked by a cool curiosity regarding many things, including her father's devotion to tennis. Which was why she had gone down to the courts with him that day.

With condescending gentleness the doctor bounced a ball over the net to his daughter. Helen swung the racket like a nightstick and missed—and so had her first lesson in tennis technique. At the next bounce of the ball her slim fingers changed to a flexible grip, and her father knew he had an opponent.

Dawn could hardly come quick enough the next morning for little Helen, who scampered away to the country club and banged balls merrily for hours. Within a month the little lady of the lithe hands could trounce her father.

That was the beginning, and the end was far away. At fifteen Helen Wills won the junior singles championship of her native state, California. Then she journeyed to Forest Hills and captured chief honors in the national tourney. And before she was eighteen she swept back the viking attack of Molla Bjursdtedt Mallory and became champion of the United States—to stand face to face, two years later, with the turbaned and temperamental Lenglen in a brilliant but losing fight for the championship of the world.

There is a summary of social evolution in the spectacle of two young women holding the eyes of the civilized world with a contest of skill and physical endurance. Unattended by formal and farcical prizering ballyhooing, the event was easily the dominant sport high spot of the year.

HERSELF AGAIN

I saw Helen at Forest Hills after she had passed through two of the major crises in her young life—the emotional crisis of her glorious defeat and the physical ordeal of an operation for appendicitis.

Batteries of movie and still cameras were lined up on the greensward of the practice courts, many of the photographers being veterans of five years who had first photographed Helen with braids down her back. She strode into the sun, although strode is hardly the word; her pace is meticulous to the point of mincing. A vision in white and pink, her mauve-gray eyes were guarded by the visor without which she is rarely photographed, although it subtracts from the chiseled beauty of her face.

Helen gazed unconcernedly into the camera, took off a jacket as light and pink as peach skin, strode to the court and played her first full hour of tennis since she had left Wimbledon for an operating table in Paris.

EXCITED—ONCE

A male professional opposed her—Helen always practices with the most vigorous opposition available. She stood, poised and ready, a serenely alert figure of strength, her arms two pistoning columns of white muscle as she volleyed back the whirlwind service that searched out every corner of the court she defended.

The man player was dynamic, a strenuous athlete, running back and forth, leaping from side to side, the blade of his racket swishing aggressively. Helen gave only an impression of static calm. When the professional smashed a liner his face contorted, teeth bristling with the effort. Helen received it and retorted—a smash as hard as his, more accurately placed, without a twinge of muscle, lips level and unmoved. During one rapid-fire exchange the ball shot to and fro without touching the green—like a bullet catapulted from gun to gun. She gave no impression of quick action, no rush of fleet feet or swing of graceful body from side to side. Yet when her opponent's attack shifted to oscillate between extreme boundary lines, her reply was always instant, always deadly.

After a fusillade that left the professional panting and perspiring this girl remained at ease, her breathing imperceptible. Those who have watched her from the first day she walked to the Forest Hills courts a precociously self-possessed child, to whack her way through the ranks of all America's young tennis players, say that this imperturbable energy, this miracle of motion that produces a final image of dainty stateliness, is characteristic of Helen. It has earned for her the court cognomen, "Little Poker Face."

"That," she said—in the gently dropping modulation of a high-school girl: a diffident high-school girl mildly amused at the turning of armies of heads to watch her progress from the field—"is what tennis has done for me. It can do the same thing for any girl, for anybody—develop physical control, which is quite as important as sheer muscular strength.

"I was not robust as a child," she went on, passing before a crowded porch of staring eyes as though the massed onlookers were no more than a painted back drop. "I first took up swimming as an exercise. That helped me. Then my father bought me a horse, and riding helped my health. But when I took up tennis I really began to develop.

"It is more strenuous than swimming, more vigorous than horseback riding, and if there were any way of measuring the output of energy in the different forms of athletics, tennis, I believe, would prove to call for more stamina than any, save perhaps rowing."

She sipped a glass of water minus ice—water, with milk drinks and an occasional cup of coffee and tea, is the extent of her beverage consumption.

"I have never," she said, her eyes direct, unsmiling with the studious immobility that marks her conversational attitude, "taken a lesson in tennis or any other sport. What I know I have learned through observation of others and actual practice and contest. I used to play frequently with William Johnston, who has been nearly champion often enough to get it some day. Playing against men is the best training for women players—the men are naturally stronger, although not always more deft."

"Little Miss Poker Face," published in Collier's by John B. Kennedy on September 18, 1926, provides a well-rounded portrait of Wills on the tennis court and in her personal life. Through Kennedy's observations and Wills's comments, this interview describes her talents, interests, opinions, and idiosyncrasies.

Source: Kennedy, John B. "Little Miss Poker Face." Collier's 78, no. 10, Sept. 18, 1926.

She talked of this player and that, assaying them in neat, simple phrases, expressing only admiration for them, especially when they happened to be opposed to her in singles or doubles. I learned that if this impregnably placid young woman had ever experienced acute excitement it was not when two worlds watched her battle with the champion of France on a French court, but when she defeated Mrs. McKane, the English champion, in England.

HELEN ON HER CONTEMPORARIES

"That was the most thrilling contest I have ever had," she said. "There were many moments when the score stood tied and one false stroke would have brought the loss of a set and perhaps eventual defeat. I drove with all the force and skill I could command, but it seemed to me that always Mrs. McKane was on the spot to pick up the ball and fire it back. Toward the end of the final set I thought I could go no further. The crowd sensed it. They were not noisy; the English crowds have always been particularly generous to me. Mrs. McKane crowded me, giving no chance for respite. Finally, when she had forced me back to the extreme edge of the court, I was able to whip over a transverse shot she could not do much damage to.

"The newspapers were good enough to say I played a cool, heady game, but it was the only time in my life that I momentarily lost confidence, only to reclaim it with one fortunate stroke."

I was eager to hear much of her views on tennis and tennis players, but more eager to delve into the personality that graces the vanguard of America's women athletes.

America, she thinks, will always have her most potent tennis rival in France. The French women and men are nervous, high-strung, but they work at their games. The English don't, although Englishwomen take their tennis, for instance, more seriously than the men. Helen says bluntly—and she can be very blunt—that the Englishwomen are better players than the men. She discovered everywhere in Europe a wholesome admiration for American female athletic prowess. . . .

BRAINS AND BEAUTY

Helen knows how to use those brows. Her face has little to say outside of those gently molded arches. One of the ubiquitous Hollywood gentlemen, who, rightly or wrongly, think all things from earthquakes to eggnogs are measurable in screen value, tried to lure Helen with large sums to the screen. She declined.

"The only by-products of the game I care for are writing and drawing," she said. "I like to write. It helps me in my study of English. And I like to draw."

Another thing Helen likes is quick business dealing and scrupulous honesty. The gentlemen who handle her syndicated articles declare that she knows how to drive a deal shrewdly, assaying with finesse the value of her work. She will not permit any professional writer to masquerade under her name. Everything she signs she writes, and that is something new under the sun.

Socially she insists on remaining a home girl. The glare of publicity flatters her not. During tournaments at home and abroad she eschews parties—Lenglen and the other players of note are beyond her years: their diversions are not hers. She would do almost anything but miss her night's rest—eight hours, from ten-thirty to six-thirty—and that does not vary even on the eve of a titular contest. "Helen," said her mother, which was all she said, "is a champion sleeper."

Her principal diversion is reading.

"I like Conrad, Lewis, Wells, and the serious authors," she said. "Such a balance is necessary when one's public life is crowded with sport talk and sport events."

Brains and beauty—the rarest of alternatives—Helen has both. And something more she has, which, by the clock I watched, I would have sworn was not hers—the gift of hearty laughter.

I told her how her dusky namesake, Harry Wills of the unemployed punch, was welcomed by bearded notables in Prague, Czechoslovakia, and hailed as the famed brother of a famed sister.

She threw back her chin, and rich laughter cascaded through trim white rows of teeth.

"That," I said, "is a pleasant sound, for which you are not famous."

And her answer surprised me.

"The secret of mirth," she said sagely, "is to keep it secret. Most of my laughing is done on the tennis courts in brisk fights."

"But nobody has noticed it."

"That is one of the reasons why I laugh."

"Emancipated Legs Mean Better Sports" by Helen Wills (1927)

In "Emancipated Legs Mean Better Sports," published in April 1927 by The Ladies' Home Journal, Wills discusses her decision to cast aside outmoded "fussiness" in favor of modern "simplicity" in women's athletic wear. She specifically uses Suzanne Lenglen and herself as models of smart fashion in tennis

From the past of long, swirling skirts and countless petticoats, simplicity has emerged, sleek and slim. And we of today, concerned with the smartness as well as the suitability of our clothes, realize that in simplicity lies beauty.

Perhaps nowhere else so definitely as in the realm of sports has the simple costume come into its own. Long, slender lines and absence of the old-time "fussiness" mark every portion of the modern wardrobe, but in the clothes we wear for sports—whether of the active or the sideline variety—the doctrine of simplicity has reached its highest point.

In tennis particularly—the sport which interests me most—the change has been most drastic. It wasn't so many years ago that girls wore skirts which brushed the court and corsets that hampered every move. How on earth could they have run without tripping on their hems and getting thoroughly out of breath? Tennis must have been dangerous then—or perhaps the problem was solved by not running at all! No wonder women's tennis has advanced so remarkably.

Today we choose our tennis clothes for comfort, yet we sacrifice nothing of smartness in so doing.

Mademoiselle Lenglen, with her simple, sleeveless frocks, round-necked and plaited as to skirt, has proved that no tennis dress can be too simply cut, too short of sleeve or skirt, if it enables the player to express herself and make the most of her ability. Type, figure and weight are, of course, important factors, and only the slender person can safely wear the Lenglen type. I myself prefer the two-piece dress, with camisole skirt that stays in place even during the most vigorous rally; but both types are smart and pleasing, with their choice depending only on the style and build of the player.

A colored sweater always adds a gay note to the ensemble, and is a necessity as well as a smart supplement to the frock. Mademoiselle Lenglen has a collection of delightfully colored silk sweaters, but lightweight wool and cashmere ones are more practical, I believe. White shoes and stockings are an unwritten law in women's tennis, and horrified whispers of the American woman who wore black stockings on the court at Wimbledon were still rife when I was there not long ago. I have found that silk stockings are best, with perhaps a light-weight wool foot coming just to the top of the shoe, if the court surface is of clay or asphalt.

As to tennis headgear, I have a particular dislike, although an altogether unreasonable one, for the narrow satin ribbons that some players tie about their heads. The georgette crepe of Mademoiselle Lenglen's famous bandeau is attractive as well as practical, but for myself I like an eye shade, because it protects the eyes, prevents wrinkles from forming about them, holds the hair in place, and keeps away some of the sunburn.

Sports clothes on the sidelines follow the same rules as those on the court—they are simple, practical and suitable. I think everyone agrees that the really smart woman, the world over, is never conspicuously dressed. The fact that one sees pictures of overdressed women who are said to be wearing "fashion's latest Parisian creations" merely proves that every country has some women of bad taste.

The elimination of fussy detail, the cultivation of simplicity, the harmony of the ensemble—these are things for which we should aim. Perfect simplicity can come only through study. Today sophistication spells simplicity.

and considers how women's new attire has improved both their style and sport. Yet, even though women like Wills and Lenglen achieved a new level of respect for their athleticism in the 1920s, their appearance still played an important role in their public image.

Source: Wills, Helen. "Emancipated Legs Mean Better Sports." *The Ladies' Home Journal*, April 1927. ©April 1927, Meredith Corporation. All rights reserved. Used with the permission of *Ladies' Home Journal*.

HELEN WILLS PLAYING TENNIS (1935)

This photo illustrates Wills's skill as she effortlessly completes a backhand in Wimbledon, England.

Source: From the collections of the Library of Congress.

Woodrow Wilson

Woodrow Wilson, a strong and idealistic president, reluctantly led the United States into World War I to make the world "safe for democracy." Following the war, he struggled to establish a just and peaceful world order through the Treaty of Versailles.

Thomas Woodrow Wilson was born in Staunton, Virginia, on December 28, 1856, the son and grandson of Presbyterian ministers, and was raised in Georgia and the Carolinas. From an early age he harbored a strong ambition to serve as a public statesman. Keenly interested in British political history, he entered the College of New Jersey (now Princeton University) in 1875, where he excelled in debate. In 1883, Wilson entered graduate school at Johns Hopkins University and studied constitutional and political history. He wrote his first book, *Congressional Government* (1885) and was awarded a doctorate in 1886.

In June 1885 he married Ellen Louise Axson, whom he had met in Rome, Georgia, in 1883. They would have three daughters. He taught at Bryn Mawr College and Wesleyan University; in 1890 he returned to

From the collections of the Library of Congress.

Princeton as a professor of jurisprudence and political economy. A popular professor, he was unanimously elected president of Princeton in 1902; he introduced several structural reforms to make teaching more efficient and the university more democratic.

Through his lecture tours and books, Wilson had built a national reputation as a political thinker, and his championing of reforms at Princeton caught the eye of New Jersey Democratic Party bosses. In the handsome, articulate college president they saw a governor, even a president; thinking him politically naïve and manipulable, they encouraged him to run for governor. Wilson won by a large margin and quickly showed his independence from the party machine by pushing through the New Jersey state assembly a corrupt practices act, a public utilities act, an employers' liability act, and laws that improved working conditions for women and children. Wilson quickly won national press attention as a progressive governor who got results.

After repeated losses in presidential elections, the national Democratic Party by 1912 was desperate for a candidate who could win. Wilson had the influential support of **William Jennings Bryan**, a progressive leader of the Democratic Party who had lost three presidential elections but still commanded immense respect nationwide. With Republicans split between William Howard Taft and former Republican president Theodore Roosevelt (running on the new Progressive Party, or "Bull Moose" ticket), Wilson won 42 percent of the popular vote (to Roosevelt's 27 and Taft's 23 percent) and a commanding 435 electoral votes to Roosevelt's 88.

In his inaugural address on March 4, 1913, President Wilson set forth an ambitious agenda, known as the "New Freedom," for banking and tariff (tax) reform, trust (monopolies) and labor legislation, conservation, and regulation of "the larger economic interests of the nation." He repaid his political debt to Bryan by naming him secretary of state, an appointment that pleased Democrats and helped unite the party to pass a remarkable series of reform initiatives. On April 8, Wilson went to Capitol Hill to personally deliver a message to Congress, a gesture no president had made since John Adams. He pressed for lowered taxes on imported goods to stimulate trade, restore competition, and weaken monopolies' chokehold on American business. On October 13, 1913, Wilson happily signed the Underwood Tariff Act.

His next major initiative was possibly the most important financial legislation since the days of Alexander Hamilton and the establishment of the first Bank of the United States. Over the protests of big bankers, Wilson signed the Federal Reserve Act (1913), which established a system of 12 regional banks under a Federal Reserve Board to stabilize the national economy by regulating the money supply, taking away Wall Street's monopoly on credit, and establishing an "elastic" currency resistant to the wild fluctuations in value caused by financial panics (such as the devastating Panic of 1907). In 1914 he pushed through

Congress the Federal Trade Commission Act and the Clayton Antitrust Act, which defended labor unions' right to strike, boycott, and picket. Wilson was at first reluctant to endorse woman suffrage, but spoke out for it in 1915 and made women's voting rights a campaign issue in 1916.

The president was heartbroken by the death of his wife on August 6, 1914. Only days later, war broke out in Europe. The president declared American neutrality and tried repeatedly to encourage a diplomatic settlement, but was spurned by the Allied Powers (England, France, and Russia) and by the Central Powers (Germany, Austria-Hungary, and, for a while, Italy). From 1914 to 1917, Wilson struggled to balance the nation's neutrality with its right to trade with belligerents and its citizens' safety on the high seas. When a German U-boat sunk the British passenger liner *Lusitania* on May 7, 1915, drowning more than a thousand passengers, including 128 Americans, Wilson warned Germany that American maritime and commercial rights must not be imperiled by submarine warfare. Bryan, a pacifist, caused a stir by resigning rather than sign Wilson's second, stronger note.

Wilson was narrowly reelected in 1916 with the slogan, "He has kept us out of the war." Most Americans had no wish to get involved in a European conflict, but public opinion changed and the president's choices narrowed in early 1917 with the sinking of three more American ships by German submarines and the publicized discovery of a secret telegram, known as the Zimmermann note, in which Germany sought a military alliance with Mexico against the United States.

Wilson appeared before a special session of Congress on April 2, 1917, to assert that "the world must be made safe for democracy." On April 6 Congress declared war against Germany. Wilson appointed Gen. **John J. Pershing** to command the American Expeditionary Force (AEF) in Europe, and on May 18 he signed the Selective Service Act, which required all men between the ages of 21 and 31 to sign up for the military (the U.S. Army at this time numbered fewer than 110,000 men). Emergency war powers authorized by Congress in the Lever Act (1917) gave the government unprecedented control over industrial production, labor, and transportation, and also control over civil liberties with the Espionage Act (1917) and the Sedition Act (1918)—laws that silenced antiwar protesters like **Emma Goldman** and provided grounds for deportations during the "Red Scare" of 1919–20.

Wilson addressed Congress in January 1918 to set forth the principles for which the Allies were fighting—known as the "Fourteen Points." This speech, the most important single statement on the war aims, boosted morale, strengthened Allied cohesiveness, and laid out terms for an eventual peace settlement, such as the crushing of German militarism, reduction of armaments, establishment of freedom of the seas, open diplomacy, and a league of nations to maintain international peace.

United States troops began arriving in Europe in mid-1917, but the "Yanks" didn't join in active fighting until May and June 1918. The Americans' two major offensives, the Battle of St. Mihiel and the Meuse-Argonne offensive, began in September. By early October 1918, Germany was appealing to Wilson for a suspension of hostilities on the basis of the Fourteen Points. An armistice was signed on November 11, 1918.

In December 1918, Wilson and his representative Edward M. House sailed to France for the Paris Peace Conference; it was the first time that a U.S. president had traveled to Europe while in office. Wilson had high hopes for a just peace, but negotiations were complex and exhausting. He urged Britain and France not to punish Germany and insisted that a league of nations be written into the peace agreement, the Treaty of Versailles. The Covenant of the League of Nations sought the reduction of armaments, judicial settlement of international disputes, and collective response to acts of aggression.

Congress hesitated to commit to settling conflicts in distant lands and feared losing sovereignty to an international decision-making body, but Wilson refused to compromise; his trip to Paris had put him out of touch with political developments in the United States. At the urging of Senator **Henry Cabot Lodge**, the Senate rejected the ratification of United States membership in the League of Nations. Further, the Senate refused to ratify the Treaty of Versailles; rather, in 1921, it declared the war with Germany at an end. In the treaty, Britain and France managed to impose upon Germany harsh, punitive terms that are generally credited with causing that nation's economic crisis in the 1920s, which made possible the later rise of Adolf Hitler, and, thus, World War II.

Wilson was traveling in the United States on a campaign to build public support for the League when he collapsed from exhaustion on September 25, 1919, in Pueblo, New Mexico. He was brought back to Washington and on October 2 suffered a massive stroke. He lived and served out the rest of his term, but his administration was essentially paralyzed. His second wife (the president had remarried in December 1915) and his doctor severely restricted visitors, and communications with his cabinet were less than minimal. Wilson died in Washington, D.C., on February 3, 1924.

For his efforts to restore order to a war-torn world, Wilson was awarded the Nobel Prize for Peace in 1919, and his legislative achievements such as the Federal Reserve Act continued to hold the nation steady. For his idealism and reform efforts, Wilson is remembered as one of the most influential "activist" presidents of the twentieth century.

Mark LaFlaur

For Further Reading
Auchincloss, Louis. *Woodrow Wilson*. New York: Viking Press, 2000.
Cashman, Sean Dennis. *America Ascendant: From Theodore Roosevelt to FDR in the Century of American Power, 1901–1945.* New York: New York University Press, 1998.
Heckscher, August. *Woodrow Wilson*. New York: Scribners, 1991.
Link, Arthur S. *Wilson.* 5 vols. Princeton, N.J.: Princeton University Press, 1947–65.

INAUGURAL ADDRESS by Woodrow Wilson (March 4, 1913) [EXCERPT]

During his inaugural address on March 4, 1913, President Wilson outlined his "New Freedom" agenda.

Source: The Papers of Woodrow Wilson. Vol. 27, 1913. Edited by Arthur S. Link. Princeton, N.J.: Princeton University Press, 1978.

There has been a change of government. It began two years ago, when the House of Representatives became Democratic by a decisive majority. It has now been completed. The Senate about to assemble will also be Democratic. The offices of President and Vice President have been put into the hands of Democrats. What does the change mean? That is the question that is uppermost in our minds today. That is the question I am going to try to answer, in order, if I may, to interpret the occasion. . . .

We have itemized with some degree of particularity the things that ought to be altered, and here are some of the chief items: A tariff which cuts us off from our proper part in the commerce of the world, violates the just principles of taxation, and makes the government a facile instrument in the hands of private interests; a banking and currency system based upon the necessity of the government to sell its bonds fifty years ago and perfectly adapted to concentrating cash and restricting credits; an industrial system which, take it on all its sides, financial as well as administrative, holds capital in leading strings, restricts the liberties and limits the opportunities of labor, and exploits without renewing or conserving the natural resources of the country; a body of agricultural activities never yet given the efficiency of great business undertakings or served as it should be through the instrumentality of science taken directly to the farm, or afforded the facilities of credit best suited to its practical needs; watercourses undeveloped, waste places unreclaimed, forests untended, fast disappearing without plan or prospect of renewal, unregarded waste heaps at every mine. We have studied as perhaps no other nation has the most effective means of production, but we have not studied cost or economy as we should either as organizers of industry, as statesmen, or as individuals.

Nor have we studied and perfected the means by which government may be put at the service of humanity, in safeguarding the health of the nation, the health of its men and its women and its children, as well as their rights in the struggle for existence. This is no sentimental duty. The firm basis of government is justice, not pity. These are matters of justice. There can be no equality of opportunity, the first essential of justice in the body politic, if men and women and children be not shielded in their lives, their very vitality, from the consequences of great industrial and social processes which they cannot alter, control, or singly cope with. Society must see to it that it does not itself crush or weaken or damage its own constituent parts. The first duty of law is to keep sound the society it serves. Sanitary laws, pure food laws, and laws determining conditions of labor which individuals are powerless to determine for themselves are intimate parts of the very business of justice and legal efficiency.

These are some of the things we ought to do, and not leave the others undone, the old-fashioned, never-to-be-neglected, fundamental safeguarding of property and of individual right. This is the high enterprise of the new day: to lift everything that concerns our life as a nation to the light that shines from the hearthfire of every man's conscience and vision of the right. It is inconceivable that we should do this as partisans; it is inconceivable we should do it in ignorance of the facts as they are or in blind haste. We shall restore, not destroy. We shall deal with our economic system as it is and as it may be modified, not as it might be if we had a clean sheet of paper to write upon; and step by step we shall make it what it should be, in the spirit of those who question their own wisdom and seek counsel and knowledge, not shallow self-satisfaction or the excitement of excursions whither they cannot tell. Justice, and only justice, shall always be our motto.

And yet it will be no cool process of mere science. The nation has been deeply stirred, stirred by a solemn passion, stirred by the knowledge of wrong, of ideals lost, of government too often debauched and made an instrument of evil. The feelings with which we face this new age of right and opportunity sweep across our heartstrings like some air out of God's own presence, where justice and mercy are reconciled and the judge and the brother are one. We know our task to be no mere task of politics but a task which shall search us through and through, whether we be able to understand our time and the need of our people, whether we be indeed their spokesmen and interpreters, whether we have the pure heart to comprehend and the rectified will to choose our high course of action.

This is not a day of triumph; it is a day of dedication. Here muster, not the forces of party, but the forces of humanity. Men's hearts wait upon us, men's lives hang in the balance; men's hopes call upon us to say what we will do. Who shall live up to the great trust? Who dares fail to try? I summon all honest men, all patriotic, all forward-looking men, to my side. God helping me, I will not fail them, if they will but counsel and sustain me!

War Message by Woodrow Wilson (April 2, 1917) [Excerpt]

Gentlemen of the Congress:

I have called the Congress into extraordinary session because there are serious, very serious, choices of policy to be made, and made immediately, which it was neither right nor constitutionally permissible that I should assume the responsibility of making. . . .

The present German submarine warfare against commerce is a warfare against mankind.

It is a war against all nations. American ships have been sunk, American lives taken, in ways which it has stirred us very deeply to learn of, but the ships and people of other neutral and friendly nations have been sunk and overwhelmed in the waters in the same way. There has been no discrimination. The challenge is to all mankind. Each nation must decide for itself how it will meet it. The choice we make for ourselves must be made with a moderation of counsel and a temperateness of judgment befitting our character and our motives as a nation. We must put excited feeling away. Our motive will not be revenge or the victorious assertion of the physical might of the nation, but only the vindication of right, of human right, of which we are only a single champion. . . .

With a profound sense of the solemn and even tragical character of the step I am taking and of the grave responsibilities which it involves, but in unhesitating obedience to what I deem my constitutional duty, I advise that the Congress declare the recent course of the Imperial German Government to be in fact nothing less than war against the Government and people of the United States; that it formally accept the status of belligerent which has thus been thrust upon it, and that it take immediate steps not only to put the country in a more thorough state of defense but also to exert all its power and employ all its resources to bring the Government of the German Empire to terms and end the war. . . .

While we do these things, these deeply momentous things, let us be very clear, and make very clear to all the world what our motives and our objects are. My own thought has not been driven from its habitual and normal course by the unhappy events of the last two months, and I do not believe that the thought of the nation has been altered or clouded by them I have exactly the same things in mind now that I had in mind when I addressed the Senate on the 22d of January last; the same that I had in mind when I addressed the Congress on the 3d of February and on the 26th of February. Our object now, as then, is to vindicate the principles of peace and justice in the life of the world as against selfish and autocratic power and to set up amongst the really free and self-governed peoples of the world such a concert of purpose and of action as will henceforth ensure the observance of those principles. Neutrality is no longer feasible or desirable where the peace of the world is involved and the freedom of its peoples, and the menace to that peace and freedom lies in the existence of autocratic governments backed by organized force which is controlled wholly by their will, not by the will of their people. We have seen the last of neutrality in such circumstances. We are at the beginning of an age in which it will be insisted that the same standards of conduct and of responsibility for wrong done shall be observed among nations and their governments that are observed among the individual citizens of civilized states. . . .

We are accepting this challenge of hostile purpose because we know that in such a government, following such methods, we can never have a friend; and that in the presence of its organized power, always lying in wait to accomplish we know not what purpose, there can be no assured security for the democratic governments of the world. We are now about to accept gage of battle with this natural foe to liberty and shall, if necessary, spend the whole force of the nation to check and nullify its pretensions and its power. We are glad, now that we see the facts with no veil of false pretense about them, to fight thus for the ultimate peace of the world and for the liberation of its peoples, the German peoples included: for the rights of nations great and small and the privilege of men everywhere to choose their way of life and of obedience. The world must be made safe for democracy. Its peace must be planted upon the tested foundations of political liberty. We have no selfish ends to serve. We desire no conquest, no dominion. We seek no indemnities for ourselves, no material compensation for the sacrifices we shall freely make. We are but one of the champions of the rights of mankind. We shall be satisfied when those rights have been made as secure as the faith and the freedom of nations can make them.

Just because we fight without rancour and without selfish object, seeking nothing for ourselves but what we shall wish to share with all free peoples, we shall, I feel confident, conduct our operations as belligerents without passion and ourselves observe with proud punctilio the principles of right and of fair play we profess to be fighting for. . . .

It will be all the easier for us to conduct ourselves as belligerents in a high spirit of right and fairness because we act without animus, not in enmity towards a people or with the desire to bring any injury or disadvantage upon them, but only in armed opposition to an irresponsible government which has thrown aside all considerations of humanity and of right and is running amuck. We are, let me say again, the sincere friends of the German people, and shall desire nothing so much as the early reestablishment of intimate relations of mutual advantage between us—however hard it may be for them, for the time being, to believe that this is spoken from our hearts. We have borne with their present government through all these bitter months because of that friendship—exercising a patience and forbearance which would otherwise have been impossible. We shall, happily, still have an opportunity to prove that friendship in our daily attitude and actions towards the millions of men and women of German birth and native sympathy, who live amongst us and share our life, and we shall be proud to prove it towards all who are in fact loyal to their neighbours and to the

On April 2, 1917, President Wilson delivered this message in a Special Session of Congress, following the sinking of three American ships by German submarines and the discovery of the Zimmermann note. In his message, Wilson asserts that "the world must be made safe for democracy."

Source: Wilson, Woodrow. *War Messages. Congressional Record.* 65th Cong., 1st sess. 1917, Senate Doc. 5, no. 7264.

Government in the hour of test. They are, most of them, as true and loyal Americans as if they had never known any other fealty or allegiance. They will be prompt to stand with us in rebuking and restraining the few who may be of a different mind and purpose. If there should be disloyalty, it will be dealt with with a firm hand of stern repression; but, if it lifts its head at all, it will lift it only here and there and without countenance except from a lawless and malignant few.

It is a distressing and oppressive duty, gentlemen of the Congress, which I have performed in thus addressing you. There are, it may be, many months of fiery trial and sacrifice ahead of us. It is a fearful thing to lead this great peaceful people into war, into the most terrible and disastrous of all wars, civilization itself seeming to be in the balance. But the right is more precious than peace, and we shall fight for the things which we have always carried nearest our hearts—for democracy, for the right of those who submit to authority to have a voice in their own governments for the rights and liberties of small nations, for a universal dominion of right by such a concert of free peoples as shall bring peace and safety to all nations and make the world itself at last free. To such a task we can dedicate our lives and our fortunes, everything that we are and everything that we have, with the pride of those who know that the day has come when America is privileged to spend her blood and her might for the principles that gave her birth and happiness and the peace which she has treasured. God helping her, she can do no other.

"FOURTEEN POINTS" by Woodrow Wilson (January 8, 1918) [EXCERPT]

A listing of the "Fourteen Points," that President Wilson presented in a famous speech to Congress on January 8, 1918. These points would become crucial in the postwar peace negotiations for the Treaty of Versailles.

Source: Asinof, Eliot. *1919: America's Loss of Innocence.* New York: Donald I. Fine, 1990.

. . .We entered this war because violations of right had occurred which touched us to the quick and made the life of our own people impossible unless they were corrected and the world secure once for all against their recurrence. What we demand in this war, therefore, is nothing peculiar to ourselves. It is that the world be made fit and safe to live in; and particularly that it be made safe for every peace-loving nation which, like our own, wishes to live its own life, determine its own institutions, be assured of justice and fair dealing by the other peoples of the world as against force and selfish aggression. All the peoples of the world are in effect partners in this interest, and for our own part we see very clearly that unless justice be done to others it will not be done to us. The program of the world's peace, therefore, is our program; and that program, the only possible program, as we see it, is this:

I. Open covenants of peace, openly arrived at, after which there shall be no private international understandings of any kind but diplomacy shall proceed always frankly and in the public view.

II. Absolute freedom of navigation upon the seas, outside territorial waters, alike in peace and in war, except as the seas may be closed in whole or in part by international action for the enforcement of international covenants.

III. The removal, so far as possible, of all economic barriers and the establishment of an equality of trade conditions among all the nations consenting to the peace and associating themselves for its maintenance.

IV. Adequate guarantees given and taken that national armaments will be reduced to the lowest point consistent with domestic safety.

V. A free, open-minded, and absolutely impartial adjustment of all colonial claims, based upon a strict observance of the principle that in determining all such questions of sovereignty the interests of the populations concerned must have equal weight with the equitable claims of the government whose title is to be determined.

VI. The evacuation of all Russian territory and such a settlement of all questions affecting Russia as will secure the best and freest cooperation of the other nations of the world in obtaining for her an unhampered and unembarrassed opportunity for the independent determination of her own political development and national policy and assure her of a sincere welcome into the society of free nations under institutions of her own choosing; and, more than a welcome, assistance also of every kind that she may need and may herself desire. The treatment accorded Russia by her sister nations in the months to come will be the acid test of their good will, of their comprehension of her needs as distinguished from their own interests, and of their intelligent and unselfish sympathy.

VII. Belgium, the whole world will agree, must be evacuated and restored, without any attempt to limit the sovereignty which she enjoys in common with all other free nations. No other single act will serve as this will serve to restore confidence among the nations in the laws which they have themselves set and determined for the government of their relations with one another. Without this healing act the whole structure and validity of international law is forever impaired.

VIII. All French territory should be freed and the invaded portions restored, and the wrong done to France by Prussia in 1871 in the matter of Alsace-Lorraine, which has unsettled the peace of the world for nearly fifty years, should be righted, in order that peace may once more be made secure in the interest of all.

IX. A readjustment of the frontiers of Italy should be effected along clearly recognizable lines of nationality.

X. The peoples of Austria-Hungary, whose place among the nations we wish to see safeguarded and assured, should be accorded the freest opportunity to autonomous development.

XI. Rumania, Serbia, and Montenegro should be evacuated; occupied territories restored; Serbia accorded free and secure access to the sea; and the relations of the several Balkan states to one another determined by friendly counsel along historically established lines of allegiance and nationality; and international guarantees of the political and economic independence and territorial integrity of the several Balkan states should be entered into.

XII. The Turkish portion of the present Ottoman Empire should be assured a secure sovereignty, but the other nationalities which are now under Turkish rule should be assured an undoubted security of life and an absolutely unmolested opportunity of autonomous development, and the Dardanelles should be permanently opened as a free passage to the ships and commerce of all nations under international guarantees.

XIII. An independent Polish state should be erected which should include the territories inhabited by indisputably Polish populations, which should be assured a free and secure access to the sea, and whose political and economic independence and territorial integrity should be guaranteed by international covenant.

XIV. A general association of nations must be formed under specific covenants for the purpose of affording mutual guarantees of political independence and territorial integrity to great and small states alike. . . .

"THEY WON'T DOVETAIL" POLITICAL CARTOON (1919)

This political cartoon, published in the San Francisco Chronicle in 1919, reflects the United States' reluctance to accept the League of Nations, on which Wilson refused to compromise.

Source: From the collections of the Library of Congress.

Anna May Wong

1907–1961
Chinese-American Movie Star

Anna May Wong was the world's first female Asian movie star, overcoming tremendous odds in an industry that discriminated against her sex and race.

Born on January 3, 1907, in Los Angeles, California, she was named Wong Liu Tsong, meaning "Frosted Yellow Willow." A third-generation Chinese American, she endured racial slurs at an early age from her classmates at California Street School. Early on, she dreamed of becoming a movie star. She sometimes skipped Chinese school in the evenings to attend the local nickelodeon, admiring actors like Pearl White in *The Perils of Pauline* (1914). At age 12, Wong seized the opportunity to play an extra in the 1919 production *The Red Lantern,* an event she kept secret from her family. When more bit parts followed, Wong pursued a career on the silver screen despite the disapproval of her traditional parents.

Wong earned her first screen credit in *Bits of Life* (1922) and appeared in one of the first full-length Technicolor features, *The Toll of the Sea* (1922). In this variation on *Madame Butterfly,* she

From the collections of the Library of Congress.

shone in the role of a Chinese villager who drowns herself in the sea when her white lover returns to America. The strikingly beautiful Wong was then chosen for the part of an exotic "Mongol slave" girl in Douglas Fairbanks's 1924 epic, *The Thief of Bagdad.* This fantasy picture gained her international acclaim and numerous movie offers. She went on to play Keko in *The Alaskan* (1924) and Tiger Lily in *Peter Pan* (1924). Wong's brief yet stunning performances should have made her a star, but unfortunately, producers withheld major Hollywood roles from her because she was Chinese. Following World War I, a growth in racism, radical activities, and isolationist sentiments led to a marked increase in the fear of foreigners and the desire to create more restrictive immigration laws. Asian communities were specifically targeted with the Immigration Act of 1917, which established an Asiatic Barred Zone—a geographic region from which immigrants would be denied entry to the United States. California suffered from a pro-

longed history of anti-Chinese sentiments and riots protesting the use of cheap Chinese labor. The movie industry reflected the same biased attitudes prevalent throughout the United States at this time.

During the 1920s, Hollywood producers typically cast ethnic minorities as stock characters. African-American and Asian actors were forced to settle for demeaning roles that reinforced ethnic stereotypes, while the few ethnic leads that existed were played by heavily made-up Caucasians. The films *Mr. Wu* (1927), with French actor Renee Adoree, and *The Crimson City* (1928), with American actor Myrna Loy, exemplify this studio practice; Wong serves as a supporting performer to Caucasian females in Chinese roles. Most often her parts reflected Hollywood's stereotypes of the Asian woman—the mysterious dancer, seductive temptress, and deceptive dragon lady. In films about China and the Far East, such as *Old San Francisco* (1927), *The Chinese Parrot* (1927), *The Devil Dancer* (1927), *Across to Singapore* (1928), and *Chinatown Charlie* (1928), Wong is depicted more as exotic ambiance than a realistic character. Dissatisfied with her screen opportunities, Wong left Hollywood after *Chinatown Charlie* to embark on an acting career in Europe. Later, Wong wrote, "I was so tired of parts I had to play. Why is it that the screen Chinese is always the villain of the piece?"

Overseas Wong learned to speak fluent German and French and flourished as an international star. She immediately gained recognition in Germany for her film *Song* (1928), astonishing critics with her flawless German dialogue, which many believed had been dubbed. In 1929, Wong was radiant as a conniving nightclub performer in the British film *Piccadilly* with costar Charles Laughton. She also made her stage debut opposite Laurence Olivier in *The Circle of Chalk,* an adaptation of a classic Chinese drama written especially for Wong. Although these roles did not differ radically from Hollywood stereotypes, they did offer greater prominence and appreciation. Like African-American performer **Josephine Baker**, Wong enjoyed critical praise and a sophisticated lifestyle in Europe, mingling with the social elite and residing at London's stylish Claridge's Hotel.

After starring in the international release *The Flame of Love* and the Viennese opera *Tschuin Tschi (Springtime),* Wong returned to the United States in 1930 for a part in the Broadway show *On the Spot.* Signing a contract with Paramount, she finally landed major Hollywood roles in melodramas like *Daughter of the Dragon* (1931), and her most notable American picture, *Shanghai Express* (1932). Wong worked in the United States and abroad for the next few years, and in 1936, she traveled to China to visit her father's first wife and son and explore her cultural heritage. On her 10-month sojourn, she discovered that a number of her films had been banned in China for their negative portrayal of Asian women. Wong, who was perceived to be too Western for Chinese theater and too ethnic for American producers, felt culturally displaced and deeply saddened.

In 1942, during World War II, she retired from films and volunteered for the United China Relief Fund and United Service Organizations (USO). Almost two decades later Wong made a guest appearance in her final film *Portrait in Black* (1960). On February 3, 1961, she died of a heart attack in Santa Monica, California.

Anna May Wong possessed the beauty and the talent of a leading lady but her ethnicity limited her to supporting roles in the United States. Whereas Hollywood largely ignored Wong's talent, European countries offered her distinct screen and stage opportunities. This international success brought her new appreciation in Hollywood; still, she was never considered "star material" like her white contemporaries. Despite these limitations, Wong appeared in nearly 50 films during her career, becoming the first female Asian star.

Renée Miller

For Further Reading
"Anna May Wong: Combination of East and West," *New York Herald-Tribune,* November 9, 1930.
Davis, Mac. "Fled from Fame for 5 Years," *New York Enquirer,* February 18, 1957.
Mok, Michel. "Anna May Wong with Chinese Courtesy Makes Newspaper Photographer Blush," *New York Post,* 26 April 1939.
Parish, James Robert, and William T. Leonard. *Hollywood Players: The Thirties.* New Rochelle, N.Y.: Arlington House Publishers, 1976.

SECTION 3 OF THE IMMIGRATION ACT OF 1917 (1917) [EXCERPT]

SEC. 3. That the following classes of aliens shall be excluded from admission into the United States: . . . unless otherwise provided for by existing treaties, persons who are natives of islands not possessed by the United States adjacent to the Continent of Asia, situate south of the twentieth parallel latitude north, west of the one hundred and sixtieth meridian of longitude east from Greenwich and north of the tenth parallel of latitude south or who are natives of any country, province, or dependency situate on the Continent of Asia west of the one hundred and tenth meridian of longitude east from Greenwich and east of the fiftieth meridian of longitude east from Greenwich and south of the fiftieth parallel of latitude north, except that portion of said territory situate between the fiftieth and the sixty-fourth meridians of longitude east from Greenwich and the twenty-fourth and thirty-eighth parallels of latitude north, and no alien now in any way excluded from or prevented from entering, the United States shall be admitted to the United States. The provision next foregoing, however, shall not apply to persons of the following status or occupations: Government officers, ministers or religious teachers, missionaries, lawyers, physicians, chemists, civil engineers, teachers, students, authors, artists, merchants, and travelers for curiosity or pleasure, nor to their legal wives or their children under sixteen years of age who shall accompany them or who subsequently may apply for admission to the United States, but such persons or their legal wives or foreign-born children who fail to maintain in the United States a status or occupation placing them within the excepted classes shall be deemed to be in the United States contrary to law, and shall be subject to deportation as provided in section nineteen of this Act. . . .

The Immigration Act of 1917 sought to specifically exclude most Asians from entry into the United States by creating the Asiatic Barred Zone, a geographic region that included South Asia, Southeast Asia, and the Pacific Islands. Congress passed the act on February 5, 1917.

Source: Immigration Act of 1917. Congressional Record. 64th Cong. 2d sess. 1918, 54.

REVIEW OF *THE TOLL OF THE SEA* from *New York Times* (December 4, 1922) [EXCERPT]

There are a number of things to say about "The Toll of the Sea," the photoplay at the Rialto this week. First, it is entirely in colors, and, so far as the records show, it is the second full-length dramatic film of its kind, its predecessor being "The Glorious Adventure," which J. Stuart Blackton made in England with Lady Diana Manners in the leading role.

And, of course, comparison between the two is unavoidable. So, in order next is the report that the color work of "The Toll of the Sea" is noticeably superior to that of "The Glorious Adventure." The earlier film had a number of effective scenes and nothing can deprive it of its prestige as first in the field, but, taken as a whole, it must rank below "The Toll of the Sea" as a chromatic production. Whether the superiority of the latter film is due to a superiority of the Technicolor process by which it was made or to a more discriminating selection of color subjects and use of light, or both, is a question, but it does not seem amiss to distribute credit for the results obtained among Professors Daniel C. Comstock and Herbert D. Kaimus, who developed the process, and J. A. Ball, the photographic director of the film. All of them, surely, deserve special recognition.

Wong appeared in one of her few leading Hollywood roles and one of the first full-length Technicolor features in The Toll of the Sea. Aside from praising the picture's use of color, this 1922 New York Times review compliments Wong's natural acting ability and predicts her future screen success.

Source: New York Times, December 4, 1922.

And not merely for making a picture whose colors are better than those of another production, but for making a picture whose colors are independently good. The scenes of "The Toll of the Sea" are nearly all satisfying to the eye and many of them are distinctly pleasing. For the most part they are clear, true and bright without being harsh. There are delicate, as well as strong, shades in them, and they are nicely, sometimes exquisitely, detailed. They are enjoyable in themselves and promise the further and furthering development of chromatic cinematography.

The producers of the picture have been wise in selecting as their subject a story which lends itself to colored treatment. It is based on an old Chinese legend, it is said, and most of its scenes are in gay gardens and by the sea. Here are settings just waiting for reproduction in colors, and in them are Chinese people whose costumes of elaborate and finely embroidered silks and severely plain cotton permit richness and the effective variety of contrast. Also the story had been suitably photographed outdoors. Even its few interior scenes seem to have been made in the sunlight, which, apparently, gives the best results with the color camera.

As a photoplay in colors, then, "The Toll of the Sea" may be counted a distinct achievement. And as a photoplay it is also good. Though it lacks the recommendation of originality, being simply another version of "Mme. Butterfly," it possesses the quality of genuineness and is convincingly acted. So nothing is to be marked against it because it is not new. There are stories fundamentally true, or truly sentimental, which can stand repeated retelling and become persuasive anew whenever they are well told. And "The Toll of the Sea" is exceedingly well told.

Chester M. Franklin, the dramatic director of the piece, and Frances Marion, the scenarist, deserve credit for this, of course. They brought to the production skill and sympathy and, most unusual among moviemakers, restraint, which, above all things, is needed for such a story as that with which they dealt.

But their best efforts would have gone for little or nothing with a heavy, heaving movie emoter of the usual kind in the leading role, which gives special point to the report that nothing they did has been lost and much has been added to their efforts by the actress who has the central part, Anna May Wong, naturally Chinese and exactly, easily natural, even in her most tormented scenes. As the trusting child of a carelessly considered race whose roving American husband, like the Captain of "Mme. Butterfly," returns to his home for a "real" wife, Miss Wong stirs in the spectator all the sympathy her part calls for, and she never repels one by an excess of theatrical "feeling." She has a difficult role, a role that is botched nine times out of ten, but hers is the tenth performance. Completely unconscious of the camera, with a fine sense of proportion and remarkable pantomimic accuracy, she makes the deserted little Lotus Flower a genuinely appealing, understandable figure. She should be seen again and often on the screen.

The others in the cast are entirely satisfactory. A majority of them are real Chinese, who, being capable actors as well, strengthen the story's appearance of reality. The only person, in fact, who seems to have had anything against the picture is the title writer, who did all he could to destroy a number of scenes by detailing them explicitly in words before they had a chance to speak for themselves. . . .

"THE TRUE LIFE STORY OF A CHINESE GIRL" by Anna May Wong (August 1926) [EXCERPT]

A third-generation Chinese American, Wong often felt torn between her Chinese ethnicity and American environment. Although Wong remained proud of her heritage, she absorbed the values and attitudes of Western culture. In this excerpt from her memoir, "The True Life of a Chinese Girl," the first of two 1926 installments in Pictures, she describes the conflicting influences of her heritage, childhood, and career path to stardom.

Source: Wong, Anna May. "The True Life Story of a Chinese Girl, Part I." Pictures, August 1926.

A lot of people, when they first meet me, are surprised that I speak and write English without difficulty. But why shouldn't I? I was born right here in Los Angeles and went to the public schools here. I speak English without any accent at all. But my parents complain that the same cannot be said of my Chinese. Although I have gone to Chinese schools, and always talk to my father and mother in our native tongue, it is said that I speak Chinese with an English accent!

An Oriental child, raised in a Chinese home in an American city is apt to have a few peculiarities, I guess. Especially when she turns out to be a motion picture actress. My parents nearly had a fit when I went into pictures. They're used to it now, and don't object any longer, but it wasn't an easy thing to overcome their prejudice. They wanted me to stay at home, and get married while I was still young to some nice Chinese boy. But I wanted a career. And I haven't found the Chinese man yet whom I would marry.

But I'll speak of this marriage problem, which a Chinese girl like myself faces, in a later installment.

I don't know much about writing an autobiography. At first I thought I couldn't do it, but the Editor of Pictures believes that my position in Hollywood, or in any American environment, for that matter, is unique and will prove of interest to the motion picture fans and the public at large. So I'll try to do the best I can on this story. I'll explain as best I can how it feels to be an American-born Chinese girl—proud of her parents and of her race, yet so thoroughly Americanized as to demand independence, a career, a life of her own. . . .

My sister was named Wong Lew Ying, but her arrival was not the signal for any rejoicing in the family. In fact, when father found out that his first child was a girl he was so disgusted that he didn't come home for days, mother says. And when he did come home, he wouldn't even look at the baby for some time. Lew Ying was certainly considered a total loss.

Then, to make matters worse, I was born second in the family, on January 3, 1905. Not only did my father have two girls on his hands, but mother, my sister and myself all contracted the measles as a crowning insult. It is a wonder father ever did get over that. Luckily he had four sons born later, or he might never have become reconciled to his Los Angeles family.

I was named Wong Lew Song, which means Frosted Yellow Willows. A rather unusual name, isn't it. Most Chinese children have names, which, interpreted into English, sound rather attractive, though they wouldn't do for everyday use. They are all right in poetry, but I wouldn't want to be called Frosted Yellow Willows by my acquaintances. It sounds altogether too quaint for a modern Chinese girl.

Probably my earliest memory is of playing with some English children who lived next door to us for several years. Until I went to public school it never occurred to me that I wasn't of the same nationality as all the children in the neighborhood. We all played games together and romped around with no thought of color or creed to disturb us. . . .

I spoke English from my earliest childhood, and when my sister and I grew old enough, we entered the California Street School, one of the public schools in Los Angeles.

I was very much thrilled to be going to school, not realizing that it was going to mean torture to me before very long. My parents bought me slates, pencils and books with pictures of bright red apples and gaily colored birds—goodness knows what all, in them. I learned the alphabet, and how to write "This is a Cat— This is a Dog." I learned to write my name, laboriously, in English. With a whole-souled devotion I bent over my books as, I had been taught, a proper student should do.

Having played always with white children, it seemed perfectly natural to me to be surrounded by them in school. I had straight black hair and black eyes. They had brown, blonde or red hair, blue, hazel or gray eyes. This meant nothing to me. The children in school looked just about like my playmates next door. I was certain that I would enjoy knowing them, when I overcame my shyness enough to mingle with them. They could come to my house and, if they liked, play with my toys. My mother would give them cookies. My father would always welcome them, even show them the delightful mysteries of his laundry. My father has always been kind to children.

Yes, I was going to enjoy school very much. I would learn my lessons well, and be an obedient student, so that my teachers as well as my parents would feel that I fully appreciated my opportunities.

Then came the knife stab which, even today, has left a scar on my heart.

My sister and I, after school, used to trudge home together, talking about our studies, what we had learned in this class and that, how pleased our parents would be over our progress. We had not yet made friends with our schoolmates, but as we were both shy we expected that it would take time to do that. Then, one day, on our homeward way, the world came crashing down around us.

A group of little boys, our schoolmates, started following us. They came nearer and nearer, singing some sort of a chant. Finally they were at our heels.

"Chink, Chink, Chinaman," they were shouting. "Chink, Chink, Chinaman."

They surrounded us. Some of them pulled our hair, which we wore in long braids down our backs. They shoved us off the sidewalk, pushing us this way and that, and all the time keeping up their chant: "Chink, Chink, Chinaman. Chink, Chink, Chinaman."

When finally they had tired of tormenting us, we fled for home, and once in our mother's arms we burst into bitter tears. I don't suppose either of us ever cried so hard in our lives, before or since.

We asked our father, sobbingly, what it all meant. Why had the little boys pulled our hair, slapped us, driven us from the sidewalk? We had done nothing wrong. We had tried always to behave in a proper manner. We had been polite to our schoolmates, respectful toward our teachers, as our parents instructed us to be. What was wrong?

Perhaps our father was sad at heart, to find that social ostracism had come to us so early. Perhaps he was resentful. But he showed nothing of this as he took us, one on each knee. He explained to us, gently, that it was no disgrace to be Chinese, that indeed we must be proud always of our people and our race. But, he told us, our position in an American community must at times be a difficult one. Perhaps it was as well for us to find this out now, while we were still so young, he said.

"Accept everything in life as it comes," he instructed us. "Hold no malice in your hearts toward anyone."

So, the next day, we went back to school again, even though we felt that we were suddenly thrust into a new and terrifying world. And it proved to be just that. What some of the older boys had started, the others now continued. The girls joined them, too. At recess, at noon, after school, the great game was to gather around my sister and myself to torment us. We never fought back. Our father had told us to hold no malice in our hearts. We never cried before our schoolmates. Our father had told us that we must be too proud to cry, and show that we were hurt.

We tried to walk unconcernedly home from school, always with a larger and larger crowd of our tormentors around us shouting, "Chink, Chink, Chinaman. Chink, Chink, Chinaman." Yanking our "pigtails" as they called our straight black braids of hair. Pushing us off the sidewalk into the street. Pinching us. Slapping us.

We hurried along toward home as fast as they would permit, our eyes downcast, our lips tightly closed. Sometimes we had to bite our lips very hard to keep from crying.

Presently, of course, it became unbearable. Every day was one of torture for us. We lived in such terror that we couldn't keep our minds on our lessons. We became ill with fright. All our bright dreams of making friends with our schoolmates, of standing well in our lessons, of winning the approbation of our teachers, vanished. We were just two hunted, tormented little creatures, and presently our parents realized that they must find some escape for us.

So, to our tremendous relief, we were taken out of the California Street School and placed in the Chinese Mission School in Chinatown. Here, though our teachers were American, all our schoolmates were Chinese. We were among our own people. We were not tormented any longer.

STILL FROM *THE CRIMSON CITY* (1928)

Wong consistently played Asian stereotypes and supporting characters in Hollywood during the 1920s. In this photo from the 1928 film Crimson City, Wong appears with Caucasian actor Myrna Loy, who played the lead role of the Chinese girl Onoto. Later that year, Wong, frustrated with the studio system, left Hollywood for a more appreciative Europe.

Source: Culver Pictures.

The Appendices,
Bibliography, and Index

Appendix One Document List

Armstrong, Edwin
Article "The Man Who Made Broadcasting Possible" from *The Literary Digest* (1922)
Photo Edwin Armstrong and Marion MacInnis (1923)
Speech From the Institute of Radio Engineers (1934)

Armstrong, Louis
Letter From Louis Armstrong to Isadore Barbarin (1922)
Lyrics "Heebie Jeebies" (1926)
Photo Louis Armstrong and the Carroll Dickerson Orchestra (1929)

Baker, Josephine
Photo Josephine Baker in *Chocolate Dandies* (1924)
Poster *La Revue Negre* (1925)
Article "The Negro Dance: Under European Eyes" by André Levinson (1927)
Article "Topic of the Day" by Josephine Baker (1927)
Poem Autobiographical Prose Poem by Josephine Baker (1931)

Baldwin, Roger Nash
Speech "Conscience at the Bar" by Roger Baldwin (1918)
Photo Reunion at Caldwell Penitentiary (1923)
Article "American Civil Liberties Union" from *Reds in America* by Richard Merrill Whitney (1924)

Barton, Bruce
Poster Salvation Army Poster (1918)
Book Excerpt *The Man Nobody Knows* by Bruce Barton (1925)
Article "There Are Two Seas" by Bruce Barton (1928)

Bow, Clara
Film Review *The Plastic Age* from *Variety* (1926)
Film Review *Mantrap* from *Variety* (1926)
Photo Still of Clara Bow and Antonio Moreno from *It* (1927)
Article "Clara Bow: My Life Story, Part Three" by Clara Bow (1928)

Brandeis, Louis
Article "A 'People's Lawyer' for the Supreme Court" from *The Literary Digest* (February 12, 1916)
Political Cartoon "The Blow That Almost Killed Father" (1916)
Speech Delivered at a Convention for the Zionist Organization of America (1918)
Dissenting Opinion Dissent by Louis Brandeis in *Schaefer* v. *United States* (1920)

Bryan, William Jennings
Speech "Cross of Gold" by William Jennings Bryan (July 8, 1896)
Political Cartoon "Gathering Data for the Tennessee Trial" (1925)
Speech "Mr. Bryan's Last Speech" from the Scopes Trial (1925)
Photo Anti-Evolution League Book Sale (1925)
Essay "Bryan and the Dogma of Majority Rule" by Walter Lippmann (1926)

Cannon, Annie Jump
Article "Friend to the Stars" by Kate M. Tucker (June 14, 1924)
Photo Annie Jump Cannon with Other Harvard College Observatory Staff (c. 1925)

Article "The Award of the Draper Medal to Dr. Annie J. Cannon" from *Scientific Monthly* (1932)

Capone, Al
Amendment Eighteenth Amendment Text (January 29, 1919)
Police Record Rap Sheet of Al Capone (1919–31)
Photo St. Valentine's Day Massacre (1929)
Photo Mug Shot of Al Capone (1931)
Article "Walter Winchell on Broadway: Portrait of a Man Talking to Capone" by Walter Winchell (1931)

Catt, Carrie Chapman
Essay "Woman Suffrage Must Win" by Carrie Chapman Catt (1915)
Poster "Stand by the Country" (1917)
Brochure *Declaration of Principles* from the Southern Women's League (c. 1917)
Brochure *Women in the Home* (c. 1917)
Political Cartoon "Southern Chivalry Isn't What It Used To Be" (1920)
Amendment Nineteenth Amendment Text (1920)

Chaplin, Charlie
Film Review *The Tramp* from *Little Review* (1915)
Film Review *The Kid* from *Variety* (January 21, 1921)
Photo Charlie Chaplin Movie Posters (1925)
Photo Still from *The Gold Rush* (1925)

Coolidge, Calvin
Photo National Guards during Boston Police Strike (1919)
Speech Calvin Coolidge's First Inaugural Address (March 4, 1925)
Speech "Third Annual Message" by Calvin Coolidge (December 8, 1925)
Essay "Calvin Coolidge: Puritanism De Luxe" by Walter Lippmann (1926)
Speech "Fifth Annual Message" by Calvin Coolidge (December 6, 1927)

Darrow, Clarence
Letter To the *Chicago Tribune* (July 4, 1923)
Speech "Mercy for Leopold and Loeb" by Clarence Darrow (1924)
Photo Clarence Darrow at the Scopes Trial (1925)
Editorial "Darrow's Eloquent Appeal" by H. L. Mencken (July 14, 1925)

Debs, Eugene V.
Speech From Canton, Ohio, Socialist Party Convention by Eugene V. Debs (June 16, 1918)
Photo Eugene V. Debs Delivering Speech in Canton, Ohio (June 16, 1918)
Campaign Button Eugene V. Debs's Presidential Campaign Button (1920)
Photo Terre Haute Citizens Signing Petitions (1921)

Dempsey, Jack
Statistics Jack Dempsey's Fight Record (1914–27)

Essay "The Negro Artist and the Racial Mountain" by Langston Hughes (June 23, 1926)

Review "Review of *Fine Clothes to The Jew*" by J. A. Rogers (1927)

Review "Review of *Fine Clothes to The Jew*" by Lewis Alexander (1927)

Hurston, Zora Neale

Anthology *The Eatonville Anthology* by Zora Neale Hurston (1926)

Essay "How it Feels to be Colored Me" by Zora Neale Hurston (1928)

Book Review *Jonah's Gourd Vine* by Andrew Burris (1934)

Photo Zora Neale Hurston Interviewing Eatonville Residents (1935)

Song Lyrics "Mule on De Mount" from *Mules and Men* (1935)

Jackson, Shoeless Joe

Statistics Player Statistics of Shoeless Joe Jackson (1910–20)

Testimony The Grand Jury Testimony of Shoeless Joe Jackson (September 28, 1920)

Telegram From Charles Comiskey (1920)

Commentary Hugh Fullerton's Commentary from *New York Evening World* (1920)

Kennedy, Joseph P.

Photo Joseph P. Kennedy (1914)

Letters From Joseph P. Kennedy to Albert Garceau (1921) and Matthew Brush (1922)

Letters From Joseph P. Kennedy to Grenville McFarland (1921) and Louis B. Mayer (1928)

Article "Joe Kennedy Has Never Liked Any Job He's Tackled" by John B. Kennedy (May 1928)

La Follette, Robert Marion

Political Cartoon "The Only Adequate Award" (March 7, 1917)

Written Message From Robert La Follette to the Conference for Progressive Political Action (1924)

Photo Robert La Follette Giving Radio Speech (1924)

Obituary "La Follette" from *The Outlook* (July 1, 1925)

Lasker, Albert

Business Creed From Lord & Thomas (1917)

Advertisement California Sunkist Oranges (1924)

Article "Is Advertising Read?" from Lord & Thomas (1927)

Advertisement Lucky Strike Cigarettes (1929)

Lindbergh, Charles

Report Report by Charles Lindbergh (1925)

Photo Charles Lindbergh's Medal (1927)

Photo Le Bourget Airfield before Charles Lindbergh's Landing (1927)

Photo Charles Lindbergh and *Spirit of St. Louis* (1927)

Song Lyrics "Lindbergh—Eagle of the USA" by the High Hatters (1927)

Lodge, Henry Cabot

Letter From Woodrow Wilson to Henry Cabot Lodge (August 15, 1919)

Senate Proposal The Fourteen Reservations by Henry Cabot Lodge (1919)

Political Cartoon "Refusing to Give the Lady a Seat" (c. 1919)

Treaty Four-Power Pacific Treaty (December 13, 1921)

Mayer, Louis

Article "$65,000,000 Movie Merger Completed" from the *New York Times* (April 1924)

Photo Still from Chariot Race in *Ben-Hur* (1925)

Film Review *Ben-Hur* from *Variety* (1926)

Photo Leo the Lion (1928)

McPherson, Aimee Semple

Letter To Aimee Semple McPherson (1923)

Statement Defense Statement of Aimee Semple McPherson (1926)

Poem "An Evangelist Drowns" by Upton Sinclair (1926)

Article "Vaudeville at Angelus Temple" by Sheldon Bissell (May 23, 1928)

Photo Aimee Semple McPherson's 25th Anniversary Pageant (1935)

Mencken, H. L.

Essay "The Woman Voter" by H. L. Mencken (1922)

Essay "On Being an American" by H. L. Mencken (1922)

Book Review "H. L. Mencken: A Review of His Notes on Democracy" by Walter Lippmann (1926)

Interview "Mencken Sees Tranquility Arise in U.S. from Ashes of Prohibition" by Sheilah Graham (November 12, 1933)

Palmer, A. Mitchell

Photo A. Mitchell Palmer's House after Bomb Explosion (1919)

Article "The Case Against the 'Reds'" by A. Mitchell Palmer (1920)

Essay Introduction of *To the American People* from the National Popular Government League (1920)

FBI Document Exhibit 12, "Instructions to Agents," from *To the American People* (1920)

Parker, Dorothy

Poem "A Well-Worn Story" by Dorothy Parker (1927)

Book Review *Enough Rope* by Edmund Wilson (1927)

Short Story Excerpt "Big Blonde" by Dorothy Parker (1929)

Paul, Alice

Article "Colby Proclaims Woman Suffrage" from the *New York Times* (August 27, 1920)

Photo Photo of Alice Paul (1920)

Amendments Texts of the Equal Rights Amendment (1923 and 1943)

Flyer "How New Jersey Laws Discriminate Against Women" (1926)

Political Cartoon "The Liberty Belle—She's Cracked" (1926)

Pershing, John J.

Political Cartoon "The Announcement" (1915)

Telegram Zimmermann Telegram (January 19, 1917)

Poster U.S. Food Administration War Poster (1918)

Article Article Describing Pershing's Victory Parade from the *New York Times* (September 11, 1919)

Report Final Report of Gen. John J. Pershing (1920)

Rankin, Jeannette

Article "The First Woman Elected to Congress" from *The Outlook* (November 22, 1916)

Photo Jeannette Rankin and Carrie Chapman Catt (1917)

Article "What We Women Should Do" by Jeannette Rankin (1917)

Speech Speech by Jeannette Rankin (1917)

Rockne, Knute

Statistics Knute Rockne's Game Record as Head Coach of Notre Dame (1918–30)

Photo The "Four Horsemen" (1924)

Letter From Knute Rockne to Jerome J. Crowley (1928)

Speech   To Studebaker Corporation by Knute Rockne (1931)

Rogers, Will

Photo   Publicity Photo of Will Rogers (Undated)

Article   "Duck Al! Here's Another Open Letter" by Will Rogers (October 29, 1927)

Article   "How To Be Funny" by Will Rogers (1929)

Ruth, Babe

Statistics   Babe Ruth's Baseball Record (1914–35)

Contract   Boston Red Sox and New York Yankee Agreement (December 26, 1919)

Radio Transcript   From World Series (1926)

Photo   The "Called Shot" Home Run (October 1, 1932)

Sacco, Nicola, and Bartolomeo Vanzetti

Speech   Speech of Nicola Sacco to Judge Webster Thayer (April 9, 1927)

Editorial   "Justice Underfoot" by Oswald Garrison Villard (August 17, 1927)

Letter   Bartolomeo Vanzetti's Letter to Dante Sacco (August 21, 1927)

Photo   Demonstration in New York City (1927)

Sanger, Margaret

Letter   Letter from Margaret Sanger to *Woman Rebel* Subscribers (1914)

Handbill   Handbill for First Birth Control Clinic (1916)

Court Transcript   Margaret Sanger's Trial (1917)

Debate   Debate on Birth Control Between Winter Russell and Margaret Sanger (1921)

Article   "The Case for Birth Control" by Margaret Sanger (February 23, 1924)

Letter   Letter to Margaret Sanger (January 5, 1925)

Smith, Alfred E.

Speech   Given by Alfred E. Smith at New York State Democratic Convention (1924)

Political Cartoon   "Have a Heart!" (c. 1920s)

Letter   "An Open Letter to the Honorable Alfred E. Smith" by Charles C. Marshall (1927)

Letter   "Catholic and Patriot: Governor Smith Replies" by Alfred E. Smith (1927)

Smith, Bessie

Photo   Publicity Photo of Bessie Smith (1923)

Article   "Singer Began at Seven Years Old" by Mabel Chew (March 27, 1926)

Poster   Columbia Records Advertising "Race Records" (1928)

Stein, Gertrude

Painting   Portrait of Gertrude Stein by Pablo Picasso (1906)

Poem   "Susie Asado" by Gertrude Stein (1922)

Lecture   "Composition as Explanation" by Gertrude Stein (1926)

Essay   "Everybody Is a Real One" by Katherine Anne Porter (January 16, 1927)

Essay   "Tests for Counterfeit in the Arts" by Wyndham Lewis (1927)

Stieglitz, Alfred

Photo   Portrait of Georgia O'Keeffe by Alfred Stieglitz (1920)

Article   "A Photographer Challenges" by Herbert J. Seligman (February 16, 1921)

Photo   "Equivalent" by Alfred Stieglitz (1923)

Wills, Helen

Statistics   Tennis Record of Helen Wills (1922–38)

Photo   Suzanne Lenglen and Helen Wills (1926)

Interview   "Little Miss Poker Face" by John B. Kennedy (September 18, 1926)

Article   "Emancipated Legs Mean Better Sports" by Helen Wills (1927)

Photo   Helen Wills Playing Tennis (1935)

Wilson, Woodrow

Speech   Inaugural Address by Woodrow Wilson (March 4, 1913)

Speech   War Message by Woodrow Wilson (April 2, 1917)

Speech   "Fourteen Points" by Woodrow Wilson (January 8, 1918)

Political Cartoon   "They Won't Dovetail" (1919)

Wong, Anna May

Congressional Act   Section 3 of the Immigration Act of 1917 (1917)

Film Review   *The Toll of the Sea* from *New York Times* (December 4, 1922)

Article   "The True Life Story of a Chinese Girl" by Anna May Wong (August 1926)

Photo   Still from *The Crimson City* (1928)

June 1914—Austrian Archduke Francis Ferdinand is assassinated in Sarajevo (in present-day Bosnia and Herzegovina), leading to World War I.

August 1, 1914—**Marcus Garvey** founds the Universal Negro Improvement Association (UNIA) in Jamaica. In 1917 he moves the center of operations to Harlem in New York City; by the end of the decade chapters have been established around the world. The UNIA will spearhead Garvey's efforts to achieve equality for black people by encouraging economic initiatives and political independence, operating a trading company called the Black Star Line, and entering into negotiations with the Liberian government to repatriate black citizens of the New World to Africa.

September 26, 1914—The Federal Trade Commission Act is passed to regulate business.

October 6, 1914—**Edwin Armstrong** is issued a patent for the regeneration circuit, an improvement on the audion tube invented by Lee De Forest in 1906, and the key technical innovation that makes radio possible. De Forest will later sue Armstrong, claiming patent rights to the circuit should belong to him. Ten years and as many courts later, the Supreme Court awards the rights to De Forest; the scientific community, however, continues to regard Armstrong as the true "father of radio."

October 15, 1914—Congress passes the Clayton Antitrust Act, which is intended to prevent monopolies and foster competition. An important supplement to the Sherman Antitrust Act of 1890, it expanded and specified the kinds of illegal behavior for which businesses could be prosecuted.

March 3, 1915—**D. W. Griffith**'s *Birth of a Nation* premieres in New York City. At nearly three hours long, the film becomes a blockbuster, setting attendance and box office records across the nation. Its innovative techniques reveal cinema's potential as an art form, even as its racist story—centering around the heroic exploits of the Ku Klux Klan—draws protests from the National Association for the Advancement of Colored People (NAACP).

March 4, 1915—The Seaman's Act is signed into law. Sponsored by Senator **Robert Marion La Follette**, the bill improves working conditions of sailors by protecting their wages, increasing rations, and requiring a nine-hour working day while in port. It also increases the safety of passengers—requiring, for instance, that ships provide enough lifeboats for all passengers and crew.

May 1915—British ocean liner the *Lusitania* is sunk by a German submarine. Almost 2,000 people are killed, including 128 Americans. The incident turns United States opinion against Germany.

November 1915—**Albert Einstein** completes his theory of general relativity, one of the foundations of modern physics.

March 1916—In response to a raid by the soldiers of Pancho Villa on Columbus, New Mexico, the U.S. Army sends a force of 10,000 soldiers into Mexico to hunt down Villa. Led by Brigadier General **John J. Pershing**, the punitive expedition fails to find Villa but is an important testing ground for the army, shaping Pershing's tactics in World War I.

June 1, 1916—The Senate confirms the appointment of **Louis Brandeis** to the Supreme Court by a vote of 47 to 22. He becomes the first Jew to sit on the high court.

June 6, 1916—National Women's Party is formed with **Alice Paul** as its leader. The following January the group will begin picketing the White House. Paul's radical approach causes strife within the suffragist movement, but attracts attention to the cause and exerts pressure on congressional leaders to work with the suffragists.

October 1916—**Margaret Sanger** opens the world's first birth control clinic in Brooklyn, New York. On the tenth day of business, every staff member is arrested under Section 1142 of the New York Penal Code, which forbids access to contraceptive information. Sanger's subsequent appeal and a great deal of publicity resulted in a slight relaxation of restrictions on dissemination of birth control information and devices in New York State.

November 1916—**Jeannette Rankin**, representative from Montana, becomes the first woman elected to Congress.

February 5, 1917—Congress passes the Immigration Act of 1917, Section 3 of which creates an Asiatic Barred Zone, a geographic region that includes South Asia, Southeast Asia, and the Pacific Islands. This act significantly curtails Asian immigration.

March 1, 1917—The Zimmerman Telegram, promising the return of Texas, Arizona, and New Mexico to Mexico if it allied itself with Germany, is published by the U.S. press, causing public outrage. Diplomatic ties with Germany had been severed in February; President **Woodrow Wilson** asks Congress to declare war on April 2.

March 2, 1917—Czar Nicholas II of Russia abdicates after widespread rioting; an unpopular provisional government is instituted, throwing the Russian war effort into disarray.

April 6, 1917—Congress declares war on Germany.

May 18, 1917—Congress passes the Selective Service Act, requiring that all men between the ages of 21 and 31 (later expanded to those between ages 18 and 45) report to their local draft board to register for military service.

June 1917—**Emma Goldman** founds the No Conscription League in response to the Selective Service Act passed by Congress. The

League holds protest rallies and passes out over 100,000 antidraft flyers and pamphlets. On June 15, Goldman is arrested and charged with conspiracy to obstruct the draft.

June 1917—Espionage Act is passed by Congress. This new law creates stiff penalties for individuals who interfere with troop recruitment or who release information damaging to national security and the war effort. Although derided as unconstitutional, the law is used to suppress the antiwar movement and arrest leftist activists such as **Eugene V. Debs**.

October 6, 1917—Congress passes the Trading with Enemies Act, which recognizes the existence of enemies of the United States residing within the nation's borders and authorizes the president to control the monetary transactions of these internal enemies.

November 6, 1917—Bolshevik Revolution overthrows provisional government of Russia and creates the United Soviet Socialist Republic, the world's first communist government.

January 1918—President **Woodrow Wilson** presents his Fourteen Points in a message to Congress.

March 1918—Russia withdraws from World War I after negotiating the Treaty of Brest-Litovsk with the Central Powers (Germany, Austria-Hungary, the Ottoman Empire, and Bulgaria).

May 1918—Congress passes the Sedition Act. An amendment to the Espionage Act of 1917, the Sedition Act makes it a crime to criticize the United States government or the Constitution; it results in the arrest and deportation of hundreds of radical activists, including **Emma Goldman**.

October 1918—Spanish flu epidemic reaches peak, with the death rate in the city of Philadelphia 700 times higher than normal. By the time the disease has run its course, 500,000 Americans (estimated 30 million people worldwide) will have died of influenza, more than three times the number killed in World War I.

November 11, 1918—Armistice is declared, bringing an end to World War I.

January 17, 1919—The Eighteenth Amendment, which prohibits the manufacture, sale, and transportation of alcoholic beverages, is ratified.

February 5, 1919—United Artists Corporation is formed by **D. W. Griffith**, Douglas Fairbanks, Mary Pickford, and **Charlie Chaplin**.

March 3, 1919— In *Schenck* v. *the United States*, a freedom-of-speech case arising from alleged violations of the wartime Espionage Act, Supreme Court Justice **Oliver Wendell Holmes, Jr**. delivers the Court's decision to uphold the Espionage Act. In a famous text that will be cited in many subsequent trials, Holmes states that rights such as free speech may be abridged when a person's attempt to exercise such rights "create[s] a clear and present danger."

June 1919—First luncheon of the Algonquin Round Table is held in New York City; the group of prominent 1920s intellectuals includes **Dorothy Parker**.

June 28, 1919—The Treaty of Versailles is signed in France, officially ending World War I.

August 1, 1919—Attorney General **A. Mitchell Palmer** creates the General Intelligence Division (GID) of the Justice Department to collect information about radicals.

September 1919—The Boston police walk off the job after the police commissioner denies them the right to unionize. After looting and riots break out across the city, **Calvin Coolidge**, governor of Massachusetts at the time, brings in 5,000 National Guardsmen to restore order; this incident brings him to national prominence.

October 28, 1919—The National Prohibition Act (the Volstead Act) is passed into law. Named for its author, Representative Andrew J. Volstead, the act makes the enforcement of the Eighteenth Amendment possible and truly ushers in Prohibition.

1920—**Roger Nash Baldwin** and others found the American Civil Liberties Union (ACLU) in New York City, dedicated to protecting United States citizens' constitutional rights. The ACLU will be involved in some of the most famous court cases of the decade, including the Scopes "Monkey" trial and the obscenity proceedings against James Joyce's *Ulysses*.

January 1920—Red Sox owner Harry Frazee trades **Babe Ruth** to the New York Yankees for $125,000.

January 2, 1920—At the height of the Red Scare, the Justice Department, under Attorney General **A. Mitchell Palmer**, rounds up thousands of radicals in what becomes known as the Palmer Raids.

March 19, 1920—The U.S. Senate, under the leadership of **Henry Cabot Lodge**, refuses to ratify United States membership in the League of Nations.

May 1920—In Matewan, West Virginia, attempts by the United Mine Workers to organize coal miners result in a fierce gun battle between miners and private detectives hired to evict them. Twelve people are killed in the Matewan Massacre; within a month, 10,000 coal miners go on strike.

August 1920—J. T. Thompson's portable submachine gun is demonstrated at a national gun show in Ohio. Beloved of gangsters, the "Tommy gun" becomes an emblem of the rise in violent crime during Prohibition.

August 18, 1920—With Tennessee's ratification of the Nineteenth Amendment, women get the right to vote.

August 26, 1920—The Nineteenth Amendment becomes a part of the Constitution of the United States.

September 28, 1920—In what becomes known as the "Black Sox" Scandal, eight White Sox players are accused of conspiring to throw the 1919 World Series: Chick Gandil, Eddie Cicotte, Swede Risberg, Fred McMullin, Lefty Williams, Buck Weaver, Happy Felsch, and **Shoeless Joe Jackson**.

November 2, 1920—**Warren G. Harding**, after conducting his famous "front porch" campaign following his presidential nomination in June 1920, is elected president. Harding defeats Democrat James Cox and Socialist **Eugene V. Debs**. Debs, running for his fifth and final time while in prison for violating the Espionage Act, receives over 900,000 votes, his best showing ever.

November 2, 1920—KDKA of Pittsburgh becomes the first commercially licensed radio station to broadcast; its first reports are on the presidential election results. By the end of the decade, radio stations are set up across the country, and radio listening has become the nation's favorite pastime.

May 19, 1921—The Immigration Quota Act limits immigration. Yearly quotas are set based on 3 percent of the number of people of specific nationalities present in the United States in 1910.

June 1, 1921—Some of the most destructive race riots in United States history take place in Tulsa, Oklahoma. White mobs burn down the black neighborhood of Greenwood, leaving dozens dead and reducing 36 city square blocks to cinders.

July 14, 1921—**Nicola Sacco and Bartolomeo Vanzetti**, Italian laborers and acknowledged anarchists, are convicted of murdering and robbing two men on April 15, 1920. The prejudicial comments and obvious bias of the trial judge incite a firestorm of public protest.

September 1921—Virginia Rappe, an aspiring film actress, dies of a ruptured bladder after passing out at a party in San Francisco four days earlier. The popular comedian Roscoe "Fatty" Arbuckle is accused of raping the unconscious girl. Tried three times for rape and murder, Arbuckle is eventually acquitted of all charges, but his career is destroyed and the scandal helps spur the creation of the "Hays Office" whose production code will be used to censor movies for the next four decades.

September 7–8, 1921—The first Miss America Pageant is held in Atlantic City, New Jersey. Sixteen-year-old Margaret Gorman from Washington, D.C., is chosen as the first "Miss Washington," and, after competing with other women and girls, is also crowned "America's Most Beautiful Bathing Girl." The two titles were eventually combined and Gorman became the first "Miss America."

November 10, 1921—**Margaret Sanger** founds the American Birth Control League (ABCL) at the First American Birth Control Conference in New York City. The goals of the ABCL include education, legislative reform, and research in the field of women's contraception.

1922—The Jamaican-born poet Claude McKay publishes *Harlem Shadows*, a volume of verse considered to mark the start of the Harlem Renaissance.

February 1922—James Joyce's *Ulysses* is published by Sylvia Beach's Shakespeare and Company in Paris. The book is banned in the United States and becomes the subject of a lengthy indecency trial; the scandal only adds to its success. Joyce's stream-of-consciousness style heralds the arrival of Modernism in the arts and will shape literature throughout the twentieth century.

April 1922—An oil field owned by the U.S. Navy and called the Teapot Dome is leased secretly to Harry F. Sinclair, president of the

Mammoth Oil Company, by Secretary of the Interior Albert B. Fall; Fall makes similar shady deals with the Elk Hills Oil Reserve a few weeks later. The "Teapot Dome" affair and the corruption it reveals in the **Warren G. Harding** administration will become one of the longest running scandals of the 1920s.

September 21, 1922—Congress passes the Fordney-McCumber Tariff, raising duties to an average of 38 percent. It was intended to protect domestic industries, particularly the chemical and drug industries that developed during World War I, by imposing the highest duties ever on imports.

November 7, 1922— Archaeologist Howard Carter and his sponsor, the Earl of Carnarvon, open the tomb of King Tutankhamun in the Valley of the Kings in Luxor, Egypt. The cache in King Tut's tomb remains the greatest trove of ancient Egyptian artifacts ever discovered, inspiring lasting worldwide interest in archaeology and ancient Egypt, and influencing contemporary Western art and fashion, particularly art deco.

November 25, 1922—Benito Mussolini becomes leader of Italy and institutes the world's first fascist government. The rise of fascism will shape the coming decades and plunge the world into war in 1939.

December 4, 1922—The U.S. House of Representatives passes an antilynching bill in response to postwar racial violence, but a filibuster by the southern states causes it to be withdrawn from the floor of the Senate.

February 15, 1923—The "Empress of the Blues," **Bessie Smith**, makes her first recordings with Columbia Records in New York City.

April 1923—The flow of rural southern blacks to the North and its factories—described by historians as the Great Migration—peaks. In Georgia, 13 percent of sharecroppers leave; the Labor Department estimates that 500,000 blacks have left the South by the end of 1923.

August 2, 1923—President **Warren G. Harding** dies in San Francisco and is widely mourned; posthumous revelations of corruption in his administration and scandalous personal behavior will eventually tarnish his image. Vice President **Calvin Coolidge** takes office.

Early 1924—Only 2,000 strong in 1920, membership in the Ku Klux Klan reaches its highest levels in early 1924, with an estimated five million recruited.

March 17, 1924—The first around-the-world flight is attempted. Four U.S. Army airplanes take off in California; only two successfully complete the trip, landing in Seattle 351 hours later after making 57 stops.

Spring 1924—The Charleston, a dance invented in 1913, becomes the rage nationally and internationally after appearing in the 1924 all-black musical revue *Runnin' Wild*; the popularity of the dance is such that its very name is used to evoke the era and its youthful, rebellious flappers.

April 26, 1924—**Louis B. Mayer** merges his company with Metro Pictures Corporation and Goldwyn Pictures Corporation to create

Metro-Goldwyn-Mayer; the new company celebrates its founding at its studio headquarters in Culver City, California.

May 10, 1924—At age 29, J. Edgar Hoover is appointed director of the corruption-ridden Bureau of Investigation. Hoover reforms and heads the Bureau—renamed the Federal Bureau of Investigations, or F.B.I.—for the next 50 years. He is responsible for hunting down some of the century's most wanted criminals, as well as for the creation of secret F.B.I. files on some of the country's most prominent figures.

May 26, 1924—Amendments to the Immigration Quota Act of 1921 reduce the percentage of immigrants of a given nationality permitted into the United States from 3 to 2, using census statistics from 1890 rather than 1910, thus curtailing Italian and other Southern and Eastern European immigrants; the Oriental Exclusion Act ends most Asian immigration. The Japanese Consulate protests, but to no avail.

Summer 1924—The National Democratic Convention is held in New York City. William Gibbs McAdoo of Tennessee emerges as the favorite of the southern, rural, Prohibition-supporting block, while **Alfred E. Smith** of New York, a Prohibition opponent, is backed by the northern big-city political bosses. A fierce battle ensues, resulting in the longest convention to date; after 103 ballots, the practically unknown compromise candidate, John W. Davis, emerges with the Democratic nomination.

September 10, 1924—Leopold and Loeb are sentenced to life in prison. On May 22, 1924, Nathan Leopold, Jr., 19, and Richard Loeb, 18, kidnapped and murdered 14-year-old Robert Franks in an attempt to commit "the perfect crime." Both killers were the wealthy, gifted, and remorseless sons of prominent Chicago families; they escaped the noose only through the brilliant, precedent-setting work of defense attorney **Clarence Darrow**.

November 2, 1924—Having served over a year as president following the death of **Warren G. Harding**, **Calvin Coolidge** is elected president with 54 percent of the popular vote.

November 7, 1924—In a five-year high, 2.33 million shares are traded on the New York Stock Exchange.

November 9, 1924—Nellie Ross is elected governor of Wyoming, the first woman governor in the United States.

February 17, 1925—Harold Ross publishes the first issue of *The New Yorker* magazine, an urbane weekly that captures the spirit of New York during the 1920s; Ross employs **Dorothy Parker** and Robert Benchley as critics and publishes some of the decade's most important fiction.

March, 1925—**Alfred Stieglitz**'s art exhibit "Seven Americans," featuring work by Paul Strand, Charles Demuth, John Marin, Marsden Hartley, Arthur Dove, Georgia O'Keeffe, and himself, opens. These artists' experiments in painting, sculpture, and photography will go on to form the core of the Modernist art movement in the United States in the following decades.

March 1925—After an assassination attempt and a voluntary nine-month jail sentence, gangster Johnny Torrio leaves Chicago for New York, handing over control of the Chicago mob to **Al Capone**, whose brutality, wealth, and fame will far surpass his mentor's.

May 1925—In one of the most famous encounters of twentieth-century literary history, **Ernest Hemingway** and **F. Scott Fitzgerald** meet for the first time at the Dingo Bar in Paris.

May 25, 1925—Victorious Allies sign Paris agreement to force more reparations from Germany; Germany is to pay $1 billion to the United States for costs associated with the U. S. Army's occupation.

May 25, 1925—High school teacher John T. Scopes is indicted in Dayton, Tennessee, for violating state law by teaching evolution. The subsequent Scopes "Monkey" trial captures national attention, not only because of the religious controversy surrounding the theory of evolution itself, but also because it features the clash of defense attorney **Clarence Darrow** and the prosecution's famous orator **William Jennings Bryan**. Bryan's unswerving faith gains local sympathy, but he is unable to effectively counter the piercing interrogation of Darrow. Scopes is eventually convicted of violating the law and fined. The conviction is later overturned on a technicality, but the law stayed on the books until 1967.

July 1925—Physicists W. K. Heisenberg and Niels Bohr develop quantum mechanics, a key concept in modern physics.

July 28, 1925—Microbiologists **George and Gladys Dick** obtain their patent for the "Dick test," which indicates an individual's immunity or susceptibility to scarlet fever.

Fall 1925—Alain Locke publishes *The New Negro*, an anthology of essays, fiction, poetry, and art that calls on black people to reclaim their African heritage. The anthology, featuring work by **Langston Hughes**, Claude McKay, Countee Cullen, and **Zora Neale Hurston**, has a strong influence on the Harlem Renaissance.

October 1925—**Josephine Baker** and *La Revue Nègre* take Paris by storm. Breaking free from the artistic and moral constraints imposed on black performers in America, Baker's sensuous "jungle" dances inspire fascination across Europe.

1926—The Division of Trade Practice Conference, a new Federal Trade Commission division, is created to encourage businesses to comply voluntarily with the antitrust provisions of the Sherman and Clayton Antitrust Acts—rather than prosecuting them for violations. This decision reflects the friendly attitude toward business of President **Calvin Coolidge**'s administration.

February 1926—Crime becomes so prevalent in Chicago that local business leaders plead in desperation with the Senate to set up a federal investigation into the city's gangsters.

April 7, 1926—A New York report estimates the U.S. bootlegging industry (the illegal production and distribution of alcohol during Prohibition) to be worth $3.6 billion. More than 32,000 speakeasies are operating in New York City alone—double the number of legal taverns in the city before Prohibition.

May 1926—The mysterious disappearance, and subsequent bizarre reappearance, of radio evangelist **Aimee Semple McPherson** absorbs the nation. McPherson claims to have been kidnapped and to have escaped, a story that elicits sympathy from her faithful followers and draws scorn and disbelief from the world at large. The incident prompts a grand jury investigation for fraud by Los Angeles County; McPherson is never indicted, but remains under a cloud of suspicion.

August 6, 1926—American Gertrude Ederle becomes the first woman to swim the English Channel. Upon her return to New York City, she receives a ticker tape parade.

September 25, 1926—An eight-hour day and five-day week are instituted at **Henry Ford**'s auto plants, an important step in advancing workers' rights.

1927—*It*, starring **Clara Bow**, is released. Based on a novel by Elinor Glyn, the quality referred to as "it" describes a type of girl who had an unforgettable, indescribable combination of sexual allure and brazen independence. Bow, as the "It Girl," embodies that combination for a generation, becoming one of the silent film era's biggest stars.

March 7, 1927—A Texas law preventing blacks from voting in primary elections is declared unconstitutional by the Supreme Court.

April 9, 1927—Complaints by the Society for the Suppression of Vice result in Mae West being found guilty of obscenity in New York City for the suggestive script (and her even more risqué ad libs) of her popular Broadway show, *Sex*. She is sentenced to 10 days in jail, but gains much fame from the incident and goes on to a successful career on stage and film.

May 21, 1927—**Charles Lindbergh** completes the first solo flight across the Atlantic from New York to Paris.

August 23, 1927—**Nicola Sacco and Bartolomeo Vanzetti** are electrocuted in the Charlestown State Prison near Boston despite many unsuccessful appeals and public protests.

September 7, 1927—Philo T. Farnsworth demonstrates his invention, the television, in San Francisco. Other inventors had transmitted images through electronic signals before, but Farnsworth's prototype will be the basis of the television boom of the 1940s and 1950s.

September 22, 1927—In a much anticipated bout, boxer **Jack Dempsey** attempts to regain his heavyweight title from Gene Tunney. The rematch—and its "The Long Count"—was forever marked by controversy when, in the seventh round, Dempsey knocked down Tunney and then hovered over his fallen opponent for a few seconds before retreating to a neutral corner. The delay caused the referee to restart his count, giving Tunney crucial time to recover; Tunney went on to win the match by unanimous decision. Many boxing fans were disappointed by the decision and Dempsey retired after the defeat without ever regaining the heavyweight championship.

September 30, 1927—**Babe Ruth** hits his 60th home run, a record thought unbreakable at the time; in 1961 Roger Maris hits 61 home runs. Some baseball fans contend that Maris's achievement does not equal Ruth's because the baseball season was eight games longer in 1961 than in 1927.

October 6, 1927—*The Jazz Singer*, starring Al Jolson, premieres. Although sound had been used before in pictures, *The Jazz Singer* is commonly acknowledged as the first "talkie" for its use of sound to record dialogue, not just for effects or music. With box office receipts of $3 million, it is a smash hit and signals the end of the silent era in film.

December 1927—The Cotton Club in Harlem, New York City, hosts **Duke Ellington** and his orchestra; they stay on for four box-office shattering years, while the Duke begins to make his name as one of the most innovative composers in jazz.

May 1928—German scientists Ernst Ruska and Max Knoll invent the electron microscope. This tool permits scientists to study viruses, which are too small to be seen by conventional microscopes.

May 1928—President **Calvin Coolidge** again vetoes the McNary-Haugen bill, which would have established price controls to aid farmers. The veto confirms Coolidge's sympathy for business; the plight of American farmers is mostly ignored by the country.

June 1928—Amelia Earhart becomes the first woman to successfully fly an airplane across the Atlantic; she later completes the feat alone and becomes the first woman to make a solo transcontinental flight. In 1937, she mysteriously disappears while attempting to circle the globe.

July 1928—At the summer Olympic Games in Amsterdam, women are allowed to compete in track and field events for the first time. The Americans fare especially well, taking home 56 medals, with the women winning medals in 4 out of 5 track and field events.

August 27, 1928—Fifteen nations—eventually joined by many more—sign the Kellogg-Briand Treaty in Paris, a peace pact designed to prevent the use of "war as an instrument of national policy." However, the treaty, which excluded civil war, wars of self-defense, and mutual-defense pacts from its provisions, and contained no articles specifying how it was to be enforced, proves ineffectual.

Fall 1928—The Chrysler Corporation reveals its plan to build the world's tallest building for its new headquarters in midtown Manhattan. At 68 stories (800 feet), the Chrysler Building will also be the world's largest example of the new art deco style.

November 6, 1928—Herbert Hoover is elected president of the United States, defeating Democratic candidate **Alfred E. Smith**, who was the first Roman Catholic to run for the presidency.

November 18, 1928—Walt Disney's *Steamboat Willie*, featuring Mickey Mouse, premieres at the Colony Theatre in New York City; it is the first cartoon in which sound effects are synchronized with the images.

February 14, 1929—In an attempt to eliminate rival gangster George "Bugs" Moran, **Al Capone** orders the St. Valentine's Day

Massacre. His hit men, disguised as police officers, arrive at a Chicago warehouse owned by Moran and kill seven members of Moran's mob—one of the most bloody assassination attempts in Mafia history; Moran, however, escapes.

March 1929—Fats Waller's *Hot Chocolates*, featuring such classic songs as "Ain't Misbehavin'" and "Black and Blue," premieres at Connie's Inn in Harlem.

March 26, 1929—The New York Stock Exchange trades 8.2 million shares in a single day, setting a record.

Spring 1929—The Gerber Company introduces prepared baby food.

May 1929—President Herbert Hoover appoints a national commission to study Prohibition's relation to rising crime.

May 16, 1929—In Hollywood, California, the Academy of Motion Picture Arts and Sciences hosts its first awards show to honor the movies of 1927 and 1928. The Academy Awards, or Oscars, will later become a world-famous showcase for the glamour of Hollywood.

May 27, 1929—In an important test of the Espionage Act, the Supreme Court rules that Hungarian immigrant Rosika Schwimmer may be barred from citizenship because of her pacifism. Justice **Oliver Wendell Holmes, Jr.**, in a renowned dissent, argues that the ability to hold and voice unpopular ideas is an important freedom guaranteed by the United States Constitution.

October 24, 1929—The stock market crashes on Thursday the 24th, or Black Thursday. A small downturn in stock prices creates a panic on the market floor and 13 million shares are sold. By Tuesday, October 29, Black Tuesday, the market appears to have hit bottom, with 16 million shares sold. Slight recovery occurs over the next few days, but share prices soon fall again, reaching their lowest level on November 13. Rampant speculation and margin investing (buying stocks with borrowed money) had driven the boom during the 1920s. When the crash comes, investors' stocks are worthless, and they no longer have the money to repay their debt. The crash affects stocks worldwide and helps bring about the Great Depression, 10 years of hardship and struggle very different from the frivolity of the decade that preceded them.

Bibliography

OVERVIEWS OF THE 1920S

Akin, William E. *Technocracy and the American Dream: The Technocrat Movement, 1900–1941.* Berkeley: University of California Press, 1977.

Allen, Frederick Lewis. *Only Yesterday: An Informal History of the 1920's.* New York: Perennial Classics, 2000.

Boardman, Fon Wyman, Jr. *America and the Jazz Age: A History of the 1920's.* New York: H. Z. Walck, 1968.

Braeman, John, Robert H. Bremner, and David Brody, eds. *Change and Continuity in Twentieth Century America: The 1920's.* Columbus: Ohio State University Press, 1968.

Carter, Paul Allen. *The Twenties in America.* 2d ed. Arlington Heights, Ill.: Harlan Davidson, 1987.

Cashman, Sean Dennis. *America Ascendant: From Theodore Roosevelt to FDR in the Century of American Power, 1901–1945.* New York: New York University Press, 1998.

———. *America in the Age of the Titans: The Progressive Era and World War I.* New York: New York University Press, 1988.

———. *America in the Twenties and Thirties: The Olympian Age of Franklin Delano Roosevelt.* New York: New York University Press, 1989.

Dumenil, Lynn. *The Modern Temper: American Culture and Society in the 1920s.* New York: Hill and Wang, 1995.

Gilbert, Martin. *A History of the Twentieth Century: 1900–1933.* Vol. 1. New York: W. Morrow, 1998.

Goldberg, David Joseph. *Discontented America: The United States in the 1920s.* Baltimore, Md.: Johns Hopkins University Press, 1999.

Goodman, Paul, and Frank Otto Gatell. *America in the Twenties: The Beginnings of Contemporary America.* New York: Holt, Rinehart and Winston, 1972.

Jenkins, Alan. *The Twenties.* New York: Universe Books, 1974.

Leuchtenburg, William E. *The Perils of Prosperity, 1914–1932.* 2d ed. Chicago: University of Chicago Press, 1993.

Link, William A., and Arthur S. Link. *American Epoch: A History of the United States Since 1900.* 7th ed. 2 vols. New York: McGraw-Hill, 1993.

McCoy, Donald R. *Coming of Age: The United States during the 1920's and 1930's.* Baltimore, Md.: Penguin Books, 1973.

Mowry, George E., ed. *The Twenties: Fords, Flappers and Fanatics.* Englewood Cliffs, N. J.: Prentice-Hall, 1963.

Perrett, Geoffrey. *America in the Twenties: A History.* New York: Simon & Schuster, 1982.

Shannon, David A. *Between the Wars: America, 1919–1941.* 2d ed. Boston: Houghton Mifflin, 1979.

Stevenson, Elizabeth. *Babbitts and Bohemians: From the Great War to the Great Depression.* New Brunswick, N. J.: Transaction Publishers, 1998.

Sullivan, Mark. *Our Times: America at the Birth of the Twentieth Century.* Edited and with new material added by Dan Rather. Abridged ed. New York: Scribner, 1996.

ADVERTISING AND CONSUMERISM

Calder, Lendol Glen. *Financing the American Dream: A Cultural History of Consumer Credit.* Princeton, N. J.: Princeton University Press, 1999.

Consumer Society in American History: A Reader. Edited and with an introduction and bibliographic essay by Lawrence B. Glickman. Ithaca, N. Y.: Cornell University Press, 1999.

Cross, Gary S. *An All-Consuming Century: Why Commercialism Won in Modern America.* New York: Columbia University Press, 2000.

Ewen, Stuart. *Captains of Consciousness: Advertising and the Social Roots of the Consumer Culture.* New York: McGraw-Hill, 1976.

Fox, Stephen R. *The Mirror Makers: A History of American Advertising and Its Creators.* Urbana: University of Illinois Press, 1997.

Glickman, Lawrence B. *A Living Wage: American Workers and the Making of Consumer Society.* Ithaca, N. Y.: Cornell University Press, 1997.

Goodrum, Charles A., and Helen Dalrymple. *Advertising in America: The First 200 Years.* New York: Harry N. Abrams, 1990.

Laird, Pamela Walker. *Advertising Progress: American Business and the Rise of Consumer Marketing.* Baltimore, Md.: Johns Hopkins University Press, 1998.

Leach, William. *Land of Desire: Merchants, Power, and the Rise of a New American Culture.* New York: Pantheon Books, 1993.

Lears, T. J. Jackson. *Fables of Abundance: A Cultural History of Advertising in America.* New York: Basic Books, 1994.

Marchand, Roland. *Advertising the American Dream: Making Way for Modernity, 1920–1940.* Berkeley: University of California Press, 1985.

———. *Creating the Corporate Soul: The Rise of Public Relations and Corporate Imagery in American Big Business.* Berkeley: University of California Press, 1998.

Morello, John A. *Selling the President, 1920: Albert D. Lasker, Advertising & the Election of Warren G. Harding.* Westport, Conn.: Greenwood Publishing, 2001.

Pendergast, Tom. *Creating The Modern Man: American Magazines and Consumer Culture, 1900–1950.* Columbia: University of Missouri Press, 2000.

Sivulka, Juliann. *Soap, Sex, and Cigarettes: A Cultural History of American Advertising.* Belmont, Calif.: Wadsworth, 1998.

Strasser, Susan. *Satisfaction Guaranteed: The Making of the American Mass Market.* New York: Pantheon Books, 1989.

Susman, Warren I. *Culture as History: The Transformation of American Society in the Twentieth Century.* New York: Pantheon Books, 1984.

ART, LITERATURE, MUSIC, AND THOUGHT

Anderson, Paul Allen. *Deep River: Music and Memory in Harlem Renaissance Thought.* Durham, N. C.: Duke University Press, 2001.

Bell, Bernard W., Emily Grosholz, and James B. Stewart. *W.E.B. Du Bois on Race and Culture: Philosophy, Politics, and Poetics.* New York: Routledge, 1996.

Bourgeois, Anna Stong. *Blueswomen: Profiles of 37 Early Performers, With an Anthology of Lyrics, 1920–1945.* Jefferson, N.C.: McFarland, 1996.

Callaghan, Morley. *That Summer in Paris: Memories of Tangled Friendships with Hemingway, Fitzgerald and Some Others.* New York: Coward McCann, 1963.

Carpenter, Humphrey. *Geniuses Together: American Writers in Paris in the 1920s.* Boston: Houghton Mifflin, 1988.

Connor, Celeste. *Democratic Visions: Art and Theory of the Steiglitz Circle, 1924–1934.* Berkeley: University of California Press, 2001.

Cowley, Malcolm. *Exile's Return: A Literary Odyssey of the 1920's.* New York: Viking Press, 1973.

——. *A Second Flowering: Works and Days of the Lost Generation.* New York: Penguin Books, 1980.

Curtiss, Thomas Quinn. *The Smart Set: George Jean Nathan and H. L. Mencken.* New York: Applause, 1998.

Evans, Nicholas M. *Writing Jazz: Race, Nationalism, and Modern Culture in the 1920s.* New York: Garland Publishing, 2000.

Fitch, Noel Riley. *Sylvia Beach and the Lost Generation: A History of Literary Paris in the Twenties and Thirties.* New York: Norton, 1983.

Furia, Philip. *The Poets of Tin Pan Alley: A History of America's Great Lyricists.* New York: Oxford University Press, 1990.

Geismar, Maxwell David. *The Last of the Provincials; the American Novel, 1915–1925: H. L. Mencken, Sinclair Lewis, Willa Cather, Sherwood Anderson, F. Scott Fitzgerald.* New York: Hill and Wang, 1959.

George Eastman House. *Photo-secession: Stieglitz and the Fine-art Movement in Photography.* With a foreword by Beaumont Newhall. New York: Dover Publications, 1978.

Greenough, Sarah, et al., eds. *Modern Art and America: Alfred Stieglitz and His New York Galleries.* Washington, D.C.: National Gallery of Art; Boston: Bulfinch Press, 2001.

Harrison, Daphne Duval. *Black Pearls: Blues Queens of the 1920's.* New Brunswick, N.J.: Rutgers University Press, 1988.

Hull, Gloria T. *Color, Sex & Poetry: Three Women Writers of the Harlem Renaissance.* Bloomington: Indiana University Press, 1987.

Jasen, David A. *Tin Pan Alley.* New York: Dutton/Plume, 1989.

Lucas, John. *The Radical Twenties: Writing, Politics, and Culture.* New Brunswick, N.J.: Rutgers University Press, 1999.

Mordden, Ethan. *Make-Believe: The Broadway Musical in the 1920s.* New York: Oxford University Press, 1997.

Morgan, Thomas L., and William Barlow. *From Cakewalks to Concert Halls: An Illustrated History of African American Popular Music From 1895 to 1930.* Washington, D.C.: Elliott & Clark, 1992.

Moses, Wilson Jeremiah, ed. *Classical Black Nationalism: From the American Revolution to Marcus Garvey.* New York: New York University Press, 1996.

Nash, Roderick. *The Nervous Generation: American Thought, 1917–1930.* Chicago: Rand McNally, 1970.

Ogren, Kathy J. *The Jazz Revolution: Twenties America & The Meaning of Jazz.* New York: Oxford University Press, 1989.

Scruggs, Charles. *The Sage in Harlem: H. L. Mencken and the Black Writers of the 1920s.* Baltimore, Md.: Johns Hopkins University Press, 1984.

Singleton, Marvin Kenneth. *H. L. Mencken and the American Mercury Adventure.* Durham, N.C.: Duke University Press, 1962.

Stansell, Christine. *American Moderns: Bohemian New York and the Creation of a New Century.* New York: Metropolitan Books/Henry Holt, 2000.

Tolson, Melvin Beaunorus. *The Harlem Group of Negro Writers.* Edited by Edward J. Mullen. Westport, Conn.: Greenwood Press, 2001.

Tracy, Steven C. *Langston Hughes & the Blues.* Urbana: University of Illinois Press, 2001.

Turner, Elizabeth Hutton. *In the American Grain: Arthur Dove, Marsden Hartley, John Marin, Georgia O'Keeffe, and Alfred Stieglitz: The Stieglitz Circle at the Phillips Collection.* Washington, D.C.: Counterpoint, 1995.

Ward, Geoffrey C. *Jazz: A History of America's Music.* Based on a documentary film by Ken Burns written by Geoffrey C. Ward, with a preface by Ken Burns. New York: Alfred A. Knopf, 2000.

Zamir, Shamoon. *Dark Voices: W.E.B. Du Bois and American Thought, 1888–1903.* Chicago: University of Chicago Press, 1995.

BUSINESS, INDUSTRY, AND THE ECONOMY

Batchelor, Ray. *Henry Ford, Mass Production & Design.* Manchester, England: Manchester University Press, 1995.

Beaudreau, Bernard C. *Mass Production, the Stock Market Crash, and the Great Depression: The Macroeconomics of Electrification.* Westport, Conn.: Greenwood Press, 1996.

Diamond, William. *The Economic Thought of Woodrow Wilson.* New York: AMS Press, 1982.

Douglas, Alan. *Radio Manufacturers of the 1920s: RCA to Zenith.* Lanham, Md.: Madison Books, 1991.

Hooker, Clarence. *Life in the Shadows of the Crystal Palace, 1910–1927: Ford Workers in the Model T Era.* Bowling Green, Ohio: Bowling Green State University Popular Press, 1997.

Israel, Paul B. *From Machine Shop to Industrial Laboratory: Telegraphy & the Changing Context of American Invention, 1830–1920.* Baltimore, Md.: Johns Hopkins University Press, 1992.

Keller, Morton. *Regulating a New Economy: Public Policy and Economic Change in America, 1900–1933.* Cambridge, Mass.: Harvard University Press, 1990.

Koistinen, Paul A. C. *Planning War, Pursuing Peace: The Political Economy of American Warfare, 1920–1939.* Lawrence: University Press of Kansas, 1998.

Lewis, Tom. *Empire of the Air: The Men Who Made Radio.* New York: E. Burlingame Books, 1991.

Morello, John A. *Selling the President, 1920: Albert D. Lasker, Advertising & the Election of Warren G. Harding.* Westport, Conn.: Greenwood Publishing, 2001.

Patterson, Robert Trescott. *The Great Boom and Panic, 1921–1929.* Chicago: Regnery, 1965.

Potter, Jim. *The American Economy Between the World Wars.* Rev. ed. London: Macmillan, 1985.

Sobel, Robert. *The Great Bull Market: Wall Street in the 1920s.* New York: Norton, 1968.

Tolliday, Steven. *The Rise and Fall of Mass Production.* Northampton, Mass.: Edward Elgar Publishing, 1998.

HARLEM RENAISSANCE

Anderson, Paul Allen. *Deep River: Music and Memory in Harlem Renaissance Thought.* Durham, N.C.: Duke University Press, 2001.

Bascom, Lionel C., ed. *A Renaissance in Harlem: Lost Voices of an American Community.* New York: Bard, 1999.

Fabre, Geneviève, and Michel Feith, eds. *Temples for Tomorrow: Looking Back at the Harlem Renaissance.* Bloomington: Indiana University Press, 2001.

Helbling, Mark Irving. *The Harlem Renaissance: The One and the Many.* Westport, Conn.: Greenwood Press, 1999.

Huggins, Nathan Irvin. *Harlem Renaissance.* New York: Oxford University Press, 1971.

Hughes, Langston. *Remember Me to Harlem: The Letters of Langston Hughes and Carl Van Vechten, 1925–1964.* Edited by Emily Bernard. New York: Alfred A. Knopf, 2001.

Hull, Gloria T. *Color, Sex & Poetry: Three Women Writers of the Harlem Renaissance.* Bloomington: Indiana University Press, 1987.

Marks, Carole, and Diana Edkins. *The Power of Pride: Stylemakers and Rulebreakers of the Harlem Renaissance.* New York: Crown Publishers, 1999.

Nathiri, N. Y., ed. *Zora! Zora Neale Hurston: A Woman & Her Community.* Lincolnwood, Ill.: NTC/Contemporary Publishing, 1991.

Tolson, Melvin Beaunorus. *The Harlem Group of Negro Writers.* Edited by Edward J. Mullen. Westport, Conn.: Greenwood Press, 2001.

Tracy, Steven C. *Langston Hughes & the Blues.* Urbana: University of Illinois Press, 2001.

Wall, Cheryl A. *Women of the Harlem Renaissance.* Bloomington: Indiana University Press, 1995.

Watson, Steven. *Circles of the Twentieth Century: The Harlem Renaissance.* New York: Pantheon Books, 1995.

Wintz, Cary D. *Black Culture and the Harlem Renaissance.* Houston, Tex.: Rice University Press, 1988.

———, ed. *Remembering the Harlem Renaissance.* New York: Garland Publishing, 1996.

HOLLYWOOD AND FILM

Altman, Diana. *Hollywood East: Louis B. Mayer and the Origins of the Studio System.* New York: Carol Publishing, 1992.

Basinger, Jeanine. *Silent Stars.* New York: Alfred A. Knopf, 1999.

Bernstein, Matthew, ed. *Controlling Hollywood: Censorship and Regulation in the Studio Era.* New Brunswick, N.J.: Rutgers University Press, 1999.

Calistro, Paddy, and Fred E. Basten. *The Hollywood Archive: The Hidden History of Hollywood in the Golden Age.* New York: Universe, 2000.

Cameron, Kenneth M. *America on Film: Hollywood & American History.* New York: Continuum International Publishing, 1997.

Carr, Steven Alan. *Hollywood and Anti-Semitism: A Cultural History up to World War II.* New York: Cambridge University Press, 2001.

DeCordova, Richard. *Picture Personalities: The Emergence of the Star System in America.* Champaign: University of Illinois Press, 1990.

Everson, William K. *American Silent Film.* New York: Oxford University Press, 1978.

Gunning, Tom. *D. W. Griffith and the Origins of American Narrative Film: The Early Years at Biograph.* Urbana: University of Illinois Press, 1994.

Higham, Charles. *Merchant of Dreams: Louis B. Mayer, M.G.M., and the Secret Hollywood.* New York: D. I. Fine, 1993.

Hill, John, and Pamela Church Gibson, eds. *American Cinema and Hollywood: Critical Approaches.* Consulting editors Richard Dyer, E. Ann Kaplan, Paul Willemen. Oxford: Oxford University Press, 2000.

Marks, Martin Miller. *Music and the Silent Film: Contexts and Case Studies, 1895–1924.* New York: Oxford University Press, 1997.

Robinson, David. *From Peep Show to Palace: The Birth of American Film.* New York: Columbia University Press, 1996.

———. *Hollywood in the Twenties.* New York: A. S. Barnes, 1968.

Sklar, Robert. *Movie-made America: A Cultural History of American Movies.* Rev. ed. New York: Vintage Books, 1994.

Slide, Anthony. *Early American Cinema*. New York: A. S. Barnes, 1970.

———. *The New Historical Dictionary of the American Film Industry*. Lanham, Md.: Scarecrow Press, 1998.

Wollstein, Hans J. *Vixens, Floozies and Molls: 28 Actresses of Late 1920s and 1930s Hollywood*. Jefferson, N.C.: McFarland, 1999.

LABOR

Bernstein, Irving. *The Lean Years: A History of the American Worker, 1920–1933*. Boston: Houghton Mifflin, 1960.

Brown, Cliff. *Racial Conflicts and Violence in the Labor Market: Roots in the 1919 Steel Strike*. New York: Garland Publishing, 1998.

Buhle, Paul. *From the Knights of Labor to the New World Order: Essays on Labor and Culture*. New York: Garland Publishing, 1997.

———. *Taking Care of Business: Samuel Gompers, George Meany, Lane Kirkland, and the Tragedy of American Labor*. New York: Monthly Review Press, 1999.

Buhle, Paul and Alan Dawley. *Working for Democracy: American Workers from the Revolution to the Present*. With a foreword by Herbert G. Gutman. Urbana: University of Illinois Press, 1985.

Dubofsky, Melvyn. *We Shall Be All: A History of the Industrial Workers of the World*. Edited by Joseph A. McCartin. Abridged ed. Urbana: University of Illinois Press, 2000.

Duus, Masayo. *The Japanese Conspiracy: The Oahu Sugar Strike of 1920*. Translated by Beth Cary and adapted by Peter Duus. Berkeley: University of California Press, 1999.

Hall, Greg. *Harvest Wobblies: The Industrial Workers of the World and Agricultural Laborers in the American West, 1905–1930*. Corvallis: Oregon State University Press, 2001.

Hooker, Clarence. *Life in the Shadows of the Crystal Palace, 1910–1927: Ford Workers in the Model T Era*. Bowling Green, Ohio: Bowling Green State University Popular Press, 1997.

Kimeldorf, Howard. *Battling for American Labor: Wobblies, Craft Workers, and the Making of the Union Movement*. Berkeley: University of California Press, 1999.

Montgomery, David. *The Fall of the House of Labor: The Workplace, the State, and American Labor Activism, 1865–1925*. Cambridge: Cambridge University Press, 1987.

Nelson, Bruce. *Divided We Stand: American Workers and the Struggle for Black Equality*. Princeton, N.J.: Princeton University Press, 2001.

Renshaw, Patrick. *The Wobblies: The Story of the IWW and Syndicalism in the United States*. Rev. ed. Chicago: Ivan R. Dee, 1999.

Robertson, David Brian. *Capital, Labor, and State: The Battle for American Labor Markets from the Civil War to the New Deal*. Lanham, Md.: Rowman & Littlefield Publishers, 2000.

Tentler, Leslie Woodcock. *Wage-earning Women: Industrial Work and Family Life in the United States, 1900–1930*. New York: Oxford University Press, 1979.

Zieger, Robert H. *American Workers, American Unions*. 2d ed. Baltimore, Md.: Johns Hopkins University Press, 1994.

———. *Republicans and Labor, 1919–1929*. Lexington: University of Kentucky Press, 1969.

NATIVISM, ANTI-SEMITISM, AND RACISM

Baldwin, Neil. *Henry Ford and the Jews: The Mass Production of Hate*. New York: Public Affairs, 2001.

Carr, Steven Alan. *Hollywood and Anti-Semitism: A Cultural History up to World War II*. New York: Cambridge University Press, 2001.

Chalmers, David Mark. *Hooded Americanism: The History of the Ku Klux Klan*. 3rd ed. Durham, N.C.: Duke University Press, 1987.

Dinnerstein, Leonard. *The Leo Frank Case*. Athens: University of Georgia Press, 1987.

Ginger, Ray. *Six Days or Forever? Tennessee v. John Scopes*. New York: Oxford University Press, 1958.

Higham, John. *Strangers in the Land: Patterns of American Nativism, 1860–1925*. 2d ed. New Brunswick, N.J.: Rutgers University Press, 1992.

Jackson, Kenneth. *The Ku Klux Klan in the City, 1915–1930*. New York: Oxford University Press, 1967.

Larson, Edward J. *Summer for the Gods: The Scopes Trial and America's Continuing Debate over Science and Religion*. New York: Basic Books, 1997.

Lewis, Earl, and Heidi Ardizzone. *Love On Trial: An American Scandal in Black and White*. New York: Norton, 2001.

MacLean, Nancy. *Behind the Mask of Chivalry: The Making of the Second Ku Klux Klan*. New York: Oxford University Press, 1994.

Madigan, Tim. *The Burning: Massacre, Destruction, and the Tulsa Race Riot of 1921*. New York: St. Martin's Press, 2001.

Schneider, Mark Robert. *We Return Fighting: The Civil Rights Movement in the Jazz Age*. Boston: Northeastern University Press, 2001.

Wade, Wyn Craig. *The Fiery Cross: The Ku Klux Klan in America*. New York: Oxford University Press, 1998.

POLITICS

Andersen, Kristi. *After Suffrage: Women in Partisan and Electoral Politics before the New Deal*. Chicago: University of Chicago Press, 1996.

Bates, James Leonard. *The Origins of Teapot Dome: Progressives, Parties and Petroleum*. Orig. pub. 1963. Reprint, Westport, Conn.: Greenwood Publishing, 1978.

Burton, David Henry. *Taft, Holmes, and the 1920s Court: An Appraisal*. Madison, N.J.: Fairleigh Dickinson University Press, 1998.

Busch, Francis X. *Enemies of the State: An Account of the Trials of the Mary Eugenia Surratt Case, the Teapot Dome Cases, the Alphonse Capone Case, the Rosenberg Case*. Orig. pub. 1954. Reprint, Buffalo, N.Y.: William S. Hein, 1998.

Chambers, John Whiteclay. *The Tyranny of Change: America in the Progressive Era, 1890–1920*. 3rd ed. Piscataway, N.J.: Rutgers University Press, 2000.

Cooper, John Milton. *Breaking the Heart of the World: Woodrow Wilson and the Fight for the League of Nations*. New York: Cambridge University Press, 2001.

Ferrell, Robert H. *The Presidency of Calvin Coolidge*. Lawrence: University Press of Kansas, 1998.

Ford, Linda G. *Iron-Jawed Angels: The Suffrage Militancy of the National Woman's Party, 1912–1920*. Lanham, Md.: University Press of America, 1991.

Gordon, Ernest. *To End All Wars*. North Pomfret, Vt.: Trafalgar Square, 2001.

Grant, Robert B., and Joseph Katz. *The Great Trials of the Twenties: The Watershed Decade in America's Courtrooms*. Rockville Centre, N.Y.: Sarpedon, 1998.

Haynes, John Earl, ed. *Calvin Coolidge and the Coolidge Era: Essays on the History of the 1920s*. Washington, D.C.: Library of Congress, 1998.

Irons, Peter H. *A People's History of the Supreme Court*. New York: Viking, 1999.

Irwin, Inez Haynes. *The Story of Alice Paul and the National Woman's Party*. Fairfax, Va.: Denlinger's Publishers, 1977.

Milkis, Sidney M., and Jerome M. Mileur. *Progressivism and the New Democracy*. Amherst: University of Massachusetts Press, 1999.

Miller, Karen A. J. *Populist Nationalism: Republican Insurgency and American Foreign Policy Making, 1918–1925*. Westport, Conn.: Greenwood Press, 1999.

Morin, Isobel V. *Women of the United States Congress*. Minneapolis, Minn.: Oliver Press, 1994.

Mugridge, Ian. *The View from Xanadu: William Randolph Hearst & United States Foreign Policy*. Montreal: McGill-Queen's University Press, 1995.

Murray, Robert K. *The Harding Era: Warren G. Harding & His Administration*. Orig. pub. 1969. Reprint, Newtown, Conn.: American Political Biography, 2000.

———. *The Politics of Normalcy: Government Theory and Practice in the Harding-Coolidge Era*. New York: W. W. Norton, 1973.

Ostrower, Gary B. *League of Nations from 1919–1929*. New York: Penguin Putnam, 1996.

Rehnquist, William H. *The Supreme Court*. Rev. ed. New York: Knopf, 2001.

Schneider, Dorothy, and Carl J. Schneider. *American Women in the Progressive Era, 1900–1920*. New York: Doubleday, 1994.

Stid, Daniel D. *The President As Statesman: Woodrow Wilson and the Constitution*. Lawrence.: University Press of Kansas, 1998

Widenor, William C. *Henry Cabot Lodge and the Search for an American Foreign Policy*. Berkeley: University of California Press, 1980.

Wynn, Neil A. *From Progressivism to Prosperity: World War I & American Society*. New York: Holmes & Meier Publishers, 1986.

PROHIBITION

Behr, Edward. *Prohibition: Thirteen Years that Changed America*. New York: Arcade, 1996.

Bergreen, Laurence. *Capone: The Man and the Era*. New York: Simon & Schuster, 1994.

Clark, Norman H. *Deliver Us from Evil: An Interpretation of American Prohibition*. New York: Norton, 1976.

Engelmann, Larry. *Intemperance: The Lost War against Liquor*. New York: Free Press, 1979.

Hamm, Richard F. *Shaping the Eighteenth Amendment: Temperance Reform, Legal Culture, and the Polity, 1880–1920*. Chapel Hill: University of North Carolina Press, 1995.

Kerr, K. Austin. *Organized for Prohibition: A New History of the Anti-saloon League*. New Haven, Conn.: Yale University Press, 1985.

Kobler, John. *Ardent Spirits: The Rise and Fall of Prohibition*. New York: Da Capo Press, 1993.

Kyvig, David E. *Repealing National Prohibition*. 2d ed. Kent, Ohio: Kent State University Press, 2000.

Pegram, Thomas R. *Battling Demon Rum: The Struggle for a Dry America, 1800–1933*. Chicago: Ivan R. Dee, 1998.

Rose, Clifford. *Four Years with the Demon Rum, 1925–1929: The Autobiography and Diary of Temperance Inspector Clifford Rose*. Edited with an introduction by E. R. Forbes and A. A. MacKenzie. Fredericton, Neb.: Acadiensis Press, 1980.

RADICALISM

Avrich, Paul. *Anarchist Voices: An Oral History of Anarchism in America*. Princeton, N.J.: Princeton University Press, 1995.

———. *Sacco and Vanzetti: The Anarchist Background*. Princeton, N. J.: Princeton University Press, 1991.

Barrett, James R. *William Z. Foster and the Tragedy of American Radicalism*. Chicago: University of Illinois Press, 1999.

Buhle, Paul, and Edmund B. Sullivan. *Images of American Radicalism*. With a foreword by Howard Fast. Hanover, Mass.: Christopher Publishing House, 1998.

Cottrell, Robert. *Roger Nash Baldwin and the American Civil Liberties Union*. New York: Columbia University Press, 2001.

Diggins, John P. *The Rise and Fall of the American Left*. New York: W. W. Norton, 1992.

Draper, Theodore. *American Communism and Soviet Russia: The Formative Period*. New York: Viking Press, 1963.

Gengarelly, W. Anthony. *Distinguished Dissenters and Opposition to the 1919–1920 Red Scare*. Lewiston, N.Y.: Edwin Mellen Press, 1996.

Glassgold, Peter. *Anarchy!! An Anthology of Emma Goldman's Mother Earth*. Washington, D.C.: Counterpoint Press, 2001.

The Letters of Sacco and Vanzetti. Edited by Marion Denman Frankfurter and Gardner Jackson, with an introduction by Richard Polenberg. New York: Penguin Books, 1997.

Lucas, John. *The Radical Twenties: Writing, Politics, and Culture.* New Brunswick, N.J.: Rutgers University Press, 1999.

Marsh, Margaret S. *Anarchist Women: 1870–1920.* Philadelphia: Temple University Press, 1981.

Meyer, Robert S. *Peace Organizations Past and Present.* Jefferson, N.C.: McFarland, 1988.

Murray, Robert K. *Red Scare: A Study in National Hysteria, 1919–1920.* Minneapolis: University of Minnesota Press, 1955.

Preston, William. *Aliens and Dissenters: Federal Suppression of Radicals, 1903–1933.* With a foreword by Paul Buhle. 2d ed. Urbana: University of Illinois Press, 1994.

Rosenstone, Robert A. *Romantic Revolutionary: A Biography of John Reed.* New York: Knopf, 1975.

Schlesinger, Arthur Meier, Jr. *The Crisis of the Old Order, 1919–1933.* Boston: Houghton Mifflin, 1957.

Schmidt, Regine. *Red Scare: FBI & the Origins of Anti-Communism in the United States.* Copenhagen: Museum Tusculanum Press, 2000.

Shull, Michael S. *Radicalism in American Silent Films, 1909–1929: A Filmography and History.* Jefferson, N.C.: McFarland, 2000.

Walker, Samuel. *In Defense of American Liberties: A History of the ACLU.* New York: Oxford University Press, 1990.

SCIENCE AND TECHNOLOGY

Batchelor, Ray. *Henry Ford, Mass Production & Design.* Manchester, England: Manchester University Press, 1995.

Berg, A. Scott. *Lindbergh.* New York: Putnam's, 1998.

Douglas, Alan. *Radio Manufacturers of the 1920s: RCA to Zenith.* Lanham, Md.: Madison Books, 1991.

Flink, James J. *The Car Culture.* Cambridge, Mass.: MIT Press, 1975.

Han, M. Y. *Quarks and Gluons: A Century of Particle Charges.* River Edge, N.J.: World Scientific, 1999.

Holton, Gerald. *Einstein, History, and Other Passions: The Rebellion Against Science at the End of the Twentieth Century.* Reading, Mass.: Addison-Wesley Publishing, 1996.

Israel, Paul B. *From Machine Shop to Industrial Laboratory: Telegraphy & the Changing Context of American Invention, 1830–1920.* Baltimore, Md.: Johns Hopkins University Press, 1992

Kass-Simon, G., and Patricia Farnes, eds. *Women of Science: Righting the Record.* Bloomington and Indianapolis: Indiana University Press, 1993.

Leary, William M. *Aviation's Golden Age: Portraits From the 1920s and 1930s.* Iowa City: University of Iowa Press, 1989.

Lewis, Tom. *Empire of the Air: The Men Who Made Radio.* New York: E. Burlingame Books, 1991.

Millbrooke, Anne M. *Aviation History.* Englewood, Colo.: Jeppesen Sanderson, 1999.

Pais, Abraham. *"Subtle is the Lord": The Science and the Life of Albert Einstein.* New York: Oxford University Press, 1982.

Rossiter, Margaret W. *Women Scientists in America: Struggles and Strategies to 1940.* Baltimore, Md.: Johns Hopkins University Press, 1982.

Scott, Phil. *The Pioneers of Flight: A Documentary History.* Princeton, N.J.: Princeton University Press, 1999.

Smulyan, Susan. *Selling Radio: The Commercialization of American Broadcasting, 1920–1934.* Washington, D.C.: Smithsonian Institution Press, 1994.

Yost, Edna. *American Women of Science.* Philadelphia: Lippincott, 1955.

SPORTS

Ashe, Arthur. *A Hard Road to Glory: A History of the African-American Athlete, 1919–1945.* New York: Warner Books, 1988.

Asinof, Eliot. *Eight Men Out: The Black Sox and the 1919 World Series.* New York: Henry Holt, 2000.

Creamer, Robert W. *Babe: The Legend Comes to Life.* New York: Simon & Schuster, 1992.

Engelmann, Larry. *The Goddess and the American Girl: The Story of Suzanne Lenglen and Helen Wills.* New York: Oxford University Press, 1988.

Evensen, Bruce J. *When Dempsey Fought Tunney: Heroes, Hokum, and Storytelling in the Jazz Age.* Knoxville: University of Tennessee Press, 1996.

Fleitz, David L. *Shoeless: The Life and Times of Joe Jackson.* Jefferson, N.C.: McFarland, 2001.

Gardner, Robert, and Dennis Shortelle. *The Forgotten Players: The Story of Black Baseball in America.* New York: Walker, 1993.

Gropman, Donald. *Say It Ain't So, Joe!: The True Story of Shoeless Joe Jackson.* Rev. ed. New York: Carol Publishing, 1995.

Harper, William A. *How You Played the Game: The Life of Grantland Rice.* Columbia: University of Missouri Press, 1999.

Kahn, Roger. *A Flame of Pure Fire: Jack Dempsey and the Roaring 20s.* New York: Harcourt Brace, 1999.

King, Billie Jean, and Cynthia Starr. *We Have Come a Long Way: The Story of Women's Tennis.* New York: McGraw Hill, 1988.

Levine, Peter. *Ellis Island to Ebbets Field: Sport and the American Jewish Experience.* New York: Oxford University Press, 1992.

Pope, S. W. *Patriotic Games: Sporting Traditions in the American Imagination, 1876–1926.* New York: Oxford University Press, 1997.

Riess, Steven A. *City Games: The Evolution of American Urban Society and the Rise of Sports.* Urbana: University of Illinois Press, 1989.

———. *Sport in Industrial America, 1850–1920.* Wheeling, Ill.: Harlan Davidson, 1995.

Roberts, Randy. *Jack Dempsey, The Manassa Mauler.* Baton Rouge: Louisiana State University Press, 1979.

Wakefield, Wanda Ellen. *Playing to Win: Sports and the American Military, 1898–1945.* Albany: State University of New York Press, 1997.

Wallace, Joseph, Neil Hamilton, and Marty Appel. *Baseball: 100 Classic Moments in the History of the Game.* New York: Dorling Kindersley, 2000.

WOMEN AND SUFFRAGE

Andersen, Kristi. *After Suffrage: Women in Partisan and Electoral Politics before the New Deal.* Chicago: University of Chicago Press, 1996.

Bourgeois, Anna Stong. *Blueswomen: Profiles of 37 Early Performers, With an Anthology of Lyrics, 1920–1945.* Jefferson, N.C.: McFarland, 1996.

Brown, Dorothy M. *Setting a Course: American Women in the 1920s.* Boston: Twayne, 1987.

Chafe, William Henry. *The Paradox of Change: American Women in the 20th Century.* New York: Oxford University Press, 1991.

Chesler, Ellen. *Women of Valor: Margaret Sanger and the Birth Control Movement in America.* New York: Anchor Books, 1993.

Cott, Nancy F. *The Grounding of Modern Feminism.* New Haven, Conn.: Yale University Press, 1987.

DuBois, Ellen Carol. *Harriot Stanton Blatch and the Winning of Woman Suffrage.* New Haven, Conn.: Yale University Press, 1997.

Duniway, Abigail Scott. *"Yours For Liberty": Selections from Abigail Scott Duniway's Suffrage Newspaper.* Edited by Jean M. Ward and Elaine A. Maveety. Corvallis: Oregon State University Press, 2000.

Ford, Linda G. *Iron-Jawed Angels: The Suffrage Militancy of the National Woman's Party, 1912–1920.* Lanham, Md.: University Press of America, 1991.

Gurko, Miriam. *The Ladies of Seneca Falls: The Birth of the Woman's Rights Movement.* New York: Schocken Books, 1976.

Harrison, Daphne Duval. *Black Pearls: Blues Queens of the 1920's.* New Brunswick, N.J.: Rutgers University Press, 1988.

Hull, Gloria T. *Color, Sex & Poetry: Three Women Writers of the Harlem Renaissance.* Bloomington: Indiana University Press, 1987.

Irwin, Inez Haynes. *The Story of Alice Paul and the National Woman's Party.* Fairfax, Va.: Denlinger's Publishers, 1977.

King, Billie Jean, and Cynthia Starr. *We Have Come a Long Way: The Story of Women's Tennis.* New York: McGraw Hill, 1988.

Lunardini, Christine A. *From Equal Suffrage to Equal Rights: Alice Paul and the National Woman's Party, 1910–1928.* New York: New York University Press, 1986.

Marsh, Margaret S. *Anarchist Women: 1870–1920.* Philadelphia: Temple University Press, 1981.

Marshall, Susan E. *Splintered Sisterhood: Gender and Class in the Campaign against Woman Suffrage.* Madison: University of Wisconsin Press, 1997.

Marwick, Arthur. *Women at War: 1914–1918.* London: Croom Helm, 1977.

Morin, Isobel V. *Women of the United States Congress.* Minneapolis, Minn.: Oliver Press, 1994.

Schneider, Dorothy, and Carl J. Schneider. *American Women in the Progressive Era, 1900–1920.* New York: Doubleday, 1994.

Stevens, Doris. *Jailed for Freedom: American Women Win the Vote.* Edited by Carol O'Hare, with a foreword by Edith Mayo. Rev. ed. Troutdale, Ore.: NewSage Press, 1995.

Tentler, Leslie Woodcock. *Wage-earning Women: Industrial Work and Family Life in the United States, 1900–1930.* New York: Oxford University Press, 1979.

Terborg-Penn, Rosalyn. *African American Women in the Struggle for the Vote, 1850–1920.* Bloomington: Indiana University Press, 1998.

Wall, Cheryl A. *Women of the Harlem Renaissance.* Bloomington: Indiana University Press, 1995.

Weatherford, Doris. *Foreign and Female: Immigrant Women in America, 1840–1930.* Rev. ed. New York: Facts On File, 1995.

———. *A History of the American Suffragist Movement.* With a foreword by Geraldine Ferraro. Santa Barbara, Calif.: ABC-CLIO, 1998.

Wheeler, Marjorie Spruill. *New Women of the New South: The Leaders of the Woman Suffrage Movement in the Southern States.* New York: Oxford University Press, 1993.

———. *One Woman, One Vote: Rediscovering the Woman Suffrage Movement.* Troutdale, Ore.: NewSage Press, 1995.

Wiltsher, Anne. *Most Dangerous Women: Feminist Peace Campaigners of the Great War.* Boston: Pandora Press, 1985.

WORLD WAR I

Ambrosius, Lloyd E. *Wilsonian Statecraft: Theory and Practice of Liberal Internationalism during World War I.* Wilmington, Del.: SR Books, 1991.

Early, Frances H. *A World without War: How U.S. Feminists and Pacifists Resisted World War I.* Syracuse, N.Y.: Syracuse University Press, 1997.

Eisenhower, John S. D. *Yanks: The Epic Story of the American Army in World War I.* With Joanne Thompson Eisenhower. New York: Free Press, 2001.

Eksteins, Modris. *Rites of Spring: The Great War and the Birth of the Modern Age.* Boston: Houghton Mifflin, 2000.

Ferrell, Robert H. *Woodrow Wilson and World War I, 1917–1921.* New York: Harper & Row, 1985.

Fussell, Paul. *The Great War and Modern Memory.* New York: Oxford University Press, 2000.

Gallagher, Jean. *The World Wars Through the Female Gaze.* Carbondale: Southern Illinois University Press, 1998.

Harris, Stephen L. *Duty, Honor, Privilege: New York's Silk Stocking Regiment and the Breaking of the Hindenburg Line.* Washington, D.C.: Brassey's, 2001.

Hawley, Ellis. *The Great War and the Search for a Modern Order: A History of the American People and Their Institutions, 1917–1933.* 2d ed. New York: St. Martin's Press, 1992.

Keegan, John. *The First World War.* New York: A. Knopf, 1999.

Keene, Jennifer D. *Doughboys, the Great War, and the Remaking of America.* Baltimore, Md.: Johns Hopkins University Press, 2001.

Kennedy, David M. *Over Here: The First World War and American Society.* New York: Oxford University Press, 1980.

Link, Arthur S. *Woodrow Wilson: Revolution, War, and Peace.* Arlington Heights, Ill.: H. Davidson, 1979.

Marwick, Arthur. *Women at War: 1914–1918.* London: Croom Helm, 1977.

Schaffer, Ronald. *America in the Great War: The Rise of the War Welfare State.* New York: Oxford University Press, 1991.

Smith, Daniel M. *The Great Departure: The United States and World War I, 1914–1920.* New York: Knopf, 1965.

Strachan, Hew. *The First World War.* New York: Oxford University Press, 2001.

——, ed. *The Oxford Illustrated History of the First World War.* New York: Oxford University Press, 1998.

Tuchman, Barbara Wertheim. *The Guns of August.* With a new foreword by Robert K. Massie. New York: Ballantine, 1994.

Weintraub, Stanley. *Silent Night: The Story of the World War I Christmas Truce.* New York: Free Press, 2001.

Wiltsher, Anne. *Most Dangerous Women: Feminist Peace Campaigners of the Great War.* Boston: Pandora Press, 1985.

Wynn, Neil A. *From Progressivism to Prosperity: World War I and American Society.* New York: Holmes & Meier, 1986.

Index

Page numbers in **boldface** indicate article titles. Those in *italics* indicate illustrations.